About the Author

Richard W. Paul, Director of the Center for Critical Thinking, and Chair of the National Council for Excellence in Critical Thinking Instruction, is widely recognized as a major leader in the national and international critical thinking movements. He has published over forty articles and five books on critical thinking in the last five years. He has written books on how to foster critical thinking at every grade level (K–3, 4–6, 6–9, High School, and University). He has regularly taught courses in critical thinking, advanced critical thinking, and theory of critical thinking for the last 14 years. He has given hundreds of workshops at the K–12 level and made a series of eight critical thinking video programs for PBS. His views on critical thinking have been canvassed in The New York Times, Education Week, The Chronicle of Higher Education, American Teacher, Educational Leadership, Newsweek, U.S. News and World Report, and Reader's Digest. Besides publishing extensively in the field, he has organized two national and nine international conferences on critical thinking. He has given invited lectures at many universities and colleges, including Harvard, University of Chicago, University of Illinois, The University of Amsterdam, and the Universities of Puerto Rico and Costa Rica, as well as workshops and lectures on critical thinking in every region of the U.S. He has been active in helping to develop the concept of critical thinking used to design tests in critical thinking (K–12) by the State Department of Education in California and is working with Edward M. Glaser in revising the Watson-Glaser Critical Thinking test. Working with Gerald Nosich, he has developed a model for the national assessment of critical thinking at the post-secondary level for the U.S. Department of Education.

Professor Paul has been the recipient of numerous honors and awards, including "Distinguished Philosopher" (by the Council for Philosophical Studies, 1987), O. C. Tanner Lecturer in Humanities (by Utah State University 1986), Lansdowne Visiting Scholar (by the University of Victoria, 1987), and the Alfred Korsybski Memorial Lecturer (by the Institute for General Semantics, 1987). He is actively sought as a keynote speaker and staff development leader.

About the Center for Critical Thinking

The Center conducts advanced research and disseminates information on critical thinking and moral critique. It has been working closely with the Foundation for Critical Thinking, The National Council for Excellence in Critical Thinking Instruction, California State Department of Education, the College Board, numerous school districts, the Association for Supervision and Curriculum Development, the National Education Association, and the U. S. State Department of Education to facilitate implementation of high standards of critical thinking instruction from kindergarten through the university.

Its major work includes:

- International Conferences on Critical Thinking
  Each summer, in early August, the Center hosts the oldest and largest critical thinking conference with registrants from virtually every state of the union and numerous foreign countries. Over 300 distinguished experts in the field present over 300 sessions on critical thinking and critical thinking instruction over four days. These sessions are designed to meet the needs of the widest variety of educational levels and concerns from kindergarten through graduate school. A variety of subject matters and subject fields are used as examples of critical thinking infusion. The two days preceding the conference are used for intensive sessions that lay a foundation for the conference and for critical thinking instruction.

- Staff Development Services
  The Center provides staff development services at every level of education from kindergarten through graduate school (see inside back cover). Staff development programs emphasize the critique and redesign of instruction to infuse critical thinking principles into subject matter instruction.

About the Foundation for Critical Thinking

The Foundation for Critical Thinking is an independent, non-profit, institution not associated with Sonoma State University. It publishes a variety of critical thinking resources.

- *Resources for Instruction*
  - PBS Videotapes
  - Ground-Breaking Books
  - Four Grade-Level Critical Thinking Handbooks
  - The Leaders of the Critical Thinking Movement on Audio and Videotape
  - Audio and Videotapes for Critical Thinking Staff Development

For more information, contact:

The Center for Critical Thinking &
Moral Critique
Sonoma State University
Rohnert Park, CA 94928
(707) 664–2940

The Foundation for Critical Thinking
4655 Sonoma Mountain Road
Santa Rosa, CA 95404
(707) 546–4926

Critical Thinking

WHAT EVERY PERSON NEEDS TO SURVIVE
IN A RAPIDLY CHANGING WORLD

Critical Thinking:

What Every Person Needs to Survive in a Rapidly Changing World

RICHARD W. PAUL

edited by A. J. A. Binker

Foundation for Critical Thinking

1992

Acknowledgments

"The Critical Thinking Movement in Historical Perspective", originally appeared as, "The Critical Thinking Movement: A Historical Perspective", in *National Forum,* Winter 1985.

"Critical Thinking in North America", originally appeared as, "Critical Thinking in North America: A New Theory of Knowledge, Learning, and Literacy", in *Argumentation* 3, 1989.

"Critical Thinking in the Strong Sense and the Role of Argumentation in Everyday Life", appeared in *Argumentation: Across the Lines of Discipline, Proceedings of the Conference on Argumentation 1986,* 1987.

"Critical Thinking: Fundamental to Education for a Free Society", and "Ethics without Indoctrination", originally appeared in *Educational Leadership,* September 1984, May 1988.

"Critical Thinking and the Critical Person", originally appeared in *Thinking: The Second International Conference,* Lawrence Erlbaum, 1987.

"Dialogical Thinking: Critical Thought Essential to the Acquisition of Rational Knowledge and Passions", appeared in *Teaching Thinking Skills: Theory and Practice,* W. H. Freeman, Co., 1987.

"Dialogical and Dialectical Thinking", will be forthcoming in *Developing Minds,* ASCD, second edition, 1990.

"Teaching Critical Thinking in the Strong Sense: A Focus on Self-Deception, World Views, and a Dialectical Mode of Analysis", and "Background Logic, Critical Thinking, and Irrational Language Games", appeared in Informal Logic, May 1982 and Winter 1985.

"Critical Thinking Staff Development: The Lesson Plan Remodelling Approach", originally appeared as, "Staff Development for Critical Thinking: Lesson Plan Remodelling as the Strategy", in *Journal of Staff Development,* Fall 1987.

"Critical Thinking and Learning Centers", originally appeared as "Critical Thinking and Learning: A Maximalist Versus Minimalist Approach", in *Journal of College Reading and Learning,* 1988, vol. 21.

"McPeck's Mistakes: Why Critical Thinking Applies Across Disciplines and Domains", originally appeared as, "McPeck's Mistakes", in *Informal Logic,* Winter, 1985.

"Bloom's Taxonomy and Critical Thinking Instruction: Recall is Not Knowledge", originally appeared as, "Bloom's Taxonomy and Critical Thinking Instruction", in *Educational Leadership,* May, 1985.

"Critical Thinking and General Semantics: On the Primacy of Natural Languages", was originally a talk entitled, "Critical Thinking and the Way We Construct the Meaning of Things", presented at the 36th Annual Alfred Korzybski Memorial Lecture, October 30, 1987.

"Philosophy and Cognitive Psychology: Contrasting Assumptions" and "The Contributions of Philosophy to Thinking", are forthcoming as one paper, "Critical and Reflective Thinking: A Philosophical Perspective", in *Dimensions of Thinking and Cognitive Instruction: Implications for Educational Reform,* Lawrence Erlbaum, 1990.

"Critical Thinking, Human Development, and Rational Productivity", originally appeared as, "Human Factors in Learning", in the *Proceeding of the 6th Annual Rupert N. Evans Symposium April 25–26, 1985,* 1985.

ISBN number: 0–944583–07–5

Library of Congress number: 90–80195

© 1990, 1992 Foundation for Critical Thinking

To *Edward Glaser*, friend and scholar,
whose foundational book,
<u>An Experiment in the Development of Critical Thinking</u> (1941),
laid the cornerstone for the critical thinking movement

Table of Contents

I: What Is Critical Thinking?

History and Overview

Intellectual Standards and Assessment: The Foundation for Critical Thought

Critical Thinking in the Strong Sense

The Affective and Ethical Dimension

II: How to Teach for It

Instruction

Staff Development

III: Grasping Connections—Seeing Contrasts

Contrasting Viewpoints

Critical Thinking and Academic Subjects

Appendix

✦✦ Acknowledgement

I would like to take this opportunity to thank Gerald Nosich for helping me to develop my thinking through many hours of dialogue. His ability to ask just the right question, put just the right objection, question just the right concept, call attention to just the right implication, introduce just the right distinction... has been a continual delight and wonder to me. He is living proof of the value of a genuinely critical mind in creative production. His analytic philosophical skills never created an impasse, but always were a stimulus to my thought. My thinking did not bog down but rather flourished in the face of his independent thought. Furthermore, writing papers together proved to be as successful as sharing ideas on independent papers. By mutually critiquing each other's ideas in a spirit of openness, we were able to work amicably and productively. His year in residence at the Center for Critical Thinking has proven to be invaluable.

✦✦ Foreword

Although the papers included in this volume have been written at different times and for a variety of occasions, they have a unity that explains their collection into a single book. All have been written with the express purpose of persuading educators and others concerned with education of the need to place critical thinking at the heart of educational reform. They represent a point of view too often at the periphery of the discussion of what is wrong with education. Their scope reflects something of the breadth with which critical thinking ought to be conceived.

Of course, this book in no way contains the last word on critical thinking. Indeed, it is merely one of many opening salvos in a field just now beginning to emerge. In the future the field will draw, as it is just now beginning to do, illuminating contributions from sociologists, anthropologists, historians, economists, scientists, and mathematicians, as well as from psychologists and philosophers, who now dominate the field. Critical thinking will be the first field in intellectual history, I believe, that crosses fields at the same time that it draws its contributing scholars from the very fields it crosses. As such it will, I hope, provide for the intellectual perspective and synthesis so typically and significantly absent today from both education, its theory and practice, and research generally, irrespective of the field in which it is conducted.

Perceptive readers may discern in these papers many influences including but not limited to Plato, Aristotle, Aquinas, Bacon, Descartes, Tom Paine, Jefferson, John Stuart Mill, John Henry Newman, Freud, Marx, Thoreau, Max Weber, William Graham Sumner, Piaget, John Dewey, C. Wright Mills, Erving Goffman, Bertrand Russell, Wittgenstein, John Wisdom, Gilbert Ryle, and J. L. Austin. Certainly there is no idea in it that does not have many historical predecessors. Nevertheless, it seems to me that a rich appreciation of what it would take to cultivate fairminded critical persons in fairminded critical societies is just now beginning to form. I hope this book contributes to this raw beginning.

✦✦ Forward to Second Edition

I am gratified by the speed with which the first edition of *Critical Thinking* sold out. This is a tribute, in my view, not to the manner in which the first edition was written — for the various chapters were written for different audiences and occasions and quickly assembled — but rather to the growing recognition that we as a society need to get clear about what critical thinking is in order to incorporate its power into everyday learning and decision-making. We increasingly recognize that rote memorization is as obsolete as a mode of academic learning as uncritical problem-solving is as a means of mastering the challenges of everyday life.

The first edition was rushed into print because of demand for a comprehensive volume, and the second edition is following it at the same pace and for the same reason. I regret I do not have time to recast the text as a whole into one continuous argument which progressively moves, in logical stages, through each domain that the various chapters represent. I therefore leave some of the overlapping and criss-crossing of the first edition intact. The reader will still experience some redundancy. Yet I am not disconsolate, for I am still convinced that there is one significant advantage to preserving some of the criss-crossing and redundancy. And I shall express that advantage in a moment, but only after I set out the ways in which the second edition is new.

The second edition is different from the first in the following ways:

1) Some of the redundancy has been reduced by eliminating five of the papers which most significantly overlapped the remaining papers.

2) An essay on the relation between critical and creative thinking has been added, as well as an interview which I did for *Think* magazine.

3) Most important of all, a new section has been added entitled, "Intellectual Standards and Assessment: The Foundation for Critical Thought." Three new papers are included in this section: "A Model for the National Assessment of Higher Order Thinking", "Using Intellectual Standards to Assess Student Reasoning", and "Why Students — and Teachers — Don't Reason Well". The first paper provides a detailed model and justification for an approach to the assessment of higher order thinking and was written at the request of the U.S. Department of Education. The second provides an analysis of the interface between the most basic elements of reasoning (purpose, question at issue, information, conclusion, reasons, concepts, assumptions, implications, and point of view) and the fundamental intellectual criteria (clarity, accuracy,

precision, relevance, consistency, depth, breadth,...), with special attention to the appropriate way to give students feedback on their reasoning. The third paper provides an analysis of the role of reasoning in figuring out the logic of things and includes the research findings and a variety of examples that demonstrate the problems that both students and teachers face in the development and assessment of reasoning.

4) A new paper entitled, "The Art of Redesigning Instruction" is added to the section on how to teach for critical thinking. The paper provides a detailed philosophy of redesign and includes some detailed examples to go along with the theory. It introduces the concept of a critical thinking "move" analogous to "moves" that a basketball or chess player might make, or even those of a ballet dancer. It explains how, whenever there is a domain of interrelated skills and abilities, there are also three variables at work: broad principles, skilled moves, and appropriate standards.

Like the first edition, the book is constructed with the view that the concept of critical thinking is not easily grasped, at least not in a way that admits to its practical mastery. It is because of the deceptiveness of our inner sense that we already understand critical thinking that we require an introduction to it that comes at it from many different angles and gives us, through that process, a healthy respect for its complexities. After all, the basic concept of critical thinking and the fundamental concepts that underlie it are intimately related to every human condition under which the mind attempts to grasp, or believes it does grasp, the logic of something. The conceptual framework that underlies critical thinking requires a rich rather than a parsimonious introduction. One has to live with, and slowly reason through, its myriad implications and connections. These are not internalized quickly as the result of one swift reading of a logically tight argument. Some redundancy, some overlapping is to the good.

Furthermore, since we have all subconsciously internalized some of the popular, if incoherent, ideologies of the day, such as, for example, the notion that all knowledge is a subjective social construct or that the natural languages we speak (German, French, English...) are largely a reflection of social ideologies; or that all language users have their own definitions for every word they use; or that language in itself — rather than some one particular person's use of it on some particular occasion — is vague; or that all intellectual criteria are relative to a specific domain of knowledge; or that there are no general, only domain-specific, abilities; or that intellectual standards are a reflection of gender, race, or ethnicity; or... or... — since we have all taken in some of these notions — it is clear that we will grasp only with difficulty the objective basis of critical thinking. These popular notions of the day stand as significant impediments to practical insight into the nature and dimensions of critical thinking. And, unfortunately, because we did not think our way into them, we must now laboriously and painfully think our way out of them. We must root them out now by intellectual labor as bothersome pre- suppositons, not as explicit constructions and conclusions, of our thought.

Furthermore, we live in an age in which intellectual discipline is rare and in which schooling and the media are as rich in trivial information as they are devoid, or virtually devoid, of reasoned discourse. We are simultaneously put upon by a multiplicity of cultural voices — not to mention an army of academ- ic and professional specialists — and left in ignorance of the tools that could make sense of that multiplicity. We are given no guide to a common ground or to common standards upon the basis of which we might form our judgment and build our vision. We are perplexed and unsure as to how to construct a comprehensive view that would enable us to gain perspective on diversity in culture, language, and knowledge, or worse, we blindly accept hollow models we have picked up from the platitudes, truisms, and arrogance of everyday clatter as substitutes for a well-reasoned, comprehensive view.

One major obstacle to the successful construction of that comprehensive view is a lack of understanding of the basis for intellectual criteria and stan- dards. What are the criteria we use in the everyday assessment of our own thought and that of others? Where did we get those criteria and the stan- dards we set by means of them? What intellectual criteria should we instead use and how can we justify them? These issues are, as I suggest above, more prominent in the second edition than they were in the first. However, they are treated in a way that will probably not satisfy everyone, for there is no attempt made to couch the analysis in the jargon of a particular discipline nor in the light of some traditional or specialized mode of argumentation. I am, almost always, more concerned to address those who think across multi- ple disciplinary lines than those who bury themselves within the boundaries, the jargon, and the presuppositions of one.

Educational Virtue:
Becoming a Critical Thinker

by Gerald Nosich

*W*hat Richard Paul presents us with in this book is a massive, and massively different, vision of what education should be. It is a vision fundamentally different not just from contemporary practice in our schools, but from our present-day educational ideal. The breadth of this vision, and the specific details of working it out, are what distinguishes Paul's book from other books either on education or on critical thinking. It does not just present us with a program for how our educational goals can be better achieved through critical thinking. It is not really a treatise on present educational practices and their inadequacy, nor is its aim primarily to get students and teachers to think better, more critically. To construe the book in any (or all) of these ways would be natural, but it would fail to get at the revolutionary nature of what Paul is proposing.

Even if our school system, from kindergarten up, were to turn out students who by *its* standards were ideal, by Paul's standards those students would not, except by accident, be well-educated. That is, they would not be critical thinkers. They would have acquired a great deal of knowledge (at least as measured by standardized achievement tests), a few skills, and even, if they happened to sign up for a reasoning course, an ability to do a slash-and-burn demolishing critique of positions they disagreed with. This is not the ideal product of the education Paul has in mind.

Many of us would be willing to settle for knowledgeable and skilled students, of course, but it is not really our choice. Our school system in fact turns out precious few of them, and not very many near facsimiles either. And the reason is partly that we have had the wrong goal in mind from the beginning; those students who have succeeded in becoming critical thinkers have done so in the teeth of the educational system — both practice *and* theory.

What then is a critical thinker for Paul? It is someone who is able to think well and fairmindedly not just about her own beliefs and viewpoints, but about beliefs and viewpoints that are diametrically opposed to her own. And not just to think about them, but to explore and appreciate their adequacy, their cohesion, their very reasonableness vis-a-vis her own. More, a person who thinks critically is not just willing and able to explore alien, potentially threatening viewpoints, but she also *desires* to do so. She questions her own deeply-held beliefs, and if there are no opposing viewpoints ready at hand, she seeks them out or constructs them herself.

Exploring opposing points of view is just one example — though an important one — of thinking critically, but notice that it involves far more than skills. It involves attitudes and passions as well. It is not just something you do in school and then go home and get on with your life. To the extent that a person acquires the skills, attitudes, and passions of a critical thinker, it will permeate her life. It is not the kind of complex that lends itself to compartmentalization.

Paul sums up this interlocking complex of skills, attitudes, passions (and more besides) in the phrase *critical thinking.* But it is important to see that *critical thinking,* in Paul's hands, is not exactly a species of thinking; rather it is a species of living. It is living, in Socrates' phrase, an examined life, a *deeply* examined life. To become a critical thinker is not, in the end, to be the same person you are now, only with better abilities; it is, in an important sense, to become a different person.

Take another attribute of being a critical thinker: the willingness to suspend judgement. Suppose someone asks you a question, and you don't know the answer. What should you reply? The obviously reasonable response is "I don't know." And that's probably the reasonable response even if the question is a deep one, or one that you have guesses about, or one that everyone has opinions on, or one that's in the news everyday. "Why is there so much more violent crime in the U.S. than in other countries?" Chances are, unless you've really investigated the issue, the only reasonable response is "I don't know" (or maybe, tenuously, "I don't know, but it could possibly be ...."). And that is not only the reasonable *external* response, but the internal one as well. You should *feel* ignorant.

Suspending judgment, in this case as well as in innumerable similar cases, is an awkward, uncomfortable, almost unnatural response. It is far more immediately satisfying to plump down for *some* answer, however unexamined. It is more gratifying to be unreasonable.

A critical thinker suspends judgment. How are we to clarify this? The willingness and ability to suspend judgment is not a skill or a passion exactly, though both of those are involved. It is closer to an attitude, but that doesn't really capture it either because it is the kind of attitude that exists only in concert with a host of other attitudes: humility enough to recognize that you don't know, self-confidence enough to assert it, morality enough to feel that there is something wrong in acting as if you know when you don't. It is part of a way of living your life, how you respond, think, feel about the issue, other people, you yourself. This is the kind of person that Paul wants education to try to produce.

For all the breadth of its educational ideal, this is not in the least a head-in-the-air book. It is far more a practical, down-to-earth exploration of the countless avenues involved in implementing the vision: how to set up a staff development program, the necessity of administrative participation, how to get students to discover "answers" themselves, how to promote socialization and dialogue among students, how to get students to relate subject matter to their own lives and to other courses, what kinds of questions to ask, even down to how to teach maps and charts in social studies. The book is far more a practical guide, though of an unusual kind, than it is an abstract or visionary treatise. Teachers can find concrete suggestions and techniques in practically every chapter.

The problem with practical guides generally is that you can become so involved with the details, so involved with, say, asking the right question, that you lose sight of the goal in mind, and your performance slides into a mechanical, uncritical one. That is especially easy to do with critical thinking, where the techniques or applications are often so intrinsically interesting that we can forget they are *merely* techniques and applications, never the end itself. What Paul does is to infuse the goals into every technique, every discussion, so that in the end, to the extent that the book has been useful to you, you will no longer need it. You will be actively engaged in critical thinking and so will be able to (and have the skills, passions, and attitudes to want to) come up with your own techniques and applications, which may well fit your situation better than Paul's do. That, I think, is very close to the guiding principle of the book: to get other people to do it better than he does.

The papers that constitute this volume have expanded the field into areas of inquiry where, just ten years ago, few people in critical thinking had ventured. And in broadening the field, Paul — more I think than any single individual — has helped to transform it, from an almost exclusive concentration on argument to the multifaceted enterprise it is today. Consider his list of critical thinking strategies. On page 307 he gives 35 such strategies, each followed by a brief explanation and application. Of these only the last seven (plus a few scattered earlier) are "traditional" strategies in teaching reasoning. Several of these are flexible enough to provide guidelines for teaching math, composition, literature, history, and other courses whose subject matter often has little to do with argumentation. Elsewhere in the book, Paul talks about topics as far-ranging as the structure of questioning, the "logic" of learning, critical approaches to viewing and sometimes changing one's life, personality, and culture.

Or, again, consider his elucidations of basic concepts (weak sense/strong sense, monological/multilogical, for example) or the straightforward introduction of moral categories into critical thinking. Moral concepts, of course, have *always* been implicit in critical thinking (even before there was a field so called), just as they have always lurked in the background of academic fields generally: there is *value* (and it is more than adventitious value) in being reasonable. But what Paul has done in these papers is to bring them out into the open, both as explicit goals to be striven for, and as objects of critical discussion. What *are* the values inherent in this "standard" history of the Renaissance? In our account of Jacobean drama? In this handbook of managerial techniques? Following Paul's guidelines, such questions would be nearly obligatory in any subject-matter course that teaches critical thinking.

Many of Paul's points, it should be noted, are controversial. It remains to be seen, for instance, whether the concept of *multilogical* can be worked out epistemologically, or how much weight should be given to the weak sense/ strong sense distinction.

Take the multilogical issue. The essence of the monological/multilogical distinction is that the logic of some questions, monological questions, allows only one correct answer, with a single or convergent logic of justification for it. (Think of the word problems at the end of the chapter in a physics text.) Multilogical questions, on the other hand, allow more than one rationally defensible answer, and the justifications for answers are frequently divergent. (Think of social or cultural problems, for example.) The controversy centers around whether there is ultimately a single, convergent, complete answer to the latter questions as well. The key word is "ultimately," for both sides in the controversy agree that we certainly do not, at present, have such answers, that there is little prospect for discovering them in the near future, and that we, humans, may in fact never actually discover them.

What is the controversy, then? It is whether there *is* such an answer, a *knowable* answer, regardless of whether it will ever in fact be known to us. Could there be, say, an ideal sociology which would answer all questions about human social behavior, and to which every reasonable person would assent? To this, Paul gives a qualified No, while others give (on metaphysical or epistemological grounds) a Yes.

The controversy is too complex and ambiguous to discuss further here, but what is clear is that even if Paul is mistaken on this epistemological question — and I for one grow less and less convinced that he *is* wrong — the perspectival view he is committed to is not a crude one. To maintain that there is not a single, convergent, complete answer to multilogical questions is not at all to say that one answer is as good as another; it is not to say that "it all depends on your point of view."

As Paul repeatedly insists, *rational* discussion — reasons, arguments, explorations of consequences and motives, crucial tests where possible — is the deciding factor. Critical thinking is never mere discussion: it is always reason-backed discussion. It is subjecting one's point of view to critical scrutiny (and perhaps refutation).

My own way of putting the point is that there is an asymmetry between true and false, or, if you like, between establishing *as* true and establishing *as* false. With multilogical questions, the total amount of evidence, plus interpretations, may leave us rationally unable to establish one of two viewpoints as true; but whether the question is monological *or* multilogical, considerations of evidence can and often do give us conclusively good reasons to reject some points of view as false, even points of view that are sincerely and deeply held. In such cases, intellectual integrity should compel the critical thinker to admit that her point of view was mistaken, false. The dodge to saying "Well, it's still my point of view" is just that — an intellectual dodge — and one that is certainly not sanctioned by Paul's concept of the multilogical.

A resolution of the epistemological controversy (were it not question-beg-ging, I would be tempted to say that issue too is multilogical) thus does not bear on the educational point at hand: our ignorance of the ultimate truth (perhaps invincible ignorance), together with considerations about the logic of discovery, dictates that we *teach* (and learn) multilogically, perspectivally. In that sense, the difference between math and physics on the one hand, and social studies on the other, may not be so much that the former are monologi-cal while the latter are multilogical; rather, the apparent differences may be the result of the amount of expertise and knowledge required before one reaches the multilogical threshold in a field. It takes a certain amount of knowledge and familiarity to discuss questions intelligently and critically, to entertain contrasting theories and follow out their consequences. We begin to collect information (or misinformation) about the human-related matters that are the topics of social studies by the time we start using language. A ten-year-old can rationally argue some (though not all) points of view about personal identity or the causes of crime: she has reached the multilogical threshold on the basis of "common knowledge" and reasoning skills. But even an upper-level undergraduate cannot typically engage in a similar level of informed rational discussion about the big-bang theory. Physics and math majors themselves are just beginning to acquire the familiarity — with quarks or singularities, or the rudiments of super-computer-generated math-ematical proofs — that will allow them, several years down the line, to get to the multilogical thresholds of those fields.

If this speculation is right, it meshes nicely with the techniques Paul details of teaching multilogical vs. monological subject matter in courses. The differing teaching techniques are grounded not in an inherent difference in the fields as such, but in the level at which students are operating. So though Paul *may* be wrong in some of what *may* be his epistemological assumptions (I emphasize *"may"*), in an educational sense I think he is right, even profoundly right.

Whether he is talking about such distinctions, or about educational theory or practice, or, for that matter, about how to teach parts of speech to a fourth-grad-er, one major impression Paul leaves is that the results often seem disconcert-ingly obvious. In that respect the conclusions in the book are like the conclu-sions of most good, careful, original thinking: the obviousness of them is patent — but only by hindsight. I find myself responding to a chapter I read yesterday: "But *obviously* those are the strategies I should use. Of *course* that's the goal I should have in mind when I teach" — when the truth is that as recently as the day before yesterday the question had not even occurred to me. (By tomorrow, it will have become so natural that I may no longer think of it as having originat-ed in Paul's book.) This reaction occurs because of what Paul has done through-out the book: guided us to think the questions out ourselves — so the results seem just as much a product of our own critical thinking as his.

Thus, more than anything, the book demonstrates the great versatility and fecundity of critical thinking itself. It is a guidebook, of both theory and practice, in two different senses. In the conventional sense, it guides us by

providing techniques and applications that are the product of Paul's expertise as a critical thinker. But it is also a guidebook in a very different sense
(the one, I think, that Paul primarily intends): it guides us along through the
argumentation and the thought processes to arrive at conclusions ourselves.

University of New Orleans, New Orleans
December 10, 1989

✦✦ Introduction

$\mathcal{B}$ ecause we do not come to our experience with a blank slate for a mind, because our thinking is already, at any given moment, moving in a direction, because we can form new ideas, beliefs, and patterns of thought only through the scaffolding of our previously formed thought, it is essential that we learn to think critically in environments in which a variety of competing ideas are taken seriously. There is no way around the need for minds to think their way to knowledge. Thought is the key to knowledge. Knowledge is discovered by thinking, analyzed by thinking, organized by thinking, transformed by thinking, assessed by thinking, and, most importantly, *acquired* by thinking. There is no way to take the thinking out of knowledge, or the struggle out of thinking, just as there no way to create a neat and tidy step-by-step path to knowledge that all minds can mindlessly follow.

If we want to learn science we must start to think scientifically; if we want to learn math we must start to think mathematically. It is scientific thinking that gains, mathematical thinking that gains, historical thinking that gains, scientific, mathematical, and historical knowledge. But thinking requires counter-thinking, opposition and challenge, as well as support. We need reasons meaningful to us, some persuasive logic, to move our minds from one set of ideas or beliefs to another. In other words, we must "argue" ourselves out of our present thinking and into thinking that is more or less novel to us if we are to gain genuine knowledge.

We need others, therefore, to help us in this "argument", to probe and question our thinking, to present their thinking as a contrast that enlivens and stimulates our's. When we talk as if knowledge could be divorced from thinking, and thinking divorced from struggle, something gathered up by one person and given to another in the form of a collection of sentences to remember, we distort the nature of knowledge and the conditions under which it is acquired. Knowledge is not to be confused with belief nor with those things, like printed texts or spoken lectures, which represent knowledge. Humans are quite capable of believing things that are false, or things that are true, without actually knowing them to be so. A book contains knowledge only in a derivative sense, only because minds can analytically and thoughtfully read it and through that active critical process, and only thus, gain knowledge. Opinion alone is available to the uncritical reader.

To this day we have refused to face these facts about knowledge, thought, and learning. To this day we commonly teach as if mere recall were equivalent to knowledge, and/or we foolishly assume critical thinking to be present when, typically, it is not. For example, we routinely assume critical thinking is available to anyone who, at any given moment, wills to use it. Hence parents, teachers, and other authorities regularly order those under their charge to "Think!" In fact, reading, writing, listening, and speaking can all be done critically or uncritically and it is only when done in a critical manner that any of these modes of communication become bona fide instruments of knowledge or truth.

The nature of thinking and the manner and conditions under which it can be disciplined to acquire knowledge is just one of many things about which we regularly deceive ourselves. In fact, as creatures in the world we humans are best defined not as "the rational" but as "the self-deceiving animal". We consistently deceive ourselves about the state of, the degree of, and the nature of our knowledge, our freedom, and our character. We are the only creatures whose life and activity, including much of our language usage, obscures and distorts who and what we are. Our fervent beliefs we confuse with knowledge or proof, our emotionally-held opinions with convictions, our stubbornness with determination, our judgmentalism with judgment, our point of view with reality. At the same time we confound fact and opinion, data and interpretation, evidence and conclusion, information and knowledge. And we do all this with ease, with skill if you will, both individually and collectively. Social life effortlessly and skillfully fosters collective illusions while personal life fosters individual ones.

Yet this is not how we perceive ourselves or the world. Verbal, even behavioral, commitments to the ideal of reasonability are pervasive in daily life. Virtually every human action is implied to be "reasonable"in context. When people act we expect them to be receptive to requests for reasons and we expect their responses to be themselves reasonable, to make logical sense of what they have done. At the same time whatever is commonly believed is taken by most to be self-evidently true. So when schools teach what is commonly believed, they are taken to be teaching the truth. If they were to teach what flies in the face of common belief, and they virtually never do, they would be taken to be biased or narrow. The result is that subjects like social studies become an undisciplined amalgam of what is so and what we wish were so (but is not). Having knowledge is reduced to believing what those around us believe. Being free is reduced to acting as we would *like* to act, which turns out suspiciously similar to acting as those around us act, which turns out amazingly like acting as we have been conditioned to act. The "real" options become the commonly believed options. The "right" choice the commonly believed choice. Thinking is reduced to responding, reasoning to psychological association. Hence, it is not surprising, should not be surprising, that all societies view themselves as committed to objectivity, reason and rational learning, while only a feeble minority in each culture recognize the rarity of these values and the presence of dominant forms of irrationality and collective self-delusion. For most, dissent fills them with amazement or mild to vehement disgust. For most, what would appear irrational to a rational person appears rational. The result in all cultures is self-perpetuating cycles of irrationality. Growth in authentic knowledge and freedom, growth in social justice and discipline of mind, are consistently impeded thereby.

Education, so called, is a classic example. No culture sees itself as indoctrinating its young or discouraging intellectual development. Each sees itself as concerned with education worthy of the name. The rhetoric of reason and objective learning is everywhere. Yet classroom instruction around the world, at all levels, is typically didactic, one-dimensional, and indifferent, when not antithetical, to reason. Blank faces are taught barren conclusions in dreary drills. There is nothing sharp, nothing poignant, no exciting twist or turn of mind and thought, nothing fearless, nothing modest, no struggle, no conflict, no rational give and take, no intellectual excitement or discipline, no pulsation in the heart or mind. Students are not expected to ask for reasons to justify what is presented to them for belief. They do not question what they see, hear, or read, nor are they encouraged to do so. They do not demand that subject matter "make sense" to them. They do not challenge the thinking of other students nor expect their thinking to be challenged by others. Indeed, they do not expect to have to think at all. They mechanically repeat back what they were told, or what they think they were told, with little sense of the logicalness or illogicalness of what they are saying. Education for most is drab, empty, passive, and sluggish, a mass of permissions, rules, sanctions, and authorizations. And, if truth be told, educators are not typically disturbed by these facts. Indeed, they are disturbingly comfortable with them. Equally undisturbing is the fact that what teachers teach very often does not even make logical sense to the teachers themselves. Typically they cannot explain the logic of their own subject matter except at a superficial level. Very often they did not, when they were students, question what was presented to them for belief. Very often their own academic learning was heavily dependent, as it is now for their students, on rote memorization and superficial recall. Though not yet common, some few teachers are making this discovery:

> After I started teaching, I realized that I had learned physics by rote and that I really did not understand all I thought I knew about it. My thinking students asked me questions for which I always had the standard textbook answers, but for the first time it made me start thinking for myself, and I realized that these canned answers were not justified by my own thinking and only confused my students who were showing some ability to think for themselves. To achieve my academic goals I had to memorize the thoughts of others, but I had never learned or been encouraged to learn to think for myself.

It is not for nothing that the meaning of the word 'docile' has gone from its original meaning of 'teachable' to its present, ironic, meaning of "passive, lacking initiative, easily managed". Teaching has historically cultivated, and continues to this day to cultivate, intellectual deficiencies in the name of knowledge and skill. As early as the 17th Century, insightful commentators began to think along the lines of, though not necessarily as vehemently as Commenius, who summed up the schools of his day as "the slaughter house of the mind". Genuine knowledge is not gained, and the capacity for freedom is stunted, in the wearisome, the tedious, the humdrum environment that exists in most schools today.

Social and personal prejudice is another classic example. At the level of public discourse everyone is opposed to prejudice. Publically we scorn and ridicule it. As a practical matter, however, we show little interest in understanding or eradicating it, and more often than not we react to anyone who disagrees with us as if they, simply because they do not share our view, are prejudiced. At the same time we routinely assume our own views to be true and unprejudiced. No social group in any culture has yet made a real commitment to eradicate its own prejudices precisely because no social group thinks of itself in action as acting on prejudices. The common general admission to being prejudiced is merely a matter of lip service, of saying what one is expected to say, a misleading facade, a mere mask of social humility. Hence, when the newspapers of every country of the world selectively record and interpret events to square with the world view and prejudices of their own culture, the readers, whose world views and prejudices are presupposed as self-evident facts, do not object. People are apparently opposed only to the prejudices of others against them, not to their own prejudices against others. To put the point briefly, in schools around the world, and in the broader societies whose orientation they routinely and uncritically reflect, issues and events, which to be approached fairly must be approached from many points of view, are one-sidedly analyzed and answered within one, or at most two, socially dominant point(s) of view. Prejudiced conclusions are taken to be knowledge based on insight, and a mode of pseudo freedom results as people define only those options as reasonable which square with preconceived beliefs. "Free" choice, manipulated choice, and prejudiced choice, become one and the same phenomenon.

Educational reform focused on explicit consciousness of the comprehensive need for fairminded critical thinking offers hope for the gradual elevation of human life and practice from the irrational to the rational. Only if we raise children to think critically, as a matter of course, about their use of language, the information they take in, the nature of propaganda which surrounds them, the multiple prejudices assumed to be self-evident truths; only if we educate children to probe the logical structure of thought, to test proposed knowledge against experience, to scrutinize experience from alternative perspectives; only if we reward those who think for themselves, who display intellectual courage, humility, and faith in reason; only then do we have a fighting chance that children will eventually become free and morally responsible adults and hence help eventually to create, through their example and commitments, genuinely free and moral societies.

Knowledge, freedom and morality are not gifts that can be casually passed on from generation to generation. They must each be achieved, created, won, person by person, society by society. Even to this day robust freedom and morality are still largely unachieved human ideals. Their future realization depends on a deeper, more realistic commitment to what has not yet been significantly cultivated: societies that genuinely value fairminded thought and just action.

Finally, the ideal of rationality and fairminded critical thought is essential to global social and economic development and prosperity. Irrational productivity is a major problem in the global village. Rational productivity is not a matter of manufacturing more and more stuff to accumulate or consume. It is a matter, ultimately, of serving human good and preserving a precarious environment. The standards for assessing the utility of production are changing at an accelerating rate and increasingly require critical re-examination. We can no longer afford the kind of schooling that at best transforms students into narrow specialists and at worst leaves them without job skills, functional literacy, or self-confidence.

The conditions for and the nature of productivity are not things-in-themselves, but products of multitudes of human decisions embodied in human life and behavior. But again, the human world we have created has been created so far with a minimum of self-directed critical thought, a minimum of public rationality. We are always to some extent acting in ways that negate human good, that undermine our own long-range best interest. In the West, the tensions between democracy, unbridled capitalism, and the public good have not yet been faced. In the East, the tensions between democratization, capitalism, nationalism, ethnicity, and new versions of socialism are just now beginning to be faced. Both East and West, not to mention the underdeveloped world, desperately need a more genuinely educated, more well-informed, more cosmopolitan, more rational, citizenry. Economic life cannot be separated from political, social, and personal life. Each and every dimension of life has implications for the quality of life of every other dimension.

Harnessing social and economic forces to serve the public good and the good of the biosphere while encouraging and rewarding individual initiative requires mass publics around the world skilled in cooperative, fairminded, critical discourse. Such publics do not yet exist, except in embryo. Their cultivation has not yet been taken seriously by any culture.

For all of these reasons it is essential that we foster a new conception of self-identity, both individually and collectively, and a new practical sense of the value of self-disciplined, openminded thought. As long as we continue to feel threatened by those who think differently from us, we will listen seriously only to those who start from our premises, who validate our prejudices, and end up with our conclusions. We will continue to stereotype, to distort — in order to reject — what the "others", the "outsiders", say. We must learn, in other words, something quite new to us: to identify not with the content of our beliefs but with the process by which we arrived at them. We must come to define ourselves, and actually respond in everyday contexts, as people who reason their way into, and can be reasoned out of, beliefs. Only then will we feel unthreatened when others question our beliefs, only then will we welcome their questions as a reminder of the need to be ready to test and re-test our beliefs daily at the bar of reason, only then will we learn to think within multiple points of view, with a sense of global perspective.

Perhaps the glasnost that Gorbachev has tried to bring to the Soviet Union, openly inviting criticism that questions the dominant viewpoint and practices of Soviet society, welcoming changes that transform social arrangements and the structure of power, can eventually become a world-wide educational and social phenomenon. The notion that this openness is now widespread in any culture is, of course, an illusion. In the Soviet Union, as everywhere else, the nature and success of such a process depends on the rationality of the public discourse that ensues. Free and informed discussion does not result simply because those in power say "Let it be!". In every country of the world, conformity to the thinking of the dominant social group is still heavily rewarded; autonomous thought, especially when it questions dominant beliefs and practices, is still routinely penalized.

The problem of knowledge, freedom, and productivity requires that we, for the first time in our history, take true intellectual discipline and the "fitness" of our minds seriously. We must create new conditions in school and society under which intellectual virtues long ignored — - intellectual courage, intellectual humility, intellectual perseverance, intellectual integrity, faith in reason, and fairmindedness — can develop. We must learn to be comfortable with, indeed to value, for the first time, rational self-criticism. We must, for the first time, begin to devote as much time to intellectual habits as we now do to physical ones., and admit, finally, that rationality and openness of mind are not automatic or "natural" states that can be left to themselves to emerge and flourish. To begin to do this, we must reconceptualize the nature of teaching and learning in every context of life.

In short, knowledge, freedom, and social progress are deeply intertwined. Education has a crucial role to play in fostering these critical values. Yet, though there is growing insight into the nature of this role and the importance of the task it represents, and though the pressure for change in this direction is growing progressively, we should harbor no illusions about the nature of the task ahead. Only through slow, painful change, with much frustration and circling about, only with multiple misunderstandings and confusion, will we work our way, eventually, into rational lives in rational societies.

RICHARD. W. PAUL

Center for Critical Thinking and Moral Critique, Rohnert Park
February 14, 1990

Part I:

What Is Critical Thinking?

History and Overview

✦✦ Chapter 1

The Critical Thinking Movement in Historical Perspective

Abstract

In this paper, originally published in National Forum (1985), Richard Paul discusses the history of education in the United States from the standpoint of critical thinking. He stresses the traditional U.S. emphasis, evident from the earliest days of education, on passive learning, training, and indoctrination. He begins with a characterization of 17th century attitudes and then traces the dominant view of education from initial European settlers to 20th Century critiques of education.

*T*he "critical thinking movement" is beginning to have a palpable effect on the day-to-day life of American schooling. California is a bellwether in this regard. Four years ago, the massive 19-campus California State University system instituted a graduation requirement in critical thinking intended to achieve:

> ... an understanding of the relationship of language to logic, leading to the ability to analyze, criticize, and advocate ideas, to reason inductively and deductively, and to reach factual or judgmental conclusions based on sound inferences drawn from unambiguous statements of knowledge or belief.

Within two years the even larger community college system established a parallel requirement. And now, two years further down the line, the California State Department of Education is preparing to test all 8th grade students in three areas: reading and written expression, math, and social studies. Remarkably, and representing a strikingly new testing emphasis, approximately one-third of the items were designed to test critical thinking skills. David Gordon, California's Associate Superintendent of Public Instruction, recently said that he considered the state at the very beginning of a series of reforms in this direction, including textbooks, curriculum, staff development, and teacher education.

Until recently the movement was no more than a small scattered group of educators calling for a shift from a didactic paradigm of knowledge and learning to a Socratic, critically-reflective one. It's early stirrings can be traced back to and beyond Edward Glaser's *An Experiment in the Development of Critical Thinking* (1941) and his development with Watson of the *Watson-Glaser Critical Thinking Appraisal* (1940).

Of course, its deepest intellectual roots are ancient, traceable to the teaching practice and vision of Socrates 2,400 ago who discovered by a method of probing questioning that people could not rationally justify their confident claims to knowledge. Confused meanings, inadequate evidence, or self-contradictory beliefs often lurked beneath smooth but largely empty rhetoric. Since his time, Socrates' insight has been variously articulated by a scattering of intellectuals, certainly by the 18th, and increasingly in the 19th and 20th Centuries; Voltaire, John Henry Newman, John Stuart Mill, and William Graham Sumner are a few that come readily to mind. Consider Mill:

> ... since the general or prevailing opinion on any object is rarely or never the whole truth, it is only by the collision of adverse opinions that the remainder of the truth has any chance of being supplied. (*On Liberty,* 1859)

Or Newman:

> ... knowledge is not a mere extrinsic or accidental advantage, ... which may be got up from a book, and easily forgotten again, ... which we can borrow for the occasion, and carry about in our hand ... (it is) something intellectual ... which reasons upon what it sees ... the action of a formative power ... making the objects of our knowledge subjectively our own. (*Idea of A University,* 1852)

Or Sumner:

> The critical habit of thought, if usual in a society, will pervade all its mores, because it is a way of taking up the problems of life. People educated in it cannot be stampeded by stump orators and are never deceived by dithyrambic oratory. They are slow to believe. They can hold things as possible or probable in all degrees, without certainty and without pain. They can wait for evidence and weigh evidence, uninfluenced by the emphasis and confidence with which assertions are made on one side or the other. They can resist appeals to their dearest prejudices and all kinds of cajolery. Education in the critical faculty is the only education of which it can be truly said that it makes good citizens. (*Folkways,* 1906)

This view of knowledge and learning holds that beliefs without reason and the judgment of the learner behind them are for that learner mere prejudices, and that critical reflection on the part of each and every learner is an essential precondition of knowledge and of rational action. Until now this view has made little headway against a deeply if unconsciously held contrary mind-set. The everyday world — especially in the U.S.A. where the agenda has been filled with one pragmatic imperative after another, a nation with a "mission" to perform and a "destiny" to fulfill — provides little time for self-formed, self-reasoned beliefs.

Let us not forget that schools in the U.S. were established precisely to transmit by inculcation self-evident true beliefs conducive to right conduct and successful "industry". The best seller of 17th Century North America was Michael Wigglesworth's *Day of Doom,* a detailed description of the terrifying fate of condemned sinners. To question this fate was heresy. In 1671, governor Sir William Berkeley of Virginia could say with pride:

> ... there are no free schools, nor printing in Virginia, for learning has brought disobedience, and heresy ... into the world, and printing has divulged them .... God keep us from both!

"Free schools" were set up, as in Massachusetts (1647), "to teach all children to read and write ... (to combat) that old deluder Satan," or, (1675) to ensure that "children and servants" are "catechized". In Plymouth Colony (1671) "Education of Children" was mandated because "Children and Servants" were " ... in danger (of) growing Barbarous, Rude, or Stubborn" and hence were becoming "pests". This was hardly the climate in which analytic thinking and critical questioning could thrive. All questioning began and ended with a *"Nil desperandum, Christo duce."* (Don't despair, Christ is leading us.) This sense of having a mission or mandate from God has discouraged self-reflective questioning. At times it has generated arrogant self-delusion.

As late as 1840, U.S. schools taught the ordinary students nothing but the three R's, some basic catechism, and a smattering of patriotic history. The school term was short and attendance irregular. In 1800, for example, the average American attended school only 82 days out of their entire lives. By 1840 it had increased to only 208 days.

When the time in school increased, it was not because of a demand for critical thinking but for better reading and writing, skills increasingly necessary in the commercial and industrial activities of the day. To get a sense of the quality of reading instruction, one need only hear the assessment of Horace Mann:

> I have devoted especial pains to learn, with some degree of numerical accuracy, how far the reading, in our schools, is an exercise of the mind in thinking and feeling and how far it is a barren action of the organs of speech upon the atmosphere. My information is derived principally from the written statements of the school committees of the respective towns — gentlemen who are certainly exempt from all temptation to disparage the schools they superintend. The result is that more than 11/12ᵗʰs of all the children in the reading classes do not understand the meanings of the words they read; and that the ideas and feelings intended by the author to be conveyed to, and excited in, the reader's mind, still rest in the author's intention, never having yet reached the place of their destination. (Second report to the Massachusetts Board of Education, 1838.)

The increasing use of machinery, the rapid expansion of transportation, and the new waves of non-Anglo-Saxon immigrants, not a change in the basic U.S. mind set, were the main causes of expansion of schooling. For a long time the McGuffy readers, with their parables about the terrific fate of those who gave in to sloth, drunkenness, or wastefulness were as close as the average student got to reflective thinking. Of course, if they wanted, students could cogitate on their own on the higher level questions implicit in this passage:

> Remember, that time is money, ... that credit is money ... that money is of the prolific, generating nature, that six pounds a year is but a groat a day ... that the good paymaster is lord of another man's purse. (Ben Franklin, 1770.)

In 1860 the average North American spent little more than a year in school, and by 1900 spent little more than 2 years. In 1880, 17 percent of the population still could not read or write. Increasingly in this time period the question of empire was before the public and the electorate was expected to decide, for example, whether or not it was justifiable to "rule a people without their consent". Those, like Senator Beveridge, who favored imperialism, as did the majority of voters, easily formulated a logic whose fallaciousness was not penetrated by the voting majority:

> The opposition tells us that we ought not to govern a people without their consent. I answer: The rule of liberty, that all just government derives its authority from the consent of the governed, applies only to those who are capable of self-government. I answer: We govern the Indians without their consent, we govern our territories without their consent, we govern our children without their consent .... Shall we save them ... to give them a self-rule of tragedy? It would be like giving a razor to a babe and telling it to shave itself. It would be like giving a typewriter to an Eskimo and telling him to publish one of the great dailies of the world. (U.S. Senator Albert Beveridge, 1899.)

Senator Beveridge could link, without fear of significant dissent from an electorate of thinking people, the voice of liberty, Christ's gospel, and our profit:

> Ah! as our commerce spreads, the flag of liberty will circle the globe and the highways of the ocean — carrying trade to all mankind — will be guarded by the guns of the republic. And, as their thunders salute the flag, benighted peoples will know that the voice of liberty is speaking, at last for them; that civilization is dawning, at last, for them, — liberty and civilization, those children of Christ's gospel, who follow and never precede the preparing march of commerce. It is the tide of God's great purposes made manifest in the instincts of our race, whose present phase is our personal profit, but whose far-off end is the redemption of the world and the Christianization of mankind.

It should be no surprise therefore that William Graham Sumner, one of the founding fathers of anthropology, was appalled by the manner in which history was taught and the level of uncritical thinking that followed it:

> The examination papers show the pet ideas of the examiners .... An orthodoxy is produced in regard to all the great doctrines of life. It consists in the most worn and commonplace opinions .... It is intensely provincial and philistine ... (containing) broad fallacies, half-truths, and glib generalizations. (We are given) ... orthodox history ... (so) ... that children shall be taught just that one thing which is "right" in the view and interest of those in control and nothing else .... "Patriotic" history ... never can train children to criticism. (*Folkways*, 1906)

Higher education was little better. It began in the 17th and 18th centuries in primarily upper class "seminaries", providing a classical education though not, of course, in the Socratic sense. Students were drilled in Latin and Greek and Theology. Inculcation, memorization, repetition, and forensic display were the order of the day. Not until the latter half of the 19th Century was higher education possible for someone not in the upper class, and then only at the new Land Grant Colleges (150 new colleges opened between 1880 and 1900), established to promote "education of the industrial classes in the several pursuits and professions in life". Their emphasis was "agriculture and the mechanic arts". Students graduated with an agricultural, commercial, technical, industrial, scientific, professional, or theological focus. Higher education turned out graduates fit to enter farms, businesses, professions, or the clergy. Their "civic" education was not fundamentally liberal but nationalistic, not fundamentally emancipatory but provincial.

The history of teaching fits into this picture like a perfectly carved puzzle piece. In the early days teachers were selected from those who had no other job and could read, write, and cipher. From the start teaching was a low prestige, low paying job. Normal schools did not begin springing up until after 1830, and then their curriculum mainly consisted of a review of the subjects taught in elementary school, such as reading, writing, arithmetic, and spelling. Eventually, and in the spirit of industrialism, science, and technology, education — still conceived fully within the traditional U.S. world view — came to be considered, and is still largely considered, a "science" of methods of "delivery". At no point along the way, even to this day, were, or are, prospective teachers expected to demonstrate their ability to lead a discussion Socratically, so that, for example, students explore the evidence that can be advanced for or against their beliefs, note the assumptions upon which they are based, their implications for, or consistency with, other espoused beliefs. Neither were, or are, they expected to demonstrate ability to think analytically or critically about the issues of the day. The state of affairs (circa 1920-35) is satirically suggested by H. L. Mencken:

> The art of pedagogics becomes a sort of puerile magic, a thing of preposterous secrets, a grotesque compound of false premises and illogical conclusions. Every year sees a craze for some new solution of the teaching enigma, an endless series of flamboyant arcana. The worst extravagances of *private dozent* experimental psychology are gravely seized upon; the uplift pours in its ineffable principles and discoveries; mathematical formulae are marked out for every emergency; there is no sure-cure so idiotic that some superintendent of schools will not swallow it. The aim seems to be to reduce the whole teaching process to a sort of automatic reaction, to discover some master formula that will not only take the place of competence and resourcefulness in the teacher but that will also create an artificial receptivity in the child. Teaching becomes a thing in itself, separable from and superior to the thing taught. Its mastery is a special business, a sort of transcendental high jumping. A teacher well grounded in it can teach anything to any child, just as a sound dentist can pull any tooth out of any jaw. (Baltimore Sun, 1923)

One final sobering thought. When, between 1917 and 1934, inductees into the armed forces were systematically tested using the *Army Alpha Tests* (an I.Q. test based on the Stanford Benet) it was estimated that the average U.S. citizen was probably somewhere between 13 or 14 years of age intellectually —

the same intellectual age to which, I understand, most present day T.V. programming is geared. Can we conclude then that most North Americans are intellectually incapable of rising above childish reasoning, or should we rather hypothesize that as a nation both socially and scholastically we have not yet challenged most people to think for themselves beyond the most primitive levels? Are we, and if so will we remain, what William J. Lederer characterized us as being in the 1960's, *A Nation of Sheep?* If Boyer, Sizer, Adler, Bloom and others are right, if the Rockefeller Commission on the Humanities, the International Educational Achievement Studies, the College Board, The Education Commission of the States, the National Assessment of Educational Progress, and the Association of American Medical Colleges are right, then our overemphasis on "rote memorization and recall of facts" does not serve us well. We must exchange our traditional picture of knowledge and learning for one that generates and rewards "active, independent, self-directed learning" so that students can "gather and assess data rigorously and critically". We need to abandon "methods that make students passive recipients of information" and adopt those that transform them into "active participants in their own intellectual growth". Perhaps some old-fashioned intellectuals like Emerson Shideler had *something* of practical value to say after all:

> Education is training in *how* to think rather than in *what* to think; it is a confrontation, a dialogue between ways of assessing evidence and supporting conclusions. It implies that the teacher's primary job is that of making clear the bases upon which he weighs the facts, the methods by which he separates facts from fancies, and the ways in which he discovers and selects his ultimate norms .... This concept of teaching ... requires that the purported facts be accompanied by the reasons why they are considered the facts. Thereby the teacher exposes his methods of reasoning to test and change. If the facts are in dispute ... then the reasons why others do not consider them to be facts must also be presented, thus bringing alternative ways of thinking and believing into dialogue with each other.

Perhaps we, as most people, are constitutionally incapable of learning a lesson until its point becomes a long-drawn-out and painful imperative. But isn't nearly 400 years of "mis-education" imperative enough? Aren't we threatened enough on all sides by prejudice, parochialism, egocentricity, self-righteous ignorance, and an overabundance of miscellaneous gobbledygook and humbug, to consider investing for the first time in our history in the critical faculties of our citizens and in their potential as rational, autonomous thinkers and doers? If I read the signs correctly (including a mass of scathing educational reports), then finally, the time has come. If so, we should think of it, in the spirit of Churchill's oft-quoted remark: "Now this is not the end. It is not even the beginning of the end. But it is, perhaps, the end of the beginning."

✦✦ Chapter 2

Critical Thinking: Basic Questions and Answers

Abstract

In this interview for Think *magazine (April '92), Richard Paul provides a quick overview of critical thinking and the issues surrounding it: defining it, common mistakes in assessing it, its relation to communication skills, self-esteem, collaborative learning, motivation, curiosity, job skills for the future, national standards, and assessment strategies.*

Question: Critical thinking is essential to effective learning and productive living. Would you share your definition of critical thinking?

Paul: First, since critical thinking can be defined in a number of different ways consistent with each other, we should not put a lot of weight on any one definition. Definitions are at best scaffolding for the mind. With this qualification in mind, here is a bit of scaffolding: critical thinking is thinking about your thinking while you're thinking in order to make your thinking better. Two things are crucial: 1) critical thinking is not just thinking, but thinking which entails self-improvement and 2) this improvement comes from skill in using standards by which one appropriately assesses thinking. To put it briefly, it is self-improvement (in thinking) through standards (that assess thinking).

To think well is to impose discipline and restraint on our thinking — by means of intellectual standards — in order to raise our thinking to a level of "perfection" or quality that is not natural or likely in undisciplined, spontaneous thought. The dimension of critical thinking least understood is that of intellectual standards. Most teachers were not taught how to assess thinking through standards; indeed, often the thinking of teachers themselves is very "undisciplined" and reflects a lack of internalized intellectual standards.

Question: Could you give me an example?

Paul: Certainly, one of the most important distinctions that teachers need to routinely make, and which takes disciplined thinking to make, is that between reasoning and subjective reaction. If we are trying to foster quality thinking, we don't want students simply to assert things; we want them

7

to try to reason things out on the basis of evidence and good reasons. Often, teachers are unclear about this basic difference. Many teachers are apt to take student writing or speech which is fluent and witty or glib and amusing as good thinking. They are often unclear about the constituents of good reasoning. Hence, even though a student may just be asserting things, not reasoning things out at all, if she is doing so with vivacity and flamboyance, teachers are apt to take this to be equivalent to good reasoning. This was made clear in a recent California state-wide writing assessment in which teachers and testers applauded a student essay, which they said illustrated "exceptional achievement" in reasoned evaluation, an essay that contained no reasoning at all, that was nothing more than one subjective reaction after another.

The assessing teachers and testers did not notice that the student failed to respond to the directions, did not support his judgment with reasons and evidence, did not consider possible criteria on which to base his judgment, did not analyze the subject in the light of the criteria, and did not select evidence that clearly supported his judgment. Instead the student *1)* described an emotional exchange, *2)* asserted — without evidence — some questionable claims, and *3)* expressed a variety of subjective preferences. The assessing teachers were apparently not clear enough about the nature of evaluative reasoning or the basic notions of criteria, evidence, reasons, and well-supported judgment to notice the discrepancy. The result was, by the way, that a flagrantly mis-graded student essay was showcased nationally (in ASCD's *Developing Minds*), systematically misleading the 150,000 or so teachers who read the publication.

Question: Could this possibly be a rare mistake, not representative of teacher knowledge?

Paul: I don't think so. Let me suggest a way in which you could begin to test my contention. If you are familiar with any thinking skills programs, ask someone knowledgeable about it the "Where's the beef?" question, namely, "What intellectual standards does the program articulate and teach?" I think you will first find that the person is puzzled about what you mean. And then when you explain what you mean, I think you will find that the person is not able to articulate any such standards. Thinking skills programs without intellectual standards are tailor-made for mis-instruction. For example, one of the major programs asks teachers to encourage students to make inferences and use analogies, but is silent about how to teach students to *assess* the inferences they make and the strengths and weaknesses of the analogies they use. This misses the point. The idea is not to help students to make *more* inferences but to make *sound* ones, not to help students to come up with *more* analogies but with more *useful* and *insightful* ones.

Question: What is the solution to this problem? How, as a practical matter, can we solve it?

Paul: Well, not with more gimmicks or quick-fixes. Not with more fluff for teachers. Only with quality long-term staff development that helps the teachers, over an extended period of time, over years not months, to work on their own thinking and come to terms with what intellectual standards are, why they are essential, and how to teach for them. The city of Greensboro, North Carolina has just such a long-term, quality, critical thinking program. [See Chapter 28, "The Greensboro Plan: A Sample Staff Development Plan".] So that's one model your readers might look at. In addition, there is a new national organization, the National Council for Excellence in Critical Thinking Instruction, that is focused precisely on the articulation of standards for thinking, not just in general, but for every academic subject area. It is now setting up research-based committees and regional offices to disseminate its recommendations. I am hopeful that eventually, through efforts such as these, we can move from the superficial to the substantial in fostering quality student thinking. The present level of instruction for thinking is very low indeed.

Question: But there are many areas of concern in instruction, not just one, not just critical thinking, but communication skills, problem solving, creative thinking, collaborative learning, self-esteem, and so forth. How are districts to deal with the full array of needs? How are they to do all of these rather than simply one, no matter how important that one may be?

Paul: This is the key. Everything essential to education supports everything else essential to education. It is only when good things in education are viewed superficially and wrongly that they seem disconnected, a bunch of separate goals, a conglomeration of separate problems, like so many bee-bees in a bag. In fact, any well-conceived program in critical thinking requires the integration of all of the skills and abilities you mentioned above. Hence, critical thinking is not a set of skills separable from excellence in communication, problem solving, creative thinking, or collaborative learning, nor is it indifferent to one's sense of self-worth.

Question: Could you explain briefly why this is so?

Paul: Consider critical thinking first. We think critically when we have at least one problem to solve. One is not doing good critical thinking, therefore, if one is not solving any problems. If there is no problem there is no point in thinking critically. The "opposite" is also true. Uncritical problem solving is unintelligible. There is no way to effectively solve problems unless one thinks critically about the nature of the problems and of how to go about solving them. Thinking our way through a problem to a solution, then, is critical thinking, not something else. Furthermore, critical thinking, because it involves our working out afresh our own thinking on a subject, and because our own thinking is always a unique product of our self-structured experience, ideas, and reasoning, is intrinsically a new "creation", a new "making", a new set of cognitive and affective structures of some kind. All thinking, in short, is a creation of the mind's work, and when it is disciplined so as to be well-integrated into our experience, it is a new creation precisely because of the inevitable novelty of that integration. And when it helps us to solve problems that we could not solve before, it is surely properly called "creative".

The "making" and the "testing of that making" are intimately interconnected. In critical thinking we make and shape ideas and experiences so that they may be used to structure and solve problems, frame decisions, and, as the case may be, effectively communicate with others. The making, shaping, testing, structuring, solving, and communicating are not different activities of a fragmented mind but the same seamless whole viewed from different perspectives.

Question: How do communication skills fit in?

Paul: Some communication is surface communication, trivial communication — surface and trivial communication don't really require education. All of us can engage in small talk, can share gossip. And we don't require any intricate skills to do that fairly well. Where communication becomes part of our educational goal is in reading, writing, speaking and listening. These are the four modalities of communication which are essential to education and each of them is a mode of reasoning. Each of them involves problems. Each of them is shot through with critical thinking needs. Take the apparently simple matter of reading a book worth reading. The author has developed her thinking in the book, has taken some ideas and in some way represented those ideas in extended form. Our job as a reader is to translate the meaning of the author into meanings that we can understand. This is a complicated process requiring critical thinking every step along the way. What is the purpose for the book? What is the author trying to accomplish? What issues or problems are raised? What data, what experiences, what evidence are given? What concepts are used to organize this data, these experiences? How is the author thinking about the world? Is her thinking justified as far as we can see from our perspective? And how does she justify it from her perspective? How can we enter her perspective to appreciate what she has to say? All of these are the kinds of questions that a critical reader raises. And a critical reader in this sense is simply someone trying to come to terms with the text.

So if one is an uncritical reader, writer, speaker, or listener, one is not a good reader, writer, speaker, or listener at all. To do any of these well is to think critically while doing so and, at one and the same time, to solve specific problems of communication, hence to effectively communicate. Communication, in short, is always a transaction between at least two logics. In reading, as I have said, there is the logic of the thinking of the author and the logic of the thinking of the reader. The critical reader reconstructs (and so translates) the logic of the writer into the logic of the reader's thinking and experience. This entails disciplined intellectual work. The end result is a new creation; the writer's thinking for the first time now exists within the reader's mind. No mean feat!

Question: And self esteem? How does it fit in?

Paul: Healthy self-esteem emerges from a justified sense of self-worth, just as self-worth emerges from competence, ability, and genuine success. If one simply feels good about oneself for no good reason, then one is either arrogant (which is surely not desirable), or, alternatively, has a dangerous sense of misplaced confidence. Teenagers, for example, sometimes think so well of themselves that they operate under the illusion that they can safely drive while drunk or safely take drugs. They often feel much too highly of their own competence and powers and are much too unaware of their limitations. To accurately sort out genuine self-worth from a false sense of self-esteem requires, yes you guessed it, critical thinking.

Question: And finally, what about collaborative learning? How does it fit in?

Paul: Collaborative learning is desirable only if grounded in disciplined critical thinking. Without critical thinking, collaborative learning is likely to become collaborative mis-learning. It is collective bad thinking in which the bad thinking being shared becomes validated. Remember, gossip is a form of collaborative learning; peer group indoctrination is a form of collaborative learning; mass hysteria is a form of speed collaborative learning (mass learning of a most undesirable kind). We learn prejudices collaboratively, social hates and fears collaboratively, stereotypes and narrowness of mind, collaboratively. If we don't put disciplined critical thinking into the heart and soul of the collaboration, we get the mode of collaboration which is antithetical to education, knowledge, and insight.

So there are a lot of important educational goals deeply tied into critical thinking just as critical thinking is deeply tied into them. Basically the problem in the schools is that we separate things, treat them in isolation and mistreat them as a result. We end up with a superficial representation, then, of each of the individual things that is essential to education, rather than seeing how each important good thing helps inform all the others.

Question: One important aim of schooling should be to create a climate that evokes children's sense of wonder and inspires their imagination to soar. What can teachers do to "kindle" this spark and keep it alive in education?

Paul: First of all, we kill the child's curiosity, her desire to question deeply, by superficial didactic instruction. Young children continually ask why. Why this and why that? And why this other thing? But we soon shut that curiosity down with glib answers, answers to fend off rather than respond to the logic of the question. In every field of knowledge, every answer generates more questions, so that the more we know the more we recognize we don't know. It is only people who have little knowledge who take their knowledge to be complete and entire. If we thought deeply about almost any of the answers which we glibly give to children, we would recognize that we don't really have a satisfactory answer to most of their questions. Many of our answers are no more than a repetition of what we as children heard from adults. We pass on the misconceptions of our parents and those of their parents. We say what we heard, not what we know. We rarely join the quest with our children. We rarely admit our ignorance, even to ourselves. Why does rain fall from the sky? Why is snow cold? What is electricity and how does it go through the wire? Why are people bad? Why does evil exist? Why is there war? Why did my dog have to die? Why do flowers bloom? Do we really have good answers to these questions?

Question: How does curiosity fit in with critical thinking?

Paul: To flourish, curiosity must evolve into disciplined inquiry and reflection. Left to itself it will soar like a kite without a tail, that is, right into the ground! Intellectual curiosity is an important trait of mind, but it requires a family of other traits to fulfill it. It requires intellectual humility, intellectual courage, intellectual integrity, intellectual perseverance, and faith in reason. After all, intellectual curiosity is not a thing in itself — valuable in itself and for itself. It is valuable because it can lead to knowledge, understanding, and insight, because it can help broaden, deepen, sharpen our minds, making us better, more humane, more richly endowed persons. To reach these ends, the mind must be more than curious, it must be willing to work, willing to suffer through confusion and frustration, willing to face limitations and overcome obstacles, open to the views of others, and willing to entertain ideas that many people find threatening. That is, there is no point in our trying to model and encourage curiosity, if we are not willing to foster an environment in which the minds of our students can learn the value and pain of hard intellectual work. We do our students a disservice if we imply that all we need is unbridled curiosity, that with it alone knowledge comes to us with blissful ease in an atmosphere of fun, fun, fun. What good is curiosity if we don't know what to do next, how to satisfy it? We can create the environment necessary to the discipline, power, joy, and work of critical thinking only by modeling it before and with our students. They must see our minds at work. Our minds must stimulate theirs' with questions and yet further question, questions that probe information and experience, questions that call for reasons and evidence, questions that lead students to examine interpretations and conclusions, pursuing their basis in fact and experience, questions that help students to discover their assumptions, questions that stimulate students to follow out the implications of their thought, to test their ideas, to take their ideas apart, to challenge their ideas, to take their ideas seriously. It is in the totality of this intellectually rigorous atmosphere that natural curiosity thrives.

Question: It is important for our students to be productive members of the work-force. How can schools better prepare students to meet these challenges?

Paul: The fundamental characteristic of the world students now enter is ever-accelerating change, a world in which information is multiplying even as it is swiftly becoming obsolete and out of date, a world in which ideas are continually restructured, retested, and rethought, where one cannot survive with simply one way of thinking, where one must continually adapt one's thinking to the thinking of others, where one must respect the need for accuracy and precision and meticulousness, a world in which job skills must continually be upgraded and perfected — even transformed. We have never had to face such a world before. Education has never before had to prepare students for such dynamic flux, unpredictability, and complexity, for such ferment, tumult, and disarray. We as educators are now on the firing line. Are we willing to fundamentally rethink our methods of teaching? Are we ready for the 21st Century? Are we willing to learn new concepts and ideas? Are we willing to learn a new sense of discipline as we teach it to our students? Are we willing to bring new rigor to our own thinking in order to help our students bring that same rigor to theirs? Are we willing, in short, to become critical thinkers so that we might be an example of what our students must internalize and become?

These are profound challenges to the profession. They call upon us to do what no previous generation of teachers was ever called upon to do. Those of us willing to pay the price will yet have to teach side by side with teachers unwilling to pay the price. This will make our job even more difficult, but not less exciting, not less important, not less rewarding. Critical thinking is the heart of well-conceived educational reform and restructuring because it is at the heart of the changes of the 21st Century. Let us hope that enough of us will have the fortitude and vision to grasp this reality and transform our lives and our schools accordingly.

Question: National standards will result in national accountability. What is your vision for the future?

Paul: Most of the national assessment we have done thus far is based on lower-order learning and thinking. It has focused on what might be called surface knowledge. It has rewarded the kind of thinking that lends itself to multiple choice machine-graded assessment. We now recognize that the assessment of the future must focus on higher – not lower – order thinking, that it must assess more reasoning than recall, that it must assess authentic performances, students engaged in bona fide intellectual work.

Our problem is in designing and implementing such assessment. In November of this last year, Gerald Nosich and I developed and presented, at the request of the U.S. Department of Education, a model for the national assessment of higher order thinking. [Included as Chapter 6.] At a follow-up meeting of critical thinking, problem-solving, communication, and testing scholars and practitioners, it was almost unanimously agreed that it is possible to assess higher-order thinking on a national scale. It was clear from the commitments of the Departments of Education, Labor, and Commerce that such an assessment is in the cards. [See figure 1, "Today's and Tomorrow's Schools".]

The fact is we must have standards and assessment strategies for higher-order thinking for a number of reasons. First, assessment and accountability are here to stay. The public will not accept less. Second, what is not assessed is not, on the whole, taught. Third, what is mis-assessed is mis-taught. Fourth, higher-order thinking, critical thinking abilities, are increasingly crucial to success in every domain of personal and professional life. Fifth, critical thinking research is making the cultivation and assessment of higher-order thinking do-able.

The road will not be easy, but if we take the knowledge, understanding, and insights we have gained about critical thinking over the last twelve years, there is much that we could do in assessment that we haven't yet done — at the level of the individual classroom teacher, at the level of the school system, at the level of the state, and at the national level. Of course we want to do this in such a way as not to commit the "Harvard Fallacy", the mistaken notion that because graduates from Harvard are very successful, that the teaching at Harvard necessarily had something to do with it. It may be that the best prepared and well-connected students coming out of high school are going to end up as the best who graduate from college, no matter what college they attend. We need to focus our assessment,

---

Today's and Tomorrow's Schools

Schools of Today	Schools of Tomorrow
• Focus on development of basic skills	• Focus on development of thinking skills
• Testing separate from teaching	• Assessment integral to teaching
• Students work as individuals	• Cooperative problem solving
• Hierarchically sequenced — basics before higher order	• Skills learned in context of real problems
• Supervision by administration	• Learner-centered, teacher-directed
• Elite students learn to think	• All students learn to think

figure 1   From "What Work Requires of Schools" *A Scans Report for America 2000,* The Secretary's Commission on Achieving Necessary Skills, U.S. Department of Labor, June 1991

in other words, on how much value has been added by an institution. We need to know where students stood at the beginning, to assess the instruction they received on their way from the beginning to the end. We need pre- and post-testing and assessment in order to see which schools, which institutions, which districts are really adding value, and *significant* value, to the quality of thinking and learning of their students.

Finally, we have to realize that we already have instruments available for assessing what might be called the fine-textured micro-skills of critical thinking. We already know how to design prompts that test students' ability to: identify a plausible statement of a writer's purpose; distinguish clearly between purposes, inferences, assumptions, and consequences; discuss reasonably the merits of different versions of a problem or question; decide the most reasonable statement of an author's point of view; recognize bias, narrowness, and contradictions in the point of view of an excerpt; distinguish evidence from conclusions based on that evidence; give evidence to back up their positions in an essay; recognize conclusions that go beyond the evidence; distinguish central from peripheral concepts; identify crucial implications of a passage; evaluate an author's inferences; draw reasonable inferences from positions stated; and so on.

With respect to intellectual standards, we are quite able to design prompts that require students to: recognize clarity in contrast to unclarity; distinguish accurate from inaccurate accounts; decide when a statement is relevant or irrelevant to a given point; identify inconsistent positions as well as consistent ones; discriminate deep, complete, and significant accounts from those that are superficial, fragmentary, and trivial; evaluate responses with respect to their fairness; distinguish well-evidenced accounts from those unsupported by reasons and evidence; tell good reasons from bad.

With respect to large scale essay assessment we know enough now about random sampling to be able to require extended reasoning and writing without having to pay for the individual assessment of millions of essays.

What remains is to put what we know into action: at the school and district level to facilitate long-term teacher development around higher-order thinking, at the state and national level to provide for long-term assessment of district, state, and national performance. The project will take generations and perhaps in some sense will never end. After all, when will we have developed our thinking far enough, when will we have enough intellectual integrity, enough intellectual courage, enough intellectual perseverance, enough intellectual skill and ability, enough fairmindedness, enough reasonability? One thing is painfully clear. We already have more than enough rote memorization and uninspired didactic teaching, more than enough passivity and indifference, cynicism and defeatism, complacency and ineptness. The ball is in our court. Let's take up the challenge together and make, with our students, a new and better world.

✦✦ Chapter 3

The Logic of Creative and Critical Thinking

Abstract

In this paper Richard Paul develops an extended explication of the relationship between creative and critical thinking. He does so by first setting out the relationship in general, arguing that both are perfections of thought which are, in fact, inseparable in everyday reasoning. "Creativity", according to Paul, masters a process of "making" or "producing", "criticality" a process of "assessing" or "judging". He then argues that insofar as the mind — in thinking — is thinking well, it must, virtually simultaneously, both produce and assess, make and judge that making.

Having set out this relationship in general, Paul works out the details with respect to a series of theoretically basic structures and processes: 1) thinking through the logic of things, 2) taking command of reasoning and logic, 3) making fundamental assumptions about learning and knowing, 4) understanding the logic of concepts, 5) understanding the logic of academic disciplines, 6) the logic of language, 7) the logic of questions, 8) the logic of student thinking, 9) the logic of teaching, 10) the logic of reading, writing, speaking, and listening, and 11) the logic of logic. Throughout, the underlying theme of the paper is sustained: that intellectual discipline and rigor are not only quite at home with originality and productivity but that both so-called "poles" of thinking are really inseparable aspects of excellence of thought.

Beyond exploring the relation of creativity and criticality, this paper is one of the best in the collection for giving the reader a unified sense of the importance to critical thinking of the concept, "the logic of..." On Paul's analysis, this concept is indispensable and, if one reads with a sensitivity to it, one will find that it plays a role in virtually everything he writes.

✦ Introduction

C reative and critical thinking often seem to the untutored to be polar opposite forms of thought, the first based on irrational or unconscious forces, the second on rational and conscious processes, the first undirectable and unteachable, the second directable and teachable. There is some, but very little, truth in this view. The truth in it is that there is no way to generate creative geniuses, nor to get students to generate highly novel ground-breaking ideas, by some known process of systematic instruction. The dimension of "creativity", in other words, contains unknowns, even mysteries. So does "criticality" of course. Yet there are ways to teach simultaneously for both creative and critical thinking in a down-to-earth sense of those terms. To do so, however, requires that we focus on these terms in practical everyday contexts, that we keep their central meanings in mind, and that we seek insight into the respect in which they overlap and feed into each other, the respect in which they are inseparable, integrated, and unitary. This paper will develop these insights.

OVERVIEW

Good thinking is thinking that does the job we set for it. It is thinking that accomplishes the purposes of thinking. If thinking lacks a purpose, that is, is aimless, it may chance upon something of value to the thinker, but more often it will simply wander into an endless stream of unanalyzed associations from one's unanalyzed past: "hotdogs remind me of ball games, ball games remind me of Chicago, Chicago of my old neighborhood, my old neighborhood of my grandmother, of her pies, of having to eat what I didn't like, which reminds me ... which reminds me ... which reminds me...." Few people need training in aimless thinking such as this, or in daydreaming or fantasizing. For the most part we are "naturals" at aimless thinking.

Where we have trouble is in purposeful thinking, especially purposeful thinking that involves figuring things out, thinking, in other words, that poses problems to be solved and intricacies to reason through. "Criticality" and "creativity" have an intimate relationship to the ability to figure things out. There is a natural marriage between them. Indeed, all thinking that is properly called "excellent" combines these two dimensions in an intimate way. Whenever our thinking excels, it excels because we succeed in designing or engendering, fashioning or originating, creating or producing results and outcomes appropriate to our ends in thinking. It has, in a word, a *creative* dimension.

But to achieve any challenging end, we must also have *criteria:* gauges, measures, models, principles, standards, or tests to use in judging whether we are approaching that end. What is more, we must apply our criteria (models, gauges, measures, models, principles) in a way that is discerning, discriminating, exact, fastidious, judicious, and acute. We must continually monitor and assess how our thinking is going, whether it is plausibly on the right track, whether it is sufficiently clear, accurate, precise, consistent, relevant, deep, or broad for our purposes.

We don't achieve excellence in thinking with no end in view. We don't design for no reason, fashion and create without knowing what we are trying to fashion and create. We don't originate and produce with no sense of why we are doing so. Thinking that is random, thinking that roams aimlessly through half-formed images, that meanders without an organizing goal is not a candidate for either "creativity" or "criticality". It is not a candidate for excellence.

Why? When the mind thinks aimlessly, its energy and drive are typically low, its tendency is commonly toward inertness, its results usually barren. What is aimless is also normally pointless and moves in familiar alliance with indolence and dormancy. But when thinking takes on a challenging task, the mind must then come alive, ready itself for intellectual labor, engage the intellect in some form of work upon some intellectual object — until such time as it succeeds in originating, formulating, designing, engendering, creating, or producing what is necessary for the achievement of its goal. Intellectual work is essential to *create* intellectual products, and that work, that production, involves intellectual standards *judiciously* applied, ... in other words, creativity and criticality interwoven into one seamless fabric.

Like the body, the mind has its own form of fitness or excellence. Like the body, that fitness is caused by and reflected in activities done in accordance with standards (criticality). A fit mind can successfully engage in the designing, fashioning, formulating, originating, or producing of intellectual products worthy of its challenging ends. To achieve this fitness, the mind must learn to take charge of itself, to energize itself, press forward when difficulties emerge, proceed slowly and methodically when meticulousness is necessary, immerse itself in a task, become attentive, reflective, and engrossed, circle back on a train of thought, recheck to ensure that it has been thorough, accurate, exact, and deep enough.

Its generativeness and its judiciousness can only be artificially separated. In the process of actual thought they are one. Such thought is systematic when being systematic serves its end. It can also cast system aside and ransack its intuitions for a lead — when no clear maneuver, plan, strategy, or tactic comes to mind. Nor is the generative, the productive, the creative mind without standards for what it generates and produces. It is not a mind lacking judiciousness, discernment, and judgment. It is not a mind incapable of acuteness and exactness. It is not a mind whose standards are unclarity, imprecision, inaccuracy, irrelevance, triviality, inconsistency, superficiality, and narrowness. The fit mind generates and produces precisely because it has high standards for itself, because it cares about how and what it creates.

Serious thinking originates in a commitment to grasp some truth, to get to the bottom of something, to make accurate sense of that about which it is thinking. This "figuring out" cannot simply be a matter of arbitrary creation or production. There must be specific restraints and requirements to be met, something outside the will to which the will must be bent, some unyielding objectivity we must painstakingly take into account and neither ignore nor thrust aside. It is exactly the severe, inflexible, stern fact of reality that forces intellectual criticality and productivity into one seamless whole. If there were no "objectivity" outside our process of "figuring out", then we would have literally nothing to figure out. If what we figure out can be anything we want it to be, anything we fantasize it as being, then there is no logic to the expression "figure out".

In a sense, of course, all minds create and produce in a manner reflective of their fitness or lack thereof. Minds indifferent to standards and disciplined judgment tend to judge inexactly, inaccurately, inappropriately, prejudicially. Prejudices, hate, irrational jealousies and fears, stereotypes and misconceptions — these too are "created", "produced", "originated" by minds. Without minds to produce them, they would not exist. Yet they are not the products of "creative" minds. They reflect an undisciplined, an uncritical mode of thinking and therefore are not properly thought of as products of "creativity". In short, except in rare circumstances, creativity presupposes criticality and criticality creativity. This is the essential insight behind this paper.

In what follows, therefore, we shall explore the intimate connection between a well-grounded sense of creativity in thinking, the sense of thinking as a *making,* as a process of *creating* thought, as a process that *brings thoughts into being* to organize, shape, interpret, and make sense of our world — thinking that, once developed, enables us to achieve goals, accomplish purposes, solve problems, and settle important issues we face as humans in a world in which rapid change is becoming the only constant. This sense of *thought as a creative making* is the most important sense of creativity, pedagogically speaking, and cannot be understood, as I have briefly argued, separate from understanding the development of "critical judgment" and a critical mind. When a mind does not systematically and effectively embody intellectual criteria and standards, is not disciplined in reasoning things through, in figuring out the logic of things, in reflectively devising a rational approach to the solution of problems or in the accomplishment of intellectual or practical tasks, that mind is not "creative". In this sense, there is a reciprocal logic to both intellectual creation and critical judgment, to the intellectual "making" of things and to the on-going "critique" of that making. Let us examine that reciprocal logic more closely.

✦ Thinking That Grasps the Logic of Things

All intellectual products, in order to be intellectually assessed and validated, require some logic, some order or coherence, some intellectual structure that makes sense and is rationally defensible. This is true whether one is talking of poems or essays, paintings or choreographed dances, histories or anthropological reports, experiments or scientific theories, philosophies or psychologies, accounts of particular events or those of general phenomena or laws. A product of intellectual work that makes no sense, that cannot be rationally analyzed and assessed, that cannot be incorporated into other intellectual work, or used — and hence that cannot play a role in any academic tradition or discipline — is unintelligible. Whether we are designing a new screw driver, figuring out how to deal with our children's misbehavior, or working out a perspective on religion, we must order our meanings into a system of meanings that make sense to us, and so, in that respect, have a logic.

This is to say that there is an important role for reason and reasoning, for constructing and working within a logic, for creative producing and critical assessing of what is produced, in every intellectual enterprise. Let us now explore that role in brief.

WHAT IS REASONING? WHAT IS LOGIC?

The words 'reasoning' and 'logic' each have both a narrow and a broad use. In the narrow sense, 'reasoning' is drawing conclusions on the basis of reasons, and, in the narrow sense, 'logic' refers simply to the principles that apply to the assessment of that process. But in the broad sense, 'reason' and 'reasoning' refer to the total process of figuring things out, and hence to every intellectual standard relevant to doing that. And parallel to this sense is a broad sense of 'logic' which refers to the basic structure that one is, in fact, figuring out (when engaged in reasoning something through).

One can draw conclusions about poems, microbes, numbers, historical events, languages, social settings, psychological fears, everyday situations, character traits — indeed, about anything whatsoever. And this drawing of conclusions is part of a broader process of reasoning things through. The particular inferences made have a specific logic that can be assessed and the total process of reasoning things through has a general logic that also can be assessed. In this broad sense of 'logic', one focuses on the logic of the poem or the logic of a microbe or the logic of numbers or the logic of a historical event or the logic of a language, and so forth. In the narrow sense, one focuses on the logic of this or that inference within a given poem or about a given microbe or within some train of mathematical thought. Hence, Sherlock Holmes tries to figure out the logic of the murder by making a number of specific inferences from the available evidence. The broader logic contains the narrower logic.

WHAT MAKES GOOD REASONING GOOD REASONING (IN THE BROAD SENSE)?

Becoming adept at drawing justifiable conclusions on the basis of good reasons is more complex than it appears. This is because drawing a conclusion is always the tip of an intellectual iceberg. It is not just a matter of avoiding a fallacy in logic (in the narrow sense). There is much more that is implicit in reasoning than is explicit, there are more components, more "logical structures" that we do not express than those we do. To become skilled in reasoning things through we must become practiced in making what is implicit explicit so that we can "check out" what is going on "beneath the surface" of our thought.

Thus, when we draw a conclusion, we do so in some circumstances, making inferences (that have implications and consequences) based on some reasons or information (and assumptions), using some concepts, in trying to settle some question (or solve some problem) for some purpose within some point of view.

Good reasoners can consider and plausibly assess any of these elements as they function in their thought in any act of reasoning something out. Good reasoners therefore use good logic in both the narrow and the broad sense.

Furthermore, in most circumstances in which we are *using* logic we are *creating* it simultaneously. This needs explanation.

✦ *Whenever We Are Reasoning Something Through We Are Ipso Facto Engaged in Creative Thinking*

In the broad sense, all reasoned thinking is thinking within a logic, and when we have not yet learned a given logic — e.g., not yet learned the logic of the internal combustion engine, the logic of right triangles, or the logic of dolphin behavior — our minds must bring that logic into being, create it in the fabric, within the structure, of our established ways of thinking. Hence, when we are thinking something through for the first time, to some extent, we create the logic we are using. We bring into being new articulations of our purposes and of our reasons. We make new assumptions. We form new concepts. We ask new questions. We make new inferences. Our point of view is worked out in a new direction, one in which it has never been worked out before.

Indeed, there is a sense in which all reasoned thinking, all genuine acts of figuring out anything whatsoever, even something previously figured out, is a new "making", a new series of creative acts, for we rarely recall our previous thought whole cloth. Instead we generally remember only some part of what we figured out and figure out the rest anew, based on the logic of that part and other logical structures more immediately available to us. We continually create new understandings and re-create old understandings by a similar process of figuring.

In what follows, I will articulate a frame of reference that highlights the intimate interplay between creative and critical thinking, between the thinking that creates a set of logically interrelated meanings and the thinking that assesses the logic being created. I will begin with a basic assumption that underlies the model being developed. The theme that shall run throughout is as follows:

In all contexts that demand the reasoned figuring out of something, there are, as it were, *three logics* involved: *1)* the logic to be figured out (the logic it is our aim to create), *2)* the logic we use to do the figuring (chosen by us from the logics we have already learned), and *3)* the logic that results, in the end, from our reasoning (and which needs to be assessed for its "fit", for the degree to which it has captured the logic to be figured out). For example, I may use my understanding of the logic of one D.H. Lawrence novel (say, *Sons and Lovers*) as an initial framework for understanding the logic of another (say, *Lady Chatterley's Lover*). The understanding I end up with may or may not fully make sense of the actual story. The logic I make of it may be inadequate. Or again, in studying history, I may use my understanding of the logic of one economic crisis (say that of the thirties in the USA) to understand another one (say that of the nineties in the USA). The reconstruction I come up with may or may not make sense of the logic of what was actually going on economically in the nineties. In all our learning we must seek out provisional models (mini logical systems) for figuring out what we are trying to learn (the system we are trying to grasp). We then end up with a product of thought, a system we create. That system may or may not be adequate to the task.

A Basic Assumption

In all of our behavior we assume there is order, regularity, and potential intelligibility in everything; that every portion of "reality" can sooner or later be figured out, explained, and related to other portions; that our innate capacity to form conceptions of, and make inferences about, ourselves and the things around us is adequate for our purposes. This basic assumption implies that in some sense there is a discoverable logic to each dimension of reality. Of course, in making this assumption, we need not also assume that what we discover about the logic of things, from our various concepts and inferences, is some form of "Absolute Truth", nor that our knowledge of things exhausts, completely spells out, or totally captures the ultimate nature of things, or even that things have an "ultimate" nature. For one thing, our knowledge is always limited by the perspectives that are inherent in our various ways of forming concepts and making inferences. We are limited, not infinite, creatures; humans, not gods.

✦ The Logic of ...

To say that something has a logic, then, is to say that it can be understood by use of our reason, that we can form concepts that accurately — though not necessarily thoroughly — characterize the nature of that thing. Only when we have conceptualized a thing in some way, and only then, can we reason through it. Since nature does not tell us how to conceptualize it, we must create that conceptualization, individually or socially. Once conceptualized, a thing is integrated by us into a network of ideas (since no concept ever stands alone) and, as such, becomes the subject of many possible inferences.

Furthermore, once we begin to make inferences about something, we can do so either well or poorly, justifiably or unjustifiably, in keeping with the meaning of the concept and the nature of what we know of the thing conceptualized, or not so in keeping. If we are not careful, for example, we may (and very often do) infer more than is implied. If I hear a sound at the door and conceptualize it as "scratching at the door", I may then infer that it is my dog wanting to come in. I have used my reason (my capacity to conceptualize and infer) to interpret the noise as a "scratch" and I have assumed, in the process, that the only creature in the vicinity who could be making that scratch at my door is my dog... my reasoning may be off. I may have mis-conceptualized the noise as a "scratch" (I may even have misheard where the noise is coming from) or I may have wrongly assumed that there are no other creatures around who might make it. Notice that in these acts, I create the conceptualizations that are at the root of my thinking.

We approach virtually everything in our experience as something that can be thus "decoded" by the power of our minds to create a conceptualization and to make inferences on the basis of it (hence to create further conceptualizations). We do this so routinely and automatically that we don't typically recognize ourselves as engaged in processes of reasoned creation. In our everyday life we don't first experience the world in "conceptless" form and then deliberately place what we experience into categories in order to make sense of things.

Rather, it is as if things are given to us with their "names" inherent in them. So we see "trees", "clouds", "grass", "roads", "people", "men", "women", and so on. We apply these concepts intuitively, as if no rational, creative act were involved. Yet, if we think about it, we will realize that there was a time when we had to learn names for things and hence, before we knew those names, we couldn't possibly have seen these phenomena through the mediation of these concepts. In learning these concepts we had to create them in our own minds out of the concepts we already had learned.

I want to highlight the importance of this power of creative conceptualization and inference in human life, for it is precisely this power of mind that we must take charge of in forming disciplined habits of thought, thought which we summarize with the expression 'thinking critically'. In thinking critically we take command of our conceptual creations, assessing them more explicitly than is normally done. Concepts, like all human creations, can be well or poorly designed. Critical judgment is always relevant to the process of design and construction, whether that construction be conceptual or material.

For example, we study living organisms to construct "bio-logic", that is, to establish ways to conceptualize and make valid inferences about life forms. We study social arrangements to construct "socio-logic", that is, to establish ways to conceptualize and make valid inferences about life in society. We study the historical past to construct "the logic of history", ways to conceptualize and make valid inferences about the past. Since no one is born with these logical structures at his or her command, everyone must "create" them.

THE LOGIC OF CONCEPTS

In this paper, we are using the word 'concept' to mean simply "a generalized idea of a class of things". We understand "conceptualization" to be a process by which the mind infers a thing to be of a certain kind, to belong properly to some given class of things. Hence, if I call something, or interpret something to be, an apple, I have placed it into a generalized class of things (the class of all apples). Our minds understand any particular aspect of things in relation to generalized ideas that highlight perceived similarities and differences in our experience. For example, the word 'dog' represents one concept, the word 'cat' another, the word 'cloud' a third, the word 'laughter' a fourth. We reason about, and so interpret the world, by putting the objects of our experience into "categories" or "concepts" each one of which highlights some set of similarities or differences for us, links the thing up with other concepts, and validates a certain set of inferences. For example, if I see a creature before me and take it to be a dog — that is, if I place it mentally into the category of 'dog' — I can reasonably infer that it will bark rather than meow or purr. Of course, I cannot reasonably infer that it will not bite me if I attempt to chase it away. Furthermore, by placing something into the concept of 'dog' I locate the thing in relation to other concepts, such as 'animal', 'furry', 'muzzle', 'paw', 'tail', and so forth.

In learning to speak our native language, we learn thousands of concepts which, when properly used, enable us to make countless legitimate inferences about the objects of our experience. Unfortunately, there is nothing in the way we ordinarily learn to speak a language that forces us to use concepts carefully or that prevents us from making unjustifiable inferences while engaged in their use. Indeed, a fundamental need for critical thinking is given by the fact that as long as the mind remains undisciplined in its use of concepts, it is susceptible to any number of illegitimate inferences.

The process of learning the concepts implicit in a natural language like English, is a process of creating facsimiles of the concepts implicit in the language usage, to which we are exposed. However, we cannot give anyone the meaning of a word or phrase; that meaning must be individually created by every person who learns it. When we mis-learn the meaning of a word, we create in our own minds a meaning that it doesn't have.

THE LOGIC OF ACADEMIC DISCIPLINES

We can now understand each academic discipline to represent a domain in which humans are creating specialized concepts (and inferences that follow from those concepts) that enable them to approach that domain through an ordered set of logical relationships structured by human reason. Critical judgment is essential to all of the acts of construction; all acts of construction are open to critical assessment. We not only assess *what* we create; we assess as we create.

Each student who would learn the logic of a discipline has to create that logic in his or her own mind. Each moment of that creation requires the presence of critical thought and judgment. There is no way to create the logic for the student or simply to "give", transfer, or inject the logic in pre-fabricated form. By the same token, the logic of a text within a discipline enters the student's thinking only through the mediation of the logic of the student's thinking. But the logic of the student's thinking must be continually re-shaped and modified. The logic the student fashions in learning represents, if done well, an analytically modified logic, the result of a process of measured accommodation, not simply one of uncritical assimilation.

Hence, if a student reads a text within a discipline well, that is, critically, the logic he or she creates through reading matches the logic of the text well. Reading proficiently is both a creative task (a making, a creating) and a critical task (an assessing, a judging). The making and the assessing, the creating and the judging are integral to one seamless process of good reasoning. We create the logic of the text in our minds as we critically dialogue with it. We raise and answer probing questions as we read, generating and fashioning ideas and meanings in and through our responses.

This picture is complicated by those domains in which competing logics develop, each rationally defended by different, apparently equally expert, apparently equally rational, proponents. To some extent, of course, questions which call for the adjudication of competing logics emerge in all disciplines. On the other hand, some disciplines, namely those which attempt to conceptualize and make sense of human realities, seem to be inescapably "multi-logical": history, psychology, sociology, philosophy, anthropology, economics, literature, fine arts, and so forth. In these domains, seminal thinkers continue to emerge with alternative and conflicting ideas for reasoning about basic questions in the field. In this case, students have to create and reason within conflicting logics. Problems of confusion abound in this circumstance.

The creativity in reasoning one's way into disciplines which are multi-logical demands exacting and discriminating restraint and self-regulation. In reading, for example, the writings of Freud, Adler, and Jung, I must create in my mind three overlapping systems of thought, systems which complexely agree and disagree. If I come to understand what I have read, I have come to develop the ability to think within three different systems of thought. Only I, through a process of disciplined intellectual work, can generate, fabricate, engender in my mind Freudian, Adlerian, and Jungian thoughts. Only I can create the inner understandings which enable me to draw fine distinctions among their views, fine distinctions which honor the multiple logics they collectively developed. Instruction should provide incentives for students to actively create the logics of these conflicting perspectives and to critically assess that creation at one and the same time.

THE LOGIC OF LOGIC

Critical thinking can now be understood as a deep interest in *the logic of logic,* the art of taking charge of the large variety of ways in which we create concepts and make inferences by means of them, the various ways, in other words, in which we use human reason well or poorly in attempting to make sense of things and our created interpretations of them. Critical thinkers, on this view, attempt to heighten their awareness of the conditions under which their self-created conceptualizations — and inferences from them — are rationally justified. They not only use their innate capacity to reason, they also study how to improve the use of their reason, to discipline and "perfect" it (to make it more clear, precise, accurate, relevant, logical, consistent, respectful of evidence, responsive to good reasons, open to new ideas, and so forth). They habitually, therefore, reason about their reasoning. They routinely scrutinize their thinking as an act of on-going creation which must be continually monitored and checked for its "match".

In this way, critical thinkers maintain an acute and abiding interest in their own intellectual self-improvement. They carefully attend to their personal concept-creating and concept-using practices. They exercise special discipline in taking charge of their thinking by taking charge of the ideas that direct that thinking, by close examination of the ideas which they are generating and using to create an ordered set of meanings.

THE LOGIC OF LANGUAGE

Many of our ideas or concepts come from the languages we have learned to speak (and in which as a matter of course we do our thinking). Embedded in the educated use of words are criteria or standards that we must respect in order to think clearly and precisely by means of those words. We are free, of course, to use a particular word in a special way in special circumstances, but only if we have good reason for modifying its meaning. Such special stipulations should proceed from a clear understanding of established educated use. We are not free, for example, to use the word 'education' as if it were synonymous with the word 'indoctrination' or 'socialization'. We are not free to equate pride with cunning, truth with belief, knowledge with information, arrogance with self-confidence, desire with love, and so on. Each word has its own established logic, a logic that cannot, without confusion or error, be ignored.

Though each word has an established logic, we still have to recreate that logic in our thinking, and we must base that creation on meanings we have previously created. Learning the meaning of a word is therefore not a simple task because in each case we must create a new concept in our minds out of modified old understandings. This requires that our creation be ordered, restrained, regulated, and controlled. The undisciplined creation of meaning in the context of learning the logic of language is nothing more nor less than the mis-learning of that logic.

THE LOGIC OF STUDENT THINKING

Unfortunately many students do not understand the significant relationship between care and precision in language usage and care and precision in thought. Students often say, when talking about the nature of language, that people have their own meanings for all the words they use, not noticing that, were this true, we would not be able to understand each other. Students often speak and write in vague sentences because they have no criteria for choosing words other than that one word rather than another occurred to them. They do not seek to put their sentences into clear logical relationships to one another because they do not recognize any responsibility to do so nor any clear idea of what that would entail. They do not read, write, speak, or listen well because they have never had to think clearly about the logic of reading, writing, speaking, or listening.

All of the rational processes of mind are assumed by them to take care of themselves, automatically and effortlessly. Or better, they are unaware that there are any rational processes of mind to be tended to, in the first place. It goes without saying that students do not generally have any grasp of the creative dimension of all learning. They do not see themselves designing, fashioning, or shaping meanings. They think of themselves as simply absorbing meanings, as simply receiving what is being given to them by the teacher, the textbook, or experience itself.

The result of this common mind-set is that students find it very difficult, if not impossible, to master any well-developed or refined set of conceptual relationships. The logic of their own thinking is vague, fragmented, often contradictory, highly egocentric, typically sociocentric, pervasively undisciplined, and lacking in foundational insights. Since one begins to develop critical thinking significantly only insofar as one begins to discipline one's own thinking with respect to at least one framework of concepts, and since one learns a new set of concepts only by means of a set of previously learned concepts, the development of student thinking must take place over an extended period of time and must be heavily dialogical. Only by moving back and forth between their own undisciplined thought and some set of disciplined concepts, can they work their minds into disciplined thought.

Furthermore, there is the very real danger that, once developed, their emerging discipline in one domain will remain isolated and segregated from the rest of their thinking. Even expert thinkers in one domain are often atrocious in another. The human mind does not necessarily develop as an integrated whole. This is one of the reasons why it is important to emphasize critical thinking as critical thinking, in its most generalizable form. Hence, when learning to think with discipline in one domain of concepts, it is highly useful to be exposed to logically illuminating parallel examples from other domains.

Finally, lacking the discipline of critical thinking and judgment, the creative dimension of student thinking is commonly quite undistinguished. What they "create" is typically poorly designed and constructed. For example, since their own thinking is vague and fragmented, they routinely generate vague and fragmented meanings in the process of learning; their minds bring into being disjointed meanings which often have no single, definite logic whatsoever. It is important to recognize that in a literal sense there is no necessary virtue in "creating" meaning. Prejudices, self-delusions, distortions, misconceptions, and caricatures are all products of the mind as maker and creator.

THE LOGIC OF QUESTIONS

Every question, when well put, imposes specific demands upon us, demands implicit in the logic of the words of the question and in the contexts in which those words are intelligibly used by educated speakers of the language. If I ask, "What is the sum of 434 and 987?", the question requires an answer consonant with the established logic of the word 'addition'. If I ask, "Is Jack your friend or merely an acquaintance?", the question requires an answer in keeping with the logic of the established distinction between the words 'friend' and 'acquaintance'. If I ask you "To what extent are your students learning to think critically?", the question requires that you *1)* understand precisely what is implied by the expression 'thinks critically' and *2)* assess your students' thinking by some means appropriate to determining the relative standing of your students either with respect to a fixed ideal of critical thinking or some standardized norm to which your students' performances (of thinking) can appropriately be compared. An appropriate answer is one that is constructed in accordance with the logical demands of the question.

Very often, people are cavalier in their putting and answering of questions. They rarely put their own questions precisely, and, when answering the questions of others, they often respond impressionistically or otherwise inappropriately, without care, discipline, or sensitivity to what is implied by the established logic of the question (or by the context in which the question is asked). When called upon to sharpen their questions or to respond more carefully and precisely, many respond with irritation or annoyance, exasperated that they are expected to be clear or precise or accurate or relevant or consistent in their question-asking or -answering behaviors.

This general insensitivity to the logic of questions is part of the broader phenomenon of insensitivity to the logic of language, which is itself part of the even broader phenomenon of insensitivity to the need for care and discipline in our use of reason — our use of concept and inference — in figuring out the logic of the world within and around us. All of these, in turn, are part of the general insensitivity to the need to discipline our mind's creative productions, to shape them in accord with restraining conditions. Sometimes these restraining conditions are given by the logic of language, sometimes by the logic of the material world.

✦ *The Elements of Thought*

As soon as we move from thought which is purely associational and undisciplined, to thought which is conceptual and inferential, which attempts in some intelligible way to figure something out, to use the power of creative reason, then it is possible, and helpful, to think about what might be called "the elements of thought", the basic building-blocks of thinking, the essential dimensions of all reasoning whenever and wherever it creates meaning. There is, in other words, a general logic to the use of reason. We can deduce these elements, these essential dimensions of reasoning, by paying close attention to what is implicit in the attempt on the part of the mind to figure anything out whatsoever. Once we make these elements of thought clear, it will be obvious that each of them can serve as an important touchstone or point of assessment in our critical analysis and assessment of the constructed process and products of our thinking. As meaning makers we must be exacting, discriminating, and fastidious. Without a guiding logic, thinking is aimless and random. Productive thinking needs some structure, some basic logic to follow.

We have already noticed that the attempt to render something intelligible requires the construction of concepts, the creation of interpretations and understandings based on them, and inferences drawn from them. We can now set out the basic set of conditions implicit in these creative, critical acts of the mind, whenever they occur. They are as follows:

1) *Purpose, Goal, or End in View:* Whenever we reason, we reason to some end, to achieve some purpose, to satisfy some desire or fulfill some need. One source of problems in reasoning is traceable to "defects" at the level of goal, purpose, or end. If our goal itself is unrealistic, contradictory to other goals we have, confused or muddled in some way, then the reasoning we use to achieve it is problematic. The goal, purpose, or end of our thinking is something our mind must actively create.

2) *Question at Issue (or Problem to Be Solved):* Whenever we attempt to reason something out, there is at least one question at issue, at least one problem to be solved. One area of concern for the reasoner should therefore be the very formulation of the question to be answered or problem to be solved. If we are not clear about the question we are asking, or how the question relates to our basic purpose or goal, then it is unlikely that we will be able to find a reasonable answer to it, or one that will serve our purpose. The question at issue in our thinking is something our mind must actively create.

3) *Point of View or Frame of Reference:* Whenever we reason, we must reason within some point of view or frame of reference. Any defect in our point of view or frame of reference is a possible source of problems in our reasoning. Our point of view may be too narrow or too parochial, may be based on false or misleading analogies or metaphors, may not be precise enough, may contain contradictions, and so forth. The point of view which shapes and organizes our thinking is something our mind must actively create.

4) *The Empirical Dimension of Our Reasoning:* Whenever we reason, there is some "stuff", some phenomena about which we are reasoning. Any defect, then, in the experiences, data, evidence, or raw material upon which our reasoning is based is a possible source of problems. We must actively decide which of a myriad of possible experiences, data, evidence, etc. we will use.

5) *The Conceptual Dimension of Our Reasoning:* All reasoning uses some ideas or concepts and not others. Any defect in the concepts or ideas (including the theories, principles, axioms, or rules) with which we reason, is a possible source of problems. The concepts and ideas which shape and organize our thinking must be actively created by us.

6) *Assumptions* — The Starting Points of Reasoning: All reasoning must begin somewhere, must take some things for granted. Any defect in the starting points of our reasoning, any problem in what we are taking for granted, is a possible source of problems. Only we can create the assumptions on the basis of which we will reason.

7) *Inferences:* Reasoning proceeds by steps called inferences. To make an inference is to think as follows: "Because this is so, that also is so (or probably so)". Any defect in the inferences we make while we reason is a possible problem in our reasoning. Information, data, and situations do not determine what we shall deduce from them; we create inferences through the concepts and assumptions which we bring to situations.

8) *Implications and Consequences* — Where Our Reasoning Takes Us: All reasoning begins somewhere and proceeds somewhere else. No reasoning is static. Reasoning is a sequence of inferences that begin somewhere and take us somewhere else. Thus all reasoning comes to an end, yet could have been taken further. All reasoning has implications or consequences beyond those the reasoner has considered. Any problem with these (implications that are false, undesirable consequences), implies a problem in the reasoning. The implications of our reasoning are an implicit creation of our reasoning.

If we taught each school subject in such a way that students had to reason their way into the subject, and if we routinely questioned students so they came to habitually look into each basic dimension of their thinking — purpose, question at issue, point of view, data, concepts, assumptions, inferences, implications and consequences — they would progressively become more disciplined in their reasoning, more self-critical and self-directed in the process and products of their thinking.

THE LOGIC OF READING, WRITING, SPEAKING, AND LISTENING

Reading, writing, speaking, and listening are all "dialogical" in nature. That is, in each case there are at least two logics involved, and there is an attempt being made by someone to translate one logic into the terms of another. Consider reading and listening. In both of these cases we are attempting to make sense of the logic or reasoning of another person. Whatever is written must, if it is reasoned, contain all of the elements of thought, and as a critical reader one can question the text as one goes seeking to determine: What is the central purpose of the writer of the text, what problems or issues does she raise? Within what point of view is she reasoning? What is she assuming or taking for granted? What evidence, information, or data is presented to us? How is that evidence interpreted or conceptualized? What are the key concepts or ideas in the text? What lines of reasoning are formulated? What key inferences are made? Where is the reasoning taking us? What is implied by it? If this reasoning were taken seriously and made the basis for action or policy, what consequences would follow? Furthermore, each of these dimensions of reasoning could be looked at from the point of view of the "perfections" of thought, those intellectual standards which individually or collectively apply to all reasoning. (Is it clear, precise, accurate, relevant, consistent, logical, broad enough, based on sound evidence, utilizing appropriate reasons, adequate to our purposes, and fair, given other possible ways of conceiving things?)

It is this disciplined process of critical analysis that enables one to create in one's mind the logic of the text, to construct a system of meanings that mirror, to the best of one's ability, the system of meanings inherent in the text.

✦ *Intellectual Standards*

All intellectual standards are derived from some humanly created logic or are implied in the very nature of things themselves, including *universal criteria* implicit in intellectual history and educated discourse within that history, *the logic of concepts and words* implicit in educated usage, *the logic of questions* implicit in academic practice and educated usage, and *the logic of subject matter* implicit in the nature of things themselves. For example, it would be unintelligible to say, "I want to reason well but I am indifferent as to whether or not my reasoning is clear, precise, accurate, relevant, logical, consistent, based on appropriate evidence and reasons, ..." By the same token, it would be unintelligible — unless very special circumstances prevailed — to say "I am trying to determine whether or not I am a 'selfish' person, but I am not concerned with what the word 'selfish' implies." The logic of the question, "Is Jack a selfish person?" is basically revealed by understanding the established uses of the word 'selfish' in educated discourse.

✦ *The Logic of Teaching*

(Assuming that the most basic goal of education is to foster the general, reasoned, intellectual development of students.) To teach a student critically is to devise activities and an environment conducive to the general, reasoned, intellectual development of students. By the model we present, the goal will be seen to entail cultivating students' ability to reason "creatively and critically" (viewed as inseparable dimensions of good thinking) with respect to the logic of any subject matter they study, in such a way as to maximize the development, over an extended period of time, of general intellectual standards and disciplined minds, minds strongly motivated to reason rigorously and analytically with respect to any problem, issue, or intellectual task to which they afterward set themselves. The ability to read, write, speak, and listen as forms of disciplined reasoning, as forms of disciplined questioning, become central goals on the model because each is a basic modality of reason through which we learn much of what we learn. As teachers committed to the intellectual development of our students, we introduce our students not only to the logic of what they are studying but also to the very logic of logic, i.e., critical thinking, so that they begin as soon as possible to discipline their minds in a general and not simply in a subject-specific way. Through that discipline, the created products of their thinking become useful products, products fashioned, to the degree that they develop critical judgment, with acute discrimination and fastidious discernment. That minds will create meanings is not in doubt; that they will create meanings that are sound, insightful, or profound is.

✦ Conclusion

Creativity, as a term of praise, involves more than a mere haphazard or uncritical making, more than the raw process of bringing something into being. It requires that what is brought into being meet criteria intrinsic to what it is we are trying to make. Novelty alone will not do, for it is easy to produce worthless novelty. Intellectual standards and discipline do not stand in the way of creativity. Rather, they provide a way to begin to generate it, as it must be generated: slowly and painfully, one student at a time, one problem at a time, one insight at a time. If we can engage each of our students passionately in genuine intellectual work on genuine intellectual problems worthy of reasoned thought and analysis, and continually help each student to become a more judicious critic of the nature and quality of his or her thought, we have done all we can do to make likely both the critical and the creative development of each student. It is stimulating intellectual work that develops the intellect simultaneously as both a creator and evaluator: as a creator that evaluates and as an evaluator that creates. Fitness of mind, intellectual excellence, is the result.

Chapter 4

Critical Thinking in North America

Abstract

In this paper, Richard Paul sets out his conception of the emerging critical theory of education, in contrast to the standard didactic theory of education. "The root concept of the educated literate person as critical thinker is not theoretically new .... What is new is its progressive development across a variety of academic domains and its unifying foundation as a basis for addressing a variety of emerging educational, social, and economic concerns."

Students are not learning "to work by, or think for, themselves." "Neither are they learning how to gather, analyze, synthesize, and assess information, how to analyze questions and problems, how to enter sympathetically into the thinking of others, how to deal rationally with conflicting points of view. They do not use their native languages clearly, precisely, or persuasively." Most importantly, Paul argues, students gain little knowledge since, for the most part, they could not explain the basis for what they believe. They do not, therefore, become "literate," in Paul's conception of the word.

Paul names the source of these problems as a didactic conception of education — simplistic, fragmented, and inaccurate — which has shaped instructional theory and practice, and which primarily arose from schools' historical role of indoctrinating people to fit into narrow, isolated societies, a situation changing in the modern world of global communication and interdependence. Research and theoretical work on numerous fronts are developing and reflecting a contrasting theory of education which Paul explicates and links to critical thinking. The broadness and complexity of the emerging concept of critical thinking can be seen in the variety of definitions of it. After setting out numerous definitions, Paul sets out one of his own in some detail and explores its key features: perfections of thought, elements of thought, and domains of thought. Paul closes by citing research that supports his view of critical teaching.

✦ Introduction

*T*here is a critical thinking movement gaining momentum at all levels of education today. Its epicenter is in North America but its influence is being felt in Europe and beyond. It is manifested in a burgeoning variety of research projects and papers, in educational manifestoes and mandates, in new curriculum articulations, in far-reaching philosophical critique, and in a spate of efforts to "restructure" schools.

The root concept of the educated literate person as critical thinker is not theoretically new but can be traced to the ancient Socratic model of the learner as a systematic, probing questioner and dialectical reasoner striving to live a reflective and rational life. (Paul, 1987) (Siegel, 1980, 1988) What is new is its progressive development across a variety of academic domains and its unifying foundation as a basis for addressing a variety of emerging educational, social, and economic concerns.

On the economic front, developed nations must increasingly generate workers who can think critically for a living. Evidence of this growing perception is illustrated in an open letter, drafted by the president of Stanford University, Donald Kennedy, co-signed by 36 other college leaders from across the U.S., and sent to 3,000 college and university presidents (Sept. 18, 1987). It warned of "a national emergency ... rooted ... in the revolution of expectations about what our schools must accomplish:"

> It simply will not do for our schools to produce a small elite to power our scientific establishment and a larger cadre of workers with basic skills to do routine work.... Millions of people around the world now have these same basic skills and are willing to work twice as long for as little as one-tenth our basic wages.... To maintain and enhance our quality of life, we must develop a leading-edge economy based on workers who can think for a living.... If skills are equal, in the long run wages will be too. This means we have to educate a vast mass of people capable of thinking critically, creatively, and imaginatively.

On the social and political fronts, both developed and underdeveloped nations face complex problems that cannot be solved except with significant conceptual shifts on the part of large masses of people. Such large-scale shifts presuppose increased reflective and critical thought about deep-seated problems of environmental damage, human relations, over-population, rising expectations, diminishing resources, global competition, personal goals, and ideological conflict. Simultaneously, as war and preparation for war waste more and more resources, the battle for world political hegemony, which fuels this waste, becomes increasingly unacceptable. One result is an increasing drive to challenge the world-wide academic *status quo,* a *status quo* whose outdated and simplistic theoretical underpinnings invite serious attack, and to build in its place modes of education better suited to the demands of emerging world problems. A multi-dimensional, interdependent world cannot be fathomed by people schooled in fragmented, monological specialties or steeped in nationalist myopia. Most problems are multi-dimensional, logically messy, require interdisciplinary analysis and synthesis, deeply involve values and priorities, and demand sympathetic consideration of conflicting points of view or frames of reference.

Monological analysis will not solve multilogical problems. Specialists whose main *forte* is reductive thinking within a discipline offer little toward solving such problems. The lay person, bombarded with diverse contradictory explanations and prescriptions, retreats to simplistic pictures of the world. The growing mass media feed this demand for simple-minded answers. A new concept of knowledge, learning, and literacy more in tune with the modern world is emerging, however; one designed to engender people comfortable with dialogical and dialectical thinking, at home with complexity and ambi-guity, who can adjust their thinking to accelerating changes, who do not fix-ate on their present beliefs, people not easily manipulated or taken in by pro-paganda. (Scriven 1985) The theoretical foundation for this need and its fulfillment is now accumulating a solid research base. Its academic imple-mentation is merely beginning; its full development around the world is years in the future.

✦ *Two Conflicting Theories of*
Knowledge, Learning, and Literacy:
The Didactic and the Critical

Most instructional practice in most academic institutions around the world presupposes a didactic theory of knowledge, learning, and literacy, ill-suited to the development of critical minds and literate persons. After a superficial exposure to reading, writing, and arithmetic, schooling is typically fragment-ed into more or less technical domains each with a large vocabulary and an extensive content or propositional base. Students "take in" and reiterate domain-specific details. Teachers lecture and drill. Students rarely integrate their daily non-academic experiences. Teachers spend little time stimulating student questions. Students are rarely encouraged to doubt what they hear in the classroom or read in their texts. Students' personal points of view or philosophies of life are considered largely irrelevant to education. In most classrooms teachers talk and students listen. Dense and typically speedy cov-erage of content is usually followed by content-specific testing. Students are drilled in applying formulas, skills, and concepts, then tested on nearly identi-cal items. Instructional practices fail to require students to *use* what they learn when appropriate. Practice is stripped of meaning and purpose.

Interdisciplinary synthesis is ordinarily viewed as the personal responsi-bility of the student and is not routinely tested. Technical specialization is considered the natural goal of schooling and is correlated with getting a job. Few multi-logical issues or problems are discussed or assigned and even fewer teachers know how to conduct such discussions or assess student par-ticipation in them. Students rarely engage in dialogical or dialectical reason-ing and few teachers can analyze such reasoning. Knowledge is viewed as verified intra-disciplinary propositions and well-supported intra-disciplinary theories. There is little or no discussion of the nature of prejudice or bias, lit-tle or no discussion of metacognition, little or no discussion of what a disci-plined, self-directed mind or self-directed thought require. We expect stu-dents to develop into literate, educated persons from years of content memorization and ritual performance.

The above dominant pattern of academic instruction and learning assumes an uncritical theory of knowledge, learning, and literacy coming under increasing critique by those concerned with instruction fitted to new interpretations of the emerging economic and social conditions and changing conditions for human survival. (Passmore, 1967) (Scheffler 1973, 1965) Those whose teaching reflects the didactic theory rarely formulate it explicitly. Some would deny that they hold it, though their practice implies it. In any case, it is with the theory implicit in practice that we are concerned.

Now let's examine the two opposing theories systematically in terms of specific contrasting assumptions.

Theory of Knowledge, Learning, and Literacy

Didactic Theory	Critical Theory
1. The fundamental needs of students	
That the fundamental need of students is to be taught more or less *what* to think, not *how* to think (that is, that students will learn how to think if they can only get into their heads what to think). ◆ Students are "given" or told details, definitions, explanations, rules, guidelines, reasons to learn.	That the fundamental need of students is to be taught *how* not *what* to think; that it is important to focus on significant content, but this should be accomplished by raising live issues that stimulate students to gather, analyze, and assess that content.
2. The nature of knowledge	
That knowledge is independent of the thinking that generates, organizes, and applies it. ◆ Students are said to *know* when they can repeat what has been covered. Students are given the finished products of someone else's thought.	That all knowledge of "content" is generated, organized, applied, analyzed, synthesized, and assessed by thinking; that gaining knowledge is unintelligible without engagement in such thinking. (It is *not* assumed that one can think without some content to think about, nor that all content is equally significant and useful.) ◆ Students are given opportunities to puzzle their way through to knowledge and explore its justification, *as part of* the process of learning.
3. Model of the educated person	
That educated, literate people are fundamentally repositories of content analogous to an encyclopedia or a data bank, directly comparing situations in the world with facts that they carry about fully formed as a result of an absorptive process. That an educated, literate person is fundamentally a true believer, that is, a possessor of truth, and therefore claims much knowledge.	That an educated, literate person is fundamentally a repository of strategies, principles, concepts, and insights embedded in processes of thought rather than in atomic facts. Experiences analyzed and organized by critical thought, rather than facts picked up one-by-one, characterize the educated person. Much of what is known is constructed by the thinker *as needed* from

Theory of Knowledge, Learning, and Literacy	
Didactic Theory	***Critical Theory***
♦ Texts, assignments, lectures, discussions, and tests are detail-oriented, and content dense.	context to context, not *prefabricated* in sets of true statements about the world. That an educated, literate person is fundamentally a seeker and questioner rather than a true believer, therefore cautious in claiming knowledge. ♦ Classroom activities consist of questions and problems for students to discuss and discover how to solve. Teachers model insightful consideration of questions and problems, and facilitate fruitful discussions.

4. The nature of knowledge

That knowledge, truth, and understanding can be transmitted from one person to another by verbal statements in the form of lectures or didactic teaching. ♦ For example, social studies texts present principles of geography and historical explanations. Questions at the end of the chapter are framed in identical language and can be answered by repeating the texts. "The correct answer" is in bold type or otherwise emphasized.	That knowledge and truth can rarely, and insight never, be transmitted from one person to another by the transmitter's verbal statements alone; that one cannot directly give another what one has learned — one can only facilitate the conditions under which people learn for themselves by figuring out or thinking things through. ♦ Students offer their own ideas and explore ideas given in the texts, providing their own examples and reasons. Students come to conclusions by practicing reasoning historically, geographically, scientifically, etc.

5. The nature of listening

That students do not need to be taught skills of listening to learn to pay attention and this is fundamentally a matter of self-discipline achieved through will power. Students should therefore be able to listen on command by the teacher. ♦ Students are told to listen carefully and are tested on their abilities to remember details and to follow directions.	That students need to be taught how to listen critically — an active and skilled process that can be learned by degrees with various levels of proficiency. Learning what others mean by what they say requires questioning, trying on, testing, and, hence, engaging in public or private dialogue with them, and this involves critical thinking. ♦ Teachers continually model active critical listening, asking probing and insightful questions of the speaker.

Theory of Knowledge, Learning, and Literacy

Didactic Theory	*Critical Theory*

6. The relationship of basic skills to thinking skills

That the basic skills of reading and writing can be taught without emphasis on higher order critical thinking. ♦ Reading texts provide comprehension questions requiring recall of random details. Occasionally, "main point," "plot," and "theme" lessons cover these concepts. Literal comprehension is distinguished from "extras" such as inferring, evaluating, thinking beyond. Only after basic literal comprehension has been established is the deeper meaning probed.

That the basic skills of reading and writing are inferential skills that require critical thinking; that students who do not learn to read and write critically are ineffective readers and writers, and that critical reading and writing involve dialogical processes in which probing critical questions are raised and answered. (For example, What is the fundamental issue? What reasons, what evidence, is relevant to this issue? Is this source or authority credible? Are these reasons adequate? Is this evidence accurate and sufficient? Does this contradict that? Does this conclusion follow? Is another point of view relevant to consider?) ♦ Teachers routinely require students to *explain* what they have read, to reconstruct the ideas, and to evaluate written material. Students construct and compare interpretations, reasoning their way to the most plausible interpretations. Discussion moves back and forth between what was said and what it means.

7. The status of questioning

That students who have no questions typically are learning well, while students with a lot of questions are experiencing difficulty in learning; that doubt and questioning weaken belief.

That students who have no questions typically are not learning, while having pointed and specific questions, on the other hand, is a significant sign of learning. Doubt and questioning, by deepening understanding, strengthen belief by putting it on more solid ground. ♦ Teachers evaluate their teaching by asking themselves: Are my students asking better questions — perceptive questions, questions which extend and apply what they have learned? ("Is that why ...?" Does this mean that ...?" "Then what if ...?")

Theory of Knowledge, Learning, and Literacy	
Didactic Theory	**Critical Theory**

8. The desirable classroom environment

That quiet classes with little student talk are typically reflective of students learning while classes with a lot of student talk are typically disadvantaged in learning.	That quiet classes with little student talk are typically classes with little learning while classes with much student talk focused on live issues is a sign of learning (provided students learn dialogical and dialectical skills).

9. The view of knowledge (atomistic vs. holistic)

That knowledge and truth can typically be learned best by being broken down into elements, and the elements into sub-elements, each taught sequentially and atomically. Knowledge is additive. ♦ Texts provide basic definitions and masses of details, but have little back-and-forth movement between them. They break knowledge into pieces, each of which is to be mastered one by one: subjects are taught separately. Each aspect is further broken down: each part of speech is covered separately; social studies texts are organized chronologically, geographically, etc.	That knowledge and truth is heavily systemic and holistic and can be learned only by many on-going acts of synthesis, many cycles from wholes to parts, tentative graspings of a whole guiding us in understanding its parts, periodic focusing on the parts (in relation to each other) shedding light upon the whole, and that the wholes that we learn have important relations to other wholes as well as their own parts and hence need to be frequently canvassed in learning any given whole. (This assumption has the implication that we cannot achieve in-depth learning in any given domain of knowledge unless the process of grasping that domain involves active consideration of its relation to other domains of knowledge.) That each learner creates knowledge. ♦ Education is organized around issues, problems, and basic concepts which are pursued and explored through all relevant subjects. Teachers routinely require students to relate knowledge from various fields. Students compare analogous events or situations, propose examples, apply new concepts to other situations.

Theory of Knowledge, Learning, and Literacy

Didactic Theory	**Critical Theory**

10. The place of values

That people can gain significant knowledge without seeking or valuing it, and hence that education can take place without significant transformation of values for the learner. ♦ For example, texts tend to inform students of the importance of studying the subject or topic covered, rather than proving it by *showing* its immediate usefulness and having students use it.	That people gain only the knowledge they seek and value. All other learning is superficial and transitory. All genuine education transforms the basic values of the person educated, resulting in persons becoming life-long learners and rational persons. ♦ Instruction poses problems meaningful to students, requiring them to use the tools of each academic domain.

11. The importance of being aware of one's own learning process

That understanding the mind and how it functions, its epistemological health and pathology, are not important or necessary parts of learning. To learn the basic subject matter of the schools one need not focus on such matters, except perhaps with certain disadvantaged learners.	That understanding the mind and how it functions, its health and pathology, are important and necessary parts of learning. To learn subject matter in-depth, we must gain some insight into how we as thinkers and learners process that subject matter.

12. The place of misconceptions

That ignorance is a vacuum or simple lack, and that student prejudices, biases, misconceptions, and ignorance are automatically replaced by their being given knowledge. ♦ Little if any attention is given to students' beliefs. Material is presented from the point of view of the authority, the one who knows.	That prejudices, biases, and misconceptions are built up through actively constructed inferences embedded in experience and must be broken down through a similar process; hence, that students must reason their way dialogically and dialectically out of their prejudices, biases, and misconceptions. ♦ Students have many opportunities to express their views in class, however biased or prejudiced, and a non-threatening environment to argue their way out of their internalized misconceptions. Teachers cultivate in themselves genuine curiosity about how students see things, why they think as they do, and the structure of students' thought. The educational process starts where students are, and walks them through to insight.

Theory of Knowledge, Learning, and Literacy

Didactic Theory	*Critical Theory*

13. The level of understanding desired

That students need not understand the rational ground or deeper logic of what they learn to absorb knowledge. Extensive but superficial learning can later be deepened. ♦ For example, historical and scientific explanations are presented to students as givens, not as having been reasoned to. In language arts, skills and distinctions are rarely explicitly linked to such basic ideas as 'good writing' or 'clear expression.'

That rational assent is an essential facet of all genuine learning and that an in-depth understanding of basic concepts and principles is an essential foundation for rational concepts and facts. That in-depth understanding of root concepts and principles should be used as organizers for learning within and across subject matter domains. ♦ Students are encouraged to discover how the details relate to basic concepts. Details are traced back to the foundational purposes, concepts, and insights.

14. Depth versus breadth

That it is more important to cover a great deal of knowledge or information superficially than a small amount in depth. That only after the facts are understood, can students discuss their meaning; that higher order thinking can and should only be practiced by students who have mastered the material. That thought-provoking discussions are for the gifted and advanced, only.

That it is more important to cover a small amount of knowledge or information in depth (deeply probing its foundation) than to cover a great deal of knowledge superficially. That all students can and must probe the significance of and justification for what they learn.

15. Role definition for teacher and student

That the roles of teacher and learner are distinct and should not be blurred.

That we learn best by teaching or explaining to others what we know. ♦ Students have many opportunities to teach what they know, to formulate their understanding in different ways, and to respond to questions from others.

Theory of Knowledge, Learning, and Literacy

Didactic Theory	*Critical Theory*
16. The correction of ignorance	
That the teacher should correct the learners' ignorance by telling them what they do not know.	That students need to learn to distinguish for themselves what they know from what they do not know. Students should recognize that they do not genuinely know or comprehend what they have merely memorized. Self-directed recognition of ignorance is necessary to learning. ♦ Teachers respond to mistakes and confusion by probing with questions, allowing students to correct themselves and each other. Teachers routinely allow students the opportunity to supply their own ideas on a subject before reading their texts.
17. The responsibility for learning	
That the teacher has the fundamental responsibility for student learning. Teachers and texts provide information, questions, and drill.	That progressively the student should be given increasing responsibility for his or her own learning. Students need to come to see that only they can learn for themselves and that they will not do so unless they actively and willingly engage themselves in the process. ♦ The teacher provides opportunities for students to decide what they need to know and helps them develop strategies for finding or figuring it out.
18. The transfer of learning to everyday situations	
That students will automatically transfer the knowledge that they learn in didactically taught courses to relevant real-life situations. ♦ For example, students are told to perform a given skill on a given group of items. The text will *tell* students when, how, and why to use that skill.	That most knowledge that students memorize in didactically taught courses is either forgotten or rendered "inert" by their mode of learning it, and that the most significant transfer is achieved by in-depth learning which focuses on experiences meaningful to the student and aims directly at transfer.
19. Status of personal experiences	
That the personal experience of the student has no essential role to play in education.	That the personal experience of the student is essential to all schooling at all levels and in all subjects; that it is a crucial part of the content to be processed (applied, analyzed, synthesized, and assessed) by the student.

Theory of Knowledge, Learning, and Literacy

Didactic Theory	**Critical Theory** ✦

20. The assessment of knowledge acquisition

That a student who can correctly answer questions, provide definitions, and apply formulae while taking tests has proven his or her knowledge or understanding of those details. Since the didactic approach tends to assume, for example, that knowing a word is knowing its definition (and an example), didactic instruction tends to overemphasize definitions. Students practice skills by doing exercises, specifically designed as drill. Successfully finishing the exercise is taken to be equivalent to having learned the skill.	That students can often provide correct answers, repeat definitions, and apply formulae while yet not understanding those questions, definitions, or formulae. That proof of knowledge or understanding is found in the students' ability to explain in their own words, with examples, the meaning and significance of the knowledge, why it is so, and to *spontaneously* recall and use it when relevant.

21. The authority validating knowledge

That learning is essentially a private, monological process in which learners can proceed more or less directly to established truth, under the guidance of an expert in such truth. The authoritative answers that the teacher has are the fundamental standards for assessing students' learning.	That learning is essentially a public, communal, dialogical, and dialectical process in which learners can only proceed indirectly to truth, with much "zigging and zagging" along the way, much back-tracking, misconception, self-contradiction, and frustration in the process. In this process, authoritative answers are replaced by authoritative standards for engagement in the communal, dialogical process of enquiry.

✦ *A Glimpse at the Historical and Social Background of Didactic Instruction and Uncritical Learning*

The didactic theory of knowledge, learning, and literacy, though unsuited to in-depth learning or critical thinking, has been functional to some extent for the maintenance of routine life in what have been to date largely uncritical societies. Schooling has been first and last a social process, reflecting ascendant social forces and thinking largely subservient to them. Much of what happens in schools results from social and economic decisions made predominantly by non-academics. Epistemo-logic is traditionally subordinate to socio-logic.

We must remember that knowledge, however extensive, is a highly limited social construction out of an infinitude of possible such constructions. Although all humans live in a veritable sea of potentially expressible truths, they express only a few of them, only a few become knowledge. The constraints that we must live within inevitably limit the social production of knowledge. We are therefore highly selective and directional in that production. We don't randomly express truths. We systematically seek the knowledge which serves our interests, meets our needs, and solves our problems. The human mind and social life being what it is, we generate a good deal of pseudo-knowledge intermixed with the genuine. We also avoid producing and disseminating knowledge that might undermine our social engagements and vested interests. Not all learning is ipso facto rational, and irrational practices are often deeply embedded in day-to-day social life. We do this spontaneously and naturally, without guile or conscious malice. We are not *truth* seekers by nature but *functional knowledge* seekers. And widely accepted pseudo-knowledge is often quite functional. Hence, to take an obvious example, in a racist society it is functional to be racist. Rationally unjustified beliefs often enable us to get ahead and stay out of trouble. Ordinary social life, whether we like it or not, is filled with innumerable functional falsehoods.

As long as societies functioned primarily as self-contained systems independent of each other and the repercussions of economic, social, and political conflicts were manageable, functional falsehoods and suppressed knowledge (the avoidance of unpleasant truth) was tolerable. We should remember that the systematic search for particular dimensions of knowledge as an organized and specialized endeavor is itself quite recent in human history. It is at most 2,000 years old while the species is somewhere between 1,000,000 and 3,000,000 years old. Most disciplines have emerged as significant endeavors only within the last 300 or so years. Wholesale mass schooling is only about 100 years old. Schools and socialization historically have armed the mass of people with minimum levels of superficial knowledge, functional falsehoods, and socially approved biases. Only a few were encouraged to approach the ideal of critical thought, and even these only in a limited way. As scientific disciplines emerged it became necessary for some to understand particular disciplines deeply. What Kant called *scientific ignorance* — knowing clearly what we do not yet know — became necessary for advancing intra-disciplinary progress. But most people were not expected to contribute to the advances in specialized disciplines, only to use in a limited way some tools that a technological application of those advances made possible.

Furthermore, the overwhelming majority of people were each expected to find a particular niche within the complex structures of social life, not to engage in social critique, not to detect social contradictions, not to expose pseudo-knowledge or to articulate suppressed knowledge. That learning was all of a piece for the typical (uncritical) learner — truth, half-truth, bias, and falsehood blended together — created no insoluble economic or social problems for society. Problems aplenty there were, but on the whole people in the same societies shared the same basic beliefs, true or false, rational or irrational. Anarchy did not result from the fact that "Truth" meant no more in the last analysis to ordinary people than "We believe it" or "It agrees with our beliefs" or "It was said by someone with authority and prestige."

But the relative homogeneity and isolation of societies began to break down with the advent of science and the emergence of a technological world. More and more individuals became, are increasingly becoming, aware of differences in belief, not just of people outside but of people inside their societies as well. And interdependence has dramatically and increasingly emerged. What were previously local decisions with nothing more than local consequences are becoming international matters. Knowledge production and dissemination can no longer be premised on an intra-societal world and humanity cannot survive indefinitely with masses of people whose ultimate *de facto* test of knowledge is personal desire or social conformity.

✦ *What, Then, Is Critical Thinking?*

It is certainly of the nature of the human mind to think — spontaneously, continuously, and pervasively — but it is not of the nature of the human mind to think critically about the standards and principles guiding its spontaneous thought. It has no built-in drive to question its innate tendency to believe what it wants to believe, what makes it comfortable, what is simple rather than complex, and what is commonly believed and socially rewarded. The human mind is ordinarily at peace with itself as it internalizes and creates biases, prejudices, falsehoods, half-truths, and distortions. Compartmentalized contradictions do not, by their very nature, disturb those who take them in and selectively use them. The human mind spontaneously experiences itself as in tune with reality, as directly observing and faithfully recording it. It takes a special intervening process to produce the kind of self-criticalness that enables the mind to effectively and constructively question its own creations. The mind spontaneously but uncritically invests itself with epistemological authority with the same ease with which it accepts authority figures in the world into which it is socialized.

Learning to think critically is therefore an extraordinary process that cultivates capacities merely potential in human thought and develops them at the expense of capacities spontaneously activated from within and reinforced by normal socialization. It is not normal and inevitable or even common for a mind to discipline itself within a rational perspective and direct itself toward rational rather than egocentric beliefs, practices, and values. Yet it is possible to describe the precise conditions under which critical minds can be cultivated. The differences between critical and uncritical thought are increasingly apparent.

Nonetheless, because of the complexity of critical thinking — its relationship to an unlimited number of behaviors in an unlimited number of situations, its conceptual interdependence with other concepts such as the critical person, the critical society, a critical theory of knowledge, learning, and literacy, and rationality, not to speak of the opposites of these concepts — one should not put too much weight on any particular definition of critical thinking. Distinguished theoreticians have formulated many useful definitions which highlight important features of critical thought. Harvey Siegel has defined critical thinking as "thinking appropriately moved by reasons". This definition highlights the contrast between the mind's tendency to be shaped by phenomena other than reasons: desires, fears, social rewards and punishments, etc. It points up the connection between critical thinking and the classic philosophical ideal of rationality. Yet clearly the ideal of rationality is itself open to multiple explications. Similar points can be made about Robert Ennis' and Matthew Lipman's definitions.

Robert Ennis defines critical thinking as "rational reflective thinking concerned with what to do or believe". This definition usefully calls attention to the wide role that critical thinking plays in everyday life, for, since all behavior depends on what we believe, all human action depends upon what we in some sense *decide* to do. However, like Siegel's definition it assumes that the reader has a clear concept of rationality and of the conditions under which a decision can be said to be "reflective". There is also a possible ambiguity in Ennis' use of 'reflective'. As a person internalizes critical standards the application of these standards to action becomes more automatic, less a matter of conscious effort, hence less a matter of overt "reflection", assuming that Ennis means to imply by 'reflection' a special consciousness or deliberateness.

Matthew Lipman defines critical thinking as "skillful, responsible, thinking that is conducive to judgment because it relies on criteria, is self-correcting, and is sensitive to context". This definition is useful insofar as one clearly understands the difference between responsible and irresponsible thinking, as well as what the appropriate self-correction of thought, the appropriate use of criteria, and appropriate sensitivity to context mean. Of course, it would be easy to find instances of thinking that were self-correcting, used criteria, and responded to context *in one sense* and nevertheless were *uncritical* in some other sense. One's criteria might be uncritically chosen, for example, or the manner of responding to context might be critically deficient in numerous ways.

I make these points not to deny the usefulness of these definitions, but to point out limitations in the process of definition itself when addressing a complex concept such as critical thinking. Rather than to work solely with one definition of critical thinking, it is better to retain a host of definitions, for two reasons: *1)* to maintain insight into the various dimensions of critical thinking that alternative definitions highlight, and *2)* to help oneself escape the limitations of each. In this spirit I will present a number of my definitions of the cluster of concepts whose relationship to each other is fundamental to critical thinking. These concepts are: critical thinking, uncritical thinking, sophistic critical thinking, and fair-minded critical thinking. After so doing, I will analyze one definition at length.

CRITICAL THINKING

    a) the art of thinking about your thinking while your're thinking so as to make your thinking more clear, precise, accurate, relevant, consistent, and fair

    b) the art of constructive skepticism

    c) the art of identifying and removing bias, prejudice, and one-sidedness of thought

    d) the art of self-directed, in-depth, rational learning

    e) thinking that rationally certifies what we know and makes clear wherein we are ignorant

UNCRITICAL THINKING

    a) thought captive of one's ego, desires, social conditioning, prejudices, or irrational impressions

    b) thinking that is egocentric, careless, heedless of assumptions, relevant evidence, implications, or consistency

    c) thinking that habitually ignores epistemological demands in favor of its egocentric commitments

SOPHISTIC CRITICAL THINKING

    a) thinking which meets epistemological demands insofar as they square with the vested interests of the thinker

    b) skilled thinking that is heedless of assumptions, relevance, reasons, evidence, implications and consistency only insofar as it is in the vested interest of the thinker to do so

    c) skilled thinking that is motivated by vested interest, egocentrism, or ethnocentrism rather than by truth or objective reasonability

FAIRMINDED CRITICAL THINKING

    a) skilled thinking which meets epistemological demands regardless of the vested interests or ideological commitments of the thinker

    b) skilled thinking characterized by empathy into diverse opposing points of view and devotion to truth as against self-interest

    c) skilled thinking that is consistent in the application of intellectual standards, holding one's self to the same rigorous standards of evidence and proof to which one hold's one's antagonists

    d) skilled thinking that demonstrates the commitment to entertain all viewpoints sympathetically and to assess them with the same intellectual standards, without reference to one's own feelings or vested interests, or the feelings or vested interests of one's friends, community or nation

It is important not only to emphasize the dimension of skills in critical thinking, but also to explicitly mark out the very real possibility of a one-sided use of them. Indeed, the historical tendency for skills of thought to be systematically used in defense of the vested interests of dominant social groups and the parallel tendency of all social groups to develop one-sided thinking in support of their own interests, mandates marking this tendency explicitly. We should clearly recognize that one-sided critical thinking is much more common than fairminded critical thought.

With these cautionary remarks in mind I will provide a definition of critical thinking which lends itself to an analysis of three crucial dimensions of critical thought:

      1) the perfections of thought
      2) the elements of thought
      3) the domains of thought

THE DEFINITION:

> Critical thinking is disciplined, self-directed thinking which exemplifies the perfections of thinking appropriate to a particular mode or domain of thinking. It comes in two forms. If the thinking is disciplined to serve the interests of a particular individual or group, to the exclusion of other relevant persons and groups, I call it *sophistic* or *weak sense* critical thinking. If the thinking is disciplined to take into account the interests of diverse persons or groups, I call it *fairminded* or *strong sense* critical thinking.

To this definition should be added the following gloss:

> In thinking critically we use our command of *the elements of thinking* to adjust our thinking successfully to the logical demands of a type or *mode of thinking*. As we come to habitually think critically in the strong sense we develop special *traits of mind*: intellectual humility, intellectual courage, intellectual perseverance, intellectual integrity, and confidence in reason. A sophistic or weak sense critical thinker develops these traits only in a restricted way, consistent with egocentric and sociocentric commitments.

I shall now list examples of what I mean by the perfections and imperfections of thought, the elements of thought, and the domains of thought. In each case I will comment briefly on the significance of these dimensions.

The Perfections and Imperfections of Thought

clarity	vs	unclarity
precision	vs	imprecision
specificity	vs	vagueness
accuracy	vs	inaccuracy
relevance	vs	irrelevance
consistency	vs	inconsistency
logicalness	vs	illogicalness
depth	vs	superficiality
completeness	vs	incompleteness
significance	vs	triviality
fairness	vs	bias or one-sidedness
adequacy (for purpose)	vs	inadequacy

Each of the above are general canons for thought. To develop one's mind and to discipline one's thinking to come up to these standards requires extensive practice and long-term cultivation. Of course coming up to these standards is relative and often has to be adjusted to a particular domain of thought. Being *precise* while doing mathematics is not the same thing as being precise while writing a poem or describing an experience.

Furthermore, one perfection of thought may come to be periodically incompatible with the others: *adequacy to the purpose*. Because the social world is often irrational and unjust, because people are often manipulated to act against their interests, because skilled thought is often used to serve vested interest, thought adequate to these purposes may require skilled violation of the common standards for good thinking. Skilled propaganda, skilled political debate, skilled defense of a group's interests, skilled deception of one's enemy may require the violation or selective application of any of the above standards. The perfecting of one's thought as an instrument for success in a world based on power and advantage is a different matter from the perfecting of one's thought for the apprehension and defense of fairminded truth. To develop one's critical thinking skills merely to the level of adequacy for success is to develop those skills in a lower or *weaker* sense. It is important to underscore the commonality of this weaker sense of critical thinking, for it is dominant in the everyday world. Virtually all social groups disapprove of members who make the case for their competitors or enemies however justified that case may be. Skillful thinking is commonly a tool in the struggle for power and advantage, not an angelic force that transcends this struggle. It is only as the struggle becomes mutually destructive and it comes to be the advantage of all to go beyond the onesidedness of each that a social ground is laid for fairmindedness of thought. There is no society yet in existence that in a general way cultivates fairness of thought in its citizens.

THE ELEMENTS OF THOUGHT

Both sophistic and fairminded critical thinkers are skilled compared to uncritical thinkers. The uncritical thinker is often unclear, imprecise, vague, illogical, unreflective, superficial, inconsistent, inaccurate, or trivial. To avoid these imperfections in thought requires some command of the elements of thought. These include an understanding of and an ability to formulate, analyze and assess these elements:

1) The problem or question at issue
2) The purpose or goal of the thinking
3) The frame of reference or points of view involved
4) Assumptions made
5) Central concepts and ideas involved
6) Principles or theories used
7) Evidence, data, or reasons advanced
8) Interpretations and claims made
9) Inferences, reasoning, and lines of formulated thought
10) Implications and consequences involved

The principles of thought that underlie command of these elements may be formulated and grouped in a variety of ways. I favor a formulation that highlights the intimate relation between the component skills of critical thinking with the *traits* of a critical thinker. These abilities to command the elements of thought must be reflected in the critical thinkers' insights into the diverse demands of differing question types and domains of thought.

THE DOMAINS OF THOUGHT

The ability to command the elements of thought to achieve the perfections of thought depends on a thinker's ability to adjust his or her thinking to differing question types and domains of thought. Of course there is no *one* way to classify questions into types or thinking into domains. In fact, critical thinkers must be comfortable adjusting their thinking not only to different question types, but also to conceptualizing each question from various analytic points of view. Often one should understand a question from a "subject-matter" point of view: to grasp, for example, that it is biological, or psychological, or mathematical, or economic. But this is rarely enough, for the same subject area may contain questions of different types, may have more than one conceptual framework within it, and many of the most important questions we face are multi-disciplinary or interdisciplinary in nature. Or one question may be analyzed from different perspectives within the logic of questions. For example, virtually all questions can be analyzed from the perspective of the distinction between empirical, conceptual, and evaluative components. Some questions are more empirical than conceptual or more evaluative than empirical. Sometimes we need to adjust our thinking about a question to take these parameters into account. Few students, for example, can address fundamentally conceptual questions; for example, questions like these:

Is a whale a fish?
Is a human fetus a person?
Is Communism compatible with democracy?
Is Capitalism compatible with democracy?
Can one ever be certain about what is right?
Are humans essentially rational or irrational?
What is the difference between freedom fighters and terrorists?
Are there such things as male and female qualities or are all such qualities a matter of social conditioning?
Can computers think?
Do animals have language?

And this is by no means all, for sometimes one must know whether a question is being raised against the background of a given social system, a given socio-logic. I have alluded to this variable before in terms of the use within social systems of "functional falsehoods". What is justified as an answer to a question, given one social system as the defining context, may very well be different within the logic of another social system. We need to know, therefore, whether we must reason within the logic of a given social system or more broadly. A question may be answerable within one system and not within another, or not in the same sense, or in the same sense but with a different answer.

Going still further, one may have to recognize, in asking a question, whether we are framing it within the logic of a technical or natural language. The question, "What is fear?" asked with the technical language of physiology and biology in mind, may well be a different question from that same interrogative sentence asked in ordinary English, a *natural* language.

Finally we often need to know, when reasoning about a question, whether it is most appropriately treated within an established logic (monological issues), or whether it is plausible to approach it from diverse points of view (multilogical issues). If one dominant theory or established procedure or algorithm exists for settling a question, it is rational to use it. Many of the routine problems of everyday life as well as many of the standard problems in highly technical or scientific disciplines are of this sort. However, students must learn how to identify those higher order problems to which multiple theories, frames of reference, or competing ideologies apply, and hence which cannot legitimately be approached monologically. Instruction rarely addresses these multilogical issues, even though most of the pressing problems of everyday social, political, and personal life are of this kind. Moreover, there is good reason to use a multilogical approach even to monological issues, when students initially approach them. I shall return to this important point presently.

Schooling, as structured today, lacks *organized* emphasis on any of these dimensions of thought: its perfections, its elements, or its typology. Educators assume good thinking follows from the systematic coverage of content and problem-solving algorithms and the memorization that traditional didactic instruction inevitably fosters. The result is students who do not think about the general perfections, the elements, or the typology of thought, students who think about knowledge and learning solely within the traditional didactic model and, as a result, can function comfortably only with lower-order, monological problems. As Lauren Resnick has put it:

> Mass education was, from its inception, concerned with inculcating routine abilities: simple computation, reading predictable texts, reciting religious or civic codes. It did not take as goals for its students the ability to interpret unfamiliar texts, create material others would want and need to read, construct convincing arguments, develop original solutions to technical or social problems. The political conditions under which mass education developed encouraged instead the routinization of basic skills as well as the standardization of teaching and education institutions. (p. 5)

Resnick characterizes the kind of (higher order) thinking typically neglected in the schools as follows:

- Higher order thinking is *nonalgorithmic*. That is, the path of action is not fully specified in advance.

- Higher order thinking tends to be *complex*. The total path is not "visible" (mentally speaking) from any single vantage point.
- Higher order thinking often yields *multiple solutions*, each with costs and benefits, rather than unique solutions.
- Higher order thinking involves *nuanced judgment* and interpretation.
- Higher order thinking involves the application of *multiple criteria*, which sometimes conflict with one another.
- Higher order thinking often involves *uncertainty*. Not everything that bears on the task at hand is known.
- Higher order thinking involves *self-regulation* of the thinking process. We do not recognize higher order thinking in an individual when someone else calls the plays at every step.
- Higher order thinking involves *imposing meaning*, finding structure in apparent disorder.
- Higher order thinking is *effortful*. There is considerable mental work involved in the kinds of elaborations and judgments required. (p. 3)

Important consequences follow from this tendency of schools to emphasize lower order thinking: *1)* students do not learn how to think in an interdisciplinary way, *2)* they are uncomfortable thinking within multiple points of view, *3)* they tend to look for recipes and algorithmic procedures for settling questions, *4)* they tend to do poorly when faced with unfamiliar issues, and *5)* they tend to gravitate toward an uncritical dogmatism or an equally uncritical relativism. Not only do most students fail to achieve any sense of how to adjust their thinking to the nature of the issue or domain about which they are thinking, but their spontaneous "lower order" thinking prevents them from developing into autonomous thinkers and independent learners.

✦ *The Logic of Learning Versus the Logic of Proof*

Higher order (multilogical) thinking applies to two basic conditions: *1)* when the question at issue is multilogical and *2)* when one is unfamiliar with the logic of the question at issue and hence must think one's way into its background logic. Standard instruction is ill-suited to both of these conditions. Multilogical issues are usually ignored and monological domains are presented as finished products. Students seldom have an opportunity to think their way into a new domain of knowledge, but are instead expected to learn to think within finished procedures, algorithms, or concepts. Most mathematics instruction illustrates this point. Rather than being introduced to problems that bridge the gap between familiar and novel problem types, students are introduced to finished algorithms and procedures. Consequently most students have large gaps in their thinking, since the algorithms they learn are only superficially understood. They are rarely expected to *think* their way to these algorithms. They learn to identify the need for one by recognizing the form in which problems are (artificially) framed in their texts.

History instruction illustrates a parallel point. Students read the finished products of professional historians rather than problems and data which enable them to think historically. Students have little sense of how to engage in historical thinking and so do not recognize the historical dimension of the problems they face in everyday life. What they learn in history class seems totally unrelated to their concerns or values.

We need a shift to higher-order thinking in every domain of learning: in monological domains like mathematics, so that students *think* their way non-algorithmically into mathematical systems, and in multilogical domains like history and sociology so that they come to appreciate the true (multilogical) nature of these domains.

The main point is this, higher-order thinking is required for all deep-seated original learning, even within domains that, once mastered, can routinely be canvassed in a lower order, monological way. To genuinely grasp a new logical domain, one must thoughtfully transfer logical structures that one does understand to the new domain and use the familiar logic analogically to mentally construct the unfamiliar one. This requires higher order thinking on the part of all learners in all original learning. It requires argumentation pro and con as students explore alternative analogies and strategies. Standard schooling has yet to assimilate this insight.

A couple of examples from research into math and science instruction will illustrate this point. Math and science provide paradigms of monological disciplines. Algorithms and quantifiable laws abound. Most textbooks contain no theoretical disputes. Students are mainly expected to learn established procedures, technical definitions, and practices. Yet even here we are discovering the importance of having students *think* their way, on their own terms, with much theoretical disputation, to comprehension and insight. The work of Easley at Illinois (1983a, 1983b, 1984a, 1984b) Schoenfeld at Berkeley, (1979, 1985, 1986, 1987, in press), and many others [Collins, Brown, and Newman (in press), Crosswhite (1987), Kilpatrick (1987), Driver (1978, 1986, 1987), Smith (1987b, 1987a, 1983), and Roth (1984, 1986, 1987)] demonstrate this need.

Schoenfeld puts the claim bluntly: "I believe that most instruction in mathematics is, in a very real sense, deceptive and possibly fraudulent." He supports this claim by citing cases in which it can be demonstrated that even advanced students of mathematics have fundamental misconceptions about the mathematical symbols and algorithms they manipulate:

> I taught a problem-solving course for junior and senior mathematics majors at Berkeley in 1976. These students had already seen some remarkably sophisticated mathematics. Linear algebra and differential equations were old hat. Topology, Fourier transforms, and measure theory were familiar to some. I gave them a straightforward theorem from plane geometry (required when I was in the tenth grade). Only two of eight students made any progress on it, some of them by using arc length integrals to measure the circumference of a circle. (Schoenfeld, 1979) Out of the context of normal course work these students could not do elementary mathematics. (pp. 28–29)

> In sum, all too often we focus on a narrow collection of well-defined tasks and train students to execute those tasks in a routine, if not algorithmic fashion. Then we test the students on tasks that are very close to the ones they have been taught. If they succeed on those problems we and they congratulate each other on the fact that they have learned some powerful mathematical techniques. In fact, they may be able to use such techniques mechanically while lacking some rudimentary thinking skills. To allow them and ourselves, to believe that they "understand" the mathematics is deceptive and fraudulent. (p. 29)

Schoenfeld compares stereotypical standard practice with multilogical mathematics instruction that focuses on class discussion, debate, argumentation, and interdisciplinary application. He cites Harold Fawcett's geometry classes at the Ohio state University laboratory school, described in the 1938 NCTM Yearbook, *The Nature of Proof*:

> Simply put, Fawcett believed that mathematics can help you think — in particular, that a course in geometric proof can help students to learn to reason clearly about a wide range of situations. Following Dewey, Fawcett hoped to help his students develop "reflective thinking" — "active, persistent and careful consideration of any belief or supposed form of knowledge in the light of the grounds that support it and the further conclusions to which it tends". Following Christofferson, Fawcett sought to develop in his students "an attitude of mind which tends always to analyze situations, to understand their interrelationships, to question hasty conclusions, to express clearly, precisely, and accurately non-geometric as well as geometric ideas". Among his goals for students were that in situations sufficiently important to them, his students would: ask that important terms be defined; require evidence in support of conclusions they are pressed to accept; analyze the evidence and distinguish fact from assumption; recognize stated and unstated assumptions; evaluate them; and finally, evaluate the arguments, accepting or rejecting the conclusion. Moreover, they would do so reflectively, constantly re-examining the assumptions behind their beliefs and that guide their actions. (p. 37–8 Schoenfeld)

Katherine Roth (in press) comments on the problem of science instruction in a similar way:

> Students memorize facts and formulae, they plug in these facts and formulae to pass tests, and they use these to solve "textbook" problems. However, they do not use these facts and formulae to explain real-world phenomena that they observe and experience. To students, the facts and formulae are school knowledge, perhaps a third vine to add to the Pines and West (1983) metaphor. Students use this vine of knowledge to "get by" in school. However, this vine is unconnected with really making sense of their disciplinary vine, and it is totally irrelevant to students' everyday ways of thinking — their intuitive knowledge vine. Thus, students end instruction still finding their intuitive theories, or misconceptions, as most useful in explaining their world. Connections between their own understandings and the disciplinary concepts are rarely made. (p. 23)

She and others doing similar research continually call for an approach that requires much classroom "debate" and hence multilogical thinking:

> Most of the teachers using conceptual conflict as an instruction strategy frequently encouraged students to debate among themselves. They did not easily cave in to students' desires to be told the "right" answer. Instead, the teachers asked questions to help students clarify their explanations and to develop better support for their thinking. (ibid)

We should not assume, of course, that the change required is simply in a manner of teaching on the part of the teacher. It also requires a fundamental change in the teachers' thinking about their own learning. Consider this letter from a teacher with a Master's degree in physics and mathematics, with 20 years of high school teaching experience in physics:

> After I started teaching, I realized that I had learned physics by rote and that I really did not understand all I knew about physics. My thinking students asked me questions for which I always had the standard textbook answers, but for the first time it made me start thinking for myself, and I realized that these canned answers were not justified by my own thinking and only confused my students who were showing some ability to think for themselves. To achieve my academic goals I had to memorize the thoughts of others, but I had never learned or been encouraged to learn to think for myself.

✦ Conclusion

The pace of change in the world is accelerating, yet educational institutions have not kept up. Indeed, schools have historically been the most static of social institutions, uncritically passing down from generation to generation out-moded didactic, lecture-and-drill-based, models of instruction. Predictable results follow. Students, on the whole, do not learn how to work by, or think for, themselves. They do not learn how to gather, analyze, synthesize, and assess information. They do not learn how to analyze the diverse logics of the questions and problems they face and hence how to adjust their thinking to them. They do not learn how to enter sympathetically into the thinking of others, nor how to deal rationally with conflicting points of view. They do not learn to become critical readers, writers, speakers, or listeners. They do not learn how to use their native languages clearly, precisely, or persuasively. They do not, therefore, become "literate", in the proper sense of the word. Neither do they gain much genuine knowledge since, for the most part, they could not explain the basis for their beliefs. They would be hard pressed to explain, for example, which of their beliefs were based on rational assent and which on simple conformity to what they have heard. They do not see how they might critically analyze their own experience or identify national or group bias in their own thought. They are much more apt to learn on the basis of irrational than rational modes of thought. They lack the traits of mind of a genuinely educated person: intellectual humility, courage, integrity, perseverance, and faith in reason.

Fortunately, there is a movement in education today striving to address these problems in a global way, with strategies and materials for the modification of instruction at all levels of education. It arises from an emerging new theory of knowledge, learning, and literacy which recognizes the centrality of independent critical thought to all substantial learning, which recognizes the importance of higher order multilogical thinking for childhood as well as adult learning, to foundational learning in monological as well as multilogical disciplines. This educational reform movement does not propose an educational miracle cure, for its leading proponents recognize that many social and historical forces must come together before the ideals of the critical thinking movement will be achieved. Schools do not exist in a social vacuum. To the extent that the broader society is uncritical, so, on the whole, will society's schools. Nevertheless the social conditions necessary for fundamental changes in schooling are increasingly apparent. The pressure for fundamental change is growing. Whether and to what extent these needed basic changes will be delayed or side-tracked, and so require new periodic resurgences of this movement, with new, more elaborate articulations of its ideals, goals, and methods — only time will tell.

✦ References

Collins, A., Brown, J. S., & Newman, S. (in press). "The New Apprenticeship: Teaching Students the Craft of Reading, Writing, and Mathematics." In L. B. Resnick (Ed.), *Cognition and Instruction: Issues and Agendas.* Hillsdale, J. N.: Erlbaum.

Crosswhite, F. J. (1987). "Cognitive Science and Mathematics Education: A Mathematics Educator's Perspective." In A. Schoenfeld (Ed.), *Cognitive Science and Mathematics Education,* pp. 256–277. Hillsdale, NJ: Erlbaum.

Driver, R. (1986). *Restructuring the Physics Curriculum: Some Implications of Studies on Learning for Curriculum Development.* Invited paper presented at the International Conference on Trends in Physics Education, Tokyo, Japan.

Driver, R. (1987). "Promoting Conceptual Change in Classroom Settings: The Experience of the Children's Learning in Science Project". in J. D. Novak (Ed.), *Proceeding of the Second International Seminar on Misconceptions and Educational Strategies in Science and Mathematics.* Ithaca, NY: Cornell University.

Driver, R., & Easley, J. (1978). "Pupils and Paradigms: A Review of Literature Related to Concept Development in Adolescent Science Students. *Studies in Science Education, 5,* 61–84.

Easley, J. (1983a). "A Japanese Approach to Arithmetic." *For the Learning of Mathematics,* 3 (3).

Easley, J. (1983b). "What's There to Talk about in Arithmetic?" *Problem Solving* (Newsletter, The Franklin Institute Press) 5.

Easley, J. (1984a). "Is There Educative Power in Students' Alternative Frameworks?" *Problem Solving* (Newsletter, The Franklin Institute Press), 6.

Easley, J. (1984b). "A Teacher Educator's Perspective on Students' and Teachers' Schemes: Or Teaching by Listening." Unpublished paper, presented at the *Conference on Thinking, Harvard Graduate School of Education.*

Ennis, Robert H. "Goals For A Critical-Thinking/Reasoning Curriculum" Illinois Critical Thinking Project. University of Illinois, Champaign. 1985.

Kilpatrick, J. (1987) "Problem Formulating: Where do Good Problems Come From?" In A. Schoenfeld (Ed.), *Cognitive Science and Mathematics Education,* pp. 123–148. Hillsdale, J. N.: Erlbaum.

Lipman, Matthew. (March, 1988) "Critical Thinking and the Use of Criteria" *Inquiry,* Newsletter of the Institute for Critical Thinking, Montclair State College, Upper Montclair.

Passmore, John. "On Teaching to be Critical." *The Concept of Education,* Routledge & Kegan Paul, London: 1967. pp. 192–211.

Paul, Richard W. *Critical Thinking Handbook: K–3, A Guide for Remodelling Lesson Plans in Language Arts, Social Studies and Science,* Co-authors: A. J. A. Binker, Marla Charbonneau. Center for Critical Thinking and Moral Critique, Sonoma State University, Rohnert Park. 1987.

Paul, Richard W. *Critical Thinking Handbook: 4–6, A Guide for Remodelling Lesson Plans in Language Arts, Social Studies and Science,* Co-authors: A. J. A. Binker, Karen Jensen, Heidi Kreklau. Center for Critical Thinking and Moral Critique, Sonoma State University, Rohnert Park. 1987.

Paul, Richard W. "Teaching Critical Thinking in the Strong Sense: A Focus on Self-Deception, World Views, and a Dialectical Mode of Analysis," *Informal Logic,* May 1982, J. Anthony Blair and Ralph Johnson, editors.

Paul, Richard W. "The Critical Thinking Movement: A Historical Perspective," *National Forum,* Winter 1985, Stephen White, editor.

Paul, Richard W. "Critical Thinking and the Critical Person," *Thinking: Progress in Research and Teaching,* Lawrence Erlbaum Associates, Inc. 1987 Hillsdale, J. N., Perkins, Bishop, and Lochhead, editors.

Paul, Richard W. "Dialogical Thinking: Critical Thought Essential to the Acquisition of Rational Knowledge and Passions," *Teaching Thinking Skills: Theory and Practice,* W. H. Freeman Company, Publishers, NY, NY, 1987, Joan Baron and Robert Steinberg, editors.

Paul, Richard W. "Critical Thinking: Fundamental to Education for a Free Society," *Educational Leadership,* September 1984, Ronald Brandt, editor.

Paul, Richard W. "Ethics Without Indoctrination," *Educational Leadership,* May 1988, Ronald Brandt, editor.

Resnick, Lauren, *Education & Learning to Think,* National Academy Press, Washington DC, 1987.

Roth, K. J. (1984). "Using Classroom Observations to Improve Science Teaching and Curriculum Materials." In C.W. Anderson (Ed.), *Observing Science Classrooms: Perspectives from Research and Practice.* (1984 Yearbook of the Association for the Education of Teachers in Science.) Columbus, OH: ERIC Center for Science, Mathematics, and Environmental Education.

Roth, K. J. (1985). *Food for Plants: Teacher's Guide.* (Research Series No. 153). East Lansing, MI: Michigan State University, Institute for Research on Teaching.

Roth, K. J. (1986). "Conceptual-Change Learning and Student Processing of Science Texts." (Research Series 167). East Lansing, MI: Institute for Research on Teaching, Michigan State University.

Roth, K. J. (1987). *Helping Science Teachers Change: The Critical Role of Teachers' Knowledge about Science and Science Learning.* Paper presented at the annual meeting of the American Educational Research Association, Washington, DC.

Schoenfeld, A. H. (1985). *Mathematical Problem Solving*. New York: Academic Press.

Schoenfeld, A. H. (1986). "On Having and Using Geometric Knowledge." in J. Hiebert (Ed.), *Conceptual and Procedural Knowledge: The Case of Mathematics,* pp. 225–264. Hillsdale, NJ: Erlbaum.

Schoenfeld, A. H. (1987). "What's All the Fuss About Metacognition?" in A. Schoenfeld (Ed.), *Cognitive Science and Mathematics Education,* pp. 189–215. Hillsdale, NJ: Erlbaum.

Schoenfeld, A. H. (In press). "When Good Teaching Leads to Bad Results: The Disasters of 'Well Taught' Mathematics Classes." *Educational Psychologist.*

Scriven, Michael "Critical For Survival" *National Forum* Winter 1985. pp. 9–12.

Scheffler, Israel *Reason and Teaching.* Bobbs-Merrill, New York: 1973.

Scheffler, Israel *Conditions of Knowledge,* Scott Foresman, Chicago. 1965.

Siegel, Harvey *Educating Reason: Rationality, Critical Thinking, and Education,* Routledge. 1988.

Siegel, Harvey "Critical Thinking As an Educational Ideal," *The Educational Forum,* November 1980, pp. 7–23.

Smith, E. L., (1983). "Teaching for Conceptual Change: Some Ways of Going Wrong." In H. Helm and J. Novak (Eds.), *Proceeding of the International Seminar on Misconceptions in Science and Mathematics.* Ithaca, NY: Cornell University.

Smith, E. L., and Anderson, C. W. (1987a). *The Effects of Training and Use of Specially Designed Curriculum Materials on Conceptual Change Teaching and Learning.* Paper presented at the annual meeting of the National Association for Research in Science Teaching, Washington, DC.

Smith, E. L., (1987b). "What Besides Conceptions Needs to Change in Conceptual Change Learning?" In J. D. Novak (Ed.), *Proceedings of the Second International Seminar on Misconceptions and Educational Strategies in Science and Mathematics.* Ithaca, J. N.: Cornell University.

✦✦ Chapter 5

Background Logic, Critical Thinking, and Irrational Language Games*

Abstract

In this, the most technical of his papers, written for the Second International Sympo-sium on Informal Logic *in Windsor, Canada (1985), Richard Paul develops, at length, the concept of background logic: the notion that the reasoning and thinking which we overtly express can best be understood as surface manifestations of a complex system of thought which is, for the most part, implicit, presupposed, and unexpressed. With this view, Paul implies that comprehending the words and actions of other people and our selves is best understood as the problem of deciphering the use of three logics: the logic of natural lan-guages (such as, English or French), the logic of society (for example, everyday U.S. cul-tural practices), and personal logic (our personal system of assumptions and meanings). There are three major patterns of life-style that emerge from the ways people orchestrate these logics in pursuing their ends: idealizing, rationalizing, and reasoning. The first option, idealization, is dominant in the lives of uncritical persons. The second, rational-ization, is dominant in the lives of selfishly critical persons. The third, fairminded reason-ing, is dominant in the lives of fairmindedly critical persons. Most people act, on Paul's view, with minimal awareness of the social and personal meanings that dominate their lives, with little sense of how their minds have been shaped and in turn shape their experi-ence and action. Paul believes that "irrational" language usage is rampant in everyday life. The consequence is far-reaching: "When background logic is left in the background, unformulated, we are dominated rather than freed by the logic of our own thought and social transactions."*

Everywhere and always the quota of generally accepted rules and opin-ions weighs, however lightly, on the individual spirit, and it is only in theory that the child of 12–14 can submit all rules to a critical examination. Even the most rational of adults does not subject to his 'moral experience' more than an infinitesimal proportion of the rules that hedge him round. Anxious though he was to escape from his 'provisional morality', Descartes retained it to the end of his days.

Jean Piaget, *The Moral Judgment of the Child*

---

* This essay is somewhat more difficult than most of the others. The reader might defer reading it until most of the others are clearly understood.

✦ *Introduction*

$\mathcal{E}$ very human thinks. Thinking is intrinsic to human life. Thought is necessary to and implicit in all human activities. Everything that humans do is "thought-full". So deep-seated and intrinsic to our being is it that we can't stop thinking even if we want to. It is our nature to think. But we do little thinking *about* our thinking. And what we do is rarely fruitful. It is difficult to do, it must be systematically encouraged, and easily degenerates into worry, speculation, or daydreaming. At this point in our evolution as a species we have not learned how to take command of our thinking by mastering the art of thinking about our thinking.

Why is this so? Besides being thinking beings, we are also egocentric ones. When we think, our thought is spontaneously egocentric. This means that our thought is continually oriented toward the goal of getting what we want. We spontaneously form ideas that serve our selfish interests, including a self-serving image of ourselves.

This image is partially conscious and partially unconscious. The conscious part, or much of it, helps obscure that part which is unconscious. Put another way, part of what it means to be egocentric is to project an image of ourselves which conflicts with what we are. This results in strong resistance to seeing ourselves as we are. We naturally and spontaneously resist thinking about how we think, for doing so would disclose self-deceptive and ego-protective acts.

To maintain a positive self-image, we often resist admitting any inconsistency, hypocrisy, or contradiction. When we sense that our actions conflict with our ideals, we tend to respond defensively or hostilely. We often hide our inconsistencies and shortcomings, even from ourselves. To defend our behavior, we often distort not only our motives but their consequences. We routinely defend our distortions. We work hard to maintain the illusion that we are what we are not.

A second reason we generally lack command of our thought is that we are sensual-perceptual beings. We are deeply involved in a world we can see, touch, smell, hear, and taste. And though we freely fabricate mythical entities in our minds, most are entities we can "picture" in sensual terms. But our thought processes cannot be "observed" in sensual-perceptual terms. We cannot look into our minds and simply watch what takes place. Our mind is not a *place* and so we cannot turn to it. Special skills are necessary for thinking about our thinking. These are not observational skills but rather *analytic* ones. We think about our thinking not by looking in a new place, but by using new ways of dissecting what we say and do. We do not need new experiences but insight into what is implicit in our experiences.

Thinking about our thinking is partly a set of linguistic skills. We cannot effectively think about our thinking unless we learn to use words with discipline. This requires that we learn to distinguish educated use from social misuse. Thinking about thinking is partly a set of social skills. We cannot effectively think about our thinking unless we learn to analyze the social settings in which we think, to recognize how our thought is often embedded in our action in a social world.

Thought is logical. That which is logical has logical *components,* logical *relations,* and logical *direction.* For example, one cannot think without beginning one's thought "somewhere", that is, by setting off from *premises* that embody *assumptions.* Secondly, having "begun somewhere", thought proceeds in some *direction* and for some *purpose,* leaving a trail of logical *connections* and relations.

While we are thinking we do not fully know *why* or *how* we think. We do not completely know the functions of our thought, our total set of premises and assumptions, what logical connections we are developing, and the conclusions toward which our thought is tending. Yet the more we learn to think about our thinking the more we come to identify, in the very process of thinking, the logical ingredients of our thought.

✦ *Background Logic*

Most critical thinking pedagogy and theory focuses on the part of thinking actually spoken or written — what we call "manifest logic". What we say or write, however, is only a small portion of the thinking process — the proverbial tip of the iceberg. Surrounding any line of thought is a large substructure of *background thought, logical connections* not lying on the surface of reasoning, but prior to it, underlying it, or implied by it. In the background of all thinking are foundational concepts, assumptions, values, purposes, experiences, implications, and consequences — all embedded in lines of thought radiating outward in every direction.

These background connections often emerge only after extended dialogical discussion. Two people may begin with a specific question: Was the President right to order the bombing of ...? The discussion predictably moves to other questions, topics, and subjects: Should any country be bound by international law if its interests are served by violating it? What does history tell us about the likely consequences of an action such as this? Does our country have a special historic responsibility to intervene in the affairs of other countries if democracy is threatened? How can we evaluate the motives of public figures in distant countries? Are there universal ethical principles?

Disputants will probably raise points regarding other foreign policy decisions and will discuss further historical background and psychological considerations, domestic policy, news coverage, and so on. Such a broadening movement from sub-issue to sub-issue is often necessary to fully canvass the original issue. While trying to persuade the other, each arguer cites evidence, interpretations, principles, etc., which the other may or may not accept, and so must sometimes be argued. Thus, points that at first blush seem unrelated to the original question become relevant as each reasoner explores the conflicting background thinking surrounding the beliefs of the other.

People engaged in such discussions are often surprised at what the other says. Arguments that to each seem compelling, the other finds weak. The other can provide reasons to defend a seemingly indefensible position, or answer an apparently unanswerable objection. We are all largely unaware of the substructure of belief and thought that underlies what we overtly assert.

One of the reasons we ignore the importance of background logic in our thought is that our schooling did not teach us how to explicate it. In fact for most people background thought doesn't exist. They respond to the surface of what is said or done, oblivious of what is not staring them in the face.

Another reason why background thinking is not taken seriously is our over-fascination with formal procedures and what we take to be scientific objectivity. In an age of science it seems to many that all important problems are questions that should be settled by some objective scientific process that transcends the "subjectivity" of thought. Our obsession with scientific formalism, our scientism, is actually quite old, ultimately traceable perhaps to Aristotle's deductive logic.

Plato's method of intellectual give-and-take, of dialogical exchange between opposing viewpoints, was relegated by many to an inferior role, and formal syllogistic reason officially accepted as the exclusive means of acquiring true knowledge. In place of argumentation between conflicting points of view Aristotle's followers held that definite methods should be developed that lead more or less directly and objectively to the truth. This laid a foundation for a long history of formal approaches to logic: logic largely divorced from context, from the conceptual problems of everyday life and dispute, and from the practical problems faced in an irrational, multi-faceted, deeply disguised world.

Philosophy, in contrast to science, maintained dialectic as its fundamental means of inquiry. Bring opposing philosophers together and it is usually necessary to test each of their views against the objections of the other. This process is at its roots informal, for there are no hard-and-fast rules or formulas for deciding how and when to object to an opposing philosophical position. This point can be generalized to any assessment of reasoning within one point of view by reasoning from another. When one is engaged in multi-dimensional argumentation, one disputes not only the proper answer to a question but often the nature of the question itself. One must often develop new ideas, not simply use established ones. Because the ground rules typically used by a perspective for settling its own questions come under dispute, one cannot use them to adjudicate differences. Informal give-and-take, not formal or procedural skills, become primary and crucial.

Unfortunately, however, the history of "informal" argumentation within philosophy has had no perceptible influence on common practice in everyday life. Philosophy remains an elite subject, largely abstracted from everyday life and practical concerns, at least in the minds of most non-philosophers. Hence the background logic of everyday beliefs and thought is rarely systematically explored, formally or informally. In everyday life it seems anything goes, any move one can get away with is maintained as legitimate thought.

The intellectual discipline most philosophers exercise seems irrelevant, pedantic, and unintelligible to most people tackling everyday issues.

Some time after philosophers retreated from the marketplace to their own inner circles, science began its slow but steady development. With it came the emergence of more narrowly defined technical disciplines with increasingly refined procedural approaches, testifying to the power of procedure in settling narrowly defined one-dimensional questions. By the 20th Century even some philosophers began a systematic attempt to make their work "scientific". This meant to many that traditional philosophical argumentation should give way to precise and formalized method. General, comprehensive, philosophical skills seemed to many in need of replacement. Specialized, formal procedures, parallel to those used by the physical sciences, seemed necessary for philosophy itself. Philosophy, it was thought by many, should become specialized and scientific.

This demand that philosophy "professionalize" itself, and thus substitute disciplined *procedure* for freewheeling *dialectic* has diminished in the last 20 years. Likewise, educators increasingly recognize that education based on training in unconnected and isolated disciplines does not prepare one well for most of the issues one faces in everyday life. Furthermore, many concede that an overly narrow or fragmented education — the kind associated with an emphasis on specialization — engenders minds that compartmentalize and cannot easily adapt or generalize specialized understandings. There is also an increasing recognition that narrowly skilled persons may be as irrational in much of their lives as unschooled people tend to be.

Similarly, there is a growing recognition that the comprehensive thinking of a rational person cannot be equated with formal reasoning or the following of narrow rules and procedures. The crucial problems we face in the complexities of everyday life are increasingly recognized to be multi-faceted and resistant to single-discipline approaches.

Unfortunately, the fragmented schooling of today leaves little room for intellectual give-and-take or for interdisciplinary thinking. Too often questions which do not submit to disciplinary procedures are defined away or ignored. People leave school with few of the skills necessary to plumb the background logic of their own beliefs and thought, and so with few convictions, and little sense of the many contradictions that underlie their thoughts, words, and deeds. Most importantly, they lack the ability to strip off surface language and consider alternative ways to talk; little sense of what it would be to question basic labels and categories on the basis of which inferences and meanings are multiplied.

Most people unconsciously internalize the basic world view of their peer group and society with little or no conscious awareness of what it would be to rationally decide upon alternative ways to conceptualize everyday situations, persons, and events. Utterances, by themselves and others, are taken at their face value, or twisted by egocentric inclinations and vested interests. Similarly, most people are responsive to and awed by social rituals and the trappings of authority, status, and prestige. They live their lives, as it were, in surface structures. They reduce complex situations to self-serving verbalizations. Thus, not surprisingly, most people do not know how to explicate and clarify an issue, how to enter sympathetically into points of view they have consciously or unconsciously rejected. Deeply insecure, most people are only concerned with injustices inflicted upon themselves personally or upon those they ego-identify with. They easily dehumanize those who thwart, or appear to thwart, their vested interests; they typically resent those whose beliefs conflict with their own. Their reasoning is often infantile at root.

It is tendencies, qualities, and dispositions such as these which give rise to the problem of "uncritical thought". They define the obstacles against which proposed critical thinking pedagogy must be measured. The problem of teaching critical thinking to essentially rational persons in a rational society differs greatly from the problem of teaching it to irrational persons in an unconsciously irrational society. In a society that uncritically defines itself and its social, political, economic, and personal rituals as civilized, rational, and free, there is no impetus to probe beneath the surface of public discourse. When the most fundamental logical structures, the most basic concepts, assumptions, beliefs, inferences, and category-decisions are typically unexpressed, unconscious, and irrational, then the problem of background logic assumes new proportions and the language games implicit in everyday life are in need of a fundamental reconstrual. A society incapable of exploring the roots of its own thought and action is not a free society, properly so called. People cannot be said to have freely chosen what they do not recognize to exist. The rest of this paper tries to make a modest contribution to reversing this incapacity, this inability to grasp the foundations and substructure of thought and action.

✦ Some Principles

1) All human behavior is intelligible to us finally only in terms of some background of concepts and distinctions, values and meanings, associations and assumptions, purposes and goals. This background is embedded ultimately, as Wittgenstein put it, in concrete forms of life — in behavior. Yet there is little awareness of the background logics in use. We absorb these structures uncritically through socialization. We are not encouraged to explicate and assess them.

2) Often background systems of meanings are misused or confused, resulting in a multitude of category mistakes in which persons radically mis-describe their experience. For example, because we commonly characterize ourselves as free, reasonable, just, and caring, we assume that our behavior matches what these words imply. In fact words often substitute for realities named by them. Fundamental contradictions or inconsistencies in our lives typically go unquestioned. Yet to this day no adequate the-

ory of background logic has been developed and the concept remains in need of foundational analysis and clarification.

3) The inferences we make depend upon the concepts we use. Some concepts, being more basic, are implicit in unmonitored inferences that shape our behavior in many domains of life. Three important categories of background logic influence our point of view or perspective as individuals: the natural language we speak (English, French, etc.), the technical languages we study in school (the language of biology, zoology, anthropology, mathematics, etc.), and the social practices that shape the meanings fostered in social situations, the sociocentric logic of our peer group or culture. Presently I will explain how we selectively internalize these networks to define our personal philosophy, our world view, the filter through which we interpret or construct our experience. It is crucial to recognize the differences between these background domains, particularly between the logic of natural languages and that of social behavior. Social behavior often incorporates ordinary language in distorting ways. We learn how to gain advantage by a systematic misuse of everyday language. Before we consider how everyday irrationalities are obfuscated in social practices, however, it is useful to set out four dimensions of background logic implicit in every instance of reasoning.

✦ *Four Dimensions of Background Logic*

Whenever we reason and express our thinking in words, there are four background dimensions of our thought which can be probed. Each of these dimensions expresses a different point of reference and a different order of analytic fact: *1)* the dimension of our thinking *temporally prior to* what we have expressed, *2)* the dimension of our thinking *logically presupposed by* what we have expressed, *3)* the dimension of our thinking *implied by* what we have expressed, and *4)* the dimension of our *thinking developed when our thinking is challenged* by others.

The basic idea behind these distinctions is simple. Before we formulate our reasoning on a subject we must decide on our purpose and how to describe what we think is the central issue or problem we are facing. We do some *pre-thinking,* in other words. Moreover, once we formulate our thinking there is a *substructure* to it — foundational concepts and assumptions — and a *direction* to it — implications and consequences unexpressed or not fully expressed. Finally, any line of reasoning inevitably *conflicts* with other lines of reasoning. The moves that can be made in exploring any of these conflicts are important "background logic" to understand when attempting to come to terms with any reasoning set out for our assessment. When we look into the background logic of a line of reasoning, therefore, we look into various domains presupposed by it: its pre-thinking, its substructure, its implications, and its possible defense in relation to conflicting lines of thought. We analyze background logic because we recognize that we must delve into these unexpressed domains to come to terms with that part of the thought which is expressed.

This approach can be likened to coming to understand new acquaintances. We learn something of their prior lives, something of their deeper thoughts, something of where they are headed, and something of how they respond to challenges from others. We use what people overtly say and do as guides or indicators of their "background". We understand what people say or do not only by examining directly what they say or do, but also by finding out what lies in the background of what they say and do — how they came to these actions from their past, what is presupposed by these actions at the moment, where these actions take us if we follow them out to their logical consequences, and how these actions stand-up under critique from divergent standpoints.

THE DOMAIN OF PRE-THINKING

Before we reason with respect to an issue or goal, we must frame a goal or formulate an issue or problem. In other words, we must define a problem before we can look for a solution. The problem of deciding on one issue rather than another and of wording an issue one way rather than another goes a long way toward shaping reasoning with respect to it. If, in other words, all reasoning consists in an attempt to settle a question, then all reasoning presupposes an issue to settle, an issue shaped through the thinking of the reasoner. Before we argue with our spouses about some aspect of our marriage, we pre-think the situation or problem. We define it in some way, even if merely to define it as "problematic" rather than "unproblematic". We often fail to notice that the situation did not present itself as a problem, our thinking (our "pre-thinking" in other words) concluded it to be so. Perhaps we began with a feeling of disquiet or frustration then leapt to the conclusion that this particular aspect of the other person or the relationship is problematic. The reasoning behind our interpretation of the original discomfort as arising from this particular thing is often unconscious. We are not aware of having reasoned at all, but seem to have perceived the root of the problem directly.

Or, to take a more scholastic example, consider the history of philosophy. It can fruitfully be viewed as a series of disagreements regarding how best to frame philosophical questions, and hence disagreements about what specifically is at issue. Philosophers, we could say, are intensely concerned with prior questions and prior reasoning. They are invariably concerned with the issues buried in the pre-thinking of actions, judgments, and decisions.

THE DOMAIN OF SUBSTRUCTURE

Just as the domain of pre-thinking spans the initial choices of goals, problems, and issues, the substructural domain spans the concepts and assumptions presupposed in the reasoning. It is not explicit in the manifest logic since few people explicitly discuss their assumptions in their expressed thought. They use but do not focus on them. We need to probe beneath a person's reasoning to make their most fundamental concepts and assumptions explicit.

For example, to understand whether disagreements in manifest thought can be resolved, we must often use skills that probe the "inner" logic of that thought. We must often determine whether assumptions that underlie two lines of thought are reconcilable. We must often explore whether their funda-mental ideas are consistent or inconsistent. For example, if an advocate of market capitalism is debating an economic issue — say, "Should the capital gains tax be reduced?" — with an advocate of democratic socialism, the basic concepts and assumptions of capitalism and socialism underlie the reasoning of the debaters. Under what conditions is "competition" more fruitful than "cooperation", or "private interest" the best guide to "public interest"? Explor-ing issues such as these helps lay bare what I call the substructural dimen-sion of thought. Of course how far we probe into these deeper, underlying issues depends upon our purpose in discussing the issue in the first place. Practical considerations may restrict us to a more superficial analysis, to dis-cussing the manifest logic alone.

Once we begin to explore the concepts and assumptions presupposed in two lines of thought we are often driven to consider background facts and information, the empirical or experiential support for those concepts and assumptions. Hence, advocates of capitalism if pressed to defend the concept of competition will cite a variety of "facts" and "experiences" which they believe justify the concept. If pressed they will cite cases to argue for the con-cept of competition in *general*. Focus on surface facts — the facts cited in support of positions on the *original* issue — gives way to focus on "infralogi-cal facts", the empirical considerations advanced when probing into founda-tional concepts and assumptions. We begin talking about a current economic problem; we are then driven to talk about our foundational ideas and what supports them; we then move back to the original issue with a broader sense of perspective, a broader sense of the background logic of both positions.

THE DOMAIN OF IMPLICATIONS

Another domain of background logic we may need to consider, another way we may need to go beyond what is "manifest" in reasoning, is that of implica-tions and consequences. Thinking not only has a pre-history and a substruc-ture, it also has a *direction*. It leads us one way rather than another. It takes us from one set of beliefs to other beliefs that "follow from" the first. Further-more, beliefs acted upon have consequences, for different things happen when we act on different beliefs. No one can fully explore the implications and consequences of his or her reasoning. We are often circumscribed by pressures to decide and act. Nevertheless implications and consequences are always implicit in what we say and do. Unfortunately few have been taught to recognize anything but the most obvious implications and consequences and many frequently don't even recognize them.

```
┌─────────────────────────────────────────────────┐
│              Intellectual Conflict               │
│   How the reasoning stands up against or compares to │
│   competing lines of reasoning: answers to objections and │
│          objections to competing views.         │
└─────────────────────────────────────────────────┘
                         ↑
┌──────────────┐   ┌──────────────┐   ┌──────────────┐
│ Pre-thinking │   │  The belief, │   │ Implications │
│  The origin or │ →│ statement, or│ →│ Beliefs that follow │
│   source of the │  │  conclusion. │   │ from the belief and │
│ belief, its purpos- │ └──────────────┘  │ the consequences │
│  es, goals, and the │      ↑           │ of acting on the │
│  definition of the │                   │     belief.     │
│  problem or issue. │                   └──────────────┘
└──────────────┘
                         ↑
┌─────────────────────────────────────────────────┐
│                  Substructure                    │
│ Support, reasons, evidence, concepts, assumptions, and │
│  the reasons and evidence for the foundational concepts │
│              and assumptions.                    │
└─────────────────────────────────────────────────┘
```

Background Logic

There are four directions in which thought can be pursued.

THE DOMAIN OF INTELLECTUAL CONFLICT

A fourth domain of background logic for a line of reasoning is revealed when we set it into conflict with competing lines of thought. Coming to understand the strengths and weaknesses of reasoning in relation to opposing thought adds a further dimension to our grasp of the reasoning. Hence Kant's reasoning adds a dimension to our understanding of the logic of Descartes and Hume, while their reasoning contributes to our understanding of his. By the same token, different stages in the development of a discipline constitute background logic that contributes to the intelligibility and definition of each. We have a much clearer and well-developed sense of the assumptions of Newtonian physics since Einstein and quantum theory. Often then we conclude that we had not fully understood a point of view until it was superseded by another. However confident in a given line of reasoning, however attentive to the basic shaping of issues, however focused on our basic principles, concepts, and assumptions, however conscientious in explicating further implications and collateral consequences, we do not fully understand reasoning until we grasp its force in conflict with other reasoning.

✦ *Toward a Richer Understanding of Background Logic*

There is no reason, of course, why a portion, even a significant portion, of what is background logic in one context cannot become foreground or manifest logic in another. Indeed an essential characteristic of the critical mind is its passion to penetrate, explicate, and dialectically assess competing background logics. Once background logic is formulated it becomes part of manifest logic. Of course there is no way that one can formulate all the background logic for a line of reasoning, just as there is no way to describe all aspects of a person. We can go as far as we please, but we do not run out of further places to explore in all the directions that follow outward from our thought.

To begin to make effective use of our knowledge of background logic, we must develop a taxonomy of background logical distinctions in addition to the four dimensions above. For example, we must distinguish technical one-dimensional (monological) background logics, specified in fine detail, narrowly defined and procedurally developed, — for example, chemistry or algebra — from the background logic one unconsciously absorbs, for example, in the socialization process. Raised in the United States, we internalize different concepts, beliefs, and assumptions about ourselves and the world than we would have had we been raised in China or Iran, for example.

Furthermore, we must distinguish both technical and cultural background logics from the background logic of natural languages. Natural languages are a resource for virtually unlimited conceptual possibilities. They are much more flexible than technical languages. They are more neutral than the belief systems of cultural groups. As critical thinkers, we should be cog-

Dialectical Background Logic

To understand our thinking, we should appreciate the multiple dimensions in which it contrasts and sometimes conflicts with the thinking of others.

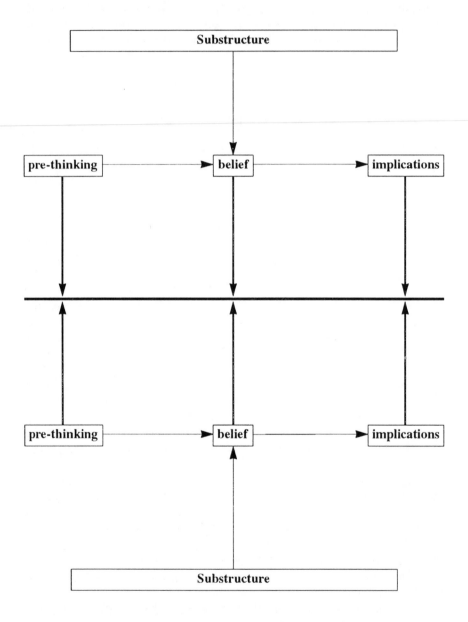

nizant, in other words, of the extent to which we are reasoning within the technical concepts of a specialized discipline, within the concepts implicit in our cultural relationships and experience, or within the concepts implicit in the language we speak. Of course, our reasoning might use concepts from all three of these dimensions simultaneously. Critical thinking requires sensitivity to the conceptual problems that may arise from this blending of domains. We will see something more of the importance of these distinctions in the next section of the paper.

✦ *Background Logic and Language Games*

The logic of the English language, and of all other known natural languages, should not be confused with the background logic of the egocentric mind or, for that matter, of the sociocentric mind. All human existence is necessarily multi-dimensional, not only because it involves beings whose nature and behavior can never be reduced to one category alone, but also because it involves some necessary intersection of personal, social, and linguistic background logics. Every interpretation of language usage, in other words, is a complex act in which we respond to cues that reflect three variously-related background logics, that of the egocentric individual, that of the social group, and that of the natural language of the user. Hence sometimes a communication is idiosyncratic, and its meaning can only be understood correctly if one understands something about the specific history or background of the speaker. For example, only if you understand something of the history of the conflict between two people, may you be able to recognize the significance of a given utterance. What may seem a compliment to an outsider may in fact be an insult.

Or, to highlight another background logic, it may be more illuminating to interpret what is said as a social or in-group performance, as a communication that presupposes familiarity with the ideology or rituals of a social group. For example, within a given society, though the leader may ask whether anyone disagrees with his or her view, it may be socially unacceptable to express such disagreement.

Or finally, one might best understand what is being said as expressing straightforwardly what is implied by the words as used by educated speakers of the language, irrespective of the society in which they were raised or of their personal idiosyncrasies. For example, a Japanese person, having learned proficient English in a Japanese school, may express his "Japanese" ideas in English. Language learning in itself does not transform the culture of the person speaking the language. It may be the occasion for such learning but does not necessarily include it.

Psychoanalysts aim at developing facility in decoding highly idiosyncratic utterances, and of disclosing thereby primitive assumptions and concepts which patients unconsciously hold about themselves, about people close to them, or about the nature of their world. All the sophisticated defense mechanisms, so called, can consequently be viewed as various forms of irrational, but highly functional language games by which people fend off unpleasant reality and maintain their unconscious world views. Thus, for an individual, weight-loss may represent a "promised land" of unreal expectations of perfection, and unhealthy eating habits may represent the safety of the familiar, protection from sexual advances, an escape, or an excuse for problems, shortcomings, and unhappiness. Neither food nor weight have these meanings socially or in the natural language: food is sustenance, nutrition, relieves hunger, and can taste good or bad. These idiosyncratic meanings may develop in our minds without our awareness of their development.

The sociocentric or in-group background logic and associated language games are easier to decode than idiosyncratic background logic, since they are more public. If one belongs to the in-group, or if one has studied the world view or perspective presupposed in given social interactions, one can render these meanings explicit, as sociologists do. However, the nature of sociocentric logic, like egocentric logic, is not ordinarily formulated as such, and for good reason. If you paid enough attention to the language which maintains and expresses the inner dynamics of group power to construct a dictionary of basic meanings, you would have a text more like Ambrose Bierce's *Devil's Dictionary,* than like the *Oxford English Dictionary.* You would find at least two layers of meaning at work simultaneously: meanings implied by surface verbalizations and, in contrast, meanings implied by behavior, with frequent contradictions between the two. An outsider or naive person would take the surface meaning to be the sole meaning. The sophisticated in-group member however would respond not simply to the surface meaning but also to latent cues and implied meanings. Goffman's *The Presentation of Self in Everyday Life* presents numerous examples of these contrasting levels of meaning.

A business party, for example, though explicitly defined as a party, and with all of its external forms and trappings — hence a time to relax, have fun, socialize, let your hair down, be yourself without the pressure of having to meet expectations — is not a party in the normal sense. It imposes limitations on behavior, and has innumerable hidden rules and agendas. The poor, naive junior executives who behave appropriately for a more genuinely *social* gathering — friendly teasing, eccentric behavior, careless flirtations — will wonder why they do not get the promotions due them given their job performance. They don't realize that actions at parties *are* part of their job performance.

If there is a split within a society between two opposing behavioral logics, and so between two social groups or classes whose action embodies those logics, then the discrepancy between verbally and behaviorally implied meanings may become a subject for discussion, analysis, and critique. But as long as the "hypocrisy", "deception", or duplicity is more or less universal within a group, it is rarely noticed as such. Things go quite as expected, no disturbances highlight contradictions.

One can distinguish three different modes of living that represent different values and different skills of analysis with respect to decoding language usage within these background systems. Some tend to idealize social interactions, routinely accepting fostered impressions and surface language usage. These people, let us dub them naive idealizers, tend to accept the ideology of their society as descriptive of reality. Their horizons are conceptually and pragmatically limited. They are not adept at manipulating situations to their advantage, since they are minimally aware of the transactions going on beneath overt meanings and behaviors. They tend to be easily manipulated by those sensitized to the deeper levels of transaction.

Clearly, idealizers are not critical thinkers, since they cannot get beyond surface logic. The rationalizers of this world, on the other hand, penetrate the surface level and identify meanings and pay-offs. They function comfortably within meanings not disclosed to the naive. They get used to reading between the lines and to taking advantage of the opportunities for gaining advantage thereby. Those who design political campaigns, with their double messages and manipulative meanings, are an excellent case in point.

Being engaged in manipulations to further their self-interest, rationalizers tend to ignore the discrepancies and inconsistencies in the unspoken social ideology they use to their advantage. Having discovered how to play a game that advances their interests, they see no value in making the game public. Besides, like all humans, rationalizers need to maintain a positive view of themselves. This would be difficult if their manipulative use of other people were made explicit. To put this another way, uncritical idealization invites manipulation, and rationalizers take advantage of openings for power and gain. Idealizers, oblivious of the struggle for power and advantage lurking beneath the surface of social transactions are tailor-made for those seeking advantage. Rationalizers are empowered to get what they want through their deeper understanding of how to use social masks to obtain private ends.

This leaves one final life-style choice with respect to the socio-linguistic activities of everyday life: interesting one's self in making hidden dimensions of discourse explicit, striving to decode as fully as possible the real, deeper, meanings and contradictions in social transactions. I would dub this third choice of life-style that of the reasoner, the genuinely fairminded, critical thinker, the person striving to transform blind conformity into rational conviction. Admittedly a tiny minority, this group is a force for progressive social change and transformation.

Reasoners or fairminded critical thinkers, on this view, learn to see their behavior in terms of the tacit infrastructure of thinking that underlies it. This necessarily requires a willingness to undergo stress, to face personal and social contradictions, to develop rational passions, and, on the whole, to engage in self-transformation. On this view, no one can become fairminded and avoid the "hot" issues that underlie personal and social life, or the necessity of facing, indeed the necessity of *constructing,* some opposition to the social status quo. Most importantly, then, fairminded critical thinking requires a passion for social disclosure not simply for abstract theorizing about social interaction, a passion for synthesis that takes into account the specific relations between, and the problems of overcoming, unformulated but lived, and formulated but unlived logical systems. Insightful critical thinking requires understanding how language is systematically misused to achieve unexpressed, self-serving social and personal ends. Since such activity requires courage and concern for social justice, it is intrinsically a moral activity.

✦ Synthesis

At the same time that our everyday experience presupposes and reflects continual and spontaneous acts of logical synthesis that transcend any particular academic category, our conscious knowledge remains logically fragmented. Our everyday action is socially more sophisticated than our conscious thinking implies. We seem able to take into account at the behavioral level more than we analyze at the intellectual level. Consider this example taken from the research of Hans Toch and Henry Clay Smith:

> Any perception is an awareness that emerges as a result of a most complicated weighing process an individual goes through as his mind takes into account a whole host of factors or cues. It must be emphasized at the very outset how tremendously complex even the simplest perception is — for example, the perception of a star point. For it can be demonstrated that, in perceiving a star point as such, a whole host of indications are weighed and integrated to give us our final experience ... the integration of all these factors is accomplished in a faction of a second and is, more frequently than not, entirely unconscious.

This spontaneous weighing and totalizing process applies in everyday experience to our perception of individuals, groups, ideologies, religions, and any manner of complex or "simple" events. We instantly know how to respond to any number of people playing diverse social roles. Unfortunately, because most of our *de facto* skills of synthesis reflect background logical systems that are egocentric, sociocentric, or both, our skills of *rational* synthesis are not enhanced thereby. The paradox is that while our irrational mind easily uses background logical systems to integrate, synthesize, and structure behavior and events, our rational mind is still highly compartmentalized, reinforced by an academic world whose fundamental interest is narrow and non-synthetic, an interest in keeping disciplinary categories unintegrated and free of dialectical and interdisciplinary thought. The academic world, it would seem, is convinced that there is no significant loss from traditional academic specialization. But we cannot face situations in everyday life in the terms in which we are academically trained. The real world of human action is not compartmentalized into academic categories. The social, the psychological, the philosophical, and the economic are, in the real world, often so entwined that it makes no sense to try to explain any one dimension without explaining the roles of the others.

Consequently, we cannot turn to isolated disciplines for an answer to the problem of uncritical thought in everyday life. The only "neutral" background logic we have at our critical disposal is that of natural languages themselves. Academic or technical languages, in contrast, presuppose the compartmentalizations they themselves have created. We can ask, for example, whether what we in the U.S. call "democratic" is consistent with what the word 'democratic' implies in the English language. We can reflect upon whether modern elections with their well-funded campaigns and reliance on manipulative practices, are consistent with the belief that the people are ruling. The concepts of the English language allow us to abstract from ideologies, academic agendas, and social presuppositions.

We can take any word that expresses an important human value — friendship, love, intimacy, honesty, integrity, equality, justice — analyze what its use implies to educated speakers of the language, and then compare these verbal implications to the world as we find it. We can learn to resist assuming that social situations commonly described by value-laden words really do merit the characterization. To do so requires a disciplined awareness of the difference between what is linguistically implied by given words in the English language and what is commonly described as such within social groups that happen to use English to talk about events in their everyday life. Unfortunately, however, few people can distinguish those uses of language which twist or distort social reality from those which reveal it.

We need to forge critical thinking abilities that focus on a command of background logics. Special intellectual skills are required, both destructive and constructive: on the one hand ability to question the on-going stream of fostered definitions and social conceptualizations, choices of basic concepts and categories that uncritically shape our daily thought and experience, and on the other hand, ability to synthesize across these concepts and categories so that our "totalization", our summing up of people, facts, and events, represents characterizations to which we can give, and do give, conscious assent. We have a responsibility to educate people to have a disposition to see social life as a whole, especially its living contradictions and hypocrisies, to look beyond surface meanings and compartmentalized academic categories, to see not only how everyday life is structured but how it might be structured were we to commit ourselves to live by the moral values we have long verbally espoused.

✦ Some Unresolved Questions

Since all reasoning, all thought, presupposes questions at issue, and since fundamental questions require critical explication of background logic, we need a fuller exploration and specification of what this entails, especially in contrast to discipline-specific training. We need to decide how to frame background logical questions and how to make this deeper mode of questioning socially acceptable. We must not forget that the social world is a real world, one whose background logic transforms the lives and minds of people. When Background logic is left in the background, unformulated, we are dominated rather than freed by the logic of our own thought and social transactions. If we think egocentrically and sociocentrically, we stifle our capacity for insight, intellectual freedom, and self-command.

This brings us to an important question, a question to which our concrete lives provide an answer, even if our words do not: is it rational to be rational in an irrational world? Less paradoxically, is it rational to give up the advantage for personal gain provided by the many who allow themselves to be manipulated? One can gain status, prestige, money, power, easy self-satisfaction, and ego-gratification only if one's actions at least *appear* to validate socially dominant views. Is it worthwhile to make contradictions and hypocrisies public to achieve abstract goals such as intellectual and moral integrity? The wisdom of the world, the answer suggested by those most heavily engaged in it, would seem to be,

> No, it is not worth it. To be rational is to be a successful rationalizer, accepting and using the ascendant social ideology, to be skilled in personal self-deception, able to question fostered appearances only when personally advantageous, and if anything else, adept in helping your friends and hurting your enemies.

Socrates and Plato might have won the academic debate against sophistry but history demonstrates they did not win the battle for the hearts and minds of people. The everyday world of social action is shot through with sophistry and hypocrisy.

✦ Summary & Conclusion

Academic disciplines with their compartmentalization of thought fail to provide a plausible approach to everyday uncritical thought. We live as inferential beings enveloped in unformulated systems. The logical systems of the schools frequently have little to do with the logic we live. We are often controlled and confused by, and consequently have never consciously assented to, the inner logic we ourselves create in our behavior. We don't know how to get perspective, how to critically analyze and synthesize what lies behind our behavior. In contrast, our inner world, the world of our self-constituted experience is heavily synthesized, but unconsciously, egocentrically, and sociocentrically so. We have not yet developed insight into the importance of background logic. We have not yet learned how to probe it and bring it under our intellectual self-command. We have not yet grasped how unformulated dimensions of thought and action dominate us. We are so fixated on action, on the agendas of our lives, that we have not yet interested ourselves in the thought embedded in our action. To come to a deeper understanding of the unformulated thinking buried in our lives, we must make background logic accessible to our conscious thought. Instead of impugning the motives of others, we should learn how to explore the background meanings that make social and personal contradictions and hypocrisies intelligible.

In any case, a fundamental distinction must be drawn between the logic of natural languages and egocentric or sociocentric uses of them. Because of his failure to note the latter two, Wittgenstein failed to distinguish irrational from rational language games. He failed to see that many socially common uses of words are not innocuous. He failed to see how social groups systematically misuse language for self-serving ends. He failed to see, for example, how often we "confuse" concepts to obscure our own hypocrisies, while calling attention to the hypocrisies of our opponents, the hypocrisies of the "enemy". He failed to recognize the need to probe the unformulated dimensions of our lives to see patterns that reveal who we really are, how much we live three significantly distinct forms of life: that of the idealizer, that of the rationalizer, and that of the reasoner.

If there are idealizers in the world, given to idiosyncratic speech acts, presumably with thoughts to match, it follows that they live in narrow, self-enclosed worlds, highly vulnerable to manipulation and frustration. If there are rationalizers in the world, given to sociocentric speech acts, presumably again with thoughts to match, it follows that, whatever advantages they gain, they cannot fully assent to the character of their own behavior. If there are fairminded thinkers in the world, with a passion to transcend egocentric or sociocentric life worlds and the irrational language games which define them, it follows that they would strive to engage in discourse which does not presuppose egocentric or sociocentric concepts and values, that they would use words with a rich sense of their implications. If these three life worlds are in some sense logical possibilities for every person, then interpretation of language usage requires an ability to distinguish egocentric, sociocentric, and rational discourse. Because these distinctions cannot be made except in reference to background logical considerations that may not be immediately apparent, and because those background logics may be hidden and denied, the problem of analysis and explication is difficult.

To become a reasoner or fairminded critical thinker requires skills of analysis and synthesis as yet underdeveloped. We get little help from the academic world with its pervasive fragmentation and specialization. We need new skills in the art of totalizing experience, and in the dialectical testing of competing ways to conceptualize experience. We need to see that human social life is still at an uncritical stage of development. Full fledged critical thought is nevertheless possible for the future. It has not yet become socially acceptable except in circumscribed ways under constraining conditions. We cannot yet embrace it. We do not yet know *how* to embrace it. We have not yet learned to live as rational persons.

We need more knowledge of the logic of questions, of background systems of thought, of the power and inner attraction of egocentrism and sociocentrism, and of how to combat the "wisdom of the world", which, till now, meets emerging critical thought with disdain, ignores or suppresses it, and thus answers with a resounding "No!" the question, "Is it rational to be rational in an irrational world?"

Intellectual Standards and Assessment: The Foundation for Critical Thought

Chapter 6

A Model for the National Assessment of Higher Order Thinking

with Gerald M. Nosich

Abstract

This paper, co-authored by Richard Paul and Gerald Nosich, was commissioned by the United States Department of Education, Office of Educational Research and Improvement of the National Center for Education Statistics. It provides exactly what its title implies: a model for the national assessment of higher order thinking. The paper consists of a preface and five main sections.

The preface delineates the problem of lower order learning, summarizes the state of research into critical thinking and educational reform, and explains the five-part structure of the paper. The first main section of the paper states and explicates 21 criteria for higher order thinking assessment. The second section makes the case for how a "rich, substantive concept of critical thinking" meets those criteria. In making this case, Paul and Nosich spell out the dangers of a non-substantive concept of critical thinking. The third section of the paper spells out four domains of critical thinking: elements of thought, abilities, affective dimensions, and intellectual standards. The fourth section of the paper makes substantive recommendations regarding how to assess the various domains of critical thinking, the test strategies that may be used, the value of the proposed strategy for the reform of education, and the suggested implementation of the proposal.

✦ Preface:
The Problem of Lower Order Learning

*V*irtually all informed commentators agree that schooling today does not foster the "higher order thinking skills and abilities" which represent the "basics" of the future. America 2000, President Bush's education initiative, seeks to bring schooling in line with changing global and economic conditions, to engender sweeping educational reform in what are now admittedly largely static institutions, systems highly resistant to substantial change. America 2000 raises the following vital question: "How can we reverse the pervasive emphasis in education on lower rather than on higher order learning, on recall rather than on reasoning, on students merely 'reproducing' rather than 'producing' knowledge?"

The state of research regarding this problem was summarized recently by Mary Kennedy in an article for the Kappan:

> ...national assessments in virtually every subject indicate that, although our students can perform basic skills pretty well, they are not doing well on thinking and reasoning. American students can compute, but they cannot reason.... They can write complete and correct sentences, but they cannot prepare arguments.... Moreover, in international comparisons, American students are falling behind ... particularly in those areas that require higher order thinking.... Our students are not doing well at thinking, reasoning, analyzing, predicting, estimating, or problem solving.

In this summary, Dr. Kennedy linked the problem to the established mode of instruction:

> ...teachers are highly likely to teach in the way they themselves were taught. If your elementary teacher presented mathematics to you as a set of procedural rules with no substantive rationale, then you are likely to think that this is what mathematics is and that this is how mathematics should be studied. And you are likely to teach it in this way. If you studied writing as a set of grammatical rules rather than as a way to organize your thoughts and to communicate ideas to others, then this is what you will think writing is, and you will probably teach it so.... By the time we complete our undergraduate education, we have observed teachers for up to 3,060 days.

Though not as commonly realized, this problem of the dominance of lower order learning is as serious in post-secondary as it is in primary and secondary education. In both undergraduate and graduate programs students are typically enrolled in content heavy courses taught by professors who feel a greater obligation to cover subject matter through lecture than to generate thought-provoking activities or assignments that may seriously reduce what they can cover or significantly add to their work load, or both.

Alan Schoenfeld has explored this problem with respect to both pre-secondary and post-secondary mathematics instruction. To illustrate the detailed nature of what Schoenfeld's research is disclosing, here is a summary from one of his studies:

> At the University of Rochester 85% of the freshman class takes calculus, and many go on ... [but] most of these students will never apply calculus in any meaningful way (if at all) in their studies, or in their lives. They complete their studies with the impression that they know some very sophisticated and high-powered mathematics. They can find the maxima of complicated functions, determine exponential decay, compute the volumes of surfaces of revolution, and so on. But the fact is that these students know barely anything at all. The only reason they can perform with any degree of competency on their final exams is that the problems on the exams are nearly carbon copies of problems they have seen before; the students are not being asked to think, but merely to apply well-rehearsed schemata for specific kinds of tasks. Tim Keiter and I studied students' abilities to deal with pre-calculus versions of elementary word problems.... We were not surprised to discover that only 19 of 120

attempts at such problems ... yielded correct answers, or that only 65 attempts produced answers of any kind.

Schoenfeld summarizes the results, in general, of research into mathematics instruction as follows:

> In sum: all too often we focus on a narrow collection of well-defined tasks and train students to execute those tasks in a routine, if not algorithmic fashion. Then we test the students on tasks that are very close to the ones they have been taught. If they succeed on those problems, we and they congratulate each other on the fact that they have learned some powerful mathematical techniques. In fact, they may be able to use such techniques mechanically while lacking some rudimentary thinking skills. To allow them, and ourselves, to believe that they 'understand' the mathematics is deceptive and fraudulent.

There is good reason, in our view, to link instructional reform with the need for a special emphasis on critical thinking, problem solving, and communication skills, for it is precisely these higher order thinking skills that are routinely sacrificed when coverage and lower order recall dominate the classroom at either the pre- or post-secondary level, as they now do.

✦ The State of Research into Critical Thinking and Instructional Reform

One major value of the last ten years of research into critical thinking is the focus on the need for reform of instruction at all levels: on the need for students to reason mathematically in mathematics courses, to reason historically in history courses, to reason scientifically in science courses, to reason sociologically in sociology courses. Indeed, critical thinking research has emphasized three basic needs for all learning: for all students to reason out all basic concepts and understandings, to reason to all basic conclusions and solutions, and to reason through and across the curriculum.

This emphasis has been embedded in the structure of the 11 major international conferences on research into critical thinking and educational reform (1980–1991) held at Sonoma State University. The 1991 Conference attracted 1400 registrants from 20 countries and featured over 300 sessions representative of education from kindergarten through graduate school. This same emphasis is reflected in the 25 or so other conferences focused on critical thinking in the last ten years (at Harvard, the University of Chicago, Montclair State, Oakton College, and elsewhere) and in most of the articles published concerning critical thinking.

What is more, the research into critical thinking has focused not only on the cultivation of reasoning in all subjects and at all educational levels, but also on generalizable standards for the assessment of reasoning as well. The concepts and distinctions embedded in critical thinking research are, as a result, well-suited for the design of a process to assess higher order thinking.

In this paper, we shall set out both the conceptual foundations for such a process as well as a viable model for carrying out that process.

Before we spell out the detailed structure of this paper, however, it is important to note that the concept of critical thinking has not played a central role in the design of educational assessment instruments to date, principally because the concept has been developed extensively only over the last ten years, and therefore has not had time to permeate already developed assessment tools. Now that we possess a rich, substantive concept, however, we have an unprecedented opportunity to assess central rather than peripheral aspects of critical thinking, and to do so in an authentic and representative way. If anything less than this concept and its central aspects is assessed, the ultimate goal of fostering higher order thinking as an academic, social, and vocational need will be ill served.

✦ The Structure of the Paper

The substance of this paper is divided into four sections, each focused on a major question, as follows:

Section One: What should be the main objectives of a process to assess higher order thinking?

Section Two: How does a rich, substantive concept of critical thinking meet these criteria?

> *a)* What is included in a rich, substantive concept of critical thinking?
>
> *b)* How, specifically, does this concept meet the criteria?
>
> *c)* What, specifically, are the dangers of a non-substantive concept of critical thinking?

Section Three: What are the four component domains of critical thinking and the implications of each of these domains for the assessment of higher order thinking?

Section Four: What is the most workable solution to the design of a process to assess higher order thinking, given the findings in the three sections above?

The first section of the paper formulates 21 objectives that should be met by any process adequate to the task. The second outlines the basic concept of critical thinking which informs the paper and explains how a rich, substantive concept of critical thinking, grounded in the research on critical thinking, provides a plausible foundation for accomplishing these objectives. The third section of the paper explicates the four domains essential to critical thinking:

> *A)* The *Elements of Thought* (eight essential dimensions of all reasoning crucial for understanding and assessing reasoning),

B) *Abilities* (basic modes of reasoning — including reading, writing, speaking, and listening — that represent modal "orchestrations" of the elements of thought),

C) *Traits of Mind* (the affective dimensions without which critical thinking skills are merely episodically used, and often in a limiting rather than an expansive manner), and

D) *Universal Intellectual Standards* (presupposed by critical thinking).

As we give a brief explication of the elements of thought, the abilities, essential traits of mind, and intellectual standards, we briefly comment on the implications for assessment purposes of each conception.

In the fourth and final section of the paper, we lay out our recommendations for a process and a time-table for assessing higher order thinking.

✦ *Section One: Objectives*

What should be the main objectives of a process to assess higher order thinking?

1) It should assess students' skills and abilities in analyzing, synthesizing, applying, and evaluating information.

2) It should concentrate on thinking skills that can be employed with maximum flexibility, in a wide variety of subjects, situations, contexts, and educational levels.

3) It should account for both the important differences among subjects and the skills, processes, and affective dispositions that are crucial to all the subjects.

4) It should focus on fundamental, enduring forms of intellectual ability that are both fitted to the accelerating pace of change and deeply embedded in the history of the advancement of the disciplines.

5) It should readily lead to the improvement of instruction.

6) It should make clear the inter-connectedness of our knowledge and abilities, and why expertise in one area cannot be divorced either from findings in other areas or from a sensitivity to the need for interdisciplinary integration.

7) It should assess those versatile and fundamental skills that are essential to being a responsible, decision-making member of the workplace.

8) It should be based on clear concepts and have well-thought-out, rationally articulated goals, criteria, and standards.

9) It should account for the integration of communication skills, problem-solving, and critical thinking, and it should assess all of them without compromising essential features of any of them.

10) It should respect cultural diversity by focusing on the common-core skills, abilities, and traits useful in all cultures.

11) It should test for thinking that is empowering and that, when incorporated into instruction, promotes (to quote the September, 1991 Kappan) "the active engagement of students in constructing their own knowledge and understanding."

12) It should concentrate on assessing the fundamental cognitive structures of communication, for example:

with reading and listening, the ability to

- create an accurate interpretation,
- assess the author's or speaker's purpose,
- accurately identify the question-at-issue or problem being discussed,
- accurately identify basic concepts at the heart of what is said or written,
- see significant implications of the advocated position,
- identify, understand, and evaluate the assumptions underlying someone's position,
- recognize evidence, argument, inference (or their lack) in oral and written presentations,
- reasonably assess the credibility of an author or speaker,
- accurately grasp the point of view of the author or speaker,
- empathetically reason within the point of view of the author or speaker.

with writing and speaking, the ability to

- identify and explicate one's own point of view and its implications,
- be clear about and communicate clearly, in either spoken or written form, the problem one is addressing,
- be clear about what one is assuming, presupposing, or taking for granted,
- present one's position precisely, accurately, completely, and give relevant, logical, and fair arguments for it,
- cite relevant evidence and experiences to support one's position,
- see, formulate, and take account of alternative positions and opposing points of view, recognizing and evaluating evidence and key assumptions on both sides,
- illustrate one's central concepts with significant examples and show how they apply in real situations,
- empathetically entertain strong objections from points of view other than one's own.

13) It should assess the skills, abilities, and attitudes that are central to making sound decisions and acting on them in the context of learning to

understand our rights and responsibilities as citizens, as well-informed and thinking consumers, and as participants in a symbiotic world economy.

14) It should avoid any reductionism that allows a multi-faceted, theoretically complex, and authentically usable body of abilities and dispositions to be assessed by means of oversimplified parts that do not adequately reflect the whole.

15) It should enable educators to see what kinds of skills are basic for the future.

16) It should be of a kind that will assess valuable skills applied to genuine problems as seen by a large body of the populace, both inside and outside of the educational community.

17) It should include items that assess both the skills of thoughtfully choosing the most reasonable answer to a problem from among a pre-selected set and the skills of formulating the problem itself and of making the initial selection of relevant alternatives.

18) It should contain items that, as much as possible, are examples of the real-life problems and issues that people will have to think out and act upon.

19) It should be affordable.

20) It should enable school districts and educators to assess the gains they are making in teaching higher order thinking.

21) It should provide for a measure of achievement against national standards.

✦ Section Two: Critical Thinking and Criteria for Assessment

✦ What Is Included in a Rich, Substantive Concept of Critical Thinking?

Most of the language we shall use is drawn from draft statements of the *National Council for Excellence in Critical Thinking Instruction.* The National Council has been established precisely to articulate standards in critical thinking by 50 key leaders in critical thinking research and 105 leading educators. It is in the process of establishing regional offices and setting up 75 research-based committees to articulate the state of research in the field.

NATIONAL COUNCIL DEFINITION

Critical thinking is the intellectually disciplined process of actively and skillfully conceptualizing, applying, analyzing, synthesizing, or evaluating information gathered from, or generated by, observation, experience, reflection, reasoning, or communication, as a guide to belief and action.

This is the working definition of the National Council for Excellence in Critical Thinking Instruction. Though the definition as well as the other draft statements of the Council are subject to modification and refinement, the basic idea is one that is common to practitioners and researchers in critical thinking.

GLOSS ON THE DEFINITION

"In its exemplary form, [critical thinking] is based on universal intellectual values that transcend subject-matter divisions: clarity, accuracy, precision, consistency, relevance, sound evidence, good reasons, depth, breadth, and fairness." (National Council Draft Statement)

a) "It entails the examination of those structures or elements of thought implicit in all reasoning: purpose; problem, or question-at-issue; assumptions; concepts; empirical grounding; inferences; implications and consequences; objections from alternative viewpoints, and frame of reference." (National Council Draft Statement)

b) It entails larger-scale abilities of integrating elementary skills in such a way as to be able to apply, synthesize, analyze, and evaluate complicated and multidimensional issues. These include such abilities as clarifying issues, transferring insights into new contexts, analyzing arguments, questioning deeply, developing criteria for evaluation, assessing solutions, refining generalizations, and evaluating the credibility of sources of information. Among the abilities are included also the central forms of communication: critical reading, writing, speaking, and listening. Each of them is a large-scaled mode of thinking which is successful to the extent that it is informed, disciplined, and guided by critical thought and reflection. (Paraphrased from National Council Draft Statement.)

c) Critical thinking entails the possession and active use of a set of traits of mind and affective dimensions: independence of thought, fairmindedness, intellectual humility, intellectual courage, intellectual perseverance, intellectual integrity, curiosity, confidence in reason, and the willingness to see objections, to enter sympathetically into another's point of view, and to recognize one's own egocentricity or ethnocentricity. (Paraphrased from National Council Draft Statement.)

Critical thinking — in being responsive to variable subject areas, issues, and purposes — is incorporated in a family of interrelated modes of thinking, among them: scientific thinking, mathematical thinking, historical thinking, anthropological thinking, economic thinking, moral thinking, and philosophical thinking (National Council Draft Statement).

✦ *How Does a Rich, Substantive Concept of Critical Thinking Meet the 21 Criteria?*

In our view, a rich, substantive concept of critical thinking, and it alone, provides an intelligible and workable means of meeting all 21 criteria. In this section we will briefly consider each objective in turn, not as a definitive response to the criteria, but merely to suggest the fuller response in Section Three below.

CRITERION # 1

Can it be used to test information processing skills? Critical thinking includes at its core "a set of information and belief generating and processing skills and abilities."

CRITERION # 2

Can it be used to test flexible skills and abilities that can be used in a wide variety of subjects, situations, contexts, and educational levels? Since the art of critical thinking "entails proficiency in the examination of those structures or elements of thought implicit in all reasoning — purpose, problem or question-at-issue, assumptions, concepts, empirical grounding, reasoning leading to conclusions, implications and consequences, objections from alternative viewpoints and frames of reference" — it provides for maximum flexibility of use. It can be used in any subject, with respect to any situation to be figured out, in any context in which reasoning is germane, and, if adapted to the proficiency of students, at any educational level.

CRITERION # 3

Can it account for important differences among the subject areas? Subjects differ not because some make assumptions and others do not, not because some pose questions or problems and others do not, not because some have purposes and others do not, but rather because each has somewhat different purposes, and hence asks somewhat different questions, poses somewhat different problems, gathers somewhat different evidence, uses somewhat different concepts, etc. Critical thinking highlights these differences while underlining common structural features.

CRITERION # 4

Can it be used to focus on fundamental abilities fitted to the accelerating pace of change and embedded in intellectual history? Basic critical thinking skills and abilities are readily shown to be implicit in the rational development and critique of ideas at the core of intellectual history. They explain, for example, how new disciplines emerge from established ones: that is, by asking new questions, pursuing new purposes, framing new concepts, gathering new data, making new assumptions, reasoning in new directions, etc. They also explain how it is that a new field of study can ground itself, even at the outset, on definite intellectual standards that transcend any particular academic field: clarity, precision, accuracy, relevance, consistency, evidentiary force, valid reasoning, consistency . . . (standards implicit in the history of critical thinking and rational discourse in every domain).

CRITERION # 5

Can it be used to improve instruction? Critical thinking is not an isolated good, unrelated to other important goals in education. Rather it is a seminal goal which, done well, simultaneously facilitates a rainbow of other ends. It is best conceived, therefore, as the hub around which all other educational ends cluster. For example, as students learn to think more critically, they become more effective readers, writers, speakers, and listeners because each ability requires well-reasoned thought. They increase their mastery of content because all content is embedded in a system of understandings which, to be grasped, must be reasoned through. They become more proficient in — because they must be practiced within — a variety of modes of thinking: for example, historical, scientific, and mathematical thinking. Self-confidence increases with the intellectual empowerment critical thinking engenders. Finally, they develop skills, abilities, and traits of mind (intellectual discipline, intellectual perseverance, intellectual humility, intellectual empathy, intellectual integrity, ...) crucial to success in the educational, professional, and everyday world.

CRITERION # 6

Can it make clear the inter-connectedness of our knowledge and abilities, and why expertise in one area cannot be divorced either from findings in other areas or from a sensitivity to the need for interdisciplinary integration? In learning to think critically, one learns to transfer what one has learned about the logic of questions in one field to logically similar questions in other fields. Typically this begins with a recognition of the need to ask questions based on logical parallels between all fields of study, for example, skilled practice in questioning concepts and theories, in questioning data, in questioning the source or interpretation of data, in questioning the nature or organization of data, in questioning inferences, in questioning assumptions, in questioning implications and consequences, in questioning points of view and frames of reference, etc.

CRITERION # 7

Can it be used to assess those versatile and fundamental skills essential to being a responsible, decision-making member of the work-place? Critical thinking skills and abilities are highly transferable to the work-place. Since in learning to think critically we learn to take increasing charge of our minds as an instrument of learning — for example, reading, writing, speaking, and listening with greater discipline and skill — we are well situated to engage in collective problem solving and goal attainment, wherever they occur. The kind of "work" increasingly required in industry and business is "intellectual", that is, it requires workers to define goals and purposes clearly, seek out and organize relevant data, conceptualize those data, consider alternative perspectives, adjust thinking to context, question assumptions, modify think-

ing in the light of the continual flood of new information, and reason to legitimate conclusions. Furthermore, the intellectual work required must increasingly be coordinated with, and must profit from the critique of, fellow workers. There is no avoiding the need, therefore, to express ideas well,
accurately represent and consider fairly the ideas of others, write clear and
precise memos and documents, and coordinate and sequence all of these so
that well-reasoned policies and decisions can be accurately understood and
effectively implemented.

CRITERION # 8

*Can it generate clear concepts and well-thought-out, rationally articulated
goals, criteria, and standards?* Since critical thinking is based on the art of
monitoring one's thinking with standards implicit in the universal structure
of thought, and since the use of these standards is implicit in intellectual history from Socrates through Einstein, there is no problem using critical thinking to generate clear concepts for testing, as well as rationally articulated
goals, criteria, and standards.

CRITERION # 9

*Can it account for the integration of adult-level communication skills,
problem-solving, and critical thinking, and legitimately assess all of them
without compromising essential features of any of them?* Shallow concepts of
critical thinking often distinguish critical thinking from problem solving and
decision making as well as from reading, writing, and speaking skills. Once
one considers a rich, substantive concept of critical thinking, however, it is
clear that each of the basic skills of critical thinking are presupposed by each
of the other skills, just as each of them is deeply interrelated to critical
thinking as a whole. Consider, does it make sense to analyze potential solutions to problems or the implications of choosing an alternative in making a
decision without using critical thinking? Clearly not. Every problem to be
solved (or question to be settled) requires a *critical* analysis of the conditions
under which it can be solved or settled. We, as problem-solvers, need to look
critically at the purpose for solving the problem, we need to critically examine contextual factors, our assumptions, our concepts, what we are using as
data, our organization of the data, the source of the data, our reasoning, the
implications of our reasoning, our point of view, objections from other points
of view. All of these are essential to higher order problem solving and decision making. Furthermore, all of these intellectual abilities are crucial to
higher order reading, writing, speaking, and listening. To read must we analyze the text and re-create its logic in our own minds. To write we must construct a logic our readers can translate into the logic of their thought. To
speak we must articulate our thoughts in such a way that our audience can
translate our thoughts into their experiences. To listen we must analyze the
logic of the thinking of the speaker. Intellectually disciplined reading, writ-

ing, speaking, and listening require, in other words, that we work explicitly with the logic we are constructing or re-constructing, using our grasp of the standards of critical thinking to communicate accurately and precisely, effectively solve problems, and rationally make decisions.

CRITERION # 10

Does it respect cultural diversity by focusing on the common-core skills, abilities and traits useful in all cultures? As the criterion presupposes, we can respect cultural diversity best by constructing tests in higher order thinking that focus on skills and abilities necessary in all modern cultures. In this way we can legitimately justify assessing it in all cultural groups. Basic critical thinking skills and abilities — because they are based on fundamental elements implicit in the structure of all reasoned thought *per se,* and because their mastery is essential to higher order thinking in all academic, professional, personal, and public life — are an appropriate foundation for assessment.

CRITERION # 11

Does it test for thinking that promotes (to quote the September, 1991 Kappan) "the active engagement of students in constructing their own knowledge and understanding?" Narrow concepts of critical thinking sometimes characterize it in negative terms, as a set of tools for detecting mistakes in thinking. A rich, substantive concept of critical thinking, however, highlights its central role in all rationally defensible thinking, whether that thinking is focused on assessing thought or products already produced, or actively engaged in the construction of new knowledge or understandings. Well-reasoned thinking, whatever its end, is a form of creation and construction. It devises and articulates purposes and goals, translates them into problems or questions, seeks data that bear upon problems or questions, interprets those data on the basis of concepts and assumptions, and reasons to conclusions within some point of view. All of these are necessary acts of the reasoning mind and must be done "critically" to be done well. Hence all require critical thinking.

CRITERION # 12

Does it concentrate on assessing the fundamental cognitive structures of communication? Each of the dimensions identified in the objective is either straightforwardly a critical thinking ability or depends on a critical thinking ability. The writer's or speaker's *purpose, implications, assumptions, point of view,* etc., are all elements of thought, and the ability to identify and assess those as one reads or listens — the ability to construct in one's mind an accurate and fertile interpretation — is simply thinking *by* listening, thinking *by* reading.

A similar reliance on elements of thought is central to writing or speaking effectively at any educational level. The knowledge of how to gather and present evidence, to make clear one's own assumptions, to see the implications of a position: these are critical thinking abilities.

All forms of communication, moreover, rely on critical thinking standards. Essays and interpretations of essays, utterances and interpretations of utterances, need to be *relevant, logical, consistently* worked out; evidence needs to be recorded and reported *accurately;* points need to be made *clearly* and with as much *precision* as the subject permits; topics need to be covered in *depth* and presented *fairly.*

CRITERION # 13

Can it be used to assess the central features of making rational decisions as a citizen, a consumer, and a part of a world economy? Both public and private life increasingly require mastery of the basic skills and abilities of critical thinking. When this mastery is absent the public degenerates into a mass society susceptible to manipulation by public relations specialists who can engineer political victories by an adroit use of mud slinging, scare tactics, shallow nationalism, fear, envy, stereotypes, greed, false idealism, and maudlin sentimentality. Modern citizenship requires basic critical thinking skills and abilities throughout. The modern citizen should be able to assess the arguments presented for his or her assent, must rationally adjudicate between conflicting points of view, must attempt to understand a culturally complex world, must assess the credibility of diverse sources of information, must translate between conflicting points of view and diverse appeals, must rationally decide priorities, must seek to understand complex issues that involve multiple domains (for example, the environmental, moral, economic, political, scientific, social, and historical domains). Without a solid grounding in critical thinking, citizens are intellectually disarmed, incapable of discharging their civic responsibilities or rationally exercising their rights.

CRITERION # 14

Can it avoid reducing a complex whole to oversimplified parts? Testing for a rich, substantive concept of critical thinking is testing for skills of reasoning in terms of elements of thought, for the ability to orchestrate those elementary skills, for the affective dimensions that make critical thinking actualizable in practice, and for universal intellectual standards, in short for a rich and complex whole rather than for fragmented parts.

CRITERION #15

Can it articulate what is central to basic skills for the future? Basic skills are constituted by the structures explicated in a rich, substantive concept of critical thinking. To teach reading is to teach the ability not merely to repeat content, but to reconceptualize that content, to see applications of the main ideas, to generalize from them, critique them, see them in context, to enter with empathy into another's point of view. To teach writing as a basic skill is to teach not merely grammar and punctuation, but the ability to arrange one's ideas logically and consistently, to anticipate reasonable objections, to transfer ideas to the page in a way that makes them decipherable in all their complexity by a reader. To teach math as a basic skill is not primarily to teach how to solve pre-selected, individual, isolated problems out of context, but to teach the ability to begin to make sense of the world mathematically, to think quantitatively, to be able to see mathematical patterns, to set up the construction of problems and then creatively go about solving them. Critical thinking abilities like these do not exist somehow *in addition to* the basic skills of life; they *constitute* the basic skills of life.

CRITERION #16

Can it provide the kind of skills that are seen as valuable outside the school as well as inside it? Critical thinking provides skills that are seen as valuable by practitioners of the academic disciplines, by responsible leaders of government, of the professions, of business, by citizens interested in their environmental, physical, and economic welfare. In all such areas what is needed are ways to adapt to rapidly changing knowledge, to recognize problems and see their implications before they become acute, to formulate approaches to their solution that recognize legitimately different points of view, to draw reasonable conclusions about what to do. Increasingly, one is hearing statements such as the one made by David Kennedy, the president of Stanford University, to 3,000 college and university presidents:

> It simply will not do for our schools to produce a small elite to power our scientific establishment and a larger cadre of workers with basic skills to do routine work. Millions of people around the world now have these same basic skills and are willing to work twice as long for as little as one-tenth our basic wages. To maintain and enhance our quality of life, we must develop a leading-edge economy based on workers who can think for a living. If skills are equal, in the long run wages will be too. This means we have to educate a vast mass of people capable of thinking critically, creatively, and imaginatively.

CRITERIA #17 AND #18

Can critical thinking be assessed in a way that requires evaluation of authentic problems in realistic contexts, where the abilities assessed include those of formulating the problem and initial screening of plausible solutions? Yes. Testing of authentic skills, abilities and dispositions in authentic contexts can be accomplished by using a combination of *a)* standard multiple-choice items, *b)* machine-gradable multiple-rating items and *c)* short essay items.

a) The standard multiple-choice part of the assessment would be an expanded version of established critical thinking tests, such as the Watson-Glaser or Cornell tests. It is suitable for assessing micro-dimensional critical thinking skills, like identifying the most plausible assumption, recognizing an author's purpose, selecting the most defensible inferences, and such like.

b) The multiple-rating part of the assessment would test more open-ended and larger-domained abilities, like thinking within opposing points of view, the willingness to suspend judgment, the ability to synthesize disparate data into a logical scheme, to take established findings and generalize them into new contexts, etc.

The multiple-rating portion of the assessment, to be reliable, must:

   i) embody a rich and substantive idea of critical thinking,

   ii) be constructed and monitored by critical thinking experts who have such a concept,

   iii) be changed often (5% annually) to assess critical thinking with respect to authentic contemporary issues.

c) The essay part of the assessment would be designed to address critical thinking abilities and traits that involve creating a logic to capture a situation rather than selecting from among possibilities suggested by the test. Examples include the ability to construct an interpretation, to make a logical outline of a text, to figure out ways to gather information, to take an unclear and complex real issue and reformulate it so as to make it more amenable to solution.

Validity on the essay part of the assessment requires that the test be:

   i) constructed by experts in critical thinking,

   ii) assembled from a large and rotating bank of short essay questions to allow for items that show no significant differences,

   iii) centrally graded by teams well-trained in a full concept of critical thinking in order to assure quality control.

CRITERION #19

Can critical thinking be assessed nationally in a way that is financially affordable? To make it affordable, the constructed response segment of the assessment should be administered not to the population of students as a whole, but rather to a representative sample of the student population of a school system. The assessment should be (a) paid for by school systems that contract to have their students tested, and (b) constructed, monitored, administered, and graded by a private agency with critical thinking credentials, or at least under the direction of scholars with a solid grounding in the research into critical thinking.

CRITERIA #20 AND #21

Can critical thinking be assessed so as to gauge the improvement of students over the course of their education and to measure the achievement of students against national standards? To evaluate students in both these dimensions requires:

a) an assessment administered as a pre-test at the 6th grade and then as a follow up at the 9th and 12th grades (to provide for value-added judgments).

b) a criterion-referenced assessment that is built on clear, consistently applied quality-norms that are derived from a rich and substantive concept of critical thinking (to provide for the measuring of national progress).

✦ *What, Specifically, Are the Dangers of a Non-Substantive Concept of Critical Thinking?*

It is important to be alert to the dangers posed by a non-substantive concept of critical thinking. Such a concept exists when, separate from a consideration of the research in the field, a person or institution presupposes *a)* that the meaning or terminology of critical thinking is intuitively obvious (hence not in need of scholarly analysis), or *b)* that each concept underlying critical thinking (such as assumption, inference, implication, reasoning, ...) can be analyzed separately from a theory that accounts for the interrelation of these concepts, or *c)* that the skills of critical thinking can be adequately cultivated without reference to the values, traits of mind, and dispositions that underlie those skills.

1) There are at least three serious problems that may result from the use of a theoretically superficial concept of critical thinking:

a) important critical thinking concepts, which must be clearly defined to be used effectively in assessment, may be used vaguely, inconsistently, incorrectly, or misleadingly,

b) a false, misleading, or simplistic over-arching concept of critical thinking may be fostered, or

c) an unrealistic strategy for the assessment and cultivation of critical thinking may be incorporated into testing and teaching.

Many examples of the unwitting use of a non-substantive concept of critical thinking could be cited — such as "thinking skills" programs devoid of intellectual standards (which, for example, systematically confuse "inferences" with "valid inferences" and "analogies" with "sound analogies"), or testing personnel who lack adequate grounding in critical thinking theory (and so, for example, frequently confuse assumptions with inferences or inferences with implications). The most far-reaching danger occurs when influential educational systems or institutions, like state departments of education, inadvertently incorporate a non-substantive concept of critical thinking into statewide curriculum standards or into statewide testing programs. This can result in significant, unintended negative consequences, for example: thousands of teachers encouraged to follow a misconceived model for the assessment of reasoning, leading to mis-instruction on a grand scale.

2) Illustration: The California Direct Writing Assessment

We shall look at one important case. Unfortunately, given the brevity of this paper, one case must stand for all. The case we have chosen concerns the

Integrated Language Arts Assessment of the California Assessment Program,
a massive statewide program that has impact not only on every student in
the public schools of California, but also, because of the leadership role of
California in assessment, on national teaching and testing practices as well.
It appears that three fundamental mistakes occurred in the design of the
direct writing assessment:

a) Though one of the goals of the program was to place an emphasis on the
quality of reasoning and critical thinking in writing, it appears that no one
with a research background in critical thinking reviewed the articulation
or implementation of the assessment prompts. (We infer this from the fact
that fundamental conceptual errors occur both in the prompts themselves
and in the application of criteria to student constructed responses.)

b) It was assumed, inappropriately, that classroom teachers without extended training in critical thinking are able to effectively assess student essays
that call for evaluative reasoning. We infer this from statements descriptive of the assessment design like:

> Teachers on the CAP writing Development Team develop all the testing and
> instructional materials for assessment. For every type of writing assessed, the
> team develops a special set of prompts ... and a scoring guide that identifies
> the thinking and writing requirements for that type of writing....
>
> Essays are scored in four to six days by several hundred teachers at four
> regional scoring centers. A special handbook for each grade level provides
> teachers with practical instructional materials for each type of writing, includ-
> ing sample prompts, illustrative essays, and related readings.

c) The resulting assessment was not monitored by anyone with a research
background in critical thinking. (We infer this from the fact that model
"strong" answers purporting to illustrate critical reasoning are showcased
that are in fact patently very weak answers, containing virtually no reasoning at all.)

Consider Figure 1 and Figure 2 used as illustrations of the nature and
quality of the writing assessment program in an article authorized and
developed by the staff of the California Assessment Program. It is entitled
"California: The State of Assessment" and was written for an important
national anthology, *Developing Minds* (more than 150,000 copies disseminated by ASCD). The show-piece article, in which these figures occur, argues
that the examples illustrate a "state-of-the-art teacher-developed writing
assessment" that is sophisticated in "its testing, scoring, and reporting systems" and designed to "include only those tasks that will stimulate high-
quality instruction."

There are a number of problems illustrated in these figures that a substantive understanding of critical thinking would have avoided:

*1) A description of subjective reactions was systematically confused with
sound evaluative reasoning.* It is important to distinguish questions like,
"Is rock music good music?" or "Does rock music excel as a form of music?"

Evaluative Essay Sample

EVALUATION. Students were asked to write an evaluative essay, make judgments about the worth of a book, television program, or type of music and then support their judgments with reasons and evidence. Students must consider possible criteria on which to base an evaluation, analyze their subject in light of the criteria, and select evidence that clearly supports their judgments. Each student was assigned one of the following evaluative tasks:

- To write a letter to a favorite author telling why they especially liked one of the author's books.
- To explain why they enjoyed one television program more than any others.
- To justify their preference for a particular type of music.

The tasks made clear that students must argue convincingly for their preferences and not just offer unsupported opinions.

This is a sample essay from a student who demonstrated exceptional achievement.

Rock Around the Clock

> *"Well, you're getting to the age when you have to learn to be responsible!"* my mother yelled out.
> *"Yes, but I can't be available all the time to do my appointed chores! I'm only thirteen! I want to be with my friends, to have fun! I don't think that it is fair for me to baby-sit while you go run your little errands!" I snapped back. I sprinted upstairs to my room before my mother could start another sentence. I turned on my radio and "Shout" was playing. I noted how true the song was and I threw some punches at my pillow. The song ended and "Control" by Janet Jackson came on. I stopped beating my pillow. I suddenly felt at peace with myself. The song had slowed me down. I pondered briefly over all the songs that had helped me to control my feelings. The list was endless. So is my devotion to rock music and pop rock. These songs help me to express my feelings, they make me wind down, and above all they make me feel good. Without this music, I might have turned out to be a violent and grumpy person.*
> *Some of my favorite songs are by Howard Jones, Pet Shop Boys, and Madonna. I especially like songs that have a message in them, such as "Stand by Me", by Ben E. King. This song tells me to stand by the people I love and to not question them in times of need. Basically this song is telling me to believe in my friends, because they are my friends.*
> *My favorite type of music is rock and pop rock. Without them, there is no way that I could survive mentally. They are with me in times of trouble, and best of all, they are only a step away.*

California classroom teachers wrote comments like these after reading and scoring students' evaluative essays:

- "Evidence of clear thinking was heavily rewarded in our scoring."
- "I am struck by how much some students can accomplish in 45 minutes; how well they can sometimes marshal the ideas; and with how much flair and sparkle they can express themselves."
- "More emphasis should be placed on critical thinking skills, supporting judgments, and tying thoughts and ideas together. Far too many papers digress, summarize, underdevelop, or state totally irrelevant facts."
- "Students generally need to develop skills in giving evidence to support their judgments. I plan to spend more time on these thinking skills next year."

Source: California State Department of Education, 1988.

figure 1   Figures 1 and 2 come from "California: The State of Assessment", Anderson, Robert L. in *Developing Minds,* edited by Art Costa, pp. 314–25.

CAP Grade 8 Direct Writing Assessment
Achievement in Evaluation

SCORE POINT	PERCENTAGE OF CALIFORNIA GRADE 8 STUDENTS*	CUMULATIVE PERCENTAGE	DESCRIPTION OF ACHIEVEMENT
6 Exceptional Achievement	0.5		The student produces convincingly argued evaluation; identifies a subject, describes it appropriately, and asserts a judgment of it; gives reasons and specific evidence to support the argument; engages the reader immediately, moves along logically and coherently, and provides closure; reflects awareness of reader's questions or alternative evaluations.
5 Commendable Achievement	8.1	8.6	The student produces well-argued evaluation; identifies, describes, and judges its subject; gives reasons and evidence to support the argument; is engaging, logical, attentive to reader's concern; is more conventional or predictable than the writer of a 6.
4 Adequate Achievement	25.5	34.1	The student produces adequately argued evaluation; identifies and judges its subject; gives at least one moderately developed reason to support the argument; lacks the authority and polish of the writer of a 5 or 6; produces writing that, although focused and coherent, may be uneven; usually describes the subject more than necessary and argues a judgment less than necessary.
3 Some Evidence of Achievement	42.4	76.5	The student states a judgment and gives one or more reasons to support it; either lists reasons without providing evidence or fails to argue even one reason logically or coherently.
2 Limited Evidence of Achievement	19.2	95.7	The student states a judgment but may describe the subject without evaluating it or may list irrelevant reasons or develop a reason in a rambling, illogical way.
1 Minimal Evidence of Achievement	3.6	99.3	The student usually states a judgment but may describe the subject without stating a judgment; either gives no reasons or lists only one or two reasons without providing evidence; usually relies on weak and general personal evaluation.
No response	0.3		
Off Topic	0.5		

*This column does not total to 100% because of rounding.

figure 2

(which call for objective evaluation) from questions like, "Do you enjoy rock music?" or "Does rock music stir powerful emotions in you?" (which call, not for reasoning, but for the description of subjective reactions). Apparently the test developers were unclear about this distinction.

2) *The assessing teachers did not notice that the student failed to respond to the directions.* The student did not develop evaluative reasoning, did not support his judgment with reasons and evidence, did not consider possible criteria on which to base his judgment, did not analyze the subject in the light of the criteria, and did not select evidence that clearly supported his judgment. Instead the student described an emotional exchange, asserted — without evidence — some questionable claims, and expressed a variety of subjective preferences (a fuller critique of the student essay is available in Chapter 8, "Why Students — and Teachers — Don't Reason Well"). The assessing teachers were apparently too confused about the nature of evaluative reasoning or the basic notions of criteria, evidence, reasons, and well-supported judgment to notice the discrepancy.

3) *The California State Department of Education assessment staff did not notice these errors once they were made.* Instead of catching the errors once made, the California Department of Education chose to use the mis-graded student essay *as a showcase model* to disseminate nationally as illustrating "exceptional achievement" in reasoned evaluation, and as a *model* of their assessment of reasoned writing. We conclude that the California Assessment Program does not use scholars with a background in critical thinking research, any of whom would surely have recognized the problem.

Fundamental misconceptions of the nature of critical thinking and reasoned discourse, such as those documented above, must not be replicated in a national assessment program. Steps should be taken to insure that a substantive concept of critical thinking and a well-supervised implementation of that concept form the basis of the finished assessment program.

✦ Section Three: The Four Domains of Critical Thinking

What are the four component domains of critical thinking and their implications for the assessment of higher order thinking?

✦ Elements of Thought

As soon as we move from thought which is purely associational and undisciplined, to thinking which is conceptual and inferential, thinking which attempts in some intelligible way to figure something out, to use the power of reason, then it is helpful to think about what can be called "the elements of thought." The elements of thought are the basic building blocks of thinking, essential dimensions of reasoning whenever and wherever it occurs. Working together, they shape reasoning and provide a general logic to reason. We can articulate these elements by paying close attention to what is implicit in the attempt on the part of the mind to figure anything out whatsoever. Once we make them clear, it will be obvious that each of them can serve as an important touchstone or point of assessment in critical analysis and in the assessment of thinking.

For each of the elements of thought there is a cluster of attendant basic thinking skills. Because they involve fundamental structures of thought, these skills can be characterized as micro-skills, those skills out of which larger-domained critical thinking abilities are built. Being able to think critically about a particular issue, then, will include the ability to identify, clarify, and argue for and against alternative formulations of the elements of thought.

The basic conditions implicit whenever we gather, conceptualize, apply, analyze, synthesize, or evaluate information — the elements of thought — are as follows:

1) *Purpose, Goal, or End in View.* Whenever we reason, we reason to some end, to achieve some objective, to satisfy some desire or fulfill some need. One source of problems in reasoning is traceable to defects at the level of goal, purpose, or end. If the goal is unrealistic, for example, or contradictory to other goals we have, confused or muddled in some way, then the reasoning used to achieve it is problematic.

An assessment of critical thinking, then, would test, at the appropriate educational level, skills of being able to state an author's purpose, to identify a plausible statement of an author's goals from a list provided, to rank formulations of an author's objectives according to which are more or less reasonable in light of a particular passage, to distinguish clearly between purposes, consequences, assumptions, and other elements of thought.

2) *Question at Issue, or Problem to be Solved.* Whenever we attempt to reason something out, there is at least one question at issue, at least one problem to be solved. One area of concern for reasoners, therefore, will be the formulation of the question to be answered or problem to be solved, whether with respect to their own reasoning or to that of others.

Assessing skills of mastery of this element of thought would test students' ability to formulate a problem in a clear and relevant way, to choose from among alternative formulations, to discuss the merits of different versions of the question at issue, to recognize key common elements in statements of different problems, to structure the articulation of problems so as to make possible lines of solution more apparent.

3) *Point of View, or Frame of Reference.* Whenever we reason, we must reason within some point of view or frame of reference. Any "defect" in that point of view or frame of reference is a possible source of problems in the reasoning. A point of view may be too narrow, too parochial, may be based on false or misleading analogies or metaphors, may contain contradictions, and so forth.

Levels of skill here would be tested with reference to being able to enunciate an author's point of view in a passage, to adjudicate between different statements of that point of view, to recognize bias, narrowness, and contradictions when they occur in the point of view, to recognize relations between the frame of reference being used and its implications, assumptions, and main concepts.

4) *The Empirical Dimension of Reasoning.* Whenever we reason, there is some "stuff", some phenomena about which we are reasoning. Any "defect", then, in the experiences, data, evidence, or raw material upon which a person's reasoning is based is a possible source of problems.

Students would be tested, again, based on their level, on their ability to distinguish evidence from conclusions based on that evidence, to give evidence themselves, to identify from a pre-selected list data that would support an author's positions, data that would oppose it, data that would be neutral, to notice the presence or lack of relevant evidence, to recognize, to be intellectually courageous in recognizing (and labeling as such) mere speculation that goes beyond the evidence.

5) *The Conceptual Dimension of Reasoning.* All reasoning uses some ideas or concepts and not others. These concepts can include the theories, principles, axioms and rules implicit in our reasoning. Any "defect" in the concepts or ideas of the reasoning is a possible source of problems.

The assessment of the relevant higher order thinking would test the ability to identify main concepts of a passage, to choose among different versions of those concepts (some perhaps equally good), to see relations among concepts, to reason about the similarity of points of view on the basis of similarity of fundamental concepts, to distinguish central from peripheral concepts, derived concepts from basic concepts, to see the implications of using one concept rather than another.

6) *Assumptions.* All reasoning must begin somewhere, must take some things for granted. Any "defect" in the assumptions or presuppositions with which the reasoning begins is a possible source of problems.

Assessing skills of reasoning about assumptions would test the ability to identify assumptions underlying given inferences, points of view, and goals, to evaluate the accuracy of different formulations of the assumptions, to distinguish between assumptions and inferences, to rank assumptions with respect to their plausibility, to be intellectually fairminded by choosing the most plausible version of assumptions underlying points of view with which they disagree.

7) *Implications and Consequences.* No matter where we stop our reasoning, it will always have further implications and consequences. As reasoning develops, statements will logically be entailed by it. Any "defect" in the implications or consequences of our reasoning is a possible source of problems.

Skills to be assessed would include the ability to identify important implications, to do so by selecting from a list of possible implications, to make fine discriminations among necessary, probable, and improbable consequences, to distinguish between implications and assumptions, to recognize the weakness of an author's position as shown by the implausibility of its implications, to exercise intellectual fairmindedness in discriminating between the likelihood of dire and mild consequences of an action to which one is opposed.

8) Inferences. Reasoning proceeds by steps in which we reason as follows: "Because this is so, that also is so (or probably so)," or "Since *this*, therefore *that*." Any "defect" in such inferences is a possible problem in our reasoning.

Assessment would test, in a way geared to their educational level, students' ability to recognize faulty and justified inferences in a passage, to rank inferences with respect to both their plausibility and their relevance, to make good inferences in their own reasoning, to discriminate among various formulations of an author's inferences with respect to which is most accurate, to take something they do not believe but to entertain it for the sake of argument and draw reasonable inferences from it.

ASSESSMENT OF ELEMENTS OF THOUGHT

Any program for the assessment of critical thinking skills must itself be assessed in terms of its validity and reliability in testing for the ability to think about, and in terms of, the elements of thought. These abilities can be successfully assessed in three related ways: by a restricted use of standard multiple-choice items, by multiple-rating items, and by short essay items. Both multiple-choice and multiple-rating items are machine-gradable, while essay items are not.

Although our recommendations about the content of the assessment will be spelled out in detail in Section Four, some of these can be anticipated here with respect to the assessment of reasoning abilities centering around the elements of thought.

Multiple-choice testing (as in the existing *Watson-Glaser Critical Thinking Appraisal* or the *Cornell Critical Thinking Tests*) is an important part of an assessment of critical thinking, but its legitimate use is restricted to testing only the most basic skills of identifying and recognizing elements of thought, and then only as they occur in relatively short and unambiguous excerpts.

Within this domain, multiple-choice questions will require students:

* to identify an author's purpose in a passage;
* to rate selected inferences as justified, probably true, insufficiently evidenced, probably false, unjustified;
* to select among formulations of the problem at issue in a passage those that are clearly reasonable, probably reasonable, probably unreasonable, clearly unreasonable;
* to recognize unstated assumptions;
* to distinguish evidence from hypotheses and conclusions;
* to rate described evidence as reliable, probably reliable, probably not reliable, unreliable.

✦ *Abilities*

The elements of thought do not exist in isolation from one another, nor — more importantly for the concept of an assessment procedure — do they exist outside a particular context of application. In the practice of good critical thinking, skills more closely associated with elements of thought are orchestrated into larger-domained abilities which are applied to thinking about complex and sometimes ambiguous issues, problems, decisions, theories, states of affairs, social institutions, and human artifacts.

These critical thinking abilities include being skillful at:

1) refining generalizations and avoiding over-simplifications,

2) comparing analogous situations: transferring insights into new contexts,

3) developing one's perspective: creating or exploring the implications of beliefs, arguments, or theories,

4) clarifying issues, conclusions, or beliefs,

5) clarifying and analyzing the meanings of words and phrases,

6) developing criteria for evaluation: clarifying values and standards,

7) evaluating the credibility of sources of information,

8) questioning deeply: raising and pursuing root or significant questions,

9) analyzing or evaluating arguments, interpretations, beliefs, or theories,

10) generating or assessing solutions,

11) analyzing or evaluating actions or policies,

12) reasoning dialogically: comparing perspectives, interpretations, or theories,

13) reasoning dialectically: evaluating perspectives, interpretations, or theories,

14) reading critically: constructing an accurate interpretation of, understanding the elements of thought in, and evaluating, the reasoning of a text,

15) listening critically: constructing an accurate interpretation of, understanding the elements of thought in, and evaluating, the reasoning of an oral communication,

16) writing critically: creating, developing, clarifying, and conveying, in written form, the logic of one's thinking,

17) speaking critically: creating, developing, clarifying, and conveying, in spoken form, the logic of one's thinking.

Abilities like these play a central role in a rich and substantive concept of critical thinking. They are essential to approaching actual issues, problems, and situations rationally. Understanding the rights and duties of citizenship, for example, requires that one at least have the ability to compare perspectives and interpretations, to read and listen critically, to analyze and evaluate policies. In fact, there is no macro-ability on the list that would not be relevant or even crucial to thinking deeply about the rights and duties of citizenship. Similarly, the capacity to make sound decisions, to participate knowledgeably in the work-place, to function as part of a global economy, to master the content in anything as complex as the academic disciplines, to apply those subject area insights to real-life situations, to make insightful cross-disciplinary connections, to communicate effectively — each of these relies in a fundamental way on having a significant number of the abilities listed. Take, for example, the capacity to make sound decisions: such decision-making is hardly possible without an attendant ability to (going down the list of abilities in order) refine generalizations, compare analogous situations, develop one's perspective, clarify issues, and so forth.

The last four abilities listed — the ability to read, write, listen, and speak, each in a critical, informed, constructive way — are best considered not as in the usual model, not as manifestations of thinking already accomplished, but as being themselves actual modes of constructive thinking. As such, they are structured amalgams of elementary skills together with any number of other abilities.

ASSESSMENT OF ABILITIES

The assessment of abilities, too often neglected, is essential to assessment of critical thinking. Since these *are* the abilities implicit in the realistic use of thinking, no assessment tool that fails to assess a significant number of these abilities could justifiably be called an assessment of higher order thinking. The assessment, moreover, needs to address such abilities *directly* (rather than through secondary indicators), *systematically* (rather than haphazardly as a result of an attempt to assess other variables like academic achievement), and in settings as *authentic* as possible given the requirement of *uniform, relevant grading*.

Assessment of abilities that meets these four criteria cannot be accomplished within the confines of a standard multiple-choice-type test. It can be accomplished, however, for all of the abilities (except those having to do with oral communication), by means of a combination of machine-gradable multiple-rating items and essay items.

For any macro-ability, there will be dimensions of the ability that are *generative* and other dimensions of it that are selective. In trying to solve a real problem, for example, much of one's thinking is devoted to *generating* a formulation of the problem that will make it more susceptible to solution. Another, and quite different, aspect of problem solving, is the ability to *select*, from among a large variety of possibilities, that avenue of thought which will most likely result in a solution. Students who are trained using a rich, substantive concept of critical thinking tend to improve in both dimensions of this ability, and both are genuine dimensions of real problem-solving.

The selective dimensions of an ability can be assessed accurately, even in complex, ambiguous, and subtle cases, using multiple-rating items. The generative dimension, on the other hand, cannot. Since it requires students to come up with their own critical thinking approaches within that macro-ability, this dimension can be assessed adequately only by carefully constructed and carefully graded essay tests. Details of the assessment and samples of assessment items will be presented in Section Four.

✦ *Affective Dimensions*

Higher order thinking requires more than higher order thinking *skills.* Critical thinking, in any substantive sense, includes more than abilities. The concept also includes, in a crucial way, certain attitudes, dispositions, passions, traits of mind. These affective dimensions are not merely important to critical thinking, they are essential to the effective use of higher order thinking in real settings.

These affective dimensions include:

1) thinking independently,

2) exercising fairmindedness,

3) developing insight into egocentricity and sociocentricity,

4) developing intellectual humility and suspending judgment,

5) developing intellectual courage,

6) developing intellectual good faith and integrity,

7) developing intellectual perseverance,

8) developing confidence in reason,

9) exploring thoughts underlying feelings and feelings underlying thoughts,

10) developing intellectual curiosity.

Without *intellectual perseverance,* one could not solve the complicated, multi-faceted problems one confronts in industry. Without *intellectual courage,* one could not maintain a defense of citizenship rights in the face of scare tactics. Without *fairmindedness,* one could not enter into another's point of view and thus would lack that empathetic understanding necessary for a reasonable approach to living in a pluralistic society. Without *developing insight into egocentricity and sociocentricity* one could employ one's reasoning skills in a merely self-serving and prejudiced way. Without *confidence in reason* one could not adequately address those complex and frequently ambiguous real-life problems that require reasonable decisions in the face of crucial uncertainties.

ASSESSMENT OF AFFECTIVE DIMENSIONS

The assessment of affective dimensions of critical thinking is an important part of an assessment of higher order thinking. An initial problem is that from the fact that all these dimensions are essential, it does not follow that all are directly testable, nor does it follow that *any* of them is *easily* testable.

For some of these affective dimensions (intellectual perseverance, for example), any testing would have to take place over an appropriately long period of time and thus could not be legitimately assessed at all during a timeframe suitable for a national test.

Nevertheless, a number of affective dimensions can be assessed in a relatively straightforward way using essay items and, especially, machine-gradable multiple-rating items.

"Reasoning Within Conflicting Points of View," a central aspect of the disposition of fairmindedness, is already being assessed on the revised version of the *Watson-Glaser Critical Thinking Appraisal*. This section of the *Appraisal* asks students to select the strongest (that is, the most defensible) argument in favor of each side of a pair of conflicting and sometimes emotionally charged points of view. Proficiency on these items indicates a fairminded willingness to distinguish the concept of *reasonable defensibility* from that of *personal belief*.

Multiple-rating items are currently being prepared that address aspects of intellectual courage, other aspects of fairmindedness, aspects of intellectual humility, and aspects of the development of insight into one's own egocentricity and sociocentricity.

✦ *Intellectual Standards*

In any domain where assessment is taking place, there are standards implicit in that assessment. Higher order thinking is thinking that meets universal intellectual standards. Thus, when assessing a student's ability to compare and evaluate perspectives (a macro-ability) and to do so with fairmindedness (a trait of mind), we would judge whether she had made such evaluations in a *relevant* and *consistent* way, with attention to *accuracy, fairness,* and *completeness* in describing each perspective, and with a sensitivity to the degree of *precision* appropriate to the topic. We would assess critical thinking about and in terms of the elements of thought in very much the same way: to judge a person's skill at recognizing the frame of reference underlying a position, we would want to judge whether she could see *relevant* alternatives, whether the frame of reference she identified fits the available *evidence*, whether her answer was *deep* or merely mechanical, *clear* or vague, *fair* or biased. Intellectual standards apply to thinking in every subject.

The process of learning to teach so as to foster critical thinking is the very process by means of which one establishes intellectual standards for assessing thinking, and, by extension, for assessing instruction itself.

Such standards are more useful if they are made explicit — to the students who are taking the test, to those doing the assessing, and to classroom teachers. Making standards explicit benefits student test-takers because they can then see that there are standards, that the standards are not arbitrary, and that understanding the standards gives them insight into what good critical thinking is. It benefits those doing the assessing because, in addition to the reasons already mentioned, it fosters both a uniformity in grading and a strong correlation between the grade and the skills being graded. Judging a response by how *clearly* and *completely* it states a position, for example, is using a critical thinking standard and dictates a certain level of assessment; judging a response by how *concisely* or how *elegantly* it states a position, on the other hand, is using a standard that is inappropriate to critical thinking assessment. Explicit standards — part of a rich and substantive concept of critical thinking — might have avoided at least some of the mistaken assessment on the *California Assessment Program,* cited earlier (see p. 94). Thus, making standards explicit promotes both the reliability and the validity of the assessment. Finally, it benefits classroom teachers because such standards can readily be built into classroom instruction. The standards, after all, are those implicit in teaching for higher order thinking; they are therefore invaluable both for teachers to use explicitly with their classes and — an essential feature of critical thinking-internalized — for students to learn to use as part of assessing themselves.

Intellectual Standards
That Apply to Thinking in Every Subject

Thinking that is: .... *Thinking that is:*

Clear	vs	Unclear
Precise	vs	Imprecise
Specific	vs	Vague
Accurate	vs	Inaccurate
Relevant	vs	Irrelevant
Plausible	vs	Implausible
Consistent	vs	Inconsistent
Logical	vs	Illogical
Deep	vs	Superficial
Broad	vs	Narrow
Complete	vs	Incomplete
Significant	vs	Trivial
Adequate *(for purpose)*	vs	Inadequate
Fair	vs	Biased or One-Sided

✦ Section Four: Recommendations of the Center for Critical Thinking

What is the most workable solution to the design of a process to assess higher order thinking?

In this section we will *1)* briefly survey existing assessment tools; *2)* make recommendations regarding the substance and format of a national assessment tool — the critical thinking domains to be assessed, the varieties of assessment strategies to be used (including sample test items), and the dual interdisciplinary and intradisciplinary scope of the assessment — *3)* appraise the value of the proposed assessment strategy for the reform of instruction, and *4)* make recommendations regarding the implementation of the assessment.

✦ Existing Assessment Tools

There are limitations in all twelve of the commercially available critical thinking tests as instruments for assessing higher order thinking:

> Cornell Class Reasoning Test, Form X (1964)
>
> Cornell Conditional Reasoning Test, Form X (1964)
>
> Cornell Critical Thinking Test, Level X (1985)
>
> Cornell Critical Thinking Test, Level Z (1985)
>
> The Ennis–Weir Critical Thinking Essay Test (1985)
>
> Judgement: Deductive Logic and Assumption Recognition (1971)
>
> Logical Reasoning (1955)
>
> New Jersey Test of Reasoning Skills (1983)
>
> Ross Test of Higher Cognitive Processes (1976)
>
> Test on Appraising Observations (1983)
>
> Test of Enquiry Skills (1979)
>
> Watson–Glaser Critical Thinking Appraisal (1980)

In addition there are limitations in all of the other available "higher studies" tests which might be taken as a possible model for the assessing of higher order thinking: the SAT, LSAT, the Test of Academic Aptitude (British), ACT, the Graduate Record Exam, the Commonwealth Secondary Scholarships Exam (Australia). We do not have the space here to review each of these tests one-by-one. Instead we will summarize the general situation as we see it.

Though aspects and dimensions of critical thinking are tested, some more and some less, in all of the above tests, none has been designed with the 21 criteria in Sections one and two in mind. Most importantly, none was designed to serve as a national assessment tool which establishes national standards in higher order thinking and as a motivation for and guide to instruction.

Behind none of these tests was there a comprehensive model for the elements of thought, the abilities of critical thinking, or the affective dispositions (as we have here provided). The relative recentness of the bulk of scholarship in critical thinking makes it unlikely that long-established tests will fill the bill.

Of course any new test for assessing higher order thinking should be based on a thorough review of established test strategies to incorporate those with significant application.

Given the need for assessment on the basis of a rich and substantive concept of critical thinking, there are two areas where competing values and objectives come into play.

The first concerns the *substance and format* of the test itself: Which domains exactly are to be covered, and with what emphases? What kinds of question will be asked? Will it include both interdisciplinary and intradisciplinary items? What kind of assessment questions best test for skills of citizenship and the challenges of the work-place?

The second area concerns the *implementation* of the test and how it is conceived: Should it be value-added or simply criterion-referenced? Who will do the assessing and who will be assessed? How much will the assessment cost and who will pay for it? How often will the test be given?

Some of these are difficult questions, with genuine values and goals on different sides, where reasonable cases can be made for more than one position. Others of these questions are clearer, especially once the objectives of the test as a whole are brought into focus.

✦ *Substance and Format*

The overall recommendations of the Center for Critical Thinking are set forward below.

1) DOMAINS TO BE ASSESSED
The national assessment of higher order thinking must test for a rich and substantive concept of critical thinking, and this testing must be geared to assessment within all four domains of critical thinking.

a) Elements of Thought
Skills of identifying, explicating, and using the elements of thought need to be assessed. They are necessary for any of the abilities to be employed with precision, depth, or accuracy. They are required if essential affective traits are to be rooted in solid, locatable, intellectual skills and the concepts they presuppose.

Lack of a solid grounding in these skills, and the concepts behind them, results in thinking which, good intentions notwithstanding, is far removed from the close, careful reasoning demanded by the rigors of higher order thinking. Among testing personnel, lack of the informed use of these concepts is part of what results in such poor assessment tools and grading as we found in the *California Direct Writing Assessment*.

Critical thinking in students requires them to be able to perform well, with an expertise appropriate to their grade level, on items testing a list of skills that center around the elements of thought:

- identify a plausible statement of a writer's purpose;
- rank formulations of an author's objectives;
- distinguish clearly between purposes, consequences, assumptions, and inferences;
- choose the most reasonable statement of the problem an author is addressing;
- discuss reasonably the merits of different versions of the question at issue;
- recognize key common elements in formulations of different problems;
- give a clear articulation of an author's point of view;
- identify the most reasonable statement of an author's point of view;
- recognize bias, narrowness, and contradictions in the point of view behind an excerpt;
- identify assumptions and implications of a writer's point of view;
- distinguish evidence from conclusions based on that evidence;
- give evidence to back up their position in an essay;
- recognize data that would support, data that would oppose, and data that would be neutral with respect to, an author's position;
- recognize conclusions that go beyond the evidence;
- note, in an evaluative essay, the presence, or the absence, of evidence in an excerpt;
- identify the main concepts in a passage;
- distinguish central from peripheral concepts;
- identify the assumption underlying a given inference;
- evaluate the aptness of different versions of an assumption;
- choose the most reasonable statement of a background theory involved in a passage;
- distinguish between inferences and assumptions;
- rank different formulations of assumptions with respect to which is the most reasonable;
- identify crucial implications of a passage;
- discriminate between consequences that are necessary, probable, and improbable;
- evaluate an author's inferences;

- make, in an evaluative essay, justified inferences;
- choose the most accurate version of an author's inferences;
- draw reasonable inferences from positions they disagree with.

b) Abilities

Abilities, grounded in a thorough familiarity with the elements of thought, are the activities we actually use to perform our higher order thinking. Abilities like clarifying values and standards, comparing analogous situations, generating and assessing solutions, analyzing and evaluating actions or policies are the stuff of reasoning. They are the means whereby decisions are to be made, problems are to be solved, thinking in the work-place is to be strengthened, and understanding of rights and responsibilities deepened.

The abilities of critical reading and critical writing are keystones of any process to assess higher order thinking in that each of them, when considered at any level, is permeated by other critical thinking abilities. It is not as if we read *and* clarify values, read *and* compare analogous situations, write *and* generate solutions. To read critically *is* to clarify values, compare analogous situations, and to exercise the other abilities as well; to write *is* to generate solutions and much more besides.

Assessment of proficiency in the abilities can be keyed to student performance on test items that are geared to as many of the abilities listed on p. 101 as is feasible given the time constraints of the test.

c) Affective Traits

Without assessing affective traits, only a diminished idea of critical thinking will be addressed.

What allows us to confront our prejudices and analytically break them down is not just abilities but a *commitment* to use them for this purpose. What allows us to solve our problems in a sufficiently diligent way as to address complicated and intricate real-life problems, is again not just cognitive abilities. It is intellectual perseverance — a drive, a disposition, an affective trait. A similar point can be made for each of the intellectual traits which are the driving force behind sound and penetrating reasoning.

Assessment of the affective dimensions will concentrate on those aspects it is plausible to test for within the constraints imposed by a national assessment. These will include aspects of fairmindedness, of the willingness to suspend judgment, of intellectual courage and intellectual integrity.

d) Intellectual Standards

Assessment has to involve explicit universal standards. If we are not testing students' abilities to be relevant, precise, logical, consistent, and the rest, then we are not assessing students' abilities to engage in higher order thinking. And if testing personnel do not employ these same explicit standards, then they are grading for something other than higher order thinking.

Relative mastery of these intellectual standards requires students to be able to

- recognize *clarity* vs. unclarity;
- distinguish *accurate* from inaccurate accounts;
- decide when a statement is *relevant* or irrelevant to a given point;
- identify inconsistent positions as well as (relatively) *consistent* ones;
- discriminate *deep, complete, and significant* accounts from those that are superficial, fragmentary, and trivial;
- evaluate responses with respect to their *fairness;*
- prefer *well-evidenced* accounts to accounts that are unsupported by evidence;
- tell *good reasons* from bad.

2) VARIETIES OF ASSESSMENT STRATEGIES

The assessment should contain three kinds of items: *A)* machine-gradable multiple-choice items; *B)* machine-gradable multiple-rating items; *C)* essay items.

A) *Multiple-Choice Items*

Legitimate use of multiple-choice items on the assessment is limited. This type of item is geared toward relatively straightforward skills of reasoning, particularly with respect to recognizing elements of thought, distinguishing one element of thought from another, and recognizing clear examples of faulty reasoning.

Two detailed samples of assessment items follow (the first, Figure 3, is on Inferences, the second, Figure 4, on Recognition of Assumptions.)

Other abbreviated samples of appropriate multiple-choice items are as follows:

1) In the following excerpt, mark E for each item that is a piece of empirical *evidence;* mark C for each item that is a *conclusion* based on evidence; mark N for each item that is neither....

2) In this test, each exercise consists of several statements (premises) followed by several suggested conclusions.... If you think the conclusion *necessarily* follows from the statements given, make a heavy black mark under *"Conclusion Follows"*; if you think it is not a necessary conclusion, put a mark under *"Conclusion Does Not Follow."*

3) The following is a list of possible findings in relation to the experiment quoted above. For each, say whether it would *support* the author's hypothesis, *oppose* the author's hypothesis, or be neutral with respect to the author's hypothesis....

4) Below is a series of questions. Each question is followed by several reasons. For the purpose of this test, you are to regard each reason as true. The problem then is to decide whether it is a *strong reason* or a *weak reason*....

Inferences

DIRECTIONS: An inference is a conclusion a person can draw from certain observed or supposed facts. For example, if the lights are on in a house and music can be heard coming from the house, a person might infer that someone is at home. But this inference may or may not be correct. Possibly the people in the house did not turn off the lights and the radio when they left the house.

In this test, each exercise begins with a statement of facts that you are to regard as true. After each statement of facts you will find several possible inferences — that is, conclusions that some persons might draw from the stated facts. Examine each inference separately and make a decision as to its degree of truth or falsity.

For each inference you will find spaces on the answer sheet labeled J, PJ, ID, PU, and U. For each inference make a mark on the answer sheet under the appropriate heading as follows:

> J if you think the inference is definitely JUSTIFIED; that it properly follows beyond a reasonable doubt from the statement of facts given.

> PJ if you think the inference is PROBABLY JUSTIFIED; that it is more likely to be true than false in the light of the facts given.

> ID if you decide that there are INSUFFICIENT DATA; that you cannot tell from the facts given whether the inference is justified or not; if the facts provide no basis for judging one way or the other.

> PU if you think the inference is PROBABLY UNJUSTIFIED; that it is more likely to be false than true in the light of the facts given.

> U if you think the inference is definitely UNJUSTIFIED; that it does not follow, either because it misinterprets the facts given, or because it contradicts the facts or necessary inferences from those facts.

Example

The first newspaper in America, edited by Ben Harris, appeared in Boston on September 25, 1690, and was banned the same day by Governor Simon Bradstreet. The editor's subsequent long fight to continue to publish his paper and print what he wished marks an important episode in the continuing struggle to maintain a free press.

1) The editor of the first American newspaper died within a few days after his paper was banned on September 25,1690.

2) Information about the first issue of Ben Harris's newspaper promptly came to Governor Bradstreet's attention.

3) The editor of this paper wrote articles criticizing Governor Bradstreet.

4) Ben Harris persisted in holding to some of his aims.

5) Governor Bradstreet objected to some of the items published in Ben Harris's paper.

In the above example:

> Inference 1 is (U) unjustified because in the facts given it mentions "the editor's long fight to continue to publish his paper..."

> Inference 2 is (J) justified because the facts state that the first newspaper appeared on September 25, 1690, and was banned the same day by the Governor.

> Regarding inference 3, there is no information given about the precise nature of the articles appearing in the paper; thus (ID) Insufficient data.

> Regarding inference 4, the facts given mention "the editor's subsequent long fight to continue to publish his newspaper and print what he wished..."; thus (J) justified.

> Inference 5 is deemed (PJ) probably justified because the Governor banned the paper the day it appeared. However this is PJ rather that J because there may have been reasons for the ban other than objections to some of the items that appeared in the paper.

figure 3

5) Which of the following conclusions is *C* completely supported by the stated evidence, *P* partially supported by the stated evidence, or *U* unsupported by the stated evidence?

6) Which of the following is an *implication* of the author's position in the passage cited?

B) Multiple-Rating Items

Though the use of multiple-choice questions is justified in assessing some micro-skills, the bulk of the machine-gradable items will be *multiple-rating*

Recognition of Assumptions

DIRECTIONS: Careful reasoners often find it necessary to complete partially stated arguments in order to evaluate those arguments. For example, someone might say, "John is selfish; we are good friends, but he never lends me money." The conclusion that "John is selfish" is supported by two explicit claims:

  1) John never lends me money.
  2) John and I are good friends.

But an important part of the argument was left out:

  3) People who never lend money to their good friends are selfish.

This third assertion is an *unstated assumption* of the argument.

In this test each exercise begins with a brief argument. Each argument is followed by three numbered statements. Examine each of the numbered statements individually and make a decision about its logical relationship to the argument. For each numbered statement there are spaces on your answer sheet labeled: EC, UA, and N. Select just one of the following alternatives for each numbered statement, and make a mark on your answer sheet under the appropriate heading:

  EC if you think the idea expressed in the numbered statement is an *explicit claim* made in the argument (even if the wording is not the same).

  UA if you think the idea expressed in the numbered statement is a probable *unstated assumption* of the argument.

  N if you think the idea expressed in the numbered statement is *neither* an explicit claim nor an unstated assumption of the argument.

Example
Argument: "We need to save time in getting there, so we'd better go by plane."

1) Going by plane will take less time than going by some other means of transportation.

[Saving time is given as a reason for going by plane; this only makes sense if the person giving the argument believes that going by plane would take less time than other available means of transportation. So the idea expressed here is an *unstated assumption* of the quoted argument.] (UA)

2) We should try to cut down how long we spend travelling to our destination.

[The idea expressed here is directly asserted, though in different words, in the argument, so it is not an unstated assumptions of the argument; rather, it is an *explicit claim* made in the argument.] (EC)

3) Travel by plane is more convenient than travel by train.

[No mention is made in the argument of either trains or convenience. The idea expressed here is *neither* an explicit claim nor an unstated assumption of the argument.] (N)

---

figure 4

rather than multiple-choice. Multiple-rating items allow one to ask questions where any number of answers from a provided list may be correct, or incorrect. It further allows students to *rank,* from a number of possibilities provided, those that are more correct. Thus students can be tested on their ability to arrange items on a continuum of reasonability. This allows much more subtle testing and grading.

The same list of possible answers can pertain to any number of independent test items. Thus, a list of twenty possibilities can be provided, and students can be asked to choose the appropriate response from that list to six different questions. There is no restriction on the number of times a given answer may be correct. Nor is there any guarantee that there will be a reasonable answer on the list to every question. Guessing, using the process of elimination, and scoring well because of test-taking skills are all but impossible.

By including clearly unreasonable choices among the multiple-rating possibilities, a grade can be much more sensitive to the *degree* of a macro-ability or to the *intensity* of an affective dimension. Thus, if there are five possible answers to a given question, they need not be graded 5, 4, 3, 2, 1. Rather, they may be graded, say, 5, 4, 1, 1, -3.

We have provided two detailed samples of multiple-rating items: Figure 5 is on Reasoning Within Conflicting Points of View (and thus is an assessment of an aspect of the affective trait of fairmindedness) and Figure 6 is on Comparing Analogous Situations (and is thus an assessment of a macro-ability). Each sample is limited here by having only four possible answers, a limitation that would not obtain on an actual test.

The following is a list of abbreviated samples of multiple-rating items, having to do with elements of thought, with abilities, with affective dimensions, and with intellectual standards.

Multiple-Rating Items, Elements of Thought

- Here is a list of formulations of the writer's objectives in this excerpt. Rank them from 1 to 5 with respect to which is the most reasonable in the light of the quoted passage....

- For each of the underlined passages in the excerpts below, mark P on the answer sheet if it is a statement of the writer's *Purpose,* C if it is a statement of the *Consequences,* A if it is a statement of the writer's *Assumptions,* and *I* if it is an *Inference* the writer is making.

- Which of the following would the author most likely give as the statement of the problem she is attempting to solve?

- Read the excerpt; then, from the following list, identify the most plausible statement of the writer's purpose.

- Of the following statements of the author's *point of view* in this passage, select the one from the following list that is both most reasonable and most relevant to the passage....

- List A below is a list of various possible statements of the writer's point of view in the quoted passage; List B is a list that includes possible assumptions and implications of those points of view. Match the items on list A with the items on list B...

- Which of the following are main *concepts* in the passage cited; which are *peripheral concepts*?

- For each inference below, decide whether the accompanying statement is *U* an unstated assumption, *A* an assertion, or *N* neither...

- Rank the following items on a scale of 1 to 5 according to how reasonable it is as a statement of the author's *assumptions*...

- Look at each of the statements below as a possible consequence of the writer's position in the excerpt cited. Rank each statement on a scale of 1 to 7, where 7 means that you consider the statement a *necessary* consequence of the passage, and 1 means that you consider the statement a *highly unlikely* consequence of the passage.

- Each of the following is an *inference* one might draw from the passage. Rank each one on a scale from 1 to 5, according to whether it is completely justified (5) or completely unjustified (1)...

Reasoning Within Conflicting Points of View

Directions: In the following questions, rank the answers in order of reasonability. In each case you are being asked to rank answers as to which is the strongest argument in favor of a position. By the strongest we mean the one that is most defensible, not necessarily the one which claims the most. To rank a defense for a position high does not mean that you actually hold that position but only that if you had to defend it before an audience of unbiased and openminded people, the options you rank higher would be easier to defend on rational grounds than the ones you rank lower.

1) Children under the age of twelve should have all of their important decisions made for them by their parents and other appropriate adults because:
    1) allowing them to make all important decisions for themselves will encourage false pride and stubbornness.
    2) allowing them to make all important decisions for themselves will undermine parental respect and authority.
    3) children are not mature enough to make all important decisions for themselves.
    4) children should not be expected to take life's problems so seriously until they grow up.
    5) children can be expected to make grave mistakes, some of which could harm them for life.

2) Children under the age of twelve should make some important decisions for themselves because:
    1) children are less prejudiced than adults and more open to the truth.
    2) children spend a lot of time watching T.V. so they know a lot about what is going on in the world.
    3) children are likely to make many reasonable decisions affecting themselves.
    4) children will become depressed if they are not allowed to make some important decisions.
    5) children will be more apt to become responsible adults if they are allowed to make some important decisions for themselves as they are growing up.

figure 5

Comparing Analogous Situations

"Having a population to study instead of an individual fossil is enormously important. No two people today are exactly alike; no two Australopithecines were either. It is for that reason that drawing conclusions from a single fossil is risky. Measurements taken of it, and theories spun off as a result of those measurements, may be misleading because the part being measured may not be typical. It is only when a large number of specimens is available that all their variations can be taken into account, and a norm derived from them. If a visitor from outer space were to describe and name *Homo sapiens sapiens* by examining one skeleton, that of a short, squat, heavy-boned New Guinea tribesman, he would certainly be excused if he set up another species on the basis of a second skeleton discovered later a few thousand miles away — that of a seven-foot, slender-boned Watutsi tribesman from central Africa." (Edey, *The Emergence of Man*, pp. 47–48)

The author of the above passage makes an analogy between an anthropologist studying fossils and a visitor from outer space studying one or two single skeletons. Rank each of the following comments 1 to 3, according to whether it would be crucial to judging the strength of the analogy for the point the author is making. Give a comment a 3 if it is CRUCIAL in judging the worth of the analogy; give it a 1 if it is IRRELEVANT to judging the worth of the analogy; give it a 2 if it lies in between.

  a) The analogy illustrates the point well because in both cases we are called upon to draw general conclusions based on a limited sample. The more items you have in your sample, the more justified your generalization will be.

  b) It is a bad analogy because the visitors from outer space would draw the same erroneous conclusion even if they had a whole population of New Guinea tribesmen to study.

  c) It is a good analogy but it shows that we need, not simply *more* fossils of Australopithecus, but fossils of it from other geographical areas.

  d) It is a bad analogy because we have no idea what visitors from outer space would conclude from seeing a skeleton of a New Guinea tribesman. The visitors might refrain from making the generalization for the same reason that makes the author say it is "risky."

figure 6

- Which of the following is the most accurate formulation of the author's *inference* in the cited passage?

Multiple-Rating Items, Abilities

- Which of the following would be relevant to deciding whether A is a *credible* source of information on the topic...?

- Here is a list of observations about the behavior of X's, made by a responsible investigator. Which of the items from the following list would be a *justified generalization* about X's?

- A has the following beliefs about astrology. Which of the questions below would be *root* or *significant questions* that A would have to answer to claim his beliefs about astrology were rational?

- A refuses to refund a customer's money and, when asked, defends her action by stating that it is "dictated by store policy". Which of the following would be *relevant* to deciding whether her action was indeed "dictated by store policy"? Which of the questions would be relevant to deciding if the store policy was rational?

- Judge A makes the following ruling in a case... Which of the following is the clearest statement of the standards Judge A is using?

- A compares the relation between managers and employees to the relation between teachers and students. Which of the following would A have to answer in order to continue using the analogy rationally?

- A gives the following argument for.... Which of the listed comments would be the *strongest objection* to her argument?

- Listen to the accompanying excerpt from an audiotape of a lecture by A. Which of the following questions would be of most help in clarifying A's views?

Multiple-Rating Items, Affective Traits

- Here are position-statements from both sides, A and B, of a controversial and inflammatory debate. From list X below, choose those items which are the most reasonable *inferences* to draw from position A; then choose those items which are the most reasonable *inferences* to draw from position B.

- Here are position-statements from both sides, A and B, of a controversial and inflammatory debate. From list X below, choose those items which state the most reasonable *assumptions* underlying position A; then choose those items which state the most reasonable *assumptions* underlying position B.

- For each of the items below, tell which is the most reasonable action to take under the circumstances described. If, in your view, there is not enough information to make a reasonable decision, you may choose the action of *suspending judgment* as the most reasonable response.

- A disposition to take a measured response rather than an exaggerated, disproportionate response will be measured by requiring students to discriminate between the likelihood of dire versus mild consequences of positions they dislike.

Multiple-Rating Items, Intellectual Standards

- The following are four definitions from *Webster's New World Dictionary.* Which of them gives the clearest definition of...?

- Rank the following definitions for their *precision* on a scale of 1 to 7. 1 means "not precise at all"; 7 means "too precise for the subject matter"; and 4 means "exactly as precise as it should be".

- Here is a list of data and a series of accounts summarizing the data. Which of the accounts is the *most accurate* summary of the data?

- For each statement below, tell whether it is *relevant* or *irrelevant* to the hypothesis in the passage cited.

- Which of the following is the *fairest* restatement of the author's position [where the author is stating a highly controversial position]?

- Rank the following statements according to which are the *best-evidenced* and which are the *least-evidenced.*

• Which of the following is a good reason for believing the statement in question? Which is a bad reason? Which is somewhere in the middle?

c) Essay Items

The full range of the use of critical thinking cannot be assessed without requiring writing on the part of the student. To confront real issues, balance competing interests, weigh objections and alternatives, and make a reasonable decision about a matter of some consequence — this is a major part of what it is to think critically.

The ability and the disposition to engage in full-fledged critical thinking is measured only in part by a person's ability to choose from among a pre-selected list. A true measure of critical thinking, and thus of a program's capacity to improve critical thinking, can be obtained only by including in the assessment *generative* as well as *selective* dimensions. Neither multiple-rating nor, obviously, multiple-choice items are adequate for testing this dimension.

Essay items will require proficiency in handling the elements of thought, in using appropriate abilities, in applying intellectual standards, and, what is more, it will require integrating these and bringing them to bear on a substantive issue.

Three detailed samples of essay items follow on the next page. Each has the same set of general directions.

In addition to full-blown essay tests, a series of short-justification items are currently being prepared. These would not ask students to write an essay on a topic, but would rather have them choose an answer from a pre-selected multiple-rating list and then justify their answer in a sentence of their own writing.

This type of test, if it were sufficiently developed, would have several advantages: it could be administered, because of the brevity and straightforwardness of students' written answers, to the student population as a whole rather than merely to a representative sample (see #1, under "Implementation", below); it would assess some, though not all, generative dimensions of critical thinking; it would allow flexibility in grading the machine-gradable keyed answers (thus, one could adjust the rating of an item up or down depending on the justification); it would be no more difficult to grade by trained personnel than the math work on currently administered standardized calculus tests.

✦ *Interdisciplinary and*
Subject-Specific

Scope of the Assessment

An assessment of the results of critical thinking instruction ought to focus both on thinking within the framework of particular academic subjects, and on thinking in the interdisciplinary contexts that are so important to functioning as an autonomous, well-informed, productive member of a democracy.

Critical Thinking, Problem Solving, & Communication Skills Essay Exam

Directions

This test is designed to assess your critical thinking, problem solving, and communication skills. Your answer will be judged for its clarity, relevance, consistency, logic, depth, coherence, and fairness. More specifically, the reader will be asking the following questions:

1) Is the question at issue well stated? Is it clear and unbiased? Does the expression of the question do justice to the complexity of the matter at issue?

2) Does the writer cite relevant evidence, experiences, and/or relevant information essential to the issue?

3) Does the writer clarify key concepts when necessary?

4) Does the writer show a sensitivity to what he or she is assuming or taking for granted (insofar as those assumptions might reasonably be questioned)?

5) Does the writer develop a definite line of reasoning, explaining well how he or she is arriving at his or her conclusions?

6) Is the writer's reasoning well-supported?

7) Does the writer show a sensitivity to alternative points of view or lines of reasoning? Does he or she consider and respond to objections framed from other points of view?

8) Does the writer show a sensitivity to the implications and/or consequences of the position he or she has taken?

ISSUE #1: ECOLOGY

The nation is facing a variety of ecological problems that have the following general form: an established practice, whether on the part of business and industry or on the part of the public, is contributing to serious health problems for a large number of people. At the same time it would be costly to modify the practice so as to reduce the health problem. People often say that the answer is one of achieving a "balance" between the amount of money we spend to correct the problem and the number of lives we would save by that expenditure. Develop a point of view and some plausible criteria for telling how one would determine this "balance." Make sure you address any dilemmas inherent in your strategy for solving such problems.

ISSUE #2: POLITICS

There is a growing number of Americans who do not vote in national and local elections. Many of them explain their non-participation by saying that their vote would not make a difference. Some go on to argue that this is true because "money plays such a large role in elections that the candidate with the highest paid, and the highest quality, media campaign wins." Most people agree that money sometimes plays an inappropriate role in determining the outcome of elections. Develop a proposed solution to this problem that takes into account the view that people and organizations with money have a right to use that money to advance political causes they believe in. If you like, you may decide to develop a position to the effect that there is no solution to the problem and that we have no choice but to accept the status quo.

ISSUE #3: MORALITY

Sociologist Erving Goffman has pointed out that all social groups, including professions, develop a protective attitude toward members of their group, even when what some of the members do is seen as morally wrong. A sense of loyalty to the group often overrides what they would otherwise deem immoral. Consider the arguments for and against exposing people with whom you are personally close or with whom you have close professional ties. Develop a position on this issue that could serve as a guide for anyone in such a position.

A basic principle of critical thinking instruction, as applied to teaching subject matter in an area, is that (to quote the National Council for Excellence in Critical Thinking Instruction) "to achieve knowledge in any domain, it is essential to think critically". A related principle is that in any domain where one is thinking well, one is thinking critically. Any example of good scientific thinking, or good historical thinking, or good anthropological thinking, or thinking in any other subject, will necessarily be an example of critical thinking: It will involve basic skills dealing with elements of thought; it will involve at least some, and probably many, of the abilities; it will involve affective traits like independent thinking and intellectual perseverance. And as far as instruction is concerned, there is a real sense in which learning biology is learning to think within and about the logic of biology.

Including critical thinking items taken from individual subject areas would also properly test those thinking skills that are more subject-specific, and it would do so in the context of presupposing a good deal of specialized knowledge. A critical thinking test in nursing or in history of art or in geology might well (in their different ways) test for skills of critical observation, while a test in sociology might assess thinking skills involved in constructing an unbiased questionnaire; a critical thinking test in English literature might well presuppose a knowledge of who Milton was, while a thinking test in physics might justifiably ask about a problem for which a knowledge of the second law of thermodynamics was taken for granted.

Even if we already had a series of critical thinking items within the various subject areas, however, we would not be testing for many of the interdisciplinary abilities we most want critical thinking for. Many of these have already been mentioned: the ability to make sound decisions in the context of understanding our rights and responsibilities as citizens, in the context of the work-place, as well-informed and thinking consumers, as members of our families, as participants in what is becoming a symbiotic and fragile world economy — the ability to reason about the gaps between subject areas, the bridges between them, and the generalizability of subjects to other areas.

To test critical thinking abilities, as they apply to these areas, what is needed are interdisciplinary questions. These are questions of broad interest, ones that shed light on the quality of and improvement in student thinking about realistic and fundamental issues; they ought to be the kind of questions which can be at least partially illuminated by well-integrated knowledge in any number of academic areas.

The national assessment we are proposing would offer a range of subject-specific items, from which students would choose those relevant to their subject-matter knowledge. The interdisciplinary items, on the other hand, would not provide choices because of the desirability of avoiding the loss of equivalency that is almost always involved. (That loss would have to be minimized in the case of subject-specific items by field testing and rewriting.)

The interdisciplinary part is constructable by experts well versed in a rich and substantive concept of critical thinking. Subject-specific critical thinking assessment items will be constructed by members of the discipline working in consultation with experts in critical thinking, perhaps the standing committees on the various disciplines of the National Council for Excellence in Critical Thinking Instruction. Both groups would work in conjunction with grade-level experts to construct appropriate levels of items, from the 6th-grade test through the college-graduate test.

✦ *The Value of the Proposed Assessment Strategy for the Reform of Instruction*

Since higher order thinking has always been considered an important object of education, and since this assessment would furnish a measure of that concept, and since performance on this assessment would have a significant impact on the standing of the school not only in the eyes of the intellectual community but in the eyes of the public as well, administrators and teachers would have a strong motivation to become familiar with the concepts and program behind the assessment. Most importantly, teachers and others in charge of instruction and the formulation of educational goals would find in it a clear model for the articulation and integration of higher order thinking across the curriculum. Note the following:

1) The concept of the elements of thought not only provides a realistic analysis of the common dimensions of reasoning in every domain, it also encourages the explicit use in instruction of those critical/analytic terms which are the common possession of the intellectual community (question-at-issue, problem, evidence, data, concept, inference, assumption, implication, conclusion, point of view, frame of reference, etc.) and makes explicit the intellectual standards implicit in every subject as well as in the closely reasoned professional work in business and industry (clarity, precision, accuracy, logic, consistency, ...)

2) By highlighting reading, writing, speaking, and listening as modes of critical reasoning, the necessity of having instruction go beyond mere didactic coverage of content would become more intelligible. As long as reading, writing, speaking, and listening skills appear the sole province of specialized subjects and at specialized levels rather than modes of reasoning intrinsic to the construction and mastery of knowledge in any subject at any level, there will continue to be a significant lack of fit between modes of instruction and modes of necessary learning.

3) By highlighting the other abilities of critical thinking, each analyzed into the same elements of thought, there would be significant transfer of emphasis to important modes of higher order thinking within a larger number of student assignments. At present, many teachers fail to notice the extent to which they either presuppose that students already grasp the nature of fundamental intellectual processes, or they make assignments which, though they appear to call for such processes, can be successfully completed by simply repeating to the teacher what was said in lecture or written in the text.

4) By highlighting a common critical/analytic language across the curriculum, students are encouraged to seek to transfer learning and intellectual discipline emphasized in one domain of learning to other domains of learning and application. The fragmentation of the subject areas, in the minds of the students if not in fact, is now a serious problem in education. This problem is mirrored, of course, in business, industry, and government in the tendency to engage in fragmented, over-specialized problem-solving which fails to address the multi-dimensional nature of many complex problems.

5) By highlighting the importance of intellectual discipline and grounding it in specific skills and abilities, teachers and other educational leaders will be given a reasonable impetus to help students make connections of a broader, more interdisciplinary nature. This will also be strongly re-enforced by the inclusion of everyday, multi-logical, interdisciplinary essay questions.

✦ *Implementation of the Proposed Assessment*

Our recommendations about implementation can be summarized as follows:

1) The essay assessment should be administered to a representative sample of the student population at each educational institution, the machine-gradable items to the total student population;

2) it should be administered at the 6th, 9th, and 12th grades, and three times during a student's college career — at entrance, at the start of the junior year, and just prior to graduation — and thus yield value-added information to schools;

3) the test should be constructed to be roughly three-hours long;

4) test items should be constructed from item shells, rather than from a simple pool of actual items;

5) it should be administered by a private agency with critical thinking credentials;

6) it should be paid for by school districts, colleges, and universities that contract to have their students tested;

7) it should provide educational institutions with detailed information about central aspects of their students' higher order thinking;

8) it should be developed according to the costs and timetables listed below.

Details of our recommendations center around the answers to five practical questions about the administration of the test:

WHO WILL BE ASSESSED?

Our *minimal* recommendation is that all portions of the assessment be given to, at the very least, a representative sample of the student population at each educational institution. Since the problems implicit in testing a random sample can be easily worked out, this recommendation avoids the expense of administering an essay test to the student population as a whole.

The assessment strategies we have proposed include two broad areas of testing: a *machine-gradable portion* that includes multiple-choice items and multiple-rating items and an *essay portion*. Both portions will assess, in their different ways and with their different emphases, micro-skills, abilities, affective traits, and intellectual standards.

There are, therefore, really two options with respect to who is assessed using the strategies we propose. First, the machine gradable portion of the assessment can be administered to the student population as a whole, while the essay portion can be administered to a representative sample of students at each institution. Second, both portions could be given only to a representative sample of the population at each institution. Both options will hold down costs, though the latter will clearly be less expensive than the former. Which option is ultimately chosen will depend on the amount of detail desired, the precise role the assessment is to play, and the funds available.

How Often Will the Assessment Take Place?

The maximum benefit to educational institutions will be provided to the extent that they are enabled to measure the progress of their students' higher order thinking during the course of their educational career. This will enable school systems not only to gauge their contribution to their students' progress, but also to measure the success of attempts to re-design their instruction so as to increase critical thinking capabilities.

These objectives can be accomplished by having students assessed often enough to reflect such progress, optimally: at the 6th, 9th, and 12th grades, and at the time of their college entrance, at the beginning of their junior year, and just before graduation from college.

How Long Will the Test Take?

The test should last about three hours in order to cover multiple-choice, multiple-rating, and essay items without becoming a speeded test to an inappropriate degree. To span all difficulty levels, it would be best to have a total of at least 30 items. While two of these could be short essay items requiring 20 minutes each to answer, the machine-gradable items would be faster to answer, and hence could be handled in 3–8 minutes.

How Will a Sufficiently Large Pool of Items Be Constructed?

While it might be possible to release a pool of items which would provide the equivalent of 6 tests at each level, hence 6 x 6 x 30, it would be better to increase flexibility by using item shells, which would be items that include identified variables, each of which could be replaced from a list of acceptable values. This would greatly increase the number of items that could be generated, but without "surprises". A pool of shells would generate over a thousand items at each level, possibly several thousand.

WHO WILL DO THE ASSESSING?

In order to avoid problems in the reliability of the assessment (like those we have seen occur in the *California Direct Writing Assessment*), the assessment needs to be monitored, administered, and graded by a private agency whose personnel have critical thinking credentials or are at least under the direction of scholars with a solid grounding in research in critical thinking.

WHO WILL BEAR THE COSTS OF THE ASSESSMENT?

The assessment should be paid for by the school systems, colleges, and universities that contract to have their students tested. This not only puts least burden on the public but represents an established precedent in distributing costs of testing.

WHAT WILL INSTITUTIONS BE ABLE TO LEARN FROM THE RESULTS OF THE ASSESSMENT?

We anticipate that educational institutions will receive an analytic report that will document all of the following:

- where their students are strongest and weakest with respect to particular micro-skills;
- where their students are strongest and weakest with respect to important abilities;
- how students stand in each of the school's subject-matter areas;
- how their students stand in relation to students at other institutions;
- how their students at one educational level stand in relation to their students at other educational levels;
- how their students stand with respect to established performance criteria.

This information would enable institutions to target instruction to remediate weaknesses and build on strengths, as well as to measure what students are gaining as a result of attending their classes.*

✦ Postscript

Dale Carlson, the head of the California Assessment Program, has recognized that the essay "Rock Around the Clock" was significantly mis-assessed and is now devising strategies to prevent this from happening in the future.

---

* The authors wish to acknowledge the invaluable advice provided us by Michael Scriven on evaluation theory in general, and, more particularly, on the logistics of test construction.

✦✦ Chapter 7

Using Intellectual Standards to Assess Student Reasoning

with Gerald M. Nosich

Abstract

In this paper, co-authored by Richard Paul and Gerald Nosich, the emphasis is on pro-viding the reader with specific examples of what is involved in applying intellectual criteria and standards to students' reasoning, especially with reference to the "elements of reason-ing" which, they explain, are the logical components of all reasoning. Paul and Nosich first explain the significance of reasoning having "elements", then the need for "standards" in assessing reasoning. They then take us through each of the elements of reasoning, giving us a general sense of the interface between elements and standards, and then, finally, provide a series of three columned charts, one for each of the elements of reasoning. Each chart briefly characterizes the differences between how good and bad reasoners handle the com-ponents of their reasoning, as well as articulating samples of the sort of feedback which we as teachers might give to students with regard to each of the components of their perfor-mance as reasoners. Their goal is clearly both theoretical and practical.

*T*o assess student reasoning requires that we focus our attention as teachers on two inter-related dimensions of reasoning. The first dimen-sion consists of the elements *of reasoning*; the second dimension consists of the *universal intellectual standards* by which we measure student ability to use, in a skillful way, each of those elements of reasoning.

Elements of reasoning. Once we progress from thought which is purely associational and undisciplined, to thinking which is conceptual and inferen-tial, thinking which attempts in some intelligible way to figure something out, in short, to reasoning, then it is helpful to concentrate on what can be called "the elements of reasoning". The elements of reasoning are those essential dimensions of reasoning whenever and wherever it occurs. Working together, they shape reasoning and provide a general logic to the use of rea-son. We can articulate these elements by paying close attention to what is implicit in the the act of figuring anything out by the the use of reason. These elements, then — purpose, question at issue, assumptions, inferences, implications, point of view, concepts and evidence — constitute a central focus in the assessment of student thinking.

Standards of Reasoning. When we assess student reasoning, we want to evaluate, in a reasonable, defensible, objective way, not just *that* students are reasoning, but *how well* they are reasoning. We will be assessing not just that they are using the elements of reasoning, but the degree to which they are using them well, critically, in accord with appropriate intellectual standards.

To assess a student response, whether written or oral, in structured discussion of content or in critical response to reading assignments, by how *clearly* or *completely* it states a position, is to assess it on the basis of a standard of reasoning. Similarly, assessing student work by how *logically* and *consistently* it defends its position, by how *flexible* and *fair* the student is in articulating other points of view, by how *significant* and *realistic* the student's purpose is, by how *precisely* and *deeply* the student articulates the question at issue — each of these is an evaluation based on standards of reasoning.

Distinct from such reasoning standards are other standards that teachers sometimes use to assess student work. To evaluate a student response on the basis of how concisely or elegantly it states a position is to use standards that are inappropriate to assessing student reasoning. Similarly unrelated to the assessment of reasoning is evaluating student work by how humorous, glib, personal or sincere it is, by how much it agrees with the teacher's views, by how "well-written" it is, by how exactly it repeats the teacher's words, by the mere quantity of information it contains. The danger is that such standards are often conflated with reasoning standards, often unconsciously, and students are assessed on grounds other than the degree to which they are reasoning well.

The basic conditions implicit whenever we gather, conceptualize, apply, analyze, synthesize, or evaluate information — the elements of reasoning — are as follows:

1) Purpose, Goal, or End in View. Whenever we reason, we reason to some end, to achieve some objective, to satisfy some desire or fulfill some need. One source of problems in student reasoning is traceable to defects at the level of goal, purpose, or end. If the goal is unrealistic, for example, or contradictory to other goals the student has, if it is confused or muddled in some way, then the reasoning used to achieve it is problematic.

A teacher's assessment of student reasoning, then, necessarily involves an assessment of the student's ability to handle the dimension of purpose in accord with relevant intellectual *standards*. It also involves giving *feedback* to students about the degree to which their reasoning meets those standards.

Is the student's purpose — in an essay, a research project, an oral report, a discussion — *clear*? Is the purpose *significant* or trivial or somewhere in between? Is the student's purpose, according to the most judicious evaluation on the teacher's part, *realistic*? Is it an *achievable* purpose? Does the student's overall goal dissolve in the course of the project, does it change, or is it *consistent* throughout? Does the student have contradictory purposes?

2) Question at Issue, or Problem to be Solved. Whenever we attempt to reason something out, there is at least one question at issue, at least one problem to be solved. One area of concern for assessing student reasoning, therefore, will be the formulation of the question to be answered or problem to be solved, whether with respect to the student's own reasoning or to that of others.

Assessing skills of mastery of this element of reasoning requires assessing — and giving feedback on — students' ability to formulate a problem in a *clear* and *relevant* way. It requires giving students direct commentary on whether the question they are addressing is an important one, whether it is *answerable*, on whether they understand the requirements for settling the question, for solving the problem.

3) Point of View, or Frame of Reference. Whenever we reason, we must reason within some point of view or frame of reference. Any "defect" in that point of view or frame of reference is a possible source of problems in the reasoning.

A point of view may be too narrow, too parochial, may be based on false or misleading analogies or metaphors, may contain contradictions, and so forth. It may be restricted or unfair. Alternatively, student reasoning involving articulation of their point of view may meet the relevant standards to a significant degree: their point of view may be *broad, flexible, fair*; it may be *clearly* stated and *consistently* adhered to.

Feedback to students would involve commentary noting both when students meet the standards and when they fail to meet them. Evaluation of students' ability to handle the dimension of point of view would also appropriately direct students to lines of reasoning that would promote a richer facility in reasoning about and in terms of points of view.

4) The Empirical Dimension of Reasoning. Whenever we reason, there is some "stuff," some phenomena about which we are reasoning. Any "defect," then, in the experiences, data, evidence, or raw material upon which a person's reasoning is based is a possible source of problems.

Students would be assessed and receive feedback on their ability to give evidence that is gathered and reported *clearly, fairly*, and *accurately*. Does the student furnish data at all? Is the data *relevant*? Is the information *adequate* for achieving the student's purpose? Is it applied *consistently*, or does the student distort it to fit her own point of view?

5) The Conceptual Dimension of Reasoning. All reasoning uses some ideas or concepts and not others. These concepts can include the theories, principles, axioms and rules implicit in our reasoning. Any "defect" in the concepts or ideas of the reasoning is a possible source of problems in student reasoning.

Feedback to students would note whether their understanding of theories and rules was *deep* or merely superficial. Are the concepts they use in their reasoning *clear* ones? Are their ideas *relevant* to the issue at hand, are their principles slanted by their point of view?

6) Assumptions. All reasoning must begin somewhere, must take some things for granted. Any "defect" in the assumptions or presuppositions with which the reasoning begins is a possible source of problems for students.

Assessing skills of reasoning involves assessing their ability to recognize and articulate their assumptions, again according to the relevant standards.

The student's assumptions may be stated *clearly* or unclearly; the assumptions may be *justifiable* or unjustifiable, *crucial* or extraneous, *consistent* or contradictory. The feedback students receive from teachers on their ability to meet the relevant standards will be a large factor in the improvement of student reasoning.

7) Implications and Consequences. No matter where we stop our reasoning, it will always have further implications and consequences. As reasoning develops, statements will logically be entailed by it. Any "defect" in the implications or consequences of our reasoning is a possible source of problems.

The ability to reason well is measured in part by an ability to understand and enunciate the implications and consequences of the reasoning. Students therefore need help in coming to understand both the relevant standards of reasoning out implications and the degree to which their own reasoning meets those standards.

When they spell out the implications of their reasoning, have they succeeded in identifying *significant* and *realistic* implications, or have they confined themselves to unimportant and unrealistic ones? Have they enunciated the implications of their views clearly and *precisely* enough to permit their thinking to be evaluated by the validity of those implications?

8) Inferences. Reasoning proceeds by steps in which we reason as follows: "Because this is so, that also is so (or probably so)," or "Since this, therefore that." Any "defect" in such inferences is a possible problem in our reasoning.

Assessment would evaluate students' ability to make sound inferences in their reasoning. When is an inference *sound*? When it meets reasonable and relevant standards of inferring. Are the inferences the student draws *clear*? Are they *justifiable*? Do they draw *deep* conclusions or do they stick to the trivial and superficial? Are the conclusions they draw *consistent*?

Purpose
(All reasoning has a purpose.)

Fundamental Standards: 1) Clarity of Purpose, 2) Significance of Purpose, 3) Achievability of Purpose, 4) Consistency

Failures of Purpose: 1) Unclear Purpose, 2) Trivial Purpose, 3) Unrealistic Purposes, 4) Contradictory Purposes

Good Reasoners:	Bad Reasoners:	Feedback to Students:
take the time to state their purpose clearly	are often unclear about their central purpose	(-) You have not made the purpose of your reasoning clear. What are you trying to achieve? Whom are you trying to persuade? (+) Your paper reflects an excellent sense of unity of purpose. It all fits together like pieces of a puzzle.

Purpose *continued*

Good Reasoners:	Bad Reasoners:	Feedback to Students:
distinguish it from related purposes	oscillate between different, sometimes contradictory purposes	(+) You do a good job of distinguishing different but related goals. (-) You seem to have a number of different purposes in mind. I am not sure how you see them as related. You seem to be going off in somewhat different directions.
periodically remind themselves of their purpose to determine whether they are straying from it	lose track of their fundamental end or goal	(-) After the second paragraph you seem to wander from your purpose. How do your 3rd and 4th paragraphs relate to your central goal? (+) I like the way you periodically show the reader how the points you are making all add up to a central conclusion.
adopt realistic purposes and goals	adopt unrealistic purposes, set unrealistic goals	(+) You make a wise decision not to try to accomplish too much. Accomplishing a little, well, is almost always better than failing in a grand and sweeping design. (-) You try to accomplish too much in so short a paper.
choose significant purposes and goals	adopt trivial purposes and goals as if they were significant	(-) Your paper would have been stronger if you had chosen a more important goal. (+) The goal of your paper is worthwhile and well-chosen.
choose goals and purposes that are consistent with other goals and purposes they have chosen	inadvertently negate their own purposes do not monitor their thinking for inconsistent goals	(-) One part of your paper seems to undermine what you are trying to accomplish in another part. You first try to persuade the reader how realistic Dickens' characters are, but after that you seem to be showing that they are caricatures. (+) Your unity of purpose is reflected in every section of your paper.
adjust their thinking regularly to their purpose	do not adjust their thinking regularly to their purpose	

Question at Issue / Central Problem

(All reasoning is an attempt to figure something out
to settle some question, solve some problem.)

Fundamental Standards: 1) Clarity of Question, 2) Significance of Question,
3) Answerability, 4) Relevance

Flawed Questions: 1) Unclear, 2) Insignificant, 3) Not answerable, 4) Irrelevant

Principle: To settle a question you must understand it and its requirements.

Good Reasoners:	*Bad Reasoners:*	*Feedback to Students:*
are clear about the question they are trying to settle	are often unclear about the kind of question they are asking	(-) The main question at issue is never made clear. (+) You do a good job of clarifying the question at issue.
can re-express a question in a variety of ways	express questions vaguely and find them difficult to reformulate	(-) You need to reformulate your question in a couple of ways to recognize the complexity of it. (+) I like the way you reformulate your question in different ways. It helps the reader see it from different points of view.
can break a question into sub-questions	are unable to break down the questions they are asking	(+) You do a good job of analyzing the main question into sub-questions. (-) It would be easier to solve your main problem if you would break it down somewhat.
have sensitivity to the kind of question they are asking routinely distinguish questions of different types	have little sensitivity to the kind of question they are asking confuse questions of different types often respond inappropriately to the questions they ask	(-) You are confusing a legal question with a moral one. (+) You do a good job of keeping the economic issues separate from the social ones.
distinguish significant from trivial questions	confuse trivial questions with significant ones	(-) You begin with a significant question but seem to wander off into some insignificant ones. (+) The problem you raise is a very significant one.
distinguish relevant questions from irrelevant ones	confuse irrelevant questions with relevant ones	(-) The questions you raise in the second part of your paper do not seem to be relevant to the main question at issue.

Questions and Problems continued

Good Reasoners:	Bad Reasoners:	Feedback to Students:
are sensitive to the assumptions built into the questions they ask	often ask loaded questions	(-) The way you put the question is loaded. You are taking for granted from the outset the correctness of your own position. (+) You put your question in a neutral and unbiased form and you don't allow yourself to be distracted by irrelevant questions.
distinguish questions they can answer from questions they can't		

Point of View

(All reasoning is done from some point of view.)

Fundamental Standards: 1) Flexibility in Point of View, 2) Fairness of Point of View, 3) Clarity of Point of View, 4) Breadth of Point of View

Defects in point of view: 1) Restricted, 2) Biased, 3) Unclear, 4) Narrow

Principle: Reasoning is better when multiple, relevant points of view are sought out, articulated clearly, empathized with fairly and logically, applied consistently and dispassionately.

Good Reasoners:	Bad Reasoners:	Feedback to Students:
keep in mind that people have different points of view, especially on issues that are controversial consistently articulate other points of view and reason from within those points of view seek other viewpoints especially when the issue is one they believe in passionately	don't realize that people approach the question at issue from different points of view are unable to see issues from points of view that are significantly different from their own personal/cultural one; i.e., are unable to reason empathetically from within alien points of view can sometimes enunciate other points of view when the question at issue is emotionally uncharged, but can no longer do so when it is an issue they are deeply committed to	(-) You haven't articulated the point of view from which you are approaching this issue. (+) You have reasoned out this controversial issue clearly from multiple relevant points of view. (-) You have characterized your own point of view, but what are the most significant aspects of the problem from X's point of view? (+)You have done an excellent job of spelling out the other side of this issue. This is especially difficult when a person is as deeply committed to one side as you are. (-) This is an unfair way of presenting X's point of view.

Good Reasoners:	Bad Reasoners:	Feedback to Students:
confine their monological reasoning to problems that are clearly monological	confuse multilogical with monological issues by insisting that there is only one frame of reference within which a particular multilogical question must be decided	(+/-) Is the question here monological or multilogical? How can you tell? (-) You are reasoning as if only one point of view is relevant to this issue.
have insight into areas and problems where they are most likely to be prejudiced	are unaware of their own prejudices	(+/-) Is this prejudice or reasoned judgment?
approach problems and issues with a richness of vision and an appropriately broad point of view	reason from within inappropriately narrow and superficial points of view	(-) Your approach to this question is too narrow. (+) You have considered this problem with the depth it requires.

Empirical Dimension
(All reasoning is based on data, information, evidence.)

Fundamental Standards: 1) Clear Evidence, 2) Relevant Information, 3) Fairly Gathered and Reported Evidence, 4) Accurate Data, 5) Adequate Evidence, 6) Consistently Applied Data

Flawed Empirical Dimension: Unclear, Unfairly or Self-Servingly Gathered, Inaccurate, Insufficient

Principle: Reasoning can only be as sound as the empirical evidence it is based on.

Good Reasoners:	Bad Reasoners:	Feedback to Students:
assert a claim only when they have sufficient evidence to back it up	assert claims without considering any evidence	(+) You have given a clear statement of the relevant data. (-) This claim can't merely be asserted. It needs to be supported by evidence or data.
can articulate and therefore evaluate the evidence behind their claims	don't articulate their evidence even when they have it, and so are less able to subject it to rational scrutiny	(+/-) I think you probably *have* evidence to support your claim here; you just haven't articulated it.
actively search for information *against* (not just *for*) their own position	gather evidence only when it supports their own point of view	(+) You have gathered and reported evidence fairly on both sides of this issue. (+/-) Where is a good place to look for evidence on the opposite side? Have you looked there?

Empirical Dimension continued

Good Reasoners:	Bad Reasoners:	Feedback to Students:
focus on relevant information and disregard information or data that is irrelevant to the question at issue	do not carefully distinguish between relevant data and irrelevant data	(+) The information you cite is relevant and to the point. (-) The data you supply is irrelevant. (+/-) How is this relevant to the claim you are making?
draw conclusions only to the extent that they are supported by the data	make inferences that go beyond what the data support	(-) Though you give some evidence to back up your claim, the claim goes beyond the evidence you've cited. (+) Your claims are well-supported by the evidence you cite.
state their evidence clearly and fairly	distort the data, or state it inaccurately	(+) This is a clear and coherent presentation of the pertinent information.

Concepts and Ideas

(All reasoning is expressed through, and shaped by, concepts and ideas.)

Fundamental Standards: 1) Clarity of Concepts, 2) Relevance of Concepts, 3) Depth of Concepts, 4) Neutrality of Concepts

Failure of Concepts: 1) Unclear, 2) Irrelevant, 3) Superficial, 4) Biased

Principle: Reasoning can only be as clear, relevant, and deep as the concepts which shape it.

Good Reasoners:	Bad Reasoners:	Feedback to Students:
are aware of the key concepts and ideas they use	are unaware of the key concepts and ideas they use	(-) The concept of democracy, central to your essay, is not analyzed in your paper. You assume that if people are in any sense allowed to vote, they are living in a democracy. You need to consider the idea of democracy more deeply. If people are systematically indoctrinated and manipulated into voting in a way contrary to their self-interest, are the "people" in charge? (+) You do well in distinguishing training, socialization, indoctrination, and education.

Good Reasoners:	Bad Reasoners:	Feedback to Students:
are able to explain the basic implications of the key words and phrases they use	do not accurately explain basic implications of their key words and phrases	(+) Yes, the word 'cunning' has negative implications that the word 'clever' does not.
are able to distinguish special, non-standard uses of words from standard uses	are not able to recognize when their use of a word or phrase departs from educated usage	(-) Where did you get your definition of this central concept? (-) You assume that abortion is murder, but you won't find a dictionary that defines it as "the murder of a very young person". Don't put your conclusion into the definition.
are aware of irrelevant concepts and ideas use concepts and ideas in ways relevant to their functions	use concepts in ways inappropriate to the subject or issue	(-) Do you think that the notion of "dog-eat-dog" applies to moral situations? Isn't the question one of moral responsibility?

Assumptions

(All reasoning is based on assumptions.)

Fundamental Standards: 1) Clarity of Assumptions, 2) Justifiability of Assumptions, 3) Consistency of Assumptions

Failure of assumptions: 1) Unclear, 2) Unjustified, 3) Contradictory

Principle: Reasoning can only be as sound as the assumptions it makes.

Good Reasoners:	Bad Reasoners:	Feedback to Students:
make assumptions that are clear	often make assumptions that are unclear	(-) It is not clear what you are assuming. (-) It is not clear what you base your main assumption on. (+) Your assumptions seem clear and reasonable.
make assumptions that are reasonable	often make assumptions that are not justified often make assumptions that are unreasonable	(-) It seems unreasonable to make assumptions about the future based on just one experience from the past.
make assumptions that are consistent with each other	often make assumptions that are contradictory	(-) The assumptions you make in the first part of your paper seem to contradict the assumptions you make in the last section of your paper.

Implications and Consequences

(All reasoning leads somewhere, has implications and consequences.)

Fundamental Standards: 1) Significance of Implications, 2) Realistic Nature of Implications, 3) Clarity of Articulated Implications, 4) Precision of Articulated Implications, 5) Completeness of Articulated Implications

Flawed Implications and Consequences: 1) Unimportant, 2) Unrealistic, 3) Unclear, 4) Imprecise, 5) Incomplete

Principle: To reason through an issue or decision, you must understand the implications and consequences that follow from it.

Good Reasoners:	Bad Reasoners:	Feedback to Students:
trace out a number of significant implications and consequences of their reasoning	trace out few or none of the implications and consequences of holding a position or making a decision	(-) You don't spell out the consequences of the action you are advocating. (+/-) If you took this course of action, what other consequences would follow.
articulate the implications and consequences clearly and precisely	are unclear and imprecise in the consequences they articulate	(+) You have spelled out the implications of your reasoning in as clear and precise a way as the subject permits. (-) You will be much clearer about whether the action is reasonable if you are more precise when you delineate the consequences likely to follow from it.
search for negative as well as for positive consequences	trace out only the consequences they had in mind at the beginning, either positive or negative, but usually not both	(+/-) You've done a good job of spelling out some positive consequences of the decision at issue, but what are some of the negative consequences?
anticipate the likelihood of unexpected negative and positive implications	are surprised when their decisions have unexpected consequences	(-) In addition to the ones you've traced out, there are several important consequences you've failed to anticipate. (+/-) Are there other factors in the decision that will probably lead to significant consequences other than those you have in mind?

Inference

(All reasoning contains inferences by which we draw conclusions and give meaning to data.)

Fundamental Standards: 1) Clarity of Inferences, 2) Justifiability of Inferences, 3) Profundity of Conclusions, 4) Reasonability of Conclusions, 5) Consistency of Conclusions

Failure of Inferences and Conclusions: 1) Unclear, 2) Unjustified, 3) Superficial, 4) Unreasonable, 5) Contradictory

Principle: Reasoning can only be as sound as the inferences it makes and conclusions it comes to.

Good Reasoners:	*Bad Reasoners:*	*Feedback to Students:*
make inferences that are clear and precise	often make inferences that are unclear	(-) It is not clear what your main conclusion is. (-) It is not clear what you base your main conclusion on. (+) Your reasoning is very clear and easy to follow.
usually make inferences that follow from the evidence or reasons presented	often make inferences that do not follow from the evidence or reasons presented	(-) The conclusion you come to does not follow from the evidence or reasons presented. (+) You justify your conclusion well with supporting evidence and good reasons.
often make inferences that are deep rather than superficial	often make inferences that are superficial	(+) Your central conclusion is well-thought-out and goes right to the heart of the issue. (-) Your conclusion is justified, but it seems superficial, given the problem.
often make inferences or come to conclusions that are reasonable	often make inferences or come to conclusions that are unreasonable	(-) It is unreasonable to infer a person's personality from their ethnic group.
make inferences or come to conclusions that are consistent with each other	often make inferences or come to conclusions that are contradictory	(-) The conclusions you come to in the first part of your paper seem to contradict the conclusions that you come to in the last section of your paper. (+) Your conclusions are reasonable, given the evidence you presented; furthermore, they are mutually consistent.

Chapter 8

Why Students — and Teachers — Don't Reason Well

Abstract

Paul begins this essay by developing the notion that all human action presupposes the use of humanly created logical systems that model, abridge, and summarize the features of the world about us, and that abstract inferential systems, and the reasoning they make possible, are as natural to us as a species as swimming is to a dolphin or flying is to a bird. As Paul puts it, we are continually "making inferences within a system we have created — about what is going on in our lives." Unfortunately, according to Paul, to reason well we must do more than simply engage in it. We must become aware of that engagement and use our knowledge of the nature of that engagement to improve it. Paul compares the good reasoner to the good ballet dancer, the good chess and tennis players. All three must explicitly study the principles and practice the moves involved (with explicit standards of performance in mind).

Having suggested what good reasoning requires, Paul presents evidence to show that most students are not good at it. What is more, he presents evidence to suggest that most teachers are not good at it either — at least not at assessing it when students are called upon to use it in their work. One of the major reasons, combining with ignorance of what reasoning requires, is a systematic confusion between intelligent subjectivity (wit, articulateness, cleverness without substance), and reasoned objectivity (careful, disciplined, reasoning about an issue), between subjective opinion (however "bright"), and reasoned judgment (however mundane).

Paul documents this problem with an analysis of a major mistake in a California Department of Education statewide assessment of reasoned evaluation in writing. He follows up this documentation of a mistake on the part of testing experts with the same mistake made by teachers. He then briefly explicates a model for the analysis and assessment of reasoning (based on the logic of the question at issue) complete with a series of samples of student reasoning, all duly analyzed for the reader.

Paul concludes the paper with a brief argument to the effect that "the logical structures implicit in an educated person's mind are highly systematized." In contrast he argues:

"When the logical structures by which a mind figures out the world are confused, a jumble, a hodgepodge, a mere conglomeration, then that figuring out is radically defective.... Then the mind begins it knows not where, takes things for granted without analysis or questioning, leaps to conclusions without sufficient evidence..., meanders without a consciousness of its point of view.... Then the mind wanders into its own prejudices and biases, its own egocentricity and sociocentricity. Then the mind is not able to discipline itself by a close analysis of the question at issue and ignores the demands that the logic of that question puts on it and us as rational, logic-creating, logic-using animals."

✦ The Ability to Reason:
A Defining Feature of Humans

Our capacity to reason is at the heart of all disciplined thinking. It explains how we alone of all the creatures of the earth have been able to develop full-fledged academic disciplines: biology, physics, botany, zoology, chemistry, geography, history, psychology, sociology, etc. We can go beyond immediate, instinctive reactions to reflective, reasoned responses precisely because we are able to develop small-scale and large-scale systems in which to intellectually operate and act. These systems enable us to mentally manipulate our possible responses to situations — to formulate them explicitly, to hold them at intellectual arm's length, to analyze and critique them, and to decide what their implications are for us. Let me explain.

We understand the various particulars of everyday life by constructing abstract models or systems that abridge and summarize their features. In simplest form, we call these models or systems *ideas*. For example, our abstract concept of a bird is a model or system for thinking about actual birds in order to make sense of their behavior — in contrast to the behavior, say, of cats, dogs, turtles, beetles, and people. As we construct these abstract systems or models, we are enabled to use the reasoning power of our minds to go beyond a bare unconceptualized noticing of things to the making of inward interpretations of them, and hence derivations from them. In short, our concepts provide our minds with systems in which to experience and think; our minds operate (reason) within them to invest the world we experience with meanings rich in implications and consequences. Much of this is done, of course, quite automatically and subconsciously.

I can reason to any number of conclusions as the result of my having one simple model for a thing. For example, if I recognize a creature to be a dog, I can quickly infer it will:

1) bark rather than meow or chirp
2) wag its tail when pleased
3) growl when irritated
4) be unable to fly
5) have no feathers
6) be unable to live under water
7) be carnivorous
8) need oxygen
9) have teeth
10) have paws rather than feet, etc.

This word ('dog') is part of a much larger logical map upon which our minds can move in virtue of our capacity to reason. As we act bodily in the world, we act intellectually in our minds. These intellectual moves guide our actions in the world. Without these maps and the capacity to locate particulars on them, we would either thrash about aimlessly or be paralyzed by the bewildering mystery of things and events before us. In every situation in our lives we "construct" a response that results from how we are modeling the situation in our minds.

Hence, put us in any situation and we start to give it meaning, to figure it out with the logical structures we have at our disposal. So quickly and automatically do we make inferences — as the result of the way we are modeling the situation in our minds — that we do not typically notice those inferences.

For example, we see dark clouds and infer rain. We hear the door slam and infer someone has arrived. We see a frowning face and infer the person is angry. Our friend is late and we infer she is being inconsiderate. We meet a tall boy and infer he is good at basketball, an Asian and infer he will be good at math. We read a book, and infer what the various sentences and paragraphs, indeed what the whole book, is saying. We listen to what people say, and make a continual series of inferences as to what they mean. As we write we make inferences as to what others will make of what we are writing. We make inferences as to the clarity of what we are saying, as to what needs further explanation, as to what needs exemplification or illustration. We could not do this without "logical structures" by means of which to draw our inferences.

Many of our inferences are justified and reasonable. But, of course, many are not. One of the most important critical thinking skills is the skill of noticing and reconstructing the inferences we make, so that the various ways in which we inferentially shape our experiences become more and more apparent to us. This skill, this sensitivity or ability, enables us to separate our experiences into analyzed parts. We learn to distinguish the raw data of our experience from our interpretations of those data (in other words, from the inferences we are making about them). Eventually we realize that the inferences we make are heavily influenced by our point of view and the assumptions we have made. This puts us in the position of being able to broaden the scope of our outlook, to see situations from more than one point of view, to become more open-minded. This requires that we recognize our point of view as a "logical system" that guides our inferences, a system that we can exchange for another (an alternative point of view), depending on our assumptions.

Often, then, different people make different inferences because they bring to situations a different point of view. They see the data differently. Or, to put it another way, they have different assumptions about what they see. For example, if two people see a man lying in a gutter, one might infer, "There's a drunken bum." The other might infer, "There's a man in need of help." These inferences are based on different assumptions about the conditions under which people end up in gutters and these assumptions are connected to the point of view about people that each has formed. The first person assumes: "Only drunks are to be found in gutters." The second person assumes: "People lying in the gutter are in need of help." The first person may have developed the point of view that people are fundamentally responsible for what happens to them and ought to be able to take care of themselves. The second may have developed the point of view that the problems people have are often caused by forces and events beyond their control. The two are modeling the situation differently. They are using a different system for experiencing it.

In any case, if we want our students to become good reasoners, we must become concerned to help them begin to notice the inferences they are making, the assumptions they are basing those inferences on, and the point of view about the world they are taking — hence the systems in which they are thinking. To help our students do this, we need to give them clear examples of simple cases, and lots and lots of practice analyzing and reconstructing them. For example, we could display the above inferences in the following way:

Person One:
Situation: "A man is lying in the gutter."
Assumption: "Only bums lie in gutters."
Inference: "That man's a bum."

Person Two:
Situation: "A man is lying in the gutter."
Assumption: "Anyone lying in the gutter is in need of help."
Inference: "That man is in need of help."

Our goal of sensitizing students to the inferences they make and to the assumptions that underlie their thinking enables them to begin to gain command over their thinking (the way they are using logical structures to model the world). Of course, it may seem odd to put any effort into making explicit such obvious examples. In the harder instances, however, the value of the explication becomes more evident. In any case, because all human thinking is inferential in nature, and all inferences are embedded in a system, we cannot gain command of our thinking unless we can recognize, one way or another, the inferences embedded in it and the assumptions that underlie it.

Consider the way in which we plan and think our way through everyday events. We think of ourselves as washing up, eating our breakfast, getting ready for work, arriving on time, sitting down at our desks, making plans for lunch, paying bills, engaging in small talk, etc. Another way to put this is to say that we are continually interpreting our actions, giving them meanings — making inferences within a system we have created — about what is going on in our lives.

And this is to say that we must choose among a variety of possible systems for thinking about things. Again, consider some simple cases. As I am sitting in my easy chair, am I "relaxing" or "wasting time"? Am I being "determined" or "stubborn", or worse, "pig-headed"? Did I "join" the conversation or "butt in"? Is Jack "laughing with me" or "laughing at me"? Am I "helping him" or "being taken advantage of"? Every time I interpret my actions within one of these systems that each word in the language represents, every time I give them a meaning, I make one or more inferences on the basis of one or more assumptions within some point of view.

As humans we continually make assumptions about ourselves, our jobs, our mates, our children, about the world in general. We take some things for granted, simply because we can't always be questioning everything. Sometimes we take the wrong things for granted. For example, I run off to the store (assuming that I have enough money with me) and arrive to find that I have left my money at home. I assume that I have enough gas in the car only to find that I have run out. I assume that an item marked down in price is a good buy only to find that it was "marked up" before it was "marked down". I assume that it will not, or that it will, rain. I assume that my car will start when I turn the key and press the starter. I assume that I mean well in my dealings with others. We make hundreds of assumptions, use hundreds of concepts, make hundreds of inferences, without noticing that we are doing so. Most of them are quite sound and justifiable. Some however are not.

The question then becomes: "How can we teach our students to begin to recognize the inferences they are making, the assumptions they are basing those inferences on, and the point of view, the perspective on the world that they are beginning to form?" That is, "How can we help students to recognize how they are reasoning about the world?"

✦ Our Students Are
Not Learning to Reason Well

Though we are "logic-creating" and "logic-using" animals, we typically operate with little awareness of this fact. We create and apply logical systems without knowing that we are doing so. Our intellectual modeling of the world is done *sub rosa,* without mindfulness. It is small wonder, then, that we often reason poorly.

Imagine a ballet dancer improving her ballet without knowing that she is a dancer or how and when she is dancing. Imagine a chess player who does not know she is playing chess. Or a tennis player who does not know she is playing tennis. We can hardly imagine people developing these physical and intellectual abilities without high consciousness of how and what they are doing in the doing of it. Yet we expect students to develop the ability to reason well without any mindfulness of the nature of reasoning, the elements of reasoning, or the criteria for assessing reasoning. We expect students to become good reasoners, in other words, without any knowledge of the logic of reasoning. Not surprisingly our approach doesn't work. Most students are very poor reasoners.

WHAT DOES RESEARCH ON LEARNING AND TEACHING TELL US?

By any measure whatsoever, most students are not learning to reason well. A recent summary of research by Mary Kennedy regarding student learning and instruction at the K–12 level documents serious reasoning deficiencies on the part of students.

FIRST FINDING: "...national assessments in virtually every subject indicate that, although our students can perform basic skills pretty well, they are not doing well on thinking and reasoning. American students can compute, but they cannot reason.... They can write complete and correct sentences, but they cannot prepare arguments.... Moreover, in international comparisons, American students are falling behind...particularly in those areas that require higher-order thinking.... Our students are not doing well at thinking, reasoning, analyzing, predicting, estimating, or problem solving."

SECOND FINDING: "...textbooks in this country typically pay scant attention to big ideas, offer no analysis, and pose no challenging questions. Instead, they provide a tremendous array of information or 'factlets', while they ask questions requiring only that students be able to recite back the same empty list."

THIRD FINDING: "Teachers teach most content only for exposure, not for understanding."

FOURTH FINDING: "Teachers tend to avoid thought-provoking work and activities and stick to predictable routines."

CONCLUSION: "If we were to describe our current K–12 education system on the basis of these four findings, we would have to say that it provides very little intellectually stimulating work for students, and that it tends to produce students who are not capable of intellectual work."

FIFTH FINDING: "... our fifth finding from research compounds all the others and makes it harder to change practice: teachers are highly likely to teach in the way they themselves were taught. If your elementary teacher presented mathematics to you as a set of procedural rules with no substantive rationale, then you are likely to think that this is what mathematics is and that this is how mathematics should be studied. And you are likely to teach it in this way. If you studied writing as a set of grammatical rules rather than as a way to organize your thoughts and to communicate ideas to others, then this is what you will think writing is, and you will probably teach it so.... By the time we complete our undergraduate education, we have observed teachers for up to 3,060 days."

IMPLICATION: "We are caught in a vicious circle of mediocre practice modeled after mediocre practice, of trivialized knowledge begetting more trivialized knowledge. Unless we find a way out of this circle, we will continue re-creating generations of teachers who re-create generations of students who are not prepared for the technological society we are becoming."

(Condensed from "Policy Issues in Teaching Education" by Mary Kennedy in the Phi Delta Kappan, May, 91, pp 661–66.)

✦ *California State-Wide Test Fiasco: Teachers and Testers Who Don't Understand Reasoning*

Before teachers will be able to help students to reason well, it is essential that they learn what reasoning is and how to assess it. A recent statewide test in California demonstrated that many teachers, and even some educational testing experts, have serious misunderstandings about the nature of reasoning and how to assess it.

Evaluative Essay Sample

EVALUATION. Students were asked to write an evaluative essay, make judgments about the worth of a book, television program, or type of music and then support their judgments with reasons and evidence. Students must consider possible criteria on which to base an evaluation, analyze their subject in light of the criteria, and select evidence that clearly supports their judgments. Each student was assigned one of the following evaluative tasks:

- To write a letter to a favorite author telling why they especially liked one of the author's books.
- To explain why they enjoyed one television program more than any others.
- To justify their preference for a particular type of music.

The tasks made clear that students must argue convincingly for their preferences and not just offer unsupported opinions.

This is a sample essay from a student who demonstrated exceptional achievement.

Rock Around the Clock

"Well, you're getting to the age when you have to learn to be responsible!" my mother yelled out.

"Yes, but I can't be available all the time to do my appointed chores! I'm only thirteen! I want to be with my friends, to have fun! I don't think that it is fair for me to baby-sit while you go run your little errands!" I snapped back. I sprinted upstairs to my room before my mother could start another sentence. I turned on my radio and "Shout" was playing. I noted how true the song was and I threw some punches at my pillow. The song ended and "Control" by Janet Jackson came on. I stopped beating my pillow. I suddenly felt at peace with myself. The song had slowed me down. I pondered briefly over all the songs that had helped me to control my feelings. The list was endless. So is my devotion to rock music and pop rock. These songs help me to express my feelings, they make me wind down, and above all they make me feel good. Without this music, I might have turned out to be a violent and grumpy person.

Some of my favorite songs are by Howard Jones, Pet Shop Boys, and Madonna. I especially like songs that have a message in them, such as "Stand by Me", by Ben E. King. This song tells me to stand by the people I love and to not question them in times of need. Basically this song is telling me to believe in my friends, because they are my friends.

My favorite type of music is rock and pop rock. Without them, there is no way that I could survive mentally. They are with me in times of trouble, and best of all, they are only a step away.

California classroom teachers wrote comments like these after reading and scoring students' evaluative essays:

- "Evidence of clear thinking was heavily rewarded in our scoring."
- "I am struck by how much some students can accomplish in 45 minutes; how well they can sometimes marshal the ideas; and with how much flair and sparkle they can express themselves."
- "More emphasis should be placed on critical thinking skills, supporting judgments, and tying thoughts and ideas together. Far too many papers digress, summarize, underdevelop, or state totally irrelevant facts."
- "Students generally need to develop skills in giving evidence to support their judgments. I plan to spend more time on these thinking skills next year."

Source: California State Department of Education, 1988. Reprinted in, "California: The State of Assessment", Anderson, Robert L. *Developing Minds,* edited by Art Costa, pp. 314–25.

The student essay above should have been graded at the lower rather than the higher end of the continuum of eight levels: "minimal evidence of achievement" or, at best, "limited evidence of achievement" rather than the highest grade of "exceptional achievement". For though the essay may have "flair and sparkle" (as one teacher expressed it), it is a poor example of evaluative reasoning, since it systematically confuses the objective goal of rea-

soned evaluation with the very different goal of explaining subjective preference, an important distinction in critical thinking which the teacher-evalua-
tors apparently missed entirely.

First of all, the instructions themselves are confused. They begin with a
clear requirement of "objective" evaluation:

"Students were asked to write an evaluative essay, make judgments about
the worth of a book, television program, or type of music and then support
their judgments with reasons and evidence. Students must consider possible
criteria on which to base an evaluation, analyze their subject in the light of
the criteria, and select evidence that clearly supports their judgments."

Unfortunately, this request for reasoned evaluation is blended in the second half of the instruction with what might possibly be taken, with a little
stretching and selective reading, as a request for the expression of a "subjective" preference:

> Each student was assigned one of the following evaluative tasks: to write
> a letter to a favorite author telling why they especially liked one of the
> author's books, to explain why they enjoyed one television program more
> than any others, or to justify their preference for a particular type of music.
> The tasks made clear that students must argue convincingly for their prefer-
> ences and not just offer unsupported opinions.

Let's look closely at this confusion. In the first place, there is still an
emphasis on objective evaluation ("The tasks made clear that students must
argue convincingly for their preferences and not just offer unsupported opinions") while the task itself is defined as the justification of a "preference".

Now most people prefer books, television programs, and types of music for
fundamentally subjective, not objective, reasons. They like a particular book,
television program, or song for no reason other than that they like it, that is,
because they enjoy it or find pleasure in it or are interested or absorbed or
excited or amused by it. Their reasons for liking what they like are not the
result of an objective evaluation. They have no relation to the objective quality of what is judged. They are about the personal responses of the experiencer, not about the objective qualities of that which is experienced.

Most people, to take the point a step further, do not have "evidence" —
other than the stuff of their subjective reactions — to justify their preferences. They prefer because of the way they feel not because of the way they
reason. To choose because of these subjective states of feeling is precisely to
lack criteria of evaluation or evidence that bears upon objective assessment.
When challenged to support subjective preferences, people usually can do little more than repeat their subjective reactions ("I find it boring, amusing,
exciting, dull, interesting, etc.") or rationalize them ("I find it exciting
because it has a lot of action in it.")

A *reasoned evaluation* of a book, a program, or a type of music requires
more than this; it requires some knowledge of the qualities of what we are
evaluating and of the criteria appropriate to the evaluation of those qualities.

One needs to be well-informed about books, about programs, about music if one is to claim to be in a position to objectively evaluate them. If one is not well-informed, one is unable to render a justified evaluative judgment, though one can always subjectively react and freely express one's subjective reactions as (mere) personal preferences. This is what the student (graded as having written an objective evaluation of "exceptional achievement") actually does. But his evaluators, not having this distinction clear in their own minds, completely miss the difference.

The sample student essay can, for analytic purposes, be divided into three parts. We shall comment briefly on each in turn. The first segment of the essay is an account of a highly emotional exchange between the student and his mother:

> "Well, you're getting to the age when you have to learn to be responsible!" my mother yelled out. "Yes, but I can't be available all the time to do my appointed chores! I'm only thirteen! I want to be with my friends, to have fun! I don't think that it is fair for me to baby-sit while you run your little errands!" I snapped back. I sprinted upstairs to my room before my mother could start another sentence.

It is clear that in this segment there is no analysis, no setting out of alternative criteria, no clarification of the question at issue, no hint at reasoning or reasoned evaluation.

In the second part, the student makes a sweeping claim about a purported causal relationship between listening to rock music and his asserted, but unsupported, ability to control his emotions. He does not consider "possible criteria on which to base an evaluation". He does not present any evidence, though he does cite two examples, one where a song prompts him to punch his pillow and one where another song prompts him to stop. This gives little credence to the notion that rock music leads to his "controlling" his emotions. If anything, his examples seem to imply that, rather than learning control from, he is learning to be controlled by, the music he listens to. His major claim that "Without this music, I might have turned out to be a violent and grumpy person" is without reasoned or evidentiary support. He merely brashly asserts that it is true:

> I turned on my radio and "Shout" was playing. I noted how true the song was and I threw some punches at my pillow. The song ended and "Control", by Janet Jackson came on. I stopped beating my pillow. I suddenly felt at peace with myself. The song had slowed me down. I pondered briefly over all the songs that had helped me to control my feelings. The list was endless. So is my devotion to rock music and pop rock. These songs help me to express my feelings, they make me wind down, and above all they make me feel good. Without this music, I might have turned out to be a violent and grumpy person.

In the third, and final, section of the essay the student closes his remarks with a series of subjective, unsupported, even irrelevant statements:

Some of my favorite songs are by Howard Jones, Pet Shop Boys, and Madonna. I especially like songs that have a message in them, such as "Stand by Me", by Ben E. King. This song tells me to stand by the people I love and to not question them in time of need. Basically this song is telling me to believe in my friends, because they are my friends.

My favorite type of music is rock and pop rock. Without them, there is no way that I could survive mentally. They are with me in times of trouble, and best of all, they are only a step away.

If this is reasoning, it is very bad reasoning: "Believe in your friends because they are your friends", "If you feel you cannot survive without rock music, then it follows that you can't." Of course, a more appropriate interpretation of what is going on is that the student is not reasoning at all but merely asserting his subjective opinions. Consider, the student doesn't examine alternative criteria on which to base an evaluation of music. He doesn't analyze rock music in the light of evaluative criteria. He doesn't provide evidence that clearly supports his judgment. His writing is vague where it needs to be precise, logically rambling where it needs to be critically reasoned. We don't really know what he means by songs "controlling" his feelings. We are not provided with any evidence on the basis of which we could assess whether there is any truth in his sweeping claims about himself, for example, that he could not survive mentally without rock music. Indeed, common sense experience strongly suggests, we believe, that the student is simply deluding himself on this point, or, alternatively, engaging in unbridled hyperbole.

When a blatantly weak essay such as this is disseminated nationally as an example of "exceptional achievement" in the writing of a *reasoned* evaluative essay, then it is clear that there are large numbers of educators who are not clear about the assessment of reasoning. Remember, the California Assessment Program of the California State Department of Education is the second largest assessment unit in the country. (I should add that Dale Carlson, the head of CAP, is now putting a major effort into rectifying this problem.)

THE MANY WAYS TEACHERS MIS-ASSESS REASONING

If many teachers take bad reasoning to be good, do they also take good reasoning to be bad? Unfortunately the answer appears to be, "Yes." This became apparent in a Center for Critical Thinking research project in which teachers were provided with a well-reasoned response to the California prompt, in addition to the poorly reasoned one. The participants were teachers enrolled in critical thinking workshops. They were given the two essays to assess after receiving a morning's instruction on critical thinking. What is significant is the myriad of confusions and misunderstandings about the assessment of reasoning that emerged and the inconsistencies in both grading and in justifying grades.

Here is the "well-reasoned response" they were asked to assess alongside the poorly-reasoned "Rock Around the Clock".

Can I Prove Rock Music is Better?

It's certainly hard to objectively judge music based on justifiable criteria because most people don't have any real standards for the music they listen to other than they like it. My friends and I are probably no different from other people. We listen to music we like because we like it. But this assignment asks me to give good reasons why we like what we like. I'm not sure I can, but I'll try.

I first wonder what would be a really good reason for liking any kind of music (other than it sounds good to you). Well, I suppose that one possible good reason for preferring one kind of music to another is that it expresses better the problems we face and what we can do to solve those problems.

Does this give me a good reason for preferring rock music to other kinds? Perhaps so. Certainly, rock music is often about problems that we have: problems of love and sex, school and parents, drugs and drink. I'm not sure, however, whether the "answers" in the songs actually are really good answers or just answers that appeal to us. They might even increase our prejudices about parents, teachers, school, and love. I'm not sure.

Another possible good reason for preferring one kind of music to another is that it is written better or more skillfully performed. Can I truthfully say that rock music is more skillfully written or performed than other kinds of music? In all honesty I cannot.

So what is my conclusion? It is this. I am unable to give any objective reason for liking rock music. My friends and I are like most people. We like the music we listen to just because we like it. For better or for worse, that's all the reason we have. What do you think? Can 15 million teenagers be wrong?

This second essay was written by one of the research staff members of the Center who made sure that it was responsive to the directions and displayed all of the critical thinking abilities called for:

1) it distinguished mere subjective preference from well-reasoned assessment,
2) it was responsive to the logic of the question at issue,
3) it formulated and discussed alternative relevant criteria,
4) it distinguished having evidence relevant to a question from lacking such evidence,
5) it displayed intellectual humility,
6) it displayed intellectual integrity,
7) it drew only those conclusions the evidence warranted.

The results highlighted the problem. On one occasion 81 teachers and administrators assessed the two essays. The poorly-reasoned essay was given an average score of 5.4 (out of 8) while the well-reasoned essay was given an average score of 3.9. Forty-nine of the teachers gave the poorly-reasoned essay a 6, 7, or 8, while only 18 teachers gave the well-reasoned essay a 6, 7, or 8.

Even more illuminating than the raw scores were the reasons given by the teachers and administrators. Multiple confusions surfaced, as I suggested above, about the nature of reasoning and the appropriate way to assess it. Let's look at some of the responses. Try to imagine students actually receiving these grades along with the often mistaken, confused, or unintelligible commentary.

I have divided teacher assessments for convenience into two groups. The first consists of those teachers who grade the poorly reasoned essay higher than the well-reasoned essay. The second consists of those teachers who grade the poorly reasoned essay lower than the well-reasoned essay. Reading the teachers' justifications for their grades reveals a great deal of misunderstanding of the nature of reasoning. [First Essay: "Rock Around the Clock" (the poorly reasoned essay) Second Essay: "Can I Prove Rock Music is Better?" (the well-reasoned essay)]

FIRST GROUP OF TEACHERS

The following teachers give a high grade to the poorly reasoned essay and a low grade to the well-reasoned essay. In virtually every case, the teachers reveal no awareness of the importance of intellectual humility, wherein one does not claim to justify a conclusion when one lacks the evidence to do so, and one rather gives good reasons for suspending judgment.

1) *A Physical Education Teacher:* [#1] "The first essay better fulfills the criteria for the assignment because the writer justifies (his or her) preference for a particular type of music. I think I would give it a 7 though because it was kind of confusing how the writer got on the subject.

[#2] "The second essay did not justify a preference for any particular type of music. So the writer did not meet the criteria for the assignment. Strangely enough it was easier to read but possibly because the way the writer feels is how I feel about music in general. I think the essay deserves a '0'."

2) *An English Teacher:* [#1] "I would give this essay a 7 because he/she gave experience from his/her life to support their opinion — gave reasons and evidence by example.

[#2] "I would give this essay a grade of 2 because he/she did not prove a point — merely rambled from one thing to another searching for a reason."

3) *A Math Teacher:* [#1] "I would give the first essay a 5 because it did not support the judgment well but did make many references.

[#2] "I would give the second essay a 3 because it is not very evaluative! It did analyze the subject but provided no real support of any judgment."

4) *A Math Teacher:* [#1] "I would give this paper a grade of 7 because criteria were evident, analysis was good and it had lots of supporting evidence.

[#2] "I would give this paper a 3 because criteria are given but nothing was analyzed and no supporting evidence."

5) *Freshman Studies Teacher:* [#1] "I would give 'Rock Around the Clock' a grade of 6 because: *a)* a more flowing style of writing than a series of loosely related points, *b)* a personal approach, *c)* specific information as to

records and effects of the songs, *d)* valid and accurate comparisons, *e)* personalization, *f)* availability, *g)* a well-supported point of view, and *h)* R&R as an avoidance tool.

[#2] "I would give 'Can I Prove Rock Music is Better?' a 3 because *a)* statement of problem OK, *b)* no exploration about 'Why we like it', *c)* discusses what it is about, not why we listen. Do we listen to the words or music?, *d)* the idea of 'better performances' not followed through on, and *e)* How do they know they are like 'most people'?"

6) *A Math Teacher: [#1]* "The first essay: grade 6. The writer has set up some criteria for his choice, the music gives him a calming influence.... Since the writer is given the opportunity to set his own criteria, this will suffice. He gives examples to justify his conclusions.

[#2] "The second essay: grade 3. An attempt is made to give reasons for supporting the music but no conclusions are made. The writer cannot make an argument for his case in any area. It is difficult, as the writer has said, to justify choice or preference, but since one can choose one's own criteria it would seem any position well-argued and justified would fulfill the assignment. The author did not succeed in doing that."

7) *Subject Taught Not Identified: [#1]* "'Rock Around the Clock' Score: 6. This student does not give any clear criteria to start off as to possible criteria to base their evaluation on. This student based their evaluation on how it made them feel or respond. It was based on reactions — not facts to choose music by, but at least this student used something to justify their preference.

[#2] "'Can I Prove Rock Music Is Better?' Score: 2 Too vague — never really makes a decision about their preference of music. This student talks about possible criteria but never really says anything about it. Shows no support to justify the preference."

8) *Former English Teacher: [#1]* "I would give this essay a grade of 8 because: *a)* essay cites specific examples, *b)* catchy opening, *c)* the criteria used was based on student's personal experience, *d)* student was asked to justify their preference. I think she did.

[#2] "I would give this essay a grade of 2 because: *a)* very generalized, *b)* few, if any, concrete examples, *c)* essay is not personalized to any extent, *d)* no specific conclusions drawn."

9) *Special Ed. Teacher: [#1]* "Point total: 7. This essay listed three criteria on which to base a judgment. It gave examples of each — maybe better examples could be found. The writer attempted to analyze a basically subjective issue in concrete terms — what the songs do for them: not objective, but a fairly concrete assessment of music's subjectivity.

[#2] "Point total: 0. This essay did not seriously attempt to answer the issue at hand. Instead it concluded, quite lamely, that no objective statement of worth could be made. While this may be accurate in the broadest sense, no effort was made to justify that position."

10) English Teacher: [#1] "I would give this essay a 7 because the author is not afraid to take a stand. Although the 'proof' is emotionally based, that was the direction of his/her argument.

[#2] "I would give this essay a 3 because the writer was not able to take a position. He/she beats around the bush and asks the reader to make the decision when that was the assignment to the writer. The insecurity and negative attitude runs through the entire paper."

SECOND GROUP OF TEACHERS

The following teachers give a low grade to the poorly reasoned essay and a high or higher grade to the well-reasoned essay. In some cases the teachers revealed some awareness of the importance of intellectual humility. Some are, however, confused or mistaken in part about reasoning and its assessment. For most, thankfully, this confusion is conjoined with some insight into reasoning. For some few others, the fact that they graded the poorly-reasoned essay lower is not based on insight but chance. This is apparent from some of the reasons they give.

1) A Library-Media Teacher: [#1] "Grade: 3 or 4. Reasons: My first thought that it wasn't a typical essay but rather starts out with a rather clever, attention-getting device. In that sense, the student did catch my attention — and also confused me somewhat. That is, it doesn't start out as a typical essay. The student is a good writer in that their word choices make sense and there are supporting reasons for why they chose rock music and pop music.... Now that I read this again, I can see that really the writer has only supplied one reason for their selection: the control/expression of feelings. Well, it's the same old problem in grading a paper, i.e., the student writes well but hasn't followed the criteria strictly.

[#2] "Grade: 7. Reasons: Just a first critical response before I re-read it. It strikes me as thoughtful and honest (which always impresses me). Now I'll see how it fits the criteria. The writer states he needs good reasons for his judgment. I don't think that 'good' is the word he wants.... Why do we like what we like? That's a provocative question!... A quickie, yes, I think they've fulfilled most of the criteria, just not in the usual fashion. Also, it's an essay (as I define one)."

2) A Special Ed. Teacher: [#1] "The student in this essay never really makes a statement that involves an evaluation of a judgment made concerning a type of music, except to say 'My favorite type of music is rock and pop rock. Without them there is no way I could survive mentally.' He does try to show what he means by this statement when he offers examples of music that affect his mood. He lacks a clear evaluation or supportive evidence toward the topic. I think his statement about surviving mentally is a bit much. I give it a 4.

[#2] "This student doesn't know what he thinks and he lets you know it continually. His closing paragraph summarizes what he is trying to put down in the essay and it is the most straightforward part of the essay. His title doesn't quite jibe with the rest of the essay. He was supposed to prove rock music is better, but what he really talked about was whether there was any justification for why people like rock music. I give it a 5."

3) *A Social Studies Teacher: [#1]* "I would give essay one a grade of 6. Essay number one lists reasons for liking rock music, but it is very superficial in analyzing them in the light of the criteria. It really does not approach the subject in a way that logically lists possible criteria as a basis for analysis and then applies the criteria to the music. The essay is generally Bull Shit with only a general connection to the instructions.

[#2] "I would give essay #2 an 8 because the possible criteria for analyzing the issue are covered...."

4) *An English Teacher: [#1]* "Score: 3. The writer in essay one has discussed how he/she feels about rock and pop music, but generalities are given and his/her statements aren't supported with evidence. The assignment is to 'justify' preference, not discuss that it makes him/her 'feel good' period. No criteria have been established, so the essay just rambles on about 'feelings' and not much else. Reasons and evidence are lacking.

[#2] "Score: 5. This essay does a little bit better in attempting an argument. The essay establishes two 'criteria' on which to base his/her essay.... Examples of 'answers' in paragraph 3 are needed as evidence.... Paragraph 4 isn't developed. Needs reasons and evidence/ examples. Weak Conclusion."

5) *A Physical Education Teacher: [#1]* "I would grade the essay 0. The essay does not show their judgment about worth with reason and evidence as asked in the directions. There are no criteria for evaluation, analysis with criteria or evidence that clearly supports the judgments.

[#2] "I would grade the essay 5. The essay attempts to set up criteria for evaluation, yet not as completely as it could have been done. There was an attempt to analyze the subject with the criteria, but not complete. There was no evidence to clearly support the judgment."

6) *A Second Grade Teacher: [#1]* "The first essay should have a 3 because the stated criterion is subjective. The conclusion comes down to, 'I like it because I like it.'

[#2] "The second essay would have a 6 because there was a search for good criteria and no evidence was found to support the good criteria."

7) A Counselor: [#1] "I would give this essay a 1 because the student did select a topic to evaluate which fit the directions. However, she reported her subjective taste (how some songs have affected her, which songs she likes) rather than evaluating 'rock music'.

[#2] "I would give this essay a 7 because: a) she selects an appropriate topic, 2) she considered what criteria would be appropriate to evaluate rock music, c) she made judgments based on the criteria she listed, 4) her conclusion was based on her criteria/judgment. However, she might have considered/used other criteria."

8) A Sixth Grade Language Arts Teacher: [#1] "A grade of 1. There was no evaluation, went strictly by senses.

[#2] "A grade of 8. The writer did a good job on a subject that is a matter of preference no matter how you look at it! He tried to objectively judge rock music, but in the end... 'We like it just because we like it.'"

9) A First Grade Teacher: [#1] "I would give 'Rock Around the Clock' a 4 because the writer did give some facts for liking rock music but wrote mostly from emotion without questioning if her facts were sound. For example, 'believe in my friends because they are my friends'.

[#2] "I would give 'Can I Prove Rock Music is Better?' a 7. The writer stated the purpose, criteria, facts, and gave a conclusion. The writer considered more than just feeling. More facts for liking rock music are needed."

✦ Introduction to the Analysis and Evaluation of Reasoning

There are two obstacles that stand in the way of fostering sound reasoning K–12: *1)* teachers must learn how to devise assignments that require reasoning, and *2)* teachers must learn how to analyze and evaluate reasoning objectively. This process will not happen overnight, but the sooner it begins, the sooner it can be achieved.

We will shortly take a look at three assignments that call for reasoning as well as at three examples of student work for each of those assignments: student work with no reasoning in it, student work with poor reasoning in it, and student work with good reasoning in it. In each case, we will provide a brief commentary to help make clear what one should look for in the reasoning. But first we will provide a brief overview of what is involved, in general, in the analysis and evaluation of reasoning.

WHAT IS INVOLVED IN ANALYZING AND EVALUATING REASONING?

The fundamental criteria to use in analyzing and evaluating reasoning comes from an analysis of the purpose of the reasoner and the logic of the question or questions raised. For example, if a person raises the question, say, as to whether democracy is failing in the USA (in the light of the dwindling number of people who vote and the growing power of vested interest groups with significant money to expend on campaign contributions), we can establish general criteria for assessing the reasoning by spelling out what in general one would have to do to settle the question. Those criteria would include such matters as the following:

1) *An Analysis of the Concept of the Ends of Democracy.* What would it be for democracy to succeed? What would it be for it to fail? What do we take the fundamental objective of democracy to be? For democracy to succeed is it enough that it simply ensure the right of the people at large to vote or must it also serve the well being of the people as well?

2) *Collection of the Facts About the Numbers of People Not Voting.* What is the actual number of people not voting? Is it growing? By what percentage?

3) *An Interpretation of the Significance of the Facts Collected in #2.* What are the reasons why growing numbers of people are not voting? What are the implications of those facts?

4) *Collection of Facts About the Number of Vested Interest Groups Influencing Elections.* How many vested interested groups are influencing elections today in comparison to the past? What is the nature and extent of their influence in money spent?

5) *An Interpretation of the Significance of the Facts Collected in #4.* What is the significance of the growing influence of vested interest groups on election outcomes? What is gained and lost by means of that influence?

6) *Synthesis of Numbers 1 through 5.* What is the overall significance of what we have found out in 1 through 5? What does it all add up to? What exactly are we gaining and losing as a result of the growing influence of vested interest groups and diminished numbers of voters? In attempting to put everything together we would want to see reflection on this issue from more than one point of view. We would want to assess how the reasoner responds to reasonable objections from other points of view.

These are some of the considerations relevant to reasoning well about the issue. A rational analysis of someone's response to this issue would involve, then, checking to see if the above considerations were reasonably addressed, to see if the reasoner had done a plausible job in analyzing the functions of democracy, collecting relevant facts and information, interpreting those facts, and putting everything together, with a sensitivity to more than one point of view, into one coherent line of reasoning.

Many of the teachers assessing the reasoning of the essays on rock music above failed to analyze or review the logic of the question at issue. Instead they read the essays impressionistically, allowing the grade they gave to be determined more by whether their impressions were positive or negative than by any close analysis of the degree to which the student responded adequately to the demands inherent in the precise question at issue.

It is the logic of the question at issue which is the "system for thinking" that should guide our reasoning. If we do not develop skill in explicating that logic, our reasoning is apt to become impressionistic, guided by our prejudices and biases, by our egocentrism and ethnocentrism, rather than disciplined by rational considerations.

✦ *Three Examples of* *Student Reasoning*

What follows below are three assignments designed to call for reasoning on the part of the students, along with three examples of student "reasoning" in response to those assignments. Two of the assignments are in history and the other in literature. The three issues the students are asked to develop their reasoning on involve: reasoning about the character of the American people, reasoning about the meaning of a poem, and reasoning about the comparative importance of inventions. It would be useful if you thought a little about your own assessment of the students' reasoning before you looked at ours'. You could then compare the two.

AMERICAN HISTORY: REASONING ABOUT THE AMERICAN CHARACTER

Question at Issue: "Are the Americans you know capable of the kind of mass hysteria which occurred in 1919 and is described in a textbook as the 'Red Scare'?"

Directions: One of the most important reasons to write our history is to discover who we are and who we are not, how we can develop ourselves, what faults we have to watch out for, and what strengths we can build upon. Read the passage in your textbook on the "Red Scare". Then write a couple of paragraphs in which you try to figure out whether the Americans you know are "capable" or "not capable" of reacting as many Americans did in 1919. (See textbook, p. 731.) Be sure you show us your reasoning. Support and explain why you think as you do.

Reading Excerpt: The "Red Scare"
(from *America: Past and Present*, by Divine, Breen, Fredrickson, and Williams;
Scott, Foreman and Company, 1984, p. 731.)

The first and most intense outbreak of national alarm came in 1919. The heightened nationalism of World War I, aimed at achieving unity at the expense of ethnic diversity, found a new target in bolshevism. The Russian Revolution and the triumph of Marxism frightened many Americans. A growing turn into communism among American radicals (especially the foreign-born) accelerated the fears, although the numbers involved were tiny — at most there were sixty thousand Communists in the United States in 1919. But they were located in the cities, and their influence appeared to be magnified with the outbreak of widespread labor unrest.

A general strike in Seattle, a police strike in Boston, and a violent strike in the iron and steel industry thoroughly alarmed the American people in the spring and summer of 1919. A series of bombings led to panic. First the mayor of strike-bound Seattle received a small brown package containing a homemade bomb; then an alert New York postal employee detected sixteen bombs addressed to a variety of famous citizens (including John D. Rockefeller); and finally, on June 2, a bomb shattered the front of Attorney General A. Mitchell Palmer's home. Although

---

the man who delivered it was blown to pieces, authorities quickly identified him as an Italian anarchist from Philadelphia.

In the ensuing public outcry, Attorney General Palmer led the attack on the alien threat. A Quaker and progressive, Palmer abandoned his earlier liberalism to launch a massive roundup of foreign-born radicals. In a series of raids that began on November 7, federal agents seized suspected anarchists and Communists and held them for deportation with no regard for due process of law. In December, 249 aliens — including such well-known radical leaders as Emma Goldman and Alexander Berkman — were sent to Russia aboard the *Buford,* dubbed the "Soviet Ark" by the press. Nearly all were innocent of the charges against them. A month later, Palmer rounded up nearly four thousand suspected Communists in a single evening. Federal agents broke into homes, meeting halls, and union offices without search warrants. Many native-born Americans were caught in the dragnet and spent several days in jail before being released; aliens rounded up were deported without hearings or trials.

For a time, it seemed that this Red Scare reflected the prevailing views of the American people. Instead of condemning their government's actions, citizens voiced their approval and even urged more drastic steps. One patriot said his solution to the alien problem was simple: "S.O.S. — ship or shoot." General Leonard Wood, the army chief of staff, favored placing Bolsheviks on "ships of stone with sails of lead," while evangelist Billy Sunday preferred to take "these ornery, wild-eyed Socialists" and "stand them up before a firing squad and save space on our ships." Inflamed by public statements like these, a group of legionnaires in Centralia, Washington, dragged a radical from the town jail, castrated him, and hanged him from a railway bridge. The coroner's report blandly stated that the victim "jumped off with a rope around his neck and then shot himself full of holes."

The very extremism of the Red Scare led to its rapid demise. Courageous government officials in the Department of Labor insisted on due process and full hearing before anyone else was deported. Prominent public leaders began to speak out against the acts of terror. Charles Evans Hughes, the defeated GOP candidate in 1916, offered to defend six Socialists expelled from the New York legislature; Ohio Senator Warren G. Harding, the embodiment of middle-class values, expressed his opinion that "too much has been said about bolshevism in America." Finally, Palmer himself, with evident presidential ambition, went too far. In April 1920, he warned of a vast revolution to occur on May 1; the entire New York City police force, some eleven thousand strong, was placed on duty. When no bombings or violence took place on May Day, the public began to react against Palmer's hysteria. Despite a violent explosion on Wall Street in September that killed thirty-three people, the Red Scare died out by the end of 1920. Palmer passed into obscurity, the tiny Communist party became torn with factionalism, and the American people tried hard to forget their momentary loss of balance.

STUDENT #1

The people I know are not like the people who lived in 1919. They obey the law and, though they might make some mistakes or do some things they ought not to, they would never hurt someone who was innocent. Most of the people I know go to church and believe in God. They are good Christians. They read the Bible. They try to raise their children to be good and avoid evil. They are kind people. So I don't believe that what happened in 1919 could ever happen again. It won't happen in my neighborhood.

Commentary on the Student's Reasoning

There is very little reasoning in this student's work and, on the whole, what there is seems uncritical and self-serving: in essence, "My friends are good. Therefore they wouldn't do anything bad." There are obvious objections to this reasoning. Presumably, most of the people in 1919 also went to church and believed in God. Presumably, they too would have thought themselves to be good Christians. Presumably, their friends thought of them as kind and as trying to raise their children to be good and to avoid evil. As a result, the student has not really responded to the logic of the question which implicitly requires that we think about mass hysteria, how it occurs, and how it influences otherwise morally sensitive people to behave in a morally insensitive way.

STUDENT #2

Certainly there are always people who go overboard. That is human nature. And it is unreasonable to think that we will ever abandon human nature. The American people rightly recognized the threat that communism posed to our way of life and fought against it. After all, if we had defeated it then we would not have to have fought the Cold War and spent so much money and resources to defeat the communists after WW II. So what is the lesson. Watch out for human nature. Don't go overboard. But on the other hand, don't forget who your enemies are and don't give up the fight against them just because some people punish them too severely or go to an extreme.

Commentary on the Student's Reasoning

There is more reasoning in this student's work, but still not very good reasoning: in essence, "It is human nature for some people to lose control. So (by implication) some of us might do so, but whether or not some of us might act as some people in 1919 did, the people in 1919 were right to fight against communists". This reasoning is weak because it largely ignores the issue raised. The question at issue is not whether it was right for the people in 1919 to oppose communism, such as it was, in the USA at the time. The question is rather how it came to pass that, as we expressed above, otherwise morally sensitive people came to behave in a morally insensitive way. The student didn't take this question seriously.

STUDENT #3

It is hard to answer the question as to what anyone is capable of. Perhaps what we are capable of is largely a result of the circumstances we are under. If we assume that all humans share human nature and that because of human nature we are capable of acting out of intense fear or insecurity or hate, then a lot depends upon whether something or someone is able to stir those things up in us. Perhaps, of course, there is a way to raise people so that they have so much good character that even when someone tries to stir up the "worst" in them, they do not give in, they resist the temptation to let their worst side take control of them. The question could then be asked whether I and my friends and neighbors are in the first or the second group. Since we have never been "tested" in a crisis situation, since we have never felt deeply threatened, I don't think I can honesty say we would pass the test. I don't know whether we would act like a "Charles Evans Hughes" or a "Billy Sunday". It's a scary thought.

Commentary on the Student's Reasoning

This is better reasoning than in either of the two passages above: in essence, "Everyone has a worse and a better side. Everyone's worse side can be appealed to. Whether you have the "character" to withstand an appeal to your worse cannot be known until you are "tested". My friends and I have not been tested. Therefore, we cannot know whether we have the character to withstand such an appeal. Therefore, we don't know whether we would or would not act as many did in 1919."

ENGLISH: INTERPRETING POEMS

Question At Issue: What is John Donne saying in his poem "Death Be Not Proud"?

Directions: Carefully read the poem below, trying to figure out what the poet is saying. Be careful to explain what your interpretation is and what exactly it is based on. Show us your reasoning. Make sure your interpretation is consistent with (all of) what the poem says.

Death Be Not Proud
(John Donne 1572–1631)

Death be not proud, though some have called thee
Mighty and dreadful, for, thou art not soe,
For, those, whom thou think'st, thou dost overthrow,
Die not, poore death, nor yet canst thou kill mee.
Much pleasure, then from thee, much more must flow,
And soonest our best men with thee doe goe,
Rest of their bones, and soules deliverie.
Thou art slave to Fate, Chance, kings, and desperate men,
And dost with poyson, warre, and sicknesse dwell,
And poppie, or charmes can make us sleepe as well,
And better then thy stroake; why swell'st thou then?
One short sleepe past, wee wake eternally,
And death shall be no more; death, thou shalt die.

STUDENT #1

I don't like this poem. It is boring and confusing. The guy does not spell correctly. He talks a lot about death but he does not say anything. I don't see why he thinks death is mighty or why he thinks it can't kill him. He says a lot of confusing things. At one time he says it gives pleasure and then talks about bones resting, which makes no sense. Then he talks about flowers and sleeping. Finally he says that death shall be no more and that it shall die. I don't get it. Why doesn't he just say what he wants to say? This is a terrible poem. Why do we have to read such stupid stuff?

Commentary on the Student's Reasoning

This student provides us with virtually no reasoning at all. Rather than attempt to figure out what the poet is saying by closely reading what is said, the student rejects the poem, dismisses it emotionally. The result is that the student flagrantly mis-reads the poem and blames his mis-reading on the poem itself and the poet. The student needs to be introduced to the concept of critical reading in which the reader uses the text as evidence to use in interpreting the meaning.

STUDENT #2

Mr. Donne says that death should not be proud. It is not mighty or dreadful. He says this because death is like sleep and when you go to sleep you rest. Therefore, because it is restful even the best people sleep, even slaves. And sleeping is better than being poisoned or being sick. Finally, he says that we only sleep a while and then we awake. And then death is gone. In fact, it is dead. He thinks this is good.

Commentary on the Student's Reasoning

There is more reasoning in this student's work but most of it ignores the evidence of what the poem says. The poem does not say or imply, for example, that "because it [death] is restful even the best people sleep, even slaves". The poem does not say or imply that "sleeping is better than being poisoned or being sick". Finally, it is clear that the student is not getting the major point of the poem, namely, that because of the promised resurrection, last judgment, and eternal life in heaven or hell, there is a sense in which "death" is not real and lasting, but only something that will "die". Like the first student, this student also needs to be introduced to the concept of critical reading in which the reader uses the text as evidence in interpreting meaning.

STUDENT #3

It is clear that Donne believes in God or at least in an afterlife. This is implied in the first four lines which I interpret as saying something like this: "Don't think you're so powerful because no one really dies but only appears to die" (People who "die" are really just awaiting their resurrection). This interpretation is supported in the next line which implies that what we call death is really a kind of "sleepe" and is not, therefore, very bad. In fact, as he says sleep often gives us "pleasure". The next lines make a different kind of point but still are a criticism of the view that death is "mighty" and "dreadful". Death, he says, is not able to control "Fate, Chance, kings, and desperate men". Furthermore, not only is it not able to control these other forces, it can't even get away from such unpleasant associates as "poyson, warre, and sicknesse". Finally, he reasons, narcotics makes us sleep as well as death does and when everyone is resurrected for final judgment (which I infer is what he means) then death itself will be gone forever, and therefore "shalt die".

Commentary on the Student's Reasoning

Finally, we have a student who illustrates the process of critical reading, carefully reasoning her way through the poem, using the words of the poem to carefully back up her interpretation.

HISTORY: REASONING ABOUT THE SIGNIFICANCE OF INVENTIONS

Question at Issue: "Of two inventions discussed in your textbook, which was the most important and why?"

Directions: The textbook for the course describes a number of important inventions, including those of Gutenberg, Edison, and George Washington Carver. Take two inventions, either from those mentioned in the book or some other inventions you know of, and compare their importance. Defend your answer by giving reasons in favor of your judgment.

STUDENT #1

An invention that is very important is the printing press. It was invented by Johann Gutenberg, who was a man that lived in Germany. He invented the printing press in the Fifteenth Century. The first book ever printed by Gutenberg was the Bible. But he soon printed many other books as well. The first printing press worked by using movable type.

Another important invention mentioned in the textbook was the dehydration of foods. This was invented by George Washington Carver. When you dehydrate foods you take the water out of them. George Washington Carver wanted many people to use his inventions, so he did not take out any patents on them. He made many other inventions besides dehydration. He even thought of more than 300 uses for the peanut, including facial cream, shoe polish, and ice cream.

Both inventions are very important. Many people read books that are printed on a printing press. Many people eat food that has been dehydrated. But to me the printing press was more important than dehydration.

Commentary on the Student's Reasoning

The student does not provide any reasoning to support his conclusion. He discusses no criteria for assessing inventions for their importance, nor any evidence to support one or the other with respect to those criteria. Most of the factual detail is irrelevant to the issue.

ESSAY #2

R-r-r-r-ring.

The first sound I hear in the morning is my alarm clock going off. It's an invention I truly hate.

R-r-r-r-ring.

It is not a pretty sound, and as soon as I hear it I feel myself getting angry. If only I didn't have to get up so early! All my muscles cry out that I want to sleep! Most mornings when I hear that sound, I even cover my ears with my pillow in the hope that I won't hear it going off.

It is an old-fashioned wind-up alarm clock that loses ten minutes a day. It is not a digital alarm clock because all the digital alarm clocks I've ever tried have alarms that are too soft to awaken a really sound sleeper. And believe me I am a *very* sound sleeper.

R-r-r-ring. But no matter what I do, or how I feel, I end up wide awake and out of bed and getting dressed for school.

Once I am awake I look at my other clock, the one that is hanging on the wall over my dresser. It is a great invention too. It's a digital clock that keeps perfect time. It has a red LED display and it glows in the dark. It has an emergency battery backup, so that even if the electricity cuts out in the night, my wall clock never loses a second.

Which of the two inventions is more important? That's the question I ask myself as I head off for school. And then the answer comes to me. No matter how perfectly the digital wall clock keeps time, without the alarm clock I wouldn't be awake to see it. So without doubt the alarm clock wins the prize as most important.

Commentary on the Student's Reasoning

The student provides some reasoning but when considered closely it is apparent that the reasoning is absurd. The notion that without the alarm clock people would never wake up is ridiculous. What does this student think happened before the alarm clock was invented? Furthermore, does she really think that loud alarms cannot be built into digital clocks? Once again, the student has not learned to think about the logic of the question at issue. Therefore, the student gives no time to reflecting on the general criteria by means of which we might assess the social worth of inventions by relating that worth to the most basic human values, like the preservation of life, the minimization of pain and suffering, the development of a more just society, and so forth. It is only in terms of the concepts of basic human values that criteria can be generated that give a solid logic to the question and hence a means to assess the reasoning which purports to settle the question.

ESSAY #3

Two inventions mentioned in the book are television and the dehydration of food. Each is important in different ways. The television set, for example, affects many people's lives. I watch television almost every night and so do all of my friends. But it's not just me and my friends. The same is true for people all across the country, and in most foreign countries as well. Television allows more people to be entertained than was ever possible before. We witness world news, nature programs, comedies and many other programs. Television lets us see much of what is going on in the world.

Dehydration of foods is important in a very different way. The main effects of dehydration are that it allows food to be kept for a long time without spoiling, and to be shipped for a lower cost. I don't know how many people in the world today use dehydrated foods, but I'm pretty sure that it's far smaller than the number of people who enjoy TV. So that seems to show that TV is more important.

And yet I don't feel right saying that one invention is more important than another simply because it has affected more people. If dehydration is used more than it is now, it could help cut down on the number of people who are starving in the world. Saving just a few people from dying of starvation is more important than taking a lot of people and entertaining them.

Commentary on the Student's Reasoning

The student provides some reasoning which might at first appear absurd, but on reflection makes good sense. This student is thinking about the logic of the question at issue and hence is reflecting on the general criteria by means of which we might assess the social worth of inventions by relating that worth to the most basic human values: like the quality or preservation of life, the minimization of pain and suffering, the development of a more just society, and so forth. To say that this student's reasoning is better than the first two students — because she does respond to the logic of the question at issue — does not mean that her reasoning is perfect, for perhaps there are yet further considerations that might be mentioned about the effects of television which might persuade us that television itself is making so large a contribution to the quality or preservation of human life that it is indeed more important than food dehydration. We may know the basic logic of a question without knowing whether we yet have the best answer to that question, the answer that best fulfills its logic.

✦ Conclusion

The whole of this book is concerned with the process of developing students who reason through what they are learning so as to grasp the logic of it, students who know clearly the difference between coming to terms with the logic of something and merely rotely memorizing it. But reasoning is not a matter to be learned once and for all. It is a matter of life-long learning, a matter of bringing insightful mindfulness into the fabric of our thinking and our action. For the teacher, it is a matter of learning how to design instruction so that students take command of the logic of their own thinking while they are thinking and through that insightful grasp, improve it.

We figure things out better if we can monitor what we are doing, intellectually, in trying to figure them out, so that we go beyond simply using logical structures, so that we go beyond simply making logical moves, so that we start to intentionally, deliberately, and willfully examine and take apart the logical structures we are using, so that we designedly, purposively, and alertly assess our use of the structures in everyday situations, and, of course, so that we do these things well: clearly, accurately, precisely, etc.

To understand logical structures is to integrate them, to establish logical connections between them, to make it possible for the mind to make an extended series of nuanced inferences, deductions, and derivations. "This is so, therefore that also is so, and that, and that." The logical structures implicit in an educated person's mind are highly systematized. The well-educated person is able to reason quite directly and deliberately, to begin somewhere, know where one is beginning, and then reason with awareness from that point to other points, all with a given question in mind, with specific evidence in mind, with specific reasons to advance, with specific conclusions to support, with consciousness of one's point of view and of contrasting points of view. The good reasoner is always reasoning within a system that disciplines and restrains that reasoning.

When the logical structures by which a mind figures out the world are confused, a jumble, a hodgepodge, a mere conglomeration, then that figuring out is radically defective, typically in any of a variety of ways: incomplete, inaccurate, distorted, muddled, inexact, superficial, rigid, inconsistent, and unproductive. Then the mind begins it knows not where, takes things for granted without analysis or questioning, leaps to conclusions without sufficient evidence to back them up, meanders without a consciousness of its point of view or of alternative points of view. Then the mind wanders into its own prejudices and biases, its own egocentricity and sociocentricity. Then the mind is not able to discipline itself by a close analysis of the question at issue and ignores the demands that the logic of that question puts on it and us as rational, logic-creating, logic-using animals.

*Critical Thinking in the
Strong Sense*

✦✦ Chapter 9

Critical Thinking:
Fundamental to Education for a Free Society

Abstract

In this paper, written for Educational Leadership *(1984), Paul argues that educational reform will not produce meaningful change unless educators explicitly grasp five inter-related truths: that students, as all people, tend to reason egocentrically; that multi-dimensional problems, traditionally ignored, ought to be central in schooling; that indoc-trination into prevailing views has inappropriately been the major academic response to real world problems; that children from the earliest years need to be encouraged to think for themselves through dialogue, discussion, and constructive debate; and, finally, that "teaching strategies need to be revamped across the board" to stress the development of dialogical and dialectical thought. Paul summarizes his thesis at the close: "An open society requires open minds. Collectively reinforced egocentric and sociocentric thought, conjoined with massive technical knowledge and power, are not the foundations for a gen-uine democracy."*

✦ *The Emerging Critical Thinking Movement*

*T*he "critical thinking movement" is now, after a long and halting start, building up a head of steam. Predictably, numerous quick-fix, miracle cures have sprung up, and turning to them is tempting, especially given the increasing variety of imperatives and mandates under which schools operate. I argue in this paper for a different understanding of how to proceed. I advo-cate both a short-term and a long-term strategy, based on an analysis of where we now stand and what we should strive for ultimately.

I argue that our strategy should reflect a realistic appraisal of the follow-ing factors: *1)* the basic cognitive and affective tendencies of the human mind in its normal, uncritical state, *2)* the categorically different problem types and the reasoning appropriate to them, *3)* the social and personal conditions under which cognitive and affective processes develop, *4)* the present critical thinking skills of teachers and students, and *5)* the fundamental intellectual, affective, and social obstacles to the further development of such skills.

I emphasize the need to recognize and highlight a fundamental difference between two distinct conceptions of critical thinking: a "weak" sense, under-stood as a set of discrete micro-logical skills extrinsic to the character of the person, skills that can be tacked onto other learning; and a "strong" sense, understood as a set of integrated macro-logical skills and abilities intrinsic ultimately to the character of the person and to insight into one's own cognitive and affective processes. If we chose the latter we concern ourselves not only with the development of *technical reason* — skills which do not transform one's grasp of one's basic cognitive and affective processes — but also with the development of *emancipatory reason* — skills and abilities which generate not only fundamental insight into, but also some command of one's own cognitive and affective processes. In the strong sense, we emphasize comprehensive critical thinking skills and abilities essential to the free, rational, and autonomous mind. In the weak sense, we are content to develop what typically comes down to "vocational" thinking skills which by themselves have little influence on a person's intellectual, emotional or moral autonomy. If we aspire to strong sense critical thinking skills and abilities for our long-term goals, and we take stock of where we now stand, careful consideration of the available evidence will, sooner or later, persuade us of something like the following points:

1) that we have deep seated tendencies to use reason to maximize getting, and justify getting, what we, often unconsciously, want, and that this means we use cognitive and affective processes to maintain self-serving or pleasant illusions, to rule out or unfairly undermine ideas in opposition to our own, to link our identity with ideas that are "ours" (and so experience disagreement as ego-threatening), and otherwise to distort or misinterpret our experience to serve our own advantage;

2) that we must distinguish two kinds of problems: problems in technical domains wherein one self-consistent, close-textured system of ideas and procedures determines the settlement of issues, and, in contrast, problems in the logically messy "real world" of everyday life, wherein opposing points of view and contradictory lines of reasoning are relevant and realities of power and self-delusion make rational settlement of issues much harder;

3) that until now, the schools, to the extent they have addressed problem-solving, have focused on technical problems and technical reason and procedures, and have either illicitly reduced real world problems to them or have tacitly inculcated into students the pre-fabricated "self-evident answers" of the dominant social majority or some favored minority;

4) that our capacity to control our cognitive and affective processes often depends on the character of our early lives both at home and school and that very special preparation is necessary for children to develop into adults comfortable with and skilled in weighing, reconciling, and assessing contradictory arguments and points of view through dialogue, discussion, and debate; and,

5) that teaching strategies need to be revamped across the board — especially in social studies and basic academic competencies — to stress the development of dialectical knowledge and skills, and thus self-formed, self-reasoned conviction.

✦ Short Term Strategy: Develop Micro-Logical, Analytic Critical Thinking Skills

The best short term strategy is to facilitate the understanding and teaching of micro-logical analytic critical thinking skills within established subject areas. This requires teaching the use of the elementary critical, analytic vocabulary of the English language, a working knowledge of such mundane terms as *premise, reason, conclusion, inference, assumption, relevant, irrelevant, consistent, contradictory, credible, doubtful, evidence, fact, interpretation, question-at-issue, problem,* etc. Teachers should be encouraged to take at least one university level course in critical thinking wherein they practice the basic micro-logical skills associated with these terms, and so learn to isolate and distinguish issues, premises, assumptions, conclusions, inferences, and master the rudiments of argument assessment.

The nationally normed tests, such as the Watson-Glaser and the Cornell Critical Thinking Tests should be available and teachers should learn how to formulate test questions modeled on them.

A full range of critical thinking books and materials, both university level and K–12, should be made available to teachers and regular brain-storming sessions established. Teachers need to begin to think critically about thinking skills, to get a handle on what makes sense to them and what they can immediately begin to do. An important caveat should be entered here, however. Unlike the domain of technical skills, teachers, and people generally, are naturally disinclined to recognize the degree to which they do not think critically. People tend to retreat to simplistic approaches that do not lay an appropriate foundation for higher level (strong sense) critical thought or to dismiss the need for any new learning at all. ("All good teachers naturally teach critical thinking.") Most people, including the most uncritical, take offense at the suggestion that they lack skill in this area. This ego-identification with critical thinking (*others* need it) is a continual obstacle to reform. To the extent that people lack critical thinking skills, they conceptualize those who have them as "prejudiced", "closedminded", "overly academic", "negative", or "nit-picky".

We must therefore emphasize from the start that the ability to think critically is a matter of degree. No one is without any critical skills whatsoever and no one has them so fully that there are *no* areas in which uncritical thinking is dominant. Openmindedness may be the proper, but it is not the "natural", disposition of the human mind. More on this presently.

Additional short term goals should include the following:

1) Getting master teachers trained in critical thinking;
2) Encouraging teachers and curriculum specialists to attend the growing numbers of critical thinking conferences;
3) Developing a school-wide attitude in which reasoning within unorthodox and conflicting points of view and respectful, reasoned disagreement is

considered essential and healthy (a very difficult goal to achieve of course);

4) Looking for what Bloom has called "latent" curricula and "unspoken" values that may undermine the critical spirit (again, very difficult); and,

5) Establishing a working relationship with at least one university critical thinking instructor.

The ideal, as I see it, is to take those first steps that initiate the teaching of relatively "self-contained" critical thinking skills — testing for inferences that do or do not follow, recognizing assumptions and clear-cut contradictions, giving initial formulations of reasons to support conclusions, considering evidence rather than relying on authority, and so forth — and that develop an environment conducive to strong sense critical thinking. In the process, wherever possible, students should have opportunities to advance ideas of their own and give reasons to support them, as well as opportunities to hear the objections of other students. If this is done carefully in an atmosphere of co-operation and while learning critical analytic terms, the students will begin to use critical distinctions to defend their ideas. When this vocabulary integration begins, a very healthy process has been set in motion which, properly nurtured, can lead to primitive emancipatory thinking skills.

✦ Long Term Strategy: Develop Macro-Logical, Integrative Thinking Skills

An effective long range strategy should have two parts: 1) an on-going explication of the obstacles to the development of strong-sense critical thought, and 2) an increasing recognition of the distinctive nature and importance of dialectical issues and how they can be brought into the curriculum. It is not enough to recognize that all human thought is embedded in human activity and all human activity embedded in human thought. We also need to recognize that much of our thinking is subconscious, automated, and irrational. The capacity to explicate the roots of the thinking "hidden" from us and to purge it when irrational are crucial. Long-term strategy must have an explicative/purgative as well as a constructive/developmental dimension. Because of the limitations of space, however, we can do no more here than set out each side of this global orientation in rough outline.

OBSTACLE ONE: THE DENIAL OF THE NEED

Without ignoring the many ways in which they intersect, consider the degree to which we live in two very different worlds: a world of technical and technological order and clarity, and a world of personal and social disorder and confusion. We are increasingly adept at solving problems in the one domain and increasingly endangered by our inability to solve problems in the other.

Various explanations have been given for this unhappy state of affairs. One of the most popular identifies the root causes to be two-fold: 1) a lack of willingness on the part of those who are right, and know they are, to "stand tall" and refuse to be pushed around by those who are wrong (and are being irrational, stubborn, or malevolent), and 2) the difficulty of getting the "others", our opposition, to see the rationality and fairmindedness of our views and the irrationality and closedmindedness (or malevolence) of their own. President Reagan, to take a recent striking example, put it succinctly when he claimed that one country, the USSR, is the "focus of all evil in the world", an "evil empire" which understands nothing but force and power and steel-eyed determination. That a one-dimensional explanation of this sort can still, not only catch the public's fancy, but seem intelligible to many national leaders, not to mention some "intellectuals", testifies, in my view, to the primitive state of much of our thinking about non-technical, non-technological human problems.

President Reagan's nationalistic expostulations remind me of a tendency to ethnocentrism deep in our own, and perhaps in all cultures. Consider this passage from a 19th century speech:

> Fellow Americans, we are God's chosen people. Yonder at Bunker Hill and Yorktown His providence was above us. At New Orleans and on ensanguined seas His hand sustained us. Abraham Lincoln was His minister, and His was the altar of Freedom the boys in blue set on a hundred battle-fields. His power directed Dewey in the East and delivered the Spanish fleet into our hands on the eve of Liberty's natal day, as He delivered the elder armada into the hands of our English sires two centuries ago. His great purposes are revealed in the progress of the flag, which surpasses the intentions of congresses and cabinets, and leads us like a holier pillar of cloud by day and pillar of fire by night into situations unforeseen by finite wisdom, and duties unexpected by the unprophetic heart of selfishness. The American people cannot use a dishonest medium of exchange; it is ours to set the world its example of right and honor. We cannot fly from our world duties; it is ours to execute the purpose of a fate that has driven us to be greater than our small intention. We cannot retreat from any soil where Providence has unfurled our banner; it is ours to save that soil for liberty and civilization. For liberty and civilization and God's promise fulfilled, the flag must henceforth be a symbol and the sign of all mankind — the flag!

Such passages bring to mind the views articulated by the children interviewed by Piaget in his study for UNESCO on the causes of war.

> *Michael M.* (9 years, 6 months old): Have you heard of such people as foreigners? *Yes, the French, the Americans, the Russians, the English ....* Quite right. Are there differences between all these people? *Oh yes, they don't speak the same language.* And what else? *I don't know.* What do you think of the French, for instance? Do you like them or not? Try and tell me as much as possible. *The French are very serious, they don't worry about anything, an' it's dirty there.* And what do you think of the Russians? *They're bad, they're always wanting to make war.* And what's your opinion of the English? *I don't know ... they're nice ....* Now look, how did you come to know all you've told me? *I don't know ... I've heard it ... that's what people say.*

Maurice D. (8 years, 3 months old): If you didn't have any nationality and you were given a free choice of nationality, which would you choose? *Swiss nationality.* Why? *Because I was born in Switzerland.* Now look, do you think the French and the Swiss are equally nice, or the one nicer or less nice than the other? *The Swiss are nicer.* Why? *The French are always nasty.* Who is more intelligent, the Swiss or the French, or do you think they're just the same? *The Swiss are more intelligent.* Why? *Because they learn French quickly.* If I asked a French boy to choose any nationality he liked, what country do you think he'd choose? *He'd choose France.* Why? *Because he was born in France.* And what would he say about who's the nicer? Would he think the Swiss and the French equally nice or one better than the other? *He'd say the French are nicer.* Why? *Because he was born in France.* And who would he think more intelligent? *The French.* Why? *He'd say that the French want to learn quicker than the Swiss.* Now you and the French boy don't really give the same answer. Who do you think answered best? *I did.* Why? *Because Switzerland is always better.*

Marina T. (7 years, 9 months old): If you were born without any nationality and you were given a free choice, what nationality would you choose? *Italian.* Why? *Because it's my country. I like it better than Argentina where my father works, because Argentina isn't my country.* Are Italians just the same, or more, or less intelligent than the Argentinians? What do you think? *The Italians are more intelligent.* Why? *I can see the people I live with, they're Italians.* If I were to give a child from Argentina a free choice of nationality, what do you think he would choose? *He'd want to stay an Argentinian.* Why? *Because that's his country.* And if I were to ask him who is more intelligent, the Argentinians, or the Italians, what do you think he would answer? *He'd say Argentinians.* Why? *Because there wasn't any war.* Now who was really right in the choice he made and what he said, the Argentinian child, you, or both? *I was right.* Why? *Because I chose Italy.*

For both the President of the United States and these children the world is nationalistically simple: the forces of good (embodied in ourselves) stand opposed by the forces of evil (those who oppose us). The need for emancipatory reason is a need of "the other", the stranger, the foreigner, the opposition.

From this perspective, the schools' job is to pass on our thought to children, exposing them to all of the reasons why our's is right and superior and unquestionable and, at the same time, developing technical abilities and technological power to defend (enforce) our views. The school's task, in short, is to inculcate cultural patriotism and facilitate vocational training.

The distinguished conservative U.S. anthropologist, William Graham Sumner, sharply challenged this view, though he had no illusions about the difficulty of transforming the schools into vehicles for human and social emancipation (1906):

SCHOOLS MAKE PERSONS ALL ON ONE PATTERN: ORTHODOXY

School education, unless it is regulated by the best knowledge and good sense, will produce men and women who are all of one pattern, as if turned in a lathe .... The examination papers show the pet ideas of the examiners .... An orthodoxy is produced in regard to all the great doctrines of life. It consists of the most worn and commonplace opinions which are current in the masses. It may be found in newspapers and popular literature. It is intensely provincial and philistine .... The popular opinions always contain broad fallacies, half-truths, and glib generalizations of fifty years before .... The boards of trustees are almost always made up of "practical men", and if their faiths, ideas, and prejudices are to make the norm of education, the schools will turn out boys and girls compressed to that pattern .... (There is a desire) that children shall be taught just that one thing which is "right" in the view and interest of those in control, and nothing else.

Sumner saw the essential link between education and critical thinking:

Criticism is the examination and test of propositions of any kind which are offered for acceptance, in order to find out whether they correspond to reality or not. The critical faculty is a product of education and training. It is a mental habit and power. It is a prime condition of human welfare that men and women should be trained in it. It is our only guarantee against delusion, deception, superstition, and misapprehension of ourselves and our earthly circumstances. It is a faculty which will protect us against all harmful suggestion .... Our education is good just so far as it produces a well-developed critical faculty ....

He even has a conception of what a society would be like were critical thinking — in what I call the strong sense — a fundamental social value:

The critical habit of thought, if usual in a society, will pervade all its mores, because it is a way of taking up the problems of life. Men educated in it cannot be stampeded by stump orators and are never deceived by dithyrambic oratory. They are slow to believe. They can hold things as possible or probable in all degrees, without certainty and without pain. They can wait for evidence and weigh evidence, uninfluenced by the emphasis and confidence with which assertions are made on one side or the other. They can resist appeals to their dearest prejudices and all kinds of cajolery. Education in the critical faculty is the only education of which it can be truly said that it makes good citizens.

Sumner's concept of a "developed critical faculty" clearly goes much beyond that envisioned by those who link it to a shopping list of atomic skills. He understands it as a pervasive organizing core of mental habits, and a shaping force in the character of a person. It is fairmindedness brought into the heart of everyday life, into all of its dimensions. As a social commitment, it transforms the very nature of how life is lived and human transactions mediated. Sumner does not tell us however how to nurture or develop this faculty and this commitment. He does not explain how it relates to strategies successful in technical domains. Finally, he does not tell us how to initiate this development, though he clearly believes it can begin very early.

OBSTACLE TWO: THE FAILURE OF COGNITIVE PSYCHOLOGY AND PROBLEM-SOLVING THEORISTS TO CALL ATTENTION TO THE LOGIC OF DIALECTICAL ISSUES

A major weakness in cognitive psychology and problem solving theory today is the failure to highlight the striking difference between the logic of technical problems and that of dialectical problems. Until one recognizes this difference one tends to reduce all problems to technical ones and so render all knowledge and all problems procedural, if not algorithmic. Both the power and the limitations of technical disciplines lie in their susceptibility to operationalism and routine procedure. Technical domains progress by severely narrowing what qualifies as appropriate subject matter and as appropriate treatment of it. All concepts are specifically designed to serve restricted disciplinary purposes. Additionally, scope is typically further limited to the quantifiable. For these reasons many of the concepts and attendant skills of application are relatively subject specific.

Consider the wide variety of disciplines that can be brought to bear on the study of humans: physics, chemistry, neurology, physiology, biology, medicine, psychology, economics, sociology, anthropology, history, and philosophy. To put this point another way, humans are physical, chemical, neurological, biological, psychological, economic, sociological, historical, and philosophical beings, all at once. Each person is one, not many. To the extent that a human problem is rendered technical, it is reduced to a relatively narrow system of exclusionary ideas; technical precision and manageability is achieved by excluding a variety of other technical and non-technical features. Specialized disciplines develop by generating ever more specialized sub-disciplines, abstracting further and further from the "wholeness" of things.

This becomes clearer when we consider those disciplines — history, psychology, sociology, anthropology, economics, and philosophy — whose study of humankind does not appear to admit, beyond a range of foundational premises, to discipline-wide unanimity. In each of these fields a variety of alternative systems or viewpoints compete. Generate a question within them and you typically generate a field of conflicting lines of reasoning and answers. Raise questions about their application to everyday life problems and debate intensifies. The issues are properly understood as dialectical, as calling for dialogical reasoning, for thinking critically and reciprocally within opposing points of view. This ability to move up and back between contradictory lines of reasoning, using each to critically cross-examine the other, is not characteristic of the technical mind.

Technical knowledge is typically developed by restriction to one frame of reference, one standpoint. Knowledge arrived at dialectically, in contrast, is like the verdict of a jury, with supporting reasoning. There is no fail-safe, technical path to it. At least two points of view must be entertained. It is not, as problem-solving theorists tend to characterize problems, a movement from an initial state through a series of transformations (or operations) to a final (answering) state.

Most of our everyday interest in people is unquestionably in the area of dialectical issues. By and large we don't know them, value them, or relate to them in terms of their technically determinable sub-features. We struggle to know them as multi-dimensional totalities, in short, as real people. We struggle to grasp the world in this same macro-integrative way. Unfortunately, we fail to see the dialectical nature of this task, the need to entertain more than one interpretation of human acts and of the human world. Indeed we rarely see that our perceptions of people and the world are inferences, based on typically unconscious assumptions, concepts, and beliefs. More on this later.

Despite this need for non-technical, dialectical, integrative thinking, most of the work in cognitive psychology and problem-solving theory assumes that all problem solving can be understood on the model of solving technical problems. Since each technical domain generates a dominant logical system and thus criteria and procedures for cognitive moves within it, theorists tend to reduce problem-solving to a technical or "scientific" model. This was true of problem-solving theory from the start.

For example, Dewey thought that one could approach all problems through the following ordered scientific steps: *1)* identify the problem, *2)* establish facts, *3)* formulate hypotheses, *4)* test hypotheses, and *5)* evaluate results. Polya formulated a similar general procedure: *1)* Understand the problem. What is the unknown? What data are given? What are the conditions? *2)* Devise a plan. Find the connection between the data and the unknown. You may be obliged to consider auxiliary problems if an immediate connection cannot be found. *3)* Carry out the plan. Check each step. Can you see clearly that the step is correct? Can you prove that it is correct? *4)* Look back. Check the result. Check the argument. Can you derive the result differently? Can you see it at a glance? We find this procedural emphasis even in a relatively recent work on problem-solving. John R. Hayes' characterization, in *The Complete Problem Solver* (1981) is typical:

> *What is a Problem?* If you are on one side of a river and you want to get to the other side but you don't know how, you have a problem. If you are assembling a mail-order purchase and the instructions leave you completely baffled about how to "put tab A in slot B" you have a problem. If you are writing a letter and you can't find the polite way to say, "No, we don't want you to come and stay a month," you have a problem. Whenever there is a gap between where you are now and where you want to be, and you don't know how to find a way to cross that gap, you have a problem.
>
> Solving a problem means finding an appropriate way to cross a gap. The process of finding a solution has two major parts: (1) representing the gap — that is, understanding the nature of the problem, and (2) searching for a means to cross it.

Though these writers have set out and described each step as checklists, the steps still require independent thought and judgment, which cannot be set out and mindlessly followed. Furthermore, the steps are not mutually exclusive. In real life there is no *one* order in which to take each step. I may begin with a vague sense of the problem which I do not thoroughly clarify until the end — *after* gathering facts, considering solutions, and so on. Defining the problem does not necessarily come first.

Most "textbook" and the "real-life" problems problem-solving theorists address are one-system problems (definable and soluble entirely within one discipline or perspective) or self-contained (soluble atomistically rather than as mutually interdependent problems). They implicitly place critical thought squarely in the center of an atomistic, information-processing model of knowledge: the finding, organizing, manipulating, and inferential transforming of technical information.

Just last month, in a *Phi Delta Kappan* article "Improving Thinking Skills — Defining the Problem", Barry Beyer identified insufficient proceduralization as a major problem in instruction in thinking skills. He expressed as self-evident the need for teachers to provide "... step-by-step instructions on how to use specific thinking skills," indeed to spell out "... exactly how to execute a skill". (Every thought that goes through your head?) He demanded that "the crucial part of teaching a skill" is "discussing its operation procedures". (For every conceivable context?) He fails to recognize that the largest and most important form of human thinking, dialectical thinking, cannot, by its very nature, be reduced to an "operational procedure". When we think dialectically we are guided by *principles* not *procedures,* and the application of the principles is often subject to discussion or debate.

The most vexing and significant "real life" problems are logically messy. They span multiple categories and academic disciplines. They are rarely "in" any one of them. The general attitude of mind, for example, that enables one with apparent peace and tranquility to confuse egocentric dogmatism with genuine conviction, to accept vague avowals as true beliefs, to take sentimental credulity for moral insight, to harmonize technical truths with pleasant delusions and superstitions, to wander in and out of a panoply of self-serving reifications, to use confusion to one's advantage, to perform social roles that one does not know one is performing — is not a problem whose solution lies in a discipline, or in a procedure, or in "finding the connection between the data and the unknown", or in "considering an auxiliary problem" or in using special "operators" or in performing a cost-benefit analysis, or in learning mnemonic techniques, or memory codes or study systems or protocol analysis. It is a problem implicit in an uncritical mode of living and so in the very structure of an uncritical mind. Furthermore, if "it works" (enables you to get what you want, perhaps even enables you to become President) is it for you a problem at all? We do not always recognize our problems *as* problems. Once in the ebb and flow of mundane life, its messy criss-crossing of categories, values, and points of view, its inevitable blending of the intellectual, the affective, and the moral, its embodying of irrationality in social practices and beliefs, there is little room for the neat and "abstract" procedures of technical reason.

We need dialogic, point-counter-point, argument for and argument against, scrutiny of individual event against the background of this or that global "totalizing" of it into one's life. We need emancipatory reason, the ability to reason "across", "between", and "beyond" the neatly marshalled data and narrowed, clear-cut concepts of any given technical domain. Because it cannot presuppose or restrict itself to any one "system" or "technical language" or "procedure", it must be dialectical. That is, it must move back and forth between opposing points of view. It must consider how this or that situation might be handled if looked at it this way, or how if looked at that way, what follows from this construal and what from that, what objection can be raised to this and what objection to that. It is the logic that is mocked in the typically closedminded exchanges of mundane human arguments about the personal and social affairs of life. It is the logic that is concept-generating as well as concept-using (since our point of view is shaped as we use it, in a way parallel to "case" law).

Precisely because it is not procedural, not susceptible to a decision-procedure or a set of technical maneuvers, there is the temptation to retreat, as I have noted, either to apodictic self-righteousness (let us pass on to our children our heritage, our wisdom — so they like us can recognize the folly of those who oppose us) or to vacuous or self-contradictory relativism (we cannot teach dialectical thinking skills for they are in the realm of opinion or faith). Both choices ignore the proper role of dialectical reason, which, used as a means of penetrating and assessing the logic of our mundane lives, alone enables us to become intellectually, emotionally, and morally autonomous.

OBSTACLE THREE: CHILDHOOD EGO-IDENTIFICATION WITH ADULT BELIEFS: A
    FOUNDATION FOR CLOSEDMINDEDNESS

If we do not control the fundamental logical structures — the assumptions, values, and beliefs — that shape our own thought, our own feeling responses, and our own moral judgments, then in a significant sense we are not free. Close scrutiny of how most children come to imbibe those structures and of the evidence that shows that most adults do not recognize them, mandates the admission that we have not yet learned how to make fundamental intellectual, emotional, and moral emancipation the likely result of parenting or schooling. The ultimate court of appeal of a free and open mind is, and must be, the principles of comprehensive reason and evidence — not external authority, ego-identification, or technical expertise — the willingness to listen to and empathize with all contending perspectives on an issue without presupposing any connection between the truth and any pre-selected line of reasoning.

The foundation for this capacity, if it is to flourish, must be laid in the early years of a child's life. It depends on which of the child's behavior is rewarded and which penalized. It depends on how the child's identity comes to be shaped. It depends on the extent that children come to be persuaded, wittingly or unwittingly, that their goodness depends on believing what those who are in authority over them believe. When love and affection are contingent on specific beliefs, then those beliefs become an integral part of the child's identity. They become egocentric extensions of children. Children are thus denied an opportunity to separate their own being from belief structures that adults impose. They literally become dependent on them — intellectually and emotionally — and cannot later, without trauma, subject them to serious critical scrutiny. They are "condemned" to closedmindedness.

Our present process of raising children and of teaching them has, in my judgment, precisely this unhappy effect. Children come to adulthood today as intellectual, emotional, and moral cripples. They are not whole or free persons, in the sense delineated in this paper, and they fail to see that they are not. Like all whose belief-states are ego-identifications they conceive those who disagree with them, however rationally, as *biased*. They may have learned how to effect an adult veneer, how to put on socially accepted masks; at root, however, infantile, egocentric identifications and commitments rule them. They do not know how to conduct a serious discussion of their own most fundamental beliefs. Indeed most do not know what those beliefs are. They cannot empathize with the reasoning of those who seriously disagree with them. If adept at conceptual moves at all, their adeptness is in dodges, such as caricaturing the reasoning of those who seriously disagree with them. They know, like politicians, how to retreat into vagueness to protect their challenged beliefs. They have learned how to avoid "understanding". They refuse to be rationally persuaded *out of* an irrational belief. They have no patience for close and exacting distinctions. They become, at best, anxious, at worst, hostile and belligerent, when their own basic assumptions or beliefs or reasonings are, even quietly and respectfully, called into question.

This fundamental failure to achieve command of one's own faculties, to grasp the root of one's own thought and emotion, has been demonstrated in many graphic studies. I shall illustrate it with one of the most stunning, the experiments of Stanley Milgram on unquestioning obedience to malevolent authority. The results he obtained go to the heart of the question of intellectual, emotional, and moral autonomy.

Most people think of themselves as free agents. They believe that their beliefs have been self-selected as a result of reasonable judgements based on experience and reflective thought. They believe that their behavior is informed by a freely chosen moral perspective and that generally they act in accordance with that perspective. Hence, they believe that though there are evil people in the world, at least people who do evil things, they do not include themselves among them. They believe that they, for example, would never, like so many Germans, have participated in the Nazi extermination of Jews. If a serious conflict arose between the demands of an authority and their own conscience, they are confident that they would follow their conscience. Let us hear the experiment summarized in Milgram's own words:

> A person comes to a psychological laboratory and is told to carry out a series of acts that come increasingly into conflict with conscience. The main question is how far the participant will comply with the experimenter's instructions before refusing to carry out the actions required of him .... Two people come to a psychology laboratory to take part in a study of memory and learning. One of them is designated as a "teacher" and the other a "learner". The experimenter explains that the study is concerned with the effects of punishment on learning. The learner is conducted into a room, seated in a chair, his arms strapped to prevent excessive movement, and an electrode

attached to his wrist. He is told that he is to learn a list of word pairs; whenever he makes an error, he will receive electric shocks of increasing intensity.

The real focus of the experiment is the teacher. After watching the learner being strapped into place, he is taken into the main experimental room and seated before an impressive shock generator. Its main feature is a horizontal line of thirty switches, ranging from 15 volts to 450 volts, in 15-volt increments. There are also verbal designations which range from Slight Shock to Danger — Severe Shock. The teacher is told that he is to administer the learning test to the man in the other room. When the learner responds correctly, the teacher moves to the next item; when the other man gives an incorrect answer, the teacher is to give him an electric shock. He is to start at the lowest shock level (15 volts) and to increase the level each time that man makes an error, going through 30 volts, 45 volts, and so on.

The "teacher" is a genuinely naive subject who has come to the laboratory to participate in an experiment. The learner, or victim, is an actor who actually receives no shock at all. The point of the experiment is to see how far a person will proceed in a concrete and measurable situation in which he is ordered to inflict increasing pain on a protesting victim. At what point will the subject refuse to obey the experimenter?

Conflict arises when the man receiving the shock begins to indicate that he is experiencing discomfort. At 75 volts, the "learner" grunts. At 120 volts he complains verbally; at 150 he demands to be released from the experiment. His protests continue as the shocks escalate, growing increasingly vehement and emotional. At 285 volts his response can only be described as an agonized scream ....

Many subjects will obey the experimenter no matter how vehement the pleading of the person being shocked, no matter how painful the shocks seem to be, and no matter how much the victim pleads to be let out. This was seen time and again in our studies and has been observed in several universities where the experiment was repeated. It is the extreme willingness of adults to go to almost any lengths on the command of an authority that constitutes the chief finding of the study and the fact most urgently demanding explanation.

A commonly offered explanation is that those who shocked the victim at the most severe level were monsters, the sadistic fringe of society. But if one considers that almost two-thirds of the participants fall into the category of "obedient" subjects, and that they represented ordinary people drawn from working, managerial, and professional classes, the argument becomes very shaky.

Not only does this experiment reveal how little most people understand the roots of their own behavior, it also reveals how much human behavior today is typically determined by external authority. Whatever schooling Milgram's participants had, and some had a great deal, that schooling had little effect on their intellectual, emotional, or moral autonomy. Furthermore, it appears that Milgram's participants were heavily influenced by their desire to maintain the approach of the experimenter giving them orders. Having been children who came to do and think what they were told to do and think, Milgram's adult participants maintain their rapport with the experimenter rather than refuse orders which apparently endangered the life of an innocent victim:

> The subjects were so concerned about the show they were putting on for the experimenter that influences from other parts of the social field did not receive much weight. This powerful orientation to the experimenter would account for the relative insensitivity of the subject to the victim ....

This need not be so. The extent to which children ego-identify with this or that belief of authorities around them can be minimized. Children can be raised to value the authority of their own reasoning. They can be encouraged to value making up their own minds thoughtfully and reflectively. They can learn comprehensive principles of rational thought. They can learn to consider it "natural" that people differ in their beliefs and points of view. And they can learn to grasp this not as a quaint peculiarity of people but as a tool for learning. They can learn how to learn from others, even from their "objections", their contrary perceptions, their different ways of thinking.

They can and should learn all this, but they will do so only if parents and teachers recognize the problem created by belief inculcation and its consequent ego-identifications, and learn to nurture and respect the dialogical process.

But how can this be done? How can these obstacles be overcome? How can we teach dialectical reasoning and pave the way for human emancipation?

✦ Teaching Basic Academic Competencies as Incipient Higher Order Thinking Skills

Unless one achieves an understanding of the relationship of language to logic one will not develop the ability to analyze, criticize and advocate ideas. We must recognize differences between the structure and purposes of technical languages, the nature and use of concepts within them, and those of natural languages such as English, German, or Swahili. The differences parallel the differences between technical and dialectical issues, and the divergent modes of reasoning they require. Teachers should realize when, on the one hand, they are teaching a technical language, and so presupposing one standpoint and a specialized, technically defined hierarchy of problems and when, on the other, they are in a domain where multiple standpoints apply, and so where concepts are used in a non-technical way, and where opposing lines of thought need to be considered.

Whenever we think, we conceptualize and make inferences from our conceptualization, based on assumptions. In technical domains like math, physics, and chemistry, however, the concepts and assumptions are *given*. They are not generally to be challenged by an alternative point of view. The logic, on the one hand, and the technical language, on the other, are opposite sides of the same coin. But the affairs of everyday life, including the inner life of the mind, are fundamentally conducted within the logic of a natural language, and the key concepts are inevitably used non-technically and (when properly handled) dialectically.

How we read, write, speak, listen, and reason varies, or should vary, in accordance with these fundamental distinctions. Do I read, write, speak, listen, and reason so as to throw myself totally into one well-defined point of view and make its rules, regulations, and operations the controlling variables in my thinking? Or do I read, write, speak, listen, and reason so as to entertain comparisons and contrasts between ideas from competing perspectives? Do I reason monologically or dialogically?

Few students have any experience in this second and crucially important mode of reading, writing, speaking, listening, and reasoning, even though many of their everyday experiences presuppose such abilities. They often talk and listen to people who look at events and situations in a variety of ways. Their parents and peers often see situations differently. They are often frustrated by their inability to come to terms with these conflicts and dilemmas.

If we understand speaking and writing as constructing a point of view, developing ideas in some logical relation to each other, and listening and reading, as entering into someone else's point of view, into *their* organization of ideas, then we can see how the basic academic competencies ought to be understood as incipient higher order thinking.

Furthermore, we will recognize that when we are listening to or reading ideas which conflict with our ego-identified belief states, we have a different problem to combat than when the difficulty is not a matter of resistance but of technical complexity. Learning how to listen to and read (without distortion) lines of reasoning whose possible truth we egocentrically wish to rule out, is an essential experience, indeed the mother's milk of educational development. As in all areas of intellectual and emotional competency, these reading and listening capacities must be built up progressively and over a long time. They are acquired by degrees. They can always be further developed.

Assignments designed to facilitate basic academic competencies may set the stage for intellectual or emotional development, indeed contribute to that development, or they may simply issue in the superficial learning of these skills. They may be learned, in other words, as lower order, or as incipient higher order thinking skills.

✦ *Teaching Social Studies*

Few recognized that the area we call "social studies" or "social science" is, when rightly conceived, a combination of technical and dialectical issues. The major justification for including them as a universal requirement however is *not* for the technical training they might provide, but for the assumed knowledge, insight, and skills that can be gleaned from their study and applied in everyday personal and social life.

However, clearly one tacit function of instruction in this area is at base "indoctrinative". By this I mean that we teach much of the subject area in a way that assumes, states, or implies (as self-evidently true) claims of a self-serving, sometimes ethnocentric, nature. Of course, the formulations of "goals" are often vague enough so that it is unclear whether a "fact" or an "ideal" is being expressed (for example, "with liberty and justice for all"). Because instruction confuses the technical, the dialectical, and the ethnocentric, and students have no tools for distinguishing them, or little sense of how to proceed to rational judgments if they did, the result is largely non-educational.

Of course, we could understand our "heritage", in another sense, as a commitment to developing the maximum degree of personal and social freedom, as a commitment to intellectual, emotional, and moral autonomy. If that is our fundamental commitment, then, we must approach education dialectically, especially in historical and social studies.

All history is history from a point of view. Alternative perspectives and interpretations of our historical past compete for our assent. Students should be exposed to some of the differing perspectives and reason dialectically between them.

The American Revolution, for example, need not be studied simply from our point of view. The same events could be seen from a British point of view, or from the point of view of a colonial loyalist, or from the point of view of a Native American, whose homeland was being systematically taken by a "foreign" race. Our attitude toward "revolution" as a justifiable political act could be compared between 1776 and now. Students should consider whether the U.S. government's present disapproval of Third World revolutions contradicts its approval of its own.

Or further, students could study the history of the Cold War itself dialectically. More and more of the national budget goes for policies premised on one unexamined interpretation of the origin and nature of the Cold War. But how often, if ever, do students reason dialectically on this issue? This means, of course, that students learn that the issue is dialectical, that interpretations differ among distinguished historians and that they developed opposing lines of reasoning to justify them, that we can empathize with the Soviet perspective, argue their case, formulate their critique of our behavior and their defense of their own, and bring the Soviet case into dialogical contest with the strongest case of the U.S. side.

Or again, students might consider some opposing analyses of the nature of our society, clarifying some of the differences between conceptualizing events from a "Right" or a "Left" perspective. Some contemporary U.S. trends could be considered from both the the the Right and the Left. Instead of seeing these perspectives as empty terms charged with positive or negative stereotypes, students could begin to translate them into analytic tools of dialogical reasoning, and therefore develop an increasingly macro-logical integrative perspective.

Of course, dialectical skills must be developed gradually. One useful teaching tool is the daily newspaper. The news, like history, is perspectival (dialectical). The news is always news from a point of view. Students now have virtually no critical reading or listening or viewing skills for the news media. This process can begin very early. Sesame Street-like skits could be developed which show young children how we take events and "re-present" them and how that "re-presentation" can serve different purposes or ends, can be constructed to convey different implications and impressions.

We are worlds away from taking this task seriously. The sooner we begin the better.

✦ Teaching Science

As elsewhere we must clearly understand the extent to which we want technical competencies and the extent to which we want global (dialectical) competencies. If we merely want to produce as many scientists and engineers as we can, then we should proceed with the strategy that best serves that end. If we doubt that most students will become scientists, engineers, or even technicians, but must live in a technological world in which science and its uses are crucial to the quality of human life, then we will use a somewhat different strategy.

Both approaches need some common foundation, but even here the emphasis may differ. Students do not inevitably understand scientific concepts better, that is, achieve global perspective with respect to them, simply because they can solve increasingly complex textbook problems. Furthermore, going in the other direction, students can gain a great deal of understanding of science, from a global perspective, without being able to solve highly complex textbook problems.

As Ronald Giere, in *Understanding Scientific Reasoning,* points out:

> Learning physics — that is, to produce solutions to problems in physics — is indeed very difficult. But if it is presented correctly, it is possible for anyone to gain some understanding of what physics, especially classical Newtonian physics, is all about. Moreover, discovering that this is so can be a very liberating experience. If you can understand Newtonian physics you can probably understand most any scientific theory presented in a reasonable manner. So learning a little about physics may give you confidence that you can understand scientific theories and even evaluate arguments for or against theoretical hypotheses. An important component in developing the skill to reason intelligently about scientific issues is simply gaining the confidence that you can do it, even if you are not an expert.

With a fuller global grasp of the uses of scientific concepts, the student is better able to think critically about the application of scientific concepts in everyday life, including such mundane issues as these:

1) media reports of scientific discoveries,
2) advertisements that make scientific claims,
3) decisions about food, nutrition, and health,
4) assessment of doctors and of the credibility of their diagnoses, etc.

Finally, only with this global grasp can students begin to aspire to Einstein's call for critical thinking about scientific concepts themselves:

The eyes of the scientist are directed upon those phenomena which are accessible to observation, upon their apperception and conceptual formulation. In the attempt to achieve a conceptual formulation of the confusingly immense body of observational data, the scientist makes use of a whole arsenal of concepts which he imbibed practically with his mother's milk; and seldom if ever is he aware of the eternally problematic character of his concepts. He uses this conceptual material, or speaking more exactly, these conceptual tools of thought, as something obviously, immutably given; something having an objective value of truth which is hardly ever, and in any case not seriously, to be doubted. How could he do otherwise? How would the ascent of a mountain be possible, if the use of hands, legs, and tools had to be sanctioned step-by-step on the basis of the science of mechanics? And yet in the interest of science it is necessary over and over again to engage in the critique of these fundamental concepts, in order that we may not unconsciously be ruled by them. This becomes evident especially in those situations involving development of ideas in which the consistent use of the traditional fundamental concepts leads us to paradoxes difficult to resolve.

✦ *Dialectical Knowledge Is Not Opinion;*
It Is Integrative Synthesis

You may think that dialectical reasoning (the reasoning required when issues cross categories or disciplinary lines, issues for which different possible points of view can plausibly be developed) limits one to *opinions*. This would be a mistake. To ask a jury to decide whether a given defendant is innocent or guilty does not imply that we seek its "opinion" as such. We are seeking the jury-members' reasoned judgment, and we expect them to use the best comprehensive canons of reasoning and evidence to reach it. We expect them to enter empathically into the arguments of both the prosecution and defense, and we want the strongest possible case to be made for both. Jurors who fulfill these standards and conclude that the accused is guilty or innocent may properly be said to know what the verdict enunciates. They may know it as well as they know this or that technical truth. The knowledge is conditional of course, but so is technical knowledge.

A scientific experiment, for example, issues in scientific knowledge to the extent that *a)* its conditions were carefully and appropriately controlled, *b)* its results were accurately recorded, and *c)* accurately interpreted.

Most of the important knowledge we have results from integrative acts of the mind, and inevitably the more we integrate the more we must scrutinize what is left out, what highlighted, and how the whole is interpreted. The process is always subject to error. There are mistakes possible in all processes that lead to knowledge. Whenever we claim to know anything, our confidence is justified to the degree we have carefully attended to possible mistakes.

Synthesis across or beyond technical categories can be well or poorly justified. When outside the purely technical, part of the dues we must pay to jus-

tify rational confidence is empathy with the strongest case against our conclusion. Unfortunately, we rarely pay them. But when we do, we are not
merely "expressing an opinion", but rendering a rational "verdict".

Dialectically achieved synthesis depends on comprehensive rational principles, not specialized procedures and concepts, "principled", not "procedural" thought. Like law, it depends on our capacity to marshal cases and evidence that illustrate principles; unlike the law, it does not require any
technical concepts or procedures to do this. It depends on our ability to
achieve command of a natural language and of ourselves, and to use both as
resources to make rational assessments, to create a perspective that is neither egocentric nor ethnocentric.

✦ A Final Plea

When, as the result of a trial, the jury comes to a verdict of guilty or innocent; when, as a result of assessing a political debate, a citizen decides to
vote for one of the candidates; when, as a result of reading the case that can
be made for alternative political systems, one concludes that one is superior
to the others; when, as a result of hearing various sides of a family argument, one becomes persuaded that one way of putting things is more justified
and accurate; when, as a result of reading many reports on the need for educational reform, one is prepared to argue for one of them; when, as a result of
entertaining various representations of national security and the building of
more nuclear weapons, one reasons to a position on the issue; when, after
reading and thinking about various approaches to raising children, one opts
for one; when, after knowing a person for a number of years and exploring
various interpretations of his or her character, one decides that he or she
would make a good spouse — *one is reasoning dialectically*. Dialectical
thought is the master-principle of all rational experience and human emancipation. It cultivates the mind and orients the person as technical training
cannot. It meets our need to bring harmony and order into our lives, to work
out an amalgamation of ideas from various dimensions of experience, to
achieve, in short, intellectual, emotional, and moral integrity. The proper
doing of it is our only defense against closedmindedness.

An open society requires open minds. Collectively reinforced egocentric
and sociocentric thought, conjoined with massive technical knowledge and
power, are not the foundations for a genuine democracy. The basic insight
formulated over a hundred years ago by John Stuart Mill is as true, and as
ignored, today as it was when he first wrote it:

> In the case of any person whose judgment is really deserving of confi-
> dence, how has it become so? Because he has kept his mind open to criti-
> cism of his opinions and conduct. Because it has been his practice to listen
> to all that could be said against him; to profit by as much of it as was just,
> and expound to himself, and upon occasion to others, the fallacy of what

was fallacious. Because he has felt that the only way in which a human being can make some approach to knowing the whole of a subject, is by hearing what can be said about it by persons of every variety of opinion, and studying all modes in which it can be looked at by every character of mind. No wise man ever acquired his wisdom in any mode but this; nor is it in the nature of human intellect to become wise in any other manner.

If the schools do not rise to meet this social need, what social institution will? If this is not the fundamental task and ultimate justification for public education, what is?

✦ References

Beveridge, Albert J., U.S. Senator. "The March of the Flag," 1898.

Beyer, Barry. "Improving Thinking Skills — Defining the Problem." *Phi Delta Kappan,* March 1984.

Bloom, Benjamin. *All Our Children Learning.* New York: McGraw-Hill. 1981, pp. 22–24.

Campbell, Sarah, ed. *Piaget Sampler: An Introduction to Jean Piaget Through His Own Words.* New York: John Wiley & Sons, 1976.

Dewey, John. cf. *How We Think.* Boston: D. C. Heath & Co., 1933.

Dewey, John. *Logic: The Theory of Inquiry.* New York: Holt, Rinehart, & Winston, 1938, Chapters VI and XXIV.

Giere, Ronald. *Understanding Scientific Reasoning.* New York: Holt, Rinehart & Winston, 1978.

Hayes, John R. *The Complete Problem Solver.* Philadelphia: The Franklin Institute Press, 1981.

Jammer, M. *Concepts of Space: The History of Theories of Space in Physics.* Cambridge: Harvard University Press, 1957. p. xi.

Milgram, Stanley. *Obedience to Authority.* New York: Harper & Row, 1969.

Mill, John Stuart. *On Liberty.* Edited by Alburey Castell. Illinois: AHM Publishing Co., 1947. p. 20.

Polya, Gyorgy. *How to Solve It.* New York: Doubleday Anchor, 1957.

Sumner, William G. *Folkways and Mores.* Edited by Edward Sagarin. New York: Schoken Books, 1959.

Chapter 10

Critical Thinking and the Critical Person

Abstract

Written for Thinking: The Second International Conference (1987), this paper explores a series of themes familiar to Richard Paul's readers: that most school learning is irrational rather than rational, that there are two different modes of critical thinking and hence two different kinds of critical persons, that strong sense critical thinking is embedded in the ancient Socratic ideal of living an examined life, and that social studies instruction today is, in the main, sociocentric. Paul illustrates this last point with items from a state department of education critical thinking test and illustrations from a popular university-level introductory political science text. Paul closes with an argument in favor of a new emphasis on developing the critical thinking abilities of teachers: "If, in our haste to bring critical thinking into the schools, we ignore the need to develop long-term strategies for nurturing the development of teachers' own critical powers and passions, we shall surely make the new emphasis on critical thinking into nothing more than a passing fad, or worse, into a new, more sophisticated form of social indoctrination and scholastic closedmindedness."

✦ Introduction

*A*s the clarion call for critical thinking instruction from kindergarten to graduate school grows louder, those responsible for classroom instruction, heavily overworked as they typically are, naturally look for simple answers to the question, "What is critical thinking?", answers that generate routine and simple in-service strategies. Few see, in fact many *resist* seeing, how much of what is deeply ingrained in standard instructional procedures and theory needs serious reformation before students truly become critical thinkers in their daily personal, professional, and civic lives.

This chapter clarifies and develops some of the theoretical and practical implications of the concept of critical thinking. I consider the work of some of the leading critical thinking theorists. I contrast my views with the general approach of cognitive psychologists. I use social studies throughout to illustrate the problem. I, along with most critical thinking theorists, believe that global insights into the multifaceted obstacles to critical reflection, inquiry, and discussion on the part of students, teachers, and people in general are crucial to sound design of critical thinking instruction. Such insights are severely limited unless one clearly and coherently grasps the "big picture". For example, few pay attention to John Passmore's claims that "being critical can be taught only by persons who can themselves freely participate in critical discussion" and that, "In many systems of public instruction ... it is a principal object of teacher training to turn out teachers who will firmly discourage free critical discussion."[1] Rarely do teachers grasp where and when "free critical discussion" is essential, what it means to conduct it, and what is required to empower students to pursue it with understanding and self-command. What follows, I hope, contributes something to those foundational understandings, to the insights on which successful critical thinking instruction depends.

✦ *Rational and Irrational Learning*

All rational learning presupposes rational assent. And, though we sometimes forget it, all learning is not automatically or even commonly rational. Much that we learn in everyday life is quite irrational. It is quite possible — and indeed the bulk of human learning is unfortunately of this character — to come to believe any number of things without knowing how or why. It is quite possible, in other words, to believe for irrational reasons: because those around us believe, because we are rewarded for believing, because we are afraid to disbelieve, because our vested interest is served by belief, because we are more comfortable with belief, because we have ego identified ourselves, our image, or our personal being with belief. In all these cases, our beliefs are without rational grounding, without good reason and evidence, without the foundation a rational person demands. We become rational, on the other hand, to the extent that our beliefs and actions are grounded in good reasons and evidence; to the extent that we recognize and critique our own irrationality; to the extent that we are not moved by bad reasons and a multiplicity of irrational motives, fears, desires; to the extent that we have cultivated a passion for clarity, accuracy, and fairmindedness. These global skills, passions, and dispositions integrated into a way of acting and thinking characterize the rational, the educated, and in my sense, the critical person.[2]

No one, in this view, is ever *fully* educated. Hence, we should view rational learning not as something completed by schooling but as something struggling to emerge against deep-seated, irrational, and uncritical tendencies and drives. Schools can be structured to foster belief without regard to rational justification. To make rational belief a probable outcome of schooling requires special design and distinctive commitment.

✦ *Thinking Critically in the "Strong" Sense*

One cannot develop a coherent concept of critical thinking without developing a coherent concept of rationality, irrationality, education, socialization,

the critical person, and the critical society, as they bear on and mutually illuminate one another. This holistic approach distinguishes the mode of theorizing of most philosophers working on the concept of critical thinking from that
commonly used by most cognitive psychologists concerned with the nature of
thinking. Cognitive psychologists often treat cognitive processes and their
"pathology" separate from any consideration of the affective, social, or political life of the thinker. The research findings of clinical and social psychologists rarely integrate self-deception, egocentricity, or ethnocentricity into the
problem definitions or conclusions of cognitive psychology.[3] Consequently,
cognitive psychologists rarely focus on messy real-life multilogical problems
that cross disciplines, instead they restrict their attention to artificial or self-
contained monological problems, problems whose solutions can typically be
found in a field-specific conceptual framework without reference to major
personal or social bias. The more basic and difficult human problems, for
whose solutions there are competing frameworks, and in which the problem
of bias and vested interest looms large, are routinely ignored.

It is hard to go very far into the core concept of the critical person, however, without recognizing the centrality of multilogical thinking, the ability to
think accurately and fairmindedly within opposing points of view and contradictory frames of reference. Multilogical problems, whose fairminded treatment requires us to suspend our egocentric tendency to confuse the framework of our own thinking with "reality" and reason within opposing points of
view, are among the most significant human problems and among those most
resistant to solution. The problems of human understanding, of war and
peace, of economic, political, and social justice, of who our friends and who
our enemies are, of what we should accept as the most basic framework of
our thinking, of our own nature, our goodness and our evil, our history and
that of those we oppose, of how we should interpret our place in the world,
and how to best satisfy our needs and critically assess our desires — all such
problems are at the heart of the basic frustrations and conflicts that plague
human life and all require multi-system thinking. We cannot justifiably
assume the correctness of any one point of view as the only perspective within which these basic human problems can be most rationally settled. Schooling should improve the student's ability to distinguish monological from multilogical problems and to address each appropriately.

On this view, we distinguish two important senses of critical thinking, a
weak sense and a *strong* one. Those who think critically only with respect to
monological issues and, as a result, consider multilogical issues with a pronounced monological bias have merely mastered weak sense critical thinking. They would lack the ability, and presumably the disposition also, to critique their own most fundamental categories of thought and analysis. They
would, as a result, lack the ability to enter sympathetically into, and reconstruct, the strongest arguments and reasons for points of view fundamentally
opposed to their own. When their monological thinking arises from an unconscious commitment to a personal point of view, their thinking is egocentric;

when it arises from an unconscious commitment to a social or cultural point
of view, their thinking is ethnocentric. In either case they think more or less
exclusively within their own frames of reference. They might use the basic
vocabulary of critical thinking with rhetorical skill — their arguments and
reasons might impress those who already shared their framework of thought
— but they would lack the basic drives and abilities of what I call *strong
sense* critical thinking: *a)* an ability to question deeply one's own framework
of thought, *b)* an ability to reconstruct sympathetically and imaginatively the
strongest versions of points of view and frameworks of thought opposed to
one's own, and *c)* an ability to reason dialectically (multilogically) to determine when one's own point of view is weakest and when an opposing point of
view is strongest.

Strong sense critical thinkers are not routinely blinded by their own
points of view. They know that they *have* a point of view and therefore recognize on what framework of assumptions and ideas their own thinking rests.
They realize they must put their own assumptions and ideas to the test of
the strongest objections that can be leveled against them. Critical proponents
of a socialist economic system, for example, can analyze economic events
from the perspective of an insightful proponent of capitalism. Critical proponents of a capitalist economic system can analyze economic events from the
perspective of an insightful proponent of socialism. This implies, by the way,
that economics should not be taught in a way which presupposes capitalism,
socialism, or any other economic system as *the* correct one. In other words,
the issue as to what economic system is most justified is a multilogical issue.

Similarly, the strong sense critical thinker's thought is disciplined to avoid
confusing concepts that belong in different categories. For example, they do
not confuse "democracy", a political concept, with "capitalism", an economic
concept. They realize that any important connection between democracy and
capitalism must be argued for, not assumed, that *free enterprise* should not
be routinely injected into U.S. social studies texts as a neutral synonym for
capitalism, any more than *people's democracy* should be routinely injected
into Soviet social studies texts as a neutral synonym for *Soviet communism.*
They can recognize when terms are used in this question-begging way. A
teacher who values strong sense critical thinking fosters these abilities.

The importance of strong sense critical thinking has been underscored,
each in his own terms, by most leading critical thinking theorists: Robert
Ennis,[4] Harvey Siegel,[5] Israel Scheffler,[6] Michael Scriven,[7] Matthew Lipman,[8]
R. S. Peters,[9] John Passmore,[10] Edward Glaser,[11] Ralph Johnson,[12] J. Anthony
Blair,[13] and others. I exemplify the point briefly with four of them: Ennis,
Siegel, Scriven and Peters.

Robert Ennis defines critical thinking as "reasonable reflective thinking
that is concerned with what to do or believe". He argues that the various
component cognitive skills essential to critical thinking cannot lead to genuine "rational reflective thinking" unless used in conjunction with, as the
manifestation of, a complex of dispositions. For example, in and of them-

selves, the component cognitive skills of critical thinking can be used to serve either closedminded or openminded thought. Those with genuine openmindedness, Ennis claims, will: *a)* Seriously consider points of view other than their own ("dialogical thinking"); *b)* reason from premises with which they disagree — without letting the disagreement interfere with their reasons ("suppositional thinking"); *c)* withhold judgment when the evidence and reasons are insufficient.[14]

Harvey Siegel argues that students cannot become genuine critical thinkers unless they develop "the critical spirit", and that students will not develop the critical spirit unless they are taught in "the critical manner":

> The critical manner is that manner of teaching that reinforces the critical spirit. A teacher who utilizes the critical manner seeks to encourage in his or her students the skills, habits, and dispositions necessary for the development of the critical spirit. This means, first, that the teacher always recognizes the right of the student to question and demand reasons; and consequently recognizes an obligation to provide reasons whenever demanded. The critical manner thus demands of a teacher a willingness to subject all beliefs and practices to scrutiny, and so to allow students the genuine opportunity to understand the role reasons play in justifying thought and action. The critical manner also demands honesty of a teacher: reasons presented by a teacher must be genuine reasons, and a teacher must honestly appraise the power of those reasons. In addition, the teacher must submit his or her reasons to the independent evaluation of the student. Teaching in the critical manner is thus teaching so as to develop in the students skills and attitudes consonant with critical thinking. It is, as Scheffler puts it, an attempt to initiate students into the rational life, a life in which the critical quest for reasons is a dominant and integrating motive.[15]

Siegel's point is that for students to develop the passions of strong sense critical thinkers (the passion for accuracy, clarity, and fairmindedness), teachers must continually model those passions in their manner of teaching. The component micro-skills of critical thinking (the ability to clarify an issue, distinguish evidence from conclusions, recognize assumptions, implications, and contradictions, and so on) do not become the skills of a (strong sense) critical thinker, except insofar as they are integrated into "a life in which the critical quest for reasons is a dominant and integrating motive."

Michael Scriven represents (strong sense) critical thinking skills as not only requiring "a whole shift of values for most of us"[16] but also as essential for survival in a world in which "the wrong decision can mean injury or long-term commitment to a disastrous form of life such as addiction or criminality or resented parenthood."[17] For students to "transfer" their critical thinking skills to such situations, they need to practice fairminded thought on controversial (multilogical) issues:

> The real case, in dealing with controversial issues is the case as put by real people who believe in what they are saying. But the schools — and to a varying but often equal extent the colleges — are not willing to let there be

that kind of serious discussion of the argument on both sides of controversial issues. Of course, they don't mind having the bad guys' position represented by someone who doesn't agree with it, in the course of dismissing it. But only the completely naive would suppose that such a presentation is likely to make the best case for the position. The notions of a fair hearing, or of confronting your accuser which are so deeply entrenched in our system of justice obviously transfer immediately to the intellectual sphere. If you want to hear the arguments for a political position other than those of the majority parties, for example the political position that the largest countries on earth espouse, you cannot possibly assume that it will be fully and fairly represented by someone to whom it is anathema.[18]

Unfortunately, many teachers will naturally fear highlighting controversial issues in the classroom. It is fair to say, I believe, few teachers have had much experience working with such issues. Many know only processes for laying out and testing for "right" answers, not assessing contradictory arguments in terms of their relative strength in dialogical or dialectical settings. There are, in other words, both affective and cognitive obstacles to the genuine fostering of fairmindedness. Some of the affective obstacles are in educators themselves.

R. S. Peters has developed the significance of the affective side of reason and critical thought in his defense of the necessity of "rational passions":

> There is, for instance, the hatred of contradictions and inconsistencies, together with the love of clarity and hatred of confusion without which words could not be held to relatively constant meanings and testable rules and generalizations stated. A reasonable man cannot, without some special explanation, slap his sides with delight or express indifference if he is told that what he says is confused, incoherent and perhaps riddled with contradictions.
>
> Reason is the antithesis of arbitrariness. In its operation it is supported by the appropriate passions which are mainly negative in character — the hatred of irrelevance, special pleading and arbitrary fiat. The more developed emotion of indignation is aroused when some excess of arbitrariness is perpetuated in a situation where people's interests and claims are at stake. The positive side of this is the passion for fairness and impartial consideration of claims.
>
> A man who is prepared to reason must feel strongly that he must follow the arguments and decide things in terms of where they lead. He must have a sense of the giveness of the impersonality of such considerations. In so far as thoughts about persons enter his head they should be tinged with the respect which is due to another who, like himself, may have a point of view which is worth considering, who may have a glimmering of the truth which has so far eluded himself. A person who proceeds in this way, who is influenced by such passions, is what we call a reasonable man.[19]

What implications does this have for students and teachers? It entails that the affective life of the student must be brought into the heart of classroom instruction and dealt with in the context of the problem of thinking fairmindedly. Students must come to terms not only with how they feel about issues both inside and outside the curriculum, but also with the rationality or irrationality of those feelings. The teacher, on the other hand, must model rational passions and set the example of showing no favoritism to particular positions. The students must become convinced that the teacher is a fair and reasonable referee, an expert in nurturing the process by which truth and understanding is sought, not an authoritative judge of what is actually true or false. Questions rather than assertions should characterize the teacher's speech. The classroom environment should be structured so that students feel encouraged to decide for themselves what is and is not so. Teachers should treat no idea or point of view as in itself absurd, stupid, or "dangerous", whatever their personal views or those of the community. They should shield their students from the pressure to conform to peers or the community. Free and open discussion should be the sacred right in all classrooms.

It should be clear that strong sense critical thinking is embedded in a personal, social, and educational ideal. It is not simply a complex of atomistic cognitive skills. To think critically in this sense requires, as Passmore points out, "initiative, independence, courage, (and) imagination".[20] Let us now look briefly at the historical foundation for his concept.

✦ Critical Thinking and the Socratic Ideal

The concept of strong sense critical thinking, of critical thought integrated into the personal and social life of the individual, is not new. It was introduced into Western intellectual tradition in the chronicles of the life and death of Socrates (470-399 BC), one of the most important and influential teachers of ancient Greece. As a teacher, he was committed to the importance of ideas and their critique in the conduct of everyday human life. It is to him that the precept "the unexamined life is not worth living" is attributed. It is in him that the ideal of conscientious civil disobedience and critical autonomy of thought is first to be found. He illustrated the possibility and the value of sharpness of mind, clarity of thought, and commitment to practical insight based on autonomous reason. He championed reason, the rational life, and a rationally structured ethic, the intimate fusion of reason and passion. He disclaimed authority on his own part but claimed the right to independently criticize all authoritative beliefs and established institutions. He made it clear that teachers cannot be educators in the fullest sense unless they can criticize the received assumptions of their social groups and are willing to nurture a climate of questioning and doubt among their students. He demonstrated the intimate connection between a passionate love of truth and knowledge, the ability to learn through the art of skilled questioning, and the willingness to face personally and socially embarrassing truths. He spoke often with those who had a sophistic (weak sense) command of critical thinking skills, who could, through their skills of persuasion and knowledge of the vulnerabilities of people, make the false appear true and the true false.

Socrates taught by joining in discussions with others who thought they knew or understood a basic or important truth, for example, what justice is, or knowledge or virtue. When questioned by Socrates — who probed the justification and foundation for the belief, examining its consistency or inconsistency with other beliefs — it became clear that his discussants did not know or understand what they at first thought they did. As a result of Socrates' mode of questioning, his "students" realized that they lacked fundamental knowledge. Of course not all of Socrates' discussants appreciated the discovery. But those who did developed a new drive to seek out knowledge. This included an appreciation of dialectical thinking, a recognition of the need to subject putative knowledge to probing questioning, especially from the vantage point of opposing points of view. Socrates' students became comfortable with and adept in the art of dialectical questioning. All beliefs had first to pass the test of critical scrutiny through dialectical challenges before they were to be accepted.

The social reaction to Socrates' mode of teaching through probing questions illustrated the inevitable antagonism between schooling as socialization into accepted beliefs and practices and schooling as education in the art of autonomous thought. Although he did not foster any doctrines of his own (other than the values of intellectual integrity and critical autonomy), he was executed for "not believing in the gods the state believes in ... and also for corrupting the young" (see Plato's *Apology*).

Socrates' practice laid the cornerstone for the history of critical thought. He provided us with our first historic glimpse into how the organizing concepts by which humans live rarely reflect the organizing concepts through which they express their thoughts publicly. We must keep this example in mind when we conceptualize and elaborate the problem of learning to think critically. If we do, we certainly will not conceive of critical thinking in narrow intradisciplinary terms, nor will we ignore the significance of the affective dimensions of thought. It is intriguing to imagine classrooms in which the example of Socrates is highlighted and encouraged as a model of education.

✦ *The Egocentrically Critical Person*

Piaget's basic model for the egocentric mind, developed by studying the thinking of children, has significant application, with appropriate translation, to much adult thinking and therefore significant application for the design of critical thinking instruction. Few adults have experience in reciprocal critical thought, that is, in reasoning within their antagonists' point of view. Few have experience in making the structure of their own thought conscious. Few, as Socrates discovered, can explain intelligibly how they came to their beliefs, or provide rational justifications for them.

The egocentrism of most adult thought parallels the egocentrism of childish thought, as Piaget characterized it in *Judgment and Reasoning in the Child*:

Egocentrism of thought necessarily entails a certain degree of unconsciousness with the egocentric thinker 'in a perpetual state of belief', (p. 137)

[The egocentric thinker:]

- [is] confident in his own ideas,
- [is] naturally...(untroubled) about the reasons and motives which have guided his reasoning process,
- [seeks] to justify himself in the eyes of others ... only under the pressure of argument and opposition...,
- [is] incapable either by introspection or retrospection of capturing the successive steps...[his] mind has taken (pp. 137–138)
- [is] not conscious of the meaning assigned to the concepts and words used ... (p. 149)
- suffers from illusions of perspective, (p. 165)
- ignorant of his own ego, takes his own point of view to be absolute, and fails to establish...that reciprocity which alone would ensure objectivity (p. 197)
- [is] intelligent without being particularly logical,
- [uses] thought ... at the service of desire,
- simply believes ... without trying to find the truth, (p. 203)
- assimilates everything he hears to his own point of view. (p. 208)

He does not try to prove whether such and such of his idea does or does not correspond to reality. When the question is put to him, he evades it. It does not interest him, and it is even alien to his whole mental attitude. (p. 247)[21]

We naturally tend to think egocentrically, especially in domains of significant personal or social interests. Egocentrism is, in some sense, as typical of adult as childish thought. It takes a special cultivated discipline to recognize and attempt to correct for it. This becomes apparent when one formulates basic safeguards against egocentric thought and attempts to cultivate an interest in students or people in general in using them. Consider, for example, the platitude "one cannot disagree with a position one does not understand," that in other words "judgment presupposes understanding". Cultivating it as a critical principle means taking steps to ensure one clearly understands what someone else is saying before one "disagrees". In my experience most people, including some with a good deal of schooling, tend to uncritically assume understanding when they have done little or nothing to test it, and as a result, are much too quick to "disagree". Most people are surprised if, after they disagree with something said, the speaker says, "What exactly did you take me to be saying that you are disagreeing with?" Often they will be puzzled and say, "Well, perhaps you should say it again," or words to that effect.

Or consider a more profound safeguard against egocentric thought, an attempt to probe the justification for one's belief by sympathetically formulating the strongest arguments for rejecting that belief from opposing points of view. After confidently stating a belief few can summarize strong arguments and reasons that have persuaded intelligent, rational others to believe in opposing positions.

Each of us, to the extent that we are egocentric, spontaneously think along lines that serve to justify our fears, desires, and vested interests. Few have developed a "Socratic" character. As a result, most everyday critical thought is egocentric. We unconsciously tend to think in the following ways: "Your thinking is well founded and insightful to the extent that it agrees with or supports my own. If it does not, then, as a matter of course, it is 'wrong' and I am obliged to criticize it." Much adult "critical" thought is not fairminded but rather egocentrically motivated and structured, lacking fairmindedness at its very core. Is it not also fair to say that few adults had opportunities in school to grapple with their own tendencies to think irrationally?

✦ *The Sociocentrically Critical Person and the Ideal of a Critical Society*

In my view, Piaget rightly identifies uncritical thought with a tendency toward egocentrism, and critical thought with a tendency toward reciprocity. He recognizes, but does not explore, how egocentricity develops into and partially merges with sociocentricity:

> The child begins with the assumption that the immediate attitudes arising out of our own special surroundings and activities are the only ones possible. This state of mind, which we shall term the unconscious egocentricity (both cognitive and affective) of the child is at first a stumbling-block both to the understanding of his own country and to the development of objective relations with other countries. Furthermore, to overcome his egocentric attitude it is necessary to train the faculty for cognitive and affective integration; this is a slow and laborious process consisting mainly in efforts at 'reciprocity', and at each new stage of the process, egocentricity re-emerges in new guises farther and farther removed from the child's initial center of interest. There are the various forms of sociocentricity — a survival of the original egocentricity — and they are the cause of subsequent disturbances or tensions, any understanding of which must be based on an accurate analysis of the initial stages and of the elementary conflicts between egocentricity and understanding of others (Reciprocity).[22]

One manifestation of the irrational mind is to uncritically presuppose the truth of beliefs and doctrines embedded in social life or values. We intellectually and affectively absorb common frames of references from the social settings in which we live. Our interests and purposes find a place within a socially absorbed picture of the world. We use that picture to test the claims of contesting others. We imaginatively rehearse situations within portions of that picture. We rarely, however, describe that picture *as* a picture, as an image constructed by one social group as against that of another. We cannot easily place that picture at arm's length, so to speak, and for a time suspend our acquiescence to it. (For example, I cannot avoid feeling uncomfortable when an acquaintance of another culture stands "too close" to me while we talk, just as that acquaintance cannot avoid feeling somewhat offended that I continually move "too far away" for conversation. To each of us, the proper distance seems obviously and objectively proper.) That our thought is often disturbed and distorted by ethnocentric tendencies is rarely an abiding recognition. At best, it occurs in most people in fleeting glimpses, to judge by how often it is recognized explicitly in everyday thought.

Although many talk about and research ethnocentrism or sociocentrism as a problem in education, there are no reasonable, effective means of combatting it. Institutions and beliefs tend to become "sacred" and "cherished"; the thinking that critiques them seems "dangerous", "subversive", or at least "disturbing" and "unsettling". Habits, customs, and faiths become deeply embedded in how we define ourselves, and intolerance, censorship, and oppression never seem to be such by those who carry them out in the name of "true belief".

Socrates is not the only thinker to imagine a society in which independent critical thought became embodied in the day-to-day lives of individuals; others, including William Graham Sumner, North America's distinguished conservative anthropologist, have formulated the ideal:

> The critical habit of thought, if usual in a society, will pervade all its mores, because it is a way of taking up the problems of life. Men educated in it cannot be stampeded by stump orators and are never deceived by dithyrambic oratory. They are slow to believe. They can hold things as possible or probable in all degrees, without certainty and without pain. They can wait for evidence and weigh evidence, uninfluenced by the emphasis or confidence with which assertions are made on one side or the other. They can resist appeals to their dearest prejudices and all kinds of cajolery. Education in the critical faculty is the only education of which it can be truly said that it makes good citizens.[23]

Until critical habits of thought pervade our society, however, schools, as social institutions, will tend to transmit the prevailing world view more or less uncritically, transmit it as reality *itself,* not as a *picture* of reality. Our ability to solve social and international problems becomes constrained by the solutions credible and plausible within our prevailing ideas and assumptions. When solutions are suggested from contrary world views, they appear patently false to us because they appear to be based on false ideas, that is, ideas that don't square with "reality" (with our ideas of reality). Of course, those who live in other societies will themselves interpret our proposed solutions as patently false because they appear to them to be based on false ideas; that is, ideas that don't square with reality (with their ideas of reality). Hence, one society's freedom-fighters are another society's terrorists, and vice versa. Each is outraged at the flagrant propaganda of the other and is forced to conclude that the other must be knowingly distorting the facts, and hence is evil to the core. Citizens in any country who question the prevailing labels commonly have their patriotism questioned, or worse.

Ideas, in other words, do not enter into school life in neutral but in socially biased ways. Helping students think critically entails developing their ability to recognize and so to question this process.

Sociocentrically critical people may use the vocabulary of critical thinking. They may develop facility in its micro-skills. But they inadvertently function as apologists for the prevailing world view, nevertheless. They may conceive of themselves as hard-headed realists, fundamentally beyond "ideology" or naive "idealism", but the lack of reciprocity in their thought demonstrates their closedmindedness.

A critical society emerges only to the extent that it becomes socially unacceptable to routinely presuppose, rather than explicitly identify and argue for, one's fundamental ideas and assumptions. In the schools of a critical society, both teachers and students would recognize multilogical issues as demanding dialogical rather than monological treatment. Reasoning within opposing points of view would be the rule, not the rare exception. Social studies instruction in particular would play a significant role in fostering reciprocal multilogical thinking and so would contribute in a special way to the nurturing in the citizenry of values and skills essential to the conduct of everyday life in a critical manner.

✦ Social Studies and the
Fostering of Rational Belief

We can assess any school program for its educative value by determining the extent to which it fosters *rational* as against *irrational* belief formation. To the extent that students merely memorize what the teacher or textbook says, or presuppose the correctness of one point of view, and so develop no sense of what would justify rational belief, to that extent the school fosters irrational learning and irrational belief.

Social studies instruction is an excellent area to canvass in this regard because societies naturally inculcate an uncritical monological nationalistic perspective, despite the multilogical nature of the major issues in the field. The tendency is natural because people within a country or culture naturally ego identify with it and hence assume rather than question the policies of its leaders. Thus, the history of those policies and of the social representation of them continually gravitates in a self-serving direction. Reason inadvertently serves an intellectually dishonorable function: the rationalization of the prevailing structure of power and the idealization of national character. Karl Mannheim identified this as the inevitable development of *ideology*.[24] Louis Wirth suggests the practical problems for thought that it engenders:

> Even today open, frank, and "objective" inquiry into the most sacred and cherished institutions and beliefs is more or less seriously restricted in every country of the world. It is virtually impossible, for instance, even in England and America, to enquire into the actual facts regarding communism, no matter how disinterestedly, without running the risk of being labelled a communist. (p. XIV, preface)[25]

Yet, the field is clearly multilogical; that is to say, the issues in the field can be intellectually defined, analyzed, and "settled" from many perspectives. There are inevitably — to put it another way — *schools* of social thought. Whether one looks at the classic theorists (Durkheim, Weber, Marx, Mannheim, Sumner, etc.), or more recent theorists (Sorokin, Parsons, Mills, Merton, Pressman, Garfinkel, Berger, etc.), clearly there is no one agreed-upon frame of reference in which social behavior can be represented and understood. Those more "conservative" inevitably come to different conclusions about people and world events than those more "liberal". There is no way to abstract all discussion and study from basic disputes arising from conflicting frames of reference. For students to rationally understand social events, they must not only recognize this but also enter the debate actively. They need to hear, and themselves make the case for, a variety of conservative, liberal, and radical interpretations of events. They need to develop the critical tools for assessing differences among these views. These skills develop only with dialectical practice. There is no alternative.

When students cover a conflict between two countries — especially when one is their own — they should hear the case not just for one but both countries' perspectives. Often other perspectives are also relevant.

U.S. textbook writers canvassing the Cold War, for example, do not identify themselves as arguing for one selective representation of it. They do not identify themselves as having a pro-U.S. bias. They do not suggest that they represent only one out of a number of points of view. They imply rather that they give an "objective" account, as though the issues were intrinsically monological and so settlable by considering merely one point of view. They imply that the reader need not consider other points of view on the Cold War. They imply that the facts speak for themselves and that they (the textbooks) contain the facts, all the facts, and nothing but the facts. There is nothing dialogical about their modes of canvassing the material nor in the assignments that accompany the account the student is inevitably led to believe.

That some of the most distinguished historians have concluded that the United Sates bears a large share of the blame for the Cold War is never, to my knowledge, even casually mentioned. It would seem bizarre to most students in the United States, and their teachers, to hear a distinguished historian like Henry Steele Commager speak of the Cold War as follows:

> How are we to explain our obsession with communism, our paranoid hostility to the Soviet Union, our preoccupations with the Cold War, our reliance on military rather than political or diplomatic solutions, and our new readiness to entertain as a possibility what was long regarded as unthinkable — atomic warfare?[26]

The notion that U.S. citizens might be obsessed or the victims of "paranoid hostility" completely contradicts how textbooks in the U.S. characterize the country, its philosophy, behavior, and values.

Or consider Arnold Toynbee's characterization:

> In examining America's situation in the world today, I can say, with my hand on my heart, that my feelings are sympathetic, not malicious. After all, mere regard for self-interest, apart from any more estimable considerations, would deter America's allies from wishing America ill .... (But) today America is no longer the inspirer and leader of the World Revolution ... by contrast, America is today, the leader of a world-wide, anti-revolutionary movement in defense of vested interests. She now stands for what Rome stood for. Rome consistently supported the rich against the poor in all foreign communities; and since the poor, so far, have always been far more numerous than the rich, Rome's policy made for inequality, for injustice, and for the least happiness for the greatest numbers. America's decision to adopt Rome's role has been deliberate, if I have gauged it right.[27]

These views would shock most U.S. citizens. Their schooling has given them no inkling that the United States' and Britain's most distinguished historians could have such a low estimation of our policies. They *would* understand the recent California State Assembly resolution, endorsed on a vote of 52–0, that the Vietnam war was waged for a noble purpose.

Similar points can be made about every major issue in history and social studies. They can all be approached from more than one point of view. All history, to put it another way, is history-written-from-a-point-of-view, just as all social perception is perception-from-a-point-of-view. There are, inevitably, different philosophies of history and society based on different presuppositions about the nature of people and human society. Different schools of historical and social research inevitably use different organizing concepts and root metaphors.

Therefore, a rational approach to historical, sociological, and anthropological issues must reflect this diversity of approach. Just as juries must hear both the pro and con cases before coming to a judgment, irrespective of the strength of the case for either, so, too, must we insist, as rational students of history and human society, on hearing the case for more than one interpretation of key events and trends so that our own view may take into account this relevant evidence and reasoning. Intellectual honesty demands this, education requires it. It is irrational to assume *a priori* the correctness of one of these perspectives, and intellectually irresponsible to make fundamental frame of reference decisions for our students.

Once students consider conflicting perspectives, they should actually argue the cases for them, role playing the thought of those who insightfully hold them. This requires students to learn how to collect the "facts" each side marshals to defend its views and analyze their divergent use of key terms. For example, what exactly differentiates those we label *freedom fighters* from those we label *terrorists*? How can we define them without presupposing the truth of someone's ideology? These crucial terms and many others current in social disputes are often used in self-serving ways by nations and groups, begging most of the crucial social and moral issues. Students need skills in breaking down ideologically biased uses of language. This requires them to develop concepts that do not presuppose specific national ideological slants. This, in turn, requires them to engage in the argumentation for and against their application in key cases.

Unfortunately, even when critical thinking becomes an explicit instructional objective and significant attention is given to formulation of curriculum, unless teachers and curriculum specialists have internalized the concept of strong sense critical thinking, instruction usually fosters sociocentric weak sense critical thinking skills rather than strong sense skills. Consider the following critical thinking writing prompts from a series of similarly constructed items for a state-wide testing program:

Critical Thinking Writing Prompt
History-Social Science

The Cold War: Cuban Missile Crisis

Directions: Read the conversation below that might have taken place between two United States citizens during the Cuban missile crisis in 1962.

Speaker 1:   These photographs in the newspaper show beyond a doubt that Russians are building missile bases in Cuba. It's time we took some strong action and did something about it. Let's get some bombers down there.

Speaker 2:   I agree that there are Russian missiles in Cuba, but I don't agree with the solution you suggest. What would the world think about America dropping bombs on a neighboring small island?

Speaker 1:   I think the only way to deal with the threat of force is force. If we do nothing, it's the same as saying it's okay to let them put in missiles that will threaten the whole hemisphere. Let's eliminate those missile bases now with military force.

Speaker 2:   The solution you propose would certainly eliminate those bases, but innocent people might be killed, and world opinion might be against us. What if we try talking to the Russians first and then try a blockade of their ships around Cuba, or something like that?

Speaker 1:   That kind of weak response won't get us anywhere. Communists only understand force.

Speaker 2:   I think we should try other less drastic measures that won't result in loss of life. Then, if they don't work, use military action.

Imagine that you are a concerned citizen in 1962. Based on the information above, write a letter to President Kennedy about the missile crisis. Take a position and explain to President Kennedy what you think should be done about the missiles in Cuba and why.

> • State your position clearly.
> • Use information from the conversation above and from what you know about the missile crisis to support your position.

Critical Thinking Writing Prompt
History-Social Science

Directions: Read the information below and answer the questions that follow.

The Cold War: Cuban Missile Crisis

In 1962 an international crisis erupted when the Soviet Union installed missile-launching equipment in Cuba. Because Cuba is only 90 miles from Florida, many Americans felt threatened by the missile bases. On October 26, 1962, President Kennedy sent the following letter to the Soviet Union's premier, Nikita Khrushchev:

"You would agree to remove these weapons systems from Cuba under appropriate United Nations' supervision ... the first ingredient is the cessation of work on missile cites in Cuba ...."

Nikita Khrushchev responded in a letter shortly thereafter by saying:

"We accept your proposal, and have ordered the Soviet vessels bound for Cuba but not yet within the area of American warships' piratical activities to stay out of the interception area."

1. Based on the information above about the Cuban missile crisis, what do you think the central issue or concern is?

2. List two facts in the information about the missile crisis.

3. Do you see any words in either President Kennedy's or Premier Khrushchev's letters that might be considered biased or "loaded"? Find which one or ones are "loaded" and list why they are "loaded".

4. Based on the information above, which side do you think is the aggressor? Why?

5. Khrushchev had spoken earlier of the need for "peaceful coexistence" between the U.S. and USSR. Is arming Cuba with missiles *consistent* with this statement about peaceful coexistence? Why or why not?

6. If you had an opportunity to interview Khrushchev in 1962, what question would you ask to find out why he placed missiles in Cuba?

_____

_____

7. President Kennedy was convinced that there actually were missile bases in Cuba. If you were President Kennedy in 1962, what information would *you* need to conclude that missile bases actually existed in Cuba?

_____

_____

8. If Cuba had been permitted to install missile bases, what affect would this have had on Cuba's relationships with other countries?

_____

_____

_____

Critical Thinking Writing Prompt

History-Social Science

The Cold War: Cuban Missile Crisis

Directions: Read the information below about missiles in Cuba and answer the questions that follow.

_____

In 1962, an international crisis erupted when the Soviet Union installed missile-launching equipment in Cuba. Some of the facts relating to the incident are:

1. Photographs of Cuba taken by United States planes show missile sites under construction in Cuba.
2. Long-range missiles are observed near the sites.
3. Russian supply ships are bringing missile base equipment and technicians to Cuba.
4. Cuba is only 90 miles from the United States.
5. The President's military advisers recommend that the missiles be removed.

_____

1. What is the central issue?

_____

2. Write one question you might want to ask the United States military advisers.

_____

3. Write one question you might want to ask Soviet Premier Khrushchev.

_____

4. What does the United States assume that Cuba will do with the missiles?

_____

_____

5. List two actions the United States might have taken in response to this crisis.

_____

_____

6. List two facts that support one of the actions identified in item 5.

_____

7. Imagine you are a concerned citizen who has been following the above events with great interest. You decide to write a letter to the editor of the local newspaper. Write your letter on this sheet of paper. In your letter, take a stand on the situation in Cuba and clearly explain your reasons.

- State your position clearly.
- Use information from the list and from what you know about the missile crisis to support your position.

Editor
Daily Bugle
Yourtown, USA

Dear Editor:

_____

_____

_____

_____

In every case, the student has *none* of the facts to which a Soviet might call attention, or any sense of how a Soviet might use them to develop an opposing line of reasoning.

Imagine, in contrast, a test item that provided a list of facts to which United States observers might allude (such as those preceding), followed by a list of facts to which Soviets might allude, including perhaps these: *a)* the United States already had placed many of its own missiles within 90 miles of the Soviet border; *b)* Cuba is a sovereign country; *c)* the United States had rejected Soviet complaints that it had put missiles too close to their borders by saying that the countries where the missiles were placed were sovereign countries.

After giving students the two lists of facts, one could give short arguments in favor of the opposed positions. Then the students might be asked to answer the same kinds of questions as the original prompt. Other contrasting lists of facts could be provided regarding many of the tense situations that have characterized the Cold War, and the students could be given a variety of dialogical writing and role-playing assignments. Through such assignments the students could come to understand how Soviets actually reason about the conflicts and tensions that have characterized the history of the two countries. They would learn not to presuppose that their country is always right. They would develop a much more realistic sense of how governments of all kinds often act in ways they themselves (the various governments) would disapprove of were "the enemy" to do what they do.

One of the major ways in which sociocentric bias is introduced into social studies texts is through the fostered illusion of "scientific" objectivity. Nothing suggests that the authors are taking a position on issues about which reasonable people could disagree, or at least that they are taking such a position only when they explicitly admit to it.

The textbook *American Democracy In World Perspective*,[28] written by four professors at the University of California for use in college political science courses, is an exemplary case in this regard. Virtually everything in its 700-plus pages is oriented toward persuading the reader that the United States has the best form of government, comes closest to "perfect" democracy, and that the fate of freedom in the world depends on the United States: "As democracy fares in the United States, so will it, in the long run, fare throughout the world."

The text divides all governments into two basic types, democratic and non-democratic, the non-democratic ones are divided into authoritarian and totalitarian ones, in accord with the figure 1.[29]

Numerous features stand out in this chart. *Democracy* is a term that we apply to ourselves (a *positive* term with which virtually all people identify). *Authoritarian* and *totalitarian* are *negative* terms with which virtually no one identifies. The United Sates is characterized by a term that expresses an ideal, whereas its enemies, the USSR and its allies, are characterized by terms that in effect condemn them. The chart, presented as purely descriptive, obscures its tendentious character. By the same token, the distinction between authoritarianism and totalitarianism provides, under the guise of pure description, a means whereby support of dictators by the United States can be justified as the "better" of two evils. It does not take too much imagination to reconstruct how an equally tendentious chart might be fabricated for a "neutral" Soviet social studies text (see figure 2).

The authors also imply that most Americans believe in *reason and experience,* whereas Communists believe in *dogmatism:*

> By using reasons and experience, man has scored impressive advances in the mastery of nature .... Democrats believe that reason and experience can be fruitfully used in the understanding and harmonious adjustment of human relations .... In contrast, dogmatists (such as Communists or Fascists) reject this belief in reason and experience.[30]

At the same time, the text gives lip service to the need for free discussion of issues in social studies.

> In trying to present a fair and balanced picture of American democracy, we have not sought to avoid controversial issues. The United States owes its existence to controversy and conflict, and throughout its history, as today, there has never been a dearth of highly controversial questions.[31]

I know of no textbook presently used in a large public school system that focuses on the multilogical issues of social studies or highlights the importance of strong sense critical thinking skills. Monological thinking that presupposes

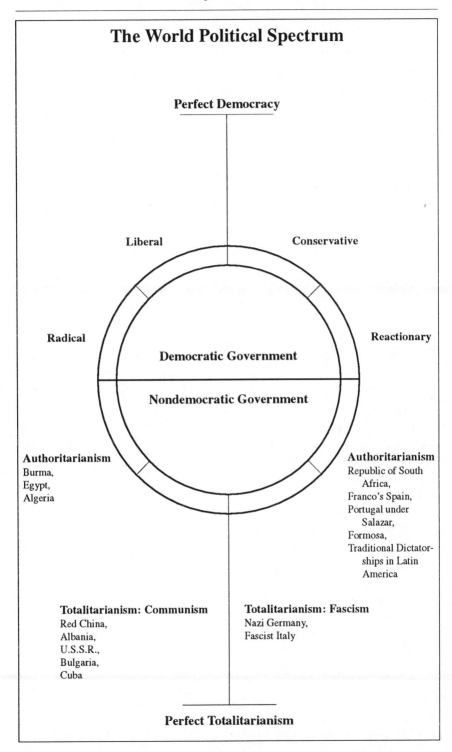

The World Political Spectrum

Perfect Democracy

Liberal

Conservative

Radical

Reactionary

Democratic Government

Nondemocratic Government

Authoritarianism
Burma,
Egypt,
Algeria

Authoritarianism
Republic of South
Africa,
Franco's Spain,
Portugal under
Salazar,
Formosa,
Traditional Dictator-
ships in Latin
America

Totalitarianism: Communism
Red China,
Albania,
U.S.S.R.,
Bulgaria,
Cuba

Totalitarianism: Fascism
Nazi Germany,
Fascist Italy

Perfect Totalitarianism

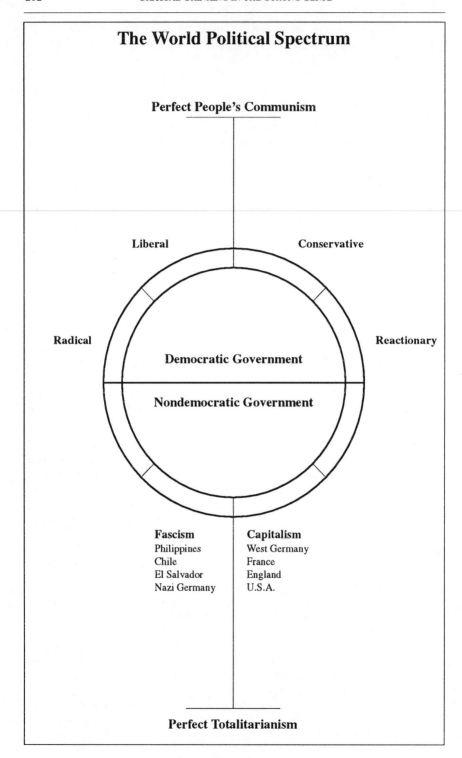

The World Political Spectrum

Perfect People's Communism

Liberal   **Conservative**

Radical   **Reactionary**

Democratic Government

Nondemocratic Government

Fascism   **Capitalism**
Philippines   West Germany
Chile   France
El Salvador   England
Nazi Germany   U.S.A.

Perfect Totalitarianism

a U.S. world view clearly dominates. At the same time, students do not recognize that they are learning, not to think, but to think like "Americans", within one out of many possible points of view.

✦ *Concluding Remarks: The Critical Teacher*

To be in the best position to encourage critical thinking in their students, teachers must first value it highly in their personal, social, and civic lives. A teacher of critical thinking must be a critical person, a person comfortable with and experienced in critical discussion, critical reflection, and critical inquiry; must be willing to make questions rather than assertions the heart of his or her contribution to student learning; must explicitly understand his or her own frame of reference and that fostered in the society at large; must be willing to treat no idea as intrinsically good or bad; must have confidence in reason, evidence, and open discussion; must deeply value clarity, accuracy, and fairmindedness; and must be willing to help students develop the various critical thinking micro-proficiencies in the context of these values and ideals. To do so, teachers must be students of human irrationality, egocentricity, and prejudice. Their interest must be both theoretical and practical. They must experience (and recognize) irrational drives and behavior in themselves as well as others. A teacher must be patient and capable of the long view, for people, schools, and society change only in the long run, never quickly, and always with some frustration, conflict, and misunderstanding.

Few now realize that the critical teacher is rare and that most of the critical thinking cultivated in students today is, at best, monological and technical, and, at worst, sociocentric and sophistic. The concept of strong sense critical thinking — of what it is to live or teach critically — has as yet had little perceptible influence on schools as a whole. If, in our haste to bring critical thinking into the schools, we ignore the need to develop long-term strategies for nurturing the development of teachers' own critical powers and passions, then we shall truly make the new emphasis on critical thinking into nothing more than a passing fad, or worse, into a new, more sophisticated form of social indoctrination and scholastic closedmindedness.

✦ *Footnotes*

[1] John Passmore, "On Teaching to be Critical," included in *The Concept of Education*, Routledge & Kegan Paul, London: 1967, pp. 192–211.

[2] For a sense of the dimensions requiring critical thinking, see the Phi Kappa Phi *National Forum* special issue on *Critical Thinking*, edited by myself, and including articles by Neil Postman, Sabini and Silver, Matthew Lipman, Edward Glaser, Robert Ennis, Michael Scriven, Ernest Boyer, and myself. Winter 1985.

See also my "Critical Thinking; Fundamental to Education For a Free Society," *Educational Leadership*, September 1984; "Teaching Critical Thinking in the Strong Sense," *Informal Logic*, 1982, Vol. 4, p. 3; and "Bloom's Taxonomy and Critical Thinking Instruction," *Educational Leadership*, May 1985.

3 "Dialogical Thinking: Critical Thought Essential to the Acquisition of Rational Knowledge and Passions," delivered at the *Connecticut Thinking Skills Conference,* March 11–13, 1985, forthcoming in *Teaching Thinking Skills: Theory and Practice,* W.H. Freeman, New York, edited by Joan Baron and Robert J. Sternberg. 1987.

4 Robert Ennis heads the Illinois Critical Thinking Project, co-authored the Cornell Critical Thinking Tests, and has written many seminal articles on critical thinking, beginning with his "A Concept of Critical Thinking," *Harvard Educational Review,* 1962, Vol. 32(1), 81–111.

5 Harvey Siegel has developed a number of ideas implicit in the writings of Israel Scheffler. Most important for critical thinking theory is Siegel's contribution "Critical Thinking as Educational Ideal," *The Educational Forum,* November 1980, pp. 7–23.

6 See Israel Scheffler's *Reason and Teaching,* Bobbs-Merrill, New York: 1973; and *Conditions of Knowledge,* Scott Foresman, Chicago: 1965.

7 See Scriven's "Critical For Survival" in the *National Forum's* special issue on critical thinking and his textbook, *Reasoning,* McGraw-Hill, New York: 1976.

8 Matthew Lipman has developed a multitude of innovative instructional strategies for bringing critical reflection into classroom discussions, third through twelfth grades, in the process of creating the *Philosophy for Children Program.*

9 See R. S. Peters' *Reason and Compassion,* Routledge & Kegan Paul, London: 1973.

10 Passmore, op. cit.

11 Edward Glaser is one of the founding fathers of the critical thinking movement in the United States. Its early stirrings can be traced back to his *An Experiment in the Development of Critical Thinking* (1941) and his development with Watson of the *Watson-Glaser Critical Thinking Test* (1940).

12,13 Ralph Johnson and J. Anthony Blair have been the major Canadian leaders in the Informal Logic/Critical Thinking movement. They have organized two major international conferences at the University of Windsor, have written many important papers in the field, edit *Informal Logic* (the major journal for those working on the theory of critical thinking), and have written an excellent text, *Logical Self-Defense,* McGraw-Hill, Toronto: 1977.

14 Ennis, "Critical Thinking," a handout developed in July 1985. *Illinois Critical Thinking Project,* University of Illinois/Champaign.

15 "Critical Thinking as Educational Ideal," op. cit., p. 11.

16 *Reasoning,* op. cit., p. ix.

17 "Critical for Survival," op. cit., p. 9

18 Ibid.

19 *Reason and Compassion,* op. cit., p. 79.

20 op. cit., p. 198

21 Piaget, Jean. *Judgment and Reasoning in the Child,* Littlefield, Adams, Totowa, NJ: 1976. Compare R. S. Peters: "The connection of being unreasonable with egocentricity is obvious enough. There is lacking even the stability in behavior that comes from acting in the light of established beliefs and practices. Beliefs tend to be infected with arbitrariness and particularity. Little attempt is made to fit them into a coherent system. A behavior is governed largely by wants and aversions of an immediate, short-term character. Little account is taken of the viewpoint or claims of others. Indeed, the behavior of others is seen largely in a self-referential way as it impinges on, threatens or thwarts the demands of the greedy, restless ego, ..." op. cit., p. 97.

22 Piaget, from "The Development in Children of the Idea of the Homeland and of Relations with Other Countries," *The International Social Science Bulletin*, Vol. III, no. 3, 1951, pp. 561–578.

23 William Graham Sumner, *Folkways,* originally 1906, reissued by Dover Publications, New York: 1959, p. 633.

24 See Karl Mannheim's magnificent classic *Ideology and Utopia,* a seminal work whose contribution to the theory of critical thinking has yet to be absorbed.

25 Ibid., Louis Wirth in his preface to Mannheim's *Ideology and Utopia.*

26 Commager, Henry Steele *The Atlantic,* March 1982.

27 Toynbee, Arnold *America and the World Revolution,* Oxford University Press, New York and London: 1962, p. 92.

28 Eberstein, Pritchett, Turner, and Mann, *American Democracy in World Perspective,* Harper & Row, New York: 1967, all quotes pp. 3–5.

29 op. cit., chart printed on inside covers.

30 op. cit., p. 5.

31 Ibid.

Chapter 11

Critical Thinking and the Nature of Prejudice

with Kenneth R. Adamson

Abstract

In this paper, originally prepared as a result of an Anti-Defamation League conference on Critical Thinking and Prejudice, *Paul and Adamson argue that there are seven basic flaws in "traditional research into the nature of prejudice". Efforts in prejudice reduction, based on traditional research, tend to merely reshape and redirect prejudice rather than to lessen it. This research problem originated in the failure of theoreticians to take seriously the groundbreaking work of William Graham Sumner in* Folkways *(1906). Sumner developed the view that prejudice is the norm rather than the exception in everyday belief formation. His concept ties in well with Piaget's research into egocentrism and sociocentrism of thought.*

Only a well-conceived critical education, Paul and Adamson argue, "an education that cultivates the rationality of students, ... liberates students from modes of thinking that limit their potential and narrow their perspective" lessens "the natural drive toward prejudice". For Paul and Adamson, "prejudice is a rich, complex, multi-dimensional phenomenon, grounded in ... the primary, instinctual nature of human thinking." Removing it, "requires the development of our secondary, more latent, nature, our capacity to develop as fairminded, rational persons." Such an emphasis "should not focus on the content of particular prejudices ... but on the mechanisms *of prejudice and their role in the struggle for power, advantage, and money." The authors conclude: "A credible program of prejudice reduction ought not focus on the prejudices of others, prejudices against us, for we are ideally situated to change our own mode of thinking, not to change the thinking of others."*

✦ Introduction

*T*raditional research into the nature of prejudice has these seven basic flaws: *1)* Researchers tend to approach prejudice as an aberration, something abnormal or atypical, something outside the normal mechanisms of thought, desire, and action — in palpable contrast to the main source, direction, and nature of human cognitive and affective life. *2)* They tend to emphasize the dysfunctional nature of prejudice, to ignore the many advantages in power, wealth, status, and peace of mind that come from prejudiced states of mind. *3)* They tend to focus on negative prejudices, "prejudices-against;" and assume that positive prejudices, "prejudices-for", are independent of negative ones and largely benign. *4)* They play down or ignore prejudices against belief systems and ideologies, as though prejudices were only against people as such. *5)* They fail to emphasize how prejudice is embedded in the pervasive problem of everyday human irrationality. *6)* They tend to focus on the content of prejudices, rather than on the mode of thinking generating them. *7)* They fail to recognize that significant prejudice reduction requires long-term strategies for developing fair and openminded persons in fair and openminded societies.

We emphasize, in contrast, the normality and universality of prejudice, its "functionality" in advancing the vested interests of favored groups, the harm in positive prejudices, the significance of prejudice against belief systems and ideologies, the embeddedness of prejudice in egocentric minds and sociocentric societies, the mode of thinking that leads to prejudice formation, and the need to focus efforts of prejudice reduction on long-term strategies for fostering openminded persons in openminded societies. We also emphasize the problem of self-serving interest in prejudice reduction: the revulsion we feel when thinking about "their" prejudices against "us;" the apathy we feel when thinking about "our" prejudices against "them".

Few in favor of prejudice reduction focus on their own prejudices, pro or con. Most grossly underestimate the strength and significance of their own prejudices while expressing anger toward and scorn for the prejudices of "others" against them. We argue that prejudice has root causes inherent not only in the human mind but also in traditional human social and cultural arrangements and practices. By largely ignoring the root causes of prejudice, contemporary approaches to prejudice reduction do little except minimize some forms of it while other forms — typically those that further vested interests — thrive. If we do not strike at the roots of prejudice, we do little to lessen the damage and injury it does, though we may shift who is damaged and to what extent.

Prejudices, on this view, are not isolatable things-in-themselves, not mental or affective atoms. Individual prejudices always spring from roots more basic than themselves. Just as a permanent underground stock of a plant continually produces and sustains the stems and leaves, so a deep-seated substratum of beliefs and drives continually creates and sustains prejudices and other irrationalities. Egocentric minds and sociocentric societies are permanent breeding grounds for prejudice. Opposing particular prejudices is pointless unless we take significant steps against what generates them in the first place. Pruning prejudiced plants does not eliminate the plant itself. To date in human history virtually all groups organized for prejudice reduction are organized to reduce particular prejudices, most notably prejudices against them. Rather than being indifferent to prejudices in favor of themselves, they actively cultivate them. Of course they cultivate them under other names such as loyalty, patriotism, or self-defense. Hence, any energy spent on prejudice reduction *reforms* rather than *reduces* prejudice, redirects rather than eradicates it. For these reasons, we argue, both research into prejudice and our conception of prejudice reduction requires a major reorientation.

✦ *The Concept of Prejudice*

The English word "prejudice" derives from the Latin stems *pre* meaning "before" and *judicium* meaning "judgment" or "sentence". Literally speaking, therefore, it means "judging or sentencing before the evidence has been considered". Its early recorded uses link it conceptually to injury, detriment, hurt, loss, or damage caused to persons by a judgment or action in which their rights were disregarded.

From the earliest uses one finds the word and its grammatical cognates used with conceptual connections to the affective and the behavioral as well as to the cognitive. Consider the following entries from the *Oxford English Dictionary:*

1. a judgment formed before due examination or consideration; a premature or hasty judgment ...

2. the action of judging an event beforehand

3. preconceived opinion; bias or leaning favorable or unfavorable

4. a feeling, favorable or unfavorable, toward any person or thing, prior to or not based on actual experience; a prepossession; a bias or leaning toward one side; an unreasoning predilection or objection

5. a preconceived idea as to what will happen

6. to affect injuriously or unfavorably by doing some act, or as a consequence of something done

7. to injure materially; to damage

Words with equivalent historical roots exist in French (préjugé), German (Vorurteil), Portuguese (preconceito), and other European languages. Each essentially refers to the human capacity to form prejudgments and preconceptions without adequate reason or before the relevant evidence is in, then to feel and act accordingly to the detriment of others. This core of meaning implies that people can be prejudiced in any dimension of thought, feeling, or action, not only with respect to ethnic or racial groups. Furthermore, the concept of prejudice formation is clearly linked to other basic concepts, such as 'bias', 'subjectivity', 'irrationality', 'narrowmindedness', 'closedmindedness', 'oversimplification', 'stereotype', 'distortion', 'rationalization', 'self-deception', 'egocentricity', 'sociocentricity', 'ethnocentricity', 'fallaciousness', and so forth. Indeed any sound empirical or theoretical work on why people tend to think, feel, or act in these flawed ways sheds light on the nature or phenomenology of prejudice.

The network of words conceptually intertwined with the word *prejudice* reenforces the seminal nature of prejudice in human life. Prejudice is not likely to become intelligible or treatable as a thing-in-itself. Rather, we should understand it as integral to our understanding of how and why humans, with the raw capacity to form beliefs and feelings upon the basis of adequate reasons and evidence, so often form them otherwise. To put this another way, the question "Why do people often think, feel, and act in a prejudiced way?" is a paraphrase of the question "Why do people often think, feel, and act in a way that does not make sense given the available evidence?" Furthermore, the tendency of people to be emotionally attached to their prejudices, to hold to them even in the face of overwhelming contrary reasons and evidence, suggests that prejudiced thought and action serve powerful motives or interests. To overturn prejudice we must overturn irrationality, narrowmindedness, self-deception, egocentricity, and sociocentricity. We must understand both the psychological and social functions of prejudiced thought, sentiment, and behavior. And most importantly we must recognize how deep-rooted prejudice is in normal human cognition in every dimension of human life.

✦ *The Status of Research Into Prejudice*

Interestingly, in one of the seminal works in the field of anthropology and sociology, *Folkways* (1906), William Graham Sumner laid a foundation for what could have (but did not) become a global account of the nature of prejudice and a systematic approach to prejudice reduction. His basic thesis was that the overwhelming majority of beliefs and sentiments, both those expressed and those acted upon, are grounded in the folkways and mores of human societies. These foundational bases for belief and sentiment, these sustaining grounds for action and reaction, according to Sumner, are not chosen by people on the basis of reason, evidence, or reflection but rather produced by "frequent repetition of petty acts" which generate "habit in the individual and custom in the group". The principal conditioners of beliefs and sentiments are "pleasure and pain". (Sumner, p. 3)

Sumner implies that prejudgments and preconceptions are inevitable because "the first task of life is to live". "Men begin with acts, not with thoughts." (Sumner, p. 2) For primitive peoples, Sumner notes,

> Custom regulates the whole of a man's action, — his bathing, washing, cutting his hair, eating, drinking, and fasting. From his cradle to his grave he is the slave of ancient usage. (p. 4)

Sumner sees little deviation from this pattern in modern life: "All men act in this way with only a little wider margin of voluntary variation."

People divide people into "ingroups" and "outgroups", forming positive prejudices toward their own group (its beliefs, sentiments, and patterns of behavior) and negative prejudices toward outgroups:

> The relation of comradeship and peace in the we-group and that of hostility and war toward others-groups are correlative to each other. The exigencies of war with outsiders are what make peace inside, lest internal discord should weaken the we-group for war. These exigencies also make government and law in the ingroup, in order to prevent quarrels and enforce discipline. Thus war and peace have reacted to each other and developed each other, one within the group, the other in the intergroup relation. (p. 12)

Sumner labels this pattern in human life "ethnocentrism" and argues that it shapes a cast of mind found in virtually all social groups:

> Ethnocentrism is the technical name for this view of things in which one's own group is the center of everything, and all others are scaled and rated with reference to it. Each group nourishes its own pride and vanity, boasts itself superior, exalts its own divinities, and looks with contempt on outsiders. (p. 13)

Sumner sees patriotism as a common manifestation of ethnocentrism, typically leading to chauvinism:

> The masses are always patriotic. For them the old ethnocentric jealousy, vanity, truculency, and ambition are the strongest elements of patriotism. Such sentiments are easily awakened in a crowd. They are sure to be popular. Wider knowledge always proves that they are not based on facts. That we are good and others are bad is never true. Every group of any kind whatsoever demands that each of its members shall help defend group interests. (p. 15)

Again and again Sumner develops the thesis that basic beliefs and sentiments, folkways and mores, wherever found, are grounded in tradition and are not subjected, except in rare circumstances, to rational reflection and critique:

> The tradition is its own warrant. It is not held subject to verification by experience. The notion of right is in the folkways. It is not outside of them, of independent origin, and brought to them to test them. In the folkways, whatever is, is right. (p. 28)

Conformity of behavior in society reflects conformity of thought and sentiment:

> All are forced to conform, and the folkways dominate social life. Then they seem true and right, and arise into mores as the norm of welfare. Thence are produced faiths, ideas, doctrines, religions, and philosophies, according to the stage of civilization and the fashions of reflection and generalization. (p. 38)

Even the mores of society, its articulated principles of right conduct, rarely reflect or stimulate reasoned belief:

> They do not stimulate thought, but quite the contrary. The thinking is already done and is embodied in the mores. They never contain their own amendment. They are not questions, but answers, to the problem of life. They present themselves as final and unchangeable, because they present answers which are offered as "the truth". (p. 79)

Or again:

> The trained reason and conscience never have heavier tasks laid upon them than where questions of conformity to, or dissent from, the mores are raised. It is by dissent and free judgment of the best reason and conscience that the mores win flexibility and automatic adjustment. Dissent is always unpopular in the group. (p. 95)

Sumner paints a picture of human life in which prejudiced sentiment and belief, highly resistant to reason and evidence, are pervasive:

> The most important fact about the mores is their dominion over the individual. Arising he knows not where or how, they meet his opening mind in earliest childhood, give him his outfit of ideas, faiths, and tastes, and lead him into prescribed mental processes. They bring to him codes of action, standards, and

> rules of ethics. They have a model of the man-as-he-should-be to which they
> mold him, in spite of himself and without his knowledge. (pp. 173–4)

Sumner's personal repugnance toward prejudiced thought and sentiment
is given in hundreds of examples that fill the nearly 700 pages of his book.
Here is one such example:

> The tyranny is greatest in regard to "American" and "Americanism". It
> follows that if anything is base and bogus it is always labeled "American". If
> a thing is to be recommended which cannot be justified, it is put under
> "Americanism". (p. 177)

Sumner, using the concepts of suggestion and pathos, explores the appara-
tus of social conditioning which universally indoctrinates people and incul-
cates beliefs and sentiments. He spells out how they are "protected from
severe examination", "cherished with such a pre-established preference and
faith that it is thought wrong to verify" them, how they work "to preclude
verification", and to "create an atmosphere of delusion". (p. 181)

In Sumner's view, and we believe his view is basically sound, belief and
sentiment usually are formed precisely as prejudgments and preconceptions.
Normally, the basic framework for belief and sentiment is prejudiced. Prejudgment and preconception is the rule, rational assent the exception. As
Sumner puts it:

> The notion that "the group thinks" deserves to be put to the side of the great
> freaks of philosophy which have been put forth from age to age. Only the elite
> in any society, or any age, think, and the world's thinking is carried on by them
> by the transplanting of ideas from mind to mind, under the stress and strain of
> clashing argument and tugging debate. If the group thinks, the thought costs
> nothing, but in truth thought costs beyond everything else .... (p. 207)

Or again:

> ... the masses always enforce conformity to the mores. Primitive taboos are
> absolute. There is no right of private judgment. Renegades, apostates, desert-
> ers, rebels, traitors, and heretics are but varieties of dissenters who are subject
> to disapproval, hatred, banishment, and death. In higher stages of civilization
> this popular temper becomes a societal force which combines with civil
> arrangements, religious observances, literature, education, and philosophy. Tol-
> eration is no sentiment of the masses for anything which they care about. What
> they believe they believe, and they want it accepted and respected. (p. 232)

In fact, Sumner titles Chapter 15, "The Mores Can Make Anything Right
and Prevent Condemnation of Anything". He closes the chapter with the
admonition that the mores of a social group form "a moral and civil atmosphere through which everything ... [is] seen and rational judgment ... made
impossible". Only in the exceptional case does Sumner allow for the formation of unprejudiced beliefs:

> It is only by high mental discipline that we can be trained to ... form
> rational judgments on current cases. This mental independence and ethical
> power are the highest products of education. (p. 532)

Of course, Sumner does not confuse *education* in the sense in which he defends it with mere *schooling:*

> School education, unless it is regulated by the best knowledge and good sense, will produce men and women who are all of one pattern, as if turned in a lathe .... An orthodoxy is produced in regard to all the great doctrines of life. It consists of the most worn and commonplace opinions which are current in the masses. It may be found in newspapers and popular literature. It is intensely provincial and philistine .... The popular opinions always contain broad fallacies, half-truths, and glib generalizations of fifty years ago. (p. 630–31)

Sumner contrasts typical schooling with genuine education based on the cultivation of critical thought:

> Criticism is the examination and test of propositions of any kind which are offered for acceptance, in order to find out whether they correspond to reality or not. The critical faculty is a product of education and training. It is a mental habit and power. It is a prime condition of human welfare that men and women should be trained in it. It is our only guarantee against delusion, deception, superstition, and misapprehension of ourselves and our earthly circumstances .... Education teaches us to act by judgment. Our education is good just so far as it produces a well developed critical faculty. (p. 632–33)

Sumner also expresses the possibility of a critical society in which the cultivation of the critical faculties would predominate over education for conformity:

> The critical habit of thought, if usual in a society, will pervade all its mores, because it is a way of taking up the problems of life. Men educated in it cannot be stampeded .... They are slow to believe. They can hold things as possible or probable in all degrees, without certainty and without pain. They can wait for evidence and weigh evidence, uninfluenced by the emphasis or confidence with which assertions are made on one side or the other. They can resist appeals to their prejudices and all kinds of cajolery. Education in the critical faculty is the only education of which it can be truly said that it makes good citizens. (p. 633)

Sumner's work, though seminal, is by no means the final word on the subject. Among other things, his book reflects many of his own prejudices. Nevertheless, *Folkways* is unequalled in the literature on prejudice in its scope as a framework for understanding the pervasive social roots of prejudice. Ironically, each of its major theses is missing from the subsequent main stream literature on prejudice:

1. that prejudgment and preconception are the dominant social roots of belief, sentiment, and behavior,
2. that prejudice-for and prejudice-against are intertwined and interdependent,
3. that only a small minority of persons have learned how to critically question their own beliefs and sentiments and to rationally restructure them,
4. that a special education or training is necessary to develop a person's critical faculties, and
5. that a critical society, though possible, has not yet emerged.

Had these theses been taken seriously, subsequent research would have focused on the nature of schooling and socialization. Instead, though the literature is voluminous, the analysis of prejudice has typically been more superficial than Sumner's profound beginnings. After Sumner, prejudgment and preconception are taken as exceptions, prejudice-for played down as innocent and innocuous, the concept of prejudice narrowed to racial and ethnic prejudices, and the bulk of attention focused on socially unpopular prejudices. Consequently, few now recognize the universality of prejudice, its "functionality" in standard social arrangements, or the profound shift needed in schooling for prejudice reduction to be a significant social commitment.

We can document these general tendencies by canvassing the review articles on prejudice in the *Encyclopedia of the Social Sciences* and the *Encyclopedic Dictionary of Psychology.* Otto Klineberg, writing on the concept of prejudice in the *Encyclopedia of the Social Sciences,* defines prejudice as "an unsubstantiated prejudgment of an individual or group, favorable or unfavorable in character, tending to action in a consonant direction". Very quickly, however, it becomes clear that Klineberg's is not the broad approach of Sumner. Klineberg moves quickly to the limited view we have been criticizing:

> Social science research has joined with popular usage in introducing two limitations to this concept. In the first place, favorable prejudices, although they undoubtedly exist, have attracted relatively little attention, perhaps on the principle that they do good rather than harm. It might, however, legitimately be argued that even favorable prejudices should be discouraged, since they too represent unwarranted generalizations, often of an irrational nature. Second, although prejudice may extend far and wide to apply to objects as disparate as trade-union leaders, women, or exotic foods, in practice it has been considered as dealing primarily, if not exclusively, with populations or ethnic groups distinguished by the possession of specific inherited physical characteristics ("race") or by differences in language, religion, culture, national origin, or any combination of these. (p. 439)

He discounts the universality of prejudice by considering it only as a derivation from psychoanalysis:

> One view of the universality of prejudice seems to derive from an erroneous interpretation of psychoanalytic theory. This theory, particularly in its orthodox form, regards hostility or aggression (Freud's Thanatos) as instinctive and universal; prejudice would then be simply one manifestation of this instinct. Not all psychoanalysts would accept this formulation, but even those who would add that although aggression must manifest itself in some form, there is no one form (for example, prejudice) which must be regarded as inevitable. There is still considerable argument as to whether hostile aggression is universal, but in any case it can be expressed in so many different ways that inference to the universality of prejudice remains exceedingly doubtful. (p. 441)

He then focuses the bulk of his article on problems concerning prejudice against minority groups. He makes a passing reference to the ease with which a "healthy" nationalism "moves into an exaggerated chauvinism which is not only for 'us' but *against* 'them'." He then treats what he calls "economic factors" in which he alludes to the commonly "motivated" nature of prejudice, how it enables

> the dominant group to maintain others in a state of subservience, to exploit them, to treat them as slaves or serfs, to reduce their power to compete on equal terms for jobs, and to keep them "in their place". (p. 443)

Quite importantly, he calls attention to the unconscious nature of prejudice and hence to the link of prejudice to self-deception:

> *They,* whom we keep in an inferior position, are happier than they would be otherwise; *they,* whom we persecute because of their beliefs, can be saved only if they accept the true (that is to say, *our*) religion; *they,* whom we destroy, are planning to destroy *us,* and we are simply exercising the right to protect ourselves. It is arguments like these, presented in all sincerity, which so often in the past, and not so rarely in the present, have given to men the conviction that what they are doing is somehow noble and beautiful, in Hooten's telling phrase, they "can rape in righteousness and murder in magnanimity". (p. 443)

But he does not follow this up with any link into standard folkways and mores or into the ways they are inculcated. Rather he implies that prejudice is abnormal rather than normal in society:

> The fact remains that under the same cultural conditions, surrounded by the same institutions and tempted by the same desire for gain, some people show prejudice and others do not. (p. 443)

He alludes to Adorno's *The Authoritarian Personality* as a possible explanation for this abnormality in development.

The limitations in the research on the nature of prejudice is mirrored in Klineberg's review of the literature on "The Reduction of Prejudice". Far from suggesting that the fundamental cause of prejudice can be found, as Sumner found it, in the inculcative, indoctrinative socialization processes which bypass and diminish a person's capacity for reflective critical thinking, Klineberg favorably mentions the possible use of propaganda techniques to reduce prejudice. He shows no sensitivity to the distinction between schooling based on inculcation and indoctrination on the one hand, and that centered on the cultivation of critical thought on the other. Indeed he ends his article on what he calls an optimistic note by ejaculating,

> There is hope, too, in the fact that "authoritarians" are conformist. If prejudice becomes unfashionable, even the hard core of resistance to change may give way to progress.

Henri Tajfel gives a similar account of the literature on prejudice in the *Encyclopedic Dictionary of Psychology:*

1. He says that the term has been narrowed, for these two reasons:

> The first is that it is generally applied to people's views about social groups and their members rather than more generally to 'persons' or 'things'.

The second is that, in practice, the term has been mainly restricted in psychological theory and research to hostile or unfavorable views about human groups other than one's own ("outgroups"). It has been used by psychologists in the context of intergroup hostility, conflicts, persecution or discrimination.

2. It focuses on discrimination and hostile attitudes toward minorities, and

3. Although Allport's approach to stereotyping as a general mode of categorizing the social world is briefly discussed, there is no mention of profound implications.

Only by admitting the profound and pervasive nature of prejudiced thought and emotion can we make intelligible the need for profound educational changes to reduce prejudice. A superficial approach to prejudice that views it narrowly, as exceptional rather than routine, cannot be used as the main fulcrum for prejudice reduction.

The best candidate for a follow-up of Sumner's, *Folkways* (1906) is Gordon Allport's *The Nature of Prejudice*. (1954) Like Sumner, Allport approaches prejudice from the broadest of perspectives, attempting to trace prejudice to a variety of roots: "economic exploitation, social structure, the mores, fear, aggression, sex conflict, or any other favored soil". (xvi) However, in attempting to deal with prejudice from a variety of points of view and to point out the limitations of each, the overall effect is diffuse. Furthermore, Allport's work underestimates, as does most of the literature, the significance of positive prejudice: "... we will be concerned chiefly with prejudice *against* ... " (p. 7)

The most significant deficiency of Allport's approach however is his relatively superficial analysis of the nature of the thinking and affect that underlie prejudice. He attempts to account for prejudiced thinking simply as a result of faulty categorization and generalization. Allport sees "irrational categories" as "formed as easily as rational categories". He does not seem to grasp the special difficulties of attempting to cultivate and nurture persons who habitually think rationally. His analysis of rational thinking is too simplistic to help him to realize the need, for example, of profound changes in schooling:

> How to combat this irrational overcategorization is a baffling problem ....
> All these obstacles are profoundly serious, representing as they do the most firmly entrenched aspects of irrationalism in people and in social groups. (Allport, p. 503)

When Allport talks about the role of critical thinking in the solution of the problem of irrationality — and he does so only by implication — his analysis is simplistic:

> Fairly early children can ... learn that Foreigner 1 is not the same as Foreigner 2. They can be shown how the law of linguistic precedence in learning (p. 305) creates dangers for them, particularly in the form of derogatory epithets such as "nigger" and "wop". Simple lessons in semantics and in elementary psychology are neither dull nor incomprehensible to children. (Allport, p. 512)

Allport's concluding comment on democracy merely points in the direction of the problem. It is a far cry from Sumner's chapter on the task of developing a critical society:

> Democracy, we now realize, places a heavy burden upon the personality, sometimes too great to bear. The maturely democratic person must possess subtle virtues and capacities: an ability to think rationally about causes and effects, an ability to form properly differentiated categories in respect to ethnic groups and their traits, a willingness to award freedom to others, and a capacity to employ it constructively for oneself. All these qualities are difficult to achieve and maintain. It is easier to succumb to oversimplification and dogmatism, to repudiate the ambiguities inherent in a democratic society, to demand definiteness, to "escape from freedom". (Allport, p. 515)

✦ Curriculum Materials Focusing on Prejudice Reduction

Curriculum materials reflect the deficiencies in the research on prejudice. Of the curriculum materials on prejudice we reviewed, one of the best is Book 2 of the series "Challenges of Our Time" entitled *Prejudice and Discrimination*. Its quality notwithstanding, this book reflects the same basic oversimplifications detailed above.

The book contains six chapters, an introduction, and a conclusion. Five of the six chapters address racial or cultural prejudice, the sixth, sexual prejudice. The aim and direction of the book is given in the Forward to the teacher's guide.

> *Prejudice and Discrimination* deals with the problems arising from the social (group-forming) nature of human beings. The prejudices, competition, and conflicts that arise between groups are discussed in terms of ethnic, sexual, racial, and religious discrimination and adjustment. Special emphasis is given to the pluralistic quality of American society: a general discussion of the theme of "a nation of immigrants" is followed by an examination of the specific situations of various ethnic minorities in the United States, including Jews, indigenous Americans (Indians), Mexican Americans, Puerto Ricans, Chinese Americans, Japanese Americans, and Afro-Americans. One chapter is devoted to anti-Semitism and Nazi persecution of the Jews and another to sexual prejudice in American society. (p. 2)

The book primarily focuses on racial prejudice. It barely touches on other forms of prejudice. It ignores the harm done by national, ideological, professional, personal, and religious prejudice. The chapter entitled "The Jewish People" might have led to a discussion of religious prejudice, but does not. Instead, when addressing the Jewish religion it concerns itself only with prejudice against the Jews culturally. It fails to address ideological prejudice anywhere, except by implication. Thus the authors not only miss the opportunity to analyze prejudice for and against political, economic, philosophical, and social systems, they also fail to address the roots of prejudice: the egocentric/sociocentric mind.

When they do hint at ideological prejudice, they ignore the ideational dimension. The term "Americanization" is introduced in chapter two, "The United States: A Nation of Immigrants", and refers to the pressure felt by immigrants to adopt the values and attitudes held by most Americans. Two questions might be asked: "To what extent was this a prejudice against other ways of seeing and understanding the world?" and, "To what extent was it a demand that all Americans learn to think alike, to share the same assumptions, the same ideas, the same world view?" The book neglects these questions. The lesson ignores how the history of U.S. prejudice involves significant prejudice against foreign *ideas* and *beliefs,* not just against foreign customs and dress, or ethnicity.

The Forward contains a list of 56 objectives for the series "Challenges of Our Time". The volume *Prejudice and Discrimination* includes the following paraphrased objectives: Students will be able to recognize various views of human nature: humans as rational and good, irrational and bad, mixture of both, the anarchist view, the racist view; students will understand the meaning of culture; students will understand the concept of groups and the basic psychological feature of group relations (in-group/out-group, or we-they attitudes.)

The few objectives cited here are quite significant, and, if ambitiously pursued, could lead students to useful and important insights into the nature of prejudiced thought, as well as into the nature of thought in general, for prejudice is grounded in the very *way* beliefs are formed. However, the book takes a less than ambitious approach and leaves untouched the heart of prejudice. For it is not enough to discover that one has this or that prejudice; one must also discover how one generates and multiplies prejudices in an ongoing way. One cannot kill poison oak merely by periodically picking a leaf off the plant. Prejudice producing modes of thinking *must* become the focus of instruction for prejudice reduction. The content of the prejudices is secondary; it does not much matter what particular prejudices particular humans have. It is their profound involvement in "prejudgment" as a habitual mode of thinking and judgment that is the key problem. Only by exposing and examining the roots of prejudice can we effectively begin to eliminate it.

This failure to recognize prejudice formation as a mode of thought is continued in the book's treatment of positive prejudice. In the student text, positive prejudice is defined as: "A preference for certain ideas, values, things, or people". (p. 5) These preferences, the student is told, are not necessarily harmful or unhealthy, and may be required to be loyal to one's group. Quoting again from the student text:

> If one is a member of a group one will usually have a prejudice in favor of it, that is, a preference for it. One will be prejudiced in favor of the group's values. If these values are sound, one's prejudice will probably be sound, too. A prejudice in favor of one's children or one's parents is a good thing in a family. (p. 5)

By approving of positive prejudice, the book potentially undermines all it attempts to accomplish. A positive prejudice is typically accompanied by a negative prejudice, for in being prejudiced in favor of particular groups we more or less automatically oppose those groups in conflict with them. In this sense, positive prejudice is rarely, if ever, harmless. Others are typically affected by our prejudices. This is certainly true of national prejudice. Our prejudice in favor of our nation tends to be accompanied by a prejudice against those nations that differ from or oppose our own. This affects our attitudes toward these nations, and our policies concerning them. We usually develop double standards to protect these prejudices, judging the actions and policies of our country differently than the actions and policies of opposing countries. Our positive prejudice may lead us to think any who say we have wronged them are either liars or fools.

Prejudice, as we have said, is located in a general mode of thinking by which beliefs are formed and maintained. Until we learn to form beliefs on the basis of rational considerations, we form them without such consideration — that is, as prejudices. Approving of positive prejudice encourages this prejudice forming process, as though it could be limited to innocent prejudices. Furthermore, in the confusion, rational preference is obscured.

To rationally prefer some belief implies that we have strong reasons and evidence to support it, and conversely, good reason to oppose conflicting beliefs. It also of course requires us to consider the case against our preferences or against the way we manifest our preference in action. *Blind* loyalty to a group is not, for example, a rational preference. Neither is the practice of giving preferred status in a society to particular ethnic and religious groups. A prejudiced preference, on the other hand, implies a preference based not on good reasons, but on considerations that will not stand up to critical assessment. Unknowingly, it is this prejudiced preference which the lesson encourages. Egocentricity and sociocentricity generate positive and negative prejudices as part of egocentric and sociocentric activities of mind, and it is these fundamental drives that must be overcome to make any significant progress toward prejudice reduction. We cannot work against prejudice if we encourage the very processes that create it.

To sum up, although this book introduces the student to some important concepts and tendencies, it is on the whole superficial, and contains fundamental confusions. Inadvertently, the book reflects the narrow focus of contemporary research on prejudice reduction.

✦ *Prejudice and Human Desire*

Human action arises from human motives and human motives arise from human desire and perceived interest. Getting what we want and what advances our prestige, wealth, power, and peace of mind naturally structures and shapes how we conceive of and understand the situations and circumstances of our daily lives. We categorize, make assumptions, interpret, and infer from within a viewpoint we routinely use to advance our personal ends and desires. We are, in a word, naturally prejudiced in our favor. We reflexively and spontaneously gravitate to the slant on things that makes it easiest to gratify our desires and justify doing so, including the desire to be correct. We naturally shrink at the thought of being wrong, and conversely, delight in the thought of being right, and so often resist the attempts of others to "correct" us, especially when this involves beliefs that are fundamental and part of our personal identity.

The thinking, then, most natural or instinctive in humans Freud called "pleasure-principle thinking". This mode of thinking requires the absence of intellectual virtues, for the presence of these virtues would prevent us from thinking one-sidedly in ways that structure or shape situations to our advantage. "How-can-I-think-of-this-situation-in-such-a-way-as-to-get-what-I-want-out-of-it?" is a reflex in the thinking of humans. Consider these two examples.

A small child who wanted to play her audio tape for a guest was told by the guest to first ask her mother if that was all right. The child ran to her mother and said, "She wants to hear my tape!" She instinctively knew not to say, "I want to play my tape. Could I play it for her?"

A toddler who was told by his mother that he could not play outside because it was raining, looked thoughtfully out the window and then ejaculated: "Yes, I can play outside. It isn't raining, its only drizzling!" Already these children are learning to structure their requests and interpret evidence in ways that help them get their way.

The extent to which these perceived interests and the means adopted to realize them are unexamined is the extent to which these ends and means are prejudices. We begin with self-serving assumptions, and from these assumptions proceed to build a system of beliefs. This system may be quite complex and sophisticated, but if the assumptions upon which it rests are a result of prejudgments, the beliefs built on them are prejudices. 'Prejudice', then, refers to the manner in which the belief is formed and held, not to its falsity. A prejudice is not necessarily a false belief, and may, on examination, be rationally defensible. Prior to this examination however it is no less a prejudice.

✦ Prejudice and the Illusion of Morality

To be prejudiced in favor of our perceived interests entails that we become prejudiced against whomever or whatever appears to oppose or stand in the way of furthering them. It is not enough to be taught to be honest, kind, generous, thoughtful, concerned with others, and respectful of human rights. The human mind can easily construe situations in ways that conceive selfish desire as self-defense, cruelty as discipline, domination as love, intolerance as conviction, and in general, evil as good. The mere conscious desire to do good does not remove prejudiced conceptions which shape perceptions to further our interests or keep us from forming such conceptions. To minimize our egocentric drives, we must develop critical thinking in a special direction. We need not only intellectual *skills* but intellectual *character* as well. Indeed, we must develop and refine our intellectual skills as we develop and refine our intellectual character, to embed the skills in our character and shape our character through the skills.

Much of our thinking is directed at deciding to perform some action from among a range of possible actions. Whatever action we decide to take will inevitably influence others in some way, often trivially, sometimes profoundly. There is, then, a distinctly moral dimension to thinking that must not be ignored. People not only *can,* but often *do* create the illusion of morality in a variety of ways. One major way is the systematic confusion of group mores with universal moral standards.

When people act in accordance with the injunctions and taboos of the group to which they belong they naturally feel righteous. They receive much praise in moral terms, and may even be treated as moral leaders, if they speak or act in a way that impresses the group. For this reason, few people distinguish moral or religious conformity or demagoguery from genuine moral integrity. Group norms are typically articulated in the language of morality and a socialized person inwardly experiences some sense of shame or guilt in violating a social taboo, and anger or moral outrage at others who do so. In other words, what commonly seems to be the inner voice of conscience is often nothing more than the internalized voice of social authority, the voice of our parents, our teachers, and other "superiors" speaking within us. Genuine moral integrity requires what might be called "intellectual character" and this requires rational assent, for moral decisions require thoughtful discrimination between what is merely socially permitted and what is genuinely morally justified.

The other major way in which humans systematically create the illusion of morality is egocentrically structured self-deception. This, as we have mentioned, is the shaping and justification of self-serving perceptions and viewpoints. When engaged in such spontaneous thought, we systematically confuse our viewpoint with reality itself. We do not experience ourselves as selecting among a range of possible perceptions; quite the contrary, it seems to us that we simply observe things *as they are.* What is really egocentric intellectual arrogance we experience as righteous moral judgment. This leads us to conceive those who disagree with us as fools, dissemblers, or worse. Since our inner voice tells us that our motives are pure, that we see things as they really are, those who set themselves against us or threaten to impede us often seem the manifestation of evil. If they use violence to advance their ends, we experience their action as aggressive, as blind to human rights and simple justice. But if we use violence, it is not even conceived as violence but as justifiable self-defense, as the restoring of law and order, as the protection of right and justice. We habitually use double standards to assess the beliefs and actions of ourselves and others. The one we apply to ourselves is sympathetic, open-ended, and forgiving, the one we apply to others is unsympathetic, rigid, and unforgiving.

✦ Prejudiced in Favor of Our Interests

Consider the common sense truth that human groups typically have vested interests and spend a significant part of their time and energy advancing them. Developing a point of view, a framework of beliefs that serve these interests, is crucial to "success". The result is that prejudiced thinking is usually functional. Fairminded thinking impedes success by diffusing effort and nurturing self-restraint that limits "profit" and "advantage". This basic truth lies at the root of much worldly prejudice. One finds it in all special interest groups, whether professional, economic, religious, ethnic, or otherwise. This can be illustrated by a recent segment of the history of the American Medical Association.

A professional association like the AMA routinely pursues the perceived vested interests of its members. This pursuit is part and parcel of developing a frame of reference and mode of thinking prejudiced in favor of these interests. For example, because the approach of the AMA to health care is predominantly pharmacological and surgical, we can predict that members will be unsympathetic to such things as home birth, holistic medicine, and chiropractic. Also, since the approach to medical practice is committed to a particular conception of free enterprise and private practice, we can be confident that the AMA will reject socialized medicine. Since the profession is based on perceived interests, on pharmacology and surgery, and on a conception of free enterprise and private practice, members of the AMA generally oppose positions that appear to negate or question views favoring these positions. They also fail to grant that there may be elements of significant truth in these opposing positions.

Consequently, few doctors read books which advocate an opposing position, such as socialized medicine or chiropractic. Thus, few doctors hear or understand the strongest arguments against the dominant thinking within their profession. They think this unnecessary because they are confident in their positions *a priori*, before the evidence. In other words, they are prejudiced in favor of views into which they were socialized by the culture of medical school and medical practice.

Consider, as an illustration, the AMA's position on chiropractic therapy. Prior to the early 1970's, some advocates of chiropractic made exaggerated claims regarding the types of disorders it could effectively treat — citing as treatable, cancer, high blood pressure, diabetes, and infectious disease. This provided a reasonable ground for AMA skepticism regarding chiropractic. However, this legitimate AMA concern for patient care soon escalated into a general caricature of chiropractic. So powerful was this negative prejudice that the AMA conspired against the chiropractic profession. It took a court ordered permanent injunction to restrain the AMA (Chester A. Wilks vs. American Medical Association). On August 27, 1987, the United States District Court decided in this case that, "the AMA and its members participated in a conspiracy against chiropractors in violation of the nation's antitrust laws". *(JAMA,* p. 81) According to the Permanent Injunction Order:

> In the early 1960's, the AMA decided to contain and eliminate chiropractic as a profession. In 1963 the AMA's Committee on Quackery was formed. The committee worked aggressively, both overtly and covertly, to eliminate chiropractic. One of the principle means used by the AMA to achieve its goal was to make it unethical for medical physicians to professionally associate with chiropractors. *(JAMA,* p. 81)

In the early 1970's, chiropractic therapy began to change, and claims of its effectiveness became more reasonable. The AMA, however, did not begin to alter its position toward chiropractic until 1977, after several lawsuits had been brought against the AMA a year earlier. Although policy had now "officially" changed, this new policy was not passed on to the members of the AMA. Quoting again from the Permanent Injunction Order:

> The AMA's present position on chiropractic, as stated to this court, is that it is ethical for a medical physician to professionally associate with chiropractors provided the physician believes that such association is in the best interests of his patients. This position has not previously been communicated by the AMA to its members. (*JAMA,* p. 81)

An initially legitimate concern for patient health became a prejudice. Of course, the initial concern may have also included a desire on the part of the AMA to "protect its turf". In the case of Wilks vs. the AMA,

> The court concluded that the AMA had a genuine concern for scientific methods in patient care, and that this concern was the dominant factor in motivating the AMA's conduct. However, the AMA failed to establish that throughout the entire period of the boycott, from 1966 to 1980, this concern was objectively reasonable .... Finally, the court ruled that the AMA's concern for scientific method in patient care could have been adequately satisfied in a manner less restrictive of competition and that a nationwide conspiracy to eliminate a licensed profession was not justified by the concern for scientific method. On the basis of these findings, the court concluded that the AMA had failed to establish the patient care defense. *(JAMA,* p. 82)

Even though "AMA witnesses, including the present Chairman of the Board of Trustees of the AMA, testified that some forms of treatment by chiropractors, including manipulation, can be therapeutic in the treatment of conditions such as back pain syndrome" *(JAMA,* p. 82), this prejudice against chiropractic persists among physicians today. Few physicians know about instances in which chiropractic manipulation of the joints and spine are, or can be, therapeutic. Few advise their patients to seek chiropractic care, and many even attempt to dissuade from visiting chiropractors those patients who express a desire to do so.

This is merely one illustration out of a virtually endless series of examples of professional prejudice. In addition to professional prejudice, of course, there are many other forms of prejudice: personal, cultural, religious, ideological, social, scientific, and national. Each, if analyzed, yields parallel insights. Later we will look at national prejudice.

The central problem of prejudice reduction in the world is that *self-announced prejudice almost never exists*. Prejudice nearly always exists in obscured, rationalized, socially validated, functional forms. It enables people to sleep peacefully at night even while flagrantly abusing the rights of others. It enables people to get more of what they want, or get it more easily. It is often sanctioned with pomp and ceremony. It sometimes appears as the very will of God. Unless we admit to these powerful tendencies in ourselves, in our social institutions, in what we sometimes take to be our most lofty actions, we will not face the problem of prejudice realistically. We will fail to attack it at its roots. We will avoid taking those measures which could empower our children to move in the direction of genuine fairmindedness. It is not mere coincidence that most groups concerned with prejudice concern themselves with the prejudices of *others*. Only on the rarest of occasions do groups focus any attention on their own prejudices for or against others.

✦ *Taking Prejudice Reduction Seriously:* *The Role of Education*

Whether in or out of school, the dominant mode of social learning is didactic, dogmatic, fragmented, and unconducive to independent critical thought. The belief that knowledge can be directly transmitted by simple statement and memorization is so embedded in the public and academic mind that instruction in this mode is a virtual addiction. Part of the reason for this is that schooling became a large scale social commitment at the turn of the century so that people might have the basic skills to fill the nation's need for manufacturing, not that people might become autonomous critical thinkers. (Tucker, 1980) The very design of schools of the day reflected that of factories. (Keating and Oakes, 1988) But the roots of the didactic paradigm of knowledge and learning long pre-dates the turn of the century.

For thousands of years most children in most societies were expected to do what their parents did, and what their parents did was essentially what their parents and their parent's parents had done for many generations. Today, parents, peer groups, mass media, and teachers transmit beliefs with little sensitivity to or explicit awareness of what it would be to give good reasons and evidence to support those beliefs.

Didacticism, the direct transmission of beliefs taken to be true, is accepted as the transmission of knowledge itself, and rote recall accepted as proof of knowledge acquisition. At all levels of schooling the main mode of instruction is didactic lecturing and the main mode of learning is reiterating what is said or written. Students memorize information and facts, but rarely think critically about what they take in, since this is not required to pass the tests. Students do not connect what they learn in school to their experience outside of school. Nor do they make interdisciplinary connections, as, for example, between what they learn in history and what they learn in civics. Since this type of instruction requires little or no critical thinking, uncritical modes of thought are undisturbed, and the modes of thought conducive to prejudice formation flourish, not only undiminished, but accelerated.

In short, the mere reiteration of facts and formulas should not be confused with assimilation of knowledge. When knowledge is separated from thinking and presented as a thing in itself, it ceases to be knowledge. One need not think about or understand what one memorizes in order to memorize it. Knowledge, on the other hand, cannot be separated from thinking minds. Knowledge is produced by thinking, grasped by thinking, transformed by thinking, and assessed by thinking. We gain genuine knowledge through disciplined dialogue, through critically analyzed experience, through controlled experiment, through careful consideration of divergent points of view, through the critical examination of assumptions, implications, and consequences, through a sensitivity to contradiction and inconsistency, and through carefully developed reasoning. To work toward these ends entails a large scale educational commitment, one largely absent from contemporary educational theory and practice.

✦ Two Modes of Thinking and Learning

There are two basic modes of learning: association and logic. The first is unmediated, spontaneous, and automatic; the second mediated, thoughtful, and deliberate. Understanding the fundamental differences between them sheds further light on the nature of education and the generation of prejudices.

ASSOCIATIONAL THINKING AND LEARNING

What we find together in our experience we associate in our minds. If we are frequently punished for not eating our spinach we associate spinach with punishment. If it often rains in the summer, we associate rain with summer. If our parents generally speak of African-Americans disparagingly, we associate negativity with African-American persons. When entertainment media portray scientists as socially dysfunctional, carpenters as ignorant, blondes as flaky, we associate those groups with those characteristics. This is the lowest and simplest kind of learning. It is effortless and automatic. However it is often unjustified. (What is "connected" in our experience might well be unconnected in fact; what was "separate" in our experience might well be connected.)

When we subconsciously and mindlessly accept our associations as the truth (What do you associate with 'blond topless waitress' or 'communist sympathizer'?), we uncritically accept what are typically stereotypes and prejudices. Mere association is in fact a classic basis for prejudgment. We do not then figure out for ourselves what underlies our conclusions, we do not then typically recognize that we are coming to conclusions at all. Our associations seem to us bare facts.

Of course, many of our associations are transitory connections that we quickly forget, precisely because we have not figured them out for ourselves. These flit in and out of our minds. As such they are not a significant problem for the mind. But others are. Others are repeated thousands of times and become deeply rooted in our subconscious thought, laying the foundation for hundreds of prejudices, pro and con. Peer group indoctrination is of this later sort.

The only way to use associative learning as a basis for genuine knowledge is to go beyond it to logic. We use logic when we figure out whether our associations have a basis in reason or fact: Does the association make sense? Do we have evidence or reasons to support it? Does it fit in with other things we know? For example, by studying climate we could come to recognize that there is no necessary relationship between rain and summer. By studying human nature and paying closer attention to the African-American persons we meet, we can break down our prejudiced association of African-Americans with negativity. And by reflecting on spinach and punishment, we can readily see there is no objective relationship between them. We can figure out why the connections we had formed through mere association do or do not make sense, do or do not stand to reason, are or are not based on sound inferences.

CRITICAL THINKING AND THE LOGIC OF THOUGHT

The word 'critical' comes from the root 'skeri': to cut, take apart, or analyze; and from the Greek word 'kriterion': a standard for judging. The word 'logic' comes from the Greek word 'logos': word, speech, account, thought, reckoning. When we think critically we do not thoughtlessly accept things as we find them. We use our power of thought to take things apart, to analyze them; we use our power of language, logos, to account for things. We set up standards for judgment and use them to give things a conscious reckoning. We do this to genuinely understand what we experience, to go beyond mere association.

When we analyze the logic of things, rather than blindly associate them, we raise our learning to a higher order through critical thought. We begin the process of developing our capacity for rational assent. We begin to develop standards for belief. We begin to question what we read, what we hear and what we subconsciously infer. We forge logical rather than simply associative connections. We often say to ourselves: "Let me see, does that make sense?" Then we talk our way through inferences, reminding ourselves of the key things we know as we proceed. Sometimes we devise an experiment or test of some kind or ask others for their thinking, which we then analyze and consider.

Much school learning relies on association rather than logic. In the rush to cover content, we give students conclusions and constructions that someone else developed. Students retreat to association to achieve recall. They rarely use their own logical powers to reflect on what is taught to them to determine whether they can make sense of it. They rarely form standards of judgment or give a personal reckoning to the conclusions they are didactically taught. They seldom take apart what is presented as connected or put together what is presented as separate. They do not therefore typically determine whether these connections make good sense to them, whether their own thought justifies them. The result is that they often mis-learn, they often forget, they often confuse, they rarely effectively use, what they learn.

Most students' work reflects associations formed about school in general or about particular subjects or assignments. These associations usually minimize higher order learning, for they represent mind-sets contrary to independent logical thought. Students do not learn to think in critically reflective and fairminded ways precisely because it is not taught, encouraged, or modeled in their instruction.

In other words, students do not expect to have to think for themselves while in school. They associate school with passivity, with someone else telling them things to remember for tests. In history classes they expect to be given names, dates, events, and their results. Fair game is asking them to repeat them. In math classes they expect to be given formulas to use according to fixed procedures. Fair game is giving them problems that can be solved by routine use of the formulas covered immediately before the test.

English classes have several operative associations. If asked to read a story students expect to be asked to recall randomly selected details or to give their subjective reactions. They do not expect to have to distill the plot, figure out the meaning of a story, or back up their subjective reactions with evidence from it. They expect the teacher ultimately to let them know the "real" meaning of the story and what if anything they should remember for the test. They expect to be given lists of words and sentences to "do" according to directions. ("Underline each noun.") If asked to write they expect either to repeat what the text or the teacher said, to copy the encyclopedia, or to write out their subjective impressions and associations as these occur to them. They have only a foggy notion of what it means to think logically. They have no sense of how to develop an idea logically. They do not realize that their thought depends on assumptions that they might probe or examine. They do not recognize that their interpretations represent inferences. They do not know how to marshal evidence for their conclusions. They do not know how to check their thinking or that of others for contradictions. They do not see that their thinking, like all thinking, takes place within a point of view or frame of reference. One might say that they are critically illiterate. The associational and impressionistic dominate their thought. Rather than form the foundation for modes of learning and thinking which undermine prejudices, the mode of instruction in schools typically fosters prejudgment and stereotypes.

✦ A Critical Education

An education that cultivates the rationality of students is a significant challenge. A critical education provides the tools and skills necessary for independent thinking and learning. It liberates students from modes of thinking that limit their potential and narrow their perspective. It appeals to reason and evidence. It encourages students to discover as well as to process information. It stimulates students to use their own thinking to come to conclusions and solutions, to defend positions on issues, to consider a wide variety of points of view, to analyze concepts, theories, and explanations, to clarify issues and conclusions, to evaluate the credibility of sources, to raise and pursue root questions, to solve non-routine problems, to transfer ideas to new contexts, to make interdisciplinary connections, to evaluate arguments, interpretations, and beliefs, to generate novel ideas, to question and discuss each others' views, to compare perspectives and theories, to compare ideals with actual practice, to examine assumptions, to distinguish relevant from irrelevant facts, to explore implications and consequences, and to come to terms with contradictions and inconsistencies. Only such a pervasive shift in instruction and school climate will get at the roots of student thinking.

A shift in classroom procedure from a didactic mode to a dialogical mode of teaching, where student questions, objections, and opinions can be freely and comfortably expressed, will of course take time, as teachers will need to learn new strategies, a new conception of knowledge and learning, and new habits of classroom response.

GETTING INTO THE LOGIC OF WHAT WE LEARN

Getting into the habit of reflecting upon the logic of what one learns is key to critical thought. Not only does this require figuring things out for oneself, it also requires pursuing the roots of what one learns until one establishes logical foundations for it. This involves tying any given thing learned into a basic logic one already understands. For example, to study history, the critical thinker does not simply memorize names, events, and dates, or thoughtlessly accept statements regarding causes and results. Nor is it enough to reflect upon alternative historical explanations. One must also reflect upon the very logic of historical thought itself: What is it to think historically? To what extent is historical thinking a dimension of all of our thinking about the world? To what extent, in other words, is all human thinking historical? This reflection need not be esoteric and distracting. The key is to recognize that everything we learn is temporally sequenced, that we continually see the present in light of how we have come to see the past, and that each of us has internalized a selective memory of what has happened to us, emphasizing what seemed to us to be significant in our experience.

When we grasp that all humans shape their present by their reading of their past and their anticipation of the future in the light of the past, we are ready to come to terms with the logic of history. We then approach not

only all historical texts but all interpretation of experience with the awareness that all recording or interpreting of the past is selective, presupposes
value judgments about what is important, and organizes what is recorded
within one out of a number of rationally defensible frames of reference or
points of view. The best basis for reasoning well within a domain of human
learning or experience is to figure out how the basic elements of thought
interrelate within that domain.

ETHICAL REASONING AND PREJUDICE

Consider the ethical domain as an example. Prejudiced thought is often
unethical, or rationalizes unethical behavior. But how are we to understand
the basic logic of moral reasoning? How are we to understand the ingredients
or elements of thought at work in everyday moral thought? We can distinguish at least these three elements:

1) General principles of morality, such as "Do not cheat, deceive, exploit,
harm, or steal from others," "Respect the rights of others, including their
freedom and well-being," "Help those most in need of help, seek the common
good, and strive to make the world more just and humane." These tend to be
shared by people everywhere, at least as expressed ideals.

2) Conflicting general perspectives of the world, such as conservatism, liberalism, theism, atheism, mainstream U.S., Soviet, Chinese, or Japanese world
views. These tend to determine how people conceptualize moral situations.

3) Data, information, or facts relevant to a particular moral issue. Our particular moral judgments are ultimately judgments about particular situations, actions, or persons. We come to our conclusions, at least in part, on the
basis of what we take to be "the facts of the case". (Paul, 1988b)

To reason more critically about moral issues, we must reason with full cog-
nizance of these elements, be able to distinguish the general moral principles
advanced, the perspective on the world into which those principles are integrated, and the factual allegations presupposed or expressed. Quite commonly, for example, people disagree in their general perspective on the world.
One is conservative, the other liberal; one approaches the issue from a mainstream French point of view, the other from a Chinese. Awareness of these
elements does not guarantee resolution of a moral issue, but it does enable
reasoners to focus more particularly on possible problem areas, and, most
importantly, gain insight into how and why their own reasoning may be
biased. For example, our personal, professional, or national perspective on
the world is often based on conditioned associations which have, over time,
become uncritically held prejudgments. As thinkers who aspire to fairmindedness we often have to probe the assumptions that underlie our reasoning;
often we find no rational foundation for them.

✦ *Traits of Mind and Modes of Learning*

The traits of mind and character we develop reflect our use of both logic and association. It makes a profound difference if and how we foster the mind's capacity for rational thought. People easily use their logical powers to justify prejudice, narrowmindedness, and intellectual arrogance. When we are prejudiced, we typically reason logically from prejudiced premises to prejudiced conclusions. Our inferences are logically flawless; these are not the problem. It is the deep seated starting points of our reasoning that are flawed.

We can see this most readily in others. Hence, when the Soviet government sent troops into Afghanistan, they had no trouble justifying their involvement logically. They reasoned as follows:

> When a government that represents the interests of the people is threatened by subversion from outside capitalist forces, it is the moral responsibility of the Soviet Union to stand by their side to protect them until they can successfully defend themselves. The government of Afghanistan represents the interests of the people and is threatened by subversion by the CIA. *Therefore*, it is the moral responsibility of the Soviet Union to protect them.

We easily see the questionableness of the assumption that the government of Afghanistan represents the interests of the people precisely because we do not share it. We are amazed that the Soviets can be so blinded by their prejudices. What we fail to see, of course, is that we are blinded by our own assumptions, which do not seem to us to be prejudices. They seem rather self-evident truths. We, for example, assume that when the CIA intervenes to overturn a government, it does so to serve the interests of its people.

To find the roots of the problem we need only review the contrary social conditioning and accompanying associations of the U.S. and U.S.S.R. U.S. citizens are conditioned to associate the United States with these images and ideas: the stars and stripes, George Washington, Abraham Lincoln, the Bill of Rights, freedom, democracy, land of opportunity, justice for all, human rights, leader of the free world, U.S. military, defense of the free world, etc. Soviets, in turn, are conditioned to associate the USSR with these images and ideas: hammer and sickle, Karl Marx, Lenin, freedom, people's democracy, land of the people, classless society, justice for all, freedom from want and exploitation, defender of the world's poor and workers, great hope for humanity and socialism, etc. The network of conditioned associations operate implicitly to generate a virtually unending series of prejudiced conclusions on both sides. Each side is prejudiced by its own positive associations with itself. Of course this is not all, since both countries also have negative associations about the other.

U.S. citizens associate the Soviet Union with bread-lines, cold and calculating bureaucrats, a monolithic power structure, slavery, totalitarianism, a drive to conquer the world for communism, Siberian labor camps, inefficiency, unhappy people, grey buildings, drab clothes, and long suffering. Soviets, in

230   CRITICAL THINKING IN THE STRONG SENSE

CRITICAL THINKING IN THE STRONG SENSE

turn, associate the United States with the wealthy dominating the poor, massive slums, malnourished poor, drug dealers, prostitutes, gangsters, racism, pornography, right-wing leadership, political corruption, greed, and a ruling-class drive to prevent the workers of the world from self-determination.

Neither side questions its own associations and the prejudices these associations spawn. Each side uses all of its logical powers to trick or outmaneuver the other. Each is self-righteous in its thought and action. Neither side is intellectually humble. Neither side is fairminded. All this is done in a spirit of confident sincerity, with neither side believing itself to have committed any breach of intellectual integrity.

As long as individuals or groups refuse to recognize the conditioned associations that operate at the base of their thinking they cannot develop the traits of mind and character necessary for a significant transcendence of prejudice. Their logical skills will mainly be used to *maintain* rather than to *critique* their prejudices. Their thinking will remain primarily associational and impressionistic, easily influenced by desire, egocentricity, and sociocentricity, typically self-serving, resistant to criticism, and characterized by a lack of intellectual and moral character.

The contrasting mode of thinking is, in a sense, unnatural, and requires a sustained effort to develop. It is primarily logical and driven by a commitment to a consistent and fair use of logical principles. The drive for integrity in thought is characterized by the intellectual virtues: intellectual humility, perseverance, courage, fairmindedness, integrity, and confidence in reason. The challenge, then, is this: to encourage a shift from an egocentric, prejudice forming mode of thinking to a critically reflective and fairminded one.

TEACHING FOR INTELLECTUAL VIRTUE

Such a shift in thinking requires that students *learn intellectual skills* as they *develop traits of mind.* These perfections of mind are acquired if students progressively recognize the importance and value of these virtues as they think in ways consonant with them. Modes of thinking and educational practices are, then, inseparable. Students cannot develop intellectual skills incompatible with classroom practice. Nor can students be expected to develop intellectual traits if these traits are not modeled in an environment favorable to their development.

Nevertheless, there are specific ways in which each of the intellectual virtues can be cultivated and encouraged. *Intellectual fairmindedness* can be fostered by encouraging students to consider evidence and reasons for positions they disagree with, as well as those with which they agree. Students can also be encouraged to show reciprocity when disputes arise or when the class is discussing issues, evaluating the reasoning of story characters, or discussing other cultures. *Intellectual humility* can be fostered in any situation in which students are not in a position to know, by encouraging them to explore the basis for their beliefs. Teachers can model intellectual humility by demonstrating a willingness to admit limits in their own knowledge and in human knowledge generally. *Intellectual courage* is fostered through a consistently openminded atmosphere. Students should be encouraged to honestly consider or doubt any belief. Students who disagree with their peers or text should be given support. Probing questions could be asked regarding unpopular ideas which students have hitherto been discouraged from considering. *Intellectual good faith* or *integrity* can be modeled and fostered by teachers' being sensitive to their own inconsistencies in the application of rules or standards, and helping students to explore their own. When evaluating or developing criteria for evaluation, students should assess both themselves and others, noting their tendency to favor themselves. *Intellectual perseverance* can be fostered by going back to previous problems to reconsider or re-analyze them, as opportunity presents itself. By reviewing and discussing the kinds of difficulties that were inherent in previous problems worked on, and exploring why it is necessary to struggle with them over an extended period, students come to see the value in pursuing important ideas at length. *Confidence in reason* can be fostered by giving students multiple opportunities to try to persuade others and by encouraging students who disagree to reason with one another. These are a few of the many ways in which the traits of mind that define intellectual virtues can be fostered.

✦ *National Prejudice*

It was stated at the beginning of this paper that there are seven fundamental deficiencies in current research on prejudice. In this and the following section we exemplify how each of these seven areas are more common than is admitted. National prejudice will be used as an illustration.

The natural drive toward prejudice is grounded, as we have argued, in egocentricity and its social extension, sociocentricity. We often make ourselves, our group, and our nation the standard by which others are compared and judged, and we do this typically on the basis of prejudgments. We do not, for example, experience a wide variety of societies and then make a comparative judgment based on independent standards. Rarely do we learn to think within the frame of reference of any group or society other than our own. Rather we begin with a host of prejudgments that we and ours are best, and then interpret and experience the events of our world upon the basis of these prejudgments. Not only our thinking but our very identity becomes shaped by thought and experience grounded in prejudgment. If someone questions or criticizes our family, religion, or nation we usually feel personally attacked and rush to the defense. Once they become part of our personal and social identity, prejudices are hard to admit and even harder to dislodge.

An uncritical national perspective is often acquired in childhood, transmitted by parents, peers, and the media. Piaget noticed this tendency and commented, " ... everything suggests that, on discovering the values accepted in his immediate circle, the child felt bound to accept the circle's opinions of

other national groups". These acquired images of other countries are typically not as favorable as that of one's own country, and are sometimes extremely
negative. An us/them dichotomy results, one typically carried into adulthood
as a network of prejudgments. We do not see beliefs based on these prejudgments as one possible perspective among many, but as the unquestionable
truth. Without realizing it, we seek to confirm our prejudgments and tend to
ignore what disconfirms them. We pay attention to what is negative about
them and positive about us. Several things follow from this.

First, we rarely see in those people and groups we dislike the positive
characteristics we take ourselves to have. Second, we rarely see in ourselves
and our favored friends the faults we identify in groups we dislike. And
third, we ascribe to ourselves and our friends intentions we withhold from
those we dislike.

Consider the first of these drives as illustrated in beliefs concerning economic and political arrangements. Western style "free enterprise" and
"democracy" are presented to the ordinary citizen as unquestionably and
obviously the best choice among economic and political structures. Most
North Americans could not persuasively argue for them, but are emotionally
attached to these beliefs regardless. In short, most Westerners are deeply
prejudiced in favor of their own economic and political arrangements and
prejudiced against those that differ from their own. Any study of these systems, say, in school, occurs within this framework and carefully protects the
favored prejudgments. Students do not learn the merits of other systems, but
continually compare them invidiously to their own beliefs, and confirm their
judgments as a result. Furthermore, we typically compare other systems'
worse points with our systems' best points, negative facts about other systems with positive ideals within ours. This is routinely done with virtually no
objection from the academic community, which itself usually reflects social
prejudices. These tendencies, unrecognized and unchecked, embed our deeply
held prejudgments in thought and action.

Prejudice also protects our viewpoints, interests, actions, and institutions
from unsettling criticism. As mentioned previously, these beliefs often constitute the bulwark of our personal and cultural identity, and we often find it
psychologically painful to think we might be wrong, especially regarding fundamentals. Prejudice gives us peace of mind, protects us from the possibility
of having to admit fundamental error, allows us to pursue vested interests,
and when others are harmed in some way by our pursuit of our interests,
enables us to continue with a clear conscience. We need only search our own
memories to find abundant examples of times we dogmatically defended
some favored position or belief, only to change our minds later. Our egocentric and sociocentric thinking prevents us from considering the merits of
other positions. Our rigid idealization of ourselves generates a rigid negation
of those who question us, oppose us, or simply stand in our way.

In addition, prejudice offers a confident and comforting retreat from the
complexities and uncertainties of life, for problems are more easily identified

and solutions more readily proposed, since there are few grey areas or complexities in prejudice. But the protection and solace of this retreat also provides for the flourishing of dogmatism, closedmindedness, double standards, oversimplification, injustice, and inequity. No one political or social system has all of the truth, neither does any political or social system contain all falsehood. But a dichotomous world view, acquired and preserved through prejudice, prevents recognition of whatever merit there might be in opposing systems. Honest and open dialogue among an array of different and opposing points of view is rare and its absence rarely noted.

Prejudice, again, is the typical, the normal state of affairs in everyday life, not an aberration; it serves a multitude of functions, from providing peace of mind to the gaining of power, wealth, and status; prejudice "for" a position is as common and potentially destructive as prejudice "against"; it is commonly directed against beliefs and ideologies as well as against ethnic and racial groups. It is one with the problem of human irrationality. National prejudice reflects this complexity. An examination of how the news media reinforces national prejudice suggests the kind of ambitious and thorough approach to prejudice reduction necessary to significantly lessen it.

✦ Prejudice and the Mainstream U.S. World View

One must first become aware of how a prejudice is expressed before one can recognize instances of it. Consider some of the more basic mainstream U.S. national prejudices.

We see ourselves as citizens of the most powerful country in the world. We see our country as moderate, peace-loving, just, democratic, free, honest in international dealings, supportive of human rights and consistently opposed to terrorism. Though subject to mistakes, the U.S. is seen as right on all fundamental issues, even when it stands alone against world opinion. Internally the country is understood to be the freest, with the greatest degree of equality of opportunity to rise to the top.

These are only a few of the many possible attitudes that could have been listed, attitudes that influence the way we view our country and its actions and policies. Since we assume that we are peace-loving, we have difficulty conceiving of our country as an aggressor in any conflict. Any who so conceive us fail to see that we are acting in self-defense, protecting ourselves, our allies, or our legitimate interests. We only "intervene" in the affairs of other countries to help them toward a more democratic government, even if they do not appreciate it at the time. We are criticized only because we are misunderstood, or because leftist propaganda has generated the criticism. Even when virtually every country of the world is against us (for example, in denying Arafat a visa) it is simply because they do not understand (in this case, because they do not grasp the threat of terrorism).

NEWS MEDIA AND NATIONAL PREJUDICE

All human thinking depends on our beliefs, beliefs that form the basis of classification, interpretation, and experience. Many of these beliefs are uncritically formed at an early age and retained and defended as prejudices. We rarely recognize how we acquired them or how they influence our perceptions. We experience but do not monitor *how* we experience events, nor do we identify what beliefs underlie which interpretations. As beliefs differ, expectations and interpretations also differ, but we do not observe this process in operation. For example, when citizens are raised to believe that the motives of their leaders are "pure" while the motives of leaders of "enemy" countries are "evil" or self-serving, events concerning these countries are experienced accordingly. The experiencer does not notice why, or link that experience to social conditioning. This difference in perspective focuses the attention of the viewer on some elements of the event and away from others, and often leads to widely disparate interpretations and experiences. News items about an intervention in *our* newspapers present interpretations of events based upon *our* assumptions and beliefs, while *their* newspapers present interpretations of the events based upon *their* assumptions and beliefs. We (and they) do not recognize that we both shape the news in a self-serving sociocentric way.

National prejudice is by no means peculiar to the United States. Every nation has its prejudiced image of itself as a nation, an image that greatly determines how events are interpreted. Consider this point made by Jerome Frank (1982), which vividly illustrates how national prejudice influences our image of other nations:

> Enemy-images mirror each other — that is, each side attributes the same virtues to itself and the same vices to the enemy. "We" are trustworthy, peace-loving, honorable, and humanitarian, "they" are treacherous, warlike, and cruel. In surveys of Americans conducted in 1942, the first five adjectives chosen to characterize both Germans and Japanese (enemies) included warlike, treacherous, and cruel, none of which appeared among the first five describing the Russians (allies); in 1966 all three had disappeared from American characterizations of the Germans and Japanese (allies), but now the Russians (no longer allies, but more rivals than enemies) were warlike and treacherous. In 1966 the Mainland Chinese predictably, were seen as warlike, treacherous, and sly. After President Nixon's visit to China, these adjectives disappeared from our characterizations of the Chinese, whom we now see as hardworking, intelligent, artistic, progressive, and practical.

Several examples illustrate how these tendencies are articulated in the media. Consider Admiral Trost's article "The Morning of the Empty Trenches: Soviet Politics of Maneuver and the U.S. Response".

> We in the West, whose ethical foundations lie on concepts of truth and justice, are frequently surprised to find that other civilizations have different ethics. In our relationship with the Soviet Union, this has had a curious inside-out effect. We have been lied to so many times that we now eagerly rush forward at the first sign that the Soviets are telling the truth. Occasionally, the Soviets may find it convenient to lie, and we must learn to deal with this.

Admiral Trost claims that the professed ethical foundations of some civilizations lie on falsehood and injustice. Clearly this is false, for all nations claim to value truth and justice. However, what a nation considers ethical often differs from what is actually ethical. Motivated by egocentricity and sociocentricity, people idealize their beliefs and actions. We value truth and justice, but so do they. We see our actions as good and just, but so do they. We differ, of course, in the things we take as being true and just.

If we or those we like engage in some activity of a questionable or negative nature, we justify the activity by appealing to motive or intent ("We meant well."). A clear example from the *San Francisco Chronicle* (1988) illustrates this:

> For the United States the war in Vietnam was humbling, draining public hubris and setting the precedent for a deficit economy. Vietnam, with Soviet support, taught America that *purity of motive* does not always prevail. (Emphasis ours.)

Though most now agree that the war in Vietnam was a tragic mistake, many still insist that our motives were "pure". Several years ago the California State Assembly passed a resolution by a vote of 52–0, that the Vietnam war was waged for a "noble purpose". However, if those we dislike engage in similar actions, we ascribe negative intent to them as easily as we do positive intent to ourselves. The Soviet involvement in Afghanistan is a recent case in point. We see *ourselves* as intervening to support a struggling democracy (South Vietnam) against an outside aggressor (North Vietnam). We see *them* as invading Afghanistan to prop up a puppet dictatorship. The Soviets see these two instances as reversed: the U.S. is the aggressor, the U.S.S.R. is the liberator. To substantiate this, consider this excerpt from the Soviet press, taken from the front page of *Pravda* dated October 14, 1986. It is written in the form of an open letter to Soviet troops returning from Afghanistan. The headline reads: "To the Soldier Internationalists Returning from the Democratic Republic of Afghanistan".

> Dear Comrades!
> We welcome you warmly, glorious sons of the Homeland. You are returning home having honorably fulfilled your internationalist duty on the soil of friendly Afghanistan.
> At the request of that country's legitimate government, you, soldiers of peace, along with your fighting friends who previously completed their terms of military service in the Democratic Republic of Afghanistan, have helped the Afghan people defend their independence and freedom and the achievements of the national democratic April Revolution, and have helped to ensure the reliable security of the southern borders of our Fatherland.
> Soviet soldiers, along with Afghan soldiers and all of the country's patriots, have courageously opposed and continue to oppose the armed aggression of hostile forces encroaching on the sovereignty of the Afghan state.

The letter continues at some length, and includes such phrases as these: "... we take pride (in) freedom and equality, culture and democracy ... " and,

"Lasting peace and reliable security for all people is our ideal." Notice the elements common to the prejudice of many nations: the (stated) love of peace, democracy, equality; disdain for aggression, terrorism, imperialism, and oppression. We defend our interventionist activities in Central America by saying that we must protect this hemisphere from the encroachment of communist influence. The U.S.S.R. defends its interventionist activities in Afghanistan similarly:

> (I)n a situation where imperialism continues to threaten the security of the socialist Fatherland and of our allies and friends and unceremoniously interferes in the affairs of others, we must be on guard.

The next two articles illustrate the use of a double standard to condemn the actions of an "enemy" country while not condemning similar actions of a "friendly" country. Both articles appeared on the front page of the "World News" section of the March 1, 1989, edition of the *San Francisco Chronicle*. The first article is titled "No Attacks on Israel: U.S. Amends Terms For Talks With PLO".

> The United States called on the Palestine Liberation Organization yesterday to refrain from attacks on Israeli military and civilian targets inside and outside Israel if it wants to continue its discussions with Washington ....
>
> In December, the United States agreed to open direct talks with the PLO after Yasser Arafat ... renounced terrorism and said he accepts Israel's right to exist.
>
> Now the United States is saying that the PLO must abstain from attacks on Israeli military targets regardless of whether such attacks fit its definition of terrorism.

In contrasting this article with the one appearing with it, the double standard becomes immediately apparent. The article is headlined "Israeli Jets Hit Bases in Lebanon 22 Children Hurt".

> Israeli jets bombed Palestinian targets southwest of Beirut yesterday, killing three people and wounding 22 school children, the police said. The police said a missile fired by one of the jets hit a school yard in the village of Ainab, wounding the children.

Nothing in this article suggests that Israel be censured for this attack. Neither is any connection made between the bombing of school yards and 'terrorism'. To exercise fairmindedness, we should imagine how this event would have been reported had Palestine attacked Israel and injured 22 Israeli school children. The action would certainly have been labeled terrorism and condemned. Instead, we condemn Palestine and declare that "the PLO must abstain from attacks on Israeli military targets," while Israel is free to "defend" its interests however it likes. Two standards are applied, a very liberal one for our ally, a strict one for their adversary.

Consider another article from the front page of *Pravda*, April 2, 1988.

> Occupied Territories: Despite the draconian repressive measures of the occupational authorities, Palestinians took to the streets in the past 24 hours to express protest against the terror unleashed on them by the aggressors. A

UN spokesman stated that on Wednesday, Land Day, the Israeli aggressors killed eight people and wounded 250 in carrying out punitive actions against the Palestinians.

We are immediately struck by several words: repressive, terror, aggressors, and punitive actions. These are words U.S. citizens normally associate with the Palestinians and their actions, not the Israelis and their actions. This article would be written very differently in our press, written to favor our friend and ally, Israel. Sociocentricity inevitably convinces us that our actions and our ally's actions are justified. This attitude is reflected in and perpetuated by the language we use to describe these events. Our choice of words give important clues in identifying prejudice: the favorable words reserved for our friends, the negative for our rivals or enemies.

Of the many forms that prejudice can take, national prejudice has perhaps the greatest potential for destruction. The prejudices of nations have global consequences. The deep-seated problems of environmental change, new complex health problems, worsening human relations, diminishing resources, overpopulation, rising expectations, global competition, and ideological conflict increasingly interact with each other to produce a host of multidimensional, logically messy problems. Our survival as a species demands that the higher potential of human critical thought be significantly tapped. The ability to recognize national prejudice and prejudiced thinking requires cultivation, as do the more general principles of critical thought.

✦ *Conclusion*

Prejudice is a rich, complex, multidimensional phenomenon, grounded in what might be called the primary, instinctual nature of human thinking. Removing prejudice requires the development of our secondary, more latent, nature, our capacity to develop as fairminded rational persons. Research into prejudice has truncated the concept while underestimating its roots, thereby delaying deep understanding of the global nature of the problem as well as of the required solution.

To understand the nature of prejudice, we must see it in relation to our basic modes of thinking, in relation to our desires and goals, in relation to our intellectual and moral traits of mind, in relation to our social groups and educational practices. Prejudice formation involves the way we think, the way we form beliefs, and the way we assess beliefs. It is fundamentally uncritical or narrowmindedly critical, governed by egocentricity and sociocentricity, reflecting double standards and inconsistencies. Obviously, humans *can* analyze, synthesize, and assess their thinking in a less than fairminded way. They can easily reshape their thinking to make it self-delusive. They create fantasies that have little relationship to reality and then live in them as though they were reality. They confuse their systems of thought, their viewpoints, ideologies, and cultural perspectives with reality itself. They embody their prejudices in cultural practices, indoctrinate children into narrow and rigid beliefs, and perpetuate closedmindedness, intolerance, and fear. They easily say one thing and do another, compartmentalize their contradictions, believe what their experience denies, ignore evidence, misuse language, value in themselves what they criticize in others, ignore and repeat their mistakes, project their faults onto others, and undermine the conditions of their own survival.

Fairminded critical thinking has always been a part of human thinking, but typically a subordinate part. Intellectuals and other intelligent people often use prejudiced thinking to advance their self-interest. Rather than exposing the narrowness of ideologies, they distinguish themselves as skilled proponents of them; rather than challenging prejudices and risking the wrath of the prejudiced, they perpetuate them; rather than taking on the worthwhile task of helping people become independent thinkers, they manipulate them, thereby advancing their self-interest. It is certainly easier to *take advantage of* prejudices and narrowmindedness than to *eradicate* them. As a result, human life and societies have often been dominated by the manipulated and the manipulators, by those largely uncritical in their thought and action and those who use their critical abilities to their narrowly conceived personal advantage. This weak form of critical thinking is the predominant mode of critical thinking developed in schools and social life.

Because the problem of prejudice formation and preservation reflects fundamental forms of thought that pervade every dimension of social and personal life, any successful effort to reduce prejudice must be systematic and foundational. A sustained and serious effort to reduce prejudice should extend into three areas of a child's life: the scholastic, the familial, and the social. Of these three, the scholastic provides the most immediate opportunity for implementing a comprehensive program of prejudice reduction. But this cannot be accomplished quickly, nor should we expect it to be. To effect changes as fundamental and sweeping as these will take years. This is an argument, not against action, but rather for a realistic strategy, for steady, deep changes over a long time. As individuals change, as their mode of thinking shifts from one that encourages prejudiced thought formation to one antithetical to it, society's folkways and mores will themselves shift, and so will familial behavior and interaction.

An educational effort to move students from prejudiced to fairminded thought processes requires critical thinking and the cultivation of intellectual traits of character. (Paul, 1987c, 1988a, 1988b.) It should not focus on the content of particular prejudices except for illustrative purposes. It should emphasize the explication of the *mechanisms* of prejudice and their role in the struggle for power, advantage, and money. It should begin with the assumption that prejudice recognition and reduction ought to begin with each of us, with our own prejudices. A credible program of prejudice reduction ought not focus on the prejudices of others, prejudices against us, for we are ideally situated to change our own mode of thinking, not to change the thinking of others.

✦ References

Allport, Gordon W. *The Nature of Prejudice*. Addison Wesley Publishing Co. Cambridge, Mass. 1954.

Frank, Jerome. "Psychological Causes of the Nuclear Arms Race." *CHEMTECH*, Aug., 1982. p. 467.

JAMA (Journal of the American Medical Association) "Special Communication: Permanent Injunction Order Against the AMA," Jan. 1, 1988. pp. 81–2.

Keating, P. and Oakes, J. "Access to Knowledge: Breaking Down School Barriers to Learning." *Denver CO: The Education Commission of the States* 1988.

Klineberg, Otto. "Prejudice" *International Encyclopedia of the Social Sciences.* Crowell Collier and MacMillan, Inc. 1968.

Paul, Richard W. (1987a) *Critical Thinking Handbook: K–3, A Guide for Remodelling Lesson Plans in Language Arts, Social Studies, and Science* Co-authors: A. J. A. Binker, Marla Charbonneau. Published by the Center for Critical Thinking and Moral Critique.

Paul, Richard W. (1987b) *Critical Thinking Handbook: 4ᵗʰ–6ᵗʰ Grades, A Guide for Remodelling Lesson Plans in Language Arts, Social Studies, and Science* Co-authors: A. J. A. Binker, Karen Jensen, and Heidi Kreklau. Published by the Center for Critical Thinking and Moral Critique.

Paul, Richard W. (1987c) "Dialogical Thinking: Critical Thought Essential to the Acquisition of Rational Knowledge and Passion," *Teaching Thinking Skills: Theory and Practice,* Joan Baron and Robert Steinberg, editors. W. H. Freeman and Co., 1987.

Paul, Richard W. (1988a) "Critical Thinking and the Critical Person," *Thinking: Progress in Research and Teaching,* by Perkins, et al., editors. Lawrence Erlbaum Associates, Inc., Hillsdale, New Jersey.

Paul, Richard W. (1988b) "Ethics Without Indoctrination," in *Educational Leadership,* Ronald Brandt, ed. May, 1988.

Paul, Richard W. (1989a) *Critical Thinking Handbook: 6ᵗʰ–9ᵗʰ Grades, A Guide for Remodelling Lesson Plans in Language Arts, Social Studies, and Science* Co-authors: A. J. A. Binker, Chris Vetrano, Heidi Kreklau Douglas Martin. Published by the Center for Critical Thinking and Moral Critique.

Paul, Richard W. (1989b) "Critical Thinking in North America: A New Theory of Knowledge, Learning, and Literacy." Forthcoming, *Argumentation,* D. Reidel Publishing Co., Dordrecht, The Netherlands.

Piaget, Jean. "The Transition from Egocentricity to Reciprocity." In Campbell, Sarah F. ed. *Piaget Sampler, An Introduction to Jean Piaget Through His Own Words,* John Wiley and Sons, New York. 1976.

Prejudice and Discrimination Book 2 of *"Challenges of Our Time,"* prepared by the Social Studies Staff of the Education Research Council of America. Allyn and Bacon, Inc., Boston. 1977.

Sumner, William Graham *Folkways* Ginn and Co., Boston. 1940.

Tajfel, Henri. "Prejudice," in *Encyclopedic Dictionary of Psychology,* Rom Harre and Roger Lamb (ed.) MIT Press, Cambridge, Mass. 1983.

Trost, C. A. H., Admiral, U.S. Navy. "The Morning of the Empty Trenches: Soviet Politics of Maneuver and the U.S. Response." *U.S. Naval Institute: Proceedings,* Aug., 1988. p. 15.

Tucker, M. S. "Peter Drucker: Knowledge, Work, and the Structure of Schools." *Educational Leadership,* 1988, 45. pp. 44–46.

The Affective and
Ethical Dimension

✦✦ Chapter 12

Ethics Without Indoctrination

Abstract

In this revised paper, originally published in Educational Leadership *(1988), Richard Paul argues that ethics ought to be taught in school, but only in conjunction with critical thinking. Without critical thinking at the heart of ethical instruction,* indoctrination *rather than ethical* insight *results. Moral principles do not apply themselves, they require a thinking mind to assess facts and interpret situations. Moral agents inevitably bring their perspectives into play in making moral judgments and this, together with the natural tendency of the human mind to self-deception when its interests are involved, is the fundamental impediment to the right use of ethical principles.*

Paul spells out the implications of this view for the teaching of ethics in literature, science, history, and civics. He provides a taxonomy of moral reasoning skills and describes an appropriate long term staff development strategy to foster ethics across the curriculum.

✦ *The Problem of Indoctrination*

$\mathcal{N}$ early everyone recognizes that even young children have moral feelings and ideas, make moral inferences and judgments, and develop an outlook on life which has moral significance for good or ill. Nearly everyone also gives at least lip service to a universal common core of general ethical principles — for example, that it is morally wrong to cheat, deceive, exploit, abuse, harm, or steal from others, that everyone has a moral responsibility to respect the rights of others, including their freedom and well-being, to help those most in need of help, to seek the common good and not merely their own self-interest and egocentric pleasures, to strive in some way to make this world more just and humane. Unfortunately, mere verbal agreement on general moral principles alone will not accomplish important moral ends nor change the world for the better. Moral principles mean something only when manifested in behavior. They have force only when embodied in action. Yet to put them into action requires some analysis and insight into the real character of everyday situations.

The world does not present itself to us in morally transparent terms. The moral thing to do is often a matter of disagreement even among people of good will. One and the same act is often morally praised by some, condemned by others. Furthermore, even when we do not face the morally conflicting claims of others, we often have our own inner conflicts as to what, morally speaking, we should do in some particular situation. Considered another way, ethical persons, however strongly motivated to do what is morally right, can do so only if they know what that is. And this they cannot do if they systematically confuse their sense of what is morally right with their self-interest, personal desires, or what is commonly believed in their peer group or community. Because of complexities such as these, ethically motivated persons must learn the art of self-critique, of moral self-examination, to become attuned to the pervasive everyday pitfalls of moral judgment: moral intolerance, self-deception, and uncritical conformity. These human foibles cause pseudo-morality, the systematic misuse of moral terms and principles in the guise of moral action and righteousness.

Unfortunately few have thought much about the complexity of everyday moral issues, can identify their own moral contradictions, or clearly distinguish their self-interest and egocentric desires from what is genuinely moral. Few have thought deeply about their own moral feelings and judgments, have tied these judgments together into a coherent moral perspective, or have mastered the complexities of moral reasoning. As a result, everyday moral judgments are often a subtle mixture of pseudo and genuine morality, moral insight and moral prejudice, moral truth and moral hypocrisy. Herein lies the danger of setting up ill-thought-out public school programs in moral education. Without scrupulous care, we merely pass on to students our own moral blindness, moral distortions, and closedmindedness. Certainly many who trumpet most loudly for ethics and morality in the schools merely want students to adopt *their* ethical beliefs and *their* ethical perspectives, regardless of the fusion of insight and prejudice those beliefs and perspectives doubtless represent. They take themselves to have *the Truth* in their pockets. They take their perspective to be exemplary of all morality rightly conceived. On the other hand, what these same people fear most is someone else's moral perspective taught as the truth: conservatives afraid of liberals being in charge, liberals of conservatives, theists of non-theists, non-theists of theists.

Now, if truth be told, all of these fears are justified. People, except in the most rare and exceptional cases, do have a strong tendency to confuse what they believe with the truth. It is always the others who do evil, who are deceived, self-interested, closedminded — never us. Given this universal blind spot in human nature, the only safe and justified basis for ethical education in the pubic schools is one precisely designed to rule out bias in favor of the substantive beliefs and conclusions of any particular group, whether religious, political, communal, or national. Indeed since one of our most fundamental responsibilities as educators is to *educate* rather than indoctrinate our students — to help them cultivate skills, insights, knowledge, and traits of mind and character that transcend narrow party and religious affiliations and help them to think beyond biased representations of the world — we must put special safeguards into moral education that prevent indoctrination. The world needs not more closedminded zealots, eager to remake the world in their image, but more morally committed rational persons with respect for and insight into the moral judgments and perspectives of others, those least likely to confuse pseudo with genuine morality.

But how is this to be done? How can we cultivate morality and character in our students without indoctrinating them, without systematically rewarding them merely because they express our moral beliefs and espouse our moral perspective?

The answer is in putting *critical thinking* into the heart of the ethical curriculum, critical thinking for both teachers and students. To bring ethics and morality into the schools in an educationally legitimate way, administrators and teachers must think critically about what to emphasize and what to avoid. Intellectually discriminating minds and morally refined sensibilities must be in charge of both initial curriculum design and its subsequent classroom implementation. This is not an unreasonable demand, for, ethics aside, skill in the art of drawing important intellectual discriminations is crucial to education in any subject or domain, and proficiency in the art of teaching critically — encouraging students to question, think for themselves, develop rational standards of judgment — is the responsibility of all classroom teachers. Any subject, after all, can be taught merely to indoctrinate students and so to inadvertently stultify rather than develop their ability to think within it. Unfortunately, we have all been subjected to a good deal of indoctrination in the name of education and retain to this day some of the intellectual disabilities that such scholastic straight-jacketing produces. To allow ethics to be taught in the public schools this narrowly is unconscionable. It is to betray our ethical responsibility as educators in the name of ethics.

✦ *Integrating Critical Thinking and Ethics*

If we bring ethics into the curriculum — and we should — we must ensure that we do so morally. This requires us to clearly distinguish between espousing the universal, general principles of morality shared by people of good will everywhere, and the very different matter of defending some particular application of these principles to actual life situations as conceived from a particular moral standpoint (liberal, conservative, radical, theistic, non-theistic, U.S., Soviet, etc.). Any particular moral judgment arises from someone conceptualizing the facts of a situation from some moral perspective or standpoint. Every moral perspective in some way embodies the same general moral principles. The integration of *principles* with purported *facts* within a particular *perspective* produces the judgment that this or that act is morally right or wrong. Precisely because we often differ about the facts or about the proper perspective on the facts, we come to differing moral judgments.

The problem is not at the level of general moral principles. No people in the world, as far as I know, take themselves to oppose human rights or stand for injustice, slavery, exploitation, deception, dishonesty, theft, greed, starvation, ignorance, falsehood, and human suffering. In turn, no nation or group has special ownership over any general moral principle. Students, then, need skill and practice in moral reasoning, not indoctrination into the view that one nation rather than another is special in enunciating these moral principles. Students certainly need opportunities to explicitly learn basic moral principles, but more importantly they need opportunities to apply them to real and imagined cases, and to develop insight into both genuine and pseudo morality. They especially need to come to terms with the pitfalls of human moralizing, to recognize the ease with which we mask self-interest or egocentric desires with high-sounding moral language.

In any case, for any particular instance of moral judgment or reasoning, students should learn the art of distinguishing *principles* (which tell us in a general way what we ought or ought not to do) from *perspectives* (which characterize the world in ways which lead to an organized way of interpreting it) and *facts* (which provide the specific information for a particular moral judgment). In learning to discriminate these dimensions of moral reasoning, we learn how to focus on the appropriate questions at issue. Sometimes the dispute will depend on the facts: (Did John actually take the watch?) But, more often, they will be a matter of perspective (If you look at it this way, Jack did not take advantage of her, but if you look at it that way, he did. Which is more plausible given the facts?) Sometimes they will be a matter of both the facts and how to interpret them. (Do most people on welfare deserve the money they get? Should white collar crime be punished more severely?).

As people, students have an undeniable right to develop their own moral perspective — whether conservative, liberal, theistic, or non-theistic — but they should be able to analyze the perspective they do use, compare it accurately with other perspectives, and scrutinize the facts they conceptualize and judge as carefully as in any other domain of knowledge. They should, in other words, become as adept in using critical thinking principles in the moral domain as we expect them to be in scientific and social domains of learning.

To help students gain these skills, teachers need to see how one adapts the principles of critical thinking to the domain of ethical judgment and reasoning (see figure #1). Teachers also need insight into the intimate interconnection of intellectual and moral virtues. They need to see that being moral is something more than abstract good-heartedness, that our basic ways of knowing are inseparable from our basic ways of being, that how we think and judge in our daily life reflects who we are, morally and intellectually. To cultivate the kind of moral independence implied in being an educated moral person, we must foster in students moral humility, moral courage, moral integrity, moral perseverance, moral empathy, and moral fairmindedness (see figure #2). These moral traits are compatible with all moral perspectives (whether conservative, liberal, theistic, non-theistic, etc.).

Students who learn to think critically about moral issues and so develop moral virtues, can then develop their moral thinking within any tradition they choose. Critical thinking does not compel or coerce students to come to any particular substantive moral conclusions or to adopt any particular substantive moral point of view. Neither does it imply moral relativism, for it emphasizes the need for the same high intellectual standards in moral reasoning and judgment at the foundation of any bona fide domain of knowledge. Since moral judgment and reasoning presupposes and is subject to the same intellectual principles and standards that educated people use in all domains of learning, one can integrate consideration of moral issues into diverse subject areas, certainly into literature, science, history, civics, and society. Let us consider each of these areas very briefly.

✦ Ethics and Literature

Good literature represents and reveals, to the reflective critical reader, the deeper meanings and universal problems of real everyday life. Most of these problems have an important moral dimension or character. They are the kinds of problems all of us must think about and solve for ourselves; no one can simply tell us the "right" answers:

> Who am I? What kind of person am I? What is the world really like? What are my parents, my friends, and other people really like? How have I become the way I am? What should I believe in? Why should I believe in it? What real options do I have? Who are my real friends? Who should I trust? Who are my enemies? Need they be my enemies? How did the world become the way it is? How do people become the way they are? Are there any really bad people in the world? Are there any really good people in the world? What is good and bad? What is right and wrong? How should I decide? How can I decide what is fair and what is unfair? How can I be fair to others? Do I have to be fair to my enemies? How should I live my life? What rights do I have? What responsibilities?

Stimulating students to reflect upon questions like these in relationship to story episodes and their own experience enables them to draw upon their own developing moral feelings and ideas, to reason about them systematically, to tie them together and see where they lead. Careful reflection on episodes in literature — characters making sound or unsound moral judgments, sometimes ignoring basic moral principles or twisting them to serve their vested interests, sometimes displaying moral courage or cowardice, often caught in the throws of a moral dilemma — helps students develop a basic moral outlook on life. Furthermore, since moral issues are deeply embedded in everyday life, they often appear in literature. One need not unnaturally force discussion of literature into a moral framework. Moral issues are inevitably implicit there for the raising. However, it is important to realize that moral issues in literature, like the moral issues of everyday life, are rarely simplistic, and involved students will typically generate opposing viewpoints about how to respond to them. This, too, reflects the nature of the real world with its variety of moral outlooks vying for our allegiance.

As teachers of literature we should not impose authoritative interpretations upon the student; we should help them develop a reasoned, reflective, and coherent approach of their own. Each perspective, of course, should be respected; however, to be considered, each perspective must be *reasoned out*, not simply dogmatically asserted. In discussion, each student must learn the art of appealing to experience and reason, not merely to authority. Each student must therefore learn to reflect upon the grounds of his or her beliefs, to clarify ideas, support them with reasons and evidence, explore their implications, and so forth. Each student must also learn how to sympathetically enter into the moral perspectives of the others, not with the view that all moral perspectives are equally sound, but rather with the sense that we cannot judge another person's perspective until we genuinely understand it. Everyone is due the respect of at least being *understood*. And just as students will feel that they have something worth saying about the moral issues facing characters in stories and want their views to be understood, so they must learn to give that same respect to the others. Students then learn the art of reasoned dialogue, how to use moral reasoning skills to articulate their concerns about rights, justice, and the common good, from whatever moral viewpoint their experience and background predisposes them.

Essay writing is an excellent means of helping students organize their thinking on moral issues in literature. It provides the impetus to formulate moral principles explicitly, to carefully conceptualize and interpret facts, and to give and consider reasons in support of their own and contending moral conclusions. Needless to say we must grade students' moral writing, not on the basis of their substantive perspectives or conclusions, but rather on grounds of clarity, coherence, and sound reasoning. A clearly thought out, well-reasoned, well-illustrated piece of "moral" writing is what we are after. Such writing need not be long and complicated. Indeed it can begin in the early years with one-sentence "essays" such as "I think Jack (in "Jack and the Bean Stalk") was greedy because he didn't need to take all the golden eggs and the golden harp, too."

✦ Ethics and Science

Students should study science to understand, evaluate, and utilize scientific information. Most students will not, of course, become scientists but nevertheless need scientific knowledge to understand and solve problems within everyday personal and vocational life, problems having to do with such diverse areas as medicine, biology, chemistry, engineering, technology, the environment, and business. Science and technology play a greater and greater role in our lives, often generating major moral issues in the process. Scientific information is not simply *used*, it is used, and sometimes misused, for a variety of purposes, to advance the interests of a variety of groups, as those interests are conceived from a variety of perspectives. Its use must always be *assessed*.

In their daily lives students, like the rest of us, are bombarded with scientific information of every kind, typically in relation to some kind of advocacy.

And they, like the rest of us, need to make decisions about the implications of that information. What are the real dangers of air pollution? Do people have a right to clean air and water? If so, how clean? What are the consequences of developing nuclear rather than solar power? To what extent should scientists be able to use animals in their experiments? Do animals have moral rights? To what extent should scientists be allowed to experiment with new viruses that might generate new diseases? Under what conditions should people be artificially kept alive? What life and death decisions should be left to doctors? What special moral responsibilities, if any, do scientists have to the broader society? These are but a few of the many weighty moral and scientific issues with which all of us as educated people are faced. Whether we develop an informed viewpoint or not, practical decisions are made everyday in each of these areas, and the public good is served or abused as a result of the rationality or irrationality of those decisions. Although many of these issues are ignored in traditional science instruction, there are good reasons not only to include but to emphasize them. First, they are more interesting and useful to most students than the more traditional "pure-science" emphasis. Second, they help students develop a more unified perspective on their values and personal beliefs and on the moral issues that science inevitably generates when applied to the real world.

✦ Ethics and History

There is no more important subject, rightly conceived, than history. Human life in all of its dimensions is deeply historical. Whatever experiences we have, the accounts that we give of things, our memories, our records, our sense of ourselves, the "news" we construct, the plans we form, even the daily gossip we hear — are historical. Furthermore, since we all have a deep-seated drive to think well of ourselves, and virtually unlimited powers to twist reality to justify ourselves, how we construct history has far-reaching ethical consequences. Not only do virtually all ethical issues have a historical component (moral judgment presupposes an account of what actually happened) but also virtually all historical issues have important ethical implications.

Issues arise among historians when they have conflicting accounts of events. Each major moral standpoint tends to *read* history differently and comes to importantly different moral conclusions as a result. The moral and the historical come together again and again in questions such as these: Morally speaking, what does the past *teach* us? What were the long-term effects of this kind of action as opposed to that? What kind of a world are we living in? What moral ideals can we actually live by and in what way? Is pacifism, for example, realistic? Are we justified in engaging in "unethical" practices in our own defense because our enemies use them to attack or harm us? What does it mean for countries to be "friendly" toward each other? How are friendships between countries like and unlike those between individuals?

To what extent have we as a nation (and I as an individual) lived in accordance with the moral ideals we have set for ourselves? For example, was the historical treatment accorded Native Americans and other ethnic groups, has our foreign policy in general, been in keeping with our traditional espoused moral values? Morally speaking, how could our founding fathers justify slavery? Should they be morally criticized for accepting this violation of human rights or are there historical reasons why our criticism should be tempered with "understanding"? If our founding fathers, who eloquently formulated universal moral principles, were capable of violating them, are we now different from them, are we morally *better*, or are we also, without recognizing it, violating basic moral values we verbally espouse?

Once we grasp the moral significance of history, as well as the historical significance of morality, and recognize that historical judgment, like ethical judgement, is necessarily selective, that facts are conceptualized from some point of view, then we are well on our way toward constructing an unlimited variety of assignments in which history is no longer an abstraction from present and immediate concerns but rather an exciting, living, thought-provoking subject. Once students truly see themselves constructing history on a daily basis and, in doing so, coming to conclusions that directly affect the well-being of themselves and others, they will have taken a giant step toward becoming historically sensitive, ethical persons. As Carl Becker said in his presidential address to the American Historical Association over 50 years ago, every person, like it or not, "is his own historian". We must make sure that our students grasp the *moral* significance of that fact.

✦ *Ethics, Civics, and the Study of Society*

Just as all of us, to be ethical, must be our own historian, so too, to ethically fulfill our civic responsibilities, we must be our own sociologists. That is to say, each of us must study the underlying realities of social events, the unwritten rules and values that unreflectively guide our behavior; otherwise how can we justify using ethical principles to judge people and situations in the real world around us? We should be more than uncritical social observers and superficial moral judges. We have to recognize, as every sociologist since William Graham Sumner has pointed out, that most human behavior is a result of unanalyzed habit and routine based on unconsciously held standards and values. These embedded standards and values often differ from, even oppose, the ideals we express, and yet the conformist thinking which socialization tends to produce resists critical analysis. This resistance was recognized even from the early days of sociology as a discipline:

> Every group of any kind demands that each of its members shall help defend group interests ... group force is also employed to enforce the obligations of devotion to group interests. It follows that judgments are precluded and criticism is silenced. (Sumner, 1906)

Even patriotism, Sumner points out, "may degenerate into a vice ... chauvinism":

> It is a name for boastful and truculent group self-assertion. It overrules personal judgment and character, and puts the whole group at the mercy of the clique which is ruling at the moment. It produces the dominance of watchwords and phrases which take the place of reason and conscience in determining conduct. The patriotic bias is a recognized perversion of thought and judgment against which our education should guard us. (Sumner, 1906)

Ironically, true patriots in a democratic society serve their country by using their critical powers to ensure governmental honesty. Intelligent distrust rather than uncritical trust is the foundation necessary to keep officials acting ethically and in the public good. It was Jefferson who said:

> It would be a dangerous delusion were a confidence in the men of our choice to silence our fears for the safety of our rights. Confidence is everywhere the parent of despotism — free government is founded in jealousy, and not in confidence.

And Madison enthusiastically agreed: "The truth is, all men having power ought to be mistrusted."

What students need in civic education, then, is precisely what they need in moral education: not indoctrination into abstracted ideals, with the tacit implication that the ideals are generally practiced, not slogans and empty moralizing, but assignments that challenge their ability to use civic ideals to assess actual political behavior. Such assignments will, of course, produce divergent conclusions by students depending on their present political leanings. But, again, their thinking, speaking, and writing should be graded on the clarity, cogency, and intellectual rigor of their work, not on the substance of their answers. All students should learn the art of political analysis, the art of subjecting political behavior to critical assessment based on civic and moral ideals, on an analysis of important relevant facts, and on consideration of alternative political viewpoints. Virtually no students graduate today with this art in hand.

This means that words like "conservatism" and "liberalism", the "right" and "left", must become more than vague jargon; they must be recognized as names of different ways of thinking about human behavior. Students need experience actually thinking within diverse political perspectives. No perspective, not even one called "moderate", should be presented as *the* correct one. By the same token, we should be careful not to lead the students to believe that all perspectives are equally justified or that important insights are equally found in all points of view. We should continually encourage and stimulate our students to think and never do their thinking for them. We should, above all, be teachers and not preachers.

✦ *Implementation Philosophy*

Bringing ethics into the curriculum is essential but difficult. Many teachers are deeply committed to didactic lectorial modes of teaching. If ethics is taught in this way, indoctrination results, and we have lost rather than gained ground. Better no ethics than dogmatic moralizing.

To successfully establish a solid framework of ethical reasoning throughout the curriculum, we need excellent supplemental resources and well-designed in-service. Whenever possible, teachers should have access to books and materials that demonstrate how ethical and critical thinking principles can be integrated into subject matter instruction. They also need opportunities to air whatever misgivings they have about the paradigm shift this model represents for many of them. Above all, one should conceive of a move such as this as part of a long-term strategy in which implementation is achieved progressively over an extended time.

Just as educators should respect the autonomy of students, so in-service design should respect the autonomy of teachers. Teachers can and should be helped to integrate a critical approach to ethics into their everyday teaching. But they must actively think their way to this integration. It should not be imposed on them.

The model I suggest is one I have used successfully in in-service for both elementary and secondary teachers on numerous occasions. I call it the "Lesson Plan Remodelling Strategy" and have written three handbooks and an article explaining it in depth.

The basic idea is simple. Every practicing teacher works daily with lesson plans of one kind or another. To remodel lesson plans is to critique one or more lesson plans and formulate one or more new lesson plans based on that critical process. Thus, a group of teachers or staff development leaders with a reasonable number of exemplary remodels with accompanying explanatory principles can design practice sessions that enable teachers to develop new teaching skills as a result of experience in lesson remodelling.

Lesson plan remodelling can become a powerful tool in staff development for several reasons. It is action oriented and puts an immediate emphasis on close examination and critical assessment of what is taught on a day-to-day basis. It makes the problem of infusion more manageable by paring it down to the critique of particular lesson plans and the progressive infusion of particular principles. It is developmental in that, over time, more and more lesson plans are remodelled, and what has been remodelled can be remodelled again.

✦ *Inservice Design*

The idea behind inservice on this model is to take teachers step-by-step through specific stages of implementation. First of all, teachers must have an opportunity to become familiar with the basic concepts of critical thinking and ethical reasoning. They should first have an opportunity to formulate and discuss various general principles of morality and then to discuss how people with differing moral perspectives sometimes come to different moral conclusions when they apply these principles to actual events. Questions like "Is abortion morally justified?" or "Under what conditions do people have a right to welfare support?" or "Is capital punishment ever morally justified?" etc., can be used as examples to demonstrate this point.

Working together, the teachers should then construct examples of how they might encourage their students to apply one or more of the moral reasoning skills listed in figure #1. One table might focus on devising ways to help students clarify moral issues and claims *(S-8)*. Another table may discuss assignments that would help students develop their moral perspective *(S-7)*. A third might focus on ways to encourage one of the essential moral *virtues,* say, *moral integrity.* Of course teachers should have examples for each of the moral reasoning skills, as well as model classroom activities that foster them. Teachers should not be expected to work with nothing more than a list of abstract labels. The subsequent examples developed by the teachers working together should be written up and shared with all participants. There should be ample opportunity for constructive feedback.

Once teachers get some confidence in devising examples of activities they can use to help students develop various individual moral reasoning skills, they should try their hands at developing a full remodel. For this, each table has an actual lesson plan and they collectively develop a critique and remodel that embodies moral reasoning skills explicitly set out as objectives of the lesson. As before, exemplary remodels should be available for teachers to compare with their remodels. The following components should be spelled out explicitly:

1. *the original lesson plan* (or an abstract of it)

2. *a statement of the objectives of the plan*

3. *a critique of the original* (Why does it need to be revised? What does it fail to do that it might do? Does it indoctrinate students?)

4. *a listing of the moral reasoning skills to be infused*

5. *the remodelled lesson plan* (containing references to where in the remodel the various moral reasoning skills are infused)

Eventually school-wide or district-wide handbooks of lesson remodels can be put together and disseminated. These can be updated yearly. At least one consultant with unquestionable credentials in critical thinking should be hired to provide outside feedback on the process and its products.

For a fuller explanation of this inservice process and a wide selection of examples, I refer the reader to either *Critical Thinking Handbook: 4th-6th Grades,* or *Critical Thinking Handbook: K-3*, both are subtitled *A Guide for Remodelling Lesson Plans in Language Arts, Social Studies & Science.* Both integrate an emphasis on ethical reasoning into critical thinking infusion, though they do not explicitly express the component critical thinking skills with a moral reasoning emphasis (as I have in figure #1). The handbook examples are easily adaptable as illustrations for the upper grade levels. In any case, handbooks or not, what we should aim at is teacher practice in critiquing and revising standard lesson plans, based on a knowledgeable commitment to critical thinking and moral reasoning. We should not expect that teachers will begin with the knowledge base or even the commitment but only that with exposure, practice, and encouragement within a well planned long-term inservice implementation, proficiency and commitment will eventually emerge.

In my own experience in conducting inservices, I have found it easy to *begin* this process working with teachers. Though the early products of the teachers are of mixed quality, all of what is produced is workable as a basis for the development of further insights and teaching skills. The difficulty is not in getting the process started; it is in keeping it going. One new lesson plan does not by itself change an established style of teaching. Like all creatures of habit, teachers tend to revert on Monday to their established teaching practices. A real on-going effort is essential for lesson plan remodelling to become a way of life and not just an interesting inservice activity.

✦ *The Need for Leadership*

I cannot overemphasize the need for leadership in this area. Teachers need to know that the administration is solidly behind them in this process, that the time and effort they put in will not only be appreciated but also visibly built upon. The school-wide or district-wide handbooks mentioned above are one kind of visible by-product that teachers should see. An excellent start is to have key administrators actively participate in the inservice along with the teachers. But the support should not end there. Administrators should facilitate on-going structures and activities to support this process: making and sharing video tapes, sending key personnel to conferences, establishing working committees, informal discussion groups, and opportunities for peer review. These are some among the many possibilities. Administrators should also be articulate defenders of an educational rather than a doctrinaire approach to morality. They should be ready, willing, and able to explain why and how critical thinking and ethics are integrated throughout the curriculum. They should make the approach intelligible to the school board and community. They should engender enthusiasm for it. They should fight to preserve it if attacked by those good hearted but closedminded people who see morality personified in their particular moral perspectives and beliefs. Above all, they should make a critical and moral commitment to a moral and critical education for all students and do this in a way that demonstrates to teachers and parents alike moral courage, perseverance, and integrity.

Figure 1
Moral Reasoning Skills

A.   Moral Affective Strategies
S-1   exercising independent moral thought and judgment
S-2   developing insight into moral egocentrism and sociocentrism
S-3   exercising moral reciprocity
S-4   exploring thought underlying moral reactions
S-5   suspending moral judgment

B.   Cognitive Strategies: Moral Macro-Abilities
S-6   avoiding oversimplification of moral issues
S-7   developing one's moral perspective
S-8   clarifying moral issues and claims
S-9   clarifying moral ideas
S-10   developing criteria for moral evaluation
S-11   evaluating moral authorities
S-12   raising and pursuing root moral questions
S-13   evaluating moral arguments
S-14   generating and assessing solutions to moral problems
S-15   identifying and clarifying moral points of view
S-16   engaging in Socratic discussion on moral issues
S-17   practicing dialogical thinking on moral issues
S-18   practicing dialectical thinking on moral issues

C.   Cognitive Strategies: Moral Micro-Skills
S-19   distinguishing facts from moral principles, values, and ideals
S-20   using critical vocabulary in discussing moral issues
S-21   distinguishing moral principles or ideas
S-22   examining moral assumptions
S-23   distinguishing morally relevant from morally irrelevant facts
S-24   making plausible moral inferences
S-25   supplying evidence for a moral conclusion
S-26   recognizing moral contradictions
S-27   exploring moral implication and consequences
S-28   refining moral generalizations

Figure 2
ESSENTIAL MORAL VIRTUES

Moral Humility: Awareness of the limits of one's moral knowledge, including sensitivity to circumstances in which one's native egocentrism is likely to function self-deceptively; sensitivity to bias and prejudice in, and limitations of, one's viewpoint. Moral humility is based on the recognition that no one should claim to know more than one actually knows. It does not imply spinelessness or submissiveness. It implies the lack of moral pretentiousness, boastfulness, or conceit, combined with insight into the strengths and weaknesses of the logical foundations of one's beliefs.

Moral Courage: The willingness to face and assess fairly moral ideas, beliefs, or viewpoints to which we have not given serious hearing, regardless of our strong negative reaction to them. This courage arises from the recognition that ideas considered dangerous or absurd are sometimes rationally justified (in whole or in part), and that moral conclusions or beliefs espoused by those around us or inculcated in us are sometimes false or misleading.

Moral Empathy: Having a consciousness of the need to imaginatively put oneself in the place of others in order to genuinely understand them. We must recognize our egocentric tendency to identify truth with our immediate perceptions or longstanding beliefs. This trait correlates with the ability to reconstruct accurately the moral viewpoints and reasoning of others and to reason from moral premises, assumptions, and ideas other than our own. This trait also requires that we remember occasions when we were morally wrong, despite an intense conviction that we were right, as well as consider that we might be similarly deceived in a case at hand.

Moral Integrity: Recognition of the need to be true to one's own moral thinking, to be consistent in the moral standards one applies, to hold one's self to the same rigorous standards of evidence and proof to which one holds one's antagonists, to practice what one morally advocates for others, and to honestly admit discrepancies and moral inconsistencies in one's own thought and action.

Moral Perseverance: Willingness and consciousness of the need to pursue moral insights and truths despite difficulties, obstacles, and frustrations; firm adherence to moral principles despite irrational opposition of others; a sense of the need to struggle with confusion and unsettled questions over an extended period of time, to achieve deeper moral understanding or insight.

Moral Fairmindedness: Willingness and consciousness of the need to entertain all moral viewpoints sympathetically and to assess them with the same intellectual standards without reference to one's own feelings or vested interests, or the feelings or vested interests of one's friends, community, or nation; implies adherence to moral standards without reference to one's own advantage or the advantage of one's group.

✦ References

Ralph W. Clark, *Introduction to Moral Reasoning,* West Publishing Company, St. Paul: 1986.

Ronald N. Giere, *Understanding Scientific Reasoning,* Holt, Rinehart, and Winston; New York: 1979.

Kuzirian and Madaras, *Taking Sides: Clashing Views on Controversial Issues in American History,* Dushkin Publishing Group; Guilford, Conn.: 1985.

Richard Paul, "Critical Thinking: Fundamental to Education for a Free Society," *Educational Leadership* 42, September, 1984.

Richard Paul, "Critical Thinking and the Critical Person," Forthcoming in *Thinking: Progress in Research and Teaching,* by Lawrence Erlbaum Associates, Inc. Publishers; Perkins, et al. editors.

Richard Paul, "Dialogical Thinking: Critical Thought Essential to the Acquisition of Rational Knowledge and Passions," *Teaching Thinking Skills; Theory and Practice,* by W.H. Freeman & Company, Publishers, Joan Baron and Robert Steinberg, editors, 1987.

Richard Paul, "Critical Thinking Staff Development: Lesson Plan Remodelling as the Strategy," *The Journal of Staff Development,* Fall 1987, Paul Burden, editor.

Paul, Binker, Jensen, and Kreklau, *Critical Thinking Handbook: 4th–6th Grades, A Guide for Remodelling Lesson Plans in Language Arts, Social Studies and Science,* Published by the Center for Critical Thinking and Moral Critique, (Sonoma State University, Rohnert Park, CA 94928) 1987.

Paul, Binker, Charbonneau *Critical Thinking Handbook: K–3, A Guide for Remodelling Lesson Plans in Language Arts, Social Studies and Science,* Published by the Center for Critical Thinking and Moral Critique, 1987.

Harvey Siegel, "Critical Thinking as an Education Ideal," *The Educational Forum,* Nov. 1980.

William Graham Sumner, *Folkways: A Study of the Sociological Importance of Usages, Manners, Customs, Mores, and Morals,* Dover Publications, Inc., New York: 1906.

Chapter 13

Critical Thinking, Moral Integrity, and Citizenship:
Teaching for the Intellectual Virtues

Abstract

Many are tempted to separate affective and moral dimensions of learning from cognitive dimensions. They argue that the cognitive and affective are obviously separate since many intelligent, well-educated people lack moral insight or sensitivity and many less intelligent, poorly-educated, or uneducated people are morally good. By distinguishing "strong" and "weak" senses of the terms 'critical thinking', 'moral integrity', and 'citizenship' Richard Paul suggests a novel answer to this objection.

Critical thinking, understood as skills alone separate from values, is often used to rationalize prejudice and vested interest. Moral integrity and responsible citizenship, understood merely as "good heartedness", are themselves susceptible to manipulation by propaganda. The human mind, whatever its conscious good will, is subject to powerful, self-deceptive, unconscious egocentricity of mind. The full development of each characteristic — critical thought, moral integrity, and responsible citizenship — in its strong sense requires and develops the others, in a parallel strong sense. The three are developed together only in an atmosphere which encourages the intellectual virtues: intellectual courage, intellectual empathy, intellectual good faith or integrity, intellectual perseverance, intellectual fairmindedness, and faith in reason. The intellectual virtues themselves are interdependent.

*E*ducators and theorists tend to approach the affective and moral dimensions of education as they approach all other dimensions of learning, as compartmentalized domains, and as a collection of learnings more or less separate from other learnings. As a result, they view moral development as more or less independent of cognitive development. "And why not!" one might imagine the reply. "Clearly there are highly educated, very intelligent people who habitually do evil and very simple, poorly-educated people who consistently do good. If moral development were so intimately connected to cognitive development, how could this be so?"

In this paper, I provide the outlines of an answer to that objection by suggesting an intimate connection between critical thinking, moral integrity, and citizenship. Specifically, I distinguish a weak and a strong sense of each and hold that the strong sense ought to guide, not only our understanding of the nature of the educated person, but also our redesigning the curriculum.

There is little to recommend schooling that does not foster what I call intellectual virtues. These virtues include intellectual empathy, intellectual perseverance, intellectual confidence in reason, and an intellectual sense of justice (fairmindedness). Without these characteristics, intellectual development is circumscribed and distorted, a caricature of what it could and should be. These same characteristics are essential to moral judgment. The "good-hearted" person who lacks intellectual virtues will act morally only when morally grasping a situation or problem does not presuppose intellectual insight. Many, if not most, moral problems and situations in the modern world are open to multiple interpretations and, hence, do presuppose these intellectual virtues.

We are now coming to see how far we are from curricula and teaching strategies that genuinely foster basic intellectual and moral development. Curricula is so highly compartmentalized and teaching so committed to "speed learning" (covering large chunks of content quickly) that it has little room for fostering what I call the intellectual virtues. Indeed, the present structure of curricula and teaching not only strongly discourages their development but also strongly encourages their opposites. Consequently, even the "best" students enter and leave college as largely mis-educated persons, with no real sense of what they do and do not understand, with little sense of the state of their prejudices or insights, with little command of their intellectual faculties — in short, with no intellectual virtues, properly so-called.

Superficially absorbed content, the inevitable by-product of extensive but shallow coverage, inevitably leads to intellectual arrogance. Such learning discourages intellectual perseverance and confidence in reason. It prevents the recognition of intellectual bad faith. It provides no foundation for intellectual empathy, nor for an intellectual sense of fair play. By taking in and giving back masses of detail, students come to believe that they *know* a lot about each subject — whether they understand or not. By practicing applying rules and formulas to familiar tasks, they come to feel that getting the answer should always be easy — if you don't know how to do something, don't try to figure it out, ask. By hearing and reading only one perspective, they come to think that perspective has a monopoly on truth — any other view must be completely wrong. By accepting (without understanding) that their government's past actions were all justified, they assume their government never would or could do wrong — if it doesn't seem right, I must not understand.

The pedagogical implications of my position include these: cutting back on coverage to focus on depth of understanding, on foundational ideas, on intellectual synthesis, and on intellectual experiences that develop and deepen the most basic intellectual skills, abilities, concepts, and virtues. A similar viewpoint was expressed by Whitehead:

> The result of teaching small parts of a large number of subjects is the passive reception of disconnected ideas, not illuminated with any spark of vitality. Let the main ideas which are introduced into a child's education be few and important, and let them be thrown into every combination possible. The

child should make them his own, and should understand their application here and now in the circumstances of his actual life. From the very beginning of his education, the child should experience the joy of discovery. The discovery which he has to make is that general ideas give an understanding of that stream of events which pours through his life. (*The Aims of Education*, p. 14)

To accomplish this re-orientation of curriculum and teaching, we need new criteria of what constitutes success and failure in school. We need to begin this re-orientation as early as possible. Integrating teaching for critical thinking, moral integrity, and citizenship is an essential part of this re-orientation.

✦ Teaching for "Strong Sense" Skills

The term "critical thinking" can be used in either a weak or a strong sense, depending upon whether we think of critical thinking narrowly, as a list or collection of discrete intellectual skills, or, more broadly, as a mode of mental integration, as a synthesized complex of dispositions, values, and skills necessary to becoming a fairminded, rational person. Teaching critical thinking in a strong sense is a powerful, and I believe necessary means to moral integrity and responsible citizenship.

Intellectual skills in and of themselves can be used either for good or ill, to enlighten or to propagandize, to gain narrow, self-serving ends, or to further the general and public good. The micro-skills themselves, for example, do not define fairmindedness and could be used as easily by those who are highly prejudiced as those who are not. Those students not exposed to the challenge of strong sense critical thinking assignments (for example, assignments in which they must empathically reconstruct viewpoints that differ strikingly from their own) will not, as a matter of abstract morality or general good-heartedness, be fair to points of view they oppose, nor will they automatically develop a rationally defensible notion of what the public good is on the many issues they must decide as citizens.

Critical thinking, in its most defensible sense, is not simply a matter of cognitive skills. Moral integrity and responsible citizenship are, in turn, not simply a matter of good-heartedness or good intentions. Many good-hearted people cannot see through and critique propaganda and mass manipulation, and most good-hearted people fall prey at times to the powerful tendency to engage in self deception, especially when their own egocentric interests and desires are at stake. One can be good-hearted and intellectually egocentric at the same time.

The problems of education for fairminded independence of thought, for genuine moral integrity, and for responsible citizenship are not three separate issues but one complex task. If we succeed with one dimension of the problem, we succeed with all. If we fail with one, we fail with all. Now we are failing with all because we do not clearly understand the interrelated nature of the problem nor how to address it.

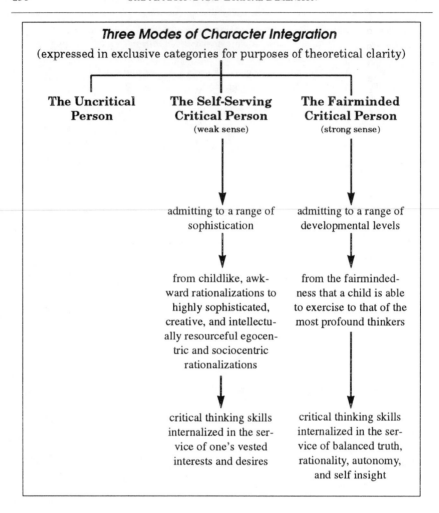

Three Modes of Character Integration

(expressed in exclusive categories for purposes of theoretical clarity)

The Uncritical Person	The Self-Serving Critical Person (weak sense)	The Fairminded Critical Person (strong sense)
	admitting to a range of sophistication	admitting to a range of developmental levels
	from childlike, awkward rationalizations to highly sophisticated, creative, and intellectually resourceful egocentric and sociocentric rationalizations	from the fairmindedness that a child is able to exercise to that of the most profound thinkers
	critical thinking skills internalized in the service of one's vested interests and desires	critical thinking skills internalized in the service of balanced truth, rationality, autonomy, and self insight

✦ The Intellectual and Moral Virtues of the Critical Person

Our basic ways of knowing are inseparable from our basic ways of being. How we think reflects who we are. Intellectual and moral virtues or disabilities are intimately interconnected. To cultivate the kind of intellectual independence implied in the concept of strong sense critical thinking, we must recognize the need to foster intellectual (epistemological) humility, courage, integrity, perseverance, empathy, and fairmindedness. A brief gloss on each will suggest how to translate these concepts into concrete examples. Intellectual humility will be my only extended illustration. I will leave to the reader's imagination what sorts of concrete examples could be marshalled in amplifying the other intellectual virtues.

Intellectual Humility: Having a consciousness of the limits of one's knowledge, including a sensitivity to circumstances in which one's native egocentrism is likely to function self-deceptively; sensitivity to bias, prejudice, and limitations of one's viewpoint. Intellectual humility depends on recognizing that one should not claim more than one actually knows. It does not imply spinelessness or submissiveness. It implies the lack of intellectual pretentiousness, boastfulness, or conceit, combined with insight into the logical foundations, or lack of such foundations, of one's beliefs.

To illustrate, consider this letter from a teacher with a Master's degree in Physics and Mathematics, with 20 years of high school teaching experience in physics:

> After I started teaching, I realized that I had learned physics by rote and that I really did not understand all I knew about physics. My thinking students asked me questions for which I always had the standard textbook answers, but for the first time it made me start thinking for myself, and I realized that these canned answers were not justified by my own thinking and only confused my students who were showing some ability to think for themselves. To achieve my academic goals I had to memorize the thoughts of others, but I had never learned or been encouraged to learn to think for myself.

This is a good example of what I call intellectual humility and, like all intellectual humility, it arises from insight into the nature of knowing. It is reminiscent of the ancient Greek insight that Socrates was the wisest of the Greeks because only he knew how little he really understood. Socrates developed this insight as a result of extensive, in-depth questioning of the knowledge claims of others. He had to think his way to this insight.

If this insight and this humility is part of our goal, then most textbooks and curricula require extensive modification, for typically they discourage rather than encourage it. The extent and nature of "coverage" for most grade levels and subjects implies that bits and pieces of knowledge are easily attained, without any significant consideration of the basis for the knowledge claimed in the text or by the teacher. The speed with which content is covered contradicts the notion that students must think in an extended way about content before giving assent to what is claimed. Most teaching and most texts are, in this sense, epistemologically unrealistic and hence foster intellectual arrogance in students, particularly in those with retentive memories who can repeat back what they have heard or read. *Pretending* to know is encouraged. Much standardized testing validates this pretense.

This led Alan Schoenfeld, for example, to conclude that "most instruction in mathematics is, in a very real sense, deceptive and possibly fraudulent". He cites numerous examples including the following. He points out that much instruction on how to solve word problems in elementary math

> ... is based on the "key word" algorithm, where the student makes his choice of the appropriate arithmetic operation by looking for syntactic cues in the problem statement. For example, the word 'left' in the problem "John had eight

apples. He gave three to Mary. How many does John have left?" ... serves to tell the students that subtraction is the appropriate operation to perform. (p. 27)

He further reports the following:

> In a widely used elementary text book series, 97 percent of the problems "solved" by the key-word method would yield (serendipitously?) the correct answer.
>
> Students are drilled in the key-word algorithm so well that they will use subtraction, for example, in almost any problem containing the word 'left'. In the study from which this conclusion was drawn, problems were constructed in which appropriate operations were addition, multiplication, and division. Each used the word 'left' conspicuously in its statement and a large percentage of the students subtracted. In fact, the situation was so extreme that many students chose to subtract in a problem that began "Mr. Left ...".

Schoenfeld then provides a couple of other examples, including the following:

> I taught a problem-solving course for junior and senior mathematics majors at Berkeley in 1976. These students had already seen some remarkably sophisticated mathematics. Linear algebra and differential equations were old hat. Topology, Fourier transforms, and measure theory were familiar to some. I gave them a straightforward theorem from plane geometry (required when I was in the tenth grade). Only two of eight students made any progress on it, some of them by using arc length integrals to measure the circumference of a circle. (Schoenfeld, 1979). Out of the context of normal course work these students could not do elementary mathematics.

He concludes:

> In sum: all too often we focus on a narrow collection of well-defined tasks and train students to execute those tasks in a routine, if not algorithmic fashion. Then we test the students on tasks that are very close to the ones they have been taught. If they succeed on those problems, we and they congratulate each other on the fact that they have learned some powerful mathematical techniques. In fact, they may be able to use such techniques mechanically while lacking some rudimentary thinking skills. To allow them, and ourselves, to believe that they "understand" the mathematics is deceptive and fraudulent.

This approach to learning in math is paralleled in all other subjects. Most teachers got through their college classes mainly by "learning the standard textbook answers" and were neither given an opportunity nor encouraged to determine whether what the text or the professor said was "justified by their own thinking". To move toward intellectual humility, most teachers need to question most of what they learned, as the teacher above did, but such questioning would require intellectual courage, perseverance, and confidence in their own capacity to reason and understand subject matter through their own thought. Most teachers have not done the kind of analytic thinking necessary for gaining such perspective.

I would generalize as follows: just as the development of intellectual humility is an essential goal of critical thinking instruction, so is the development of intellectual courage, integrity, empathy, perseverance, fairminded-ness, and confidence in reason. Furthermore, each intellectual (and moral) virtue in turn is richly developed only in conjunction with the others. Before we approach this point directly, however, a brief characterization of what I have in mind by each of these traits is in order:

Intellectual Courage: Having a consciousness of the need to face and fairly address ideas, beliefs, or viewpoints toward which we have strong nega-tive emotions and to which we have not given a serious hearing. This courage is connected with the recognition that ideas considered danger-ous or absurd are sometimes rationally justified (in whole or in part) and that conclusions and beliefs inculcated in us are sometimes false or mis-leading. To determine for ourselves which is which, we must not passive-ly and uncritically "accept" what we have "learned". Intellectual courage comes into play here, because inevitably we will come to see some truth in some ideas considered dangerous and absurd, and distortion or falsity in some ideas strongly held in our social group. We need courage to be true to our own thinking in such circumstances. The penalties for non-conformity can be severe.

Intellectual Empathy: Having a consciousness of the need to imaginatively put oneself in the place of others in order to genuinely understand them, which requires the consciousness of our egocentric tendency to identify truth with our immediate perceptions or long-standing thought or belief. This trait correlates with the ability to reconstruct accurately the view-points and reasoning of others and to reason from premises, assump-tions, and ideas other than our own. This trait also correlates with the willingness to remember occasions when we were wrong in the past despite an intense conviction that we were right, and with the ability to imagine our being similarly deceived in a case-at-hand.

Intellectual Good Faith (Integrity): Recognition of the need to be true to one's own thinking; to be consistent in the intellectual standards one applies; to hold one's self to the same rigorous standards of evidence and proof to which one holds one's antagonists; to practice what one advocates for others; and to honestly admit discrepancies and inconsistencies in one's own thought and action.

Intellectual Perseverance: Willingness and consciousness of the need to pur-sue intellectual insights and truths in spite of difficulties, obstacles, and frustrations; firm adherence to rational principles despite the irrational opposition of others; a sense of the need to struggle with confusion and unsettled questions over an extended period of time to achieve deeper understanding or insight.

Faith in Reason: Confidence that, in the long run, one's own higher interests and those of humankind at large will be best served by giving the freest play to reason, by encouraging people to come to their own conclusions by developing their own rational faculties; faith that, with proper encouragement and cultivation, people can learn to think for themselves, to form rational viewpoints, draw reasonable conclusions, think coherently and logically, persuade each other by reason and become reasonable persons, despite the deep-seated obstacles in the native character of the human mind and in society as we know it.

Fairmindedness: Willingness and consciousness of the need to treat all viewpoints alike, without reference to one's own feelings or vested interests, or the feelings or vested interests of one's friends, community, or nation; implies adherence to intellectual standards without reference to one's own advantage or the advantage of one's group.

✦ *The Interdependence of the Intellectual Virtues*

Let us now consider the interdependence of these virtues, how hard it is to deeply develop any one of them without also developing the others.

Consider intellectual humility. To become aware of the limits of our knowledge we need the *courage* to face our own prejudices and ignorance. To discover our own prejudices in turn we must often *empathize* with and reason within points of view toward which we are hostile. To do this, we must typically *persevere* over a period of time, for learning to empathically enter a point of view against which we are biased takes time and significant effort. That effort will not seem justified unless we have the *faith in reason* to believe we will not be "tainted" or "taken in" by whatever is false or misleading in the opposing viewpoint. Furthermore, merely believing we can survive serious consideration of an "alien" point of view is not enough to motivate most of us to consider them seriously. We must also be motivated by an *intellectual sense of justice*. We must recognize an intellectual *responsibility* to be fair to views we oppose. We must feel *obliged* to hear them in their strongest form to ensure that we do not condemn them out of our own ignorance or bias. At this point, we come full circle back to where we began: the need for *intellectual humility*.

Or let us begin at another point. Consider intellectual good faith or integrity. Intellectual integrity is clearly difficult to develop. We are often motivated — generally without admitting to or being aware of this motivation — to set up inconsistent intellectual standards. Our egocentric or sociocentric side readily believes positive information about those we like and negative information about those we dislike. We tend to believe what justifies our vested interest or validates our strongest desires. Hence, we all have some innate tendencies to use double standards, which is of course paradigmatic of intellectual bad faith. Such thought often helps us get ahead in the world, maximize our power or advantage, and get more of what we want.

Nevertheless, we cannot easily operate *explicitly* or overtly with a double standard. We must, therefore, avoid looking at the evidence too closely. We cannot scrutinize our own inferences and interpretations too carefully. Hence, a certain amount of *intellectual arrogance* is quite useful. I may assume, for example that I know just what you're going to say (before you say it), precisely what you are really after (before the evidence demonstrates it), and what actually is going on (before I have studied the situation carefully). My intellectual arrogance makes it easier for me to avoid noticing the unjustifiable discrepancy in the standards I apply to you and those I apply to myself. Of course, if I don't have to empathize with you, that too makes it easier to avoid seeing my duplicity. I am also better off if I don't feel a keen need to be *fair* to your point of view. A little background *fear* of what I might discover if I seriously considered the consistency of my own judgments also helps. In this case, my lack of intellectual integrity is supported by my lack of intellectual humility, empathy, and fairmindedness.

Going in the other direction, it will be difficult to maintain a double standard between us if I feel a distinct responsibility to be fair to your point of view, understand this responsibility to entail that I must view things from your perspective in an empathic fashion, and conduct this inner inquiry with some humility regarding the possibility of my being wrong and your being right. The more I dislike you personally or feel wronged in the past by you or by others who share your way of thinking, the more pronounced in my character must be the trait of intellectual integrity in order to provide the countervailing impetus to think my way to a fair conclusion.

✦ Defense Mechanisms and the Intellectual Virtues

A major obstacle to developing intellectual virtues is the presence in the human egocentric mind of what Freud has called "defense mechanisms". Each represents a way to falsify, distort, misconceive, twist, or deny reality. Their presence represents, therefore, the relative weakness or absence of the intellectual virtues. Since they operate in everyone to some degree, no one embodies the intellectual virtues purely or perfectly. In other words, we each have a side of us unwilling to face unpleasant truth, willing to distort, falsify, twist, and misrepresent. We also know from a monumental mass of psychological research that this side can be *powerful,* can dominate our minds strikingly. We marvel at, and are often dumfounded by, others whom we consider clear-cut instances of these modes of thinking. What is truly "marvelous", it seems to me, is how little we take ourselves to be victims of these falsifying thoughts, and how little we try to break them down. The vicious circle seems to be this: because we, by and large, lack the intellectual virtues, we do not have insight into them, but because we lack insight into them, we do not see ourselves as lacking them. They weren't explicitly taught to us, so we don't have to explicitly teach them to our children.

✦ Insights, Analyzed Experiences, and Activated Ignorance

Schooling has generally ignored the need for insight or intellectual virtues. This deficiency is intimately connected with another one, the failure of the schools to show students they should not only test what they "learn" in school by their own experience, but also test what they experience by what they "learn" in school. This may seem a hopeless circle, but if we can see the distinction between a critically analyzed experience and an unanalyzed one, we can see the link between the former and *insight,* and the latter and *prejudice,* and will be well on our way to seeing how to fill these needs.

We subject little of our experience to critical analysis. We seldom take our experiences apart to judge their epistemological worth. We rarely sort the "lived" integrated experience into its component parts, *raw data, our interpretation* of the data, or ask ourselves how the interests, goals, and desires we brought to those data shaped and structured that interpretation. Similarly, we rarely seriously consider the possibility that our interpretation (and hence our experience) might be selective, biased, or misleading.

This is not to say that our unanalyzed experiences lack meaning or significance. Quite the contrary, in some sense we assess *all* experience. Our egocentric side never ceases to catalogue experiences in accord with its common and idiosyncratic fears, desires, prejudices, stereotypes, caricatures, hopes, dreams, and assorted irrational drives. We shouldn't assume *a priori* that our rational side dominates the shaping of our experience. Our unanalyzed experiences are some combination of these dual contributors to thought, action, and being. Only through critical analysis can we hope to isolate the irrational dimensions of our experience. The ability to do so grows as we analyze more and more of our experience.

Of course, more important than the sheer *number* of analyzed experiences is their *quality* and *significance*. This quality and significance depends on how much our analyses embody the intellectual virtues. At the same time, the degree of our virtue depends upon the number and quality of experiences we have successfully critically analyzed. What links the virtues, as perfections of the mind, and the experiences, as analyzed products of the mind, is *insight.* Every critically analyzed experience to some extent produces one or more intellectual virtues. To become more rational it is not enough to have experiences nor even for those experiences to have meanings. Many experiences are more or less charged with *irrational* meanings. These important meanings produce stereotypes, prejudices, narrowmindedness, delusions, and illusions of various kinds.

The process of developing intellectual virtues and insights is part and parcel of our developing an interest in taking apart our experiences to separate their rational from their irrational dimensions. These meta-experiences become important benchmarks and guides for future thought. They make possible modes of thinking and maneuvers in thinking closed to the irrational mind.

✦ *Some Thoughts on How to Teach for the Intellectual Virtues*

To teach for the intellectual virtues, one must recognize the significant differences between the higher order critical thinking of a fairminded critical thinker and that of a self-serving critical thinker. Though both share a certain command of the micro-skills of critical thinking and hence would, for example, score well on tests such as the Watson-Glaser Critical Thinking Appraisal or the Cornell Critical Thinking Tests, they are not equally good at tasks which presuppose the intellectual virtues. The self-serving (weak sense) critical thinker would lack the insights that underlie and support these virtues.

I can reason well in domains in which I am prejudiced — hence, eventually, reason my way out of prejudices — only if I develop mental benchmarks for such reasoning. Of course one insight I need is that when I am prejudiced it will seem to me that I am not, and similarly, that those who are not prejudiced as I am will seem to me to be prejudiced. (To a prejudiced person, an unprejudiced person seems prejudiced.) I will come to this insight only insofar as I have analyzed experiences in which I was intensely convinced I was correct on an issue, judgment, or point of view, only to find, after a series of challenges, reconsiderations, and new reasonings, that my previous conviction was in fact prejudiced. I must take this experience apart in my mind, clearly understand its elements and how they fit together (how I became prejudiced; how I inwardly experienced that prejudice; how intensely that prejudice seemed true and insightful; how I progressively broke that prejudice down through serious consideration of opposing lines of reasoning; how I slowly came to new assumptions, new information, and ultimately new conceptualizations).

Only when one gains analyzed experiences of working and reasoning one's way out of prejudice can one gain the higher order abilities of a fairminded critical thinker. What one gains is somewhat "procedural" or sequential in that there is a *process* one must go through; but one also sees that the process cannot be followed out formulaically or algorithmically, it depends on principles. The somewhat abstract articulation of the intellectual virtues above will take on concrete meaning in the light of these *analyzed experiences*. Their true meaning to us will be given in and by these experiences. We will often return to them to recapture and rekindle the insights upon which the intellectual virtues depend.

Generally, to develop intellectual virtues, we must create a collection of analyzed experiences that represent to us intuitive models, not only of the pitfalls of our own previous thinking and experiencing but also processes for reasoning our way out of or around them. These model experiences must be charged with meaning for us. We cannot be *indifferent* to them. We must sustain them in our minds by our sense of their importance as they sustain and guide us in our thinking.

What does this imply for teaching? It implies a somewhat different content or material focus. Our own minds and experiences must become the subject of our study and learning. Indeed, only to the extent that the content of our own experiences becomes an essential part of study will the usual subject matter truly be learned. By the same token, the experiences of others must become part of what we study. But experiences of any kind should always be critically analyzed, and students must do their own analyses and clearly recognize what they are doing.

This entails that students become explicitly aware of the logic of experience. All experiences have three elements, each of which may require some special scrutiny in the analytic process: *1)* something to be experienced (some actual situation or other); *2)* an experiencing subject (with a point of view, framework of beliefs, attitudes, desires, and values); and *3)* some interpretation or conceptualization of the situation. To take any experience apart, then, students must be sensitive to three distinctive sets of questions:

1) What are the raw facts, what is the most neutral description of the situation? If one describes the experience this way, and another disagrees, on what description *can* they agree?

2) What interests, attitudes, desires, or concerns do I bring to the situation? Am I always aware of them? Why or why not?

3) How am I conceptualizing or interpreting the situation in light of my point of view? How else might it be interpreted?

Students must also explore the interrelationships of these parts: How did my point of view, values, desires, etc., affect what I noticed about the situation? How did they prevent me from noticing other things? How would I have interpreted the situation had I noticed those other things? How did my point of view, desires, etc., affect my interpretation? How *should* I interpret the situation?

If students have many assignments that require them to analyze their experiences and the experiences of others along these lines, with ample opportunity to argue among themselves about which interpretations make the most sense and why, then they will begin to amass a catalogue of critically analyzed experiences. If the experiences illuminate the pitfalls of thought, the analysis and the models of thinking they suggest will be the foundation for their intellectual traits and character. They will develop intellectual virtues because they had thought their way to them and internalized them as concrete understandings and insights, not because they took them up as slogans. Their basic values and their thinking processes will be in a symbiotic relationship to each other. Their intellectual and affective lives will become more integrated. Their standards for thinking will be implicit in their own thinking, rather than in texts, teachers, or the authority of a peer group.

✦ Conclusion

We do not now teach for the intellectual virtues. If we did, not only would we have a basis for integrating the curriculum, we would also have a basis for integrating the cognitive and affective lives of students. Such integration is the basis for strong sense critical thinking, for moral development, and for citizenship. The moral, social, and political issues we face in everyday life are increasingly intellectually complex. Their settlement relies on circumstances and events that are interpreted in a variety of (often conflicting) ways. For example, should our government publish misinformation to mislead another government or group which it considers terrorist? Is it ethical to tolerate a "racist" regime such as South Africa, or are we morally obligated to attempt to overthrow it? Is it ethical to support anti-communist groups that use, or have used, torture, rape, or murder as tools in their struggle? When, if ever, should the CIA attempt to overthrow a government it perceives as undemocratic? How can one distinguish "terrorists" from "freedom fighters"?

Or, consider issues that are more "domestic" or "personal". Should deliberate pollutors be considered "criminals"? How should we balance off "dollar losses" against "safety gains"? That is, how much money should we be willing to spend to save human lives? What is deliberate deception in advertising and business practices? Should one protect incompetent individuals within one's profession from exposure? How should one reconcile or balance one's personal vested interest against the public good? What moral or civic responsibility exists to devote time and energy to the public good as against one's private interests and amusements?

These are just a few of the many complex moral, political, and social issues that virtually all citizens must face. The response of the citizenry to such issues defines the moral character of society. These issues challenge our intellectual honesty, courage, integrity, empathy, and fairmindedness. Given their complexity, they require perseverance and confidence in reason. People easily become cynical, intellectually lazy, or retreat into simplistic models of learning and the world they learned in school and see and hear on TV. On the other hand, it is doubtful that the fundamental conflicts and antagonisms in the world can be solved or resolved by sheer power or abstract good will. Goodheartedness and power are insufficient for creating a just world. Some modest development of the intellectual virtues seems essential for future human survival and well-being. Whether the energy, the resources, and the insights necessary for this development can be significantly mustered remains open. This is certain: we will never succeed in cultivating traits whose roots we do not understand and whose development we do not foster.

✦✦ Chapter 14

Dialogical Thinking:
Critical Thought Essential to the Acquisition of
Rational Knowledge and Passions

Abstract

*Passions, Paul argues, can be rational or irrational. To become a rational person we must develop rational passions: "a passionate drive for clarity, accuracy, and fairmindedness, a fervor for getting to the bottom of things, to the deepest root issues, for listening sympathetically to opposition points of view, a compelling drive to seek out evidence, an intense aversion to contradiction, sloppy thinking, inconsistent application of standards, a devotion to truth as against self-interest." These emotional commitments are essential to the development of rationality, and only intensive dialogical and dialectical thinking over years will produce them. Paul develops this thesis at length in one of his most popular papers (*Teaching Thinking Skills: Theory and Practice *1987).*

We all have a natural tendency toward egocentricity — a tendency to assume our perspectives to be the only (or only plausible) one, to resist considering issues from the perspectives of others. This tendency is reinforced rather than combatted by approaches to problem-solving and critical thinking which are technical or monological in nature. Here, as elsewhere, Paul argues for the importance of teaching students the art of dialogical thinking. He notes that most "real-life" problems are multilogical in nature, and thus require consideration from multiple points of view.

The main thrust of the argument in this paper is pedagogical, in that, when students compare and defend multiple points of view on issues, exploring and testing them, they become more truly convinced of what they learn, and thus take that knowledge to heart. Even subjects which are, or can be seen to be, technical should be taught dialogically, since students need to reason back and forth between their own ideas about subjects (e.g., ideas about numbers or about the physical world) and the ideas being presented to them by their teacher, the textbook, or other students. Teaching all subjects through a dialogical approach, Paul emphasizes, encourages students to make their ideas explicit and to critique them, making their own ideas more sophisticated, rather than superimposing "inert school knowledge" upon "activated student ignorance". Students, in other words, need to reason their way to knowledge. Otherwise, their own deep-seated preconceptions will remain alive and ultimately displace what they passively "learned" in the classroom.

*W*hen psychologists concerned with cognitive psychology and problem solving want to test their theories, they choose different kinds of problems than those generally chosen by philosophers concerned with critical thinking and rationality. Cognitive psychologists like to analyze and generalize about problems defined, explored, and settled in a fundamentally self-contained way. They prefer atomic problems, especially those having to do with technology, math, science, and engineering. Mathematical and verbal puzzles are a favorite. They choose problems that can be represented and settled in a definitive way within one frame of reference, for example,

1. A man once offended a fortune-teller by laughing at her predictions and saying that fortune telling was all nonsense. He offended her so much, in fact, that she cast a spell on him which turned him into both a compulsive gambler and, in addition, a consistent loser. That was pretty mean. We would expect the spell would shortly have turned him into a miserable, impoverished wreck. Instead, he soon married a wealthy businesswoman who took him to the casino every day, gave him money, and smiled happily as he lost it at the roulette table. They lived happily ever after. Why was the man's wife so happy to see him lose?

2. You are visiting a strange country in which there are just two kinds of people — truth tellers and liars. Truth tellers *always* tell the truth and liars *always* lie. You hail the first two people you meet and say, "Are you truth tellers or liars?" The first mumbles something you can't hear. The second says, "He says he is a truth teller. He is a truth teller and so am I." Can you trust the directions that these two may give you?

3. Ten full crates of walnuts weigh 410 pounds, whereas an empty crate weighs 10 pounds. How much do the walnuts alone weigh?

4. In how many days of the week does the third letter of the day's name immediately follow the first letter of the day's name in the alphabet?

I call these problems (adapted from Hayes, 1940) and the means by which they are solved *monological*. This implies that they are settled within one frame of reference with a definite set of logical moves. When the right set of moves is made, the problem is settled. The proposed answer or solution can be shown to be the "right" answer or solution by standards implicit in the frame of reference.

Philosophers concerned with critical thinking and rationality are drawn to a very different kind of problem. They tend to choose non-atomic problems, problems that are inextricably joined to other problems and form clusters, with some conceptual messiness about them and often important values lurking in the background. When the problems have an empirical dimension, that dimension tends to have a controversial scope. One must argue how the facts ought to be considered and interpreted and how to determine their significance. When they have a conceptual dimension, there tend to be arguably different ways to pin the concepts down.

Consequently, the problem's precise identification and definition depend upon some arguable choice among alternative frames of reference. I call these questions *multilogical*. More than one kind of incompatible logic can be advanced for their settlement. Indeed, more than one frame of reference can be used to argue their construal.

Since more than one frame of reference is contending for their construal and settlement, we must somehow "test" the frames of reference themselves. To test whole frames of reference without begging the question one must set the frames of reference against each other dialectically, and test the logical strength of one against the logical strength of the rest by appealing to standards not peculiar to any.

If we do not know how to make the case for an answer proposed from a contending frame of reference, we can find a proponent to make the case for it. Then we listen to the case made from a competing frame of reference. Most especially, we try to determine how successfully each constructed logic answers the objections framed from opposing perspectives. A trial by jury with opposing arguments of prosecution and defense illustrates a traditional approach to multilogical issues.

However, if no informed proponents of opposing points of view are available, we have to reconstruct the arguments ourselves. We must enter into the opposing points of view on our own and frame the dialogical exchange ourselves. I contend that this skill of empathy and reciprocity is essential to the development of the rational mind. Only such activity forces us outside our own frame of reference, which, given the primary nature of the human mind, tends to become an inflexible mind set. Unless we counter this tendency early on, it begins a process that becomes progressively harder to reverse.

Even though the lives of children are deeply involved in multilogical questions, and how children respond to these questions has a profound influence on how they later define and address the central issues they will face as adults, children rarely have a real opportunity in school to reflect upon these questions in mutually supportive dialogical settings. I have in mind questions *like* the following (although not necessarily these *precisely*):

> Who am I? What am I like? What are the other people around me like? What are people of different backgrounds, religions, and nations like? How much am I like others? How much am I unlike them? What kind of a world do I live in? When should I trust? When should I distrust? What should I accept? What should I question? How should I understand my past, the past of parents, my ethnic group, my religion, my nation? Who are my friends? Who are my enemies? What is a friend? How am I like and unlike my enemy? What is most important to me? How should I live my life? What responsibilities do I have to others? What responsibilities do they have to me? What responsibilities do I have to my friends? Do I have any responsibilities to people I don't like? To people who don't like me? To my enemies? Do my parents love me? Do I love them? What is love? What is hate? What is indifference? Does it matter if others do not approve of me? When does it matter? When should I ignore what others think? What rights do I have? What rights should I give to others? What should I do if others do not respect my rights? Should I get what I want? Should I question what I want? Should I take what I want if I am strong enough or smart enough to get away with it? Who comes out ahead in this world, the strong or the good person? Is it worthwhile to be good? Are authorities good or just strong?

Questions like these underlie most of the satisfactions and frustrations of childhood. The deepest orientation of the person to self and life depends on how the individual responds to them.

✦ Background Principles

Before proceeding with my argument for the need for dialogical thinking to develop rational knowledge and passions, I would like to introduce the following background principles:

1. A reasonable person solves problems or settles questions about what to do or believe by adjusting his or her thinking to the nature of each question. Different questions require different modes of thinking. If a question's settlement presupposes the gathering of some empirical data, a reasonable person uses his or her thinking to facilitate that gathering. If that gathering requires examining sources arguing from more than one point of view, the person looks at multiple sources and listens to the case for more than one point of view. If reasonable doubts can be raised about the accuracy, relevance, completeness, or implications of these data, they raise them. If there are values or purposes implicit in the problem-solving activity that a reasonable person would clarify or question, he or she clarifies or questions them.

2. People have both a primary and a secondary nature. Our primary nature is spontaneous, egocentric, and strongly prone to irrational belief formation. It is the basis for our instinctual thought. People need no training to believe what they want to believe, what serves their immediate interests, what preserves their sense of personal comfort and righteousness, what minimizes their sense of inconsistency, and what presupposes their own correctness. People need no special training to believe what those around them believe, what their parents and friends believe, what they learn from religious and school authorities, what they often hear from or read in the media, and what is commonly believed in the nation in which they are raised. People need no training to think that those who disagree with them are wrong and probably prejudiced. People need no training to assume that their own most fundamental beliefs are self-evidently true or easily justified by evidence. People naturally and spontaneously identify with their own beliefs and experience most disagreement as personal attack, adopting as a result a defensiveness that minimizes their capacity to empathize with or enter into points of view other than their own.

On the other hand, people need extensive and systematic practice to develop their secondary nature, their implicit capacity to function rationally. They need extensive and systematic practice to recognize their tendencies to form irrational beliefs. They need extensive practice to develop a dislike of inconsistency, a love of clarity, a passion to seek reasons and evidence and to be fair to points of view other than their own. People need extensive practice to recognize that they indeed have a point of view, that they live *inferentially,* that they do not have a direct pipeline to reality, that one can easily have an overwhelming inner sense of the correctness of one's views and still be wrong.

3. Instruction that does not further the development of human rationality, though it may properly be called training, is not *education.* The cultivation of the educated mind and person presupposes the cultivation of rational skills and passions. Insofar as schooling furthers, uses, or reinforces irrational belief formation, it violates its responsibility to *educate.* A society of uneducated persons is incompatible with democracy.

Unfortunately, the rule rather than the exception in schooling today is that students are continually encouraged to believe that there are more or less authoritative answers readily available for most of the important questions and decisions we face, or at least, authoritative frames of reference through which such answers can be pursued. Students are led to believe that they are surrounded by experts whose command of knowledge enables them to definitively settle the important issues they face socially and personally. Students tend to ego-identify with the monological answers of their parents, teachers, or peers. They have no real experience with dialogical thinking.

✦ Most Important Issues of Everyday Life Are Multilogical and Human

We do not live in a disembodied world of objects and physical laws. Instead, we live in a humanly contrived and constructed world. And there is more than one way to contrive and construct the world. Not only our social relations but our inner cognitive and affective lives are inferential in nature. We do not deal with the world-in-itself but the the world-as-we-define-it in relation to our interests, perspective, and point of view. We shape our interests and point of view in the light of our sense of what significant others think, and so live in a world that is exceedingly narrow, static, and closed. To protect ourselves, we assume our view is moral and objective. For the most part, our viewpoints are in fact amoral and subjective. Consider Goffman's (1959) explanation.

> In their capacity as performers, individuals will be concerned with maintaining the impression that they are living up to the many standards by which they and their products are judged. Because these standards are so numerous and so pervasive, the individuals who are performers dwell more than we might think in a moral world. But, *qua* performers, individuals are concerned not with the moral issue of realizing these standards, but with the amoral issue of engineering a convincing impression that these standards are being realized. Our activity, then, is largely concerned with moral matters, but as performers we do not have a moral concern with them. (p. 19)

This is not, as Whitehead (1929) shrewdly points out, how we *describe* ourselves,

> It does not matter what men say in words, so long as their activities are controlled by settled instincts. The words may ultimately destroy the instincts. But until this has occurred, words do not count.

As young children we begin to internalize images and concepts of what we and others are like, of what, for example, Americans are like, of what atheists, Christians, communists, parents, children, business-people, farmers, liberals, conservatives, left-wingers, right-wingers, salespeople, foreigners, patriots, Palestinians, Kiwanis Club members, cheerleaders, politicians, Nazis, ballet dancers, terrorists, union leaders, guerrillas, freedom fighters, doctors, Marines, scientists, mathematicians, contractors, waitresses, are *like*. We then ego-identify with our conceptions, we assume them to be accurate, and spontaneously use them to guide our day-to-day decisions.

Unwittingly, we begin as children — and, unless we get extensive dialogical practice, we continue as adults — to use egocentric and self-serving theories of people and the world. We organize our experience and make judgments from the perspective of assumptions and theories we would not admit to having if questioned. Studies in social perception demonstrate this in detail. Toch and Smith (1968) summarize it as follows:

> The process of reaching a value-judgment, the unconscious weighing that man's brain is able to make of numerous cues during a fraction of a second, is by no means a random and chaotic procedure. The weighing process, resulting in a perception, goes on for a purpose, whether that purpose is seeking food, adjusting one's footsteps to a curbing, picking up a book, reading or underlining certain passages in a book, joining some gang or group, or accepting or rejecting some political ideology. (p. 6)
>
> We see people as instant wholes. A "theory" is commonly viewed as something used exclusively by scientists. The discussion, however, emphasizes that everyone has, and inevitably uses, theories about people. These theories guide the wholes they perceive and the parts that they fit into the wholes. (p. 10)
>
> We all use theories in dealing with people: We invent concepts, assume relationships between them, and make predictions from our assumptions. Our theories are not, however, useful in the scientific sense, for they are implicit rather than explicit. That is, we are only dimly aware of our theories. As a result, we rarely make any real effort to test them. Yet they rule our impressions and our judgments. (p. 13)

People from different ethnic groups, religions, social classes, and cultural allegiances tend to form different but equally egocentric belief systems and use them equally unmindfully. These different construals of the world represent alternative settlements of the same basic set of issues all people continually face. We must all decide who we are as individuals and members of a community. We must construct a history, a place in time. We must envision an emergent future. We must decide who our friends and enemies are. We must invest our time, energy, and resources in some projects and not others.

We must decide what is *ours* and *why* it is ours. We must decide what is just and unjust and what grievances and grudges we have. We must decide to whom to give and from whom to withhold credibility. We must decide what is possible and impossible, what to fear and what to hope for.

All of these decisions determine our fundamental life-style and, ultimately, our destiny. They all presuppose answers to multilogical issues. Yet few of us realize how we internalize and construct a logic, a point of view, an organized way of experiencing, reasoning, and judging. Most of us, unfortunately, think of the world in terms of a monological definition of reality. How we see things simply seems *the correct way* to see them. How others see them simply seems wrong or prejudiced.

This can be illustrated by the flagrant differences between the colonial and British perceptions of the so-called Boston Massacre. The accounts at the time testify to the way in which people automatically presuppose the correctness of their ethnocentric perceptions:

1. A colonial onlooker, standing 20 yards from the colonists, gave sworn testimony to the justices of the peace on April 23, 1775, that the British fired the first shot.

2. A colonial Tory (a sympathizer with the British) wrote on May 4, 1775, to General Gage (the British commander in Boston), that the colonists fired the first shot.

3. A young British lieutenant wrote in his diary on April 19, 1775, that the colonists fired one or two shots, then the British returned the fire without any orders.

4. The commander of the colonial militia, John Parker, in an official deposition on April 25, 1775, said that he ordered the militia to disperse and not to fire, but the British fired on them without any provocation.

5. The *London Gazette* stated on June 10, 1775, to its British readers that the colonists fired on the British troops first.

Most teachers, I suspect, simply assume the account that favors their nation and then teach it as fact. Thus, students are taught to think monologically about historical events.

Consequently, most students (and their teachers) fail to grasp the essentially multilogical character of history. Since they don't see that all history is history-from-a-point-of-view, students fail to recognize appropriate logical parallels, for example, that all news is news-from-a-point-of-view. The result is that students do not learn how to read history or the news critically.

✦ *Inert Knowledge and Activated Ignorance*

Whitehead described the problem of inert knowledge — knowledge that we in some sense *have* but do not use when logically relevant, knowledge that just sits there in our minds, as it were, without activating force. Typically, this inability to put knowledge to work is viewed as an inability to *transfer*. In light of the above, I suggest instead that the problem is mainly due to our already having *activated* beliefs firmly entrenched in instinctual egocentric thinking.

The young child does not come to school with an empty head ready to be filled with new ideas and knowledge. The egocentric mind abhors a vacuum. The capacity to suspend judgment pending evidence is a higher order, secondary-nature, skill. The problem of inert knowledge is equivalent to the problem of *activated ignorance*. Children do not *transfer* the knowledge they learn in school to new settings because they already have activated ideas and beliefs to use in those settings.

The child's own emerging egocentric conceptions of children, teachers, parents, fun, work, play, and the physical world are much more activated and real than any alternative conceptions fostered by classroom instruction or textbooks. Only by bringing out the child's own ideas in dialogical and dialectical settings can the child begin to reconstruct and progressively transcend these conceptions. As long as school learning is simply superimposed on top of the child's own activated ignorance, that ignorance will continue to rule in the life-world of the child; scholastic learning will remain largely inert. Perhaps this is partly why so many adults, including those in high positions, often seem to act or talk like egocentric children.

There are, therefore, at least two fundamental justifications for giving children extensive dialogical practice in school: *1)* such practice is essential for all of the intrinsically multi-logical issues that the child must face, and *2)* such practice is essential for the child to come to discover, reconstruct, and ultimately transcend those ideas and beliefs uncritically and unconsciously internalized. A case can be made for the value of dialogical reasoning even with monological issues, as will be shown by the work of Jack Easley on math and science education. But first, let me be more explicit about the nature of dialogical thinking.

✦ *Dialogical Thinking in Early School Years*

Children begin developing an egocentric identity, point of view, and frame of reference through which they experience, think about, and judge the world. Many of their beliefs come from those around them. Nevertheless, from their earliest days, they come up against opposing points of view, differing interpretations of events, contradictory judgments, and incompatible lines of reasoning. First their parents and peers, later their teachers and other authorities, often disagree with them and thwart their egocentric desires.

But instruction does little to provide children with a way of entering into thoughts and feelings other than their own. Of course, they *hear* what others say, but they do not experience the inner logic of alternative points of view. That children can develop in this direction is demonstrated in their play: "You can be the mommy. I'll be the daddy. And my sister can be the baby." But schools do not, by and large, take advantage of this tendency and use it to construct exercises wherein students present reasons and evidence for alternative conclusions.

Children often use their capacity to think up reasons for and against an idea or decision only when they are already egocentrically for or against it. Of course, they must often bow to the superior power or authority of a parent, teacher, or older peer. But they rarely do so by entering into the point of view of the other and rationally assenting to it. As a result, they do not grasp that they themselves have a point of view. Rather, they tend to make absolute moral judgments about themselves and others. They frequently develop hostile feelings (often repressed) toward themselves or toward those who force them, rightly or wrongly, to accept their point of view. They do not have an opportunity to work out their own thoughts and discover ways of judging *reasons* without judging the *worth of the person* advancing them.

Children need assignments in multilogical issues. They need to discover opposing points of view in nonthreatening situations. They need to put their ideas into words, advance conclusions, and justify them. They need to discover their own assumptions and those of others. They need to discover their own inconsistencies and those of others. They do this best when they learn how to role-play the thinking of others, advance conclusions other than their own, and construct reasons supporting them.

Children need to do this for the multilogical issues — the conflicting points of view, interpretations, and conclusions — that they inevitably face in their everyday lives. But perhaps we should go further. All or most of what we learn rationally requires dialogical exchanges and opportunities to judge between conflicting points of view. The work of Jack Easley on math and science education suggests this thesis.

✦ Should Dialogical Instruction Be Used for Monological Issues?

In a series of articles on mathematics and science education, Jack Easley (1983a, b; 1984a) argues that children should learn how to solve virtually all problems — even the most monological and formalistic ones — dialogically or dialectically. He argues that studies indicate that primary school teachers *1)* cannot *transmit* knowledge, *2)* should therefore leave most discussion of math and science content to pupils, *3)* should choose and present appropriately challenging problems and tasks to the pupils, *4)* should train group leaders to facilitate dialogical exchanges, and *5)* should serve, fundamentally, as moderators of class communication. Most important, children should work in small but heterogeneous groups, trying to convince and understand each other. Through arguing, children discover their own views' strengths and weaknesses and also discover contrasts between their views and the views of others. Here are some of the ways Easely (1984b) formulates these points:

Primary teachers in the U.S., at least, should leave most discussion of mathematics and physical science content to their pupils. *a)* Cognitive research shows that young children develop and test alternative rational explanations which authoritative exposition can't displace. *b)* The conflicts that arise between presentations by teachers and texts and the pupil's unexamined math-science concepts generate severe anxieties about mathematics and science in most children....

Only by reflection on the alternative schemes in the light of conflicts with standard schemes can revisions be produced....

Those few students who do truly master mathematical or scientific subjects do so through a long process of doubting and challenging authority which few teachers are willing to take the time to do, even in pre-service training....

Teachers of regular primary grade classes should train group leaders on a regular basis to provide appropriate challenges for every member of their group....

Primary children should strive first to develop expression in some form by working in heterogeneous groups, trying to convince each other by clear speaking and writing....

They should also learn to say in advance what kind of contribution to the dialogue they are trying to make: an objection, an alternative view, a supporting point, etc....

I became convinced that teachers should be accepted by school reformers as the persons who are effectively in charge of instruction and who can change only as their perceptions of the classroom context are opened up through dialogues which respect the perceptions they have built from their own experience....

In Kitamaeno School, use of peer group dialogues helped children recognize alternative schemes and deal with them. Organizing children into small working groups around pre-selected appropriately challenging tasks required group leaders with confidence and some training in what to do when things went wrong....

The teachers' role was to present, often very dramatically, the challenging problem they had selected for the lesson, and almost totally abstaining from demonstrating or explaining how to solve it and to serve as master of ceremonies to see that every child had ample opportunity to be heard and took the responsibility to express ideas and to listen critically to those of others....

As children discover they have different solutions, different methods, different frameworks, and they try to convince each other, or at least to understand each other, they revise their understanding in many small but important ways....

As you can see, Easley argues that, irrespective of whether we have a precise and thoroughly defensible monological system for settling certain types of problems, children must work their way to that mono-logic through dialogic. Since students have alternative beliefs and frames of reference, even regarding scientific and mathematical concepts, they need to confront them or they will remain implicit, unchallenged, and unreconstructed. If we do not provide an environment for children to discover their own *activated* ideas, they may become and remain invincibly ignorant when it comes to putting knowledge into action. Their biases, stereotypes, distortions, illusions, and misconceptions will not dissolve without the purging power of dialogical exchange. They will simply superimpose adult beliefs on top of unreconstructed but still highly activated infantile ones.

Students leave school not only with unreconstructed mathematical and physical ideas but with unreconstructed personal, social, moral, historical, economic, and political views. Students leave school not knowing what they *really* — that is *deeply* — believe. Students leave school with much inert knowledge and even more activated ignorance. Therefore, students do not understand how to write, think, or speak in ways that organize and express what they believe, or read or listen in ways that allow them to understand and assess the thought of another. Students do not know how they respond to the mass media and to what extent it reinforces their subconscious egocentric or sociocentric views. They do not grasp how to read a newspaper or a book critically or how to listen to a lecture critically. They have no *rational* passions. They feel deeply only about egocentric concerns, justifying getting what they want and avoiding what they do not want. If dialogical thinking enables students to reconstruct mathematical and scientific ideas, it is most certainly called for on personal, social, moral, historical, economic, and political ones.

✦ Dialogical Thinking as a Strategy for Breaking Down Egocentric Identifications and Mind Sets

Children must experience dialogical thinking because such thinking is essential for rationally approaching the most significant and pervasive everyday human problems, and without it they will not develop the intellectual tools essential for confronting their own instinctual egocentric thought. Until we discover our own egocentric thinking, we cannot monitor or work through it. Indeed, to hold beliefs egocentrically is to hold them in nontestable ways. As Piaget (1976) puts it:

> Many adults are still egocentric in their ways of thinking. Such people interpose between themselves and reality an imaginary or mystical world, and they reduce everything to this individual point of view. Unadapted to ordinary conditions, they seem to be immersed in an inner life that is all the more intense. Does this make them conscious of themselves? Does egocentrism point the way to a truer introspection? On the contrary, it can easily be seen that there is a way of living in oneself that develops a great wealth of inexpressible feelings, of personal images and schemas, while at the same time it impoverishes analysis and consciousness of self. (p. 209)

Like egocentric children, egocentric adults assimilate everything they hear or experience to their own point of view. They learn how to affect reciprocity — to create the appearance of entering into points of view other than their own. But when there is conflict, they "enter" them only to negate or refute. They never genuinely leave their own mind set.

I am reminded of a distinction drawn by the sociologist, C. Wright Mills (1962), illuminating how people relate to their belief systems. Mills argued that there were three types of believers — vulgar, sophisticated, and "plain" (critical). Vulgar believers can only operate with slogans and stereotypes within a point of view with which they egocentrically identify. Vulgar Marxists use slogans like "Power to the people!" "Smash the state!" "Down with the capitalist pigs!" to badger their would-be opponents. They are not interested in reading books on capitalism or by capitalists, but consider them only as the enemy.

In contrast, sophisticated Marxists do read books on capitalism or by capitalists only to refute them. They stand on their heads if necessary to show that Marxism is in all senses and respects superior to capitalism. They might be intellectually creative, but they use their creativity to further one and only one point of view.

Only critical believers would, in Mills's sense, enter sympathetically into opposing points of view, for only they recognize weaknesses in their own. If they become Marxists, it is because they read Marx as Marx read others — sympathetically and critically. They learn from criticism and are not egocentrically attached to their point of view. They understand they must continually develop and refine it by a fuller and richer consideration of the available evidence and reasoning, through exposure to the best thinking in alternative points of view.

If Mills is right, we also have vulgar, sophisticated, and critical capitalists; vulgar, sophisticated, and critical Christians; vulgar, sophisticated, and critical North Americans, Frenchmen, and Soviets; vulgar, sophisticated, and critical Freudians, and so on. Given their fundamental mode of thinking, their shared capacity to enter into points of view other than their own and to learn from criticism, critical Marxists, capitalists, Christians, Muslims, North Americans, Frenchmen, Soviets, Freudians, and Skinnerians share more in common with each other than they do with their vulgar or sophisticated counterparts.

A fundamental problem of schooling today is that schools in all societies tend to produce vulgar and sophisticated, rather than critical, believers. This problem is mainly due to the lack of dialogical thinking. Most instruction is monological, with various *authoritative* perspectives being nurtured and inculcated. When the inculcated perspective is incompatible with the child's egocentric beliefs, the academically learned perspective is simply superimposed as a facade or veneer. This veneer may itself be egocentrically defended, but the defense is merely *verbal,* because the primary and more primitive system is maintained in behavior. Hence, people can vehemently defend Christianity and yet continually behave in a most un-Christian fashion, apparently and self-righteously oblivious to their contradictions. Or they can defend democracy with passion and abandon, and yet act to undermine all possibility of its being practiced. This is true of any system of beliefs, whether scientific, religious, social, political, or personal. Wherever we find people, we find blatant contradictions between word and deed. Wherever we find people, we find a great deal of ego-defensive self-delusion.

✦ Teaching Critical Thinking in the Strong Sense: School as Purgatory

I would like to use a religious metaphor to characterize the problem of education. For a Catholic, there are three possible divine dispensations as a result of how one lives. In addition to heaven or hell, one may be sent to purgatory, a place in which one must work one's way back to God. The assumption is that one can die with one's thoughts and will still somewhat resistant to God. One then must go through a process of purging one's sinful tendencies. This process involves some pain and struggle, but issues ultimately in a purification of heart and will, a rooting out of one's sinful tendencies, and a reconstruction of one's inner thought.

This concept is apt for understanding what schooling would be if we were to cultivate that very rare breed — the educated, rational person. If we want persons who believe critically, who are neither vulgar nor sophisticated in their beliefs, then we waste our time by trying to make school heaven — all fun and games, all pleasant and satisfying, all positive reinforcement, all sweetness and light, with no confusion, struggle, or dispute. Of course, I take it for granted that we will get nowhere by going to the other extreme and making it hell. The challenge is to foster a process whereby students progressively and over a long period of time rid themselves of their egocentric and sociocentric beliefs and attachments. Presently, it appears that schooling does little more than make people's instinctual egocentrism a bit more sophisticated, at least with respect to those issues, that involve our collective egos.

However, this does not mean that schools that foster dialogical or dialectical thinking would be hotbeds of strident argument, closedminded debate, or personal trauma. Our experience of argument, debate, and controversy occurs now in the context of unreconstituted egocentric attachment. People now typically argue for egocentric purposes and with egocentric ends in view. They argue now to score points, *defeat* the other person, make their point of view *look* good. They experience "argument" as *battle,* not as a mutual or cooperative search for a fuller understanding.

Yet I know from years of working with students that they *can* learn to reason dialogically in mutually supportive ways, that they can learn to experience dialogical thought as leading to discovery, not victory. To achieve this end we must first ensure that, as soon as possible, they learn to argue for and against each and every important point of view and each basic belief or conclusion that they are to take seriously. We must also raise issues that they care about and which engage their egocentric thoughts and beliefs. We should begin with beliefs that are mildly egocentric and work slowly to those that are deeply embedded in the ego. Then the dialogical thinking we nurture helps develop critical thinking in the strong sense.

Teaching critical thinking in the strong sense means teaching so that students explicate, understand, and critique their own deepest prejudices, biases, and misconceptions, thereby encouraging students to discover and contest their own egocentric and sociocentric tendencies. Only if we experientially contest our inevitable egocentric and sociocentric habits of thought can we hope to genuinely think rationally. Only dialogical thinking about basic issues that matter to the individual provides the kind of practice and skill essential to strong-sense critical thinking. I grant that every student needs to develop the particular skills that Robert Ennis and others have delineated, but I am arguing that *how* these skills are nurtured is crucial.

Students need to develop all critical thinking skills in dialogical settings to develop ethically, rationally, that is, to develop genuine fairmindedness. If simply taught as atomic skills apart from empathically entering into points of view students fear or dislike, critical thinking will in the end simply be used to rationalize prejudices and preconceptions, or convince people that their point of view is *the* correct one. Students will then merely be transformed from vulgar to sophisticated, but not to *critical* thinkers.

✦ *Fact, Opinion, and Reasoned Judgment*

Unfortunately, many programs designed to enhance critical thinking fail to give students insight into the nature of multilogical issues and the need for dialogical thinking. They often teach as if all questions are reducible either to matters of fact (where science, math, engineering, and technical learning are dominant) or matters of opinion (where personal taste, culture, religion, preference, and faith are dominant). This happens when students are told to divide beliefs or statements into facts and opinions. Neither category allows dialogical thinking. It is presumably unnecessary with facts, because scientific, mathematical, and technological procedures and methods presuppose relatively agreed-upon frames of reference and modes of issue settlement. It is useless with opinions, because presumably one cannot reason in matters of pure taste: *De gustibus non est disputandem.* Schools under the sway of this view take as their first and foremost responsibility teaching students *the facts,* and then secondarily, passing on the shared values and beliefs of the culture.

Unfortunately, a taxonomy that divides all beliefs into either facts or opinions leaves out the most important category: *reasoned judgment.* Most important issues are not simply matters of fact, nor are they essentially matters of faith, taste, or preference. They call for our reasoned judgment. They can be understood from different points of view through different frames of reference. People approach them with different assumptions, concepts, priorities, and ends in view. When analytically applied to these perspectives in dialectical contexts, the tools of critical thinking enable us to grasp genuine weaknesses. The dialectical experience enables us to gain this perspective.

For example, it is exceedingly difficult to judge the case made by a prosecutor in a trial *until* we have heard the arguments for the defense. Only by stepping out of the perspective of the prosecutor and actually organizing the evidence in language designed to make the strongest case for the defense, can we begin to grasp the true strength and weakness of the prosecutor's case. This approach is the only proper way to approach the important issues we face in our lives, and I am amazed that we and our textbooks refuse to recognize it. The most basic issues simply do not reduce to unadulterated fact or arbitrary opinion. True, they often have a factual dimension. But often some of the alleged facts are questionable. And we often must decide which facts are *most* important, which should be made central, and which should be deemed peripheral or even irrelevant. Then, typically, there are alternative arguable interpretations and implications. Make your own list of the ten most important issues and see if this is not true (but beware of the tendency to see your own answers to these issues as self-evident facts!).

✦ The Cultivation of Rational Passions

To grasp the problem of teaching critical thinking skills in a strong sense, we must challenge the reason-versus-emotion stereotype, which fosters the view that a rational person is cold, unfeeling, and generally without passion, whereas an irrational person is passionate but unintellectual. A false dichotomy is set up between reason and passion, and we are forced to choose between the two as incompatible opposites.

But this point of view is profoundly misleading. All action requires the marshaling of energy. All action presupposes a driving force. We must *care* about something to do something about it. Emotions, feelings, and passions of some kind or other underlie all human behavior. What we should want to free ourselves from is not emotion, feeling, or passion *per se*, but irrational emotions, irrational feelings, and irrational passions. A highly developed intellect can be used for good or ill either at the service of rational or irrational passions. Only the development of rational passions can prevent our intelligence from becoming the tool of our egocentric emotions and the point of view embedded in them. A passionate drive for clarity, accuracy, and fairmindedness, a fervor for getting to the bottom of things, to the deepest root issues, for listening sympathetically to opposition points of view, a compelling drive to seek out evidence, an intensive aversion to contradiction, sloppy thinking, inconsistent application of standards, a devotion to truth as against self-interest — these are essential commitments of the rational person. They enable us to assent rationally to a belief even when it is ridiculed by others, to question what is passionately believed and socially sanctioned, to conquer the fear of abandoning a long and deeply held belief. There is nothing passive, bland, or complacent about such a person.

Emotions and beliefs are always inseparably wedded together. When we describe ourselves as driven by irrational emotions, we are also driven by the irrational *beliefs* that structure and support them. When we conquer an irrational emotion through the use of our reason, we do it by using our rational passions. To put this another way and link it more explicitly with the earlier sections of this chapter, our primary egocentric nature is a complex mixture of belief, values, drives, and assumptions. It is an integrated cognitive and affective system. It generates a total frame of reference through which we can come to perceive, think, and judge. When we develop our secondary nature, we develop a countervailing system, equally complex and complete. We may of course experience intense internal struggles between these incompatible modes of being. Both systems can become highly *intellectualized* so that intelligence per se is not what distinguishes them. It is quite possible to find highly intelligent but essentially irrational persons, as well as basically rational ones of limited intelligence. In this way, a highly intelligent but sophisticated (i.e., sophistic) thinker can create the illusion of defending a more rational point of view than that defended by a thinker who is basically rational but not as clever.

Therefore, as educators we should embrace the nurturing of rational passions as an essential dimension in the development of the *thinking* of our students. Teachers must model rational passions. This, of course, presupposes that teachers genuinely have them. It will do no good for a teacher to pretend. This is not a matter of *technique*. This is an important reason why successful critical thinking instruction cannot be achieved as the result of a few weekend in-service workshops.

✦ Critical and Creative Thinking

Just as it is misleading to talk of developing a student's capacity to think critically without facing the problem of cultivating the student's rational passions — the necessary driving force behind the rational use of all critical thinking skills — so too is it misleading to talk of developing a student's ability to think critically as something separate from the student's ability to think creatively. All rational dialogical thinking requires creativity, because dialogical thinking is a series of reciprocal creative acts wherein we move up and back between categorically different imagined roles. We must first of all imagine ourselves in a given frame of reference. Then we must imaginatively construct some reasons to support it. Next we must step outside it and imagine ourselves responding to those reasons from an opposing point of view. Then we must imagine ourselves back in the first point of view to respond to the opposition we just created. Next we must change roles again and create a further response, and so on. The imagination and its creative powers are continually called forth. Each act must fit the unique move preceding it. In dialogical exchange, we cannot predict in advance what another, or indeed what we, will say. Yet what we say, to be rational, must respond to the logic of what the other just said. Furthermore, integrating the strengths of opposing views, and eliminating weak points are also creative and constructive acts. One must creatively develop a new point of view.

Students need not begin by playing both sides of a dialogue simultaneously. But we should continually nurture their ability to frame dialogical exchanges, first brief, then extended ones. Their creative imagination will be continually challenged to develop through this process.

✦ Conclusion

People become educated, as opposed to trained, insofar as they achieve a grasp of critical principles and the ability and passion to choose, organize, and shape their own ideas and living beliefs by means of them. Education is not merely piling up more and more bits and pieces of information. It is a process of autonomously distinguishing true from false. It calls for self-motivated action on our own mental nature and active participation in forming our own character. It requires us to learn to open our mind, correct and refine it, and enable it to learn rationally, thereby empowering it to analyze, digest, master, and rule its own knowledge, gain command over its own faculties, and achieve flexibility, fairmindedness, and critical exactness.

This process cannot be accomplished when learning is viewed monologically. The process of gaining knowledge is at its roots dialogical. Our minds are never empty of beliefs and never without a point of view. They cannot function framelessly. Since our instinctive intellectual drives are initially egocentric, and then typically ethnocentric, we must learn to bring our implicit ideas and reasonings into open dialogical conflict with opposing ones to decide rationally, as best we can, upon their merit as candidates for mindful belief. Our implicit everyday theories of ourselves, our friends and neighbors, our nation and religion, our enemies and antagonists, and our hopes, fears, and premonitions must become overtly known to us that we might learn to continually re-assess them as we enter empathically into more or less alien belief systems.

Children begin by engaging in mere collective monologue, but early on they also begin to respond to the points of view of others. Their play suggests that they enjoy taking on the role of others and acting as though they were someone else. This initial drive must not be allowed to wither away, but must be cultivated, expanded, and reshaped. Whether we begin with empathy into the thinking and predicaments of characters in children's stories, lead children into reflective philosophical discussions, or provide challenging ethical questions and dilemmas for them to think about, we must lead students to the point that they begin to get comfortable dealing with dialogical issues rationally. Progressively, the issues that students deal with should get more and more complex.

Baby Bear had the smallest bowl.

"Why do I have the smallest bowl?" he said.

"Because you are the smallest bear." said his mother.

"Is that fair?" said Baby Bear.

- *Did Baby Bear <u>need</u> as much as the big bears? Why?*
- *Could he eat as much as the big bears? Why?*
- *Did he* deserve *as much as the big bears? Why?*
- *Do you think it is fair for Baby Bear to have a smaller bowl? Why?*
- *What problems have you seen like the one in this story?*

figure 1

Discussion Plan: Friends

1. Can people talk together a lot and still not be friends?
2. Can people hardly ever talk together and still be friends?
3. Are there some people who always fight with their friends?
4. Are there some people who never fight with their friends?
5. Are there some people who have no friends?
6. Are there people who have friends, even though they have hardly anything else?
7. Do you trust your friends more than anyone else?
8. Are there some people whom you trust more than your friend?
9. Is it possible to be afraid of a friend?
10. What is the difference between friends and family?
11. Are there animals you could be friends with, and other animals you could never be friends with?

figure 2

WHAT DID SARA LEARN?

Making Things Right

The children had damaged the wall. Sara thought they should *make things right.* One way was for them to put a new coat of paint on the wall.

The children's parents might have to pay to have new paint put on the wall. Sara thought that might be another way to *make things right.*

- *What would be fair? Why?*
- *What problems like this have you seen?*
- *What does MAKING THINGS RIGHT have to do with being fair?*

figure 3

For each of the following issues, identify reasons that support each side of the issue.

Issue

Students' grades should be based not only on how much they learn, but also on how hard they try.

Students' grades should be based only on how much they learn.

Supporting Reasons

1. This policy will encourage students who learn slowly.

2. _____

3. _____

Supporting Reasons

1. Teachers don't always know how hard a student is trying.

2. _____

3. _____

Issue

The best way to deal with crime is to give long prison sentences.

Long prison sentences will not reduce crime.

Supporting Reasons

1. _____

2. _____

3. _____

Supporting Reasons

1. _____

2. _____

3. _____

figure 4

"If a man destroy the eye of another, they shall destroy his eye."
Hammurabi, about 1950 B.C.

Convicted of theft, Mustafa was taken into the public square where, before a fascinated crowd, the executioner chopped off his right hand with a sword.

The court ordered Sarah to pay $5,500 for damages to Paul's car and $8,376 in medical bills for injuries to Paul after she crashed into his car while he was stopped for a red light.

Three members of a teen-aged gang beat and robbed a 60-year-old woman standing at a bus stop. The woman was hospitalized for two months and permanently crippled by the beating. The boys were arrested and placed in Juvenile Hall for six months where they were given psychological counseling, released, and placed on probation for one year.

Each of the above situations involves an issue of *corrective justice*. Corrective justice refers to the fairness of responses to wrongs or injuries.

What Do You Think?

1. *What is fair or unfair about each of the above responses to wrongs or injuries?*
2. *What values and interests, other than fairness, might be important to take into account in deciding what might be a proper response to a wrong or injury?*

figure 5

More and more, students should have assignments that challenge their ability to identify and analyze frames of reference and points of view — the frames of reference in their texts, various subject areas, TV programs, news broadcasts and daily papers, the language of their peers and teachers, political speeches and personal discussions, and everyday decisions and ways of living. And they should do this to discover, not that everything is relative and arbitrary, or a matter of opinion, but that all beliefs and points of view are subject to rational analysis and assessment. As they achieve increasing success in this process, their rational passions will develop by degrees and their egocentric defensiveness will concomitantly decrease.

Students will not become progressively more unruly and hard to handle. On the contrary, they will become more and more amenable to reason and the power of evidence. They will, of course, eventually question us and our points of view, but they will do so rationally and hence help us to develop as well. Ideally, the process will pervade the school climate and be reflected in the deepest structures of school life. By this means, schools can perhaps begin to become leading institutions in society, paradigms of rationality, by helping an irrational society become what it itself has said is its own highest goal: a free society of free and autonomous persons.

✦ *References*

Easley, Jack. (1983a). "A Japanese Approach to Arithmetic," in *For the Learning of Mathematics,* 3 (3).

Easley, Jack. (1983b). "What's there to Talk About in Arithmetic?" in *Problem Solving* (Newsletter, The Franklin Institute Press) 5.

Easley, Jack. (1984a). "Is there Educative Power in Students' Alternative Frameworks?" in *Problem Solving* (Newsletter, The Franklin Institute Press), 6:1–4.

Easley, Jack. (1984b). "A Teacher Educator's Perspective on Students and Teachers' Schemes: Or Teaching by Listening." Unpublished paper, presented at the Conference on Thinking, Harvard Graduate School of Education.

Goffman, Erving. (1959). *The Presentation of Self in Everyday Life.* Garden City, N.J.: Doubleday.

Hayes, J. (1940). *The Complete Problem Solver.* Philadelphia: The Franklin Institute Press.

Mills, C. Wright. (1962). *The Marxists.* New York: Dell.

Piaget, Jean. (1976). *Judgment and Reasoning in the Child.* Totowa, N.J.: Littlefield, Adams.

Toch, H., & Smith, H. C. (Eds.). (1968). *Social Perception.* New York: Van Nostrand.

Whitehead, Alfred. (1929). *The Aims of Education and Other Essays.* New York: Dutton.

* Figures 1, 3, and 5 are from *Justice,* a series produced by *Law in a Free Society,* 5115 Douglas Fir Drive, Calabasas, CA 91302. Figure 2 is from *Pixie: Looking for Meaning,* by Matthew Lipman, in *Philosophy for Children,* Institute for the Advancement of Philosophy for Children, Montclair State College, Montclair, N.J. Figure 4 is from *Thinking Critically,* by John Chaffee, 1985, Houghton Mifflin, Boston.

✦✦ Chapter 15

Power, Vested Interest, and Prejudice:
On the Need for Critical Thinking in the Ethics
of Social and Economic Development

Abstract

In this paper, presented at the International Conference on The Ethics of Development, *held at the University of Costa Rica (1987), Richard Paul argues that mass education is essential to ethically sensitive economic and social development. There are two main reasons Paul advances to support this view:* 1) *politicians, despite their rhetoric to the contrary, do not typically respond to ethical concerns unless those concerns square with their vested interests, and* 2) *the mass media in each country — the main source of information regarding development for most people — must be critically analyzed to understand the ethical issues implicit in social and economic development options. As Paul puts it, "neither the leaders of powerful nations and groups nor their 'followers' are likely to analyze or apply the ethical principles relevant to development in a way likely to do justice to those principles. The thinking of the leaders verges toward manipulations, rationalizations, and narrow ways-and-means analysis while the thinking of the followers tends toward naivete, closedmindedness, and intellectual servitude fostered by their restricted sources of information, limited access to education, and traditional egocentric and ethnocentric prejudices."*

✦ We Have Appropriate Ethical Principles

*T*he problem of ethics in economic development is neither verbal nor philosophical, but operational. It isn't that appropriate ethical principles have never been formulated. On the contrary, one could easily identify and set out appropriate ethical principles. The problem is, rather, how to make those principles morally operational, to put them into action when policies and decisions are formulated and implemented by persons and groups in power.

In the next few paragraphs I will provide an incomplete but illustrative list of some moral principles relevant to economic development. For example, the U.S. Catholic bishops, in a pastoral letter on the economy, gave the following "basic and social moral principles" as "guidelines for economic life:"

1) Every economic decision and institution should be judged in light of whether it *protects* or *undermines* the *dignity* of the human person. The economy must be at the service of all people, *especially* the poor.

2) Human dignity can be realized and protected only in community. The obligation to "love our neighbor" has an individual dimension, but it also requires a broader commitment to the common good.

3) Everyone has *a right to participate* in the economic life of society. No person or group should be unfairly excluded or unable to contribute to the economy.

4) All members of society have a *special obligation* to the poor and vulnerable. It is our duty to speak for the voiceless, defend the defenseless, and assess lifestyles, policies, and social institutions in terms of their impact on the poor.

5) Human rights are the minimum conditions for life in community. All people have a right to life, food, clothing, shelter, rest, medical care, education, and employment.

6) Society as a whole, acting through private and government institutions, has the moral responsibility to enhance human dignity and protect human rights.

Similar or supplemental principles have been formulated in the U.N. "International Covenant on Civil and Political Rights" (U.N. General Assembly resolution 2200 of 16 December 1966) and the U.N. "International Bill of Human Rights" (U.N. General Assembly resolution 217 of 10 December 1948).

More recently, the U.N. World Commission on Environment and Development issued a report prepared by 21 commissioners who conducted public hearings on five continents, which concluded *1)* that resources must be transferred from the wealthy industrial nations to the poorer developed nations, *2)* that global military expenditures (said to be now $1 trillion a year) use resources that might be employed "more productively to diminish the security threats created by environmental conflict and the resentments that are fueled by widespread poverty," and that "sustainable human progress" can be achieved only through a system of international cooperation that treats economic growth and environmental protection as inseparable.

This report is quite consistent with the ethical principles cited in the American Catholics bishops' letter and the basic U.N. declarations of human rights. The facts upon which they base their ethical judgments are generally accepted by the scholarly community. But the steps being called for sharply contrast with the fundamental mode of operation of powerful nations and groups. Let us now consider why ethical principles are generally moot in the world of economic and political power.

✦ *There Are No Practical Incentives for the Powerful to Comply*

If actions speak louder than words, then the powerful nations and groups (for example, international corporations) tell us that there is no reason to limit the pursuit of their vested interests, profit, and advantage because of the demands of ethical principles.

The overwhelming majority of nations have condemned the Soviet invasion of Afghanistan, for example, but this condemnation has not persuaded the Soviets to withdraw. The overwhelming majority of nations and the World Court have condemned the U.S.-sponsored invasion of Nicaragua, but the condemnation has not persuaded the U.S. government to desist. Amnesty International and other organizations have documented the extensive use of torture, assassination and terrorism by many nations, but have failed to significantly reduce these ethical violations. Although powerful nations and groups attempt to maintain a positive image in the world press, clearly this image-fostering has little to do with ethical scruples or a willingness to respond to ethical critique. Furthermore, powerful nations spend a great deal of money on covert actions of their intelligence wings enabling them to evade responsibility for much of their own unethical behavior. Hence the fact, for example, that Idi Amin was brought to power by collaborative efforts by the CIA, MOSSAD (Israel), and the MI6 (Britain) is not common knowledge even though scholarly documentation is readily available. Consequently, nations can easily take a strong public stand condemning terrorism while financing it with a lot of money and technical expertise.

The amoral and immoral activities of powerful nations and groups, whether overt or covert, are often at odds with the social, political, and economic development of less powerful nations and groups, so there is a crucial link between the manner in which power is obtained and used and the problems of third world development.

Do not assume I am implying that the leaders of powerful governments and groups are self-consciously or deliberately amoral or immoral in the formulations of their policies and decisions. This I do not intend or believe. Rather my view is that many who rise to political and economic power have highly developed their capacity for rationalizing their vested interests and ignoring viewpoints or lines of reasoning which question what they do. Most discussions over pressing policy decisions focus on ways and means for advancing specific interests; to raise ethical issues in such discussions would seem to the participants "irrelevant", "idealistic", or "hopelessly philosophical". If nothing else, groups vying for power would hesitate to restrict their own use of power, based on ethical considerations, while competing groups, in their view, are not so restricted. Furthermore, since competing groups, in their view, tend to drift toward considering the competing "other" as the "enemy", restricting their activities based on ethical considerations appears to them as "folly".

Jerome Frank has described this tendency with respect to the phenomenon of war in the following way:

> The power of group relationships to determine how the members of groups perceive each other has been neatly shown by the vicissitudes of this image, which always arises when two nations are in conflict and which is

always the same no matter who the conflicting parties are. Enemy-images mirror each other — that is, each side attributes the same virtues to itself and the same vices to the enemy. "We" are trustworthy, peace-loving, honorable, and humanitarian; "they" are treacherous, warlike, and cruel. In surveys of Americans conducted in 1942, the first five adjectives chosen to characterize both Germans and Japanese (enemies) included warlike, treacherous, and cruel, none of which appeared among the first five describing the Russians (allies); in 1966 all three had disappeared from American characterizations of the Germans and Japanese (allies), but now the Russians (no longer allies, although more rivals than enemies) were warlike and treacherous. In 1966 the mainland Chinese, predictably, were seen as warlike, treacherous, and sly. After President Nixon's visit to China, these adjectives disappeared from our characterization of the Chinese, whom we now see as hardworking, intelligent, artistic, progressive, and practical.

The image of the enemy creates a self-fulfilling prophecy by causing enemies to acquire the evil characteristics they attribute to each other. In combating what they perceive to be the other's cruelty and treachery, each side becomes more cruel and treacherous itself. The enemy-image nations form of each other thus more or less corresponds to reality.

Of course much of the use of economic resources is motivated today by considerations seen as crucial to the "cold war". Economies and economic and political policies are deeply tied into the role nations and groups appear to play in relation to this struggle between the U.S. and its allies and the Soviet Union and its allies. The superpowers try to prevent anyone from remaining outside of their strategic decisions and policies.

Most citizens find it very difficult to make reasonable ethical judgments about questions of development, when most of their information comes from the public media which are heavily influenced (when not overtly controlled) by a perspective on development of powerful groups.

The picture I am painting is as follows. The leaders of powerful nations and groups are involved in an intense struggle for power, within the context of which ethical principles seem irrelevant or somehow intrinsically embedded in their own vested interests. On the other hand, the majority of citizens in the world are provided with information from sources that are tied, in large part, to these same powerful vested interests. Thus, neither the leaders of powerful nations and groups nor their "followers" are likely to analyze or apply the ethical principles relevant to development in a way likely to do justice to those principles. The thinking of the leaders verges toward practical manipulations, rationalizations, and narrow ways and means analysis while the thinking of the followers tends toward naiveté and closedmindedness fostered by their restricted sources of information, limited access to education, and traditional ethnocentric prejudices. The misinformation and disinformation fostered by the vested interests shape the media representations making the question of development a puzzle to most.

✦ There Is a Need to Foster Critical Thinking
in the Education of the Ordinary Citizen

There is little hope that the leaders of powerful nations and groups will of their own volition take ethical considerations seriously in formulating policies and practices that bear on the well-being and development of all. They must be pressured by those not deeply involved in the struggle for political and economic power. But such persons are traditionally ill-prepared to exercise the critical thinking necessary to address the problem of development. Though the relevant ethical principles have been formulated, ordinary people have not been taught those formulations. They have not been encouraged to seek out sources of information not readily accessible in their national public media nor in how to analyze the media critically. They have not developed the conceptual sophistication to see through the bias of their own groups' conceptualizations.

Unless educators in all countries can begin to foster genuine critical thinking in schools accessible to most people, or some other means is developed or generated for helping people free themselves from the self-serving manipulations of their own leaders, it is doubtful that "ethical reasoning" will play its appropriate role in social and economic development. Ethical reasoning, to be effective, cannot be "uncritical" for ethical principles must be applied in the context of human action and interest heavily polluted by distortion and one-sidedness, by vested interests portrayed in the guise of ethical righteousness.

Part II:

How to Teach for It

Instruction

✦✦ **Chapter 16**

The Critical Connection:
Higher Order Thinking That Unifies Curriculum, Instruction, and Learning

Abstract

"Though education by its very nature comprises a set of high order goals, actual school learning, given established practice, culminates in a set of lower order results." "The problem," in Paul's view, "is unambiguous. How can we reconceptualize and restructure what we presently do to narrow the gap between goals and results, to make high order goals a practical reality? ... What sorts of changes do we need so that in math classes students learn to think mathematically, in history classes they learn to think historically, in science classes they learn to think scientifically, and so that in general, not only in school but in their everyday lives as well, students begin to think critically in a disciplined, self-directed fashion?" Paul traces the problem to a tacit but large-scale acceptance of a network of uncritically held assumptions about instruction, knowledge, and learning. He argues for an alternative set of assumptions and spells out the kinds of changes needed in curricula and staff development for these more critically held assumptions about instruction, knowledge, and learning to become embedded in practice. Paul argues for long-term commitment to this process because of the deep-seated nature of the changes needed and the depth of resistance that can be expected.

✦ Introduction

*T*he fundamental problems in schooling today at all levels are fragmentation and lower order learning. Both within and between subject areas there is a dearth of connection and depth. Atomized lists dominate curricula, atomized teaching dominates instruction, and atomized recall dominates learning. What is learned are superficial fragments, typically soon forgotten. What is missing is coherence, connection, and depth of understanding.

Recognition of the economic implications of the pervasiveness of lower order learning is illustrated in an open letter drafted by the president of Stanford University, Donald Kennedy, co-signed by 36 other college leaders from across the USA and sent to 3,000 college and university presidents (Sept. 18, 1987). It warned of,

> a national emergency ... rooted ... in the revolution of expectations about what our schools must accomplish ....

293

It simply will not do for our schools to produce a small elite to power our scientific establishment and a larger cadre of workers with basic skills to do routine work. Millions of people around the world now have these same basic skills and are willing to work twice as long for as little as one-tenth our basic wages. To maintain and enhance our quality of life, we must develop a leading-edge economy based on workers who can think for a living. If skills are equal, in the long run wages will be too. This means we have to educate a vast mass of people capable of thinking critically, creatively, and imaginatively.

There are reasons why teaching and learning are lower order and reasons why they could and should be higher order. In this paper I explore both.

The bottom line, as we all well know, is not what is taught but what is learned. Students often learn something very different from what is taught. This dichotomy leads Alan Schoenfeld, the distinguished math educator, to conclude that math instruction is on the whole "deceptive and fraudulent". He uses strong words to underscore a wide gulf between what math teachers think their students are learning and what in fact they are. (Schoenfeld, 1982) He elaborates as follows:

> All too often we focus on a narrow collection of well-defined tasks and train students to execute those tasks in a routine, if not algorithmic fashion. Then we test the students on tasks that are very close to the ones they have been taught. If they succeed on those problems, we and they congratulate each other on the fact that they have learned some powerful mathematical techniques. In fact, they may be able to use such techniques mechanically while lacking some rudimentary thinking skills. To allow them, and ourselves, to believe that they "understand" the mathematics is deceptive and fraudulent. (p. 29)

Schoenfeld cites a number of studies to justify this characterization of math instruction and its lower order consequences. He also gives a number of striking examples, at the tertiary as well as at the primary and secondary levels:

> At the University of Rochester 85 percent of the freshman class takes calculus, and many go on. Roughly half of our students see calculus as their last mathematics course. Most of these students will never apply calculus in any meaningful way (if at all) in their studies, or in their lives. They complete their studies with the impression that they know some very sophisticated and high-powered mathematics. They can find the maxima of complicated functions, determine exponential decay, compute the volumes of surfaces of revolution, and so on. But the fact is that these students know barely anything at all. The only reason they can perform with any degree of competency on their final exams is that the problems on the exams are nearly carbon copies of problems they have seen before; the students are not being asked to think, but merely to apply well-rehearsed schemata for specific kinds of tasks. Tim Keifer and I studied students abilities to deal with pre-calculus versions of elementary word problems such as the following:
>
> *As 8-foot fence is located 3 feet from a building. Express the length L of the ladder which may be leaned against the building and just touch the top of the fence as a function of the distance X between the foot of the ladder and the base of the building.*

We were not surprised to discover that only 19 of 120 attempts at such problems (four each for 30 students) yielded correct answers, or that only 65 attempts produced answers of any kind. (p. 28)

Schoenfeld documents similar problems at the level of elementary math instruction. He reports on an experiment in which elementary students were asked questions like, "There are 26 sheep and 10 goats on a ship. How old is the captain?" 76 of the 97 students "solved" the problem by adding, subtracting, multiplying, or dividing. (Schoenfeld, 1989)

Schoenfeld cites many similar cases, including a study that demonstrated that "word problems", which are supposed to require thought, tend to be approached by students mindlessly with the *key word algorithm,* that is, by reading problems like "John had eight apples. He gave three to Mary. How many does John have left?" and looking for words like 'left' to tell them what operation to perform. As Schoenfeld puts it, "... the situation was so extreme that many students chose to subtract in a problem that began 'Mr. Left'." (Schoenfeld, 1982) This tendency to approach math problems and assignments with robotic lower order responses becomes obsessive in most students.

Robotic lower order learning is not, of course, peculiar to math. It is the common mode of learning in every subject area. This results in a kind of global self-deception that surrounds teaching and learning, often with the students clearer about what is really being learned than the teachers. Many students, for example, realize that in their history courses they merely learn to mouth names, dates, events, and outcomes whose significance they do not really understand and whose content they forget shortly after the test. Our stated goal may be to prepare students to think historically when dealing with public and private issues and problems, but that is not what happens. That is not the bottom line.

In other words, though education by its very nature comprises a set of higher order goals, actual school learning, given established practice, culminates in a set of lower order results. The problem is unambiguous. How can we reconceptualize and restructure what we presently do to narrow the gap between goals and results, to make higher order goals a practical reality, to reduce lower order goals to what they should be: mere means for higher order ends. What sorts of changes do we need to make so that in math classes students learn to think mathematically, in history classes they learn to think historically, in science classes they learn to think scientifically, and so that in general, not only in school but in their everyday lives as well, they begin to think critically in a disciplined, self-directed fashion?

✦ *The Root of the Problem Is Our Confidence in Didactic Teaching*

Fundamental changes are needed, ones that require insight into a host of interrelated conditions. Consider some of the connections we need to grasp. We can improve student performance only by improving their thinking. We can improve their thinking only by creating opportunities and incentives for them to think. We can provide them with opportunities and incentives to think only if their teachers have time to thoughtfully redesign their instruction. We can give teachers time to thoughtfully redesign their instruction only if they do not feel compelled to cover huge amounts of subject matter. We can reduce the obsession to cover huge amounts of subject matter only if the curriculum is restructured to focus on basic concepts, understandings, and abilities. We can restructure the curriculum to focus on basic concepts, understandings, and abilities only if we understand why such a focus is essential to higher order learning. We will understand why such a focus is essential to higher order learning only if we clearly understand the profound differences between the present didactic model of education, which confuses acquiring knowledge with memorization, and the critical model of education which recognizes that acquiring knowledge intrinsically and necessarily depends on higher order critical thought.

In education the whole is greater than the sum of the parts. We need to forge connections that shape the parts to form a coherent educational whole. To achieve this, nothing is more important than a clear conception of education explicitly embedded in curriculum, inservice, and instruction. No significant reform of education can occur unless we face the didactic lower order conception of education that informs daily practice. Present instruction implies that parroting information is equivalent to the acquisition of knowledge. Hence, teachers often feel compelled to cover information, even though they realize their students do not really understand and will soon forget it. Behind this practice is a network of uncritically held assumptions that need to be made explicit and unequivocally refuted, namely:

1) that students learn *how* to think when they know *what* to think,

2) that knowledge can be given directly to students without their having to think it through for themselves,

3) that the process of education is, in essence, the process of storing content in the head like data in a computer,

4) that quiet classes with little student talk are evidence of student learning,

5) that students gain significant knowledge without seeking or valuing it,

6) that material should be presented from the point of view of the one who knows,

7) that superficial learning can later be deepened,

8) that coverage is more important than depth,

9) that students who correctly answer questions, provide definitions, and apply formulae demonstrate substantial understanding, and

10) that students learn best by working alone.

One who understands and values education as higher order learning holds a very different set of assumptions, namely:

1) that students learn *what* to think only as they learn *how* to think,

2) that one gains knowledge *only* through thinking,

3) that the process of education is the process of each student gathering, analyzing, synthesizing, applying, and assessing information for him or herself,

4) that classes with much student talk, focused on live issues, is a better sign of learning than quiet classes focused on a passive acceptance of what the teacher says,

5) that students gain significant knowledge only when they value it,

6) that information should be presented so as to be understandable from the point of view of the learner, hence continually related to the learner's experiences and point of view,

7) that superficial learning is often mis-learning and stands as an obstacle to deeper understanding,

8) that depth is more important than coverage,

9) that students can often provide correct answers, repeat definitions, and apply formulas while not understanding those answers, definitions, or formulas, and

10) that students learn best by working together with other students, actively debating and exchanging ideas.

These contrasting assumptions about education, knowledge, teaching, and learning have contrasting implications for how textbooks should be written, how teachers should teach, and how students should go about learning. Indeed they have very different implications for every dimension of school life. The first set of statements collectively define a *didactic* conception of education, the second a *critical* one. The first set encourages lower order learning, the second higher order. We must make a paradigm shift from a didactic to a critical model of education to make higher order thinking a classroom reality. This shift is like a global shift in our eating habits and lifestyle. It cannot be achieved in a one-day inservice or by any other short-term strategy. It must come over an extended period of time and be experienced as something of a conversion, as a new way of thinking about every dimension of schooling. Let us now consider some of the basic changes that must be made to effect this shift.

✦ Step One: Reconceive and
Redesign the Curriculum

Curricula play a significant role in school life. Instruction arises from goals and objectives stated in them. When they are heavily loaded with lower order objectives and content, when higher order objectives are vaguely defined, when assessment is tied to content recall and lower order skills, a didactic conception of education, complete with extensive lower order teaching and learning, results.

As things now stand many teachers are — usually without knowing it — obsessed with the notion that they must cover so much content that they have no time to focus on depth of understanding at any point along the way, let alone at every point along the way. This compulsion blocks redesign of instruction. Teachers feel they have no time to focus on higher order learning and therefore on what has recently been called "high" content — the most basic ideas and issues within a content area approached in such a way that students think them through for themselves.

Only through an explicit shift to a critical conception of education, with an explicit critique and rejection of the assumptions of didactic education, can we achieve significant reform. Consider one of the conclusions of the studies conducted at the National Center on Effective Secondary Schools concerning teaching effectiveness in higher order thinking. These studies focus on high school social studies departments which have made an explicit commitment to teaching higher order critical thinking. They found, among other things, that even in departments with a special interest in higher order thinking numerous teachers lapse into didactic teaching and end up focusing more on coverage than depth. What is more, not only do didactic teachers score poorly on the teaching of higher order thinking, this failure correlates with their obsession with coverage:

> A careful interpretation of the above findings suggests that lower scorers, unlike high scorers, are caught in a contradiction. That is, lower scorers make the general statement that breadth of coverage is detrimental to thinking, yet at the same time: a) claim that specific breadth-oriented lessons enhance students' thinking, and b) impose coverage pressure on themselves equal to or greater than the coverage demands articulated by the department or district. (Newmann, 1988)

Similar conclusions are emerging in the field studies headed by Rexford Brown for the Policy and the Higher Literacies Project of the Education Commission of the States. Results of this sort underscore the need to attack the didactic model directly and explicitly. Subconscious habits of thought and instruction, internalized over many years of schooling, are not easily changed. Even with careful critique, ingrained habits of thought and behavior can only be abandoned by degrees as new ones take their place. The shift from a lecture-drill-recall paradigm to one focused upon engaged-deep-processing can only be achieved through long-term evolution. If we want a focus on *high content* we must make the implications of that commitment explicit and detailed. With this in mind, let us consider the connection to curricula.

Since most complete curricula contain a complex of elements — philosophy, goals, standards, objectives, assessment, and instructional examples — their formulation provides an important opportunity to confront the didactic model head on, and make the shift from low to high content inescapable. Unfortunately the philosophy expressed in most district curricula is typically little more than a set of empty platitudes, not an articulate analysis of the general conditions necessary for knowledge acquisition and learning. Given vagueness at the outset, a crucial opportunity is missed to nail down and avoid the misconceptions about knowledge and learning embedded in most didactic teaching. Nothing is done to forestall common misconceptions because there is no significant awareness that such misconceptions need to be forestalled. Nothing is done to make high content a priority.

As a result, teachers typically interpret the various goals and objectives as so many bits and pieces of information to be implanted in the students' minds by didactic instruction. Furthermore, systematic assessment often concentrates on recall and lower order skills. The result: higher order critical thinking lost in the rush to cover extended lists of content in preparation for testing. For this reason a major emphasis needs to be put on a detailed formulation of philosophy, one which highlights the essential role of thinking in the acquisition of knowledge, and contrasts lower order with higher order learning. Let us see how this might be stated as philosophy in the curriculum.

✦ *Demonstrate How Knowledge Is Embedded in Thought: A Sample Curricular Statement*

Imagine the following included under "philosophy" in a curriculum:

> Higher order learning can be cultivated in almost any academic setting. By focusing on the rational capacities of students' minds, by designing instruction so that students explicitly grasp the sense, the logicalness, of what they learn, we can make all additional learning easier for them. Higher order learning multiplies comprehension and insight; lower order rote memorization and performance multiply misunderstanding and prejudice. Higher order learning stimulates and empowers, lower order discourages and limits the learner. Good teaching focuses on high content, basic ideas and issues taught in ways which actively engage student reflection and thought. Though very little present instruction deliberately aims at lower order learning, most results in it. "Good" students have developed techniques for short term rote memorization; "poor" students have none. But few know what it is to think analytically through the content of a subject, few use critical thinking as a tool for acquiring knowledge.
>
> We often talk of knowledge as though it could be divorced from thinking, as though it could be gathered up by one person and given to another in the form of a collection of sentences to remember. When we talk in this way we forget that knowledge, by its very nature, depends on thought. Knowledge is

produced by thought, analyzed by thought, comprehended by thought, organized, evaluated, maintained, and transformed by thought. Knowledge exists,
properly speaking, only in minds that have comprehended and justified it
through thought. And when we say *thought* we mean *critical thought*.
Knowledge must be distinguished from the memorization of true statements.
People can easily blindly memorize what they do not understand. A book
contains knowledge only in a derivative sense, only because minds can
thoughtfully read it and, through this analytic process, gain knowledge. We
systematically forget this and design instruction as though recall were equivalent to knowledge.

We need to remember that all knowledge exists in and through critical
thought. All the disciplines — mathematics, physics, chemistry, biology,
geography, sociology, anthropology, history, philosophy, and so on — are
modes of thinking. We know mathematics, not to the extent that we can
recite mathematical formulas, but only to the extent that we can think mathematically. We know science, not to the extent that we can recall sentences
from our science textbooks, but only to the extent that we can think scientifically. We understand sociology only to the extent that we can think sociologically, history only to the extent that we can think historically, and philosophy only to the extent that we can think philosophically.

When we teach each subject in such a way that students pass courses
without thinking their way into the knowledge that these subjects make possible, students leave those courses with no more knowledge than they had
when they entered them. *When we sacrifice thought to gain coverage, we
sacrifice knowledge at the same time.*

There are numerous forms of lower order learning we must avoid. We can
understand them by understanding the relative lack of student comprehension
characteristic of them. Paradigmatically, lower order learning is learning by
sheer association or rote. Hence students come to think of history class, for
example, as a place where you hear names and dates and places; where you
try to remember them and state them on tests, where you read that this event
had this cause and that result. Math comes to be thought of as numbers, symbols, and formulas, mysterious things you mechanically manipulate as the
teacher told you to get the right answer. Literature is often thought of as uninteresting stories to remember along with what the teacher said is important
about them. Science means measuring, counting, and filling out graphs.

Consider history taught as a mode of thought. Viewed from the paradigm
of a critical education, blindly memorized content ceases to be the focal
point. Learning to think historically becomes the order of the day. Students
learn historical content by thinking historically about historical questions and
problems. They learn through their own thinking and classroom discussion
that history is not a simple recounting of past events, but also an interpretation of events selected by and written from someone's point of view. In recognizing that each historian writes from a point of view, students begin to
identify and assess points of view leading to various historical interpretations. They recognize, for example, what it is to interpret the American Revolution from a British as well as a colonial perspective. They role-play different historical perspectives and master content through in-depth historical
thought. They relate the present to the past by discussing how their own
stored-up interpretations of the events of their own lives shape their respons-

es to the present and their plans for the future. They come to understand the daily news as a form of historical thought shaped by the profit-making agendas of news collecting outlets. They come to recognize that gossip is a kind of historical thought often shaped by bias.

Learning to think historically is, in short, a very different and much deeper approach to history than that adopted traditionally. The one-dimensional didactic approach, wherein students quickly forget what the teacher or text said, is abandoned as a misconceived anachronism. When students learn to think historically, they not only acquire information and higher order knowledge, but also insights, skills, abilities, and values — learnings that serve them well in grappling with real problems in a historically complex world. They learn that history is not principally what is found in dusty books, but what is actively embedded in people's minds as they interpret and shape events in the world about them.

Including language such as this in curriculum philosophy would go far toward flagging the problem of didactic lower order teaching, sensitizing teachers to the crucial shift needed. Of course we must follow up this curriculum philosophy with a redesigned articulation of curriculum goals, standards, objectives, assessment, and instructional examples.

✦ Step Two: Give Teachers Time to Thoughtfully Redesign their Instruction

As teachers become increasingly aware of the difference between a didactic and a critical conception of education, and have a curriculum which articulates a coherent understanding of and commitment to higher order learning and high content for all students, they need the time and the incentive to thoughtfully redesign or remodel their own instruction. This is no simple, one-shot task. It must address deep-seated teaching habits and ways of thinking. It requires incremental change. It requires on-going critical thinking on the part of teachers and administrators. It requires long term planning. It requires a set of strategies for transforming instruction as well as an understanding of the nature of higher order thinking and of the conditions under which it can occur.

Consider this statement of what characterizes higher order thinking which Lauren Resnick made in a recent report on the research on the subject for the National Research Council (Resnick, 1987):

1) Higher order thinking is *nonalgorithmic.* That is, the path of action is not fully specified in advance.

2) Higher order thinking tends to be *complex.* The total path is not "visible" (mentally speaking) from any single vantage point.

3) Higher order thinking often yields *multiple solutions,* each with costs and benefits, rather than unique solutions.

4) Higher order thinking involves *nuanced judgment* and interpretation.

5) Higher order thinking involves the application of *multiple criteria*, which sometimes conflict with one another.

6) Higher order thinking often involves *uncertainty*. Not everything that bears on the task is known.

7) Higher order thinking involves *self-regulation* of the thinking process. We do not recognize higher order thinking in an individual when someone else "calls the plays" at every step.

8) Higher order thinking involves *imposing meaning*, finding structure in apparent disorder.

9) Higher order thinking is *effortful*. There is considerable mental work involved in the kinds of elaborations and judgments required.

This characterization warns us against conceptions of critical thinking that imply it can be proceduralized for students, reduced to predictable steps in a predictable order. Critical thinking needs to be understood globally not mechanistically. For example, we need to recognize that assignments that compel students to think their own way through the logic of the content, using their own experience, their own assumptions, their own ideas, call upon them to think in a higher order fashion virtually every step along the way. We also need to see that in doing such assignments no two students think it through in exactly the same way.

We cannot escape the brute fact that there are no algorithms for doing one's own thinking. Critical thinking is by its very nature *principled* not procedural thinking. Critical thinking requires thinkers to continually *monitor* their thinking by means of questions that test for clarity, accuracy, specificity, relevance, consistency, logic, depth, and significance. Since critical thinking often involves thinking within *multiple points of view and frames of reference,* it often yields multiple possible solutions. Since critical thinking enables a person to achieve *genuine knowledge* rather than mere recall, and since what one learns is always integrated into one's personal experience and previous knowledge, it always involves the *imposition of meaning.*

Critical thinking, in the deepest and fullest meaning of that phrase, is equivalent to higher order thinking. It engages us in an evolving process in which we progressively take control of our own thinking, disciplining it by degrees, making it more and more responsive to evidence and reason, and extending it to ever more domains and situations. We naturally use it to create, build upon, reform, modify, and redesign our beliefs and behavior. Teachers need time to assimilate this conception, to tie it into their experience, to try it out in their everyday life, to integrate it into their own thinking, to translate it into strategies for instructional reform.

Let us now look briefly at both the cognitive and affective dimensions, and the insights that underlie them. This will clarify the sort of reflective process teachers must go through.

✦ *Provide Opportunities for Teachers to Learn How to Teach for the Affective Dimensions of Higher Order Thinking*

No one learns what they do not in some sense value. Knowledge has value because of its use. Consider, for example, things that students value, how quickly they learn them, how much they know about them, and how well they retain and use what they know. A list would include sports, music, television, movies, fashions, styles, video games, and so on. Taking any one of these, say skateboarding, we can easily see the connection between the cognitive and the affective. Students who value skateboarding spend much time and energy learning the differences between available wheels, trucks, and boards, the advantages and disadvantages of each, the kind of riding best suited to each, and how these components work together. They then use this knowledge to assemble a board appropriate to the kind of riding they prefer. Difficulties do not dampen their enthusiasm.

If we want students to learn to think in higher order ways we need to cultivate the traits essential to such thinking. Consider, for example, the most fundamental disposition necessary for all higher order thinking: the drive, disposition, or will to think independently. It is always easier in the short run to try to get someone else to do our thinking for us, for someone else to tell us what to do, for someone else to solve our problems for us, for someone else to figure out life for us. Students habitually expect the teacher or text to solve their scholastic problems for them — though they rarely expect teachers or texts to solve their real-world problems. In school, they look for algorithms, formulas, and fail-safe recipes or procedures. They expect to act robotically. Faced with problems at home or on the street they often, in contrast, show real independence of thought. Yet teachers rarely tap this independence. They rarely harness or discipline it. They cave in to the students' demand for mindless short-cuts, re-enforcing the students' expectations that they ought to have them. Indeed, teachers continually look for algorithms, formulas, and fail-safe recipes or procedures. They wrongly feel that this helps their students. Ironically and painfully, many teachers today are now looking for robotic procedures to teach higher order thinking.

Of course there are many ways teachers *can* cultivate independence of thought in their students, though none of these strategies involve formulas or mindless rules. Consider the following examples:

1) Rather than simply having students discuss ideas found in their texts, have them brainstorm their own ideas and argue among themselves about problems and the solutions to problems.

2) Routinely ask students for their point of view on issues, concepts, and ideas.

3) Before reading a section of text that explains a map, chart, time-line, or graph, have the students read and discuss what the map, etc., shows.

4) Whenever possible give students tasks that call upon them to develop their own categories and modes of classification instead of being provided with them in advance. For example, rather than providing them with ways of classifying literature, lead a discussion on how students *do* classify what they read, calling upon them to justify whatever labels they already use.

5) When giving written assignments, give the students a larger role in gathering and assembling information, in analyzing and synthesizing it, and in formulating and evaluating the conclusions or interpretations of others.

6) In science classes, have students devise their own hypotheses and experiments or seek out what they take to be examples of pseudo science, explaining how they came to this conclusion.

7) In math classes, devise activities that lead students to argue and debate various possible ways to solve standard math problems before you give them access to algorithms and formulas.

Teachers can devise innumerable such scenarios for the cultivation of every essential trait or disposition available. When teachers understand the importance of the affective dimension of thought and have some start-up examples, they are very creative in devising such strategies. Every teacher can devise ways of cultivating fairmindedness, intellectual humility, intellectual courage, intellectual perseverance, intellectual integrity, and confidence in reason, but only if they understand them, see them as important, and feel free to take the time to do so.

Of course, lest we be taken to be fostering an atomization of higher order thinking, it should be emphasized that the affective traits and dispositions we advocate are interdependent. Consider intellectual humility. To become aware of the limits of our knowledge, we need courage to face our prejudices and ignorance. To discover our prejudices, in turn, we often must empathize with and reason within points of view toward which we are hostile. To achieve this end, we must typically persevere over a period of time, for learning to empathically enter a point of view against which we are biased takes time and significant effort. That effort will not seem justified unless we have the confidence in reason to believe we will not be "tainted" or "taken in" by whatever is false or misleading in the opposing viewpoint. Furthermore, merely believing we can survive serious consideration of an "alien" point of view is not enough to motivate most of us to consider it seriously. We must also be motivated by an intellectual sense of justice. We must recognize an intellectual responsibility to be fair to views we oppose. We must feel obliged to hear them in their strongest form to ensure that we do not condemn them out of our own ignorance or bias. At this point, we come full circle back to where we began: the need for intellectual humility.

For a large catalog of examples K–12 the reader may want to consult the *Critical Thinking Handbook* series published by the Center For Critical Thinking and Moral Critique. They provide a "principled" rather than a "procedural" approach throughout.

The crucial point is this. Teachers need time to become aware of the variety of strategies available for cultivating the affective traits of mind essential to higher order thinking. They also need incentives for cultivating these traits. Ultimately, of course, teachers must come up with their own particular redesigned lessons. They must develop confidence in their own thinking, their own capacity to take a new idea and make it a reality in practice. Teachers who do not think independently and critically about their own instruction will never be able to teach independent critical thought to their students. No formulas, procedures, or recipes can substitute for independent critical thinking on the part of each and every teacher and, of course, each and every student.

✦ *Provide Opportunities for Teachers to Learn How to Teach for Higher Order Cognitive Abilities*

There are a variety of critical thinking principles which can be transformed into teaching strategies for fostering higher order cognitive abilities and skills. These principles apply on the micro as well as the macro level. That is, in addition to developing the skills of identifying assumptions, evidence, conclusions, implications and consequences, and so forth, students have to learn to orchestrate those skills into more extended thought processes. They need to be able to read and write critically, to engage in Socratic discussions, to reason dialectically, to pursue root questions, and so forth. The upshot is that teachers have to learn how to teach for higher order cognitive abilities and skills. To do this they need to have the principles that underlie them spelled out with examples of the sorts of classroom activities and assignments that foster them.

Consider, for example, the concept of critical reading. Some people think of it as reading in an argumentative mind frame. This misses the essence of the process. Though critical readers do read with a healthy skepticism, their fundamental purpose is to understand the text, to grasp what is being said from the point of view of the person writing. They appreciate how, when humans think, they think within a point of view. Unless we sympathetically enter into the perspective of a writer we cannot make the best and most accurate sense of what is being said. Furthermore, a critical reader recognizes that whenever important ideas are dealt with they have important connections that a critical reader needs to determine. For example, all writers have a basic goal or purpose, make fundamental assumptions, reason from the assumptions they make, come to conclusions, and generate implications and consequences. Hence, a critical reader reads with a view to identifying these important elements, reads so as to better understand what precisely is being said, what portion should be accepted and what should be questioned and followed up with further reading.

When teachers have this principle of critical reading in mind, there are a number of things they can do to foster critical reading on the part of their students:

1) Call attention to the difference between uncritical impressionistic reading, on the one hand, and critical reading on the other, pointing out the differences between the two so that students begin to think about their own reading habits with a greater sense of what specific things they might try to do.

2) Have student's identify the author's point of view, purpose, conclusions, reasons given, assumptions made, issues raised, basic ideas used, and so forth.

3) Teach students to question as they read: "Can I summarize the last paragraph in my own words? Can I relate it to my experience? Can I see what the author is implying? Can I see reasons for what is said? Are there objections I might raise? Is this consistent with other things I know or believe?"

4) Lead a discussion on the relation of reading and listening. Compare asking questions of a speaker to asking questions while one reads.

5) Show by demonstration examples of poor and good reading.

6) Read aloud expressing your own questions as you proceed, using provisional answers expressed aloud to guide you in interpreting the text. Make your own critical reading explicit by thinking aloud. Have students take turns doing the same.

Teachers can take strategies such as these and work out the details with their own students, recognizing thereby that there are no formulas or pat procedures for producing critical readers. Each teacher committed to critical reading develops somewhat different ways of encouraging it. When teachers have time to exchange ideas on how to cultivate critical reading, they learn from each other and achieve higher levels of success.

✦ Step Three: Take the Long View

Short-term reform can do no more than foster surface reform. Deep change takes time, patience, perseverance, understanding, and commitment. This is not easy in an educational world saturated with glossy, superficial, quick-fixes and plagued historically by a very short attention span. Nevertheless, a well-devised long-term educational reform program, focused on the progressive ameliorization of instruction through the development of the critical thought of teachers, promises the kind of multiple long term payoffs that make in-depth reform cost-effective. Furthermore, the amount of money invested is in fact secondary, if the motivation and leadership are present.

A case in point is the Greensboro Plan, a reasoning and writing project which began in the city of Greensboro in the spring of 1986 and has been gathering momentum ever since. It was initially proposed by Associate

Superintendent Sammie Parrish and approved by the Greensboro board of education as the spearhead of a commitment to infuse critical thinking and writing into K–12 curriculum. To ensure that the reform project had a life of its own, two full-time facilitators were hired: Kim DeVaney, an experienced elementary school teacher, and Janet Williamson, a high school teacher who had just completed a doctorate with a special emphasis on critical thinking. Williamson and DeVaney nurtured the project as a creature of the teaching staff. From the start they knew that the project needed a solid foundation. Accordingly, they began with a small group of 14 volunteers. These 14 read widely and diversely about critical thinking, developing their own thinking as they critically analyzed a variety of proposals for infusion. (For details about the Greensboro plan, see Chapter 27.)

I have included the Greensboro Plan in this anthology for a reason. It illustrates well the style, flavor, and thrust of a well-devised, well-run reform effort, tuned into the multiple connections that must be made to carry it through. Furthermore, Greensboro is not a wealthy suburban district. It is a medium sized urban district with 21,000 students and 1,389 classroom teachers. The students come from diverse economic and racial backgrounds. 46% of the student population is White; 52% Black; and 2% Asian, Hispanic, or Native American. Almost 28% of the student population has a family income low enough for them to receive either free or discounted lunches.

The Greensboro teachers and administrators know that even though they have been working hard for some three years, they are still, comparatively speaking, at the beginning of fundamental change. This is not a source of discouragement but of strength, of knowing what real change requires and how it comes to pass.

✦ Conclusion

There are a number of connections we must make conceptually and pragmatically to successfully reform education. All fundamental school practices presently cluster around or emerge from a didactic conception of education. The dominance of lower order learning is inevitable given this fact. Unless teachers and administrators come to terms with this dominance and its foundation in a mistaken conception of education, they will never be able to make the shift to higher order teaching and learning. Curricula will remain cluttered with details, superficial content, and low level skills. Schooling will remain a hurried race through undigested content. Students will remain largely passive and indifferent.

Substantial change can occur only by restructuring math classes so that students learn to think mathematically, history classes so that students learn to think historically, science classes so that students learn to think scientifically, and so that in general, not only in school but in everyday life as well, students — and teachers — begin to think critically in a deeply internalized, self-directed fashion. This requires that curricula be reconceptualized and recast by a critical model of higher order teaching and learning. It also requires long-term, in-depth staff development programs that remain focused on higher order learning for the forseeable future. Teachers need years of practice critiquing and remodelling their instruction, to grow out of deeply ingrained compulsive didacticism. The obsession with didactic instruction is such that many will periodically relapse and begin again to treat the basic acquisition of knowledge as a mode of lower order memorization.

In this process it is important to involve the widest possible spectrum of people in discussing, articulating, and implementing the effort to infuse critical thinking. This includes teachers, administrators, board members, and parents. Incentives must be provided to those who move forward in the implementation process. Many small changes will be necessary before larger changes take place. Do not rush implementation. A slow but steady progress with continual monitoring and adjusting of efforts is best. Provide for refocusing on the long-term goal and ways of making the progress visible and explicit. Work continually to institutionalize the changes made as the understanding of higher order thinking grows, making sure that the goals and strategies being used are deeply embedded in school-wide and district-wide statements and articulations. Honor individual differences among teachers. Maximize the opportunities for teachers to pursue critical thinking strategies in keeping with their individual differences.

As you pursue these evolutionary changes, you will recognize additional implications and connections attendant on the process: a natural link with cooperative learning, with professionalizing teaching, with responsible assessment, with teacher involvement in school and district management decisions, and, not least, with preparing students to participate in a world — vocationally, personally, politically, and socially — in which fundamental change, adaptability, and higher order thinking are pressing needs in every dimension, in every conceivable domain of thought and action.

Chapter 17

Dialogical and Dialectical Thinking

Abstract

This paper is divided into two sections. Part I is theoretical. In it, Richard Paul discusses the importance of dialogical and dialectical thinking. He argues that students learn best in dialogical and dialectical situations, when their thinking involves dialogue or extended exchange between different points of view or frames of reference. Part II is pedagogical. In it, Paul discusses what can be done in a classroom to engage student thought dialogically and dialectically. He discusses how to distinguish multilogical issues (those having many logics) from monological issues (those having one logic). He then discusses Socratic questioning as a way to effectively involve students in a discussion and engage their thinking about an issue or topic. The value of cooperative learning is then discussed. Paul stresses that dialectical discussions are disciplined, that students must "learn how to bring intellectual standards into their work, how to hold themselves and their classmates to standards of good reasoning and analysis."

◆ Part I: Theory

◆ Introduction

*W*hen as the result of a trial, the jury comes to a verdict of guilty or innocent; when as a result of political debate, a citizen decides to vote for one of the candidates; when as a result of reading the case that can be made for alternative political systems, one concludes that one is superior to the others; when as a result of hearing various sides of a family argument, one becomes persuaded that one side is more justified and accurate; when as a result of reading many reports on the need for educational reform, one is prepared to argue for one of them; when as a result of entertaining various representations of national security, one reasons to a position of one's own; when after reading and thinking about various approaches to the raising of children, one concludes that one is better than the others; when after interacting with a person for a number of years and entertaining various conflicting interpretations of her character, one decides that she would make a good marriage partner — *one is reasoning dialectically.*

Whenever students discuss their ideas, beliefs, or points of view with other students or the teacher; whenever students have to role play the thinking of others; whenever students have to use their thinking to figure out the thinking of another (say, that of the author of a textbook or of a story); whenever students have to listen carefully to the thoughts of another and try to make sense of them; whenever students, whether orally or in writing, have to arrange their thoughts in such a fashion as to be understood by another; whenever students have to enter sympathetically into the thinking of others or reason hypothetically from the assumptions of others, *they are reasoning dialogically.*

An open society requires open minds. One-sided egocentric and sociocentric thought, joined with massive technical knowledge and power, are not the foundations of a genuine democracy. The basic insight, formulated over a hundred years ago by John Stuart Mill, is as true today, and as ignored, as it was when he first wrote it:

> In the case of any person whose judgment is really deserving of confidence, how has it become so? Because he has kept his mind open to criticism of his opinions and conduct. Because it has been his practice to listen to all that could be said against him; to profit by as much of it as was just, and expound to himself, and upon occasion to others, the fallacy of what was fallacious. Because he has felt that the only way in which a human being can make some approach to knowing the whole of a subject, is by hearing what can be said about it by persons of every variety of opinion, and study.

This is the dialogical ideal. Dialogical and dialectical thinking involve dialogue or extended exchange between different points of view or frames of reference. Both are multilogical (involving *many* logics) rather than monological (involving *one* logic) because in both cases there is more than one line of reasoning to consider, more than one "logic" being formulated. Dialogue becomes dialectical when ideas or reasonings come into conflict with each other and we need to assess their various strengths and weaknesses.   ·

In general, students learn best in dialogical situations, in circumstances in which they must continually express their views to others and try to fit others' views into their own. Even when dealing with monological problems (like many found in math and science) students need to move dialogically between their own thinking and "correct" thinking on the subject before they come to appreciate the one "right" (monological) way to proceed. They cannot simply leap directly to "correct" thought; they need to think dialogically first.

Unfortunately, the dominant mode of teaching at all levels is still didactic: teaching by telling, learning by memorizing. The problem it creates is evident in this excerpt from a letter by a teacher with a Master's degree in physics and mathematics:

> After I started teaching, I realized that I had learned physics by rote and that I really did not understand all I knew about physics. My thinking students asked me questions for which I always had the standard textbook answers, but for the first time made me start thinking for myself, and I realized that these canned answers were not justified by my own thinking and only confused my

students who were showing some ability to think for themselves. To achieve my academic goals I had memorized the thoughts of others, but I had never learned or been encouraged to learn to think for myself.

Didactic teaching encourages monological thinking from beginning to end. There is little room for dialogical or dialectical thinking in the mind of the didactic teacher. Rather the teacher, usually focused on content coverage, tells students directly what to believe and think about subject matter, while students, in turn, focus on remembering what the teacher said in order to reproduce it on demand. In its most common form, this mode of teaching falsely assumes that one can directly give a person knowledge without that person having to think his or her way to it, that knowledge can directly be implanted in students' minds through memorization. It confuses *information* with *knowledge*. It falsely assumes that knowledge can be separated from understanding and justification. It confuses the ability to *state* a principle with *understanding* that principle, the ability to *supply a definition* with *comprehending* a concept. Didactic instruction flourishes when it appears that life's problems can be solved by one-dimensional answers and that knowledge is ready-made for passive absorption. Most teachers teach as if this were so without recognizing it.

Students today have very little experience in school of reasoning within opposing points of view. Indeed students today have little experience with reasoning at all. Most students do not know what inferences are, what it is to make assumptions, what it is to reason from an assumption to one or more conclusions. In the didactic classroom of today, the teacher is engaged in inculcating information. Classroom monologue (students passively listening) rather than active dialogue (students thoughtfully engaged) is the paradigm. Unfortunately, students then come away with the impression that knowledge can be obtained without struggle, without having to hear from more than one point of view, without having to identify or assess evidence, without having to question assumptions, without having to trace implications, without having to analyze concepts, without having to consider objections.

The result: students with no real sense of what the process of acquiring knowledge involves, students with nothing more than a jumble of information and beliefs, students with little sense of what it is to reason one's way to knowledge. The result: teachers oblivious of the fact that knowledge must be earned through thought, who teach as if knowledge were available to anyone willing to commit information to short-term memory. The result: school as a place where knowledge is didactically dispensed and passively acquired, something found principally in books, something that comes from authorities.

But if gaining knowledge really is a fundamental goal of education — and all curricula say it is — then most students should be spending most of their time actively reasoning. That is, most of the students most of the time should be gathering, analyzing, and assessing information. They should be considering alternative competing interpretations and theories. They should be identifying and questioning assumptions, advancing reasons, devising hypotheses, thinking up ways to experiment and test their beliefs. They should be following out implications, analyzing concepts, considering objections. They should be testing their ideas against the ideas of others. They should be sympathetically entering opposing points of view. They should be role playing reasoning different from their own. In short, they should be *reasoning dialogically and dialectically.*

Only when students have a rich diet of dialogical and dialectical thought, do they become prepared for the messy, multi-dimensional real world, where opposition, conflict, critique, and contradiction are everywhere. Only through a rigorous exposure to dialogical and dialectical thinking, do students develop intellectually fit minds.

✦ *Absolutistic Thinking in Early School Years*

Young children do not recognize that they have a point of view. Rather, they tend to make absolute judgments about themselves and others. They are not usually given an opportunity to rationally develop their own thoughts. Their capacity to judge reasons and evidence is usually not cultivated. Their intellectual growth is stunted.

As a result, young children uncritically internalize images and concepts of what they and others are like, of what, for example, Americans are like, of what atheists, Christians, communists, parents, children, business-people, farmers, liberals, conservatives, left-wingers, right-wingers, salespeople, foreigners, patriots, Palestinians, Kiwanis Club members, cheerleaders, politicians, Nazis, ballet dancers, terrorists, union leaders, guerrillas, freedom fighters, doctors, Marines, scientists, mathematicians, contractors, waitresses, are like. They then ego-identify with their conceptions, which they assume to be accurate, spontaneously using them as guides in their day-to-day decision making.

Children need assignments in multilogical issues to break out of their uncritical absolutism. They need to discover opposing points of view in non-threatening situations. They need to put their ideas into words, advance conclusions, and justify them. They need to discover their own assumptions as well as the assumptions of others. They need to discover their own inconsistencies as well as the inconsistencies of others. They do this best when they learn how to role-play the thinking of others, advance conclusions other than their own, and construct reasons to support them. Children need to do this for the multilogical issues — issues involving conflicting points of view, interpretations, and conclusions — that they inevitably face in their everyday lives. But they also need to do so for the disciplined monological questions that they must of necessity approach from within the context of their own undisciplined minds.

Because children are not exposed to dialogical and dialectical activities, children do not learn how to read, write, think, listen, or speak in such a way as to rationally organize and express what they believe. They do not learn how uncritically they are responding to the mass media nor to what extent it is reinforcing their subconscious egocentric or sociocentric views. They feel deeply primarily about egocentric concerns, justifying getting what they want, and avoiding what they do not want. If school is to prepare students for life as it is, if it is to empower children to become rational persons, it must cultivate dialogical engagement and reasoned judgment from the outset.

✦ *Fact, Opinion, and Reasoned Judgment*

When critical thinking is introduced into the classroom — and very often it is not — it is often approached monologically, for example, by having students divide a set of statements into "facts" and "opinions".

Unfortunately, a taxonomy that divides all beliefs into either facts or opinions leaves out the most important category: reasoned judgment. Most important issues are not simply matters of fact, nor are they essentially matters of faith, taste, or preference. They are matters that call for reasoned reflection. They are matters that can be understood from different points of view through different frames of reference. We can, and many different people do, approach them with different assumptions, ideas and concepts, priorities, and ends in view. The tools of critical thinking enable us to grasp genuine strengths and weaknesses in thought only when they are analytically applied to divergent perspectives in dialectical contexts. Dialogical and dialectical experience enables us to develop a sense of what is most reasonable. Monological rules do not.

For example, it is exceedingly difficult to judge the case made by a prosecutor in a trial until we have heard the arguments for the defense. Only by stepping out of the perspective of the prosecutor and actually organizing the evidence in language designed to make the strongest case for the defense can we begin to grasp the true strength and weakness of the prosecutor's case.

This approach is the only proper way to deal with the important issues we face in our lives, and I am amazed that we and our textbooks refuse to recognize it. The most basic issues simply do not reduce to unadulterated fact or arbitrary opinion. True, they often have a factual dimension. But characteristically, some of what is apparently empirically true is also arguable. And we are often faced with the problem of deciding which facts are most important, which should be made central, and which should be deemed peripheral or even irrelevant. Finally, despite the common view, facts do not speak for themselves. They must be rendered meaningful by interpretation, by explanation, by construal. Make your own list of the ten most important issues and see if this is not true (but beware, of course, the tendency to see your own answers to these issues as self-evident facts!).

✦ *Part II: Pedagogy*

Everyday life, in contrast to school, is filled with multilogical problems for which there are competing answers and so require dialogical thinking. Furthermore, even when subject matter can be algorithmically and monologically expressed, students need to approach that subject matter through dialogical thought which brings their own thinking into play. Teachers do not, by and large, recognize these facts, nor when it is pointed out to them, do they know how to take them into account in the classroom. Being habituated to didactic instruction, dialogical instruction that does not result in predictable "correct" answers is a puzzle to them. They do not know how to foster it. They do not know how to assess it. They do not know how to use it to aid students in mastering content.

There are four interrelated things teachers need to learn: *1)* how to identify and distinguish multilogical from monological problems and issues, *2)* how to teach Socratically, *3)* how to use dialogical and dialectical thought to master content, and *4)* how to assess dialogical and dialectical thought. I should add that one does not master these understandings overnight, but only by degrees over an extended period of time. They cannot be taught, for example, in a one-day workshop. Let us consider each of these four learnings in order.

✦ *Learning to Identify and Distinguish*
Multilogical from Monological
Problems and Issues

This involves distinguishing problems for which there is an established step-by-step procedure for solving them — What is the square root of 653? What is the boiling point of water? In what year did the American revolution begin? — from problems and issues that can be analyzed from different points of view leading to multiple competing answers, resolutions, or solutions — Was the American revolution justified? Should the colonists have used violence to achieve their ends? When should you conform to group pressure and when should you resist that pressure? What is the meaning of this story? What would a true friend do in this situation? What caused WWII? Could it have been avoided? How important is it to get a good education? How important is it to make a lot of money? Is money the root of all evil? What kind of a person are you? What are America's real values? How can you tell what to believe and what not to believe? These kinds of questions, we should note, can be raised from the earliest school years: Who was right in your argument with your sister, she or you? When should you share your toys? Was it right for Jack (in "Jack and the Bean Stalk") to take the golden eggs and the harp as well? Should the big Billy Goat have killed the Troll (in "Billy Goat Gruff")? Is this the best rule to have to avoid accidents in the playground or can you think of a better one? Do the advertisements on TV for toys give you good information about toys, or do they mislead you about them?

Of course, though there are multiple conflicting answers possible to multilogical questions, it does not follow that each is *equally* defensible or *equally* rational. The whole point of considering the reasoning behind conflicting positions is to assess their relative merits and debits in a rational way. After analysis and dialogue, we may be able to rule out some as simplistic, recognize the partiality of others, and gain some sense of what a deeper response to the issue would include. We will come out with better answers, if not *the* answer.

✦ Socratic Questioning and Dialogical Discussion

Dialogical discussion will naturally occur if teachers learn to stimulate student thinking through Socratic questioning. This consists in teachers wondering aloud about the meaning and truth of students' responses to questions. The Socratic teacher models a reflective, analytic listener. One that actively pursues clarity of expression. One that actively looks for evidence and reasons. One that actively considers alternative points of view. One that actively tries to reconcile differences of viewpoint. One that actively tries to find out not just what people think but whether what they think is actually so.

Socratic discussion allows students to develop and evaluate their thinking in comparison to that of other students. Since inevitably students respond to Socratic questions within their own points of view, the discussion inevitably becomes multi-dimensional.

By routinely raising root questions and root ideas in a classroom setting, multiple points of view get expressed, but in a context in which the seminal ideas, which must be mastered to master the content, are deeply considered and their interrelationships established.

Over time, students learn from Socratic discussions a sense of intellectual discipline and thoroughness. They learn to appreciate the power of logic and logical thinking. They learn that all thoughts can be pursued in at least four directions:

1) *Their origin:* How did you come to think this? Can you remember the circumstances in which you formed this belief?

2) *Their support:* Why do you believe this? Do you have any evidence for this? What are some of the reasons why people believe this? In believing this aren't you assuming that such and so is true? Is that a sound assumption do you think?

3) *Their conflicts with other thoughts:* Some people might object to your position by saying .... How would you answer them? What do you think of this contrasting view? How would you answer the objection that ...? and,

4) *Their implications and consequences:* What are the practical consequences of believing this? What would we have to do to put it into action? What follows from the view that ...? Wouldn't we also have to believe that ... in order to be consistent? Are you implying that ...?

Before a Socratic discussion, teachers should pre-think the issues and connections that underlie the area or subject to be discussed. Whenever possible they should figure out in advance what the fundamental ideas are and how they relate to fundamental problems. For example, before leading a Socratic discussion on the question "What is history?", teachers should pre-think the issue so that they are clear about the essential insights that the Socratic discussion is to foster, for example, that history is selective (it is not possible to include all of the past in a book), that historians make value judgments about what to include and exclude, that history is written from a point of view, and that historians with different view points often come to different historical judgments. Teachers should also recognize various related insights, for example, that all human thinking has a historical dimension (in that all our thinking is shaped by our life and times), that memory is a kind of internal historian, that the news is like the history of yesterday, that gossip is a form of historical thought, etc. This pre-thinking enables teachers to look for opportunities in discussion to help students to make connections and see the implications of their own thinking about history and things historical. Through Socratic discussion we do not teach students *our* view of history, but the ingredients in all historical views, however they may be particularized.

Of course, teachers must also follow up on the insights that are fostered through Socratic discussion. Hence, once a Socratic discussion has been held on the nature of history, students should be encouraged to raise questions about their history text. (What sorts of things would you guess were left out of this account of the battle? What point of view does the writer seem to have? Which of the sentences in this paragraph state facts? Which of the sentences interpret the facts or draw a conclusion from them? If you were a Native American do you think you would agree with this conclusion in your history text?...) Students should also have follow-up assignments which require them to further develop the insights being fostered. (For example, "I'd like each of you to imagine that you are one of the colonists loyal to the king and to write one paragraph in which you list your reasons why you think that armed revolution is not justified.")

No matter how much pre-thinking has been done, however, actual Socratic discussion will proceed, not in a predictable or straightforward direction, but in a criss-crossing, back-and-forth movement. Because Socratic instructors continually encourage the students to explore how what they think about x relates to what they think about y and z, students' thinking moves back and forth between their own basic ideas and those being presented by the other students, between their own ideas and those expressed in a book or story, between their own thinking and their own experience, between ideas within one domain and those in another, in short, between any of a variety of perspectives. This dialogical process will sometimes become dialectical when ideas clash or are inconsistent.

✦ Using Cooperative Learning to Foster Dialogical and Dialectical Thinking

Cooperative Learning fosters dialogical and dialectical thinking since individual students will inevitably have different points of view and will need to argue out those differences. The key is students learning to assess their own thinking so that they can make logical choices among the various proposals and suggestions they meet in cooperative learning. For example, we want students in cooperative groups to Socratically question each other in a supportive way. We want them to develop confidence in their capacity to reason together to find insightful answers to important questions. To do this they must probe each other's thinking for its support and implications. Along the way they must develop a sensitivity to what they and others are assuming. Most importantly if cooperative learning is not to be *cooperative mislearning,* it is essential that students learn how to bring intellectual standards into their work, how to hold themselves and their classmates to standards of good reasoning and analysis.

✦ Assessing Dialogical and Dialectical Thinking

Since dialogical and dialectical activities focus on the process rather than the product of thinking, it is essential that both students and teachers learn how to assess thought processes. To do this it is essential that definite standards for thinking be established. Unfortunately, few teachers have had an education that emphasized the universal standards for thought. This deficiency is linked with the fact that the logic of thinking is not presently emphasized in schooling. Teachers must learn — while already in the classroom — how to distinguish and explain the difference between clear and unclear, precise and imprecise, specific and vague, relevant and irrelevant, consistent and inconsistent, logical and illogical, deep and superficial, complete and incomplete, significant and trivial, openminded and biased, adequate and inadequate ... reasoning and expression. Students, in turn, need to recognize their responsibility to express themselves in reasoning that is as clear, precise, specific, accurate, relevant, consistent, logical, deep, complete, and openminded as possible, irrespective of the subject matter. These are deep and substantial, even revolutionary, understandings. They provide an entirely new perspective on what knowledge and learning are all about.

✦ How to Use Dialogical and Dialectical Thinking to Master Content

Because students do not come to the classroom with blank slates for minds, because their thinking is already developing in a direction, because they have already formed ideas, assumptions, beliefs, and patterns of inference, because they can learn new ideas, assumptions, and beliefs only through the scaffolding of their previously formed thinking, it is essential that dialogical and dialectical thinking form the core of their learning. There is no way around the need of minds to think their way to knowledge. Knowledge is discovered by thinking, analyzed by thinking, interpreted by thinking, organized by thinking, extended by thinking, and assessed by thinking. There is no way to take the thinking out of knowledge, neither is there a way to create a direct step-by-step path to knowledge that all minds can follow. In science classes students should be learning how to think scientifically, in math classes how to think mathematically, in history classes how to think historically, and so forth. It is scientific thinking that produces scientific knowledge, mathematical thinking that produces mathematical knowledge, historical thinking that produces historical knowledge. Dialogical exchange and dialectical clash are integral to the acquisition of all these forms of knowledge. To this day we have refused to face this reality.

✦ *Conclusion*

Dialogical thinking refers to thinking that involves a dialogue or extended exchange between different points of view, cognitive domains, or frames of reference. Whenever we consider concepts or issues deeply, we naturally explore their connections to other ideas and issues within different domains or points of view. Critical thinkers need to be able to engage in fruitful, exploratory dialogue, proposing ideas, probing their roots, considering subject matter insights and evidence, testing ideas, and moving between various points of view. Socratic questioning is one form of dialogical thinking.

Dialectical thinking refers to dialogical thinking conducted in order to test the strengths and weaknesses of opposing points of view. Court trials and debates are dialectical in form and intention. They pit idea against idea, reasoning against counter-reasoning in order to get at the truth of a matter. As soon as we begin to explore ideas, we find that some clash or are inconsistent with others. If we are to integrate our thinking, we need to assess which of the conflicting ideas we will accept and which reject, or which parts of the views are strong and which weak, or, if neither, how the views can be reconciled. Students need to develop dialectical reasoning skills, so that their thinking moves comfortably between divergent points of view or lines of thought, assessing the relative strengths and weaknesses of the evidence or reasoning presented. Dialectical thinking can be practiced whenever two conflicting points of view, arguments, or conclusions are under discussion.

Because at present both teachers and students are largely unpracticed in either dialogical or dialectical thinking, it is important to move instruction in this direction slowly and carefully as part of a reflectively designed, long-term staff development plan, one with a sufficiently rich theoretical base and pedagogical translation to allow for individual teachers to proceed at their own rates. I recommend an approach that focuses on lesson remodelling and redesign, and have written four books to aid teachers in this redesign of instruction. Nevertheless, most teachers need to work with other teachers to carry through needed reforms. They need to work together with much encouragement and many incentives. Very few districts have taken up the challenge. Most have created the mere appearance of change. In most, didacticism remains — unchallenged in its arrogance, in its self-deception, and in its fruitlessness.

✦✦ Chapter 18

The Art of Redesigning Instruction

Abstract

This paper is divided into two parts. The first part is entitled, "Why Should We Redesign Instruction?" Paul begins with an argument as to why reasoning should be recognized to be the essential mode of learning, for, only if we are reasoning while we are learning, do we truly figure out what we are striving to learn, and, thereby, truly make it our own. Paul extends the argument by suggesting that in a literal sense no one can teach us anything of importance, again, because reasoning is essential to quality learning and no one can reason for us. The best they can do is reason in front of us. Paul then discusses addictive and pseudo-learning and links them to the theme of the paper.

With this background established, Paul argues for three dimensions essential to education for reasoning: learning the principles that underlie reasoning, learning the moves that those principles define, and learning the standards that one must use to assess reasoning. He then extends this analysis to include the basic elements of reasoning (the source of critical thinking moves), the abilities intrinsic to reasoning (which are the basic moves), the modes of reasoning (patterned sequences of moves), the abilities as regulated by traits of mind (the attributes that motivate making the moves), and intellectual standards (the standards used to assess the moves). He provides an extended analysis of reading as a mode of reasoning.

The second part of the paper is entitled, "How Do We Redesign Instruction?" As you might expect, the idea of redesign follows from the argument developed in the first half of the paper. The crucial question for redesign is "How can I get my students to reason more and reason better?" As a teacher, you should be interested in the basic elements of reasoning "because they represent both a basic orientation and a resource for fundamental moves in reasoning". You will be interested in the component critical thinking abilities "because they represent the kinds of moves you want students to master". You will be interested in the modes of reasoning (reading, writing, speaking, and listening, for example) "because one cannot learn to reason without them."

Paul then provides a model for "Six Forms of Decision-Making in Designing Instruction", a sample redesigned lesson, a section on patterns in teaching, and a section on general recommendations for instruction. Paul's approach to the redesign of instruction "presupposes intellectual development on three fronts, a growing recognition of: 1) what is wrong with didactic instruction, 2) the nature and dimensions of critical thinking, and 3) pedagogical strategies that can be used to effectively integrate critical thinking into instruction (based on 1 and 2)."

✦ *Why Should We Redesign Instruction?*

THE PROBLEM OF "MOTHER ROBIN TEACHING"

*B*oth teaching and learning today are desperately in need of restructuring. However, grasping the how and why of it requires rare insight into what is wrong with instruction: what is wrong with the way teachers typically go about teaching, and what is wrong with the way students typically go about learning. The essential insight requires understanding of the dual roles that teaching and learning can play in the lives of our students and how those roles correlate with very different, sometimes opposing, realities.

The most important starting point for that understanding is given in the following truth: teaching, learning, and knowledge can be either lower order or higher order, fragmented or organized, surface or deep. Though all teachers, in theory, aspire to teaching so that students gain higher order, organized, deep knowledge, the effect of most teaching is otherwise: lower order, fragmented, superficial, and often transitory. A significant part of this problem is due to what might be called "mother robin teaching".

When we teach in "mother robin" fashion — trying to mentally chew up everything for our students so we can put it into their intellectual beaks to swallow — students tend to become, if I can slightly mix my metaphor, "polly parrot" learners:

"I can't understand anything unless you tell me exactly how and what to say and think. I need you to figure out everything for me. I shouldn't have to do more than repeat what you and the textbook say."

Unfortunately, the more students grow in this direction, the more teachers try to amplify their mother robin teaching to accommodate it. Growth on either side produces a compensating growth on the other. By the middle school level, most students are deeply entrenched in learning, and teachers in teaching, nothing but lower order, fragmented, surface knowledge. Teachers feel by this level that they have no choice but to think for their students, or worse, that they should not require any thinking at all, that students are not really capable of it.

Rarely do students learn to reason well once such mutually-reinforcing, lower order habits develop. Rarely do they integrate what they are learning into what they already know or believe. Rarely do they learn to grapple with, or grasp the logic of, what they are learning. Content comes and goes as something independent of thought, dissociated from active engagement, from give-and-take, from disciplined reading, writing, speaking, or listening. Intellectual paralysis sets in. The trance-like state that students bring typically to class becomes permanent.

THE SOLUTION: REASONING AS A MODE OF LEARNING

To learn how to teach critically, teachers must abandon mother robin teaching and make every effort to discourage polly parrot learning. To learn to think critically, students must learn to use reasoning as a pervasive tool of learning.

What is reasoning? Expressed most simply, it is the art of "figuring things out for yourself". It begins when we, in effect, say to ourselves something like this:

"Let's see, how can I understand this? Is it to be understood on the model of this experience or that? Shall I think of it in this way or that? Let me see. Ah, I think I see. It is just so... but, no, not exactly. Let me try again. Perhaps I can understand it from this point of view, by interpreting it thus. OK, now I think I am getting it...."

When we reason we puzzle something out, work out our understanding of it in relationship to what we already know. Reasoning contrasts, therefore, with thoughtlessly accepting what others say. It intrinsically involves *testing as we learn* to see if this or that is so. There are two ways we go about testing as we learn, and the two often work together: physical testing and mental testing. We physically test things by trying them out in the physical world. We mentally test things by trying them out in our minds. Hence we test ideas and beliefs by ideas, beliefs, and experiences we already have. For example, you tell me that you've just met a really *perfect* person and I, by thinking of my experience of people and my conception of human nature, inwardly decide that what you are saying *cannot be true*. I have tested out what you said in my mind and what you said "failed" the test.

In everyday life, of course, we continually have to figure things out for ourselves — for example, what our mothers, fathers, brothers and sisters, friends and acquaintances are *really* like, how to deal with personal and social problems, how to get what we want and avoid what we don't want. We are forced to develop theories about the world we live in and, of course, to test them in the crucible of day by day experience. Admittedly, our tests are often ill-conceived, our criteria often irrational. Nevertheless, there is a difference between what we personally reason through and what we mindlessly take in.

There are things, of course, we don't have to figure out for ourselves, that we can pick up merely by dint of lower order absorption and blind imitation. Much of this may, of course, be dysfunctional in some respects even as it is functional in others: for example, learning to be aggressive or passive, to attack or flee, to express ourselves outwardly or to "keep it all in".

There are still other learnings between the two extremes of the thoughtful and thoughtless: things which we figure out partially by ourselves through reasoning — physical or mental testing — and partially through others by mindless imitation. The reasoned and the unreasoned are thus sometimes combined.

✦ Learning from Others vs. Learning for Yourself

Very significant consequences follow from how students learn. The depth with which they understand anything is in direct proportion to the degree to which they have engaged in intellectual labor to figure it out *for* themselves. Whatever is to have meaning *to them* must be given meaning *by them*. They must work new meanings into the network of meanings they already have. They must relate new experiences to experiences they have already had. They must relate new problems to problems they have already solved. To create new meanings, to understand new experiences, to solve new problems, they must actively and intellectually participate in the "figuring out" process, going up and back between what they have already figured out and what they have not. They must do intellectual work. They must *reason to learn* — and to learn *well* they must *reason well*.

THE ADDICTIVE ILLUSION OF LEARNING FROM OTHERS

Of course, there are limited ways in which it is possible to learn things from others. Others can often help us get started. They can frequently point to or model the way. They can create environments which help shorten the "figuring out" process. The anchor point is this: There is no way to teach *that which requires understanding* so as to eliminate the "figuring out" process for the learner. When a teaching mode attempts to by-pass the processes by which each person individually figures things out, a mere illusion of learning takes place. When students do not engage in intellectual labor, they do not meaningfully learn, their learning is falsified.

Pseudo-learning mimics genuine learning. For example, students have not really learned why the earth spins on its axis if, in the last analysis, they believe that it does because their sixth grade teacher said it does. Neither do they understand because they memorized, but can't explain in their own words, the explanation in their sixth grade science text. They understand if and only if they can think it through for themselves in terms, and in the light of experiences, meaningful to each of them individually. Good teachers arrange circumstances and design activities to facilitate this process of "thinking something through". Nevertheless, there is no way on this earth or in the heavens above to eliminate the need for the process to be significantly structured by the active intellectual labor of the learner.

Pseudo-learning is addictive precisely because it appears to provide substantial learning with little effort. It seems genuine — when only parroted responses are called for. It seems substantial — as long as no one asks the students to explain what they have learned in their own words. It seems easy — as long as no one figures out how much time is wasted teaching the same content over and over and how little students retain after their schooling is completed.

This is the most fundamental problem in education today, that most teaching fosters various forms of pseudo-learning. It is because of pseudo-learning that most elementary students add, subtract, multiply, or divide when given the following "problem": "There are 75 sheep in the field and 5 sheep dogs. How old is the shepherd?" It is because of pseudo-learning that this tendency increases the more math instruction the students asked this question have had. It is because of pseudo-learning that most students are unable to explain in their own words what makes a scientific experiment scientific. It is because of pseudo-learning that most students are unable to solve problems that require more than one inference. It is because of pseudo-learning that students soon lose interest in the subjects they are "studying." (Who wants to study what one is not understanding?)

Most teaching attempts to achieve success without realistically taking into account the only conditions under which students can *genuinely* learn — and that is when they think things through for themselves. What most teachers fail to recognize, then, is that *students* (in the last analysis) *must teach themselves*.

Good teachers are not persons who know how to get students to learn without having to think. They are persons who know how to create conditions and activities, incentives and opportunities, in which those willing to think things through for themselves can achieve what they will. The statement "If you really knew how to teach, all your students would learn well and deeply" is as false as the statement: "If you really want to, you can bypass the need for students to think for themselves. There are ways to teach which automatically inject knowledge, understanding, and skill into people without their active involvement or interested consent. Knowledge can be force-fed if you really know how to teach effectively."

Make no mistake; mother robins can be very useful to baby robins. But let us also not forget that baby robins are hungry when fed and instinctively swallow what is put into their beaks. And more. If mother robins never pushed their babies out of the nest, or expected them to do their own digging for worms, or their own chewing once found, neither they nor their species could or would survive.

Figuring things out has a crucial role in learning the simple and the complicated, the surface and the deep, the theoretical and the applied. Only a few things can be learned with a minimum of reasoning (e.g., copying the shapes of letters and numbers for the first time, practicing how to tie our shoes, learning to throw and catch a fluff ball, putting different colored objects into different colored boxes). And even though quite a few things, once learned, can be done more or less automatically and robotically — walking up and down stairs, riding a bicycle, eating with knife and fork, driving along a largely empty freeway, carrying the trash out to the trash bin — very often thoughtful interventions are essential to avoid unpredicted negatives: drunk drivers, slippery steps, holes in the road, and defective trash bags.

Furthermore, most of the curriculum of schools as well as most of the philosophy that accompanies that curriculum, if taken seriously, cannot legitimately be reduced to what can be learned automatically and robotically. Most of it, to be genuinely — i.e., meaningfully — learned, requires a lot of "figuring out" of things, a lot of good reasoning, a great deal of testing, much intellectual work. Unfortunately, research and experience tell us that good reasoning is about the last thing to expect in the typical classroom on a typical day.

There are a number of reasons for this. Most teachers are not aware of the nature and importance of reasoning — most teaching being a variation on a "mother robin" theme. And even when teachers do assign reasoning they frequently do not understand how to assess it appropriately. The result is that students rely on variations of "polly parrot" learning and save their reasoning for situations in which they must figure out how to subjectively please their teachers. ("I try to agree with my teachers, to say what pleases them.")

WHAT DO STUDENTS NEED TO LEARN — TO LEARN HOW TO REASON WELL?

We can best understand what is involved in teaching students to reason well by clarifying first what learning to reason is like. We can gain some leverage on this understanding by considering how reasoning well is analogous to doing a wide variety of things well.

Whenever one develops interrelated skills and abilities, there are three dimensions involved:

1) *broad principles* that articulate what is desirable, in general, in the light of the goals,

2) *skilled "moves"* based on "principles" that learners must practice in settings that enable them to assess the effectiveness of their performance by...

3) *appropriate "standards"*.

Unfortunately, we are more familiar with the mastery of skilled moves and strategies in the physical than in the intellectual domain. We are much better at disciplining our bodies than our minds. Let us therefore build an initial concept on this familiarity with the physical. If we keep in mind at least one clear example of the interrelation of *principles, moves,* and *standards* as formulated below, we will then have a benchmark in mind to guide us in thinking about the principles, moves, and standards to be learned in the art of reasoning well.

If students seek to join basketball, soccer, football, or tennis teams, they are well aware of the need to understand thoroughly the object of the game, the principles of sound play, the strategies and moves based on those principles, and the appropriate way to self-assess their moves in play. For example, for students to develop basketball skills and abilities, they must be willing to learn such principles as "square yourself to the basket whenever making a shot".

To learn this principle they practice by the hour doing what it calls for — squaring themselves to the basket — whenever they shoot. They also learn to integrate the skilled use of this move into a variety of strategic situations on the court. They do this with a combination of theoretical discussions and practical applications. They talk a lot about how to play the game — how to make this or that move, how to work with this or that strategy, how to counter this or that opposing strategy. And they spend a lot of time actually playing the game, trying in the process to put good theory into practice. They also spend considerable time critiquing their performance, making reference to the standards of excellent performance, as well as to the moves, principles, and strategies intrinsic to that excellence.

In tennis, students learn such principles as "always return to the ready position at the center of the court", "keep your weight distributed", "bend your knees when stroking the ball", "follow through whenever possible", "watch the ball closely when you hit it", and so forth. These principles are translated into moves on the court which are subject to assessment using the standards and strategies of good tennis play.

In learning ballet, one learns ballet principles, ballet moves, and ballet standards. In learning chess, one learns chess principles, chess moves and strategies, and chess standards. In learning architecture, one learns the principles of architecture, strategies and moves in design, and design assessment. In domain after domain, this same general pattern prevails. It holds as well for the art of sound reasoning, the art of disciplining the mind.

CRITICAL THINKING: THE ART OF TAKING CHARGE OF YOUR MIND

Learning to think critically, and to reason well as a result, is the intellectual analog of learning to play basketball, tennis, or chess well. It is analogous to learning how to dance ballet or do architecture well. As in the other domains, there are general principles and strategies intrinsic to the doing of it. There are skilled "moves" — critical thinking moves — to be learned. One must find the time to practice the moves, to talk about the principles that underlie them, to critique and assess one's own, and others', use of them. One must commit oneself to standards — intellectual standards. One must not only practice, but strive continually for excellence in practice. One must be willing to make mistakes and to learn from one's mistakes, to grow progressively in ability over an extended period of time. Insightfully conceived instruction is designed to create all of the above conditions: to facilitate students' learning the general principles and strategies intrinsic to the disciplined mastery of a body of content; to facilitate students' actively making critical thinking moves in reading, writing, speaking, and listening; to facilitate students' talking about intellectual standards, assessing their own and other students' reasoning; and to facilitate students' intellectual development over an extended period of time.

✦ What Does a Mind Need to Know About Itself to Reason Well?

It is important, then, to understand our minds as a potential repository of intellectual skills and abilities, of capacities that can be disciplined by critical thinking principles, strategies, and moves, and to begin to see why the mastery of reasoning is intrinsic to the task of taking charge of our mind and thus taking personal responsibility for the quality of our own thinking. To do this we must develop an interest in all of the components of reasoned thought:

1) basic *elements* (the source of critical thinking moves),

2) the elements combined into *abilities* (which are the basic moves),

3) the abilities in *modes of reasoning* (a patterned sequence of moves as in reading critically or writing critically or questioning Socratically, etc.)

4) the abilities as regulated by *traits* of mind (the attributes that motivate making the moves), and

5) intellectual *standards* (the standards used to assess the moves).

Each of these dimensions of reasoning is explained briefly in what follows. Each is discussed in the light of the role it plays in the intelligent redesign of instruction. Once we whet your appetite and provide some initial basis for seeing why it is that teachers tend to find it difficult both to develop assignments that require student reasoning and to assess the students' "reasoning" once completed, the stage will then be set for understanding how to go about redesigning instruction.

THE BASIC BUILDING BLOCKS OF REASONING: MASTERING THE ART OF BREAKING REASONING DOWN INTO ITS COMPONENT PARTS

As students of the art of reasoning, we must learn to take our thinking apart at the seams, to see the nuts and bolts of it, the very stuff, the elementary stuff, out of which critical thinking moves are inevitably structured. This includes nine elements:

a) the purpose that guides it

b) the questions or problems on which it is focused

c) the information it gathers and uses

d) the ideas and concepts by which it shapes the information it uses

e) the conclusions and interpretations to which it comes

f) the reasons it gives in justification

g) whatever it takes for granted

h) whatever it implies (or leads to in the way of consequences)

i) the point of view in which it is embedded as a whole

If we want to develop as critical thinkers, we need to develop an interest in making moves that probe these basic structures implicit in all our reasoning. Let me illustrate. As good reasoners we should be ever ready and disposed to probe our thinking with questions like the following, each of which constitutes a critical thinking move:

a) What am I trying to accomplish?

b) What problem or problems am I solving?

c) What information do I need and where can I get it?

d) What basic concepts do I need to clarify and carefully use?

e) What conclusion or conclusions shall I come to?

f) What do I base those conclusions on?

g) What am I taking for granted? Should I?

h) What is implied in my reasoning? To what consequences does it lead?

i) From what point of view am I reasoning? Do I need to consider others?

These are some of the most basic and fundamental considerations continually used by good reasoners to keep their reasoning functioning well.

Each of the elements of thought defines a domain of "moves" that good critical thinkers effectively make. There are a variety of moves one can make concerning one's purpose, a variety concerning the question at issue, a variety concerning information, etc.

SYNTHESIS:
MASTERING THE MOVES THAT PUT THE PARTS OF REASONING TOGETHER

Each of these elements becomes a focus of skill and ability. Each becomes a shaping force in the nature of reasoning. By taking these elements into account in a variety of orchestrated ways, we are able to articulate a variety of important critical thinking moves in the process of figuring things out. We learn how to:

- uncover significant similarities and differences
- recognize contradictions, inconsistencies, and double standards
- refine generalizations and avoid oversimplifications
- create concepts, arguments, or theories
- clarify issues, conclusions, or beliefs
- clarify and analyze the meanings of words or phrases
- develop criteria for evaluation: clarify values and standards
- evaluate the credibility of sources of information
- compare analogous situations: transfer insights to new contexts
- compare and contrast ideals with actual practice
- analyze or evaluate arguments, interpretations, beliefs, or theories
- generate or assess solutions
- analyze or evaluate actions or policies
- rethink our thinking: metacognition
- question deeply: raise and pursue root or significant questions
- make interdisciplinary connections
- explore thoughts underlying feelings and feelings underlying thoughts
- design and carry out tests of concepts, theories, and hypotheses

- reason dialogically: compare perspectives, interpretations, or theories
- reason dialectically: evaluate perspectives, interpretations, or theories

Each of these abilities, depending upon the context and mode in which it is carried out, becomes a constituent in even larger structures of reasoning. We will touch upon these next.

MODES OF REASONING: LARGER STRUCTURES OF REASONING

All of the many component abilities of critical thinking, and the variety of critical thinking moves they presuppose, can be orchestrated in a number of basic ways. For example, reading, writing, speaking, and listening are four modes of reasoning. We reason while we do them and we use any of the full variety of critical thinking abilities and moves in the process. For example, if we were reading a book we might begin, for example, by trying to figure out the author's purpose in writing the book. In doing this we might make the following moves: What does the title of the book tell me about the purpose? What can I learn from the preface and introduction? Once we began to figure out the purpose, we might try to figure out the main question at issue and the main conclusion developed in relation to that question. Following any of a number of possible strategies, we would continue to reason through the text.

Consider the following example of two students engaged in reading a text. This example is taken from an important article by Stephen Norris and Linda Phillips ("Explanations of Reading Comprehension: Schema Theory and Critical Thinking Theory" in *Teachers' College Record*, Volume 89, Number 2, Winter 1987). Clearly the student who is reading the text well is reasoning his way through the text, carefully using the words of the text as "evidence" that must be taken into account in interpreting what the text means. We can see in these two readers a striking difference between good and bad reasoning embedded in the act of reading (the questions and commentaries within the text below are those of Norris and Phillips).

> In what follows we will present, episode-by-episode, Steven's and Colleen's thinking aloud as they work through the passage. The experimenter's questions are given in brackets. We have chosen to make our example detailed, because we see this as the best route for providing specificity to otherwise vague generalizations about the relationship between reading and thinking. To simulate the task for you we present the passage without a title and one episode at a time, as was done with the children.

> EPISODE 1

> *The stillness of the morning air was broken. The men headed down the bay.*

> *Steven*
> *The men were heading down the bay, I'm not sure why yet. It was a very peaceful morning. [Any questions?] No, not really. [Where do you think*

they're going?] I think they might be going sailing, water skiing, or some-thing like that.

Colleen

The men are going shopping. [Why do you say that?] They're going to buy clothes at The Bay. [What is The Bay?] It's a shopping center. [Any questions?] No. [Where do you think they're going?] They're going shop-ping because it seems like they broke something.

Steven recognizes that there is insufficient information for explaining what the men are doing. On questioning, he tentatively suggests a couple of alterna-tives consistent with the information given, but indicates there are other possi-bilities. Colleen presents one explanation of the story, and seems fairly definite that the men are going to buy clothes at The Bay, a chain of department stores in Canada. On being queried she maintains her idea that the men are going shopping, but offers an explanation inconsistent with her first one that they are going to buy clothes. To do this she assumes that something concrete was bro-ken, which could be replaced at The Bay.

EPISODE 2

The net was hard to pull. The heavy sea and strong tide made it even dif-ficult for the girdie. The meshed catch encouraged us to try harder.

Steven

It was not a very good day as there were waves which made it difficult for the girdie. That must be some kind of machine for doing something. The net could be for pulling something out of the water like an old wreck. No, wait! It said "meshed catch." I don't know why but that makes me think of fish and, sure, if you caught fish you'd really want to get them. [Any ques-tions?] No questions, just that I think maybe the girdie is a machine for helping the men pull in the fish or whatever it was. Maybe a type of pulley.

Colleen

I guess The Bay must have a big water fountain. [Why was the net hard to pull?] There's a lot of force on the water. [Why was it important for them to pull the net?] It was something they had to do. [What do you mean?] They had to pull the net and it was hard to do. [Any questions?] No. [Where do you think they're going?] Shopping.

For both children the interpretations of Episode 2 built on those of Episode 1. Steven continues to question what the men were doing. He raises a number of alternative interpretations dealing with the context of the sea. He refines his interpretations through testing hypothetical interpretations against specific details, and hypotheses of specific word meanings against his emerging interpretation of the story. At the outset he makes an inference that a girdie is a machine, but leaves details about its nature and function unspec-ified. He tentatively offers one specific use for the net, but immediately ques-tions this use when he realizes that it will not account for the meshed catch, and substitutes an alternative function. He then confirms this interpretation with the fact from the story that the men were encouraged to try harder and his belief that if you catch fish you would really want to bring them aboard.

Finally, he sees that he is in a position to offer a more definitive but tentative interpretation of the word girdie.

Colleen maintains her interpretation of going shopping at The Bay. When questioned about her interpretation, Colleen responds in vague or tautological terms. She seems not to integrate information relating to the terms net, catch, and sea, and she seemed satisfied to remain uninformed about the nature of the girdie and the reason for pulling the net. In the end, she concludes definitively that the men are going shopping.

EPISODE 3

With four quintels aboard, we were now ready to leave. The skipper saw mares' tails in the north.

Steven

I wonder what quintels are? I think maybe it's a sea term, a word that means perhaps the weight aboard. Yes maybe it's how much fish they had aboard. [So you think it was fish?] I think fish or maybe something they had found in the water but I think fish more because of the word "catch." [Why were they worried about the mares' tails?] I'm not sure. Mares' tails, let me see, mares are horses but horses are not going to be in the water. The mares' tails are in the north. Here farmers watch the north for bad weather, so maybe the fishermen do the same thing. Yeah, I think that's it, it's a cloud formation which could mean strong winds and hail or something which I think could be dangerous if you were in a boat and had a lot of weight aboard. [Any questions?] No.

Colleen

They were finished with their shopping and were ready to go home. [What did they have aboard?] Quintels. [What are quintels?] I don't know. [Why were they worried about the mares' tails?] There were a group of horses on the street and they were afraid they would attack the car. [Any questions?] No.

Steven is successful in his efforts to incorporate the new information into an evolving interpretation. From the outset Steven acknowledges that he does not know the meaning of quintel and seeks a resolution of this unknown. He derives a meaning consistent with his evolving interpretation and with the textual evidence. In his attempt to understand the expression *mares' tails* he first acknowledges that he does not know the meaning of the expression. Thence, he establishes what he does know from the background knowledge (mares are horses, horses are not going to be in the water, there is nothing around except sky and water, farmers watch the north for bad weather) and textual information (the men are on the bay, they have things aboard, the mares' tails are in the north) and inferences he has previously made (the men are in a boat, they are fishing). He integrates this knowledge into a comparison between the concerns of Alberta farmers with which he is familiar, and what he takes to be analogous concerns of fishermen. On seeing the pertinence of this analogy he draws the conclusion that the mares' tails must be a cloud formation foreboding inclement weather. He claims support for his conclusion in the fact that it would explain the skipper's concern for the mares' tails, indicating that he did not lose sight of the overall task of understanding the story.

Colleen maintains her original interpretation but does not incorporate all the new textual information into it. She works with the information on the men's leaving and the mares' tails, but appears to ignore or remain vague about other information. For example, she says the cargo was comprised of quintels but indicates no effort to determine what these things are. She cites the fact that the men were ready to leave and suggests that they have finished their shopping, but does not attempt to explain the use of such words as skipper, cargo, and aboard in the context of shopping for clothes. She interprets mares' tails as a group of horses that possibly would attack the men, but gives no account of what the horses might be doing on the street. Basically, she appears to grow tolerant of ambiguity and incompleteness in her interpretation.

Socratic questioning and role-playing are also modes of reasoning. The Socratic questioner orchestrates questioning in a variety of ways, using any of the full variety of critical thinking moves in the process. This is more obvious, of course, if we remember that typically Socratic questioning occurs during a discussion and therefore while both speaking and listening are going on. A similar point can be made for role-playing.

CRITICALITY, CREATIVITY, AND THE STANDARDS OF GOOD THINKING

Good thinking is thinking that does the job we set for it. It is thinking that figures things out, that poses problems to be solved and intricacies to reason through and then meets the challenge it has set itself with appropriate intellectual work. "Criticality" and "creativity" have an intimate relationship to this process. There is a natural marriage between them. Indeed, all thinking that is properly called "excellent" combines these two dimensions in an intimate way. Whenever our thinking excels, it excels because we succeed in designing or engendering, fashioning or originating, creating or producing results appropriate to our ends in thinking. It has, in a word, a creative dimension.

Like the body, the mind has its own form of fitness or excellence. Like the body, that fitness is caused by and reflected in activities done in accordance with standards (criticality). A fit mind can successfully engage in the designing, fashioning, formulating, originating, or producing of intellectual products worthy of its challenging ends. To achieve this fitness the mind must learn to take charge of itself, to energize itself, press forward when difficulties emerge, proceed slowly and methodically when meticulousness is necessary, immerse itself in a task, become attentive, reflective, and engrossed, circle back on a train of thought, re-check to ensure that it has been thorough, accurate, exact, and deep enough.

In a sense, of course, all minds create and produce in a manner reflective of their fitness or lack thereof. Minds indifferent to standards and judgment tend to judge inexactly, inaccurately, inappropriately, prejudicially. Preju-

dices, hate, irrational jealousies and fears, stereotypes and misconceptions —
these too are "created", "produced", "originated" by minds. But they are not
the products of "creative" minds. They reflect an undisciplined, an uncritical
mode of thinking, and therefore are not properly thought of as products of
"creativity". In short, except in rare circumstances, creativity presupposes
criticality and criticality creativity.

INTELLECTUAL CHARACTER TRAITS

We can now begin to see why the mastery of reasoning is intrinsic to becoming a certain kind of person. At the highest level of development, the mastery
of reasoning entails the development of a variety of interrelated character
traits: intellectual humility, intellectual courage, intellectual perseverance,
intellectual civility, intellectual integrity, intellectual curiosity, intellectual
responsibility, intellectual autonomy, fairmindedness, and faith in reason.

Once we state the principles that underlie one of these traits, it becomes
apparent what sort of critical thinking moves and strategies are intrinsic to
them. Consider, for example, the principle behind intellectual humility:

> PRINCIPLE: Awareness of the limits of one's knowledge, including
> sensitivity to circumstances in which one's native egocentrism is
> likely to function self-deceptively; sensitivity to bias and prejudice in,
> and limitations of one's viewpoint. Intellectual humility is based on
> the recognition that *no one should claim more than he or she
> actually knows*. It does not imply spinelessness or submissiveness. It
> implies the lack of intellectual pretentiousness, boastfulness, or
> conceit, combined with insight into the strengths or weaknesses of
> the logical foundations of one's beliefs: knowing what evidence one
> has, how one has come to believe, what further evidence one might
> look for or examine.

Given an understanding of and commitment to this principle, critical
thinkers make moves such as the following. They question what they think
they know. They admit the limitations of their knowledge. They readily
admit to appropriate qualifications to their knowledge. They admit to mistakes when they make them. They modify their beliefs when the evidence
requires such a modification. They listen with an open mind to people who
have different experiences and perspectives. The acts of an intellectually
humble mind readily lead to the expansion of knowledge and the
development of insight. Needless to say, intellectual moves based on understanding the elements of thought, abilities, and modes are intrinsic to the
development of these intellectual character traits.

✦ *How Do We Redesign Instruction?*

The Basic Idea

The redesign of instruction is based upon a judgment as to what students are presently not learning that they should be learning. We have argued at length that the most fundamental failure in education is the failure to teach students to reason well. Reasoning, we have contended, is the only means by which people acquire knowledge, master content, and solve problems. If students become proficient in figuring things out — while reading, writing, speaking, and listening, while studying the subjects they should master, while tackling the problems of everyday life — then they get precisely what it is that schooling at its best should be "giving" them but is not.

As teachers, therefore, we should continually be asking:

How can I get my students to reason more and reason better?

How can I get my students when "studying" science to reason scientifically? How can I get them enthusiastic about and skilled in scientific reasoning? To pose scientific questions? To seek scientific data and information? To acquire scientific concepts? To question their non-scientific assumptions? To grasp scientific truths?

How can I get my students when "studying" math to reason mathematically? How can I get them enthusiastic about and skilled in mathematical reasoning? To pose mathematical questions? To seek mathematical data and information? To acquire mathematical concepts? To question their false mathematical assumptions? To grasp mathematical truths?

How can I get my students when "studying" history to reason historically? How can I get them enthusiastic about and skilled in historical reasoning? To pose historical questions? To seek historical data and information? To acquire historical concepts? To question their false historical assumptions? To grasp historical truths?

How can I get my students when "studying" geography to reason geographically? How can I get them enthusiastic about and skilled in geographical reasoning? To pose geographical questions? To seek geographical data and information? To acquire geographical concepts? To question their false geographical assumptions? To grasp geographical truths?

It is questions and concerns such as these that are essential to the successful redesign of instruction. If we put these questions continually at the center of our thinking as teachers, we will progressively move toward a model for instructional design and redesign which helps transform students into better thinkers and learners.

WHAT DOES THIS BASIC IDEA OF DESIGN ENTAIL?

If as a teacher you are continually concerned to get your students to reason while learning, in order to learn well and deeply, then you will be keenly interested in a variety of other concerns as a matter of course. You will be interested in *the basic elements of reasoning,* because they represent both a basic orientation and a resource for fundamental moves in reasoning. You will be interested in understanding the various *component critical thinking abilities,* because they represent the kinds of moves you want students to master. You will be interested in the *modes of reasoning* — reading, writing, speaking and listening — because one cannot learn without reasoning well within them. You will be interested in intellectual *traits of mind,* because without them students will be unmotivated to practice the abilities they initially learn. You will be interested in *intellectual criteria and standards,* because without them reasoning cannot be assessed.

Our idea for instructional design is built on a systematic approach that includes all of the dimensions above. The logic of the teaching process should reflect the logic by means of which students ought to learn.

✦ *Six Forms of Decision-Making in Designing or Redesigning Instruction*

There are six forms of decision-making in designing instruction:

I) Get Clear About What the Students Have to Reason About (the domain, the topic and the issue).

1) What is the domain about which the students will have to reason (e.g., within what subject or field: historical reasoning, economic reasoning, biological, anthropological, reasoning about a poem, about a short story, about...)?

2) Express, as specifically and as clearly as you can, the precise question at issue.

3) Ask yourself what sorts of things a person must do to reason well about this question (include here what sorts of facts persons must have, the understandings they must possess, the motivations or values they must have, the skills, etc.).

II) Find Something That Students Are Already Familiar With to Use as a Bridge or Crutch to Help Them Learn What They Are Not Familiar With
Decide where in their lives the students already deal with this question.

1) Once you have the problem or question-at-issue clearly in mind, scan the life-world of your students looking for questions in their lives that logically mirror or are analogous to the question at hand.

2) Two Back-Up Strategies: If for some reason you can't find a problem in the life-world of your students that mirrors the question at hand, consider two back-up strategies: *a)* Could you help them to reason to the answer on the basis of what they have already learned about the subject or *b)* Could you give them a group of examples from everyday life that they could examine and come to a conclusion about, pro or con?

III) Make Decisions About How You Are Going to Use Large and Small Groups

1) Typically you should begin with a large group Socratic discussion that helps the students to locate themselves with respect to the subject. Describe how you will do this.

2) As soon as the basic framework for the question is set in large group discussion, switch to small group discussion (groups of 3 or 4). The groups should have a specific amount of time and a specific task. They should have a clear sense of what is expected of them and of how they will have to report back.

3) You might from time to time have the groups report to another group, having the groups give feedback to each other. Describe.

IV) Get Clear About Assessment Issues

You should always think about how you are going to get the students to reason with discipline, how they are expected to get into the elements of what they are thinking about, how they are expected to use critical thinking abilities, what critical thinking standards are most important, and what traits can be cultivated. Decide on your overall plan for getting the students to reason with discipline in the lesson or unit, keeping in mind the major obstacles to disciplined reasoning about the topic.

V) Include Critical Writing as Well as Critical Speaking and Listening

The working groups should often culminate in an individual or group writing assignment. You should spell out what you want carefully and clearly, taking the time to make sure that the students understand what you are asking for and how they should assess themselves along the way.

VI) Gathering and Interpreting Information

At some point along the way, it will often be necessary to have the students gather and interpret information. When you do so, the students need to gain an appreciation of precisely what the task entails and what is expected of them. How will you do this?

NOW LET US GET CLEAR ABOUT WHY EACH OF THESE DIMENSIONS IS IMPORTANT:

1) Getting clear about what the students have to reason about forces us to become clear about the logic within which we want students to reason. The requirements for the reasoning will be importantly determined, first, by the general logic of the domain, and second, by the specific logic of the particular question at issue.

2) Finding something that students are already familiar with to use as a bridge to help them learn forces us to consider how to make the learning real and meaningful.

3) Making decisions about how we are going to use small and large groups forces us to consciously consider how to maximize the active involvement of the students in the learning process and maximize the knowledge base and idea pool available to all students.

4) Getting clear about assessment issues forces us to decide on how we are going to help the students to assess their own reasoning.

5) Getting clear about how and when students will read and write, as well as engage in Socratic questioning or role playing, forces us to decide on which of these important modes of reasoning the students will engage in.

6) Trying to find opportunities for students to gather information on their own forces us to maximize the extent to which our students will free themselves from dependence on others for information.

✦ A Sample Redesigned Lesson

Let us now look at a sample redesigned lesson to see what the end product of this process might look like.

Geographical Thinking and Human Welfare

Deep Point: Getting insight into how "geographical thinking" is essential to human welfare.

Central Concept: geographical features

Central Issue: What is the relation between geographical features and the conditions of human life?

Present Practice

> Geography is often taught, like many other subjects, as a conglomeration of factoids that students are given to memorize and be tested upon. Rarely do students have to reason geographically in such instruction.

Critique

Geographical facts and concepts play an increasingly important role in schooling, and rightly so, but when they are taught didactically, students rarely learn how to *reason geographically*. Consequently, students rarely acquire geographical insights or an enthusiastic sense of how and why geographical thinking is essential to human welfare. Etymologically, the word 'geography' means "a description of the Earth". In fact geographers are most principally concerned — in contrast to, say, geologists — with the implications for human life of facts about the Earth. In studying the Earth from the geographical standpoint, one can concern oneself with mathematical questions (about the size, shape, and movements of the Earth), about "physical" questions (about the layers of the Earth's surface and about the forces historically shaping those surfaces), or about "biological" and "human" questions (about the life conditions of plants, animals, and humans). The result is that good geographical reasoning presupposes some ability to reason geologically, astronomically, zoologically, botanically, meteorologically, and historically. The central concept is "the Earth in evolution" and the central impact of informed reasoning with respect to that concept is insight into the way in which the evolution of the Earth has shaped and transformed, and continues to shape and transform, conditions for life on Earth.

Now since all reasoning involves basic fundamental structures or elements (*elements of thought*), and since these elements are essential to reasoning well, it is important that, as we cultivate geographical thinking, we cultivate students' awareness, not only of their use, but of the need for *standards* in their use of these decisive structures. So, because all reasoning serves a *purpose* which directs it, we want our students to have a *clear* purpose in mind as they go about *reasoning geographically*. Because all reasoning generates *questions* that need to be expressed *clearly* and *precisely* in order to be answered, we want to teach in such a way that students get experience in putting their *geographical questions* into clear and precise form. Because all reasoning depends upon *accurate* and *sufficient information* about the "things" we are reasoning about, it is important that we design instruction so that students have opportunities to *gather, interpret,* and *assess geographical information.*

It is important that the specific content that we are focusing on — land forms in this case — not become an end in itself, that is, not be reduced to a series of surface facts about the shape and character of land. Finally, it is important that we not overwhelm our students with either questions or facts, nor proceed so quickly that they are not able to *reason* their way into the content on the basis of their previous *knowledge, beliefs,* and *experiences.*

Proposed Design for Instruction

I will bring some globes into class, divide my class into groups of four or five, and ask that each group figure out what they can tell about the planet from what they see on the globe itself (*collaborative learning, dialogical thinking, critical listening, independence of thought, intellectual perseverance*). I will ask, "Based on what you know right now about interpreting what you see represented on the globe, figure out what conclusions you can justifiably come to concerning the Earth and the conditions for life on it." I would stimulate thinking with more specific questions like this: "For example, are there areas of the world that you can see that you believe would have very few plants and animals? Are there areas of the Earth where people could not live except under very special circumstances?" (*Thinking aloud*), etc.

I would give the groups a set amount of time to prepare a short report on the conclusions they came to and when the groups reported I would encourage the class to question how the individual groups came to the conclusions they came to and whether or not those conclusions were, in their view, justified (*formulating questions at issue, distinguishing evidence from conclusions, assessing inferences, noticing and questioning assumptions, analyzing concepts, critical listening, critical speaking, and dialogical, perhaps even dialectical, thinking*). As the reports and probings into the reports were taking place, I would be writing on the board the geographical *concepts* that were occurring, and *questions and problems* that were arising, in the *geographical reasoning* being presented.

Subsequent to this activity, I would lead a general discussion on the *assumptions*, including the assumed geographical *ideas*, implicit in their group's *reasoning* as well as in the subsequent *questioning* of that reasoning (*Socratic questioning*). I would outline the *issues* that arose (*identifying and clarifying issues*). I would ask the class to help me divide the issues into those that have to do with the nature of the Earth as a whole and those that have to do with specific areas of the Earth (*analyzing and classifying questions*). On the basis of the division I got, I would ask the group to choose which cluster of *questions* they wished to explore in working groups (which would be assigned as library research as the basis of a further report to the class as a whole) (*critical reading, collaborative learning, dialogical thinking*). I would underscore the importance of discussing in the group what to include and why (*seeking and giving good reasons*). I would ask the students to pay attention to what questions or issues they feel they have answered or resolved and which questions or issues they have not (*intellectual humility*).

The report would be a written report and I would spell out to the class how the report should be structured and why (*critical writing, asking root questions, clarifying purpose*). In doing this last, I would periodically stop and ask the question, "Why do you think it is important to do this in writing up your report?" For example, "Why do you think it is important to identify your sources?", "Why do you think it is important to put into quotes what you take literally from outside sources?", "Why do you think it is important to separate the conclusions you come to from what you are basing your conclusions on?", "Why do you think it is important to make us a short glossary of the important technical terms that you are using in your report?" (leading to *assessing the credibility of sources, clarifying evidence, making well-reasoned inferences*).

Four copies of each report would be made and each group would now become an assessment group for the report submitted by another group (*assessing reasoning, utilizing elements of thought and intellectual standards*). Before each group proceeded with the assessment, I would hold a discussion with the class as to how to go about assessing the reports (*designing and analyzing standards for evaluation*). This would involve, ultimately, detailed suggestions as to what to look for and why. The emphasis, of course, would be on constructive suggestions as to how the report could have been made more useful to the class, including comments on what further research would be required in the light of what the report did and did not accomplish (*intellectual civility, intellectual responsibility, intellectual humility*). I would emphasize the importance of trying to figure out what further questions or issues are raised in the light of the findings of the groups (*intellectual curiosity, intellectual perseverance*).

The next activity would be the reading, by a representative of the research group, of their report to the class as a whole (*critical speaking, critical listening*). The floor would then be opened for questions (because everyone has already served as part of an assessment team on some groups' report I would expect every group report to generate some good probing questions) (*dialogical thinking, asking root questions, analyzing and assessing reasoning, clarifying concepts, identifying assumptions, tracing implications, developing one's perspective*). After each report and question and answer period, a representative of the assessment team for that report would summarize the assessment teams' findings (*critical speaking*). The class would be given an opportunity to comment on the assessment (*critical listening, analyzing and assessing reasoning*, etc.). In this period any member of the group whose report was assessed could respond as well, agreeing or disagreeing with elements of the assessment (*critical speaking, dialogical and dialectical thinking, assessing reasoning, developing one's perspective*).

In the light of the issues and questions that arose from the reports, assessments, and discussions, new clusters of problems would be generated, new groups formed, and new research projects begun, leading to new assessments, new discussions, and yet further questions and issues. From this design for teaching "land forms" it is apparent that a conception is being formed that could be generalized to a whole semester. It illustrates therefore how, given skill in the art of instructional design based on critical thinking, one can avoid detailed lesson plan design for each class, and of how well-conceived overall design strategies can simplify, when they don't obviate entirely, the tasks of day-to-day design.

✦ *Patterns in Teaching*

Every teacher teaches in a patterned way, though few teachers are explicitly aware of the patterns implicit in their teaching. For many teachers the pattern consists in nothing more than this: lecture, lecture, lecture, quiz; lecture, lecture, lecture, quiz; lecture, lecture, lecture, mid-term exam, with occasional question and answer periods focused on recall with respect to lectures and the textbook. It is important for teachers who aspire to take command of their teaching to foster higher order learning to begin to develop a sense of the patterns implicit in their own instruction, to critique those patterns, and to begin to experiment with patterns that enable them more readily to cultivate the critical thinking of their students. For one thing, once one discovers one or two powerful patterns of teaching with which one can successfully work, it is possible to structure a whole semester of teaching around that pattern.

Assuming that one has accepted the view that students must reason through what they are learning, there is a basic logic to deciding on the pattern of instruction to use. The basic logic comes in three variations (or schemas):

Schema One: Thinking to Conceptual Understandings and Insights

1) Decide upon some kind of "start-up activities" (which will help the students to begin thinking about the subject—typically this involves linking the subject with their experience).

2) Now, given that the thinking of every person is "individual" and some "diversity" of conclusions is to be expected from having thought about a topic, decide upon some way for the students to synthesize the insights, collect information together, or analyze what they have come up with, including identifying any conflicts or contradictions that have emerged.

3) Now develop an activity which will help the students to assess what they have successfully figured out and what still remains to be figured out.

On this model, our patterns of instruction should reveal many episodes of individuation, reconciliation, and assessment. The students begin their thinking on a topic, develop it, and then test it (figuring out at the end what they have learned and what is still to be learned). This pattern would hold whether or not the topic was a technical one — just so long as it required that they develop their concepts and understandings of something.

However, there are two other basic alternative schemas which we should also be aware of (in addition to the "thinking-to-conceptual-understanding" schema). The first is based on all those occasions in which we are teaching the students to think through doing "research" on a topic and those in which we are teaching them a skill or ability by modeling it for them.

Schema Two: Thinking Through Research

The research schema also has three parts: *1)* start-up thinking, *2)* fact or information gathering, and *3)* analysis and assessment of information or facts gathered.

Schema Three: Reflective Modeled Practice of Skills

The skill-development schema has three parts as well: introduction (what are we going to try to learn), modeling (I model the skill slowly and carefully in front of the students), and practice (the students try to emulate my example). The second two phases of this schema may well be repeated multiple times: "I do it — they do it — I do it — they do it — I do it — they do it."

Now consider the following variations on the three schemas above, each with different "modules" of instruction (each one of which we represent with a box).

Schema One: For a lesson on discrimination: The main objective is to have students engage in moral reasoning, we might use the following pattern:

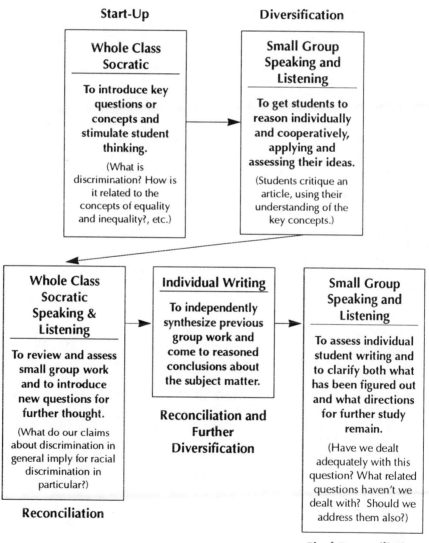

Schema Two: For a lesson on the civil war: The main objective of this lesson is to teach students how researching historical events can lead us to a better understanding of them, and how this in turn can lead us to benefit from that understanding. We might use the following pattern:

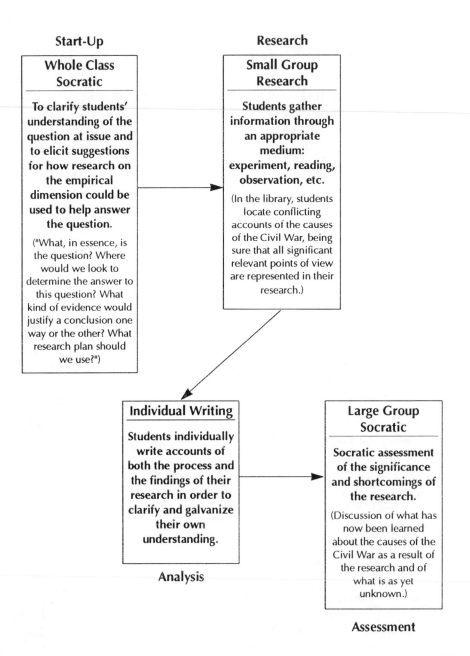

Start-Up

Whole Class Socratic

To clarify students' understanding of the question at issue and to elicit suggestions for how research on the empirical dimension could be used to help answer the question.

("What, in essence, is the question? Where would we look to determine the answer to this question? What kind of evidence would justify a conclusion one way or the other? What research plan should we use?")

Research

Small Group Research

Students gather information through an appropriate medium: experiment, reading, observation, etc.

(In the library, students locate conflicting accounts of the causes of the Civil War, being sure that all significant relevant points of view are represented in their research.)

Individual Writing

Students individually write accounts of both the process and the findings of their research in order to clarify and galvanize their own understanding.

Analysis

Large Group Socratic

Socratic assessment of the significance and shortcomings of the research.

(Discussion of what has now been learned about the causes of the Civil War as a result of the research and of what is as yet unknown.)

Assessment

Schema Three: For a lesson on critical reading: The main objective of the lesson is to get students to gain skill in critical reading through practice.

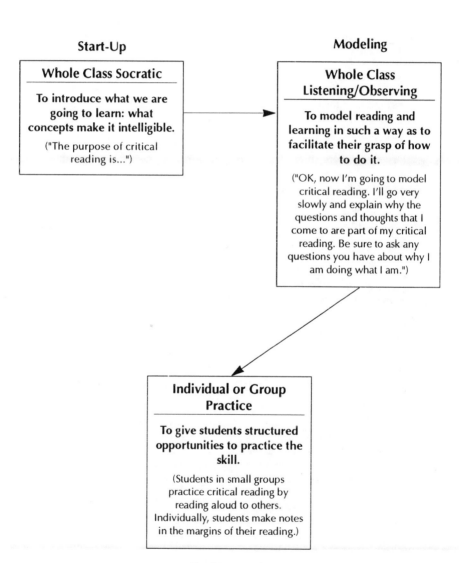

Start-Up

Whole Class Socratic

To introduce what we are going to learn: what concepts make it intelligible.

("The purpose of critical reading is...")

Modeling

Whole Class Listening/Observing

To model reading and learning in such a way as to facilitate their grasp of how to do it.

("OK, now I'm going to model critical reading. I'll go very slowly and explain why the questions and thoughts that I come to are part of my critical reading. Be sure to ask any questions you have about why I am doing what I am.")

Individual or Group Practice

To give students structured opportunities to practice the skill.

(Students in small groups practice critical reading by reading aloud to others. Individually, students make notes in the margins of their reading.)

Performance

Given the analysis of teaching and learning, the following general recommendations for instruction represent important needed changes that should now be intelligible to the reader:

TACTICAL AND STRUCTURAL RECOMMENDATIONS

1) *Design coverage so that students grasp more!* Plan instruction so students attain organizing concepts that enable them to retain more of what you teach. Cover *less* when *more* entails that they learn *less*.

2) *Speak less* so that they *think more!* (Try not to lecture more than 20% of total class time.)

3) *Don't be a mother robin* — chewing up the text for the students and putting it into their beaks through lecture! Teach them instead how to read the text for themselves, actively and analytically. Focus, in other words, on how to read the text, not on "reading the text for them".

4) *Focus on fundamental and powerful concepts with high generalizability.* Don't cover more than 50 basic concepts in any one course. Spend the time usually spent introducing more concepts applying and analyzing the basic ones while engaged in problem-solving and reasoned application.

5) *Present concepts,* as far as possible, *in the context of their use* as functional tools for the solution of real problems and the analysis of significant issues.

6) *Develop specific strategies for cultivating critical reading, writing, speaking, and listening.* Assume that your students enter your class — as indeed they do — with limited skills in these essential learning modes.

7) *Think aloud in front of your students.* Let them hear you thinking, better, *puzzling* your way slowly through problems in the subject. (Try to think aloud at the level of a good student, not as a speedy professional. If your thinking is too advanced or proceeds too quickly, they will not be able to internalize it.)

8) *Regularly question your students Socratically* — probing various dimensions of their thinking: their purpose; their evidence, reasons, data; their claims, beliefs, interpretations, deductions, conclusions; the implications and consequences of their thought; their response to alternative thinking from contrasting points of view, and so on.

9) *Call frequently on students who don't have their hands up.* Then, when one student says something, call on other students to summarize in their own words what the first student said (so that they actively listen to each other).

10) *Use concrete examples whenever you can* to illustrate abstract concepts and thinking. Cite experiences that you believe are more or less common in the lives of your students (relevant to what you are teaching).

11) *Require regular writing for class,* but grade using random sampling to make it possible for you to grade their writing without having to read it all (which you probably won't have time for). Or have the students themselves select their best work for you to assess.

12) *Spell out explicitly the intellectual standards you will be using in your grading,* and why. Teach the students, as well as you can, how to assess their own work using those standards.

13) *Break the class down frequently into small groups* (of two's, three's, four's, etc.), give the groups specific tasks and specific time limits, and call on particular groups afterward to report back on what part of their task they completed, what problems occurred, how they tackled those problems, etc.

14) *In general, design all activities and assignments, including readings, so that students must think their way through them.* Lead discussions on the kind of thinking that is required.

15) *Keep the logic of the most basic concepts in the foreground,* continually re-weaving new concepts into the basic ones. Talk about the whole in relation to the parts and the parts in relation to the whole.

16) *Let them know what they're in for.* On the first day of class, spell out as completely as possible what your philosophy of education is, how you are going to structure the class and why: why the students will be required to think their way through it, why standard methods of rote memorization will not work, what strategies you have in store for them to combat the strategies they use for passing classes without much thinking, etc.

✦ *Conclusion*

The redesign of instruction presupposes intellectual development on three fronts, a growing recognition of *1)* what is wrong with didactic instruction, *2)* the nature and dimensions of critical thinking, and *3)* pedagogical strategies that can be used to effectively integrate critical thinking into instruction (based on 1 and 2). Problems of understanding on any of these fronts can produce problems in implementation. It is not enough for our hearts to be in the right place. Nevertheless, it is possible to begin the process of moving forward on each of these fronts *simultaneously.* Indeed, that is the only way that significant progress can be made. We must continually teach with three considerations in mind: Am I falling into the traps of didactic instruction? Are the students reasoning their way through the class, or are they falling back into roles of passivity? What strategies and what patterns of instruction am I using to keep students involved in disciplined critical thinking?

✦✦ **Chapter 19**

Using Critical Thinking to Identify National Bias in the News

with Kenneth R. Adamson

Abstract

In this previously unpublished paper, Paul and Adamson present a model for teaching students how to identify national bias in the news. This model, they argue, can be extended to any form of bias in the news. They fit the task of detecting bias into a coherent theory which illuminates the logic or pattern of sociocentric thought. Possible student instructions and samples of strong and weak student work are included.

One of the most destructive forms of bias in the world today is national bias, the tendency to analyze and assess world events through a nationalistic mind set. Though many teachers recognize that much news coverage is biased in one way or another, few see clearly how to teach students to identify bias. The purpose of this article is to explain how students can become critical consumers of the news.

The ability to identify bias is an important dimension of critical thinking and, as other dimensions, requires practice. We need: *1)* a reasonably clear theory why bias exists, how it affects our thinking, and the forms it takes; and *2)* practice identifying it. We need, then, good theory and good practice. There are many forms and dimensions of bias, so it is useful to begin with one basic form. Other forms can be added as time goes on.

Teaching students to identify bias will be no easy task, for when we are biased it appears to us that we are not. We resist the notion that we might have a bias. Many students also feel reluctant to accept this. Teachers need to be aware of this tendency in themselves and their students, and their pedagogy must reflect this awareness.

✦ *The Importance of Recognizing Bias*

Bias exerts a subtle, but powerful, influence on our thinking. None of us is free of it. Some biases are personal, while others are socially shared. National

346

bias is a socially shared bias in which most citizens of a country hold a common view of themselves, their country, and the world. For example, most people in Iran believe in tenets of the Shiite Moslem religion, most people in the U.S.S.R. believe in communism, and most people in the U.S. believe in capitalism. These views are transmitted as biases to children by members of each society, most notably parents, peers, and the media. Piaget (1976) noticed this tendency and commented, "... everything suggests that, on discovering the values accepted in his immediate circle, the child felt bound to accept the circle's opinions of all other national groups". These acquired images of other countries are less favorable than one's image of one's own country, and sometimes are extremely negative. This tendency has very deep historical and psychological roots.

To quote Sam Keene (1986):

> Sadly, the majority of tribes and nations create a sense of social solidarity and membership in part by systematically creating enemies. The corporate identity of most peoples depends upon dividing the world into a basic antagonism:

Us	versus	Them
Insider	versus	Outsiders
The tribe	versus	The enemy

Those who teach social studies struggle against this acquired bias, for they want their students not only to understand their own culture and society, but also to develop an understanding of cultures and societies different from their own. To simply impart facts about these cultures to students and hope that understanding will follow, is too optimistic. If Piaget and Keene are right, we have strong reason to suspect the adequacy of the simple transmission of facts and pleas for fairness as sufficient to foster in students a genuine understanding of, not to mention an appreciation for, other countries and cultures. The us/them dichotomy pervades our cultural, political, and social thought, is passed on and reinforced overtly and covertly, becomes deeply entrenched in our and the students' minds, and cannot be dislodged by simply learning facts. These views have become part of the students' individual and social identity. This struggle for fairness, then, is a battle to be waged against egocentricity and sociocentricity. Students have to fight against their own deep-seated views, by itself a very powerful influence, and against uncritically held mainstream cultural conceptions of the world. Facts, by themselves, cannot win this battle. Neither is general encouragement to be fair sufficient for the student to actually be fair. Students need to gain insight into the nature of bias, the ways it influences their thought, and the methods by which it is passed on and reinforced. Only then can the student critically and fairly appraise the facts about "them". When we have biases, especially deep-seated ones, we need to *think* our way out of them. Someone else's thinking will not do.

✦ *The Roots of National Bias*

All of our thinking depends on our beliefs about the world. Our beliefs form the basis of how we classify, interpret, and experience things. In this sense, to have a "bias" is inevitable, for we approach all situations with some expectations and a point of view. This "inevitable bias" is compatible with objectivity *if we recognize it* and acknowledge other possible ways to classify and interpret. Indeed we become objective only to the degree that we develop this openmindedness: "I see it this way for this reason, in the light of this evidence. How do you see it? What is your point of view?"

Conversely, the illegitimately biased person regularly equates his or her point of view with *the Truth,* and so is unlikely to grant any significant truth to other systems of belief, to other perspectives. Such a person is not open-minded. To move students toward objectivity we need to help them become explicitly conscious of the beliefs they implicitly hold, so that they can become skilled in recognizing when and how those beliefs shape their experience. They need to recognize, for example, that when the members of a nation are raised to implicitly believe that the motives of their leaders are "pure" while the motives of the leaders of "enemy" countries are "evil", then, though both countries might do the same thing, say, intervene in the affairs of another country, the events will be experienced differently. Objective persons see that the events can be distinguished only to the degree that these assumptions they are making about themselves and others are truly justifiable. They can see, in other words, how news items about the intervention in *our* newspapers present interpretations of events based upon *our* assumptions and beliefs, while *their* newspapers present interpretations of events based upon *their* assumptions and beliefs. We (and they) do not recognize, and even resist recognizing, that we (and they) have a picture of the world, a picture quite different from other possible pictures. Each picture may have merit but all highlight some facts at the expense of others and no picture includes, or could include, *all* of reality.

If to "have a bias" (a partial view) is inevitable, to recognize it is essential. Consider this analogy. In bowling, the word 'bias' refers to a weight that is sometimes built into the bowling ball causing it to curve toward the weighted direction. If one uses a weighted ball, and is aware that the ball is weighted, one will bowl differently. When beginning bowlers use weighted balls they usually attribute the curve to themselves. Similarly, to fail to recognize that we have a bias increases the likelihood of our seeing other beliefs and points of view as "defective", rather than seeing the partiality in our own perspective. To be aware of our bias allows us to "bowl with a biased ball", as it were, to appreciate other points of view and learn how they structure the world.

Few of us continually recognize that we see the world from some point of view. We often see our own picture of the world as the simple truth; not merely as the *best* of possible views, but as the *only* view. Those who agree with us and hold to their views strongly and unfalteringly we see as committed and dedicated, not as opinionated and dogmatic. As a case in point, consider Oliver North and the Iran-Contra scandal. Many U.S. citizens did not review the issue in any depth, but saw North's patriotic confidence in his actions as sufficient justification of them. What North said agreed perfectly with their bias, namely, that what the United States does, and what is done in the name of patriotism, is the right thing to do, even if "questionable".

Often we do not even know exactly what we believe or why we believe it. Many things just seem true to us even if we can think of no reasons to support them. We often do not consider that there may be elements of truth in other beliefs. We need to learn, then, how to fairly and accurately assess beliefs, both our own and others'. To quote Israel Scheffler (1973), the knower "must typically earn the right to confidence in his belief by acquiring the capacity to make a reasonable case for the belief in question". This task of making a reasonable case is fatally hampered if we do not recognize how our point of view and beliefs influence our thinking.

✦ *Egocentricity: The Theory*

'Egocentricity' is the tendency to view everything in relation to one's self, viewing the world only from one's own perspective. Since we want to bolster our self-respect and protect our self-image, we often make ourselves the standard by which we judge others. Here is a familiar example. If a driver carelessly pulls in front of me, cutting me off, I see this person as a reckless driver, and I will probably be irritated or even angry. However, if I do the same, I tend to think of myself not as "cutting another person off" but only as "pulling in close". I generally have an excuse for myself. I will not see myself, as I would see another, as careless or stupid.

This egocentric tendency manifests itself in a variety of ways. We tend to think that the beliefs and values we hold are better than the beliefs and values of others. ("*My* beliefs are accurate and true; *you* are deceived.") We also tend to believe that our attitudes are more appropriate than another's ("*I* have good reason to be angry; *you* just have a bad temper."), and that our actions are more reasonable and moral than the actions of another ("I plan; you plot."). And it is psychologically understandable that we would think this way, for if we thought that another's beliefs, attitudes, or actions were in some way better than our own, we would be faced with a problem: Why do I believe or act as I do?

This tendency toward egocentric thinking provides the basis for the creation of a dichotomous view of the world and the people in it: "We are number one!" To be unaware of this tendency allows us to propagate and preserve this illusion. We then dichotomize: We are good, they are bad or evil. Our friends are seen by us as good, but not as good as we are. Our view of our enemies, however, is typically antagonistic and hostile. Of course, we are not denying that sometimes we have solid evidence and good reasons to believe that one country is better than another in some specific way. For example, we may have statistics to demonstrate that infant mortality is lower in one country than another, or that one commits fewer human rights violations. The point is that given our eagerness to believe we are best, our minds often use evidence only after the fact, to justify what we are committed to believing in advance.

✦ *Sociocentricity and National Bias: The Theory*

A perfect parallel exists between egocentricity and sociocentricity: the "I" of the individual becomes the "We" of the group, since judgments are made from the perspective of the group rather than the individual. Since sociocentricity is a direct extension of egocentricity, the reader will notice here a repetition of those tendencies of egocentricity. The same basic principles apply to the one as to the other, and very little needs to be changed. We see the beliefs, values, attitudes, and actions of our group as better than those of other groups. The groups or countries that we consider friends we view positively, while groups and countries we think of as unfriendly, as rivals, or as enemies, we view negatively. Consider this thought from Jerome Frank (1982):

> Behind the arms race and wars lies a trait humans share with all social animals: fear and distrust of members of groups other than their own. When two human groups compete for the same goal, this distrust rapidly escalates into the mutual "image of the enemy".

Taking the notion of group or sociocentric bias we can apply these tendencies to a much larger group, our nation. There is, again, a perfect parallel between egocentricity and national bias (sociocentrism). We easily extend our "group think" from that of local groups to the nation as a whole. Consider the point as made by Jerome Frank (1982), focusing on how national bias influences our choice of words:

> Enemy-images mirror each other — that is, each side attributes the same virtues to itself and the same vices to the enemy. "We" are trustworthy, peace-loving, honorable, and humanitarian, "they" are treacherous, warlike, and cruel. In surveys of Americans conducted in 1942, the first five adjectives chosen to characterize both Germans and Japanese (enemies) included warlike, treacherous, and cruel, none of which appeared among the first five describing the Russians (allies); in 1966 all three had disappeared from American characterizations of the Germans and Japanese (allies), but now the Russians (no longer allies, but more rivals than enemies) were warlike and treacherous. In 1966 the Mainland Chinese, predictably, were seen as warlike, treacherous, and sly. After President Nixon's visit to China, these adjectives disappeared from our characterizations of the Chinese, whom we now see as hardworking, intelligent, artistic, progressive, and practical.

The tendency to think egocentrically and sociocentrically, then, influences the judgments we form regarding "us" and "them", as we tend to assess the people and groups we like by different standards than those we dislike. Some predictable results follow:

A. Since we are more eager to praise those people and groups we like, we tend to notice the good things about ourselves more than we do the good things about them. We often fail to see in those people and groups we dislike the positive qualities we clearly see and readily praise in ourselves. In short, we tend to play down or ignore the good things about those we dislike, as we play up or emphasize the good things about us and those we like.

B. Since we are more eager to criticize those people and groups we dislike, we often fail to see in ourselves the negative qualities we see and readily criticize in those we dislike. In short, we tend to play up or emphasize negative qualities of those we dislike, while we tend to play down or ignore the negative qualities in ourselves.

C. Since we tend to have more positive images of ourselves and the people and groups we like, we often project into people and groups we like more noble intentions and purer motives.

It may be helpful to illustrate how these tendencies actually become articulated in the media. If we or those we like engage in some activity of a questionable or negative nature, we try to justify the activity by an appeal to motive or intent. ("We meant well.") A clear example from the *San Francisco Chronicle* (1988) illustrates this:

> For the United States the war in Vietnam was humbling, draining public hubris and setting the precedent for a deficit economy. Vietnam, with Soviet support, taught America that purity of motive does not always prevail.

While most people now consider Vietnam a tragic mistake, many believe that our motives were "pure". On the other hand, if those we dislike engage in some apparently commendable action, we tend to question their motives, often dismissing the activity as scheming or treacherous. Consider, for example, how we view the Soviet involvement in Afghanistan. For another example, consider a recent edition of "Global Affairs" (1988); in it an almost direct analogy is drawn between the Hitler of 1938 Germany and the Gorbachev of 1988 USSR:

> Despite the half century anniversary of the fatal consequences deriving from the acceptance by the Western Allies of Adolph Hitler's promises ... that he had no further political ambitions in Europe, the vision of the West is once again obscured by a smiling, apparently reasonable, and seemingly sincere authoritarian leader.

To be cautious in accepting Gorbachev's proposals is one thing, to dismiss it at the outset as Hitlerian scheming is quite another. It is easy to see the importance of an awareness of these tendencies. If unrecognized and unchecked, bias easily and quickly becomes prejudice. Only when we become sensitized to how we habitually sanitize our own behavior and negatively portray that of our "enemies", can we begin to evaluate beliefs and actions more fairly and reasonably. Only then can we see the truth in the views of others and the falsehood in our own. Only then can we see the parallels in all human behavior, the general consistency in most group rationalizations and judgments. Only then can we say that we have "earned the right to confidence in our beliefs".

✦ Language: The Importance of Precision

Many words have evaluative connotations, and when used voice our approval or censure of the subject under discussion. Rarely, however, are related words perfectly synonymous, for all words have nuances not duplicated by other words. Consider the following list of related words:

Column A:	Column B:
self-assured	arrogant
dedicated	obstinate
quiet	dull
sympathetic	indulgent
educated	indoctrinated
informed	propagandized
defenders	attackers
clever	sneaky
planners	plotters

The words in column A are related to the corresponding words in column B, but have different meanings and implications, and hence require different evidence to justify them. We use the words in column A when we approve of the subject under discussion; we use the words in column B when we disapprove. In describing ourselves or our friends we tend to use the words in column A, but in describing those we dislike, we tend to use the words in column B. "We are dedicated, they are fanatic." "We intervene to aid other countries, but they invade." "We protect our interests, but they commit acts of aggression." "We support freedom fighters, they support terrorists."

Notice that each of the examples above could have been described as an example of "sloppy" language or of misuse of terms. This is an important recognition: all biased uses of language are to that extent *incorrect* uses of language. We often use language imprecisely, allowing for the strengthening of our images of ourselves and them. To help students detect bias in language use, we must teach them how to identify misuses of words. To notice their biased language, students must learn that each word has a specific range of meaning somewhat different from every other word choice. Students must become sensitized into their use of language, they must control it as reflective, rational agents.

✦ United States' National Bias

One must first become aware of our biases before one can look for and recognize instances of it. We must, therefore, have a clear idea what mainstream United States viewpoints are, for they form the basis for our biases.

How do citizens of the U.S. see themselves and the world? Citizens of the U.S. see themselves as citizens of the greatest country in the world. They see themselves as supporting neither the extreme right or left, but as being in the well-balanced middle. They see their country as peace-loving, just, democratic and free, honest in international dealings, and abhorring terrorism. They see the United States as fundamentally right, at least on all important issues, even if the world disagrees.

It is easy to see how these attitudes influence the way we view our country and our country's actions. If we are peace-loving, it is inconceivable that we would be the aggressor in any conflict. If we intervene in the affairs of another country, it is therefore only to help them toward a more democratic government. We are there to help, even if they do not appreciate our help at the time. We are criticized only because we are misunderstood, or lied about. Even if the world is against our actions or decisions (for example, in denying Arafat a visa or invading Panama) it is because they do not understand or are unfairly set against us. With these as examples, we can move onto some classroom assignments and actual student work.

✦ *Classroom Assignments*

The long assignment given below is probably too much to give students without some prior in-class activities designed to foster their practical insight into national bias. You may decide to present these points to students in smaller chunks, passing them out only after group discussion. Here are some examples of what could be done initially:

1. Bring samples of articles displaying national bias into class. Read each aloud and ask the class to comment on how, if at all, the article reflects national bias.

2. Ask students to imagine how an article might have been written in a Soviet newspaper. Have students work in groups to rewrite it accordingly. How would the wording be different? What about the size of the article or its placement in the paper? Articles could even be selected from a Soviet paper, such as *Pravda,* without telling students its source. Most would probably immediately recognize its bias. They could then be asked *why and how* it is biased. After being told the article's source, students could be asked to suggest how it would have been written differently had it appeared in our press. Students will thus have a clear example of how much easier it is to spot another's bias than one's own.

3. Break the class into small groups of two or three students. Students could be asked to explain to the rest of the group what it means to talk about a national bias. As one student is explaining, the others could ask questions. Those asking the questions could be encouraged to argue the case for the objectivity of national news reporting. Roles could then be reversed.

4. Have students to bring newspapers to class and seek out examples of bias. They could work on this in groups. As articles are suggested by members of the group, the others could question why it was selected.

POSSIBLE STUDENT INSTRUCTIONS

1. Be cautious as you attempt to identify instances of national bias. Ask yourself: "To what extent is the article written with a sociocentric bias, slanting the news to reinforce a U.S. point of view?" Ignore other biases. Remember, you are not identifying regional, professional, religious, or any other bias but national.

2. Keep in mind that before you can identify our national bias in news stories, you must have a clear picture of how "Americans", as against, say, Soviets, see ourselves and the world. It is helpful to have a clear picture of how the Soviets see the world (as a point of contrast). A good way to test yourself is to take a story and imagine how that story might be written for *Isvestia* or *Pravda*.

2A. Be certain you are looking for the mainstream American point of view. Do not confuse this with your own point of view, or with that of some other group within the U.S. In any country there will always be some who dissent from the mainstream view, but this is not what we want.

3. Be sure you know what is meant by 'national bias'. Keep in mind that some of our biases may be shared by other countries. For example, the idea that our country is peaceful is part of our national bias, but many other countries may also see themselves as peaceful. Some biases are unique to the U.S., for example, belief in the superiority of the two-party system. Both the unique biases and the shared biases are part of our country's mainstream bias. Do not look only for biases peculiar to the U.S.

4. Make specific predictions about how some given story about "us" or "them" will be written before you actually read the story. Do this in order to look for specific bias. See the examples below, and try to think of others yourself.

4A. Remember, most countries like to see themselves as peaceful and unaggressive. We are no exception. If this is so, how might our newspapers describe the deployment and use of U.S. troops in another country? As an invasion? As an act of aggression? How would you predict our newspapers would describe the deployment and use of Soviet troops in another country? Are they there by the invitation of that country's legitimate government? Then reverse the positions. How are Soviet newspapers likely to describe the deployment and use of our troops in another country?

4B. Try to predict how the Soviets might write about, say, Israel. What words do you think they might choose to describe some of Israel's recent activities? The following article appeared on the front page of *Pravda*, April 2, 1988:

> Occupied Territories: Despite the *draconian repressive* measures of the occupational authorities, Palestinians took to the streets in the past 24 hours to express protest against the *terror unleashed on them by the aggressors*. A

UN spokesman stated that on Wednesday, Land Day, the Israeli *aggressors* killed eight people and wounded 250 in carrying out *punitive actions* against the Palestinians.

Notice the italicized words. What do they tell you about a mainstream Soviet viewpoint? How would you predict the Soviets might write about the Palestinians? How might *we* describe some of their actions?

5. Remember to pay attention to story placement. Is it on the front page, inside the paper? If a story does not support the mainstream U.S. point of view, where would we expect to find it? Will it be given much space or little space? Other than trivial "fillers" used by the press to fill space, what sorts of articles can we predict will be buried within the paper?

6. Look for key information within the article. What occurs at the beginning of the article? What at the end? For example, the *San Francisco Chronicle* once ran a front page story reporting on some Palestinian "terrorist" attacks on Israeli villages. At the end of the last paragraph, which was continued on the back page, it briefly mentioned that the Palestinians said they had done this in response to Israeli "terrorist" attacks made against them. Its placement toward the end suggests to those few who had read this far that the Palestinian allegations of Israeli terrorist attacks on Palestinians were insignificant, or even wrong.

7. What is the headline of the story? Imagine other possible headlines.

8. Pay attention to word choice, especially note charged words. Who gets the positive words? Who gets the negative words?

9. Remember the general logic of nationally biased communications:

   A. They play up what is positive about us and our allies or friends.

   B. They play down what is negative about us and our allies or friends.

   C. They play up what is negative about our enemies, their allies and friends.

   D. They play down what is positive about our enemies, their allies and friends.

10. Finally, note exceptions to this rule: When might you expect to see our news play up some positive news about "them"? If the Soviet Union is making some changes that we consider positive, for example, toward free enterprise, this may become front page news. ("They finally have to admit that free enterprise is the best economic system.") Conversely, when might you expect to see our news play up some negative news about this country? What negative news about this country can be criticized by the media, and what cannot?

11. Here is a way to try out your skills. Go through the newspaper page by page, identifying stories, editorials, advertisements, etc., that may be biased. Examine them one by one to determine whether they are biased, and if they are, whether you need to make a number of points about them, or just one. If you are making just one point, you may be able to group it with others. For example, you might group together a set of articles which are "buried" (that is, where negative information about "us" or positive information about "them" is being played down by placement).

12. When you do have a number of points to make, underline passages in the article and number them. Write your points clearly and give your reasons for them. Do this on a separate attached page, or at least make sure the reader can understand what you are saying.

13. When you have all your evidence assembled, write an introduction that explains to the reader what you have done and why. Write it so as to help the reader figure out exactly what you are presenting. Assume that the reader has never heard of national bias in the news.

✦ Examples of Student Work

As would be expected, student work will demonstrate a wide range of understanding, from superficial and impressionistic, to deep and insightful. What follows are examples of actual student work on the identification of national bias. Some of the examples betray a superficial understanding, others deep and insightful understanding. In reading both good and bad examples of work, the teacher will see the kinds of misunderstanding to anticipate, as well as the kind of work to have as a goal.

EXAMPLES OF WEAK WORK

Some students have trouble going beyond an impressionistic understanding of national bias. In the examples that follow, the students' commentaries reflect basic misunderstandings. One tendency is to go to extremes, as in the following: "If bias tends to influence us to look at the bad things about them and the good things about us, then *any* bad news about them is biased and *any* good news about us is biased."

This first example illustrates how some students see any bad news as biased. Of course, the fact that it contains negative news is not enough to suggest bias. The article quite fairly points out that the United States also has a serious drug and AIDS problem which the student, eager to see bias, failed to acknowledge.

> Quote From Article (Source not cited) The headline reads: "Heroin problem in Italy growing at alarming rate" Quotes from the article: "Overdose deaths skyrocket ... spread of AIDS among addicts ... two-thirds of those with AIDS are intravenous drug users .... Italians have cause for worry."

> *Student Commentary* "This article is plainly biased. The huge heading of Italy's drug problem says it all. Throughout the article the press is stating fact for fact how terrible Italy's drug and AIDS problem is."

This second article shows how positive news about the U.S. is seen by the student as being biased. The article, however, was not obviously biased.

> Quote From Article (Source not cited) Headline: "Even War-Torn Nations Aid Armenia, Rare Soviet Acceptance of Help." First paragraph: "From Los Angeles and New York, from Argentina and Cuba, from Britain, Scandinavia, Israel and Japan, people around the world sent food, medical supplies, and rescue equipment to victims of the earthquake in Soviet Armenia."

Student Commentary. "This front page article, with a huge heading, flashes "good deed" in front of the American readers eyes. Of course, it is a good thing for war-torn nations to aid Armenia, but as you read on in the article you notice that it is making the U.S. first on the list of contributors."

This next example shows a student making unsupported allegations. The student was probably having difficulty in finding articles with bias, and so had to "make" one with a bias. This commentary probably gives us more insight into the student's own bias than into any actual bias the article may contain.

Quote From Article (Source not cited.) The headline reads: "Abortion most cited issue". The article reads: "Despite all the T.V. ads and speeches on prison furloughs and the Pledge of Allegiance, few voters cited these as key issues. The No. 1 issue: abortion, cited by nearly a third of voters interviewed by ABC News. And those who cited abortion went for Bush. The issues that dominated the campaigns were cited less frequently, about 10 percent each on furloughs and the Pledge. One in four voters mentioned the drug problem and split nearly evenly between the candidates."

Student Commentary "The paper did not want the public to know that the issues the two candidates used against each other so viciously were not the issues that the people wanted to hear the answers to. The issue of abortion was not a commercial for Bush or Dukakis, but why is it the No. 1 danced around issue? Because the conservatives avoid the issue until the election is over in order to steal some of the votes of the liberals, then put their beliefs and views into action once elected."

EXAMPLES OF STRONG WORK

The following excerpts illustrate work in which students demonstrate a basic understanding of bias in general, and national bias in particular. The student commentary is not perfect, and should not be taken by the reader as exemplary work. It serves only to illustrate a student's first steps toward understanding and identifying national bias.

The following article is a fairly good example of a buried story, one placed in the background either because it puts us in a negative light or one of our enemies in a somewhat positive light.

Quote From Article *(Los Angeles Times,* 11–14–88 p. 12) Headline: "Grim Picture of Reagan's Legacy to U.S. Defenses" First paragraph: "Today's high technology weapons are so expensive that President Bush will not have enough money to operate them and still pay for all the new ones that President Reagan has ordered but not paid for, according to military budget analysts."

Student Commentary "This story is buried because it contradicts the popular assumption that the U.S. defense industry has been strengthened through heavy financial support by the Reagan administration .... Because it identifies fallacies in administration and defense department assumptions, and verifies the assessment of failure from normally supportive sources, this information has been buried. Though it has national significance, it runs counter to the belief of many Americans that national defense has been strengthened by the Reagan administration."

This next article illustrates how word choice influences our perception of the situation. In this example, our position is made to look better, and the "enemy" made to look worse.

> Quote From Article *(San Francisco Chronicle,* 12–01–88 p. A25) Headline: "Envoy to U.N. Downplays Flap Over Arafat." The first paragraph reads: "U.N. Ambassador Vernon Walters told a San Francisco audience yesterday that the Reagan administration is right in denying an entry visa to PLO chairman Yasser Arafat, and that the whole controversy will blow over in a couple of weeks."

> *Student Commentary* "This headline's use of the word 'flap' implies that the controversy surrounding the U.S. denial of Arafat's visa to speak before the U.N. is trivial. Other word choices could have been 'outrage' or 'protest'.... Asserting that the U.S. 'never signed an agreement allowing criminals into the country' sidesteps the fact that the U.S. signed an agreement not to impede access to the U.N. forum for any representative of an issue before that body .... Shunting attention to other issues, also biased, he attacked the Vietnamese government with emotive words, characterizing it as an 'abominable, tyrannical regime'. He follows with the assertion that the U.S. 'forced' the Soviets to realize their 'failure' as an imperialistic nation. Neither of these two last issues have any bearing on the story, but rather try to shore up a very weak position by diverting attention."

✦ From National Bias to Bias Detection in General

Once we and our students understand how to identify national bias, we should be well on the way to recognizing how to identify other forms of bias: personal, professional, religious, regional, etc. In each case we need to recognize that we do have a point of view we favor and that this commitment to one way of seeing things affects the way we represent and experience particular events.

For example, consider a professional bias — that of the American Medical Association. To recognize that doctors who belong to the AMA have a bias is to realize that they have a particular way of viewing issues which affect the medical profession, a view which supports their interests regardless of the evidence. Identifying these biases will help us predict the stance taken by the AMA on major issues. For example, the approach of the AMA to health care is generally pharmacological and surgical. We would expect, then, that they would be opposed to such things as home birth, holistic medicine and chiropractics. Furthermore, given their financial interests, we can be confident that the official position of the AMA on socialized medicine will be negative, unless at some later date it becomes possible to make more money under a national health act than under a private system.

To sum up, people typically presuppose their points of view to be the truth. This uncritical closedmindedness perpetuates prejudice. Individuals are not inclined to examine and question their own biases, unless they develop critical insight into them. Neither are they inclined to consider whether another's point of view is more accurate or insightful than their own. We must help students discover that no single point of view contains all the truth, that no single perspective is without limitations and weaknesses, that confusing one's own point of view with reality inevitably produces biases and prejudices. These recognitions require extensive practice. Only when students grasp this explicitly, and systematically begin to critically assess their own biases can they begin to correct and improve how they look at the world. It is our responsibility as teachers to design activities and assignments that directly facilitate this end.

✦ References

Frank, Jerome. "Psychological Causes of the Nuclear Arms Race." *CHEMTECH* August, 1982, p. 467.

Friedlander, Robert A. "The Munich Affliction: Will It Happen Again?" *Global Affairs,* Fall, 1988, p. 18.

Keene, Sam. *Faces of the Enemy.* Harper and Row, San Francisco. 1986 p. 18.

Piaget, Jean. "The Transition From Egocentricity to Reciprocity" *Piaget Sampler, An Introduction to Jean Piaget Through His Own Words.* Campbell, Sarah F. (ed.) John Wiley and Sons, New York. 1976 p. 48.

"Dawning of a New World Order." Briefing section, *San Francisco Chronicle,* December 8, 1988 p. 1.

Scheffler, Israel "Philosophical Models of Teaching." *Reason And Teaching,* Bobbs-Merrill and Co., Inc. New York. 1973 p. 7.

✦✦ Chapter 20

Socratic Questioning

with A. J. A. Binker

Abstract
Socratic questioning is at the heart of critical teaching. In this paper, published as a chapter in the Critical Thinking Handbook *series, Paul and Binker explain its nature and significance. Three types of Socratic questioning are described, uses of Socratic discussions are suggested, a taxonomy of Socratic questions is provided, and three extended examples of Socratic discussions are given.*

✦ Introduction

Socratic discussion, wherein students' thought is elicited and probed, allows students to develop and evaluate their thinking by making it explicit. By encouraging students to slow their thinking down and elaborate on it, Socratic discussion gives students the opportunity to develop and test their ideas — the beliefs they have spontaneously formed and those they learn in school. Thus, students can synthesize their beliefs into a more coherent and better-developed perspective.

Socratic questioning requires teachers to take seriously and wonder about what students say and think: what they mean, its significance to them, its relationship to other beliefs, how it can be tested, to what extent and in what way it is true or makes sense. Teachers who wonder about the meaning and truth of students' statements can translate that curiosity into probing questions. By wondering aloud, teachers simultaneously convey interest in and respect for student thought, and model analytical moves for students. Fruitful Socratic discussion infects students with the same curiosity about the meaning and truth of what they think, hear, and read and gives students the clear message that they are expected to think and to take everyone else's beliefs seriously.

Socratic questioning is based on the idea that all thinking has a logic or structure, that any one statement only partially reveals the thinking underlying it, expressing no more than a tiny piece of the system of interconnected beliefs of which it is a part. (See the chapter on Background Logic.) Its purpose is to expose the logic of someone's thought. Use of Socratic questioning presupposes the following points: All thinking has assumptions; makes claims or creates meaning; has implications and consequences; focuses on some things and throws others into the background; uses some concepts or

as and not others; is defined by purposes, issues, or problems; uses or
ılains some facts and not others; is relatively clear or unclear; is relatively
:p or superficial; is relatively critical or uncritical; is relatively elaborated
ındeveloped; is relatively monological or multi-logical. Critical thinking is
nking done with an effective, self-monitoring awareness of these points.

Socratic instruction can take many forms. Socratic questions can come from
: teacher or from students. They can be used in a large group discussion, in
ıall groups, one-to-one, or even with oneself. They can have different purpos-
. What each form has in common is that someone's thought is developed as a
:ult of the probing, stimulating questions asked. It requires questioners to
y on others' beliefs, to imagine what it would be like to accept them and won-
ır what it would be like to believe otherwise. If a student says that people are
lfish, the teacher may wonder aloud as to what it means to say that, how the
ıdent explains acts others call altruistic, what sort of example that student
ould accept as an unselfish act, or what the student thinks it means to say
that an act or person was unselfish. The discussion which follows could help
clarify the concepts of selfish and unselfish behavior, the kind of evidence
required to determine whether or not someone is acting selfishly, and the consequences of accepting or rejecting the original generalization. Such a discussion enables students to examine their own views on such concepts as generosity, motivation, obligation, human nature, and right and wrong.

Some erroneously believe that a Socratic discussion is a chaotic free-for-
all. In fact, Socratic discussion has distinctive goals and distinctive ways to
achieve them. Indeed, any discussion — any thinking — guided by Socratic
questioning is structured. The discussion, the thinking, is structured to take
student thought from the unclear to the clear, from the unreasoned to the
reasoned, from the implicit to the explicit, from the unexamined to the examined, from the inconsistent to the consistent, from the unarticulated to the
articulated. To learn how to participate in it, one has to learn how to listen
carefully to what others say, look for reasons and evidence, recognize and
reflect upon assumptions, discover implications and consequences, seek
examples, analogies, and objections, discover, in short, what is really known
and distinguish it from what is merely believed.

Socratic Questioning

- raises basic issues
- probes beneath the surface of things
- pursues problematic areas of thought
- helps students to discover the *structure* of their own thought
- helps students develop sensitivity to clarity, accuracy, and relevance
- helps students arrive at judgment through their own reasoning
- helps students note claims, evidence, conclusions, questions-at-issue,
  assumptions, implications, consequences, concepts, interpretations,
  points of view — the elements of thought

✦ *Three Kinds of Socratic Discussion*

We can loosely categorize three general forms of Socratic questioning and distinguish three basic kinds of preparation for each: the spontaneous, the exploratory, and the issue-specific.

SPONTANEOUS OR UNPLANNED

Every teacher's teaching should be imbued with the Socratic spirit. We should always keep our curiosity and wondering alive. If we do, we will often spontaneously ask students what they mean and explore with them how we might find out if something is true. If one student says that a given angle will be the same as another angle in a geometrical figure, we may spontaneously wonder how we might go about proving or disproving that. If one student says people in the U.S. love freedom, we may spontaneously wonder exactly what that means. (Does that mean, for example, that we love freedom more than other people do? How could we find out?) If in a science class a student says that most space is empty, we may be spontaneously moved to ask what that might mean and how we might find out.

Such spontaneous discussions provide models of listening critically as well as exploring the beliefs expressed. If something said seems questionable, misleading, or false, Socratic questioning provides a way of helping students to become self-correcting, rather than relying on correction by the teacher. Spontaneous Socratic discussion can prove especially useful when students become interested in a topic, when they raise an important issue, when they are on the brink of grasping or integrating something, when discussion becomes bogged down or confused or hostile. Socratic questioning provides specific moves which can fruitfully take advantage of the interest, effectively approach the issue, aid integration and expansion of the insight, move a troubled discussion forward, clarify or sort through what appears confusing, and diffuse frustration or anger.

Although by definition one cannot pre-plan for a particular spontaneous discussion, teachers can prepare themselves by becoming familiar and comfortable with generic Socratic questions, and developing the art of raising probing follow-up questions and giving encouraging and helpful responses. Ask for examples, evidence, or reasons, propose counter-examples, ask the other students if they agree with a point made, suggest parallel or analogous cases, ask for a paraphrase of opposing views, rephrase student responses clearly and succinctly. These are among the most common moves.

- If you see little or no relevance in a student comment, you may think, "I wonder why this student mentioned that now?" and ask, "What connection do you see between our discussion and your point that ...?" or "I'm not sure why you mentioned that now. Could you explain how it's related to this discussion?" or "What made you think of that?" Either the point is germane, and you can clarify the connection, or only marginally related, and you can rephrase it and say "A new issue has been raised." That new issue can be pursued then, or tactfully postponed, or can generate an assignment.

- If a student says something vague or general, you may think, "I wonder about the role of that belief in this student's life, the consequences of that belief, or how the student perceives the consequences, or whether it has any practical consequences at all" and so may ask, "How does that belief affect how you act? What, for example, do you do or refrain from doing because you believe that?" You might have several students respond and compare their understandings, or suggest an alternative view and have students compare its consequences.

Because we begin to wonder more and more about meaning and truth, and so think aloud in front of our students by means of questions, Socratic exchanges will occur at many unplanned moments in our instruction. However, in addition to these unplanned wonderings we can also design or plan at least two distinct kinds of Socratic discussion: one that explores a wide range of issues and one that focuses on one particular issue.

EXPLORATORY

Exploratory Socratic questioning enables teachers to find out what students know or think and to probe into student thinking on a variety of issues. Hence you may use it to learn students' impressions of a subject to assess their thought and ability to articulate it, you may use it to see what students value, or to uncover problematic areas or potential biases, or find out where students' thought is clearest and fuzziest. You may use it to discover areas or issues of interest or controversy, or to find out where and how students have integrated school material into their belief systems. Such discussions can serve as a general preparation for later study or analysis of a topic, as an introduction, as review, to see what students understood from their study of a unit or topic before a test, to suggest where they should focus study for a test, as a basis for or guide to future assignments, or to prepare for an assignment. You might have students take (or pick) an issue raised in discussion and give their own views, or have students form groups to discuss the issue or topic.

This type of Socratic questioning raises and explores a broad range of interrelated issues and concepts. It requires minimal pre-planning or pre-thinking. It has a relatively loose order or structure. You can prepare by having some general questions ready to raise when appropriate by considering the topic or issue, related issues, and key concepts. You can also prepare by predicting students' likeliest responses and preparing some follow-up questions. Remember, however, that once students' thought is stimulated no one can predict exactly where discussion will go.

Here are some suggestions and possible topics for Socratic discussions:
- "What is social studies?" If students have difficulty, ask, "When you've studied social studies, what have you talked about?" If students list topics, put them on the board. Then have students discuss the items and try to group them. "Do these topics have something in common? Are there differences between these topics?" Encourage students to discuss details they

know about the topics. If, instead of listing topics, they give a general answer or definition, or if they can give a statement about what the topics listed have in common, suggest examples that fit the definition but are not social studies. For example, if a student says, "It's about people", mention medicine. Have them modify or improve their definition. "How is social studies like and unlike other subjects? What basic questions does the subject address? How does it address them? Why study social studies? Is it important? Why or why not? How can we use what we learn in social studies? What are the most important ideas you've learned from this subject?"

- When, if ever, is violence justified? Why are people as violent as they are? What effects does violence have? Can violence be lessened or stopped?
- What is a friend?
- What is education? Why learn?
- What is most important?
- What is right and wrong? Why be good? What is a good person?
- What is the difference between living and non-living things?
- Of what sorts of things is the universe made?
- What is language?
- What are the similarities and differences between humans and animals?

Sometimes you may not know whether to call a discussion exploratory or issue-specific. Which you call it is unimportant. What is important is what happens in the discussion. For example, consider this group of questions:

- What does 'vote' mean?
    How do people decide whom to elect? How should they decide? How could people predict how a potential leader is likely to act? If you don't know about an issue or the candidates for an office, should you vote?
    Is voting important? Why or why not? What are elections supposed to produce? How? What does that require? What does that tell us about voting?
    Why have elections? Why is democracy considered good? What does belief in democracy assume about human nature?
    How do people become candidates?
    Why does the press emphasize how much money candidates have? How does having lots of money help candidates win?
    Why do people give money to candidates? Why do companies?
    Is voting the same thing as marking a ballot?

These questions could be the list generated as possible questions for an exploratory discussion. Which of them are actually used would depend on how students respond. For an issue-specific discussion, these questions and more could be used in an order which takes students from ideas with which they are most familiar to those with which they are least familiar.

ISSUE-SPECIFIC

You will often approach your instruction with specific areas and issues to cover. This is the time for issue-specific Socratic questioning. To really probe an issue or concept in depth, to have students clarify, sort, analyze and evaluate thoughts and perspectives, distinguish the known from the unknown, synthesize relevant factors and knowledge, students can engage in an extended and focused discussion. This type of discussion offers students the chance to pursue perspectives to their most basic assumptions and through their furthest implications and consequences. These discussions give students experience in engaging in an extended, ordered, and integrated discussion in which they discover, develop, and share ideas and insights. It requires pre-planning or thinking through possible perspectives on the issue, grounds for conclusions, problematic concepts, implications, and consequences. You can further prepare by reflecting on those subjects relevant to the issue: their methods, standards, basic distinctions and concepts, and interrelationships — points of overlap or possible conflict. You may also prepare by considering likeliest student answers.

All three types of Socratic discussion require developing the art of questioning. They require the teacher to develop familiarity with a wide variety of intellectual moves and sensitivity to when to ask which kinds of questions, though there is rarely one best question at any particular time.

Some Suggestions for Using Socratic Discussion

- Have an initial exploratory discussion about a complex issue in which students break it down into simpler parts. Students can then choose the aspects they want to explore or research. Then have an issue-specific discussion where students share, analyze, evaluate, and synthesize their work.
- The class could have a "fishbowl" discussion. One third of the class, sitting in a circle, discusses a topic. The rest of the class, in a circle around the others, listens, takes notes, then discusses the discussion.
- Assign an essay asking students to respond to a point of interest made in a discussion.
- Have students write summaries of their discussions immediately afterwards. They could also add new thoughts or examples, provide further clarification, etc. They could later share these notes.

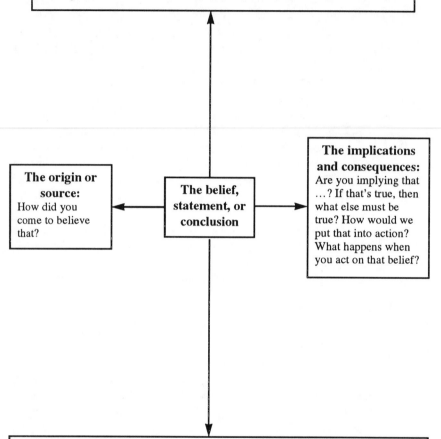

Conflicts with other thoughts and answers to objections:
How would you answer someone who said ...? What might these people say?
How could someone else look at this? Why? Why do you think your way of
looking at it is better?

The origin or source:
How did you
come to believe
that?

The belief, statement, or conclusion

The implications and consequences:
Are you implying that
...? If that's true, then
what else must be
true? How would we
put that into action?
What happens when
you act on that belief?

Support, reasons, evidence, and assumptions:
How do you know? Are you assuming that ...? Is this a good assumption? What evi-
dence do you have? Why is that relevant? How do you know your evidence is true?
How are you conceiving of, thinking about the issue? Why?

Socratic Discussion

There are four directions in which thought can be pursued.

✦ *A Taxonomy of Socratic Questions*

It is helpful to recognize, in light of the universal features in the logic of human thought, that there are identifiable categories of questions for the adept Socratic questioner to dip into: questions of clarification, questions that probe assumptions, questions that probe reasons and evidence, questions about viewpoints or perspectives, questions that probe implications and consequences, and questions about the question. Here are some examples of generic questions in each of these categories:

QUESTIONS OF CLARIFICATION

- What do you mean by _____?
- Could you give me an example?
- What is your main point?
- Would this be an example: ___?
- How does _____ relate to ___?
- Could you explain that further?
- Could you put that another way?
- Would you say more about that?
- Is your basic point _____ or _____?
- Why do you say that?
- What do you think is the main issue here?
- Let me see if I understand you; do you mean _____ or _____?
- How does this relate to our discussion (problem, issue)?
- What do you think John meant by his remark? What did you take John to mean?
- Jane, would you summarize in your own words what Richard has said? ... Richard, is that what you meant?

QUESTIONS THAT PROBE ASSUMPTIONS

- What are you assuming?
- What is Karen assuming?
- What could we assume instead?
- You seem to be assuming _____. Do I understand you correctly?
- All of your reasoning depends on the idea that ___. Why have you based your reasoning on _____ rather than _____?
- You seem to be assuming ___. How would you justify taking this for granted?
- Is it always the case? Why do you think the assumption holds here?
- Why would someone make this assumption?

QUESTIONS THAT PROBE REASONS AND EVIDENCE

- What would be an example?
- Are these reasons adequate?
- How do you know?
- Why did you say that?
- Why do you think that is true?
- What led you to that belief?
- Do you have any evidence for that?
- How does that apply to this case?
- What difference does that make?
- What would change your mind?
- What are your reasons for saying that?
- What other information do we need?
- Could you explain your reasons to us?

- But is that good evidence to believe that?
- Is there reason to doubt that evidence?
- Who is in a position to know if that is so?
- What would you say to someone who said ____?
- Can someone else give evidence to support that response?
- By what reasoning did you come to that conclusion?
- How could we find out whether that is true?

QUESTIONS ABOUT VIEWPOINTS OR PERSPECTIVES

- You seem to be approaching this issue from _____ perspective. Why have you chosen this rather than that perspective?
- How would other groups/types of people respond? Why? What would influence them?
- How could you answer the objection that _____ would make?
- What might someone who believed ___ think?
- Can/did anyone see this another way?
- What would someone who disagrees say?
- What is an alternative?
- How are Ken's and Roxanne's ideas alike? Different?

QUESTIONS THAT PROBE IMPLICATIONS AND CONSEQUENCES

- What are you implying by that?
- When you say _____, are you implying _____?
- But if that happened, what else would happen as a result? Why?
- What effect would that have?
- Would that necessarily happen or only probably happen?
- What is an alternative?
- If this and this are the case, then what else must also be true?
- If we say that *this* is unethical, how about *that?*

QUESTIONS ABOUT THE QUESTION

- How can we find out?
- What does this question assume?
- Would __ put the question differently?
- Is this the same issue as ____?
- How would ____ put the issue?
- Why is this question important?
- How could someone settle this question?
- Can we break this question down at all?
- Is the question clear? Do we understand it?
- Is this question easy or hard to answer? Why?
- Does this question ask us to evaluate something?
- Do we all agree that this is the question?
- To answer this question, what questions would we have to answer first?
- I'm not sure I understand how you are interpreting the main question at issue.

The Elements of Reasoning Within a Point of View

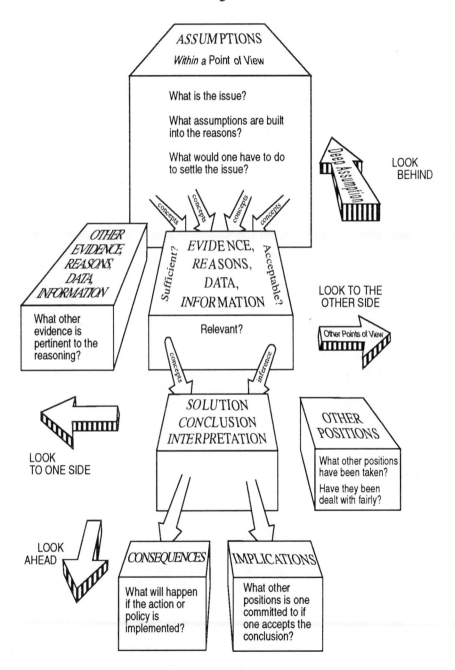

* A modified version of a schema originally devised by Ralph H. Johnson; design and layout by J. A. Blair

✦ *Wondering (and Wondering About*
Your Wonderings)

As a blossoming critical thinker, you will find yourself wondering in many directions. You will often, however, be unsure about how to share many of these wonderings with your students. You certainly don't want to overwhelm them. Neither do you want to confuse them or lead them in too many directions at once. So when do you make the wonderings explicit in the form of a question and when do you keep them in the privacy of your mind?

There is no pat formula or procedure for answering these questions, though there are some principles:

- "Test and find out." There is nothing wrong with some of your questions misfiring. You won't always be able to predict what questions will stimulate students' thought. So you must engage in some trial-and-error questioning.
- "Tie into student experience and perceived needs." You may think of numerous examples of ways students can apply what they learn, and formulate questions relating academic material to students' lives.
- "Don't give up too soon." If students don't respond to a question, wait. If they still don't respond, you could rephrase the question or break it down into simpler questions.

You should use care and caution in introducing students to Socratic questioning. The level of the questions should match the level of the students' thought. Furthermore, it should not be assumed that students will be fully successful with it, except over a considerable length of time. Nevertheless, properly used, it can be introduced in some form or other at virtually any grade level.

To participate effectively in Socratic questioning, one must:

- listen carefully to what others say
- take what they say seriously
- look for reasons and evidence
- recognize and reflect upon assumptions
- discover implications and consequences
- seek examples, analogies, and objections
- seek to distinguish what one *knows* from what one merely *believes*
- seek to enter empathetically into the perspectives or points of view of others
- be on the alert for inconsistencies, vagueness, and other possible problems in thought
- look beneath the surface of things
- maintain a healthy sense of skepticism
- be willing to helpfully play the role of devil's advocate

✦ Socratic Interludes in Class

#1 Helping Students Organize
Their Thoughts for Writing

INTRODUCTION

The following Socratic interlude represents an initial attempt to get students to think about what a persuasive essay is and how to prepare to write one. Of course, like all Socratic questioning it goes beyond one objective, for it also stimulates students to think critically in general about what they are doing and why. It helps them to see that their own ideas, if developed, are important and can lead to insights.

TRANSCRIPT
(A Reconstruction)

T: You are all going to be writing a persuasive essay, so let's talk about what you have to do to get your ideas organized. There are two ways to persuade people of something, by appealing to their reason, a rational appeal, and by appealing to their emotions, an emotional appeal. What is the difference between these? Let's take the rational appeal first, what do you do when you appeal to someone's reason?

John: You give them good reasons for accepting something. You tell them why they should do something or what they can get out of it or why it's good for them.

T: But don't they already have reasons why they believe as they do? So why should they accept your reasons rather than theirs?

Bob: Well, maybe mine are better than theirs.

T: Have you ever given someone, say your mother or father, good reasons for what you wanted to do, but they just did not accept your reasons even though they seemed compelling to you?

Susan: Yeah, that happens a lot to me. They just say that I have to do what they say whether I like it or not because they're my parents.

T: So is it hopeless to give people good reasons for changing their minds because people will never change their minds?

Grace: No, people sometimes do change their minds. Sometimes they haven't thought about things a lot or they haven't noticed something about what they're doing. So you tell them something they hadn't considered and then they change their minds ... sometimes.

T: That's right, sometimes people do change their minds after you give them a new way of looking at things or reasons they hadn't considered. What does that tell you about one thing you want to be sure to do in deciding how to defend your ideas and get people to consider them? What do you think, Tom?

Tom: I guess you want to consider different ways to look at things, to find new reasons and things.

T: Where can you find different ways to look at things? What do you think, Janet?

Janet: I would look in the library.

T: How? What would you look for, could you be more specific?

Janet: Sure. I'm going to write about why women should have the same rights as men, so I'll look for books on feminism and women.

T: How will that help you to find different ways to look at things, could you spell that out further?

Janet: I think that there will probably be different ideas in different books. Not all women think alike. Black women and white women and religious women and Hispanic women all have their own point of view. I will look for the best reasons that each gives and try to put them into my paper.

T: OK, but so far we have just talked about giving reasons to support your ideas, what I called in the beginning a 'rational appeal'. What about the emotional side of things, of appealing to people's emotions? John, what are some emotions and why appeal to them?

John: Emotions are things like fear and anger and jealousy, what happens when we feel strongly, or are excited.

T: Right, so do you know anyone who appeals to our emotions? Are your emotions ever appealed to?

Judy: Sure, we all try to get people involved in feeling as we do. When we talk to friends about kids we don't like we describe them so that our friends will get mad at them and feel like we do.

T: How do we do this, could you give me an example, Judy?

Judy: OK, like I know this girl who's always trying to get her hands on boys, even if they already have girl friends. So I tell my friends how she acts. I give them all the details, how she touches them when she talks to them and acts like a dip. We really get mad at her.

T: So what do you think, should you try to get your reader to share your feeling? Should you try to get their emotions involved?

Judy: Sure, if you can.

T: But isn't this the way propaganda works? How we get people emotional so that they go along with things they shouldn't? Didn't Hitler get people all emotional and stir up their hate?

Judy: Yeah, but we do that too when we play the national anthem or when we get excited about Americans winning medals at the Olympics.

T: *So what do you think of this Frank, should we or shouldn't we try to get people's emotions stirred up?*

Frank: If what we are trying to get people to do is good we should do it, but if what we are trying to get them to do is bad we shouldn't.

T: *Well, what do you think about Judy's getting her friends mad at a girl by telling them how she flirts with boys?*

Frank: Are you asking me? ... I think she ought to clean up her own act first. (laughter)

Judy: What do you mean by that?!

Frank: Well, you're one of the biggest flirts around!

Judy: I never flirt with boys who have girl friends and anyway I'm just a friendly person.

Frank: Yes you are, *very* friendly!

T: *OK, calm down you guys. I think you better settle this one in private. But look, there's an important point here. Sometimes we do act inconsistently, sometimes there are contradictions in our behavior, and we criticize people for doing what we do. And that's one thing we should think about when writing our papers, are we willing to live by what we are preaching to others? Or another way to put this is by asking whether our point of view is realistic. If our point of view seems too idealistic then our reader may not be persuaded.*

We don't have much time left today, so let me try to summarize what I see as implied in what we have talked about. So far, we have agreed about a number of things important to persuasive writing: 1) you need to give good reasons to support your point of view, 2) you should be clear about what your reasons are, 3) you should consider the issue from more than one point of view, including considering how your reader might look at it, 4) you should check out books or articles on the subject to get different points of view, 5) you should consider how you might reach your reader's feelings, how what you say ties into what they care about, 6) following Judy's example you should present specific examples and include the details that make your example realistic and moving, 7) in line with Frank's point, you should watch out for contradictions and inconsistencies, and 8) you should make sure that what you are arguing for is realistic. For next time I would like you all to write out the introductory paragraph to your paper in which you basically tell the reader what you are going to try to persuade him or her of and how you are going to do it, that is, how the paper will be structured. Don't worry that your first draft is rough; you will be working in groups of threes to sharpen up what you have written.

✦ #2 *Helping Students to Think More Deeply About Basic Ideas*

INTRODUCTION

We tend to pass by basic ideas quickly to get into more derivative ideas. This is part of the didactic mind set of giving-students-content-to-remember. What we need to do, in contrast, is to stimulate student's thinking right from the start, especially about the most basic ideas in a subject so that they are motivated from the beginning to use their thinking in trying to understand things, and so that they base their thinking on foundational ideas that make sense to them.

TRANSCRIPT

(A Reconstruction)

T: This is a course in Biology. What kind of a subject is that? What do you know about Biology already? Kathleen, what do you know about it?

Kathleen: It's a science.

T: And what's a science?

Kathleen: Me? A science is very exact. They do experiments and measure things and test things.

T: What other sciences are there besides biology? Marisa, could you name some?

Marisa: Sure, there's chemistry and physics.

T: What else?

Blake: There's botany and math?

T: Math ... math is a little different from the others, isn't it? How is math different from biology, chemistry, physics, and botany? Blake, what would you say?

Blake: You don't do experiments in math.

T: And why not?

Blake: I guess 'cause numbers are different.

T: Yes, studying numbers and other mathematical things is different from studying chemicals or laws in the physical world or living things and so forth. You might ask your math teacher about why numbers are different or do some reading about that, but let's focus our attention here on what are called the life sciences. Why are biology and botany called life sciences?

Peter: Because they both study living things.

T: How are they different? How is biology different from botany? Jennifer, what do you think?

Jennifer: I don't know.

T: Well, let's all of us look up the words in our dictionaries and see what it says about them.

(Students look up the words)

T: Jennifer, what did you find for biology?

Jennifer: It says: "The science that deals with the origin, history, physical characteristics, life processes, habits, etc., of plants and animals: It includes botany and zoology."

T: So what do we know about the relationship of botany to biology? Rick?

Rick: Botany is just a part of biology.

T: Right, and what can we tell about biology from just looking at its etymology. What does it literally mean? If you break the word into two parts "bio" and "logy". Blake, what does it tell us?

Blake: The science of life or the study of life.

T: So, do you see how etymology can help us get an insight into the meaning of a word? Do you see how the longer definition spells out the etymological meaning in greater detail? Well, why do you think experiments are so important to biologists and other scientists? Have humans always done experiments do you think? Marisa.

Marisa: I guess not, not before there was any science.

T: Right, that's an excellent point, science didn't always exist. What did people do before science existed? How did they get their information? How did they form their beliefs? Peter.

Peter: From religion.

T: Yes, religion often shaped a lot of what people thought. Why don't we use religion today to decide, for example, what is true of the origin, history, and physical characteristics of life?

Peter: Some people still do. Some people believe that the Bible explains the origin of life and that the theory of evolution is wrong.

T: What is the theory of evolution, Jose?

Jose: I don't know.

T: Well, why don't we all look up the name Darwin in our dictionaries and see if there is anything there about Darwinian theory.

(Students look up the words)

T: Jose, read aloud what you have found.

Jose: It says, "Darwin's theory of evolution holds that all species of plants and animals developed from earlier forms by hereditary transmission of slight variations in successive generations and that the forms which survive are those that are best adapted to the environment."

T: What does that mean to you … in ordinary language? How would you explain that? Jose.

Jose: It means the stronger survive and the weaker die?

T: Well, if that's true why do you think the dinosaurs died out? I thought dinosaurs were very strong?

Shannon: They died because of the ice age, I think.

T: So I guess it's not enough to be strong, you must also fit in with the changes in the environment. Perhaps fitness or adaptability is more important than strength. Well, in any case why do you think that most people today look to science to provide answers to questions about the origin and nature of life rather than to the Bible or other religious teachings?

Shannon: Nowadays most people believe that science and religion deal with different things and that scientific questions cannot be answered by religion.

T: And by the same token, I suppose, we recognize that religious questions cannot be answered by science. In any case, how were scientists able to convince people to consider their way of finding answers to questions about the nature of life and life processes. Kathleen, you've been quiet for a while, what do you think?

Kathleen: To me science can be proved. When scientists say something we can ask for proof and they can show us, and if we want we can try it out for ourselves.

T: Could you explain that further?

Kathleen: Sure, in my chemistry class we did experiments in which we tested out some of the things that were said in our chemistry books. We could see for ourselves.

T: That's right, science is based on the notion that when we claim things to be true about the world we should be able to test them to see if, objectively, they are true. Marisa, you have a question?

Marisa: Yes, but don't we all test things. We test our parents and our friends. We try out ideas to see if they work.

T: That's true. But is there any difference between the way you and I test our friends and the way a chemist might test a solution to see if it is acidic?

Marisa: Sure, ... but I'm not sure how to explain it.

T: Blake, what do you think?

Blake: Scientists have laboratories; we don't.

T: They also do precise measurements and use precise instruments, don't they? Why don't we do that with our friends, parents, and children? Adrian, do you have an idea why not?

Adrian: We don't need to measure our friends. We need to find out whether they really care about us.

T: Yes, finding out about caring is a different matter than finding out about acids and bases, or even than finding out about animal behavior. You might say that there are two different kinds of realities in the world, the qualitative and the quantitative, and that science is mostly concerned with the quantitative, while we are often concerned with the qualitative. Could you name some qualitative ideas that all of us are concerned with? Rick, what do you think?

Rick: I don't know what you mean.

T: Well, the word qualitative is connected to the word quality. If I were to ask you to describe your own qualities in comparison to your brother or sister, would you know the sort of thing I was asking you?

Rick: I guess so.

T: Could you, for example, take your father and describe to us some of his best and some of his worst qualities as you see them?

Rick: I guess so.

T: OK, why don't you do it. What do you think some of your father's best qualities are?

Rick: To me he is generous. He likes to help people out when they are in trouble.

T: And what science studies generosity?

Rick: I don't know. None, I guess.

T: That's right, generosity is a human quality, it can't be measured scientifically. There is no such thing as generosity units. So science is not the only way we can find things out. We can also experience qualities in the world. We can experience kindness, generosity, fear, love, hate, jealousy, self-satisfaction, friendship, and many, many other things as well. In this class we are concerned mainly with what we can find out about life quantitatively or scientifically. For next time, I want you to read the first chapter in your text book and I want you to be prepared to explain what the first chapter says. I will be dividing you up into groups of four and each group of four will develop a short summary of the first chapter (without looking at it, of course) and then we will have a spokesperson

*from each group explain your summary to the class. After that, we will
have a discussion of the ideas mentioned. Don't forget today's discussion, because I'll be asking you some questions that will see if you can
relate what we talked about today with what was said in your first
chapter. Any questions? ... OK, ... See you next time.*

✦ #3 Helping Students to Think Seriously About Complex Social Issues

INTRODUCTION

In the following extended discussion, Rodger Halstad, Homested High
School Social Studies teacher, Socratically questions students about their
views about the Middle East. He links up the issue with the deathcamps of
WWII and, ultimately, with the problem of how to correct one injustice without committing another.

PART ONE

*I thought what we'd do now is to talk a little about the Middle East. And
remember we saw a film, and title of the film was, "Let My People Go".
And in the process of seeing that film, we took a look at some of the
things that happened in the concentration camps; in the death-camps of
Nazi Germany during World War II. Remember that? It's pretty hard to
forget, so I'm sure that you do remember that. Who do you hold responsible for what happened to the Jewish people during the holocaust, the
Nazi holocaust of the 1940's and the late 1930's? Who do you hold
responsible for that? Laura?*

Laura: Everyone. Um ...

What do you mean, everyone?

Student: It started in Germany. I would ... My first thought goes to Hitler;
then it goes to the German people that allowed him to take control without ... without seeing what he was doing before it was too
late.

*Let's see if we understand. Are you talking now about what I call moral
responsibility, that they hold some moral responsibility for what happened, or are you talking about legal responsibility? What I'd like to
really have us talk about is legal responsibility. Who would you punish
for the responsibility for what happened to the Jewish people? Would
you punish all Germans? No. OK, then who would you punish?*

Student: Hitler.

*Hitler. OK, if he had been alive and we'd been able to capture him, you
would have punished him.*

Student: Absolutely.

OK. I think probably we'd all agree to that, alright? Anybody else?

Student: Probably his five top men. I ... I'm not sure ....

Well, whatever. Whether it's five or six or ten or whatever. The top guys, the SS ....

Student: (several talking) Well, that's a good question ... and, there are a lot of Nazis out there.

Well, are you sure everyone was a member of the Nazi party? Not all Germans were.

Student: Well, not all Germans were ... um ...

Want to think about it?

Student: Yeah.

How about somebody else? First of all, we all agree that somebody should have been punished, right? Alright, these are not acts that should have gone unpunished. OK, Steve?

Steve: Well, it'd be kind of hard, but, like, I think that every soldier or whatever, whoever took a life, theirs should be taken. (Several speaking)

Every person who ... every ... every Nazi soldier who was in the camps ....

Steve: Who had something to do with ...

Who had something to do with the killing of the people in the camps. The Jews, the gypsies, the opponents of Hitler, all those people. All the 12 million killed. Anybody that had a direct ... played a direct role. You would punish them. What if we had a corporal here, Steve, and the corporal said, "The reason I did this is because I was ordered to do it. And if I didn't do it, my family was going to be injured, or something was going to happen to my family." Are you going to punish that corporal?

Steve: Well, I guess ... well, I mean ... ah, they ... They still took a life, you know, but they're ... what they're ... You know, they were just following the rules. What ... (Laughter) Yes, but I mean ... I, I, I believe that, you know, if you take a life ...

What if they didn't take a life? What if they just tortured somebody?

Steve: Then they ... then ... then they should be tortured in the same way.

So you say anybody who was directly responsible for any injury, torture, murder, whatever in the camps, they themselves should get a similar kind of punishment. What about the people who were in the bureaucracy of the German government who, uh, set up the trains and the time schedule of the trains? What about the engineer on the train? You're looking at me, Amy. I'm not sure if ...

Amy: Well, yeah, I guess ....

All those people?

Amy: Yeah, because if you think about it, if they hadn't of done that, they couldn't have gotten the people there.

OK, and what about the people standing on the streets while the Jews had to get in the trucks …?

Amy: No, I think that's going a little too …

OK, so anybody who participates in any way in the arrest, the carrying out of all these activities, including even people who, uh … what about people who typed up the memos?

Amy: Yeah, I guess.

(Several Speaking)

No, says Manuel. Why not no? Why no?

Manuel: Like, for example, if they're put under a lot of duress. Like, uh, "We're going to kill your family, we're going to hurt your family, put them in a concentration camp, too …."

Yes. Yes?

Manuel: It, it's just total … you just can't hold them responsible because their family … it's just like, uh … the next, the closest thing to them, and you can't just say you have to punish them because I don't think they did it on purpose. They didn't do it because we hate the Jews, we don't like you … we're not doing it because we want to see you suffer. They're doing it because they don't want to see their family suffer.

Anybody who enjoyed what they were doing, Manny, clearly needs to be punished, in your … right? What if I do it, but I don't enjoy it? "Oh, God! I don't want to do this! Ohhh! But you made me do it."

Manuel: I don't think they should be punished.

OK, the war's over, Manny. Let's get the man in here for a second. The war's over, Manny, and we now have the rest of these people. Leslie, did you do that because you wanted to do that? (jumps to Rodger)

(Laughter)

Student: No.

No. Gail, did you do it because you wanted to do it?

Gail: No.

Did you do it because you wanted to do it, Ariel? Did you do it, Laurel? 'Cause you wanted, Brad?

Student: No.

Manny, what we got? None of them did it because they wanted to. They all did it because it was orders.

Manuel: Well, uh ...

How do we know?

Manuel: That's a good question.

You want to get off the hot seat for a second, Manny?

Manuel: Yeah.

OK, I don't know ... eeny, meeny, Stacy?

Stacy: Well, ah ... that's why I think that it should maybe just be the leadership because they're the ones ...

Just Hitler, and the ...

Stacy: Yeah, 'cause they're the ones who made up the concentration camps, and they're the ones who tell the people to do it. And some people will want to do these things, and some people won't, and you can't determine who wants to do it and who doesn't.

Student: Yeah, but how far do you go down?

Stacy: See ... Well, that's why you just do ... it'd just be those top ...

Student: What's the top ...?

Stacy: Hitler and his five or six men.

Stacy, would I gather that you agree with Manny that if somebody really enjoyed doing it and wanted to do it, 'doing it' meaning hurting, killing, torture; if they really wanted to do it and enjoyed it, those people should be punished.

Stacy: Yeah, they should, but you can't decide, you can't tell who really wanted to be ...

OK, someone who did it reluctantly, you shouldn't punish them, is that right?

Stacy: Right.

Suppose you and I are in the mafia. And suppose you and I are in the mafia, and I order you to kill ... uh, Katherine. OK?

Stacy: OK.

You happen to be ... uh, acquaintances with Kathy, and you don't want to do it, but I order you to do it. And, in fact you do, you carry it out because I tell ya, if you don't do it, I'm going to pull your fingernails out, and your toenails, and I'm going to shoot off your kneecap. And so you kill Katherine. Now, along comes Brad. He's a policeman. And he arrests you for killing Katherine, OK? And you say, "I didn't want to do it. My toenails were going to go out, my fingernails were going to go out, my kneecaps were going to go." Should we say, "You're home free, Stacy."?

Stacy: No, I'd lead them to you, is what I'd do.

So, they're going to arrest me?

Stacy: Yeah.

Alright. Now should you be arrested? Should we just say, "I'm sorry, Stacy." Should you be arrested? Should you be punished?

Stacy: Yeah, I should be arrested but maybe not .... You should be *really* punished, yeah.

Really punished?

Stacy: Yeah.

Should you be punished too?

Stacy: I'm in the Mafia, I shouldn't be in the Mafia.

So anybody who is in the camp who does these deeds because even though they did it because they did not want to do them they should also be held responsible and punished.

Stacy: You can't. There are too many of them. It's stooping to the Nazi's level by killing, by punishing all these people.

So will you let some of them go free because you can't punish all?

Stacy: Right, you can't, you can't punish a whole entire group of people that's like millions of people.

Why can't you do that?

Stacy: Because it's doing what they were doing to the Jewish people.

We'll get some disagreement here. Jeannette?

Jeannette: If you can't call a person responsible for making a decision, where does that leave society?

What kind of decision?

Jeannette: They made a decision to follow the order.

And you are saying we can't be responsible for a major ...

(voices)

Oh, I'm sorry. Oh you have to ... the front row is answering ... why must you hold them responsible?

(Laughter.)

Jeannette: Because they made the decision, they did it.

But what if they did it under duress?

Jeannette: They could've ... faced the responsibilities, you have to face responsibilities either way, you can't just do something.

Suppose, suppose I say to you, "Jeannette you, I want you to uh pull Bill's eyeballs out of his head. (Laughter) And if you don't do that, I am going to kill you, Jeannette."

Jeannette: I am responsible.

Are you responsible?

Jeannette: I'm responsible.

You're going to die!

Jeannette: I'm responsible!

So we should punish you because you do this deed even though you would have died if you hadn't done it?

Jeannette: No! it's still my decision.

Student: Yeah.

Stacy: But they, what if they were drafted into being in the Nazi camps and they were forced to do that — and they did not want to do that?

Student: How did they force ...

Stacy: Just like we had American troops in Vietnam, they were killing people.

Student: And they were drafted. A lot of people ran, though ....

Student: A lot of people didn't.

Time out! Time out, we have a real important discussion and that is the issue of the people who — what about the people who did not willingly do it, who did it because of orders, are they or are they not responsible?

Student: No.

Jody: I agree with Jeannette. They are responsible, they made the decision to do it, — they have a choice but some people, I'm sure, made the choice to die rather than to do this. I'm sure there were people that did that. And that was their decision because they could not go through with the order. You can't live with that. They went through it and made that decision. They have to live with what they did and they have to be punished for it because they took the lives of other people.

Wait a minute, no, no, no, no, no. Do you know the story of Patty Hearst at all? I know its ancient history to you. She was kidnapped by a group call the SLA. She was brainwashed and she was beaten. She was abused and eventually she joins the group and they rob a bank and she had a part in the bank robbery up in Carmichael, California, it's up near Sacramento. And in the process of doing that — after she is freed, she argued that during the bank robbery they had a gun on her and she didn't have any choice.

Now, she's arrested for the bank robbery and she's going to be put on trial. Is she responsible for her acts in that bank robbery Jody? Does she go free or do you punish her for the bank robbery?

Jody: That's a hard question. (yeah, no fair) Was it proven that there was a gun on her?

Yes, they had tape. It was not clear whether there were bullets in the gun or so forth. There is tape of a gun.

Jody: Well, if there's really proof, that's different.

What do you mean that's different?

Jody: Well, than someone who was a Nazi.

No, no, no, let's not get to Nazis yet. You're on a jury, Jody, are you going to vote guilty or innocent?

Jody: Innocent.

Why?

Jody: Because there was proof that she was forced; it wasn't a threat that something was going to happen. She was forced.

Did she do it under threat of her own life?

Student: Yes.

All right. Leslie here is a Nazi. OK, Gayle is just a neutral. Leslie tells Gayle if you don't kill Ariel the Jew, you will be punished. Gayle kills Ariel the Jew. The reason she does, is, because Leslie told her to do it.

Jody: No, I guess.

Leslie held the gun on her. Are we not going to punish Gayle — Gayle "Patty Hearst"?

Jody: No. I would probably have to say that she would have to be responsible.

Patty Hearst? Patty Hearst?

Jody: Yeah.

Because you see the inconsistency with the previous position and you want to hold the position that in fact everyone who does things even under orders and compulsion are responsible for what they do. Is that right? Would I be clear that in any future argument with your parents, you will not argue a line that might say, "The reason I did that is because somebody else told me I had to do that." You'll never argue that?

Jody: Your parents always say, "But it was your decision."

And you agree to that.

Jody: And you don't have to listen to what everyone else says.

And you believe that.

Jody: Yeah.

And you will follow it?

Jennifer.

Jennifer: Um, I agree with Janet, but I think its conditional because ...

What is conditional?

Jennifer: Well, that, that the people are ultimately responsible for their actions because in the Patty Hearst case, she umm, it was a bank robbery, and that wasn't directly, I mean that was, — you're not supposed to steal people's money and that would affect people but it's not physically, its not physical pain and it's not, you know, killing them, and so I think they should of, um, punish all the people who are in the Nazi camp because they were responsible for — physical pain and uh their deaths.

Now let's see. Let's change it just slightly to make sure we understand. So far, we have pretty wide — all the leaders get punished, right? We had some disagreement on who in the camps will be punished and some of you think all the people involved in the camps and others think not quite all the people. Anybody beyond that? What about Germans who knew what was going on and did nothing to stop it?

Student: (many voices)

Student: It's too broad.

It's too broad?

Student: Yeah.

Is there anybody in the room right now who thinks that we should punish all the Germans who knew what was going on and did nothing to stop it. OK, so obviously you would not agree to punish Americans who knew about it, right? Or the British, right? So you're keeping your level of punishment to the leaders and those who are directly involved, and you have some disagreement on who is directly involved and should be punished. Have I got it right?

PART TWO

> *You're in the U.N. It's 1947. You have now been given the legal right, whether you believe it is the moral right or not, you have been given the legal right to decide what to do with Palestine. OK, we are not talking about moral. No, we are talking about legal. You are a country, you are going to have to vote on what to do with the state of Palestine. What are you going to do?*

Student: Vote for the Arabs.

> *For the Arabs. You are going to vote that the Arabs have — why?*

Student: Additionally, I would give the Jews a piece of Germany.

> *OK, OK, Would you today be somewhat sympathetic to a Palestinian who comes to you and says, "My land has been taken wrongly from me and I have been driven off my land by a people and by an organization for an act that I had no responsibility for." Would you be sympathetic to a Palestinian who said that?*

Jeannette: Yes.

> *What would you say to the Palestinian, other than to say that I am sympathetic?*

Jeannette: I would say what my Daddy always says to me, that life is not fair.

> *So the world is not fair and life is not fair. We do the best we can. Do the Palestinians have, in your mind, some right to oppose what was done to them?*

Jeannette: Yes.

> *Do they have the right to use force to try to, uh, change what was done to them?*

Jeannette: They have a right.

> *In your mind?*

Jeannette: Yes, they do.

> *How do we get out of this dilemma?*

Jeannette: I don't know.

> *It is a real dilemma isn't it?*

Jeannette: Yeah.

> *Anybody else? John.*

John: No wait, I want to clarify a couple of things first.

> *OK.*

John: OK, the land that is, uh, that is in question, Palestine, was once the Jews'. If we go back far enough ... it was their holy land, right?

Yes. Correct.

John: And the Arabs drove them off a long time ago.

Well, actually the Romans drove them off.

John: The Romans drove them off, OK, but they've had a history of persecution, so isn't that ...

Student: The Jews?

John: Isn't that — yeah the Jews — isn't that the significance of giving them that piece of land instead of a piece of Germany is because that's originally theirs and they have pride and heritage there and they were driven off ...?

John, would you then argue the proposition that anybody who, any group of people, who have been persecuted and driven off their land, at some time in the future should be given that land back?

John: No.

That's not your proposition?

John: That's a Halstead generalization.

Well, I thought that's what you said; did I not get what you said correct?

John: I'm talking about the Jews specifically.

All right, explain it to me again, let's see if I hear it right.

John: OK, the Jews have been burned all through history.

All right.

John: You agree with that?

Yes, I do.

John: OK, and you agree that that was once their holy land.

I agree to that.

John: So, if in fact, the UN decides to give them a piece of land, which they did, the significance of giving them that land in contrast to giving them a piece of Germany is because it was once theirs and it was, it had some significance to them, in fact we're trying to compensate for 'em, not just push them into the corner, OK.

I agree to all that, now are you saying to me that you personally, if you had been a delegate in the UN would have voted to give a portion of Palestine to the Jewish people because of that argument?

John: Correct.

Is that an argument that is valid for any other group of people or is that argument only valid to the Jewish people?

John: It's, yeah, it depends.

Well, I ... suppose ... suppose I can find, John, suppose I can find another group of people who have been persecuted for a good portion of their life and had their land taken away by another group and now these people are trying to find someplace to live where they in fact can live a fruitful life, would you in fact agree to those people getting their land back?

John: Yeah.

All right, let's talk about the American Indian. Were the American Indians persecuted?

Class: Yes.

Were they driven off their land?

Class: Yes.

Were they put in reservations?

Class: Yes.

Have we taken their land away from them?

Class: Yes.

John: And I'm not saying that's right.

Are the, are the American Indians today that are alive basically on land areas where they are not able to survive fruitfully as a people? Should they be given their land back?

Student: Some.

John: Seems logical, I mean ...

Am I correct then that, John, that you're arguing, that you would agree that we in the United States should give this land back to the American Indian because of all those circumstances?

John: They should get something, in proportion to the size of their people.

They should get something, something of the United States ... and they should get something that is worthwhile and fruitful and that they can live and survive not some junk land down in the desert ... is that correct?

Class: Yes.

Would you agree perhaps maybe Santa Clara Valley? Would you personally, John, be willing to move out of your house and turn it over to the Indians?

Class laughs.

Student: Give Ohio.

> *Well, that's too easy for John to give away Ohio. Would you give away your home?*

John: I wouldn't be happy about it.

> *No you wouldn't, you would feel wronged if it happened, right?*

John: Right.

> *Would you, would you, if the government came down and said "John Rimenshutter and family, your house has just been given away to an Indian couple". Would you feel right in taking some force against that Indian couple at a later time to get your house back?*

John: Yeah.

Laurel: I wouldn't, I would ...

> *Laurel, you wouldn't what?*

Laurel: I wouldn't.

> *You wouldn't what?*

Laurel: I wouldn't feel comfortable using force to get my house back from the Indian couple. I would go to the government.

John: Well, yeah.

Laurel: And, and .... Well, but the question was, would you feel force ...

> *Laurel, you're in the UN. Would you vote to give a piece of that land to the Jewish people, or would you vote to give it to the Arabs in its entirety?*

Laurel: I really ... I want to be able to feel good about giving that homeland to the Jews.

> *All right.*

Laurel: I think they deserve it ... and I think I would vote no because the Arabs are there and it is Arab land.

> *So then what do we do with the Jews? It's 1946, 1947.*

Laurel: And you know a lot of the time ... Jody was telling me a lot of Jews didn't want to go back to their homes that they've been ... they didn't want to go back to their German homes.

> *Is that rightfully so? Would you, would you agree that there is logical reason why they would not want to go back?*

Laurel: Absolutely, oh absolutely ....

So what do we do with them maybe we've got thousands maybe hundreds of thousands of Jews who were in the camps they don't want to go back to Germany, they don't want to go back to Poland?

Laurel: Maybe ...

John has raised what is actually true, they want to go back to where is their historical place.

Laurel: Right, right.

You do not believe that's right, because the majority of the people who live there are Arabs now. So what are we going to do with the Jews?

Laurel: Somehow, uh ...

It's a heck of a dilemma, isn't it?

Laurel: Somehow, split up Israel so that, um, the Arabs, but yeah, but, but they didn't do that totally, I mean a lot of, there's like what, in Lebanon there's a lot of — there's many camps up there for, for ...

Palestinians.

Laurel: Palestinians and I don't think that that's fair.

OK.

Laurel: And, um, I think somehow both sides ...

In trying to correct one injustice have we created another injustice?

Laurel: Yes!

And do we, do we have in the Middle East, two groups of people who believe rightfully so, that they have been injured, and that there is a solution to their problem and that is that the solution to their problem, for both of them, is to have the land of Palestine? Now the Palestinians feel injured because their land was given away and their solution is to give them back Palestine, and the Jews feel that they have been injured historically and specifically the Holocaust and the solution to them is to give them Palestine. Haven't we got a heck of a dilemma on our hands? Yeah, Katherine.

Katherine: Well, not all of the Jews that live in Israel are survivors of the Holocaust.

I agree.

Laurel: I mean they're from, it's their homeland for people from all around the world so now they can practice freely and have a place, a place to be without being persecuted. And, when I was there, the feeling is that they are more than willing to live with the Arabs only as long as they can just be there, but, the Arabs, it seems that the Arabs only they want to be in there and they don't want — they don't — they aren't willing to live with the Jews.

✦✦ Chapter 21

Strategies:
Thirty–Five Dimensions of Critical Thinking

with A. J. A. Binker

Abstract
The following strategies, originally developed to help teachers remodel lessons and redesign instruction in the Critical Thinking Handbook *series, indicate how critical thinking principles can be transformed into teaching strategies. The various strategies overlap; each illuminates a dimension of critical thought.*

✦ *Introduction*

$\mathcal{T}$he purpose of this chapter is to illustrate how the concept of the autonomous, precise, fairminded thinker can be translated into classroom activities and discussions. We have broken the global concept of critical thinking down into 35 aspects or instructional strategies. Each strategy section has three parts. The "principle" provides the theory of critical thinking on which the strategy is based and links the strategy to the ideal of the fairminded critical thinker. We could have labeled it "What the Critical Thinker Does, and Why". We included it because we are convinced that one cannot do or teach critical thinking well without understanding why one should honor principles of critical thought, and to help overcome the tendency in education to treat insights and skills in isolation from each other. The "application" provides examples of when and how the strategy can be used in the classroom. Our lists of possible questions are often larger and more detailed here than in the remodels, and sometimes our remarks are general. We tried to provide some idea of when the principle could apply, to describe ways texts and some standard instructional practices can undermine or interfere with students learning the principle, and some initial suggestions to further illustrate and clarify the principle and get you started developing your own techniques for teaching it.

Here is an example. The thirteenth strategy on our list, **S–13,** is called "Clarifying Issues, Conclusions, or Beliefs". The principle that underlies it is briefly characterized as follows:

Principle

The more completely, clearly, and accurately an issue or statement is formulated, the easier and more helpful the discussion of its settlement or verification. Given a clear statement of an issue, and prior to evaluating conclusions or solutions, it is important to recognize what is required to settle it. And before we can agree or disagree with a claim, we must understand it clearly. It makes no sense to say "I don't know what you mean, but I deny it, whatever it is." Critical thinkers make sure that understanding precedes judgment. They routinely distinguish facts from interpretations, opinions, judgments, or theories. They seek to express themselves clearly and precisely.

Following the principle is an explanation of some of the ways we might teach for it:

Application

Teachers should encourage children to slow down and reflect before coming to conclusions. When discussing an issue, the teacher can ask students first, *"How would you describe the problem?"* Children should be encouraged to continually reformulate the issue in light of new information. They should be encouraged to see how the first statement of the issue or problem is rarely best (that is, most accurate, clear, and complete) and that they are in a better position to settle a question *after* they have developed as clear a formulation as possible.

When talking about an issue, teachers can have children discuss such questions as,*"Do we understand the issue? Do we know how to get an answer? Have we stated it fairly? Are the words clear? Are we evaluating anything? What? Why? How can we get the evidence we need?"*

When a statement is unclear, the class can discuss such questions as, *"How can we know whether or not this is it? Are any words or phrases unclear? Is there a clearer way to say this? Is there a more accurate way to say this? Can it be rephrased? Do the different ways of putting it say the same thing?"*

This strategy provides a way of remodelling lessons that focus on "Fact/ Opinion," or which have vague passages of text.

The reader should keep in mind the connection between the principles and applications on the one hand, and the character traits of a fairminded critical thinker on the other. Our aim is not a set of disjointed skills, but an integrated, committed, thinking person. All of the pieces of the remodelling process — understanding what critical thinking is and why one should do it; breaking the concept into teachable components; inventing ways to help students learn and practice critical thought; evaluating lessons; and improving them — all fit together. These activities are interdependent. Figuring out how to teach a particular principle helps you better understand what critical thinking is (and isn't). Analyzing and evaluating a lesson helps you see how critical thinking applies to particular situations. Clarifying the global concept of critical thinking helps you keep your focus on its most important features, and suggests ways of understanding and teaching specific principles and skills.

The strategies listed below are divided into three categories — one for the affective and two for the cognitive. This of course is not to imply that the cognitive dimension of critical thinking should be given twice as much emphasis. Indeed, the affective dimension is every bit as important to critical thinking. No one learns to think critically who is not motivated to do so. In any case, whatever dimension is emphasized, the other dimension should be integrated. We want students to continually use their emerging critical thinking skills and abilities in keeping with the critical spirit, and the critical spirit can be nurtured only when actually practicing critical thinking in some (cognitive) way. One cannot develop one's fairmindedness, for example, without actually thinking fairmindedly. One cannot develop one's intellectual independence without actually thinking independently. This is true of all the essential critical thinking traits, values, or dispositions. They are developmentally embedded in thinking itself. In teaching for critical thinking in a strong sense, the affective dimension of thinking is fully as important as the cognitive.

The List of Strategies

Affective Strategies

S-1   thinking independently

S-2   developing insight into egocentricity or sociocentricity

S-3   exercising fairmindedness

S-4   exploring thoughts underlying feelings and feelings underlying thoughts

S-5   developing intellectual humility and suspending judgment

S-6   developing intellectual courage

S-7   developing intellectual good faith or integrity

S-8   developing intellectual perseverance

S-9   developing confidence in reason

Cognitive Strategies — Macro-Abilities

S-10   refining generalizations and avoiding oversimplifications

S-11   comparing analogous situations: transferring insights to new contexts

S-12   developing one's perspective: creating or exploring beliefs, arguments, or theories

S-13   clarifying issues, conclusions, or beliefs

S-14   clarifying and analyzing the meanings of words or phrases

S-15   developing criteria for evaluation: clarifying values and standards

S-16   evaluating the credibility of sources of information

S-17   questioning deeply: raising and pursuing root or significant questions

S-18   analyzing or evaluating arguments, interpretations, beliefs, or theories

S-19   generating or assessing solutions

S-20   analyzing or evaluating actions or policies

S-21   reading critically: clarifying or critiquing texts

S-22   listening critically: the art of silent dialogue

S-23   making interdisciplinary connections

S-24   practicing Socratic discussion: clarifying and questioning beliefs, theories, or perspectives

S-25   reasoning dialogically: comparing perspectives, interpretations, or theories

S-26   reasoning dialectically: evaluating perspectives, interpretations, or theories

Cognitive Strategies — Micro-Skills

S-27   comparing and contrasting ideals with actual practice

S-28   thinking precisely about thinking: using critical vocabulary

S-29   noting significant similarities and differences

S-30   examining or evaluating assumptions

S-31   distinguishing relevant from irrelevant facts

S-32   making plausible inferences, predictions, or interpretations

S-33   giving reasons and evaluating evidence and alleged facts

S-34   recognizing contradictions

S-35   exploring implications and consequences

✦ *The Interdependence of Traits of Mind*

Just as the cognitive and affective dimensions are interdependent and intertwined, so also are the various individual strategies. For purposes of learning, we articulate separate principles and applications. In the beginning, the connections between them may be obscure. Nevertheless, eventually we begin to discover how progress with any one principle leads inevitably to other principles. To see this, let us look first at the individual strategies in the affective dimension.

Affective strategies are interdependent because the intellectual traits they imply develop best in concert with each other. Consider intellectual humility. To become aware of the limits of our knowledge, we need the courage to face our own prejudices and ignorance. To discover our own prejudices in turn, we often must empathize with and reason within points of view toward which we are hostile. To achieve this end, we must typically persevere over a period of time, for learning to empathically enter a point of view against which we are biased takes time and significant effort. That effort will not seem justified unless we have the confidence in reason to believe we will not be "tainted" or "taken in" by whatever is false or misleading in the opposing viewpoint. Furthermore, merely believing we can survive serious consideration of an "alien" point of view is not enough to motivate most of us to consider them seriously. We must also be motivated by an intellectual sense of justice. We must recognize an intellectual responsibility to be fair to views we oppose. We must feel obliged to hear them in their strongest form to ensure that we are not condemning them out of ignorance or bias on our part. At this point, we come full circle back to where we began: the need for intellectual humility.

To begin at another point, consider intellectual good faith or integrity. Intellectual integrity is clearly a difficult trait to develop. We are often motivated, generally without admitting to or being aware of this motivation, to set up inconsistent intellectual standards. Our egocentric or sociocentric tendencies make us ready to believe positive information about those we like, and negative information about those we dislike. We are likewise strongly inclined to believe what serves to justify our vested interest or validate our strongest desires. Hence, all humans have some innate mental tendencies to operate with double standards, which of course is paradigmatic of intellectual bad faith. Such modes of thinking often correlate quite well with getting ahead in the world, maximizing our power or advantage, and getting more of what we want.

Nevertheless, it is difficult to operate explicitly or overtly with a double standard. We therefore need to avoid looking at the evidence too closely. We need to avoid scrutinizing our own inferences and interpretations too carefully. At this point, a certain amount of intellectual arrogance is quite useful. I may assume, for example, that I know just what you're going to say (before you say it), precisely what you are really after (before the evidence demonstrates it), and what actually is going on (before I have studied the situation carefully). My intellectual arrogance may make it easier for me to avoid noticing the unjustifiable discrepancy between the standards I apply to you and the standards I apply to myself. Of course, if I don't have to empathize with you, that too makes it easier to avoid seeing my duplicity. I am also better positioned if I lack a keen need to be fair to your point of view. A little background fear of what I might discover if I seriously considered the consistency of my own judgments can be quite useful as well. In this case, my lack of intellectual integrity is supported by my lack of intellectual humility, empathy, and fairmindedness.

Going in the other direction, it will be difficult to use a double standard if I feel a responsibility to be fair to your point of view, see that this responsibility requires me to view things from your perspective empathically, and do so with some humility, recognizing I could be wrong, and you right. The more I dislike you personally, or feel wronged in the past by you or by others who share your way of thinking, the more pronounced in my character the trait of intellectual integrity and good faith must be to compel me to be fair.

✦ Distinguishing Macro-Abilities from Micro-Skills

Our reason for dividing cognitive strategies into macro-abilities and micro-skills is not to create a hard and fast line between the most elementary skills of critical thinking (the micro-skills) and the process of orchestrating those elementary skills, but rather to provide teachers with a way of thinking about two levels of learning. We use these two levels in most complex abilities. For intuitive examples, consider what is involved in learning to play the piano, learning to play good tennis, mastering ballet, or becoming a surgeon. In each of these areas, there is a level of skill learning which focuses on the most elementary of moves: for example, learning to practice the most elementary ballet positions at the bar, learning to play scales on the piano, or learning to hit various tennis strokes on the backboard. One must often return to this micro-level to ensure that one keeps the fundamentals well in hand. Nevertheless, dancing ballet is not practicing at the bar. Playing the piano is not simply playing scales. And hitting tennis balls against a backboard is not playing tennis. One must move to the macro level for the real thing. So, too, in critical thinking, students have to learn the fundamentals: what an assumption is, what an implication is, what an inference and conclusion are, what it is to isolate an issue, what it is to offer reasons or evidence in support of what one says, how to identify a contradiction or a vague sentence.

But thinking critically in any actual situation is typically doing something more complex and holistic than this. Rarely in thinking critically do we do just one elementary thing. Usually we have to integrate or make use of a variety of elementary critical thinking skills. For example, when we are reading (a macro-ability) we have to make use of a variety of critical thinking micro-skills, and we have to use them in concert with each other. We might begin by reflecting on the implications of a story or book title. We might then begin to read the preface or introduction and start to identify some of the basic issues or objectives the book or story is focused on. As we proceed, we might begin to identify particular sentences that seem vague to us. We might consider various interpretations of them. As we move along, we would doubt-less dip into our own experience for possible examples of what the author is saying. Or we might begin to notice assumptions the author is making. We would be making all of these individual moves as part of one integrated activity: the attempt to make sense of, to follow, what we are reading. As always, the whole is greater than and more important than the parts. We do not read to practice our critical thinking micro-skills; we use our critical thinking micro-skills in order to read, or better, in order to read clearly, pre-cisely, and accurately.

Standard instruction and many approaches to teaching critical thinking or thinking skills often fail here. They over-emphasize drill in micro-skills and neglect their use. Being able to find assumptions only when someone tells you to is of little value. Articulating and evaluating assumptions helps one only if one does it when appropriate. This requires thinkers to notice for themselves when a questionable assumption is made. Macro abilities cannot be taught through drill. They must be developed and practiced in the context of some reasoning. Keep this principle of interdependence in mind as you read through the various strategies.

✦ *Have We Left Out Any Important Strategies?*

As you begin to use the principles of critical thinking we have formulated in your teaching, you may wonder whether our list is complete. You may wonder, in other words, whether we may have left out any important critical thinking principles. The answer to this is "Yes and no." "No" in the sense that all of the important critical thinking principles are at least implicit in the ones we have formulated. "Yes" in the sense that some of what is merely implicit might properly be made explicit.

To exemplify this point, consider these insightful suggestions which we recently received from Rex Dalzell of New Zealand.

> With respect to your list of strategies, I would like to suggest, with due intellectual humility, that the list could be usefully expand-ed by the addition of a further four strategies as follows:

AFFECTIVE STRATEGIES

Developing Intellectual Curiosity

> In the affective area, I believe the development of an attitude of intellectual curiosity is of prime importance. Although there are ele-ments of this dimension in other characteristics (e.g., independence

of thought, intellectual perseverance, etc.), and while the whole notion of critical thinking implies the presence of this attribute, it seems to me sufficiently important to warrant an explicit category of its own.

Critical thinkers need to be curious about their environment, they need to seek explanations of apparent discrepancies and they need to speculate as to possible causes of these discrepancies. In short, they need to be predisposed to wonder about the world around them. This sense of wonder, this intellectual curiosity that seeks explanations and proffers solutions, is something that can be and needs to be encouraged and developed. For this reason I believe it would be helpful to include it as a separate stand-alone category in any overall schema.

Developing Social Sensitivity

In addition to developing insight into egocentricity and sociocentricity so that desirable levels of self-awareness are achieved it is also necessary, I believe, for critical thinkers to develop a high level of social sensitivity. By this I mean that critical thinkers need to become sensitive to the social situation they find themselves in so that they can judge effectively when it is and when it is not appropriate to exercise, at least overtly, their critical thinking skills. It is my experience that with some critical thinkers, particularly the "born again, evangelical" variety, they are quite insensitive to the social milieu in which they find themselves. Without due regard for the sensitivity of the situation, they launch forth with their battery of critical thinking skills and often destroy any possibility of a productive outcome.

In addition to being able to recognize the limits of their knowledge and being able to suspend judgment, critical thinkers also need to know when to put their skills into operation and when and how to articulate the results. Listing social sensitivity as a separate category would, I believe, be useful in helping critical thinkers develop this skill.

COGNITIVE STRATEGIES: MACRO-ABILITIES

Observing Critically

In addition to reading critically and listening critically, I believe it is very important for critical thinkers to learn how to observe critically. Intellectual curiosity is a necessary but not sufficient condition for critical observation to occur. Critical thinkers need to "see" as well as "look at" what is in their environment. They need to be trained to see the details of their surroundings, physical as well as social, and to accurately recall just exactly what they have seen. Most, if not all, of the micro-cognitive skills depend on this critical observation as a basis for productive application. As with intellectual curiosity and social sensitivity it seems to me that critical observation is a skill that merits recognition in its own right.

Expressing Precisely

While precision is an integral feature of all critical thinking and is highlighted by such macro skills as clarifying issues, conclusions, or beliefs, clarifying and analyzing the meanings of words and phrases, the overall emphasis is on precision of analysis rather than on precision of expression. While precision of expression is implied in many of the listed skills — how else for example, could one engage successfully in Socratic discussion or reasoned dialogue or dialectic without such precision? — it seems to me that it would be helpful to list it as a separate skill. If critical thinkers are not able to express themselves with precision then their overall effectiveness is greatly reduced.

You may decide to add these four principles to your personal list, even though we received them too late to incorporate them formally in this volume. In any case, it would be quite instructive to try to fill out these descriptions and write an "application section" for each of them. Keep this awareness alive as you begin to work out your own unique application of critical thinking principles.

Note About Applications

The purpose of the following strategy list is to further clarify the basic principles of critical thinking, but not necessarily to provide applications of each strategy for each grade level. Teachers should experiment with the applications that seem appropriate and plausible for their students. Once you understand a range of applications (some at your grade level, some not), you will be able to begin to think up applications of your own. So do not assume that every application we provide is appropriate for your class. Experiment with an assortment of strategies and you will end up with a wide variety that works for your students.

S-1 Thinking Independently

Principle

Critical thinking is autonomous thinking, thinking for oneself. Many of our beliefs are acquired at an early age, when we have a strong tendency to form beliefs for irrational reasons (because we want to believe, because we are rewarded for believing). Critical thinkers use critical skills and insights to reveal and eradicate beliefs to which they cannot rationally assent. In formulating new beliefs, critical thinkers do not passively accept the beliefs of others; rather, they analyze issues themselves, reject unjustified authorities, and recognize the contributions of justified authorities. They thoughtfully form principles of thought and action; they do not mindlessly accept those presented to them. Nor are they unduly influenced by the language of another. If they find that a set of categories or distinctions is more appropriate than that suggested by another, they will use it. Recognizing that categories serve human purposes, they use those categories which best serve their purpose at the time. They are not limited by accepted ways of doing things. They evaluate both goals and how to achieve them. They do not accept as true, or reject as false, beliefs they do not understand. They are not easily manipulated.

Independent thinkers strive to incorporate all known relevant knowledge and insight into their thought and behavior. They strive to determine for themselves when information is relevant, when to apply a concept, or when to make use of a skill. They are self-monitoring: they catch their own mistakes; they don't need to be told what to do every step of the way.

Application

A critical education respects the autonomy of the student. It appeals to rationality. Students should be encouraged to discover information and use their knowledge, skills and insights to think for themselves. Merely giving students "facts" or telling them "the right way" to solve a problem interferes with students' critiquing and modifying pre-existing beliefs with new knowledge.

Rather than having students discuss only those ideas mentioned in their texts, the teacher can have them brainstorm ideas and argue among themselves, for instance, about problems and solutions.

Before reading a section of text that refers to a map, chart, time-line, or graph, students could examine and discuss it.

Students could develop their own categories instead of being provided with them. "Types of Literature" lessons could be remodelled so that students group and discuss writings they have read, entertaining different ways to classify them. Students can classify animals before reading zoological classification systems in their texts.

Rather than asking students to place objects into pre-existing categories, for instance, the teacher can encourage students to form their own categories. Students can then discuss the reasons they had for forming each category. When different students have used different sets of categories to form groups, the teacher can ask such questions as: *When would this set of categories be most useful? When would that set be best? Why would someone else make different groupings?*

In math, instead of following directions in their texts, students can be given a task to perform or problem to solve in small groups. The class can then discuss their solutions and then compare them to what is in their text.

When a text tries to do too much of the students' thinking for them, it can be examined in depth. *"Why does the text tell you about this? Why do the authors think this (concept, skill, procedure, step) is worth knowing? Why does the text tell you to do this? What would happen if you didn't?"*

When giving written assignments, those assignments should provide many opportunities for the student to exercise independent judgment: in gathering and assembling information, in analyzing and synthesizing it, and in formulating and evaluating conclusions. Have students discuss how to organize their points in essays.

In science, students could put their own headings on charts or graphs they make, or decide what kind of graph would be most illuminating. Students can design their own experiments rather than follow directions in their texts.

Students could review material themselves, rather than relying on their texts for summaries and review questions. The teacher could routinely ask students, *"What are the most important points covered in the passage (chapter, story, etc.)?"* as a discussion beginner. The class could brainstorm about what they learned when studying a lesson, unit, or story. Only after they have exhausted their memories can the teacher try to elicit any crucial points neglected.

When discussing specific countries and periods of history, have students look at and discuss some combination of political, population distribution, physical, historical, linguistic, or land use maps before reading their texts. *"What can we tell about this country by looking at this map? What areas does it have? What kind of climate? Where do most of the people live? Why do you think they might live there? Where is the land easier to live on? Could that be why so many people live there? What languages do they speak? Who else in the world speaks that language? What can we infer from the fact that these people speak the same language as those over there? Were they in contact with each other at some point? What countries surround this country? What do we know about those countries? Judging by the physical map, would there have been much travel between this country and that, or would travel have been hard?* After students have made educated guesses, the class could discuss how they could verify their predictions. Groups of students could be assigned specific points to research. After studying their texts and hearing the results of the research, students could review the points made in this discussion, distinguishing things they were able to figure out from what they didn't know and what they were wrong about, so that the next time their predictions can be better qualified.

S-2 Developing Insight into Egocentricity or Sociocentricity

Principle

Egocentricity is the confusion of immediate perception with reality. It manifests itself as an inability or unwillingness to consider others' points of view, to accept ideas or facts which would conflict with gratification of desire. In the extreme, it is characterized by a need to be right about everything, a lack of interest in consistency and clarity, an all or nothing attitude ("I am 100% right; you are 100% wrong."), and a lack of self-consciousness of one's own thought processes. The egocentric individual is more concerned with the *appearance* of truth, fairness, and fairmindedness, than with actually *being* correct, fair, or fairminded. Egocentricity is the opposite of critical thought.

As people are socialized, egocentricity partly evolves into sociocentricity. Egocentric identification extends to groups. The individual goes from *"I* am right!" to *"We* are right!" To put this another way, people find that they can often best satisfy their egocentric desires through a group. "Group think" results when people egocentrically attach themselves to a group. One can see this in both children and adults: My daddy is better than your daddy! My school (religion, country, race, etc.) is better than yours.

If egocentricity and sociocentricity are the disease, self-awareness is the cure. In cases in which their own egocentric commitments are not supported, few people accept another's egocentric reasoning. Most can identify the socio-centricity of members of opposing groups. Yet when we are thinking egocen-trically or sociocentrically, it seems right to us (at least at the time). Our belief in our own rightness is easier to maintain because we suppress the faults in our thinking. We automatically hide our egocentricity from our-selves. We fail to notice when our behavior contradicts our self-image. We base our reasoning on false assumptions we are unaware of making. We fail to make relevant distinctions of which we are otherwise aware, and able to make (when making such distinctions does not prevent us from getting what we want). We deny or conveniently "forget" facts inconsistent with our con-clusions. We often misunderstand or distort what others say.

The solution, then, is to reflect on our reasoning and behavior; to make our assumptions explicit, critique them, and, when they are false, stop making them; to apply the same concepts in the same ways to ourselves and others; to consider every relevant fact, and to make our conclusions consistent with the evidence; and to listen carefully and openmindedly to those with whom we disagree. We can change egocentric tendencies when we see them for what they are: irrational and unjust. Therefore, the development of students' awareness of their egocentric and sociocentric patterns of thought is a crucial part of education in critical thinking.

Application

Although everyone has egocentric, sociocentric, and critical (or fairminded) tendencies to some extent, the purpose of education in critical thinking is to help students move away from egocentricity and sociocentricity, toward increasingly critical thought. Texts usually neglect obstacles to rationality, content to point out or have students point out irrationality and injustice. We recommend that students repeatedly discuss *why* people think irrationally and act unfairly.

The teacher can facilitate discussions of egocentric or sociocentric thought and behavior whenever such discussions seem relevant. Such discussions can be used as a basis for having students think about their own egocentric or sociocentric tendencies. The class can discuss conditions under which people are most likely to be egocentric and how egocentricity interferes with our ability to think and listen. By discussing what people think (and how they think) when they are being egocentric and sociocentric, students can begin to recognize common patterns of egocentric thought. The class can discuss some of the common false assumptions we all make at times (e.g., "Anyone who disapproves of anything I do is wrong or unfair. I have a right to have everything I want. Truth is what I want it to be. Different is bad. Our group (country, school, language, etc.) is better than any other.") Teachers can also have students point out the contradictions of egocentric attitudes. ("When I use something of yours without permission, it is 'borrowing'; when you use something of mine, it is 'stealing.' Taking something without asking is O.K. Taking something without asking is wrong.") Sometimes story characters illustrate egocentricity.

The most real and immediate form of sociocentricity students experience is in the mini-society of their peers. Student attitudes present a microcosm of the patterns which exist on a larger scale in societies. All of your students share some attitudes which are sociocentric. Furthermore, students divide themselves into "subcultures" or cliques, each of which is narrower than the school-wide "culture". Honest and realistic exploration of these phenomena allows students to clarify and evaluate the ways in which "group think" limits them.

Often texts attempt to discourage sociocentricity by encouraging tolerance — asking students to agree that people whose ways are different are not necessarily wrong. Yet, by keeping discussion general and not introducing specific advantages of different ways, students are left with a vague sense that they should be tolerant, rather than a clear sense that others have ways worth knowing about and learning from.

Some texts inadvertently foster sociocentricity by giving only the U.S. or European side of issues, treating rationalizations as truth, or presenting some groups in a distinctly negative light. The teacher could encourage students to recognize sociocentric bias, reconstruct and consider other views of current and historical issues, and discuss how to avoid thinking sociocentrically.

Texts include many subtle forms of sociocentricity, displaying a narrowly European or American perspective in word choice. For example, a society might be described as "isolated" rather than "isolated from contact with Europeans."

Before beginning study of another culture, the teacher could elicit students' ideas of that group, including stereotypes and misconceptions. Ask, *"What are these people like? What do you think of when you think of them? How have you seen them portrayed in movies and on T.V.?"* After study, students could evaluate these ideas in light of what they have learned, and why they had them. *"Remember what you said about these people before we studied them? Which of our original believes were false or misleading? Why did we think that way? Where did we get these ideas? How do people come to think they know what other people are like before they know anything about them? What false beliefs might other people have about us? Why?"*

S-3 Exercising Fairmindedness

Principle

To think critically about issues, we must be able to consider the strengths and weaknesses of opposing points of view; to imaginatively put ourselves in the place of others in order to genuinely understand them; to overcome our egocentric tendency to identify truth with our immediate perceptions or long-standing thought or belief. This trait correlates with the ability to reconstruct accurately the viewpoints and reasoning of others and to reason from premises, assumptions, and ideas other than our own. This trait also correlates with the willingness to remember occasions when we were wrong in the past despite an intense conviction that we were right, as well as the ability to imagine our being similarly deceived in a case at hand. Critical thinkers realize the unfairness of judging unfamiliar ideas until they fully understand them.

The world consists of many societies and peoples with many different points of view and ways of thinking. In order to develop as reasonable persons we need to enter into and think within the frameworks and ideas of different peoples and societies. We cannot truly understand the world if we think about it only from one viewpoint, as Americans, as Italians, or as Soviets.

Furthermore, critical thinkers recognize that their behavior affects others, and so consider their behavior from the perspective of those others.

Application

The teacher can encourage students to show reciprocity when disputes arise or when the class is discussing issues, evaluating the reasoning of story characters, or discussing people from other cultures.

When disputes naturally arise in the course of the day, the teacher can ask students to state one another's positions. Students should be given an opportunity to correct any misunderstanding of their positions. The teacher can then ask students to explain why their fellow student might see the issue differently than they do. *"What is Sue angry about? Why does that make her mad? Sue, is that right?"*

Students can be encouraged to consider evidence and reasons for positions they disagree with, as well as those with which they agree. For example, have students consider positions from their parents' or siblings' points of view. *"Why doesn't your mother want you to ...? Why does she think it's bad for you (wrong, etc.)? What does she think will happen?"*

Rather then always having students argue their points of view, call on a student who doesn't have a position on the issue under discussion — that is still thinking things through. Help that student clarify the uncertainty. *"What makes sense about what each side said? What seems wrong? What aren't you sure about?"*

Although texts often have students consider a subject or issue from a second point of view, discussion is brief, rather than extended, and no attempt is made to have students integrate insights gained by considering multiple perspectives. If students write a dialogue about an issue from opposing points of view, or contrast a story character's reasoning with an opposing point of view, or role play discussions, the teacher can have them directly compare and evaluate different perspectives.

When the class is discussing different cultures the teacher can encourage students to consider *why* people choose to do things differently or why other people think their ways are best. For example, ask, *"What would be some advantages to arranged marriages? Why might some people prefer that system to ours? What problems would it solve or lessen?"*

Students can be reminded of, and analyze, times that many members of a group or the class contributed something toward finding or figuring out an answer, solving a problem, or understanding a complex situation.

The class can discuss how hard it sometimes can be to be fairminded.

S-4 Exploring Thoughts Underlying Feelings and Feelings Underlying Thoughts

Principle

Although it is common to separate thought and feeling as though they were independent opposing forces in the human mind, the truth is that virtually all human feelings are based on some level of thought and virtually all thought generative of some level of feeling. To think with self-understanding and insight, we must come to terms with the intimate connections between thought and feeling, reason and emotion. Critical thinkers realize that their feelings are their response (but not the only possible, or even necessarily the most reasonable response) to a situation. They know that their feelings would be different if they had a different understanding or interpretation of that situation. They recognize that thoughts and feelings, far from being different kinds of "things", are two aspects of their responses. Uncritical thinkers see little or no relationship between their feelings and their thoughts, and so escape responsibility for their thoughts, feelings, and actions. Their own feelings often seem unintelligible to them.

When we feel sad or depressed, it is often because we are interpreting our situation in an overly negative or pessimistic light. We may be forgetting to consider positive aspects of our life. We can better understand our feelings by asking ourselves "How have I come to feel this way? How am I looking at the situation? To what conclusion have I come? What is my evidence? What assumptions am I making? What inferences am I making? Are they sound inferences? Are there other possible ways to interpret this situation?" We can learn to seek patterns in our assumptions, and so begin to see the unity behind our separate emotions. Understanding oneself is the first step toward self-control and self-improvement. This self-understanding requires that we understand our feelings and emotions in relation to our thoughts, ideas, and interpretations of the world.

Application

Whenever a class discusses someone's feelings (such as that of a character in a story), the teacher can ask students to consider what the person might be thinking to have that feeling in that situation. *"Why does he feel this way? How is he interpreting his situation? What led him to that conclusion? Would you have felt the same if you had been in his circumstances? Why or why not? What accounts for the difference? What could he have thought instead? Then how might he have felt?"*

This strategy can be used in the service of developing an intellectual sense of justice and courage. Students can discuss the thoughts underlying passionate commitment to personal or social change. *"Why was she willing to do this? Was she scared? What else did she feel that helped her ignore her fears? Why? How did she look at things that helped her endure and stick with it?"*

Students can discuss reasons for greed, fear, apathy, and other negative or hampering feelings. *"Why are people greedy? What thoughts underlie greed? Why do people feel they need more money? What does less money mean to them? Why? What assumptions underlie these attitudes? To what further thoughts do these attitudes lead?"*

When discussing a case of mixed feelings, the teacher could ask, *"What was he feeling? What else? (Encourage multiple responses.) What led to this feeling? That one? Are these beliefs consistent or contradictory? How could someone have contradictory responses to one situation? Is there a way he could reconcile these contradictions?"*

Students can also generalize about thoughts behind various emotions: behind fear, thoughts like — "This is dangerous. I may be harmed;" behind anger, thoughts like — "This is not right, not fair;" behind indifference, thoughts like — "This does not matter, no one can do anything about this;" behind relief, thoughts like — "Things are better now. This won't bother me anymore."

S-5 Developing Intellectual Humility and Suspending Judgment

Principle

Critical thinkers recognize the limits of their knowledge. They are sensitive to circumstances in which their native egocentrism is likely to function self-deceptively; they are sensitive to bias, prejudice, and limitations of their views. Intellectual humility is based on the recognition that one ought not claim more than one actually knows. It does not imply spinelessness or submissiveness. It implies the lack of intellectual pretentiousness, arrogance, or conceit. It implies insight into the foundations of one's beliefs: knowing what evidence one has, how one has come to believe, what further evidence one might look for or examine.

Thus, critical thinkers distinguish what they know from what they don't know. They are not afraid of saying "I don't know" when they are not in a position to be sure. They can make this distinction because they habitually ask themselves, "How could one know whether or not this is true?" To say "In this case I must suspend judgment until I find out x and y," does not make them anxious or uncomfortable. They are willing to rethink conclusions in the light of new knowledge. They qualify their claims appropriately.

Application

Texts and testing methods inadvertently foster intellectual arrogance. Most text writing says, "Here's the way it is. Here's what we know. Remember this, and you'll know it, too." Behind student learning, there is often little more thought than "It's true because my textbook said it's true." This often generalizes to, "It's true because I read it somewhere."

Teachers can take advantage of any situation in which students are not in a position to know, to encourage the habit of exploring the basis for their beliefs. When materials call on students to make claims for which they have insufficient evidence, we suggest the teacher encourage students to remember what is said in the materials but also to suspend judgment as to its truth. The teacher might first ask for the evidence or reasons for the claim and have students probe its strength. Students can be encouraged to explain what they would need to learn in order to be more certain. You might have students consider how reasonable people respond to gossip or the news on T.V. They hear what is said, remember what they have heard, but do not automatically believe it.

In exposing students to concepts within a field, we can help students to see how all concepts depend on other, more basic concepts and how each field of knowledge is based on fundamental assumptions which need to be examined, understood, and justified. We can help students to discover experiences in their own lives which help support or justify what a text says. We should always be willing to entertain student doubts about what a text says.

We can model intellectual humility by demonstrating a willingness to admit limits in our own knowledge and in human knowledge generally. Routinely qualify statements: "I believe," "I'm pretty sure that," "I doubt," "I suspect," "Perhaps," "I'm told," "It seems," etc. This trait can be encouraged by frequent discussion in which ideas new to the students are explored for evidence and support.

Students should discuss such experiences as getting a bad first impression, then learning they were wrong; feeling certain of something, then later changing their minds; thinking they knew something, then realizing they didn't understand it; thinking they had the best or only answer or solution, then hearing a better one.

The teacher can have students brainstorm questions they have *after* study of a topic. Students could keep question logs during the course of research projects, periodically recording their unanswered questions. Thus, they can come to see for themselves that even when they have learned what is always expected of them, there is more to learn.

S-6 Developing Intellectual Courage

Principle

To think independently and fairly, one must feel the need to face and fairly deal with unpopular ideas, beliefs, or viewpoints. The courage to do so arises from the recognition that ideas considered dangerous or absurd are sometimes rationally justified (in whole or in part) and that conclusions or beliefs inculcated in us are sometimes false or misleading. If we are to determine for ourselves which is which, we must not passively and uncritically accept what we have "learned". We need courage to admit the truth in some ideas considered dangerous and absurd, and the distortion or falsity in some ideas strongly held in our social group. It will take courage to be true to our own thinking, for honestly questioning our deeply held beliefs can be difficult and sometimes frightening, and the penalties for non-conformity are often severe.

Application

Intellectual courage is fostered through a consistently openminded atmosphere. Students should be encouraged to honestly consider or doubt any belief. Students who disagree with or doubt their peers or text should be given support. The teacher should raise probing questions regarding unpopular ideas which students have hitherto been discouraged from considering. The teacher should model intellectual courage by playing devil's advocate. *Why does this idea bother you?*

Texts often seem to suggest that standing up for one's beliefs is fairly easy; they ignore the difficulty of "doing the right thing." Students could discuss such questions as these: *"Why is it hard to go against the crowd? If everyone around you is sure of something, why is it hard to question it or disagree?*

When is it good to do so? When might you hesitate? When should you hesitate? Is it hard to question your own beliefs? Why?"

Students who have been habitually praised for uncritically accepting others' claims may feel the rug pulled out from under them for a while when expected to think for themselves. Students should be emotionally supported in these circumstances and encouraged to express the natural hesitancy, discomfort, or anxiety they may experience so they may work their way through these feelings. A willingness to consider unpopular beliefs develops by degrees. Teachers should exercise discretion beginning first with mildly unpopular rather than with extremely unpopular beliefs.

If, during the course of the year, an idea or suggestion which at first sounded "crazy" was proven valuable, students can later be reminded of it, and discuss it at length, and compare it to other events. *"How did this idea seem at first? Why? What made you change your mind about it? Have you had other similar experiences? Why did those ideas seem crazy or stupid at first?"*

S-7 Developing Intellectual Good Faith or Integrity

Principle

Critical thinkers recognize the need to be true to their own thought, to be consistent in the intellectual standards they apply, to hold themselves to the same rigorous standards of evidence and proof to which they hold others, to practice what they advocate for others, and to honestly admit discrepancies and inconsistencies in their own thought and action. They believe most strongly what has been justified by their own thought and analyzed experience. They have a commitment to bringing the self they are and the self they want to be together. People in general are often inconsistent in their application of standards once their ego is involved positively or negatively. When people like us, we tend to over-estimate their positive characteristics; when they dislike us, we tend to underrate them.

Application

Texts often inadvertently encourage the mental split between "school belief" and "real life" belief and between verbal or public belief and belief that guides action. There is an old saying to the effect that "They are good prophets who follow their own teachings." And sometimes parents say, "Do as I say, not as I do." There is often a lack of integrity in human life. Hypocrisy and inconsistency are common. As educators, we need to highlight the difficulties of being consistent in an often inconsistent world.

As teachers, we need to be sensitive to our own inconsistencies in the application of rules and standards, and we need to help students to explore their own. Peer groups often pressure students to judge in-group members less critically than out-group members. Students need opportunities to honestly assess their own participation in such phenomena.

Texts often preach. They unrealistically present moral perfection as easy when it is often not. They ask general and loaded questions ("Do you listen to other views? Is it important to treat others fairly?") to which students are likely to simply respond with a "Yes!" Such questions should be remodelled and the "dark side" explored. For example, ask, *"When have you found it difficult to listen to others?"* or *"Why are people often unfair?"*

Language Arts texts sometimes have students roundly criticize characters without taking into account the difficulties of living up to worthy ideals. Students should be encouraged to give more realistic assessments. *"Would you have done otherwise? Would it have been easy? Why or why not? Why do so few people do this?"*

Social studies texts are harsher judges of other societies than of ours. Students should evaluate their texts' consistency in evaluation. The teacher may have to help students to recognize this problem.

When evaluating or developing criteria for evaluation, have students assess both themselves and others, noting their tendency to favor themselves.

S-8 Developing Intellectual Perseverance

Principle

Becoming a more critical thinker is not easy. It takes time and effort. Critical thinking is reflective and recursive; that is, we often go back in our thoughts to previous problems to re-consider or re-analyze them. Critical thinkers are willing to pursue intellectual insights and truths in spite of difficulties, obstacles, and frustrations. They recognize the need to struggle with confusion and unsettled questions over an extended period of time in order to achieve deeper understanding and insight. They recognize that significant change requires patience and hard work. Important issues often require extended thought, research, struggle. Considering a new view takes time. Yet people are often impatient to "get on with it" when they most need to slow down and think carefully. People rarely define issues or problems clearly; concepts are often left vague; related issues are not sorted out, etc. When people don't understand a problem or situation, their reactions and solutions often compound the original problem. Students need to gain insight into the need for intellectual perseverance.

Application

Intellectual perseverance can be developed by reviewing and discussing the kinds of difficulties that were inherent in previous problems worked on, exploring why it is necessary to struggle with them over an extended period.

Studying the work of great inventors or thinkers through biography can also be of use, with students discussing why long-range commitment was necessary. In time, students will see the value in pursuing important ideas at length.

Texts discourage this trait by doing too much for students: breaking processes into proceduralized fragments and drilling the fragments. Texts try to remove all struggle from learning. Students should come to see mental struggle as crucial to learning by discovering its reward in genuine understanding. Texts often present knowledge and knowledge acquisition (for example, scientific conclusions) as simple ("this experiment proved"), rather than the result of much thought, work, dead ends, etc.

Students should have some experiences slowly reading difficult material. Prove to them that if they are careful and stick to it, examining it one word, phrase, and sentence at a time, they can master it. Such in-depth reading can be done as a class, sentence by sentence, with students interpreting and explaining as they go.

Students with hobbies, skills, or interests could discuss how they learned about them, their mistakes, failures, and frustrations along the way, and the tenacity their mastery required.

Raise difficult problems again and again over the course of the year. Design long-term projects for which students must persevere. Of course, it is important to work with students on skills of breaking down complex problems into simpler components, so that they will see how to attack problems systematically.

Students can discuss experiences they have had wherein they came to understand something that at first baffled them, or seemed hopelessly confusing and frustrating. *"What was it like to not understand or be able to do it? How did you come to understand it? What was that like? Was it worth it? Did it seem worth it at the time? What made you change your mind?"*

Texts will sometimes say of a problem that it is hard to solve, and leave it at that. This encourages an "Oh, that's very complicated. I'll never get it." attitude antithetical to the critical spirit. Life's problems are not divided into the simple and the hopeless. To help students develop the sense that they can begin to attack even complex problems, you could divide the class into groups and have them discuss various ways in which the problem could be approached, seeing if they can break the problem down into simpler components. It is important to devote considerable time to problem analysis, in order to develop student confidence in their ability to distinguish hard from easy problems and to recognize when a longer term commitment will be necessary. Students will not develop intellectual perseverance unless they develop confidence in their ability to analyze and approach problems with success. You should not overwhelm students with the task of *solving* problems so difficult that they have little hope of making progress, nevertheless, they should be expected to make some progress toward understanding and sorting out complexities.

Take a basic idea within a subject ("well-written," "justice," "culture," "life," "matter," etc.). Have students write their ideas on it and discuss them. Every month or so, have them add to, revise, or write another paper. At the end of the year, they can assess the changes in their understanding from repeated consideration over the course of the year, graphically illustrating their own progress and development achieved through perseverance.

For students to recognize the need for further study of an idea, they need to have some sense of how their present knowledge is limited. Presenting some problems that are beyond their knowledge can be useful, if the class can come to see what they would have to learn to solve them. In this context, students can successfully uncover what they don't know, thereby fostering intellectual humility as well as laying the foundation for intellectual perseverance.

Illustrate how getting answers is not the only form of progress, show students how having better, clearer questions is also progress. Point out progress made. Sympathize with students' natural frustration and discouragement.

Have students discuss the importance of sufficient thought regarding significant decisions and beliefs, and the difficulty of becoming rational and well-educated, fairminded people.

When study and research fail to settle key questions, due to the inadequacy of available resources, the class could write letters to appropriate faculty of one or two colleges. Have students describe their research and results and pose their unanswered questions. The teacher may have to explain the replies. Students can then reopen the issues for further, better-informed discussion.

S-9 Developing Confidence in Reason

Principle

The rational person recognizes the power of reason and the value of disciplining thinking in accordance with rational standards. Virtually all of the progress that has been made in science and human knowledge testifies to this power, and so to the reasonability of having *confidence* in reason. To develop this faith is to come to see that ultimately one's own higher interests and those of humankind at large will be served best by giving the freest play to reason, by encouraging people to come to their own conclusions through a process of developing their own rational faculties. It is to believe that, with proper encouragement and cultivation, people can develop the ability to think for themselves, to form reasonable points of view, draw reasonable conclusions, think coherently and logically, persuade each other by reason and, ultimately, become reasonable persons, despite the deep-seated obstacles in the native character of the human mind and in society as we know it. It is to reject force and trickery as standard ways of changing another's mind. This confidence is essential to building a democracy in which people come to genuine rule, rather than being manipulated by the mass media, special interests, or by the inner prejudices, fears, and irrationalities that so easily and commonly tend to dominate human mindsYou should note that the act of faith we are recommending is not to be blind but should be tested in everyday experiences and academic work. In other words, we should have confidence in reason, because reason works. Confidence in reason does not deny the reality of intuition; rather, it provides a way of distinguishing intuition from prejudice.

At the heart of this principle is the desire to make sense of the world, and the expectation that sense can be made. Texts often don't make sense to students, sometimes because what they say doesn't make sense, more often because students don't have opportunities to make sense out of what they are told. Being continually called upon to "master" what seems nonsensical undermines the feeling that one can make sense of the world. Many students, rushed through mountains of material, give up on this early. ("If I try to make sense of this, I'll never finish. Trying to really understand just slows me down.")

Application

As a teacher, you can model confidence in reason in many ways. Every time you show your students that you can make rules, assignments, and classroom activities *intelligible* to them so that they can see that you are doing things for well-thought-out reasons, you help them to understand why confidence in reason is justified. Every time you help them solve a problem with the use of their own thinking or "think aloud" through a difficult problem in front of them, you encourage them to develop confidence in reason. Every time you encourage them to *question* the reasons behind rules, activities, and procedures, you help them to recognize that we should expect *reasonability* to be at the foundation of our lives. Every time you display a patient willingness to hear their reasons for their beliefs and actions you encourage confidence in reason. Every time you clarify a standard of good reasoning, helping them to grasp *why* this standard makes sense, you help them to develop confidence in reason.

One reason students have little faith in reason is that they don't see reason being used in their everyday lives. Power, authority, prestige, strength, intimidation, and pressure are often used instead of reason. Students develop a natural cynicism about reason which educators should help them to overcome.

Texts often make knowledge acquisition seem mysterious, as though scholars have some sort of mystical mental powers. Make the reasoning behind what they study clear, and students will feel that knowledge and reason are within their grasp.

Give students multiple opportunities to try to persuade each other and you. Insist that students who disagree *reason* with each other, rather than using ridicule, intimidation, peer pressure, etc.

By beginning study of a new topic by discussing what they know about it, students can begin to realize that their initial knowledge is worthwhile. By allowing students to tackle problems and tasks on their own before explaining what to do, teachers help students experience the power of their own minds. By then showing them a better way that scholars have developed, students can see its superior power for themselves. Thus, as they learn, they can feel their minds grow.

Have students compare and contrast the following concepts: intimidate, convince, persuade, trick, brainwash.

S-10 Refining Generalizations and Avoiding Oversimplifications

Principle

It is natural to seek to simplify problems and experiences to make them easier to deal with. Everyone does this. However, the uncritical thinker often oversimplifies, and as a result misrepresents problems and experiences. What should be recognized as complex, intricate, ambiguous, or subtle is viewed as simple, elementary, clear, and obvious. For example, it is typically an oversimplification to view people or groups as *all good* or *all bad*, actions as *always right* or *always wrong*, one contributing factor as *the cause*, etc., and yet such beliefs are common. Critical thinkers try to find simplifying patterns and solutions, but not by misrepresentation or distortion. Making a distinction between useful simplifications and misleading oversimplifications is important to critical thinking.

One of the strongest tendencies of the egocentric, uncritical mind is to see things in terms of black and white, "all right" and "all wrong." Hence, beliefs which should be held with varying degrees of certainty are held as certain. Critical thinkers are sensitive to this problem. They understand the relationship of evidence to belief and so qualify their statements accordingly. The tentativeness of many of their beliefs is characterized by the appropriate use of such qualifiers as 'highly likely,' 'probably,' 'not very likely,' 'highly unlikely,' 'often,' 'usually,' 'seldom,' 'I doubt,' 'I suspect,' 'most,' 'many,' and 'some.'

Critical thinkers scrutinize generalizations, probe for possible exceptions, and then use appropriate qualifications. Critical thinkers are not only clear, but also *exact* or *precise*.

Application

Whenever students or texts oversimplify, the teacher can ask questions which raise the problem of complexity. For instance, if a student or text overgeneralizes, the teacher can ask for counter-examples. If a text overlooks factors by stating one cause for a problem, situation, or event, the teacher can raise questions about other possible contributing factors. If different things are lumped together, the teacher can call attention to differences. (*"Is this situation 'just like' that one? What are some differences?"*) If interconnected or overlapping phenomena are too casually separated, the teacher can probe overlaps or connections. If only one point of view is expressed, though others are relevant, the teacher can play devil's advocate, bringing in other points of view.

Texts grossly oversimplify the concept of "characterization" by having students infer character traits from one action or speech (and thus leave students with a collections of unintegrated, fragmented, contradictory snap judgments, rather than a developed, consistent, complete understanding of characters). Students should analyze the whole character by considering the variety of attitudes, actions, and statements.

Texts often state such vague generalities as "People must work together to solve this problem." Such a statement glosses over complications which could be clarified in a discussion. *"Why don't people work together on this? How should they? Why? Why wouldn't this seemingly obvious solution work? So, what else must be done? How could these needs and interests be reconciled?"*

Among the most common forms of oversimplification found in social studies texts is that of vaguely expressed explanations. Students can better understand explanations and descriptions of historical events, and peoples' reactions to them, by considering offered explanations in depth. For example, a text says that citizens of a former colony resented the rule they lived under. Students could discuss questions like the following: *Why did they resent being ruled by others? What, exactly made them unhappy with their situation? How would we feel about being conquered and ruled? What consequences might arise from our being taken over? Why? How might we respond? Why? Why would a country want to rule another group? What would it get out of it? Why wouldn't they want to give it up? What do they say are their reasons for not giving it up? Why don't the people they rule accept those reasons? Was this group's treatment of that group consistent with those reasons?*

Another common form of oversimplification in history texts occurs when texts describe *"the"* reason or cause of present or historical situations. This treatment often serves texts' sociocentric bias when discussing the causes of wars in which the U.S. has been involved; the enemy bears total responsibility. Students have had a sufficient number of experiences with conflict to be able to see how sometimes both sides are partly to blame. By discussing these experiences, and drawing analogies, students can learn to avoid simple, pat, self-serving interpretations of events. *"Did the U.S. contribute to this situation? How? Why did they do this? What might they have done instead? What result might that have had? Was only one side to blame?"*

When discussing generalizations, the teacher could ask students for counter-examples. The class can then suggest and evaluate more accurate formulations of the claim. *"Is this always the case? Can you think of a time when an x wasn't a y? Given that example, how could we make the claim more accurate?"* ("Sometimes ...." "When this is the case, that happens ...." "It seems that...." "When this *and* that are *both* true, then ....)

The teacher can encourage students to qualify their statements when they have insufficient evidence to be certain. By asking for the evidence on which student claims are based and encouraging students to recognize the possibility that alternative claims may be true, the teacher can help students develop the habits of saying "I'm not sure," and of using appropriate probability qualifiers.

Analogies and models (for example, in science) simplify the phenomena they represent. The class can examine ways such analogies and models break down. *"In what ways is this a poor analogy? How does this model break down? Why?*

What accounts for the differences? What does that tell us about our subject? Could the analogy or model be improved? How? Why is that better?"

S-11 Comparing Analogous Situations: Transferring Insights to New Contexts

Principle

An idea's power is limited by our capacity to see its application. Critical thinkers' ability to use ideas mindfully enhances their ability to transfer ideas critically. They practice using ideas and insights by appropriately applying them to new situations. This allows them to organize materials and experiences in different ways, to compare and contrast alternative labels, to integrate their understanding of different situations, and to find fruitful ways to conceptualize novel situations. Each new application of an idea enriches our understanding of both the idea applied and the situation to which it is applied. True education provides for more than one way to organize material. For example, history can be organized in our minds by geography, chronology, or by such phenomena as repeated patterns, common situations, analogous "stories", the dynamics of various kinds of change, and so on. The truly educated person is not trapped by one organizing principle, but can take knowledge apart and put it together many different ways. Each way of organizing knowledge has some benefit.

Application

Critical teaching, focussing more on basic concepts than on artificial organization of material, encourages students to apply what they have just learned to different but analogous contexts. Using similar information from different situations makes explanations clearer, less vague. For example, a conflict in literature might parallel a war or political conflict. Economic relations between nations could be compared to the economy of a household. *"How would that dynamic explain this situation?"*

When students master a new skill, or discover an insight, they can be encouraged to use it to analyze other situations. Combine the strategy with independent thought by asking students to name, recall, or find analogous situations.

Students can find analogies between historical events or beliefs and present day actions and claims. Any parallel situations can be compared, and insights into each applied to the other. *"Given what we know about our own civil war, it's causes and results, what it was like, what can we say about this other country's civil war?" "Does anything said here about the beginning of this country tell us anything about the beginning of our own country? Vice versa?"*

When students have learned a scientific law, concept, or principle, they can enrich their grasp of it by applying it to situations not mentioned in the text. *"Is air like a liquid in this way?"* By exploring student understanding in this way, teachers can also discover students' misunderstandings of what they just learned.

After an idea has been covered, it can be brought up again, when useful. For example, a passage mentions a U.S. soldier during the war with Mexico leading troops over desert on horseback. If students have discussed the principle that geography and technology affect history, they could be reminded of that insight, and discuss questions like the following: *How did the desert affect the cavalry march? Why? What other affects do deserts have on war? Have we talked about other deserts that were involved in war or war maneuvers? Compare deserts to other difficult terrain, like mountains. How would the desert have affected marching troops? What else could have affected such a march?*

S-12 Developing One's Perspective: Creating or Exploring Beliefs, Arguments, or Theories

Principle

The world is not given to us sliced up into categories with pre-assigned labels on them. There are always many ways to "divide up" and so experience the world. How we do so is essential to our thinking and behavior. Uncritical thinkers assume that their perspective on things is the only correct one. Selfish critical thinkers manipulate the perspectives of others to gain advantage for themselves. Fairminded critical thinkers learn to recognize that their own way of thinking and that of all other perspectives are some combination of insight and error. They learn to develop their point of view through a critical analysis of their experience. They learn to question commonly accepted ways of understanding things and avoid uncritically accepting the viewpoints of their peer groups or society. They know what their perspectives are and can talk insightfully about them. To do this, they must create and explore their own beliefs, their own reasoning, and their own theories.

Application

Perspective is developed through extended thought, discussion, and writing. Students who are unsure what to think can be given time to reflect and come to tentative conclusions. Students who have definite conclusions about the subject at hand can consider ideas from other perspectives, answer questions about what they think, or reflect on new situations or problems. Students can compare what they say they believe with how they act.

Texts rarely call upon students to thoughtfully react to what they read. Teachers can raise basic and important questions about what students learn, having them discover and discuss underlying principles in their thought.

One-to-one Socratic questioning may facilitate development of perspective, especially for students who think they've exhausted their ideas. This strategy will also often coincide with evaluating actions and policies, arguments, or assumptions.

Students could explain how what they have learned has changed their thinking in some way. A written assignment could be used as an opportunity for a student to explore an idea in depth, and either come to conclusions, or clarify issues and concepts.

In general, we should look for opportunities to ask students what *they* believe, how *they* see things, what reasons seem most persuasive to *them*, what theory *they* think best explains what we are trying to explain, and so forth. We should look for occasions in which they can name and describe their own perspectives, philosophies, and ways of thinking.

Explore big questions, helping students integrate details from different lessons and try to come to grips with the world. *What things are most important in life? What's the difference between important and trivial? What are people like? What kinds of people are there? What's the difference between right and wrong? What is friendship?* During such discussions, raise points made during study, and have students relate their general ideas to specifics they have studied.

S-13 Clarifying Issues, Conclusions, or Beliefs

Principle

The more completely, clearly, and accurately an issue or statement is formulated, the easier and more helpful the discussion of its settlement or verification. Given a clear statement of an issue, and prior to evaluating conclusions or solutions, it is important to recognize what is required to settle it. And before we can agree or disagree with a claim, we must understand it clearly. It makes no sense to say "I don't know what you mean, but I deny it, whatever it is." Critical thinkers recognize problematic claims, concepts, and standards of evaluation, making sure that understanding precedes judgment. They routinely distinguish facts from interpretations, opinions, judgments, or theories. They can then raise those questions most appropriate to understanding and evaluating each.

Application

Teachers should encourage students to slow down and reflect before coming to conclusions. When discussing an issue, the teacher can ask students first, *"Is the issue clear? What do you need to know to settle it? What would someone who disagreed with you say?"* Students should be encouraged to continually reformulate the issue in light of new information. They should be encouraged to see how the first statement of the issue or problem is rarely best (that is, most accurate, clear, and complete) and that they are in a better position to settle a question *after* they have developed as clear a formulation as possible.

When discussing an issue, teachers can have students discuss such questions as, *"Do we understand the issue? Do we know how to settle it? Have we stated it fairly? (Does our formulation assume one answer is correct? Would everyone involved accept this as a fair and accurate statement of the issue?)*

Are the words clear? Do we have to analyze any concepts? Do we know when the key words and phrases apply and don't apply? Do we clearly understand how they apply to this case?

Does this question ask something about facts? About the meanings of words? Are we evaluating anything? What? Why? What criteria should we use in the evaluation?

What facts are relevant? How can we get the evidence we need? How would the facts be gathered? What would researchers have to do to conduct such a study? What problems would they face? How could those obstacles be surmounted?"

When a statement is unclear, the class can discuss such questions as, *"How can we know whether or not this is true? What would it be like for this claim to be true? False? Do we clearly understand the difference? What evidence would count for it? Against it? Are any concepts (words or phrases) unclear? What does it assume? What does it imply? What does its opposite imply? Is there a clearer way to say this? Is there a more accurate way to say this? Can it be rephrased? Do the different ways of putting it say the same thing? Why would someone agree? Disagree?"*

This strategy provides a way of remodelling lessons that focus on "Fact/Opinion," or which have vague passages of text.

To encourage students to distinguish fact from interpretation, the teacher could use questions like the following: *Does this description stick to the facts, or is reasoning or response included? Is this something that can be directly seen, or would you have to interpret what you saw to arrive at this statement? Is this how anyone would describe the situation, or would someone else see it differently? What alternative descriptions or explanations are there?* Students could then examine the assumptions, inferences, and theories underlying the alternatives.

S-14 Clarifying and Analyzing the Meanings of Words or Phrases

Principle

Critical, independent thinking requires clarity of thought. A clear thinker understands concepts and knows what kind of evidence is required to justify applying a word or phrase to a situation. The ability to supply a definition is not proof of understanding. One must be able to supply clear, obvious examples and use the concept appropriately. In contrast, for an unclear thinker, words float through the mind unattached to clear, specific, concrete cases. Distinct concepts are confused. Often the only criterion for the application of a term is that the case in question "seems like" an example. Irrelevant associations are confused with what are necessary parts of the concept (e.g., "Love involves flowers and candlelight.") Unclear thinkers lack independence of thought because they lack the ability to analyze a concept, and so critique its use.

Application

There are a number of techniques the teacher can use for analyzing concepts. Rather than simply asking students what a word or phrase means, or asking them for a definition, the teacher can use one of the techniques mentioned below.

When introducing concepts, paraphrasing is often helpful for relating the new term (word or phrase) to ideas students already understand. The teacher can also supply a range of examples, allowing students to add to the list. The class should discuss the purposes the concepts serves. *Why are you learning this? When would it be useful to make this distinction? What does this concept tell us?*

When introducing or discussing a concept that is not within students' experience, the teacher can use analogies which relate the idea to one with which students are familiar. Students could then compare the concepts.

When discussing words or phrases with which students are familiar, we suggest that teachers have students discuss clear examples of the concept, examples of its opposite (or examples which are clearly not instances of the concept), and examples for which neither the word or its opposite are completely accurate (borderline cases). Have students compare the facts relevant to deciding when the term and its opposite apply. Students could also discuss the implications of the concept and why people make a distinction between it and its opposite. *"Give me examples of X and the opposite of X. Why is this an X? What is it about this that makes you call it an X? What are you saying about it when you call it that? Why would someone use this expression? Why would someone want to bring it to people's attention? What are the practical consequences of calling it that? How do we feel about or treat X's? Why?" (Do the same for the opposite.)* When discussing examples, always start with the clearest, most obvious, indisputable cases and opposite cases. Only when those have been examined at length, should discussion move to the more problematic, controversial, difficult, or borderline examples. *"Why is this case different from the others? Why do you kind of want to call it X? Why do you hesitate to call it X? What can we call this case?"*

When clarifying a concept expressed by a phrase rather than a single word, discuss cases in which the phrase applies, instead of merely discussing the individual words. For example, when clarifying the concept of a 'just law,' though a general discussion of 'justice' may be helpful, the more specific idea 'just law' should be discussed and contrasted with its opposite.

For concepts that commonly have a lot of irrelevant associations, the teacher can have students distinguish those associations which are logically related to the concept, from those which are not. Have the class brainstorm ideas associated with the term under discussion. *(What do you think of when you think of school?)* Then ask the students if they can imagine using the term for situations lacking this or that listed idea. *(If teachers and students gathered in a building to study, but there were no blackboard or desks, is it a school?)* Students may see that many of their associations are not part of the concept. They are left with a clearer understanding of what is relevant to the concept and will be less tempted to confuse mere association with it.

Whenever a text or discussion uses one term in more than one sense, the teacher can ask students to state how it is being used in each case or have students paraphrase sentences in which they occur. Then the teacher can ask students to generate examples in which one, both, or neither meaning of the term applies. For example, students could distinguish ordinary from scientific concepts of work and energy. The class could rephrase such seeming absurdities as "This solid table isn't solid," into "This table that I can't pass my hand through actually has lots of empty spaces in it."

When a text confuses two distinct concepts, students can clarify them. Students can distinguish concepts by discussing the different applications and implications of the concepts. *Can you think of an example of A that isn't B? What's the difference?* Students could rewrite passages, making them clearer. For example, a social studies text explains how 'consensus' means that everyone in the group has to agree to decisions. The teachers' notes then suggest discussion of an example wherein a group of children have to make a decision, so they vote, and the majority gets its way. The example, though intended to illustrate consensus, misses the point and confuses 'consensus' with 'majority rule.' The class could compare the two ideas, and so distinguish them. *"What did the text say 'consensus' means? What example does it give? Is this an example of everyone having to agree? What is the difference? How could the example be changed to illustrate the term?"*

S-15 Developing Criteria for Evaluation: Clarifying Values and Standards

Principle

Critical thinkers realize that expressing mere preference does not substitute for evaluating something. Awareness of the process or components of evaluating facilitates thoughtful and fairminded evaluation. This process requires developing and using criteria or standards of evaluation, or making standards or criteria explicit. Critical thinkers are aware of the values on which they base their judgments. They have clarified them and understand *why* they are values.

When developing criteria, critical thinkers should understand the object and purpose of the evaluation, and what function the thing being evaluated is supposed to serve. Critical thinkers take into consideration different points of view when attempting to evaluate something.

Application

Whenever students are evaluating something — an object, action, policy, solution, belief — the teacher can ask students what they are evaluating, the purpose of the evaluation, and the criteria they used. With practice, students can see the importance of developing clear criteria and applying them consistently. When discussing criteria as a class or in groups, rational discussion, clarity, and fairmindedness are usually more important than reaching consensus.

The class could discuss questions like the following: *What are we evaluating? Why? Why do we need an X? What are X's for? Name or describe some good X's versus bad X's. Why are these good and those bad? What are the differences? Given these reasons or differences, can we generalize and list criteria? Can we describe what to look for when judging an X? What features does an X need to have? Why.*

Much of Language Arts instruction can be viewed as developing and clarifying criteria for evaluating writing. Students should continually evaluate written material and discuss their criteria. Specific points should be explained in terms of the values they support (such as clarity).

Students could relate the evaluation of governments to their perspectives on the purposes and functions of governments. During discussions in which they evaluate specific actions or policies of some government, they could relate their evaluations to this discussion of criteria and underlying values.

S-16 Evaluating the Credibility of Sources of Information

Principle

Critical thinkers recognize the importance of using reliable sources of information when formulating conclusions. They give less weight to sources which either lack a track record of honesty, are not in a position to know, or have a vested interest in the issue. Critical thinkers recognize when there is more than one reasonable position to be taken on an issue; they compare alternative sources of information, noting areas of agreement; they analyze questions to determine whether or not the source is in a position to know; and they gather further information where sources disagree. They recognize obstacles to gathering accurate and pertinent information. They realize that preconception, for example, influences observation — that we often see only what we expect to see and fail to notice things we aren't looking for.

Application

When the class is discussing an issue about which people disagree, the teacher can encourage students to check a variety of sources representing *different points of view.* (Examining twenty sources representing the same point of view is worthless for teaching this principle.) This strategy can be used in history and news lessons.

The class can discuss the relevance of a source's past dependability, how to determine whether a source is in a position to know, and how motives should be taken into account when determining whether a source of information is credible. The teacher can ask the following questions: *Is this person in a position to know? What would someone need, to be in a position to know? Was this person there? Could he have directly seen or heard, or would he have to have reasoned to what he claims to know? What do we know about this person's expertise and experience? What experience would you need to have to be an expert? What must you have studied? What does he claim about this issue? Where did he get his information? Is there reason to doubt him?. Has he been reliable in the past? Does he have anything to gain by convincing others? Who commissioned this report? Why?*

To more fully explore the idea of expertise with respect to a particular topic, the teacher could ask,"*What subjects, perspectives, theories, what kinds of details, what sorts of analyses would someone need knowledge of, in order to develop a complete and fairminded view of this subject?*" (For example, if the subject is a political conflict, an expert would need to know the historical background of the groups, their cultures, religions, and world views — including, for example, how each group sees itself and the others, — the geography of the area, the economic system or systems under which the groups live, etc.)

Finally, the teacher can use examples from the students' personal experience (for instance, trying to determine who started an argument) and encourage students to recognize the ways in which their own motivations can affect their interpretations and descriptions of events.

S-17 Questioning Deeply: Raising and Pursuing Root or Significant Questions

Principle

Critical thinkers can pursue an issue in depth, covering germane aspects in an extended process of thought or discussion. When reading a passage, they look for issues and concepts underlying the claims expressed. They come to their own understanding of the details they learn, placing them in the larger framework of the subject and their overall perspective. They contemplate the significant issues and questions underlying subjects or problems studied. They can move between basic underlying ideas and specific details. When pursuing a line of thought, they are not continually dragged off the subject. They use important issues to organize their thought and are not bound by the organization given by another.

Application

Each of the various subject areas has been developed to clarify and settle questions peculiar to itself. (For example, history: How did the world come to be the way it is now?) The teacher can use such questions to organize and unify details covered in each subject. Perhaps more important are basic questions everyone faces about what people are like, the nature of right and wrong, how we know things, and so on. Both general and subject-specific basic questions should be repeatedly raised and used as a framework for organizing details.

Texts fail to develop this trait of pursuing root questions by presenting pre-formulated conclusions, categories, solutions, and ideals, by failing to raise crucial or thought-provoking issues (and so avoiding them), by suggesting a too-limited discussion of them, by mixing questions relevant to different issues or by pursuing their objectives in a confusing way. To rectify these problems, teachers need to provide opportunities for students to come to their own conclusions, construct their own categories, devise their own solutions, and formulate their own ideals. They need to raise thought-provoking issues, allow extended discussion of them and keep the discussion focussed, so that different issues are identified and appropriately addressed. The students, in turn, need to be clear about the objectives and to see themselves as accomplishing them in a fruitful way.

The class can begin exploration of an important topic, concept, or issue not discussed in any one place in their texts by looking it up in the table of contents, index, list of tables, etc. They can then divide up the task of reading and taking notes on the references. The class can then discuss their passages, and pose questions to guide further research using other resources, and share their findings. Each student could then write an essay pulling the ideas together.

Why do people go to war? What wars do you know about? What caused each? Why do people fight? Can we generalize from these cases?

What main concepts (distinctions, categories) are used in this subject? Why? Why is this distinction more important than that one?

When a class discusses rules, institutions, activities, or ideals, the teacher can facilitate a discussion of their purposes, importance, or value. Students should be encouraged to see institutions, for example, as a creation of people, designed to fulfill certain functions, not as something that is "just there." Thus, they will be in a better position, when they are adults, to see that it fulfills its goals. Or, for another example, ideals will be better understood as requiring specific kinds of actions, instead of being left as mere vague slogans, if the class examines their value.

When the text avoids important issues related to or underlying the object of study (such as moral implications), the teacher or students could raise them and discuss them at length. Students can go through the assigned material, and possibly other resources, using the chosen issue or issues to organize the details, for example, making a chart or issue map. Socratic questioning, it should be noted, typically raises root issues.

When a lesson does raise important questions but has too few and scattered questions, the teacher can pull out, rearrange, and add to the relevant questions, integrating them into an extended and focussed, rather than fragmented, discussion. Students can begin study with one or more significant questions and list relevant details as they read.

S-18 Analyzing or Evaluating Arguments, Interpretations, Beliefs, or Theories

Principle

Rather than carelessly agreeing or disagreeing with a conclusion based on their preconceptions of what is true, critical thinkers use analytic tools to understand the reasoning behind it and determine its relative strengths and weaknesses. When analyzing arguments, critical thinkers recognize the importance of asking for reasons and considering alternative views. They are especially sensitive to possible strengths of arguments that they disagree with, recognizing the tendency of humans to ignore, oversimplify, distort, or otherwise unfairly dismiss them. Critical thinkers analyze questions and place conflicting arguments, interpretations, and theories in opposition to one another, as a means of highlighting key concepts, assumptions, implications, etc.

When giving or being given an interpretation, critical thinkers, recognizing the difference between evidence and interpretation, explore the assumptions on which it is based, and propose and evaluate alternative interpretations for their relative strength. Autonomous thinkers consider competing theories and develop their own theories.

Application

Often texts claim to have students analyze and evaluate arguments, when all they have them do is state preferences and locate factual claims, with very limited discussion. They fail to teach most techniques for analyzing and evaluating arguments. Texts that do address aspects of argument critique tend to teach such skills and insights in isolation, and fail to mention them when appropriate and useful. (See "Text Treatment of Critical Thinking and Argumentation," in the chapter, "Thinking Critically About Teaching: From Didactic to Critical Teaching".)

Instead of simply stating why they agree or disagree with a line of reasoning, students should be encouraged to place competing arguments, interpretations, or theories in opposition to one another. Ask, *"What reasons are given? What would someone who disagreed with this argument say?"* Students should then be encouraged to argue back and forth, and modify their positions in light of the strengths of others' positions.

Students can become better able to evaluate reasoning by familiarizing themselves with, and practicing, specific analytic techniques, such as making assumptions explicit and evaluating them; clarifying issues, conclusions, values, and words, developing criteria for evaluation; recognizing and pinpointing contradictions; distinguishing relevant from irrelevant facts; evaluating evidence; and exploring implications. (See the strategies addressing these skills.) After extended discussion, have students state their final positions. Encourage them to qualify their claims appropriately.

When learning scientific theories, students should be encouraged to describe or develop their own theories and compare them with those presented in their texts. Students can compare the relative explanatory and predictive powers of various theories, whenever possible testing predictions with experiments or research.

S-19 Generating or Assessing Solutions

Principle

Critical problem-solvers use everything available to them to find the best solution they can. They evaluate solutions, not independently of, but in relation to one another (since 'best' implies a comparison). They take the time to formulate problems clearly, accurately, and fairly, rather than offering a sloppy, half-baked description and then immediately leaping to solutions. They examine the causes of the problem at length. They have reflected on such questions as, "What makes some solutions better than others? What does the solution to this problem require? What solutions have been tried for this and similar problems? With what results?"

But alternative solutions are often not given, they must be generated or thought-up. Critical thinkers must be creative thinkers as well, generating possible solutions in order to find the best one. Very often a problem persists, not because we can't tell which available solution is best but because the best solution has not yet been made available — no one has thought it up yet. Therefore, although critical thinkers use all available information relevant to their problems, including solutions others have tried in similar situations, they are flexible and imaginative, willing to try any good idea whether it has been done before or not.

Fairminded thinkers take into account the interests of everyone affected by the problem and proposed solutions. They are more committed to finding the best solution than to getting their way. They approach problems realistically.

Application

When presenting problem-solving lessons or activities, texts tend to provide lists of problem-solving steps which unnecessarily limit the process. For example, texts rarely encourage students to consider how others solved or tried to solve the same or a similar problem. They generally make "describing the problem" step one, without having students reformulate their descriptions after further examination. They do not suggest analysis of causes. Texts often break problem-solving into steps and have students memorize the steps. They then drill students on one or two steps. But students don't follow the process through. Thus, each step, practiced in isolation, has no meaning.

The best way to develop insight into problem-solving is to solve problems. If problems arise in the class — for example, if discussions degenerate into shouting matches — students should be assisted in developing and instituting their own solutions. If the first attempt fails or causes other problems, students should consider why and try again. Thus, they can learn the practical difficulties involved in discovering and implementing a workable solution.

We recommend first that the teacher have students state the problem, if that has not been done. Students should explore the causes at length, exploring and evaluating multiple perspectives. Encourage them to integrate the strong points within each view. As the process of exploring solutions proceeds, students may find it useful to reformulate the description of the problem.

Rather than simply asking students if a given solution is good, the teacher could encourage an extended discussion of such questions as, *"Does this solve the problem? How? What other solutions can you think of? What are their advantages and disadvantages? Are we missing any relevant facts? (Is there anything we need to find out before we can decide which solution is best?) What are the criteria for judging solutions in this case? (How will we know if a solution is a good one?) Why do people/have people behaved in the ways that cause the problem? Can you think of other cases of this problem or similar problems? How did the people involved try to solve them? What results did that have? Did they solve the problems? Could we use the same solution, or is our case different in an important way? How do the solutions compare with each other? Why? What are some bad ways of trying to solve the problem? What is wrong with them? Do any of these solutions ignore someone's legitimate concerns or needs? How could the various needs be incorporated? If this fact about the situation were different, would it change our choice of solutions? Why or why not?"*

Fiction often provides opportunities for analysis of problems and evaluation of solutions. Texts' treatments are often too brief, superficial, and unrealistic. They can be extended by having students clarify the problem and analyze solutions as described above.

History texts often provide opportunities for use of this strategy when they describe problems people or government attempted to solve, for instance, by passing new laws. Students can evaluate the text's statement of the problem and its causes, evaluate the solution tried, and propose and evaluate alternatives. Students should be encouraged to explore the beliefs underlying various choices of solutions.

For instance, ask, *"Why do these people favor this solution and those people that one? What does each side claim causes the problem? What does each perspective assume? What sort of evidence would support each perspective?*

What other perspectives can there be? Can the perspectives be reconciled? What is your perspective on this problem? Why?"

Social studies texts provide innumerable opportunities for exploring crucial problems. *"What problems do we have in our country or part of the country? Why? Who is involved in this? Who contributes? How? Why? Who's affected? How? Why? What should be done? Why? Why not do it? What could go wrong? What do other people think should be done? Why? How can we find out more about the causes of this? How can we find out what different people want? Can the wants be reconciled? How? Why not? What compromises are in order?"*

What does this passage say was the problem? The cause? Explain the cause. What other explanations are there? Evaluate the explanations. What else was part of the cause? What was the solution tried? (Action, law, set of laws, policy, amendment, revolt, etc.) What were the effects? Who was affected? Did it have the desired effects? Undesirable effects? What should have been done differently, or what should we do now to rectify the problems that action caused? Do we need the law (policy, etc.) now?

S-20 Analyzing or Evaluating Actions and Policies

Principle

Critical thinking involves more than analysis of reasoning; it includes analysis of behavior or policy and a recognition of the reasoning that that behavior or policy presupposes. When evaluating the behavior of themselves and others, critical thinkers are conscious of the standards they use, so that these, too, can become objects of evaluation. Critical thinkers examine the consequences of actions and recognize these as fundamental to the standards for assessing both behavior and policy.

Critical thinkers base their evaluations of behavior on assumptions to which they have rationally assented. They can articulate and rationally apply principles.

Application

The teacher can encourage students to raise ethical questions about actions and policies of themselves and others. Students can become more comfortable with the process of evaluating if they are given a number of opportunities to make and assess moral judgments: *Why did x do this? What reasons were given? Were they the real reasons? Why do you think so? What are the probable consequences of these actions? How would you feel if someone acted this way toward you? Why? What reasons were your evaluations based on? Might someone else use a different standard to evaluate? Why? Do you think the action was fair, smart, etc.? Why or why not?*

Too often history texts fail to have students evaluate the behavior and policies about which they read. Texts often assume that people's stated reasons were their real reasons. Sometimes texts describe behavior inconsistent with the stated intentions, yet fail to have students discuss these inconsistencies. *"Why did that group or government say they took this action? What did they do? What result did they say they wanted? What results did it actually have? Who was helped? Hurt? Why? Is the stated reason consistent with that behavior? Was the reason they gave their real reason? Why do you think so?"*

Students should evaluate the behavior of important people of the past. Such evaluation can be enhanced by having interested students report on the long-term consequences of past actions and policies. Future citizens of a democracy need to develop their own sense of how leaders and countries should and shouldn't behave.

Students should also be called upon to generalize, to formulate principles of judgment. *What makes some actions right, others wrong? What rights do people have? How can I know when someone's rights are being violated? Why respect people's rights? Why be good? Should I live according to rules? If so, what rules? If not, how should I decide what to do? What policies should be established and why? What are governments supposed to do? What shouldn't they do?*

These generalizations can be further analyzed and tested by having students compare them to specific cases they have judged in previous lessons. *"Is this principle consistent with that judgment you made last week about (fictional character, historical or current event, etc.)?"*

S-21 Reading Critically: Clarifying or Critiquing Texts

Principle

Critical thinkers read with a healthy skepticism. But they do not doubt or deny until they understand. They clarify before they judge. They expect intelligibility from what they read, and do not mindlessly accept nonsense. They realize that everyone is capable of making mistakes and being wrong, including authors of textbooks. They also realize that, since everyone has a point of view, everyone sometimes leaves out some relevant information. No two authors would write the same book or write from exactly the same perspective. Therefore, critical readers recognize that reading a book is reading one limited perspective on a subject and that more can be learned by considering other perspectives. Critical readers ask themselves questions as they read, wonder about the implications of, reasons for, examples of, and meaning and truth of the material. They do not approach written material as a collection of sentences, but as a whole, trying out various interpretations until one fits all of the work, rather than ignoring or distorting statements that don't fit their interpretation.

Application

Students should feel free to raise questions about materials they read. When a text is ambiguous, vague, or misleading, teachers can raise such questions as, *"What does this passage say? What does it imply? Assume? Is it clear? Explain it. Does it contradict anything you know or suspect to be true? How do you know? How could you find out? Does this fit in with your experience? In what way? Why or why not? What might someone who disagreed with it say? Does the text leave out relevant information? Does it favor one perspective? Which? Why do you suppose it was written this way? How could we rewrite this passage to make it clearer, fairer, or more accurate?"*

In Language Arts, rather than simply using recall questions at the end of fictional selections, have students describe the plot. Thus, students must pull out the main parts and understand cause and effect while being checked for basic comprehension and recall. Don't forget that students should continually evaluate what they read. *"How good is this selection? Why? Is it well written? Why or why not? Is it saying something important? What? How does it compare with other things we've read? Are some parts better than others? Which? Why?"*

Students can evaluate unit, chapter, and section titles and headings in their texts. *"What is the main point in this passage? What details does it give? What ideas do those details support, elaborate on, justify? Is the heading accurate? Misleading? Could you suggest a better heading?"*

Often passages which attempt to instill belief in important U.S. ideals are too vague to give more than the vague impression that our ideals are important. Such passages typically say that the ideals are important or precious, that people from other countries wish they had them or come here to enjoy them, that we all have a responsibility to preserve them, and so on. Such passages could be reread slowly and deeply with much discussion.

The class could engage in deeper, critical reading by discussing questions like the following: *Why is this right important? How is this supposed to help people? Does not having this right hurt people? How? Why?*

Why would someone try to prevent people from voting or speaking out? How could they? Have you ever denied someone the right to speak or be heard? Why? Were you justified? Why or why not? What should you have done?

Why is this right precious? Why are these rights emphasized? Do you have other rights? Why doesn't the text (or Constitution) say that you have the right to eat pickles? What are the differences between that right and those mentioned?

Does everyone believe in this or want this? How do you know? Have you ever heard anyone say that tyranny is the best kind of government, or free speech is bad? Why?

Is there a basic idea behind all of these rights? Why does the text say people have this responsibility? How, exactly, does this help our country? Why do some people not do this? What does it require of you? And how do you do that? Is it easy or hard? What else does it mean you should do?

The teacher could make copies of passages from several sample texts which cover the same material and have students compare and critique them.

Students can discuss their interpretations of what they read. Small groups of students can compare their paraphrases and interpretations and write better ones.

S-22 Listening Critically: The Art of Silent Dialogue

Principle

Critical thinkers realize that listening can be done passively and uncritically or actively and critically. They know that it is easy to misunderstand what is said by another and difficult to integrate another's thinking into our own. Compare speaking and listening. When we speak, we need only keep track of our own ideas, arranging them in some order, expressing thoughts with which we are intimately familiar: our own. But listening is more complex. We must take the words of another and translate them into ideas that make sense to us. We have not had the experiences of the speakers. We are not on the inside of their point of view. We can't anticipate, as they can themselves, where their thoughts are leading them. We must continually interpret what others say within the confines of our experiences. We must find a way to enter into their points of view, shift our minds to follow their trains of thought.

What all of this means is that we need to learn how to listen actively and critically. We need to recognize that listening is an art involving skills that we can develop only with time and practice. We need to learn, for example, that to listen and learn from what we are hearing, we need to learn to ask key questions that enable us to locate ourselves in the thought of another. We must practice asking questions like the following: "I'm not sure I understand you when you say ..., could you explain that further?" "Could you give me an example or illustration of this?" "Would you also say ...?" "Let me see if I understand you. What you are saying is .... Is that right?" "How do you respond to this objection?" Critical readers ask questions as they read and use those questions to orient themselves to what an author is saying. Critical listeners ask questions as they listen to orient themselves to what a speaker is saying: Why does she say that? What examples could I give to illustrate that point? What is the main point? How does this detail relate to the main point? That one? Is she using this word as I would, or somewhat differently? These highly skilled and activated processes are crucial to learning. We need to heighten student awareness of and practice in them as often as we can.

Application

The first and best way to teach critical listening is to model it. It is necessary that we actively and constructively listen to what students say, demonstrating the patience and skill necessary to understand them. We should not casually assume that we know what they mean. We should not pass by their expressions too quickly. Students rarely take seriously their own meanings. They rarely listen to themselves. They rarely realize the need to elaborate or exemplify their own thoughts. And we are often in a position to help them to do so with facilitating questions that result from close, enquiring listening.

Secondly, students rarely listen carefully to what other students have to say. They rarely take each other seriously. We can facilitate this process with questioning interventions. We can say things like: "Joel, did you follow what Diane said? Could you put what she said in your own words?" Or we can say, "Richard, could you give us an example from your own experience of what Jane has said? Has anything like that ever happened to you?"

The success of Socratic questioning and class discussion depends upon close and critical listening. Many assignments are understood or misunderstood through word of mouth. We need to take the occasion of making an assignment an occasion for testing and encouraging critical listening. In this way, we will get better work from students, because in learning how to listen critically to what we are asking them to do, they will gain a clearer grasp of what that is, and hence do a better job in doing it. Students often do an assignment poorly, because they never clearly understood it in the first place.

Students can describe discussions, videotapes, or movies in writing, then compare their versions in small groups, trying to accurately reconstruct what they heard. Whenever possible, they should watch the piece a second time to verify their accounts or settle conflicting accounts of what they saw and heard.

While watching a movie or video, students can be asked to take notes. Afterward, students can compare and discuss their notes. A teacher could periodically stop a movie or video and have students outline the main point, and raise critical questions.

S-23 Making Interdisciplinary Connections

Principle

Although in some ways it is convenient to divide knowledge up into disciplines, the divisions are not absolute. Critical thinkers do not allow the somewhat arbitrary distinctions between academic subjects to control their thinking. When considering issues which transcend subjects, they bring relevant concepts, knowledge, and insights from many subjects to the analysis. They make use of insights into one subject to inform their understanding of other subjects. There are always connections between subjects (language and logic; history, geography, psychology, anthropology, physiology; politics, geography, science, ecology; math, science, economics). To understand, say, reasons for the American Revolution (historical question), insights from technology, geography, economics, and philosophy can be fruitfully applied.

Application

Reading and writing can and should be taught in conjunction with every subject. One way to teach reading during other subjects would be to have students who cannot answer questions about what they read skim their texts to find the answer. Teachers could also have students who misunderstood a sentence in their texts find it. Either the sentence was unclearly written, in which case, students could revise it, or the students didn't read carefully, in which case the class could discuss why the sentence does not mean what the students thought.

Any time another subject is relevant to the object of discussion, those insights can be used and integrated. Some teachers allot time for coverage of topics in different subjects so that the topic is examined from the perspective of several subjects (history, literature, art, music, science). Study of the news can combine with nearly every subject — language arts, social studies, math, geography, science, health, etc.

Socratic questioning can be used to make subject connections clear. The teacher can use discussion of students' issues and problems to show the importance of bringing insights from many subjects to bear.

The class could evaluate writing in their texts from a literary or composition standpoint. *"Given what you know about good writing, is this passage well written? Organized? Interesting? Why or why not? How can it be improved? Is the quote used evocative? To the point? How does it illustrate or enhance the point made?"*

Students can evaluate the psychological, sociological, or historical accuracy or sophistication of fiction and biography.

S-24 Practicing Socratic Discussion: Clarifying and Questioning Beliefs, Theories, or Perspectives

Principle

Critical thinkers are nothing if not questioners. The ability to question and probe deeply, to get down to root ideas, to get beneath the mere appearance of things, is at the very heart of the activity. And, as questioners, they have many different kinds of questions and moves available and can follow up their questions appropriately. They can use questioning techniques, not to make others look stupid, but to learn what they think, helping them develop their ideas, or as a prelude to evaluating them. When confronted with a new idea, they want to understand it, to relate it to their experience, and to determine its implications, consequences, and value. They can fruitfully uncover the structure of their own and others' perspectives. Probing questions are the tools by which these goals are reached.

Furthermore, critical thinkers are comfortable being questioned. They don't become offended, confused, or intimidated. They welcome good questions as an opportunity to develop a line of thought.

Application

Students, then, should develop the ability to go beyond the basic what and why questions that are found in their native questioning impulses. To do this, they need to discover a variety of ways to frame questions which probe the logic of what they are reading, hearing, writing, or thinking. They need to learn how to probe for and question assumptions, judgments, inferences, apparent contradictions, or inconsistencies. They need to learn how to question the relevance of what is presented, the evidence for and against what is said, the way concepts are used, the implications of positions taken. Not only do we need to question students, we also need to have them question each other and themselves.

Classroom instruction and activities, therefore, should stimulate the student to question and help make the students comfortable when questioned, so that the questioning process is increasingly valued and mastered. Questioning should be introduced in such a way that students come to see it as an effective way to get at the heart of matters and to understand things from different points of view. It should not be used to embarrass or negate students. It should be part of an inquiry into issues of significance in an atmosphere of mutual support and cooperation. We therefore recommend that teachers cultivate a habit of wondering about the reasoning behind students' beliefs and translating their musings into questions.

The teacher should model Socratic questioning techniques and use them often. Any thought-provoking questions can start a Socratic discussion. To follow up responses, use questions like the following: *Why? If that is so, what follows? Are you assuming that...? How do you know that? Is the point that you are making that... or, ...? For example? Is this an example of what you mean..., or this,...? Can I summarize your point as...? What is your reason for saying that? What do you mean when using this word? Is it possible that...? Are there other ways of looking at it? How else could we view this matter?* (For more questions, see the chapter on Socratic questioning.)

Immediately after Socratic discussion, students can write for five minutes, summarizing the key points, raising new questions, adding analysis, examples, or clarification. Later these notes could be shared and discussion continued.

To develop students' abilities to use Socratic questioning, the teacher could present an idea or passage to students and have them brainstorm possible questions. For instance, they could think of questions to ask story or historical characters or a famous person or personal hero on a particular subject.

Pairs of students can practice questioning each other about issues raised in study, trading the roles of questioner and questioned. The teacher may provide lists of possible initial questions and perhaps some follow-up questions. Students could also be allowed to continue their discussions another day, after they've had time to think. As students practice Socratic questioning, see it modeled, and learn the language, skills, and insights of critical thinking, their mastery of questioning techniques will increase.

The direction and structure of a Socratic discussion can be made clearer by periodically summarizing and rephrasing the main points made or by distinguishing the perspectives expressed. *"We began with this question. Some of you said _____, others _____. These arguments were given .... Joan recommended that we distinguish X from Y. We've reached an impasse on X because we can't agree about two contradictory assumptions,_____ and _____. We decided we would need to find out _____. So let's take up Y."*

To practice exploring the idea of illuminating and probing Socratic questioning, students could read and evaluate different kinds of interviews, categorizing the questions asked. They could then list probing follow-up questions that weren't asked, and share and discuss their lists. *Why would you ask this? How could that be followed up? What would that tell you?*

S-25 Reasoning Dialogically: Comparing Perspectives, Interpretations, or Theories

Principle

Dialogical thinking refers to thinking that involves a dialogue or extended exchange between different points of view, cognitive domains, or frames of reference. Whenever we consider concepts or issues deeply, we naturally explore their connections to other ideas and issues within different domains or points of view. Critical thinkers need to be able to engage in fruitful, exploratory dialogue, proposing ideas, probing their roots, considering subject matter insights and evidence, testing ideas, and moving between various points of view. When we think, we often engage in dialogue, either inwardly or aloud with others. We need to integrate critical thinking skills into that dialogue so that it is as fruitful as possible. Socratic questioning is one form of dialogical thinking.

Application

By routinely raising root questions and root ideas in a classroom setting, multiple points of view get expressed and the thinking proceeds, not in a predictable or straightforward direction, but in a criss-crossing, back-and-forth movement. We continually encourage the students to explore how what they think about x relates to what they think about y and z. This necessarily requires that students' thinking moves back and forth between their own basic ideas and those being presented by the other students, between their own ideas and those expressed in a book or story, between their own thinking and their own experience, between ideas within one domain and those in another, in short, between any two perspectives. This dialogical process will sometimes become dialectical. Some ideas will clash or be inconsistent with others.

What would someone who disagreed say? Why? How could the first respond? Why? Etc.

When texts give only one side of an issue or event, the teacher could have students discuss other views. *What did the other (character, group of people) think? Why? (Take specific statements from the text.) Would others see it this way? Would they use these words? How would they describe this? Why? What exactly do they disagree about? Why? What does X think is the cause? Y? Why do they differ?*

Students could list points from multiple perspectives for reference, then write dialogues of people arguing about the issues.

Texts approach teaching dialogical thinking by having students discuss perspectives other than that presented by their texts. Yet such discussion is simply tacked on; it is not integrated with the rest of the material. Thus, the ideas are merely juxtaposed, not synthesized. Rather than separate activities or discussions about different perspectives, the teacher can have students move back and forth between points of view. *"What do the environmentalists want? Why? Factory owners? Why? Workers? Why? Why do the environmentalists think the factory owners are wrong? How do the factory owners respond to that? ... What beliefs do the sides have in common? How would ecologists look at this dispute? Economists? Anthropologists?"*

S-26 Reasoning Dialectically: Evaluating Perspectives, Interpretations, or Theories

Principle

Dialectical thinking refers to dialogical thinking conducted in order to test the strengths and weaknesses of opposing points of view. Court trials and debates are dialectical in intention. They pit idea against idea, reasoning against counter-reasoning in order to get at the truth of a matter. As soon as we begin to explore ideas, we find that some clash or are inconsistent with others. If we are to integrate our thinking, we need to assess which of the conflicting ideas we will provisionally accept and which we shall provisionally reject, or which parts of the views are strong and which weak, or how the views can be reconciled. Students need to develop dialectical reasoning skills, so that their thinking not only moves comfortably between divergent points of view or lines of thought, but also makes some assessments in light of the relative strengths and weaknesses of the evidence or reasoning presented. Hence, when thinking dialectically, critical thinkers can use critical micro-skills appropriately.

Application

Dialectical thinking can be practiced whenever two conflicting points of view, arguments, or conclusions are under discussion. Stories and history lessons provide many opportunities. Dialectical exchange between students in science classes enables students to discover and appropriately amend their preconceptions about the physical world.

The teacher could have proponents of conflicting views argue their positions and have others evaluate them. A dialogical discussion could be taped for later analysis and evaluation. Or the teacher could inject evaluative questions into dialogical discussion. *"Was that reason a good one? Why or why not? Does the other view have a good objection to that reason? What? And the answer to that objection? Does each side use language appropriately and consistently? To what evidence does each side appeal? Is the evidence from both sides relevant? Questionable, or acceptable? Compare the sources each side cites for its evidence. Which is more trustworthy? How can we know which of these conflicting assumptions is best? Is there a way of reconciling these views? The evidence? What is this side right about? The other side? Which of these views is strongest? Why?"*

S-27 Comparing and Contrasting Ideals with Actual Practice

Principle

Self-improvement and social improvement are presupposed values of critical thinking. Critical thinking, therefore, requires an effort to see ourselves and others accurately. This requires recognizing gaps between ideals and practice. The fairminded thinker values truth and consistency and, therefore, works to minimize these gaps. The confusion of facts with ideals prevents us from moving closer to achieving our ideals. A critical education strives to highlight discrepancies between facts and ideals, and proposes and evaluates methods for minimizing them. This strategy is intimately connected with "developing intellectual good faith."

Application

Since, when discussing our society, many texts consistently confuse ideals with facts, the teacher can use them as objects of analysis. Ask, *"Is this a fact or an ideal? Are things always this way, or is this statement an expression of what people are trying to achieve? Are these ideals yours? Why or why not? How have people attempted to achieve this ideal? When did they not meet the ideal? Why? What problems did they have? Why? How can we better achieve these ideals?"* Students could rewrite misleading portions of text, making them more accurate.

Sometimes this strategy could take the form of *avoiding oversimplification.* For example, when considering the idea that we in this country are free to choose the work or jobs we want, the teacher could ask, *"Can people in this country choose any job they want? Always? What, besides choice, might affect what job someone has or gets? Would someone who looked like a bum be hired as a salesman? Does this mean they don't have this freedom? Why or why not? What if there aren't enough openings for some kind of work? How can this claim be made more accurate?"*

The teacher can facilitate a general discussion of the value of achieving consistency of thought and action. Ask, *"Have you ever thought something was true about yourself but acted in a way that was inconsistent with your ideal? Did you see yourself differently then? Did you make efforts to change the behavior? Can anyone think of ways to be more consistent? Why is it often hard to be honest about yourself and the groups you belong to? Is it worth the pain?"*

Sometimes texts foster this confusion in students by asking questions to which most people want to answer yes, for example: Do you like to help others? Do you listen to what other people have to say? Do you share things? Since none of us always adheres to our principles (though few like to admit it) you might consider rephrasing such questions. For example, ask, *"When have you enjoyed helping someone? When not? Why? Did you have to help that person? When is it hard to listen to what someone else has to say? Why? Have you ever not wanted to share something? Should you have? Why or why not? If you didn't share, why didn't you?"*

Such discussion can also explore the rationalizations people use. *What were you thinking? Why? Did you know you shouldn't, or did it seem OK at the time? Why?*

Obviously, the more realistic are our ideals, the closer we can come to achieving them. Therefore, any text's attempt to encourage unrealistic ideals can be remodelled. For example, rather than assuming that everyone should always do everything they can for everyone anytime, allow students to express a range of views on such virtues as generosity.

When discussing a departure from ideals or theory, have students analyze and evaluate it. Students could write an essay in which they focus on one such point. *"How is this supposed to work in theory? Why? What result is that supposed to have? Why is that considered good? How does this really work? Why? What incorrect assumption is made in the theory? What reasons are there for accepting this as it is? For trying to make it closer to the ideal? Is the way we actually do this justified? Why or why not? If it isn't justified, how can we correct it?"*

Students who are learning about capitalism could discuss how ads affect the workings of supply and demand. *"If ads get people to buy things for irrelevant reasons, or by distorting the facts, then is it true that people tend to buy the best products at the lowest prices? How does this affect manufacturers? What if it's cheaper and more profitable to make better ads than to make products? How does that affect the economy? Productions? How might it affect salaries?"*

S-28 Thinking Precisely About Thinking: Using Critical Vocabulary

Principle

An essential requirement of critical thinking is the ability to think about thinking, to engage in what is sometimes called "metacognition". One possible definition of critical thinking is the art of thinking about your thinking while you're thinking in order to make your thinking better: more clear, more accurate, more fair. It is precisely at the level of "thinking about thinking" that most critical thinking stands in contrast to uncritical thinking. Critical thinkers can analyze thought — take it apart and put it together again. For the uncritical, thoughts are "just there". "I think what I think, don't ask me why." The analytical vocabulary in the English language (such terms as 'assume,' 'infer,' 'conclude,' 'criteria,' 'point of view,' 'relevance,' 'issue,' 'elaborate,' 'ambiguous,' 'objection,' 'support,' 'bias,' 'justify,' 'perspective,' 'contradiction,' 'consistent', 'credibility,' 'evidence,' 'interpret,' 'distinguish') enables us to think more precisely about our thinking. We are in a better position to assess reasoning (our own, as well as that of others) when we can use analytic vocabulary with accuracy and ease.

Application

Since most language is acquired by hearing words used in context, teachers should try to make critical terms part of their working vocabulary.

When students are reasoning or discussing the reasoning of others, the teacher can encourage them to use critical vocabulary. New words are most easily learned and remembered when they are clearly useful.

When introducing a term, the teacher can speak in pairs of sentences: first, using the critical vocabulary, then, rephrasing the sentence without the new term, e.g., *"What facts are relevant to this issue? What facts must we consider in deciding this issue? What information do we need?"* The teacher can also rephrase students' statements to incorporate the vocabulary. *"Do you mean that Jane is assuming that ...?"*

When conducting discussions, participating students could be encouraged to explain the role of their remarks in the discussion: supporting a point, raising an objection, answering an objection, distinguishing concepts or issues, questioning relevance, etc. *"Why were you raising that point here? Are you supporting Fred's point or ...?"*

Students could look up and discuss sets of related critical vocabulary words, and discuss relationships among them, when each can be used, and for what purposes.

S-29 Noting Significant Similarities and Differences

Principle

Critical thinkers strive to treat similar things similarly and different things differently. Uncritical thinkers, on the other hand, often miss significant similarities and differences. Things superficially similar are often significantly different. Things superficially different are often essentially the same. It is only by developing our observational and reasoning skills to a high point that we become sensitized to significant similarities and differences. As we develop this sensitivity, it influences how we experience, how we describe, how we categorize, and how we reason about things. We become more careful and discriminating in our use of words and phrases. We hesitate before we accept this or that analogy or comparison.

We recognize the purposes of the comparisons we make. We recognize that purposes govern the act of comparing and determine its scope and limits. The hierarchy of categories biologists, for instance, use to classify living things (with Kingdom as the most basic, all the way down to sub-species) reflects biological judgment regarding which kinds of similarities and differences between species are the most important *biologically,* that is, which distinctions shed the most light on how each organism is structured and lives. To the zoologist, the similarities whales have to horses is considered more important than their similarities to fish. The differences between whales and fish are considered more significant than differences between whales and horses. These distinctions suit the biologists' purposes.

Application

Texts often call on students to compare and contrast two or more things — objects, ideas, phenomena, etc. Yet these activities rarely have a serious purpose. Merely listing similarities and differences has little value in itself. Rather than encouraging students to make such lists, these activities should be proposed in a context which narrows the range of pertinent comparisons and requires some *use* be made of them in pursuit of some specific goal. For example, if comparing and contrasting two cultures, students should use their understanding to illuminate the relationship between them, perhaps to explain factors contributing to conflict or war. Thus, only those points which shed light on the particular problem need be mentioned, and each point has implications to be drawn out and integrated into a broader picture.

"What does this remind you of? Why? How is it similar? Different? How important are the differences? Why? What does this tell us about our topic? How useful is that comparison? Can anyone think of an even more useful comparison?"

Students can compare models to what they represent, and so evaluate them. *How much is the model like the real thing? Unlike it? What doesn't the model show? Why not? Could it? How or why not? What parts do they both have? Do they have analogous parts? Why or why not? How important are the missing or extra parts? How like the original thing is this part? How is this model helpful? In what ways is it misleading? What do we have to keep in mind when we look at this model? How good is this model? How could it be improved?*

When comparing characters from literature, rather than simply listing differences, students should analyze and *use* their comparisons. *Why are they different? (personality, lives, problems, current situations)* Don't let students over-generalize from differences. Texts have students make sweeping statements from one difference in attitude or action. Such differences may not reflect difference in character as much as differences in situation. Have students relate differences in characterization, to differences in perspective. Relate differences in feelings and behavior to differences in how characters see things. Relate all significant differences between characters to the theme.

S-30 Examining or Evaluating Assumptions

Principle

We are in a better position to evaluate any reasoning or behavior when all of the elements of that reasoning or behavior are made explicit. We base both our reasoning and our behavior on beliefs we take for granted. We are often unaware of these assumptions. It is only by recognizing them that we can evaluate them. Critical thinkers have a passion for truth and for accepting the strongest reasoning. Thus, they have the intellectual courage to seek out and reject false assumptions. They realize that everyone makes some questionable assumptions. They are willing to question, and have others question, even their own most cherished assumptions. They consider alternative assumptions. They base their acceptance or rejection of assumptions on their rational scrutiny of them. They hold questionable assumptions with an appropriate degree of tentativeness. Independent thinkers evaluate assumptions for themselves, and do not simply accept the assumptions of others, even those assumptions made by everyone they know.

Application

Teachers should encourage students to make assumptions explicit as often as possible — assumptions made in what they read or hear and assumptions they make. Teachers should ask questions that elicit the implicit elements of students' claims. Although it is valuable practice to have students make good assumptions explicit, it is especially important when assumptions are questionable. The teacher might ask, *"If this was the evidence, and this the conclusion, what was assumed?"* or *If this is what he saw (heard, etc.), and this is what he concluded or thought, what did he assume?* (*"He saw red fruit and said 'Apples!' and ate it." "He assumed that all red fruits are apples." or "He assumed that, because it looked like an apple, it was good to eat."*)

There are no rules for determining when to have students evaluate assumptions. Students should feel free to question and discuss any assumptions they suspect are questionable or false. Students should also evaluate good assumptions. Doing so gives them a contrast with poor assumptions.

The following are some of the probing questions teachers may use when a class discusses the worth of an assumption: *Why do people (did this person) make this assumption? Have you ever made this assumption? What could be assumed instead? Is this belief true? Sometimes true? Seldom true? Always*

false? (Ask for examples.) Can you think of reasons for this belief? Against it?
What, if anything, can we conclude about this assumption? What would we
need to find out to be able to judge it? How would someone who makes this
assumption act?

S-31 Distinguishing Relevant From Irrelevant Facts

Principle

Critical thinking requires sensitivity to the distinction between those facts
that are relevant to an issue and those which are not. Critical thinkers focus
their attention on relevant facts and do not let irrelevant considerations
affect their conclusions. Furthermore, they recognize that a fact is only relevant or irrelevant in relation to an issue. Information relevant to one problem may not be relevant to another.

Application

When discussing an issue, solution to a problem, or when giving reasons
for a conclusion, students can practice limiting their remarks to facts which
are germane to that issue, problem, or conclusion. Often students assume
that all information given has to be used to solve a problem. Life does not
sort relevant from irrelevant information for us. Teachers can encourage students to make a case for the pertinence of their remarks, and help them see
when their remarks are irrelevant. *"How would this fact affect our conclu-*
sion? If it were false, would we have to change our conclusion? Why or why
not? What is the connection? Why does that matter? What issue are you
addressing? Are you addressing this issue or raising a new one?"

Students could read a chapter of text or story with one or more issues in
mind and note relevant details. Students could then share and discuss their
lists. Students can then discover that sometimes they must *argue* for the relevance of a particular fact to an issue.

Another technique for developing students' sensitivity to relevance is to
change an issue slightly and have students compare what was relevant to
the first issue to what is relevant to the second. ("What *really* happened?"
versus "What does X *think* happened?" Or *"Can* you do this?" versus *"Should*
you do it?" Or "Which one *is* best?" versus "Which do people *think* is best?" Or
"Is this *legal?"* versus "Is this *right?"* versus "Is this *convenient?"*)

Students who disagree about the relevance of a particular point to the
issue discussed, should be encouraged to argue its potential relevance, and
probe the beliefs underlying their disagreement. *Why do you think it's rele-*
vant? Why do you think it isn't? What is each side assuming? Do these
assumptions make sense?

S-32 Making Plausible Inferences, Predictions, or Interpretations

Principle

Thinking critically involves the ability to reach sound conclusions based on observation and information. Critical thinkers distinguish their observations from their conclusions. They look beyond the facts, to see what those facts imply. They know what the concepts they use imply. They also distinguish cases in which they can only guess from cases in which they can safely conclude. Critical thinkers recognize their tendency to make inferences that support their own egocentric or sociocentric world views and are therefore especially careful to evaluate inferences they make when their interests or desires are involved. Remember, every interpretation is based on inference, and we interpret every situation we are in.

Application

Teachers can ask students to make inferences based on a wide variety of statements, actions, story titles and pictures, story characters' statements and actions, text statements, and their fellow students' statements and actions. They can then argue for their inferences or interpretations. Students should be encouraged to distinguish their observations from inferences, and sound inferences from unsound inferences, guesses, etc.

Sometimes texts will describe details yet fail to make or have students make plausible inferences from them. The class could discuss such passages. Or groups of students might suggest possible inferences which the class as a whole could then discuss and evaluate.

Teachers can have students give examples, from their experience, of making bad inferences, and encourage them to recognize situations in which they are most susceptible to uncritical thought. The class can discuss ways in which they can successfully minimize the effects of irrationality in their thought.

Science instruction all too often provides the "correct" inferences to be made from experiments or observations rather than having students propose their own. Sometimes science texts encourage poor inferences given the observation cited. Though the conclusion is correct, students should note that the experiment alone did not prove it and should discuss other evidence supporting it.

Students should interpret experiments, and argue for their interpretations. *What happened? What does that mean? Are there other ways to interpret our results? What? How can we tell which is best?*

S-33 Evaluating Evidence and Alleged Facts

Principle

Critical thinkers can take their reasoning apart in order to examine and evaluate its components. They know on what evidence they base their conclusions. They realize that unstated, unknown reasons can be neither communicated nor critiqued. They can insightfully discuss evidence relevant to the issue or conclusions they consider. Not everything offered as evidence should be accepted. Evidence and factual claims should be scrutinized and evaluated. Evidence can be complete or incomplete, acceptable, questionable, or false.

Application

When asking students to come to conclusions, the teacher should ask for their reasons. *"How do you know? Why do you think so? What evidence do you have?"* etc. When the reasons students supply are incomplete, the teacher may want to ask a series of probing questions to elicit a fuller explanation of student reasoning. *"What other evidence do you have? How do you know your information is correct? What assumptions are you making? Do you have reason to think your assumptions are true?"* etc.

When discussing their interpretations of written material, students should routinely be asked to show specifically on what in the book or passage they base that interpretation. The sentence or passage can then be clarified and discussed and the student's interpretation better understood and evaluated.

On what evidence is this conclusion based? Where did we get the evidence? Is the source reliable? How could we find out what other evidence exists? What evidence supports opposing views? Is the evidence sufficient or do we need more? Is there reason to question this evidence? What makes it questionable? Acceptable? Does another view account for this evidence?"

S-34 Recognizing Contradictions

Principle

Consistency is a fundamental — some would say the *defining* — ideal of critical thinkers. They strive to remove contradictions from their beliefs, and are wary of contradictions in others. As would-be fairminded thinkers they strive to judge like cases in a like manner. Perhaps the most difficult form of consistency to achieve is that between word and deed. Self-serving double standards are one of the most common problems in human life. Children are in some sense aware of the importance of consistency ("Why don't I get to do what they get to do?"). They are frustrated by double standards, yet are given little help in getting insight into them and dealing with them.

Critical thinkers can pinpoint specifically where opposing arguments or views contradict each other, distinguishing the contradictions from compatible beliefs, thus focussing their analyses of conflicting views.

Application

When discussing conflicting lines of reasoning, inconsistent versions of the same story, or egocentric reasoning or behavior, the teacher can encourage students to bring out both views and practice recognizing contradictions. *"What does each person say? Could both views be true? Why or why not? If one is true, must the other be false? Where, exactly, do these views contradict each other? On what do they agree?"*

Sometimes fiction illustrates contradictions between what people say and what they do. History texts often confuse stated reasons with reasons implied by behavior. They will often repeat the noble justification that, say, a particular group ruled another group for its own good, when they in fact exploited them. Students could discuss questions like the following: *What did they say? What did they do? Are the two consistent or contradictory? Why do you say so? What behavior would have been consistent with their words? What words would have been consistent with their behavior?*

When arguing opposing views, students should be encouraged to find points of agreement and specify points of dispute or contradiction. *"What is it about that view that you think is false? Do you accept this claim? That one? On what question does your disagreement turn? What, exactly, is it in this view that you doubt or disagree with?"*

The class can explore possible ways to reconcile apparent contradictions. *"Could someone hold both of these views? How might someone argue that someone can believe both?"*

S-35 Exploring Implications and Consequences

Principle:

Critical thinkers can take statements, recognize their implications (i.e., if x is true, then y must also be true) and develop a fuller, more complete understanding of their meaning. They realize that to accept a statement one must also accept its implications. They can explore both implications and consequences at length. When considering beliefs that relate to actions or policies, critical thinkers assess the consequences of acting on those beliefs.

Application

The teacher can ask students to state the implications of material in student texts, especially when the text materials lack clarity. The process can help students better understand the meaning of a passage. *"What does this imply/mean? If this is true, what else must be true? What were, or would be, the consequences of this action, policy, solution? How do you know? Why wouldn't this happen instead? Are the consequences desirable? Why or why not?"*

Teachers can have students explore the implications and consequences of their own beliefs. During dialogical exchanges, students can compare the implications of ideas from different perspectives and the consequences of accepting each perspective. *"How would someone who believes this act? What result would that have?"*

✦✦ Chapter 22

Critical Thinking in the Elementary Classroom

with A. J. A. Binker

Abstract

This paper, which originally appeared as the first in a series of articles for Teaching K–8, *introduces teachers to lesson plan remodelling by offering an example of an original lesson (about advertising), a critique and remodel of it, and lists of the "strategies used to remodel" and "objectives of the remodelled lesson."*

No matter what grade you teach, your lesson plans can be remodelled to encourage critical thinking.

I begin every inservice — whether for elementary, secondary, or university educators — by having each person choose a number between one and 28. I then have everyone read the critical thinking principle that correlates with that number on a list of critical thinking principles. Next, I ask for a show of hands of all those who feel that the principle they've just read applies to their grade level. To date, only two out of about 4,500 teachers and professors I have inserviced have answered in the negative.

The implication is obvious. It's relatively easy to articulate a list of critical thinking principles which are easily recognized as applicable to every subject and grade level. The problem is not their articulation, but their *application*.

To meet this need, I have been working with a team of researchers and practitioner-advisors at the Center for Critical Thinking at Sonoma State University on a series of handbooks that illustrate the infusion of critical thinking principles into about 100 standardized K–8 lessons. Our objective has been, not only to demonstrate that such infusion is possible, but also to help teachers learn how to infuse these principles into their own lessons. The end result is teachers who think critically about their own instruction and use their own critiques to develop remodelled lessons that foster critical thinking.

To see how a teacher might infuse critical thinking principles into his or her lessons, let's take a closer look at one of the principles:

S-17, making inferences.

Principle: Thinking critically involves the ability to reach sound conclusions based on observation and information. Critical thinkers distinguish their observations from their conclusions. They look beyond the facts to see what those facts imply, and they know what the concepts they use imply. They also distinguish cases in which they must guess from cases in which they can safely conclude. Critical thinkers recognize their tendency to make inferences that support their own egocentric world view and are therefore especially careful to evaluate inferences when their interests or desires are involved.

Application: Teachers can ask students to make inferences based on a wide variety of statements and actions. For example, students can make inferences from story titles and pictures, story characters' statements and actions, and their fellow students' statements and actions. Students should be encouraged to distinguish their observations from inferences. Teachers can have students give examples of their experience of inferring incorrectly, and encourage them to recognize situations in which they are most susceptible to uncritical thought. The class can discuss how to successfully minimize the effects of irrationality in their lives. Remember — every interpretation is based on inference, and we interpret every situation we are in.

Once teachers are familiar with these principles and can generate some applications of their own, they are ready to try remodelling some lessons. The following lesson in language arts shows the kind of before/after transformation we have in mind.

Advertising

Objectives of the remodelled plan

The students will:

- think dialogically by considering advertisements from a variety of perspectives
- practice using critical vocabulary to analyze and evaluate ads
- clarify key words in ads
- distinguish relevant from irrelevant facts in ads
- develop insight into egocentricity by exploring the ways in which ads appeal to self-image
- explore the implications of visual and audio aspects of ads
- examine assumptions in ads

Original Lesson Plan

Abstract

The student text reminds students that poets have their own ways of using language to describe, then points out that ad writers also have a unique way of using language. It emphasizes that such writers try to make products sound attractive. Students are informed that *"Advertisers use language that influences people to buy."* Students match products with sentences. (For example, strawberries: *Try our sweet vine-ripened rubies to delight a king's table.*) They make up names for products, and rewrite sentences (For example: *Our vitamins will make you feel better.*) "using the language of advertisers". They write a "Buyer's Guide".

> from *Patterns of Language,* H. Tompson Fillmer, et al. American Book Co. © 1974 pp. 80–81.

Critique

We chose this lesson for its subject: advertising. Ads are a natural tie-in to critical thinking, since many are designed to persuade the audience it needs or wants a product. Ads provide innumerable clear-cut examples of irrelevance, distortion, suppressed evidence, and vague uses of language. Students can later compare these examples with other reasoning. Analysis of ads can teach students critical thinking micro-skills, and show their use in context. This lesson, however, is not done in a way which best achieves these results.

The lesson focuses more on writing ads than critiquing them. It treats neutral and advertising language as basically equivalent in meaning, though different in effect, rather than pointing out how differences in effect arise from differences in meaning. It downplays the emptiness, irrelevance, repetition, and distortion of language in most ads. Its made-up slogans bear little resemblance to real ads. Furthermore, most of the products are not children's products, minimizing the immediate usefulness of any insights students may have.

Since most students are exposed to more television commercials than other ads, we recommend that students discuss real commercials, aimed at them. We also provide suggestions for using ads to practice use of critical vocabulary, and to discuss the visual and audio aspects of commercials.

Strategies used to remodel

S-18   evaluating arguments
S-14   clarifying the meanings of words or phrases
S-25   reasoning dialogically
S-31   distinguishing relevant from irrelevant facts
S-2   developing insight into egocentricity and sociocentricity
S-28   using critical vocabulary
S-35   exploring implications and consequences
S-30   examining assumptions

Remodelled Lesson Plan

Due to the number of ads to which students are exposed and their degree of influence, we recommend the class spend as much time as possible on the subject.

To focus on ads and language, begin by having students give complete descriptions of what is said in a variety of television commercials. Put the quotes on the board. For each commercial, the class can discuss the following questions: What ideas does it give you about the product (or service) and owning or using it? Does it give reasons for buying the product? If so, what reasons? Are they good reasons? **S-18** What are the key words? Do they have a clear meaning? What? What would be some examples of (key word)? How can you tell whether something is (key word)? **S-14** What other words could have been chosen? How might someone who wasn't trying to sell the product describe it? How might a competitor describe it? **S-25** What would you need to know to make a wise decision about whether to buy it? **S-31** Does the commercial address these points? Why or why not? Has anyone here had experience with the product? What?

When the commercials have been discussed, have students group them by the nature of the ads (repetition, positive but empty language, etc.) or of the appeals made (to the desires to: have fun, be popular, be more grown up, etc.) **S-2** Have students fill out the groups by naming similar commercials not previously discussed.

The class could also compare different ads for the same product, aimed at different audiences (e.g., fast food ads aimed at children and adults). Or the class could compare ads for different brands of the same or similar products, compare ads to what can be read on ingredients' labels, or conduct blind taste tests.

The teacher interested in developing students' critical vocabulary can have students practice while critiquing ads. Use questions like the following: **S-28** What does the ad *imply?* **S-35** Does the ad make, or lead the audience to make, any *assumptions?* **S-30** Are the assumptions *true, questionable,* or *false?* Does the ad contain an *argument?* If so, what is the *conclusion?* Is the conclusion *stated* or *implied?* Does the ad *misuse* any *concepts* or *ideas?* To judge the product, what facts are *relevant?* **S-31** Are the relevant facts presented? Does it make any *irrelevant* claims?

The class could also discuss aspects of the ads other than use of language. **S-35** What does the ad show? What effect is it designed to achieve? What is the music like? Why is it used? Do the actors and announcers use tone of voice to persuade? Facial expression? How? Are these things relevant to judging or understanding the product?

The class could hypothesize about why ad campaigns and specific techniques work as well as they do, given their unreasonableness. *S-2*

The teacher may also have the class critique ads for any stereotyping (e.g., sexual stereotyping).

I have found that most teachers are capable of remodelling lessons in this way, provided: *1)* They have access to handbooks that provide them with a wide selection of illustrations of principles, applications and remodelled lessons in a variety of subject areas; *2)* they have time and appropriate inservice in the process, and; *3)* they are systematically encouraged over an extended period of time (with follow-up inservice).

The time and effort required in this model are well worth the results, for critical thinking skills are of signal value, not only for learning academic subjects but also in every domain of everyday life: choosing one's friends and developing one's personal philosophy.

✦✦ Chapter 23

Critical Thinking in Elementary Social Studies

with A. J. A. Binker

Abstract
This paper, the second in the series on remodelling for Teaching K–8, *lists a few of the common flaws in social studies texts, then provides excerpts from a remodelled unit on* The Constitution.

$\mathcal{T}$he April issue of *Teaching K–8* included an article by me on how, in general, traditional lesson plans can be remodelled to encourage critical thinking. I shall now illustrate how this process can be applied to social studies lessons.

As you may recall, the process of remodelling lesson plans involves teachers learning how to analyze, evaluate, and re-design already existing lessons to encourage more critical thinking on the part of students. Behind the remodelling effort is a growing sense of what needs changing in present instruction.

Traditional lessons cover several important subjects within social studies: politics, economics, history, and anthropology. They stress the importance of good citizenship, emphasizing pride in country and the importance of people working together. They compare and contrast our culture with other cultures and encourage tolerance. They stress the importance of accepting a diversity of points of view in the student's peer group, community, nation, and world. The materials, however, typically fall short of teaching the subject matter in a way that best fosters critical thought. Here, for example, are some common deficiencies in social studies texts:

° Although the texts treat diversity of opinion as necessary, beliefs are not presented as subject to examination or critique. Students are encouraged to accept *that* others have different beliefs, but are not encouraged to understand *why*. Yet only by understanding how others have reached their conclusions, can students learn what other points of view have to offer, and strengthen their own views accordingly. The text writers' emphasis on simple tolerance serves to end discussion, whereas students should learn to consider judgments as subject to rational assessment.

• Most texts treat important subjects superficially. They overemphasize the outward appearance of things rather than their underlying dynamics. Many texts also tend to approach the heart of the matter and stop short of further exploration. Topics are introduced, treated briefly, and dropped. History, for instance, is presented as a series of events, narrative, chronology. Texts describe events briefly, but seldom mention how people perceived them, why they accepted or resisted them, or what ideas and assumptions influenced them and how. Texts "cover" different political systems by mentioning the titles of political offices. Most discussions of religion reflect the same superficiality. Texts emphasize names of deities, rituals, and practices. Beliefs are not explored in sufficient depth; the inner life is ignored, the personal dimension omitted.

• Texts often encourage student passivity by providing all the answers. After lengthy map skills units, students are asked to apply those skills to answer simple questions. However, they are not held accountable for providing the answers on their own. Texts usually err by asking questions students should be able to answer on their own, and immediately providing answers. Once students understand the system, they know that they don't have to stop and think for themselves, because the text will do it *for* them in the next sentence.

With these general dissatisfactions and an ideal of critical thinking instruction in mind, (see the April article), teachers with appropriate inservice and resource materials can begin to create remodels like the following:

The Constitution

Excerpts from the objectives of the remodelled lesson
The students will:
- clarify claims in the text by exploring root issues regarding the distribution of power in our government
- develop some criteria for evaluating candidates
- through Socratic questioning, understand the reasons for and assumptions underlying rights guaranteed under the Bill of Rights

Original Lesson Plan

Abstract

This chapter, "The Constitution of the United States", begins with a paragraph about the Articles of Confederation and why they failed. It then lists the leaders at the Constitutional Convention. The terms 'republic' and 'federal' are explained, and some of the powers of the national government listed. Separation of powers and the three branches of government are briefly explained. Students are asked to state which powers from a list belong to the states, and which to the federal government. Students are told about the Constitutional

Convention debate between small and large states about how the number of representatives to Congress should be allotted, and how the issue was resolved. The term 'Amendments' is explained. Students are told that some states refused to approve the Constitution until the Bill of Rights was added. A three page Summary of the Constitution follows. Students are asked questions about the Bill of Rights.

from *The United States and Its Neighbors*, Timothy M. Helmus, Val E. Arnsdorf, Edgar A. Toppin, and Norman J. G. Pounds. © 1984 by Silver Burdett Co. pp. 120-125.

Excerpts from the Critique

INTRODUCTION

We chose this lesson for its emphasis on and summary of the Constitution, because understanding the Constitution is crucial to citizenship in a democracy. Students should explore the ideas underlying important aspects of our government: how it is supposed to work, why it was structured the way it was, how the structure is supposed to preserve citizens' rights, how it could fail to do so, and why some rights are important to preserve. Critical education demands clear and well developed understanding of these points. When understanding is superficial or vague, hidden agendas and mere associations guide thought and behavior. Slogans substitute for reasons, prejudices for thought. Citizens become willing to accept the *appearance* of freedom, equality under the law, and democracy, rather than fighting for their *realization*.

Summarizing the Constitution in language 5th graders can understand is an excellent idea, though some parts of the original could also be used. On the whole, the summary is good, though flawed by its incompleteness. For students to have enough details to understand the key concepts of the lesson, more of the specific duties of the branches of government should have been mentioned.

The greatest flaw with the lesson is its size and lack of depth; not nearly enough time is given to fostering understanding of this important document. This section is only part of a chapter which includes details of battles in the Revolutionary War. The relative importance of different material should be reflected in the text space given and time spent on it. Of the six chapter review questions, only one, a recall question, addresses the Constitution. Equal space is devoted to *"What do you think was the most important battle of the Revolutionary War? Explain."* Spending insufficient time on such important ideas leads the text to treat them superficially or vaguely. Students have little opportunity to understand key ideas fully, see the whole picture, appreciate reasons for important parts of the Constitution, or develop their perspectives on government, human relations, and how to preserve their rights.

INADEQUATE EXPLANATIONS

The lesson has too few questions, no extended discussion, and many of the questions are trivial or simple recall. Some of the suggested explanations and answers are sorely incomplete, confusing, or fail to answer the questions. For instance, the text answer to the question about why the right to a jury trial was considered important, is, *"It had been denied under British rule."* This answer is inadequate. Arson wasn't allowed under British rule, yet is not guaranteed under the Bill of Rights. The right to a trial by jury was included because the writers of the Constitution thought it was among the most important human rights. Students should consider *why*.

Important explanations are undeveloped. Questions about why the system of separation of powers and the Bill of Rights were included, for instance, fail to probe the reasons. The student text explains, *"The members of the Constitutional Convention wanted a government that would protect the people's rights, not take them away. So they divided the government's power into three parts, or branches. This is called separation of power."* Checkup question 4 (p. 120) asks, *"Why were powers divided among three branches of government?"* The suggested answer, by simply reiterating the abstract claim in the text, turns a thought-provoking question into a recall question. Students are encouraged to substitute reiteration for understanding; to accept an apparently unconnected answer as an adequate explanation. The text fails to explain *how* separation of powers protects people's rights.

The given answer to, *"Why was it necessary to add a Bill of Rights to the Constitution?"* is, *"because many states insisted that the people's rights as well as the rights of the government must be written down"*. Again, the "answer" fails to answer the important questions: *Why* did people think rights should be written down? What is the advantage? Why write them into the Constitution? Does writing them into the Constitution guarantee they won't be violated? Crucial questions and connections are left unanswered. Students are not left with a clear understanding either of the connection between separation of powers and people's rights, or of the importance of the Bill of Rights ....

Strategies used to remodel
S-13 raising and pursuing root questions
S-17 clarifying or critiquing text
S-22 distinguishing facts from ideals
S-11 developing criteria for evaluation
S-19 engaging in Socratic questioning
S-9 clarifying issues and claims
S-25 examining assumptions

Excerpts from the Remodelled Lesson Plan

2) SEPARATION OF POWERS, AND CHECKS AND BALANCES

Discussion of the last point in section one (Presidential veto) can lead into a discussion of the separation of powers, and checks and balances. To probe these ideas in greater depth than the text, thereby making the reasons for our system of government clearer, you could ask, "Have you ever been in a situation where someone had too much power, or abused his or her power? Why was that a problem? How could the problem be solved? How did the authors of the Constitution try to solve it? Why not give all of the power to one branch, say, the Executive? *S-13* Why have each branch have some power over the others, rather than giving each branch complete control over its duties? What does the text say in answer to this question? *S-17* What does this mean? How could concentrating power lead to loss of people's rights? Make up an example which shows me how a system like this could prevent abuses of power. This separation of powers, and system of checks and balances is the ideal. *S-22* What could make it go wrong? (Using the checks and balances unfairly, or not using them at all.) Make up an example of how it could go wrong. Why would that be bad? What has to happen to make it work right? What should we look for in our leaders? *S-11* What sort of people should be chosen? (E.g., when voting for President, voters should consider who the candidate would appoint to important offices or whether the candidate is a good judge of character. Perhaps members of Congress who abuse or fail to use checks on the President should be reconsidered.) ...

3) THE BILL OF RIGHTS

Students may reread the Bill of Rights section in the summary. The teacher may also want to make the real Bill of Rights available, or have it read in class, and compared to the summary. Students could use the summary to generate a list of the rights covered. To foster in-depth understanding of the meaning and importance of the Bill of Rights, the teacher could conduct a Socratic discussion of each right, with questions like the following: *S-19* What does this right mean? *S-9* What does it say people should be allowed to do? How could it be violated or denied? How important is it? Why? Why would not having this right be bad? *S-13* How would it hurt the individual? Society? Are there exceptions to this right? Should there be these exceptions? Why or why not?

The class could also discuss the underlying ideas and
assumptions behind the Bill of Rights, especially the First
Amendment rights. *S-25* (The importance of following conscience, especially regarding political and religious beliefs; the
idea that when we can all discuss our ideas and consider all
alternatives, the best ideas will prevail or compromise can be
reached; people who do no wrong shouldn't have to be afraid of
their government; even people who do wrong should have
rights; trials in which both sides argue before a jury of impartial citizens will best render justice; government has an obligation to be fair to citizens — not just run things because it's
strong; etc.) You might ask, "Why did some people want these
rights written down? What are the advantages? Are there disadvantages? Are there important rights omitted? Should they
be added to the Constitution? Why or why not?" Students could
compare their answers to that given in the text. *S-17*

For this activity, the teacher could split the class into groups,
each of which could discuss one or two rights. One member of
each group could then report to the rest of the class....

✦✦ Chapter 24

Critical Thinking in Elementary Language Arts

with A. J. A. Binker

Abstract

This, the third paper in the series for Teaching K–8, *briefly discusses the relationship of critical thinking to language arts instruction, then provides an example of a remodelled lesson on a short story.*

L ast April *Teaching K–8* published an article on infusing critical thinking by remodelling lesson plans. The October issue carried an article focused specifically on remodelling social studies lessons. The present article will apply the same basic concept to language arts instruction.

Lesson plan remodelling provides a framework wherein teachers redesign existing lesson plans based on their critical assessment of them. It helps teachers clarify their concept of critical thinking and the critical person by distinguishing and clarifying principles of critical thought. Once teachers have familiarized themselves with a few of the principles and how those principles can be integrated into instruction, they then select lessons in which those principles could be infused, and thus redesign their classroom instruction.

Throughout the process, we recommend that the teacher have clearly in mind an ideal of education and of the genuinely educated person. This ideal is developed at length in the four critical thinking handbooks we have published and serves as an organizing concept in the remodelling process. For example, if teachers are clear in their own minds that a genuinely educated person can distinguish knowledge from information, then they will look for occassions in their teaching in which students are called upon to use the distinction effectively. All of the various principles of critical thinking correlate with a set of ideals that define what it is to be educated. Before turning to an example of a remodelled lesson, let's examine some basic problems with language arts texts you should watch out for. They help suggest what most needs remodelling.

Language arts instruction tends to be fragmented. As a rule, texts fail to adequately address connections between the various aspects of language arts instruction: language, reading, writing, grammar, and literature. Skills, techniques, basic concepts, and insights within each area are rarely transferred or compared to those of the others. Furthermore, instruction within each area tends to be fragmented. The logic of grammar — the basic unifying patterns underlying many rules of grammar — is routinely ignored. Skills and crucial grammatical distinctions are usually taught as mindless drill, rather than as tools, with specific functions, useful for specific tasks. Students usually learn how to use each skill only in exercises when the directions tell them to; they rarely transfer that skill to situations that require it. In reading, discussion is also usually fragmented, with questions regarding the writer's purpose, the main points, and the significant issues mixed willy-nilly with irrelevancies and trivial details. Most importantly, the fundamental idea and goal of language use — that of "clear communication with an audience" — is rarely used to unify either reading or writing instruction; it is in fact rarely mentioned. As often as possible, each detail covered in language arts instruction should be related to this basic idea with examples that students can understand.

Students are rarely asked to evaluate writing which they create or read. Thus, they do not develop and clarify their own standards of good writing, their own sense of the distinctions between what is clear and vague, gripping and boring, flowing and awkward.

Now let us look at a sample remodel.

Marvin's Manhole

Objectives of the remodelled lesson
The students will:
- select story details to support a conclusion
- discuss different interpretations of a character's behavior

Original Lesson Plan ———

Abstract

The students read "Marvin's Manhole", a story about a boy who, rejecting his mother's explanation of the purpose of a manhole, decides that there is a "scary thing" living below his street. Marvin tries to make contact with the thing, but fails. One day he finds the manhole open. After looking for the thing, Marvin climbs into the manhole, has a scare, and meets a workman who confirms his mother's explanation.

Students are asked to recall details, discuss Marvin's personality, discuss parts of Marvin's reasoning, read an emphasized word as Marvin would have said it, discuss some of the pictures, discuss Marvin's feelings, and describe what might have happened after the end of the story.

From *People Need People,*
Eldonna L. Evertts, Holt Publishing. 1977. pp. T222–231

Critique

This lesson fails to take advantage of the ambiguous nature of Marvin's story. It is unclear whether Marvin really believes in the existence of the scary thing, or is merely pretending to believe in it. Most of Marvin's behavior can be interpreted either way. This lesson misses the opportunity to have students argue for one interpretation over another, or see how each interpretation affects the reader's understanding of the details in the story.

Early in the story, when Marvin hits the manhole cover with his baseball bat and runs away, the reader could interpret his actions as bravely trying to get the scary thing to come out, or as part of a game. The faultiness of Marvin's reasoning (for example, when he concludes that the scary thing eats the bread he leaves on the street overnight) suggests that he's joking. Yet, when he discovers that the manhole is open, he behaves as though he believes in the thing.

The suggested questions do nothing to explore the possible different points of view. Only one question raises the issue of Marvin's belief, "How strongly do you think Marvin believed in the scary thing by this point in the story?" Another assumes his belief in the thing, "Do you think Marvin finally believed what his mother had told him about the manhole?" The different interpretations, then, could be the focus of the remodelled lesson.

Strategies used to remodel

S–23 evaluating arguments
S–17 making inferences
S–10 using critical vocabulary
S–3 exercising reciprocity
S–18 supplying evidence for a conclusion

Remodelled Lesson Plan ───────────

The process of sorting out the different interpretations of the story should begin with Marvin's claim that he thinks there is a scary thing in the manhole. The teacher might ask the students, "Why do you think Marvin said that there was a thing in the manhole?" Encourage a discussion of the question. Then focus on the issue, "Does Marvin really believe in the scary thing?" Keep raising this issue as the students discuss various parts of the story. Ask, "Does this part of the story support or weaken your conclusion? *S-23* How? If you think he does believe in the thing, why do you think he did this? *S-17* What did you infer from his actions? *S-10* If you think he doesn't believe in the thing, why do you think he did this? What did you infer from his actions?"

Accept any position a student may maintain. The possibilities include: Marvin believed in the thing the whole time; Marvin believed part of the time; Marvin was pretending to believe in the thing. Encourage the students to use "if-then" statements when discussing the implications of their ideas; for example, "If Marvin really believed in the thing, he didn't make a good inference when he concluded that it ate the bread." Have the students state each other's positions. *S-3*
Finally, after the story has been read and discussed, review the positions taken and assign a writing exercise. Have the students state the issue and defend their positions with details from the story. *S-18*

Chapter 25

Critical Thinking
in Elementary Science

with A. J. A. Binker

Abstract
This paper, the fourth in the Teaching K–8 *remodelling series, briefly explains the need for students to learn how to think scientifically, and why standard instruction fails to achieve this goal. It then provides a remodelled physics lesson.*

*T*he process of remodelling lesson plans to encourage critical thinking has previously been canvassed in this journal in three previous editions. The first covered a general introduction to lesson plan remodelling, the second illustrated the process of remodelling social studies lessons, and the third, the process of remodelling language arts lessons. Today you will be given a sense of how to infuse critical thinking into science lessons. Whenever we remodel a lesson we redesign it in the light of our desire to improve it by infusing more critical thinking into it.

A critical approach to teaching science is concerned less with students accumulating undigested facts than with students learning to think scientifically. As students learn to think scientifically, they inevitably do organize and internalize facts. But they learn them deeply, tied into ideas they have thought through, and hence do not have to re-learn them again and again. Education in science should combat the common assumption that "Only scientists can understand science." Scientific thinking should be a routine dimension of everyone's daily life. But students have to do something as close to real scientific thinking as possible.

Scientists are not given experiments; they begin with a problem or question, and have to figure out how to solve it through trial and error and experiment. They struggle with problems, explore blind alleys, and often do not have step-by-step routines to fall back on. Typical science texts, however, present the student with the finished products of science. These texts present information, and tell students how to conduct experiments. Thus, students rarely engage in or see themselves as able to engage in scientific reasoning. Texts also require students to practice the skills of measuring, graphing, and counting, often for no reason other than practice. Sometimes, the experiment or study has no obvious relation to the question it is presumably designed to settle. The reasons for the design of experiments and forms of presentation of data are rarely made clear. We need to teach science in a way that avoids these pitfalls.

Below we provide an example of a lesson remodelled to overcome some' of these problems.

Ah Chute

Objectives of the remodelled lesson
The students will:
- design and test parachutes
- discuss characteristics which affect the descent rates of parachutes
- transfer insights about parachutes to other falling objects
- hypothesize, test, and refine their hypotheses regarding the descent rates of objects

Original Lesson Plan

> *Abstract*
>
> This lesson focuses on the key question, *"What is the rate of descent of your parachute?"* Students design, build, and test parachutes (twice each from three different heights), calculating the rates of descent in meters per second. They then discuss the following questions: *What things affect the rate of descent? Did the rate of your chute change from one height to another? Why? Select the five slowest rates of descent and the five fastest from the class chart. Have those students display and describe their parachutes. Were there similarities? What can you conclude? How would you modify your parachute to improve its performance?*
>
> from *The Sky's the Limit* Arthur Wiebe and Larry Ecklund editors. Fresno Pacific College. Project Aims. © 1982 p. 13

Critique

A major weakness of this lesson is its failure to connect how a parachute works to the topic of falling objects in general. It misses the opportunity to teach important science concepts such as gravity, wind resistance, and inertia. This trivializes the lesson by restricting it to one narrow topic.

This lesson offers the opportunity to have students engage in extended scientific reasoning — posing questions, testing answers, posing new questions, conducting further tests, while assessing their original ideas and refining their initial generalizations. Such extended work better reflects science than a one-shot experiment. Furthermore, headway can be made on the broadened topic without elaborate preparation or difficult measurements.

Strategies used to remodel
S-10   clarifying ideas
S-15   generating or assessing solutions
S-1   exercising independent thought
S-7   transferring ideas to new contexts
S-31   refining generalizations

Remodelled Lesson Plan

Begin by asking if anyone knows what a parachute is and what it is for. Students should know that a parachute is designed to keep something from falling too quickly, that is, that it slows the rate of descent. Rather than using the key question in the text, focus attention on the discussion question of what affects rate of descent. Ask students what characteristics make a good parachute, and how they know. **S-10** Ask them to think of situations which call for using a parachute. **S-15** Ask if there are any other possible solutions for these problems. Have them consider questions like these, "What affects the rate of descent of a parachute? How could we find out? How does a parachute work? Why does it work?"

Students could then design their tests, as well as their parachutes. **S-1** Perhaps they could try to make appropriate parachutes for various specific purposes or objects. Students may repeat their tests on different days and/or in different places (e.g., windy versus protected areas) and compare results. As in the original, have them compare slow with fast parachutes, and speculate on which differences affected the descent rate. They could compare parachutes of different materials, and carrying different weights and shapes. Ask them, "What does this tell us? About air? Gravity? Objects? Why did we get the results we did? Why does the parachute fall slowly?" Students could then begin making generalizations and hypotheses, and designing experiments to test them.

You could then broaden the original question to, "What affects the rate of fall of objects, and why?" **S-7** Students could practice making and refining generalizations. **S-31** Suggest that they experiment with other kinds of falling objects, i.e., paper planes, feathers, books, rocks, pillows, etc. Students need not measure, they could simply group objects in general categories of fast-falling, slow-falling, and in-between speeds.

After each test or each few tests, discuss results. "What were you testing for? (To see if weight, size, density, etc. affect fall rate.) What did you do? (Dropped this and that from the same height at the same time and place.) Why? (If what we tested for affects fall rate, since they're the same in every way but this, then this should have fallen much more slowly than that.) What happened? (This fell much more slowly that that.) What does that mean? Could there be another explanation? Were there other differences between the two objects that could have accounted for the results? How do these latest findings compare with our earlier tests? What other questions could be asked? Is there anything else that you noticed, that would explain the results? What else could you test for? Now what would you say affects descent rates? Why? What *doesn't* affect descent rates? Why?"

The class could keep notes on the discussions, listing ideas, tests, and conclusions. The teacher could, perhaps during the summary, point out tests that failed or hypotheses which were proven wrong, but from which students learned something. Students could use the class records, sort slow, medium, and fast falling objects, and write short passages comparing the three kinds of objects, or write about other factors or conditions which affect descent rate, trying to generalize from them, and speculating on the reasons for or principles behind the results.

The material in this lesson could be related to botany with a discussion of different shaped seeds and seed containers, and how well they scatter seeds. Students could discuss objects falling on the moon. If necessary, first point out to students that the moon has less gravity and less air. Students could compare how different objects would fall on the moon as opposed to Earth. *S-7*

✦✦ Chapter 26

Teaching Critical Thinking
in the Strong Sense:
A Focus on Self-Deception, World Views,
and a Dialectical Mode of Analysis

Abstract

This revised paper, originally published in Informal Logic *in (1982), is one of the most influential of Richard Paul's writings among philosophers interested in critical thinking. In it, Paul questions some of the major assumptions that underlie much instruction in critical thinking at the college level. In so doing, Paul implicitly broadens the concept of critical thinking and links it with the problem of rationality. He links the assessment of "arguments" ultimately to the assessment of "forms of life". He argues that a world view is implicit in our behavior as well as in our public pronouncements, and further, that there are inevitable contradictions and conflicts between what we do and how we describe what we do. In this view reasoning is implicit in and intrinsic to human life and behavior. Because much of our reasoning is buried in our lives, and because there are multiple points of view possible in which to reason, the ability to enter sympathetically into divergent perspectives and to explicate the deepest substructure in reasoning are crucial to Paul's view of critical thinking. Finally, in this paper Paul emphasizes the significance of human interests, often vested interests, lurking behind, shaping, and distorting reasoning. Understanding this, it is easy to see why Paul argues against an atomistic approach to assessment of the strengths and weaknesses of reasoning, why he believes that to appreciate a line of reasoning we must appreciate how it stands up under criticism from opposing lines of reasoning, and why he so often sees strengths as implicit insights and weaknesses as distortions, as obfuscation of counter insights. For Paul there is often unexpressed motivation behind "mistakes" in reasoning. Humans often make the "mistakes" that serve their interests. We develop our ethical sensitivity only by recognizing the subtlety and pervasiveness of the dark side of human thought and reason. Given the decisions that all adults, like it or not, must make for human good or ill, it is not possible to be both intellectually naive and an ethical adult.*

... no abstract or analytic point exists out of all connection with historical, personal thought: ... every thought belongs, not just somewhere, but to someone, and is at home in a context of other thoughts, a context which is not purely formally prescribed. Thoughts ... are something to be known and understood in these concrete terms.

Isaiah Berlin, *Concepts and Categories*, xii

465

✦ *The Weak Sense: Dangers and Pitfalls*

*T*o teach a critical thinking course is to make important and often frustrating decisions about what to include and exclude, what to conceive as one's primary goals and what secondary, and how to tie all of what one includes into a coherent relationship to one's goals. There have been considerable and important debates on the value of a "symbolic" versus a "non-symbolic" approach, the appropriate definition and classification of fallacies, appropriate analysis of extended and non-extended arguments, and so forth. There has been little discussion, and as far as I know, virtually no debate, on how to avoid the fundamental dangers in teaching such a course: that of "sophistry" on the one hand (inadvertently teaching students to use critical concepts and techniques to maintain their most deep-seated prejudices and irrational habits of thought by making them appear more rational and putting their opponents on the defensive), and that of "dismissal" (the student rejects the subject either as sophistry or in favor of some supposed alternative — feeling, intuition, faith, higher consciousness, ...).

Students, much as we might sometimes wish it, do not come to us as "blank slates" upon which we can inscribe the inference-drawing patterns, analytic skills, and truth-facing motivations we value. Students studying critical thinking at the university level have highly developed belief systems buttressed by deep-seated uncritical, egocentric, and sociocentric habits of thought by which they interpret and process their experiences, whether academic or not, and place them into some larger perspective. Consequently, most students find it easy to question simply, and *only,* those beliefs, assumptions, and inferences they have already "rejected", and very difficult, often traumatic, to question those in which they have a personal, egocentric investment.

I know of no way of teaching critical thinking so that the student who learns to recognize questionable assumptions and inferences only in "egocentrically neutral" cases, *automatically* transfers those skills to the egocentric and sociocentric ones. Indeed, I think the opposite more commonly occurs. Those students who already have sets of biased assumptions, stereotypes, egocentric and sociocentric beliefs, taught to recognize "bad" reasoning in "neutral" cases (or in the case of the "opposition") become *more* sophistic rather than less so, more skilled in rationalizing and intellectualizing their biases. They are then *less* rather than *more* likely to abandon them if they later meet someone who questions them. Like the religious believer who studies apologetics, they now have a variety of critical moves to use in defense of their *a priori* egocentric belief systems.

This is not the effect, of course, we wish our teaching to have. Virtually all teachers of critical thinking want their teaching to have a global "Socratic" effect, making major inroads into the everyday reasoning of the student, enhancing to some degree that healthy, practical, and skilled skepticism one naturally and rightly associates with the *rational* person. Therefore, students need experience in seriously questioning previously held beliefs and assumptions and in identifying contradictions and inconsistencies in personal and social life. When we think along these lines and get glimpses into the everyday lives and habits of our students, most of us probably experience moments of frustration and cynicism.

I don't think the situation is hopeless, but I do believe the time has come to raise serious questions about how we now teach critical thinking. Current methods, as I conceive them, often inadvertently encourage critical thinking in the "weak" sense. The most fundamental and questionable assumption of these approaches (whether formal or informal) is that critical thinking can be successfully taught as a battery of technical skills which can be mastered more or less one-by-one without giving serious attention to self-deception, background logic, and multi-categorical ethical issues.

The usual scenario runs something like this. One begins with some general pep-talk on the importance of critical thinking in personal and social life. In this pep-talk one reminds students of the large scale social problems created by prejudice, irrationality, and sophistic manipulation. Then one launches into a discussion of the difference between arguments and non-arguments and students are led to believe that, without any further knowledge of contextual or background considerations, they can learn to analyze and evaluate arguments by parsing them into, and examining the relation between, "premises" and "conclusions". (The "non-arguments" presumably do not need critical appraisal.) To examine that relationship, students look for formal or informal fallacies, conceived as atomically determinable and correctable "mistakes". Irrationality is implied thereby to be reducible to complex combinations of atomic mistakes. One roots it out, presumably, by rooting out the atomic mistakes, one-by-one.

Models of this kind do not effectively teach critical thought. This atomistic "weak sense" approach and the questionable assumptions underlying it should be contrasted with an alternative approach specifically designed to avoid its pitfalls.

This alternative view rejects the idea that critical thinking can be taught as a battery of atomic technical skills independent of egocentric beliefs and commitments. Instead of "atomic arguments" (a set of premises and a conclusion) it emphasizes argument *networks* (world views); instead of evaluating atomic arguments it emphasizes a more dialectical and dialogical approach. Arguments need to be appraised in relation to counter-arguments. One can make moves that are very difficult to defend or ones that strengthen one's position. An atomic argument is merely a limited set of moves within a more complex set of moves reflecting a variety of logically significant engagements in the world. Argument exchanges are means by which contesting points of view are brought into rational conflict. A line of reasoning can rarely be refuted by an individual charge of fallacy, however well supported. The charge of fallacy is a move; however it is rarely logically compelling; it virtually never refutes a point of view. This approach more accurately reflects our own and the student's experience of argument exchanges.

By immediately introducing students to these more "global" problems in the analysis and evaluation of reasoning, we help them more clearly see the relationship between world views, forms of life, human engagements and interests, what is at stake (versus what is at issue), how what is at issue is often itself at issue, how the unexpressed as well as the expressed may be significant, the difficulties of judging credibility, and the ethical dimension in most important and complex human problems.

✦ Some Basic Theory: World Views, Forms of Life

Here are some basic theoretical underpinnings for a "strong sense" approach:

1) As humans we are — first, last, and always — engaged in inter-related life projects which, taken as a whole, define our personal "form of life" in relation to broader social forms. Because we are engaged in some projects rather than others, we organize or conceptualize the world and our place in it in somewhat different terms than others do. We have somewhat different *interests,* somewhat different *stakes,* and somewhat different *perceptions* of what is so. We make somewhat different assumptions and reason somewhat differently from them.

2) We also express to ourselves and others a more articulated view of how we see things, a view only partially consistent at best with the view presupposed by and reflected in our behavior. We have, then, *two* world views overlapping each other, one implicit in our activity and engagements, another implicit in how we describe our behavior. One must recognize contradictions between these conflicting views to develop as a critical thinker and as a person in good faith with one's self. Both traits are measured by the degree to which we can articulate what we live and live what we articulate.

3) Reasoning is an essential and defining operation presupposed by all human acts. To reason is to use elements in a logical system to generate conclusions. Conclusions may be explicit in words or implicit in behavior. Sometimes reasoning is explicitly cast into the form of an argument, sometimes not. However, since reasoning presupposes a system or systems of which it is a manifestation, the full implications of reasoning are rarely (if ever) exhausted or displayed in arguments in which they are cast. Arguments presuppose questions at issue. Questions at issue presuppose a point of view and interests at stake. Different points of view frequently differ, not simply in answers to questions, but in the appropriate formulations of questions themselves.

4) When we, including those of us who are logicians, analyze and evaluate arguments important to us (this includes all arguments which, if accepted, would strengthen or weaken beliefs to which we have committed ourselves in word or deed), we do so in relationship to prior belief-commitments. The

best we can do to move toward increased objectivity is to bring to the surface the set of beliefs, assumptions, and inferences from the perspective of which our analysis proceeds, and to see explicitly the dialectical nature of our task, the critical moves we might make at various points, and the various possible counter-moves to them.

5) Skill in analyzing and evaluating reasoning is skill in reciprocity, the ability to reason within more than one point of view, understanding strengths and weaknesses through comprehending the objections that could be raised at various points in the arguments by alternative points of view.

6) Laying out elements of reasoning in deductive form is useful, not principally to see whether a "mistake" had been made, but to see critical moves one might make to determine the strengths and weaknesses of the reasoning in relation to alternatives.

7) Since vested interest typically influences perception, assumptions, reasoning in general, and specific conclusions, we must become aware of the nature of our own and others' engagements to recognize strengths and weaknesses in reasoning.

   a) Only when we recognize that a given argument reflects or, if justified, would serve a given interest can we, by imaginatively entertaining a competing interest, construct an opposing point of view and so an opposing argument or set of arguments. By developing both arguments dialectically, we can see their strengths and weaknesses.

   b) Arguments are not things-in-themselves but constructions of specific people who must further interpret and develop them, for example, to answer objections. By recognizing the interests typically correlated with given arguments, we can often challenge the credibility of others' premises by alluding to discrepancies between what they say and what they do. In doing so we force them to critique their own behavior in line with the implications of their arguments, or to abandon the line of argument. There are a variety of critical moves they may make upon being so challenged.

   c) By reflecting on interests as implicit in behavior, one can often much more effectively construct the assumptions most favorable to those interests. Once formulated, one can begin to formulate alternative competing assumptions. Both can then be more effectively questioned and arguments for and against them can be entertained.

8) The total set of factual claims that buttress a world view, hence the various arguments generated by it, is usually indefinitely large and often involves shifting conceptual problems and implicit judgments of value (especially shifts in how to formulate the "facts"). The credibility of an individual claim often depends on the credibility of many other claims; very often the claims themselves are very difficult to verify "directly" and atomically. Very often then, to analyze an argument, we must judge

relative credibility. These judgments are more plausible if they take into account the vested interests and the track records of the sources.

9) The terms in which an argument is cast often reflects the biased interest of the person who formulated it. Calling into question the very concepts used or the use to which they are put is an important critical move. To become adept at this, we must practice recognizing how social groups systematically and selectively move back and forth between usage in keeping with the logic of ordinary language and that which accords with the ideological commitments of the group (and so conflicts with ordinary use). Consider the ways many people use key terms in current international debate — say, 'freedom fighter', 'liberator', 'revolutionary', 'guerrilla', 'terrorist' — and reflect on:

   a) what is implied by the *logic* of the terms apart from the usage of any particular social group (say U.S. citizens, Germans, Israelis, Soviets);

   b) what is implied by the usage of a particular group with vested interests (say, U.S. citizens, Germans, Israelis, Soviets); and

   c) the various historical examples that suggest inconsistency in the use of these by that group, and how this inconsistency depends on fundamental, typically unexpressed, assumptions. Through such disciplined reflection, one can identify predictable, self-serving inconcsistencies.

✦ *Multi-Dimensional Ethical Issues*

Teaching critical thinking in the strong sense helps students develop reasoning skills precisely in those areas where they are most likely to have egocentric and sociocentric biases. Such biases exist most profoundly in areas of their identities and vested interests. Their identities and interests are linked in turn to their unarticulated world views. One's unarticulated world view represents the person that one *is* (the view implicit in the principles which guide one's actions). One's articulated view represents the person that one *thinks* one is (the view implicit in the principles used to *justify* one's actions). Excepting honest mistakes, the contradictions or inconsistencies between these two represent the degree to which one reasons and acts in bad faith or self-deceptively.

Multi-dimensional issues involving proposed ethical justifications for behavior are ideal for teaching critical thinking. Most political, social, and personal issues which most concern us and students are of this type — abortion, nuclear energy, nuclear arms, the nature of national security, poverty, social injustices of various kinds, revolution and intervention, socialized medicine, government regulation, sexism, racism, problems of love and friendship, jealousy, rights to private property, rights to world resources, faith and intuition versus reason, and so forth.

Obviously one can cover only a few such issues, and I believe that the advantages lie in covering fewer of them deeply and intensively. I am certainly unsympathetic to inundating the student with an array of truncated arguments set up to "illustrate" atomic fallacies.

Since I teach in the United States, and since the media here as everywhere else in the world reflects, and most students have internalized, a profoundly nationalistic bias, I focus one segment of my course on identifying national bias in the news. In doing this, students must face issues that, to be approached dialectically, require them to discover that mainstream "American" reasoning and the mainstream "American" point of view on world issues is not the only dialectical possibility. I identify as mainstream American views any which have significant support with the Democratic and Republican parties. This segment of the course serves a number of purposes:

1) Though most students have internalized much media "propaganda", so that their egos are partly identified with it, they are neither totally taken in by that propaganda nor incapable of beginning to systematically question it.

2) The students become more adept at constructing and more empathetic toward alternative lines of reasoning as the *sociocentric assumptions* of mainstream media coverage come more and more to the surface — for example, the assumptions that:

   a) the U.S. government, compared to other governments, is more committted to ideals,

   b) U.S. citizens have more energy, more practical know-how, and more common sense than others;

   c) the world as a whole would be better off (freer, safer, more just) if the U.S. had *more* power;

   d) U.S. citizens are less greedy and self-deceived than other peoples;

   e) U.S. lives are more important than the lives of other peoples.

3) Explicitly addressing and constructing dialectical alternatives to political and national as well as professional and religious "party lines" and exploring their contradictions enables students to draw parallels to their personal and their peer groups' "party lines" and the myriad contradictions in their talk and behavior. Such "discoveries" explicitly and dramatically forge the beginnings of a commitment to developing the "critical spirit", the foundation for "strong sense" skills and insights.

✦ A Sample Assignment and Results

It is useful to provide one sample assignment to indicate how my concerns and objectives can be translated into assignments. The following was assigned last semester (1984) as a take-home mid-term examination, approximately six weeks into the semester. The students were allowed three weeks to complete it.

The objective of this mid-term is to determine the extent to which you understand and can effectively use the basic concepts of the course: world view, assumptions, concepts (personal, social, implicit in language, technical), evidence (empirical claims), implications, consistency, conclusions, premises, questions-at-issue.

You are to view and critically and sympathetically analyze two films: *Attack on the Americas* (a right-wing think-tank film alleging Communist control of Central American revolutionaries) and *Revolution or Death* (a *World Council of Church's* film defending the rebels in El Salvador). Two incompatible world views are presented in those films. After analyzing the films and consulting whatever background material you deem necessary to understand the two world views, construct a dialogue between two of the most intelligent defenders of each perspective. They should each demonstrate skills in explicating the basic assumptions, the questionable claims, ideas, inferences, values, and conclusions of the other side. Both should be able to make some concessions to the other point of view without conceding their basic positions. Each should be able to summarize some of the inferences of the other side and raise questions about those inferences (e.g.,"You appear to me to be arguing in the following way. You assume that .... You ignore that .... And then you conclude that ....").

In the second part of your paper, write a third-person commentary on the debate, indicating which point of view is in the strongest position logically in your view. Argue for your position; do not simply assert it. Give good reasons for rejecting or accepting whatever aspects of the two world views you reject or accept. Make clear to the reader how your position reflects your world view. The dialogue should have at least 14 exchanges (28 entries) and the commentary should be at least 4 typewritten pages.

A variety of background materials were made available, including the U.S. State Department "White Paper", an open letter from the late Archbishop of San Salvador, a copy of the Platform of the El Salvador rebels, and numerous current newspaper and magazine articles and editorials on the issue. The students were encouraged to discuss and debate the issue outside of class (which they did). The students were expected to document how the major newspapers were covering the story (e.g., that accounts favorable to the State Department position tended to be given front page coverage while accounts critical of the State Department position, say from *Amnesty International,* were de-emphasized on pages 9 through 17). There was also discussion of internal inconsistencies within the accounts.

Many of the students came to see one or more of the following points:

1) That in a conflict such as this the two sides disagree not only on conclusions but even about how the issue ought to be put. One side will put the issue, for example, in terms of the dangers of a communist takeover, the other in terms of the need for people to over-throw a repressive regime. One will see the fundamental problem as caused by Cuban and Soviet intervention, the other side by U.S. intervention. Each side will see the other as begging the essential question.

2) That a debate on how to word the issue will often become a debate on a series of factual questions. This debate will be extended into a series of historical questions. Each side will typically see the other as suppressing evidence. Those favorable to the Duarte regime, for example, will see the other side as suppressing evidence of the extent of communist involvement in El Salvador. Those favorable to the rebels will see the other side as suppressing evidence of government complicity in terrorist acts of the right. There will be disagreement about which side is committing most of the violent acts.

3) That these factual disagreements will at some point or another lead to a shifting of ground to *conceptual disagreements:* which acts should be called 'terrorist' which 'revolutionary', and which 'acts of liberation'. This debate will at some point become a debate about *values,* about which acts are reprehensible or justified. Very often the acts which from one perspective seem required by circumstances will be morally condemned by the other.

4) That at various points in the discussion the debate will become "philosophical" or "anthropological", involving broad issues concerning "the nature of man" and "the nature of human society". The side supporting the government tends to take a philosophical position that plays down the capacity of "mass man" to make rational and appropriate judgments in its own behalf, at least when under the influence of outside agitators and subversives. The other side tends to be more favorable to "mass man" and suspicious of our government's capacity or right to make what appear to them to be decisions that should be left to the people. Each side thinks the other begs important questions, suppresses evidence, stereotypes, uses unjustified analogies, uses faulty causal reasoning, misuses concepts, and so forth.

Such assignments help students appreciate the kinds of moves that typically occur in everyday argument, put them into perspective, and construct alternative arguments, precisely because they more clearly see how arguments develop in relation to each other and so in relation to a broader perspective. They give students more practical insight into the motivated nature of argument "flaws" than the traditional approach. They are therefore better able to anticipate them and more sensitive to the special probing moves that need to be made. Finally, they are much more sensitive (than I believe they would be under most "weak sense" approaches) to the profound ethical consequences of ego-serving reasoning, and to the ease with which we can fall prey to it. If we can indeed accomplish something like these results, then there is much to be said for further work and development of "strong sense" approaches. What I have described here is, I hope, the beginning of such work.

Postscript

In the five years since I wrote this paper, I have become increasingly convinced that if students are to learn to think critically in a strong sense, they must be exposed to critical thinking over an extended period of time, over years not months. To think critically in a stong sense is to become a critical person. It is to develop particular values and traits of mind in addition to particular skills and abilities. If we are committed to critical thinking, we must then be committed to major reform of education, for most schooling is didactic in nature and discourages rather than encourages critical thinking and the values and dispositions essential to it.

As time passes it becomes increasingly apparent that the field of critical thinking is only now beginning to develop. If critical thinking is to be encouraged in every discipline, every discipline must reconceptualize the manner in which students acquire its knowledge. Knowledge and thought are in a reciprocal relation. The traits of mind essential to critical thinking should be fostered in every subject area or domain, not just in selected assignments.

Staff Development

Chapter 27

Critical Thinking Staff Development:
The Lesson Plan Remodelling Approach

with A. J. A. Binker

Abstract

No one can teach critical thinking who does not think critically. Unfortunately, most teachers did not have their own critical thinking developed when they were students. Furthermore, few have time to take courses in critical thinking to develop their own thinking. The result is that staff development in critical thinking must be designed to accomplish two ends: 1) to stimulate and develop the critical thinking of teachers and 2) to help them transform their teaching from a didactic to a critical, dialogical model of education. In this paper from the Critical Thinking Handbook *series, Binker and Paul summarize "the basic idea behind lesson plan remodelling as a strategy for staff development in critical thinking."*

*T*he basic idea behind lesson plan remodelling as a strategy for staff development in critical thinking is simple. Every practicing teacher works daily with lesson plans of one kind or another. To remodel lesson plans is to critique one or more lesson plans and to formulate one or more new lesson plans based on that critical process. It is well done when the remodeller understands the strategies and principles used in producing the critique and remodel, when the strategies are well-thought-out, and when the remodel clearly follows from the critique. The idea behind our particular approach to staff development in lesson plan remodelling is also simple. A group of teachers or a staff development leader with a reasonable number of exemplary remodels and explanatory principles can design practice sessions that enable teachers to begin to develop new teaching skills as a result of experience in lesson remodelling.

When teachers have clearly contrasting "befores" and "afters", lucid and specific critiques, a set of principles clearly explained and illustrated, and a coherent unifying concept, they can increase their own skills in this process. One learns how to remodel lesson plans to incorporate critical thinking only through practice. The more one does it the better one gets, especially when one has examples of the process to serve as models.

Of course, a lesson remodelling strategy for critical thinking in-service is not tied to any particular handbook of examples, but it is easy to see the advantages of having such a handbook, assuming it is well-executed. Some teachers lack a clear concept of critical thinking. Some stereotype it as nega-tive, judgmental thinking. Some have only vague notions, such as "good thinking", or "logical thinking", with little sense of how such ideals are achieved. Others think of it simply in terms of a laundry list of atomistic skills and so cannot see how these skills need to be orchestrated or integrat-ed, or how they can be misused. Teachers rarely have a clear sense of the relationship between the component micro-skills, the basic, general concept of critical thinking, and the obstacles to using it fully.

It is theoretically possible but, practically speaking, unlikely that most teachers will sort this out for themselves as a task in abstract theorizing. In the first place, few teachers have much patience with abstract theory or little experience in developing it. In the second place, few school districts could give them the time to do so, even if they were qualified and motivated enough themselves. But sorting out the basic concept is not the only problem. Someone must also translate that concept into "principles", link the "princi-ples" to applications, and implement them in specific lessons.

On the other hand, if we simply give teachers prepackaged finished lesson plans designed by someone else, using a process unclear to them, then we have lost a major opportunity for the teachers to develop their own critical thinking skills, insights, and motivations. Furthermore, teachers who cannot use basic critical thinking principles to critique and remodel their own lesson plans prob-ably won't be able to implement someone else's effectively. Providing teachers with the scaffolding for carrying out the process for themselves and examples of its use opens the door for continuing development of critical skills and insights. It begins a process which gives the teacher more and more expertise and success in critiquing and remodelling the day-to-day practice of teaching.

Lesson plan remodelling can become a powerful tool in critical thinking staff development for other reasons as well. It is action-oriented and puts an immediate emphasis on close examination and critical assessment of what is taught on a day-to-day basis. It makes the problem of critical thinking infu-sion more manageable by paring it down to the critique of particular lesson plans and the progressive infusion of particular principles. It is developmen-tal in that, over time, more and more lesson plans are remodelled, and what has been remodelled can be remodelled again; more strategies can be system-atically infused as they become clear to the teacher. It provides a means of cooperative learning for teachers. Its results can be collected and shared, at both the site and district levels, so teachers can learn from and be encour-aged by what other teachers do. The dissemination of plausible remodels pro-vides recognition for motivated teachers. Lesson plan remodelling forges a unity between staff development, curriculum development, and student development. It avoids recipe solutions to critical thinking instruction. And, finally, properly conceptualized and implemented, it unites cognitive and affective goals and integrates the curriculum.

Of course, the remodelling approach is no panacea. It will not work for the deeply complacent or cynical, or for those who do not put a high value on students' learning to think for themselves. It will not work for those who lack a strong command of critical thinking skills and self-esteem. It will not work for those who are "burned out" or have given up on change. Finally, it will not work for those who want a quick and easy solution based on recipes and formulas. It is a long-term solution that transforms teaching by degrees as teachers' critical insights and skills develop and mature. Teachers who can develop the art of critiquing their lesson plans and using their critiques to remodel them more and more effectively, will progressively 1) refine and develop their own critical thinking skills and insights; 2) re-shape the actual or "living" curriculum (what is in fact taught); and 3) develop their teaching skills.

The approach to lesson remodelling developed by the Center for Critical Thinking and Moral Critique depends on the publication of handbooks which illustrate the remodelling process, unifying well-thought-out critical thinking theory with practical application. They explain critical thinking by translating general theory into specific teaching strategies. The strategies are multiple, allowing teachers to infuse more strategies as they clarify more dimensions of critical thought. This is especially important since the skill at, and insight into, critical thought varies.

This approach, it should be noted, respects the autonomy and professionality of teachers. *They* choose which strategies to use in a particular situation and control the rate and style of integration. It is a flexible approach, maximizing the teacher's creativity and insight. The teacher can apply the strategies to any kind of material: textbook lessons, the teacher's own lessons or units, discussion outside of formal lessons, discussion of movies, etc.

In teaching for critical thinking in the strong sense, we are committed to teaching in such a way that children, as soon and as completely as possible, learn to become responsible for their own thinking. This requires them to learn how to take command of their thinking, which requires them to learn how to notice and think about their own thinking, and the thinking of others. Consequently, we help children talk about their thinking in order to be mindful and directive in it. We want them to study their own minds and how they operate. We want them to gain tools by which they can probe deeply into and take command of their own mental processes. Finally, we want them to gain this mentally skilled self-control to become more honest with themselves and more fair to others, not only to "do better" in school. We want them to develop mental skills and processes in an ethically responsible way. This is not a "good-boy/bad-boy" approach to thinking, for people must think their own way to the ethical insights that underlie fairmindedness. We are careful not to judge the content of the student's thinking. Rather, we facilitate a process whereby the student's own insights can be developed.

The global objectives of critical thinking-based instruction are intimately linked to specific objectives. Precisely because we want students to learn how to think for themselves in an ethically responsible way we use the strategies we do – help them gain insight into their tendency to think in narrowly self-serving ways (egocentricity); encourage them to empathize with the perspectives of others; to suspend or withhold judgment when they lack sufficient evidence to justify making a judgment; to clarify issues and concepts; to evaluate sources, solutions, and actions; to notice when they make assumptions, how they make inferences and where they use, or ought to use, evidence; to consider the implications of their ideas; to identify contradictions or inconsistencies in their thinking; to consider the qualifications or lack of qualifications in their generalizations; and do all of these things in encouraging, supportive, non-judgmental ways. The same principles of education hold for staff development.

✦ Beginning to Infuse Critical Thinking

Let us now consider how to incorporate these general understandings into in-service design. Learning the art of lesson plan remodelling can be separated into five tasks. Each can be the focus of some stage of in-service activity:

1) *Clarifying the global concept* — How is the fairminded critical thinker unlike the self-serving critical thinker and the uncritical thinker? What is it to think critically? Why think critically?

2) *Understanding component principles* underlying the component critical thinking values, processes, and skills — What are the basic values that (strong sense) critical thinking presupposes? What are the micro-skills of critical thinking? What are its macro-processes? What do critical thinkers do? Why? What do they avoid doing? Why?

3) *Seeing ways to use the various component strategies in the classroom* — When can each aspect of critical thought be fostered? When is each most needed? What contexts most require each dimension? What questions or activities foster it?

4) *Getting experience in lesson plan critique* — What are the strengths and weaknesses of this lesson? What critical principles, concepts, or strategies apply to it? What important concepts, insights, and issues underlie this lesson? Are they adequately emphasized and explained? What use would the well-educated person make of this material? Will that usefulness be clear to the students?

5) *Getting experience in lesson plan remodelling* — How can I take full advantage of the strengths of this lesson? How can this material best be used to foster critical insights? Which questions or activities should I drop, use, alter, or expand upon? What should I add to it? How can I best promote genuine and deep understanding of this material?

Let us emphasize at the outset that these goals or understandings are interrelated and that achieving any or all of them is a matter of degree. We therefore warn against trying to achieve "complete" understanding of any one of them before proceeding to the others. Furthermore, we emphasize that understanding should be viewed practically or pragmatically. One does not learn about critical thinking by memorizing a definition or a set of distinctions. The teacher's mind must be actively engaged at each point in the process — concepts, principles, applications, critiques, and remodels. At each level, "hands-on" activities should immediately follow any introduction of explanatory or illustrative material. When, for example, teachers read a handbook formulation of one of the principles, they should then have a chance to brainstorm applications of it, or an opportunity to formulate another principle. When they read the critique of one lesson plan, they should have an opportunity to remodel it or to critique another. When they read a complete remodel set — original lesson plan, critique, and remodel — they should have a chance to critique their own, individually or in groups. This back-and-forth movement between example and practice should characterize the staff development process overall. These practice sessions should not be rushed, and the products of that practice should be collected and shared with the group as a whole. Teachers need to see that they are fruitfully engaged in this process; dissemination of its products demonstrates this fruitfulness. Staff development participants should understand that initial practice is not the same as final product, that what is remodelled today by critical thought can be re-remodelled tomorrow and improved progressively thereafter as experience, skills, and insights grow.

Teachers should be asked early on to formulate what critical thinking means to them. You can examine some teacher formulations in the chapter, "What Critical Thinking Means to Me". However, do not spend too much time on the general formulations of what critical thinking is before moving to particular principles and strategies. The reason for this is simple. People tend to have trouble assimilating general concepts unless they are clarified through concrete examples. Furthermore, we want teachers to develop an *operational* view of critical thinking, to understand it as particular intellectual behaviors derivative of basic insights, commitments, and principles. Critical thinking is not a set of high-sounding platitudes, but a very real and practical way to think things out and to act upon that thought. Therefore, we want teachers to make realistic translations from the general to the specific as soon as possible and to periodically revise their formulations of the global concept in light of their work on the details. Teachers should move back and forth between general formulations of critical thinking and specific strategies in specific lessons. We want teachers to see how acceptance of the general concept of critical thinking translates into clear and practical critical thinking teaching and learning strategies, and to use those strategies to help students develop as rational and fair thinkers.

For this reason, all the various strategies explained in the handbook are couched in terms of behaviors. The principles express and describe a variety of behaviors of the "ideal" critical thinker; they become applications to lessons when teachers canvass their lesson plans for places where each can be fostered. The practice we recommend helps guard against teachers using these strategies as recipes or formulas, since good judgment is always required to apply them.

✦ *Some Staff Development Design Possibilities*

1) Clarifying the global concept

After a brief exposition or explanation of the global concept of critical thinking, teachers might be asked to reflect individually (for, say, 10 minutes) on people they have known who are basically uncritical thinkers, those who are basically selfish critical thinkers, and those who are basically fairminded critical thinkers. After they have had time to think of meaningful personal examples, divide them into groups of two to share and discuss their reflections.

Or one could have them think of dimensions of their own lives in which they are most uncritical, selfishly critical, and fairminded.

2) Understanding component teaching strategies that parallel the component critical thinking values, processes, and skills

Each teacher could choose one strategy to read and think about for approximately 10 minutes and then explain it to another teacher, without reading from the handbook. The other teacher can ask questions about the strategy. Once one has finished explaining his or her strategy, roles are reversed. Following this, pairs could link up with other pairs and explain their strategies to each other. At the end, each teacher should have a basic understanding of four strategies.

3) Seeing how the various component strategies can be used in classroom settings

Teachers could reflect for about 10 minutes on how the strategies that they chose might be used in a number of classroom activities or assignments. They could then share their examples with other teachers.

4) Getting experience in lesson plan critique

Teachers can bring one lesson, activity, or assignment to the inservice session. This lesson, or one provided by the inservice leader, can be used to practice critique. Critiques can then be shared, evaluated, and improved.

5) Getting experience in lesson plan remodelling

Teachers can then remodel the lessons which they have critiqued and share, evaluate, and revise the results.

• Copy a remodel, eliminating strategy references. Groups of teachers could mark strategies on it; share, discuss, and defend their versions. Remember, ours is not "the right answer". In cases where participants disagree with, or do not understand why we cited the strategies we did, they could try to figure out why.

• Over the course of a year, the whole group can work on at least one remodel for each participant.

• Participants could each choose several strategies and explain their interrelationships, mention cases in which they are equivalent, or how they could be used together. (For example, refining generalizations could be seen as evaluating the assumption that all x's are y's.)

- To become more reflective about their teaching, teachers could keep a teaching log or journal, making entries as often as possible, using prompts such as these: What was the best question I asked today? Why? What was the most effective strategy I used today? Was it appropriate? Why or why not? What could I do to improve that strategy? What did I actively do today to help create the atmosphere that will help students to become critical thinkers? How and why was it effective? What is the best evidence of clear, precise, accurate reasoning I saw in a student today? What factors contributed to that reasoning? Did the other students realize the clarity of the idea? Why or why not? What was the most glaring evidence of irrationality or poor thinking I saw today in a student? What factors contributed to that reasoning? How could I (and did I) help the student to clarify his or her own thoughts? (From *The Greensboro Plan)*

The processes we have described thus far presuppose motivation on the part of the teacher to implement changes. Unfortunately, many teachers lack this motivation. We must address this directly. This can be done by focusing attention on the insights that underlie each strategy. We need to foster discussion of them so that it becomes clear to teachers not only *that* critical thinking requires this or that kind of activity but *why*, that is, what desirable consequences it brings about. If, for example, teachers do not see why thinking for themselves is important for the well-being and success of their students, they will not take the trouble to implement activities that foster it, even if they know what these activities are.

To meet this motivational need, we have formulated "principles" to suggest important insights. For example, consider the brief introduction which is provided in the Strategy chapter for the strategy "exercising fairmindedness:"

Principle: To think critically about issues, we must be able to consider the strengths and weaknesses of opposing points of view; to imaginatively put ourselves in the place of others in order to genuinely understand them; to overcome our egocentric tendency to identify truth with our immediate perceptions or long-standing thought or belief. This trait correlates with the ability to reconstruct accurately the viewpoints and reasoning of others and to reason from premises, assumptions, and ideas other than our own. This trait also correlates with the willingness to remember occasions when we were wrong in the past, despite an intense conviction that we were right, and the ability to imagine our being similarly deceived in a case at hand. Critical thinkers realize the unfairness of judging unfamiliar ideas until they fully understand them.

The world consists of many societies and peoples with many different points of view and ways of thinking. To develop as reasonable persons, we need to enter into and think within the frameworks and ideas of different peoples and societies. We cannot truly understand the world if we think about it only from *one* viewpoint, as North Americans, as Italians, or as Soviets.

Furthermore, critical thinkers recognize that their behavior affects others, and so consider their behavior from the perspective of those others.

Teachers reflecting on this principle in the light of their own experience should be able to give their own reasons why fairmindedness is important. They might reflect upon the personal problems and frustrations they faced when others — spouses or friends, for example — did not or would not empathically enter their point of view. Or they might reflect on their frustration as children when their parents, siblings, or schoolmates did not take their point of view seriously. Through examples of this sort, constructed by the teachers themselves, insight into the need for an intellectual sense of justice can be developed.

Once teachers have the insight, they are ready to discuss the variety of ways that students can practice thinking fairmindedly. As always, we want to be quite specific here, so that teachers understand the kinds of behaviors they are fostering. The handbooks provide a start in the *application* section following the *principle*. For more of our examples, one can look up one or more remodelled lesson plans in which the strategy was used, referenced under each. Remember, it is more important for teachers to think up their own examples and applications than to rely on the handbook examples, which are intended as illustrative only.

Lesson plan remodelling as a strategy for staff and curriculum development is not a simple, one-shot approach. It requires patience and commitment. But it genuinely develops the critical thinking of teachers and puts them in a position to understand and help structure the inner workings of the curriculum. While doing so, it builds confidence, self-respect, and professionality. With such an approach, enthusiasm for critical thinking strategies will grow over time. It deserves serious consideration as the main thrust of a staff development program. If a staff becomes proficient at critiquing and remodelling lesson plans, it can, by redirecting the focus of its energy, critique and "remodel" any other aspect of school life and activity. In this way, the staff can become increasingly less dependent on direction or supervision from above and increasingly more activated by self-direction from within. Responsible, constructive critical thinking, developed through lesson plan remodelling, promotes this transformation.

Besides devising in-service days that help teachers develop skills in remodelling their lessons, it is important to orchestrate a process that facilitates critical thinking infusion on a long-term, evolutionary basis. As you consider the "big picture", remember the following principles:

✔ *Involve the widest possible spectrum of people* in discussing, articulating, and implementing the effort to infuse critical thinking. This includes teachers, administrators, board members, and parents.

✔ *Provide incentives to those who move forward in the implementation process.* Focus attention on those who make special efforts. Do not embarrass or draw attention to those who do not.

✔ *Recognize that many small changes are often necessary before larger changes can take place.*

✔ *Do not rush implementation.* A slow but steady progress with continual monitoring and adjusting of efforts is best. Provide for refocusing on the long-term goal and ways of making the progress visible and explicit.

✔ *Work continually to institutionalize the changes made* as the understanding of critical thinking grows, making sure that the goals and strategies being used are deeply embedded in school-wide and district-wide statements and articulations. Foster discussion on how progress in critical thinking instruction can be made permanent and continuous.

✔ *Honor individual differences among teachers.* Maximize the opportunities for teachers to pursue critical thinking strategies in keeping with their own educational philosophy. Enforcing conformity is incompatible with the spirit of critical thinking.

It's especially important to have a sound long-term plan for staff development in critical thinking. The plan of the Greensboro City Schools is especially noteworthy for many reasons. *1)* It does not compromise depth and quality for short-term attractiveness. *2)* It allows for individual variations between teachers at different stages of their development as critical thinkers. *3)* It provides a range of incentives to teachers. *4)* It can be used with a variety of staff development strategies. *5)* It is based on a broad philosophical grasp of the nature of education, integrated into realistic pedagogy. *6)* It is long-term, providing for evolution over an extended period of time. Infusing critical thinking into the curriculum cannot be done overnight. It takes a commitment that evolves over years. The Greensboro plan is in tune with this inescapable truth.

Consider these features of the Greensboro plan:

> A good staff development program should be realistic in its assessment of time. Teachers need time to reflect upon and discuss ideas, they need opportunities to try out and practice new strategies, to begin to change their own attitudes and behaviors in order to change those of their students, to observe themselves and their colleagues — and then they need more time to reflect upon and internalize concepts.
>
> Furthermore, we think that teachers need to see *modeled* the teacher attitudes and behaviors that we want them to take back to the classroom. We ask teachers to participate in Socratic discussion, we ask teachers to write, and we employ the discovery method in our workshops. We do *not* imply that we have "the answer" to the problem of how to get students to think and we seldom lecture.
>
> In planning and giving workshops, we follow these basic guidelines. Workshop leaders:
>
> 1. model for teachers the behaviors they wish them to learn and internalize. These teaching behaviors include getting the participants actively involved, calling upon and using prior experiences and knowledge of the participants, and letting the participants process and deal with ideas rather than just lecturing to them.
>
> 2. use the discovery method, allowing teachers to explore and to internalize ideas and giving time for discussion, dissension, and elaboration.

3. include writing in their plans — we internalize what we can process in our own words.

Here is what Greensboro said about the remodelling approach:

After studying and analyzing a number of approaches and materials, this nucleus recommends Richard Paul's approach to infusing critical thinking into the school curriculum (which has a number of advantages).

1. It avoids the pitfalls of pre-packaged materials, which often give directions which the teacher follows without understanding why or even what the process is that she/he is following. Pre-packaged materials thus do not provide an opportunity for the teacher to gain knowledge in how to teach for and about thinking, nor do they provide opportunity for the teacher to gain insight and reflection into his/her own teaching.

2. It does not ask teachers to develop a new curriculum or a continuum of skills, both of which are time-consuming and of questionable productivity. The major factor in the productivity of a curriculum guide is how it is used, and too many guides traditionally remain on the shelf, unused by the teacher.

3. It is practical and manageable. Teachers do not need to feel overwhelmed in their attempts to change an entire curriculum, nor does it need impractical expenditures on materials or adoption of new textbooks. Rather, the teacher is able to exercise his/her professional judgment in deciding where, when, at what rate, and how his or her lesson plans can be infused with more critical thinking.

4. It infuses critical thinking into the curriculum rather than treating is as a separate subject, an "add on" to an already crowded curriculum.

5. It recognizes the complexity of the thinking process, and rather than merely listing discreet skills, it focuses on both affective strategies and cognitive strategies.

This focus on affective and cognitive strategies may seem confusing at first, but the distinction is quite valid. Paul's approach recognizes that a major part of good thinking is a person's affective (or emotional) approach, in other words, attitudes or dispositions. Although a student may become very skilled in specific skills, such as making an inference or examining assumptions, he or she will not be a good thinker without displaying affective strategies such as exercising independent judgment and fairmindedness or suspending judgment until sufficient evidence has been collected. Likewise, Paul also emphasizes such behavior and attitudes as intellectual humility, perseverance, and faith in reason, all of which are necessary for good thinking.

Paul's approach also gives specific ways to remodel lesson plans so that the teacher can stress these affective and cognitive skills. Thirty-one specific strategies are examined and numerous examples of how to remodel lesson plans using these strategies are presented. These concrete suggestions range from ways to engage students in Socratic dialogue to how to restructure questions asked to students.

A critical factor in this approach is the way that a teacher presents material, asks questions, and provides opportunities for students to take more and more responsibility on themselves for thinking and learning. The teacher's aim is to create an environment that fosters and nurtures student thinking.

This nucleus recommends that this approach be disseminated through the faculty in two ways. First, a series of workshops will familiarize teachers with the handbooks. Secondly, nucleus teachers will work with small numbers of teachers (two or three) using peer collaboration, coaching, and cooperation to remodel and infuse critical thinking into lesson plans.

Since no two districts are alike, just as no two teachers are alike, any plan must be adjusted to the particular needs of a particular district. Nevertheless, all teachers assess their lessons in some fashion or other, and getting into the habit of using critical thought to assess their instruction cannot but improve it. The key is to find an on-going process to encourage and reward such instructional critique.

Chapter 28

The Greensboro Plan:
A Sample Staff Development Plan

by Janet L. Williamson

Abstract

This chapter from the second edition of The Greensboro Plan, *written by Janet Williamson, describes the Greensboro School District's Reasoning and Writing Project, which is using the lesson plan remodelling method of bringing critical thinking into instruction. It is included in this volume as a model of staff development in critical thinking.*

G reensboro, North Carolina is a medium-sized city nestled in the rolling hills of the Piedmont, near the Appalachian Mountains. The school system enrolls approximately 21,000 students and employs 1,400 classroom teachers. Although our school system is a relatively small one, Greensboro has recently implemented a program that is beginning successfully to infuse critical thinking and writing skills into the K–12 curriculum.

The Reasoning and Writing Project began in the spring of 1986 when the school board approved the project and affirmed as a priority the infusion of thinking and writing into the K–12 curriculum. The school system hired two educators to coordinate the program. The two current facilitators are Carolyn Eller, who is a former coordinator for the Academically Gifted program, and myself, Janet L. Williamson, a former English teacher who had recently returned from a leave of absence during which I completed my doctorate with a special emphasis on critical thinking.

Carolyn and I are teachers on special assignment, relieved of our regular classroom duties in order to facilitate the project. We stress this fact; we are facilitators, not directors; we are teachers, not administrators; the project is primarily teacher directed and implemented. In fact, this tenet of teacher empowerment is one of the major principles of the project, as is the strong emphasis on and commitment to a philosophical and theoretical basis of the program.

We began the program with some basic beliefs and ideas. We combined reasoning and writing because we think that there is an interdependence between the two processes and that writing is an excellent tool for making ideas clear and explicit. We also believe that no simple or quick solution would bring about a meaningful change in the complex set of human attitudes and behaviors that comprise thinking. Accordingly, we began the project at two demonstration sites where we could slowly develop a strategic plan for the program. A small group of fourteen volunteers formed the nucleus with whom we primarily worked during the first semester of the project.

Even though I had studied under Dr. Robert H. Ennis, worked as a research assistant with the Illinois Critical Thinking Project, and written my dissertation on infusing critical thinking skills into an English curriculum, we did not develop our theoretical approach to the program quickly or easily. I was aware that if this project were going to be truly teacher-directed, my role would be to guide the nucleus teachers in reading widely and diversely about critical thinking, in considering how to infuse thinking instruction into the curriculum, and in becoming familiar with and comparing different approaches to critical thinking. My role would not be, however, to dictate the philosophy or strategies of the program.

This first stage in implementing a critical thinking program, where teachers read, study, and gather information, is absolutely vital. It is not necessary, of course, for a facilitator to have a graduate degree specializing in critical thinking in order to institute a sound program, but it is necessary for at least a small group of people to become educated, in the strongest sense of the word, about critical thinking and to develop a consistent and sound theory or philosophy based on that knowledge. There are a number of ways to develop this knowledge — read (and reread), question, develop a common vocabulary of critical thinking terms and the knowledge of how to use them, take university or college courses in thinking, seek out local consultants such as professors, and attend seminars and conferences.

In the beginning stages of our program, we found out that the importance of a consistent and sound theoretical basis is not empty educational jargon. We found inconsistencies in our stated beliefs and our interactions with our students and in our administrators' stated beliefs and their interactions with teachers. For example, as teachers we sometimes proclaim that we want independent thinkers and then give students only activity sheets to practice their "thinking skills"; we declare that we want good problem solving and decision making to transfer into all aspects of life and then tend to avoid controversial or "sensitive" topics; we bemoan the lack of student thinking and then structure our classrooms so that "guessing what is in the teacher's mind" is the prevailing rule. We also noted a tendency of some principals to espouse the idea that teachers are professionals and then declare that their faculty prefer structured activities rather than dealing with theory or complex ideas. Although most administrators state that learning to process information is more important than memorizing it, a few have acted as if the emphasis on critical thinking is "just a fad." One of the biggest contradictions we have encountered has been the opinion of both teachers and administrators that "we're already doing a good job of this (teaching for thinking)" while they admit that students are not good thinkers.

While recognizing these contradictions is important, that does not in and of itself solve the problem. In the spirit of peer coaching and collegiality, we are trying to establish an atmosphere that will allow us to point out such contradictions to each other. As our theories and concepts become more internalized and completely understood, such contradictions in thought and action become less frequent. In all truthfulness, however, such contradictions still plague us and probably will for quite a while.

We encountered, however, other problems that proved easier to solve. I vastly underestimated the amount of time that we would need for an introductory workshop, and our first workshops failed to give teachers the background they needed; we now structure our workshops for days, not hours. There was an initial suggestion from the central office that we use a "packaged program" as the basis of our program, or at least as a starting point. To the credit of central office administration, although they may have questioned whether we should use an already existing program, they certainly did not mandate that we use any particular approach. As we collected evaluations of our program, from our teachers, neighboring school systems, and outside consultants, however, there seemed to be a general consensus that developing our own program, rather than adopting a pre-existing one, has been the correct choice.

Finally, teachers became confused with the array of materials, activities, and approaches. They questioned the value of developing and internalizing a concept of critical thinking and asked for specifics, activities they could use immediately in the classroom. This problem, however, worked itself out as teachers reflected on the complexity of critical thinking and how it can be fostered. We began to note and collect instances such as the following: a high school instructor, after participating in a workshop that stressed how a teacher can use Socratic questioning in the classroom, commented that students who had previously been giving unsatisfactory answers were now beginning to give insightful and creative ones. Not only had she discovered that the quality of the student's response is in part determined by the quality of the teacher's questions, she was finding new and innovative ways to question her students. Another teacher, after having seen how the slowest reading group in her fourth grade class responded to questions that asked them to think and reflect, commented that she couldn't believe how responsive and expressive the children were. I can think of no nucleus teacher who would now advocate focusing on classroom activities rather than a consistent and reflective approach to critical thinking.

As the nucleus teachers read and studied the field, they outlined and wrote the tenets that underscore the program. These tenets include the belief that real and lasting change takes place not by writing a new curriculum guide, by having teachers attend a one day inspirational workshop at the beginning of each new year, by adopting new textbooks that emphasize more skills, or by purchasing pre-packaged programs and activity books for thinking. Rather, change takes place when attitudes and priorities are carefully and reflectively reconsidered, when an atmosphere is established that encourages independent thinking for both teachers and students, and when we recognize the complex interdependence between thinking and writing.

The nucleus teachers at the demonstration schools decided that change in the teaching of thinking skills can best take place by remodelling lesson plans not by creating new ones, and a committee dealing with thinking skills wrote a position paper adopting Richard Paul's Critical Thinking Handbook. (This committee report is included as Chapter 2.) This approach, they wrote, is practical and manageable. It allows the teacher to exercise professional judgment and provides opportunity for the teacher to gain insight into his or her own teaching. In addition, it recognizes the complexity of the thinking process and does not merely list discrete skills.

The primary-level nucleus teachers decided to focus upon language development as the basis for critical thinking; their rationale was that language is the basis for both thinking and writing, that students must master language sufficiently to be able to use it as a tool in thinking and writing, and that this emphasis is underdeveloped in many early classrooms. (A committee report is included as Chapter 3.) This group of teachers worked on increasing teacher knowledge and awareness of language development as well as developing and collecting materials, techniques, and ideas for bulletin boards for classroom use.

By the second semester, the project had expanded to two high schools. By the second year of the program, we had expanded to sixteen new schools, including all six middle schools. Now in our fourth year, we have held workshops in over thirty schools and we have conducted workshops for interested central office and school based administrators. Also, workshops have been conducted or planned that are led by the original nucleus teachers for their colleagues at a number of schools.

It is certainly to the credit of the school board and the central administration that we have had an adequate budget on which to operate. As I have mentioned, Carolyn and I are full-time facilitators of the program. Substitutes have been hired to cover classes when teachers worked on the project during school hours. We were able to send teachers to conferences led by Richard Paul and we were able to bring in Professor Paul for a very successful two day workshop. One of the Seventeen Underpinnings of Quality Critical Thinking Staff Development is:

Allocate special resources on a
permanent basis.

Without at least one full-time facilitator and resources for substitutes, conferences, a newsletter, books, and materials, the program would have had little impact.

Our teachers work individually and in pairs, and in small and large groups at various times during the day. A number of teachers have videotaped themselves and their classes in action, providing an opportunity to view and reflect on ways that they and their colleagues could infuse more thinking opportunities into the curriculum. Essentially, we have worked on three facets in the program:

1) workshops that provide baseline information,

2) follow-up that includes demonstration teaching by facilitators, individual study, collegial sharing of ideas, peer coaching, individual and group remodelling of lesson plans, teachers writing about their experiences both for their personal learning and for publication, team planning of lessons, peer observation, and

3) dissemination of materials, including our popular newsletter and the materials in our growing professional library.

As the program expands, we have found that critical thinking is not an isolated instructional methodology. Rather, as one elementary teacher recently expressed, "Critical thinking is the framework on which we build, the basis of all teaching and learning." Sound instructional techniques such as cooperative learning and integrated education naturally dovetail with our endeavors in the Reasoning and Writing Program, and we constantly talk about them and infuse them into workshops and follow-up. It is our contention that educationally sound instructional methods, such as cooperative learning, must have as their basis these assumptions: 1) knowledge can only be achieved through thinking, 2) students are active learners only when they are involved in processing information and not just memorizing factual material, and 3) students must learn how to make meaning for themselves, not passively accept the ideas which are given to them. Thus, critical thinking instruction can be an underlying assumption upon which other methods of instruction are based. Without a solid understanding of and commitment to critical thinking instruction, cooperative learning can degenerate into cooperative worksheets. With critical thinking instruction as an underlying assumption, cooperative learning can help students to think dialogically, consider other perspectives, and develop more complexity in their thinking.

Therefore, the Reasoning and Writing Program is committed to these Underpinnings of Quality Critical Thinking Staff Development:

*Formulate a comprehensive philosophy of
education focused on critical thinking,
one that makes clear that knowledge can
be achieved only through thinking.*

> *Make critical thinking the essential mode of*
> *instruction for all subjects, all students,*
> *all grade levels.*

We are expanding slowing and only on a volunteer basis. Another assumption, one of the Seventeen Underpinnings of the program, is:

> *Rely on voluntary participation. There is no*
> *gain in "forcing" teachers to teach in a*
> *way they do not favor.*

Currently, we have approximately over two hundred nucleus teachers working in over thirty schools in the system. Plans for the future should include two factions: ways for the nucleus groups to continue to expand their professional growth and knowledge of critical thinking and an expansion of the program to include more teachers. We plan to continue to build on the essential strengths of the program — the empowerment of teachers to make decisions, the thorough theoretical underpinnings of the program, the slow and deliberate design and implementation plan, and our adherence to another of the Seventeen Underpinnings of Quality Critical Thinking Staff Development:

> *Don't use a canned program or an*
> *algorithmic approach.*

Our teachers generally seem enthusiastic and committed. In anonymous, written evaluations of the program, they have given the program overwhelming support. One teacher stated:
It is the most worthwhile project the central office has ever offered....
Because
- It wasn't forced on me.
- It wasn't touted as the greatest thing since sliced bread.
- It was not a one-shot deal that was supposed to make everything all better.
- It was not already conceived and planned down to the last minute by someone who had never been in a classroom or who hadn't been in one for x years.

It was, instead,
- led by professionals who were still very close to the classroom.
- designed by us,
- a volunteer group of classroom teachers,
- who had time to reflect and read and talk after each session
- who had continuing support and information from the leaders, not just orders and instructions.

✦ 17 Underpinnings of Quality Critical Thinking Staff Development

1) Formulate a *comprehensive philosophy of education* focused on critical thinking, one that makes clear that knowledge can be achieved only through thinking.

2) Make *critical teaching the essential mode of instruction* for all subjects, all students, all grade levels.

3) Rely on *voluntary participation*. There is no gain in "forcing" teachers to teach in a way they do not favor.

4) Systematically *cultivate the critical thinking of teachers*. Do not assume that all teachers are automatically good critical thinkers.

5) *Don't use a canned program*. or an algorithmic approach.

6) Make *a long-term, system-wide, open-ended commitment to critical thinking* that provides for the different rates of growth of different teachers.

7) Create *multiple incentives* for teachers. Teachers like everyone else are busy and not likely to do what they are not rewarded for doing.

8) Allocate *special resources* on a permanent basis.

9) Find at least *one committed driving force*, one passionate critical thinking enthusiast, to head the effort.

10) Adopt *a broad and rich concept of critical thinking* that is consistent not only with the variety of subject matter areas and disciplines but with the individuality of teachers as well.

11) Provide for *diverse critical thinking staff development activities*.

12) Give each teacher a *critical thinking handbook* that contains lessons shown before and after critical thinking has been infused.

13) Set up a *library* of critical thinking books and video tapes.

14) Create a *critical thinking newsletter*.

15) Set *modest short-term goals*.

16) Provide for *on-going, site-based follow up*.

17) *Involve parents* as completely as you can.

These are the keys to quality critical thinking staff development and they are the keys to quality education as well. If critical teaching and learning are not nurtured — and today very largely they are not — then there is little chance that our young people will become critical thinkers on their own.

SHORT RANGE AND LONG RANGE GOALS

Developing and sustaining a good critical thinking program is a long-range enterprise that takes a number of years. Accordingly, we have developed both long-range and short-range goals. Truthfully, we began the program with some confusion and hesitancy about our goals; we developed many of these goals as the program progressed and we continue to redefine our priorities. However, as part of the Seventeen Underpinnings of Quality Critical Thinking Staff Development, we do include:

Set modest short-term goals.

Short Range Goals

- Provide staff development and workshops for all teachers, for school based administrators, and for central office administrators
- Develop a professional library with materials and resources which teachers have identified as useful
- Adopt an elementary writing process model which can be used by all teachers
- Adopt a secondary writing model which can be used by teachers in all disciplines
- Establish demonstration schools and demonstration classrooms
- Develop and encourage peer observations and peer coaching
- Establish a network for communicating and sharing with other school systems
- Adopt instruments that encourage self-reflection and analysis of teaching
- Adopt processes and instruments for evaluating the project
- Foster growth in knowledge and mastery of a number of programs and approaches to critical thinking as well as an expanded, common vocabulary of critical thinking terms
- Foster participation of teachers in a number of experiences of remodelling lessons and sharing these remodelled lessons with colleagues

Long Range Goals

- Develop a concept of critical thinking that allows for individual perceptions as well as for the differences between technical thinking and thinking dialectically
- Develop ways to help students transfer good thinking from discipline to discipline and from school work to out-of-school experiences
- Develop insight into our own thinking, including our biases and a consideration of contradictions in our espoused objectives and our behavior
- Develop a supportive atmosphere that fosters good thinking for teachers, administrators, and students

Chapter 29

Critical Thinking
and Learning Centers

Abstract

In this paper, originally presented as a keynote address at the annual meeting of the Western Reading and Learning Association, Richard Paul explains the relationship of critical thinking to learning. He distinguishes between student survival skills (those tactics and strategies which enable students to "beat the system", as it were) and student critical thinking skills (which enable students to master content and learn deeply). This distinction becomes the basis for a further distinction between a "minimalist" and a "maximalist" approach to structuring a learning center. In a minimalist approach, students learn the study skills that students use to get good grades, particularly short term recall strategies. In a maximalist approach, students learn to critically process and master content through critical reading, writing, and listening skills.

✦ What Is Critical Thinking

*I*t is always frustrating, and a challenge, to talk about notions as complex and rich as critical thinking. To illuminate, at the same time, particular practical concerns, in this case those of directors of learning centers, adds a further dimension of difficulty. So let me say now that I will not canvass every dimension of critical thinking. I will telescope my remarks on many fronts, for there is much more to critical thinking and evaluation than I can possibly span in one talk.

A definition of critical thinking is in order, of course, but before I give you one, let me caution against overemphasizing any particular definition, including the one I shall give. Definitions of complex realities are at best aids to the beginnings of understanding. They necessarily emphasize some features of the defined reality more than others. They are possible traps by which we sometimes convince ourselves that our depth of understanding is greater than it is. You can perhaps see my point best by remembering how misleading a three or four sentence definition of *you* would be, how little the intricate workings of your mind and character and experience could be captured in a short sequence of words. Your mother, your father, your sisters, your brothers, and your peers might all give different characterizations that would illuminate different parts, elements, or aspects of you. But no one person could give a definition which could capture you totally, as Browning once said, "root and all, and all in all". I hope you remember this essential qualification when you think later about what critical thinking is. In the last analysis, your knowledge of it, your insight into it, will grow over time as you interest yourself more and more, if you do, in helping students become critical thinkers.

In the future, when schools commit themselves more than they yet have to helping students think for themselves actively and independently, the nature and richness of critical thinking will become more commonly understood. Today the term does no more for most people than conjure up vague notions, or worse, misleading stereotypes. Hence, some people think of critical thinking as negative thinking, as fault-finding, even nit-picking or judgmentalism. Some people think of it merely as a summary term that stands for a heterogeneous list of atomistic intellectual skills. Others think of it as one of many forms of thinking, to be used on occasion. These latter sometimes contrast critical thinking with creative thinking, sometimes with problem-solving or decision-making.

From my vantage point, however, critical thinking is best understood as a global way of disciplining and taking control of one's own thinking so as to accomplish more effectively the purposes of thinking through disciplined self-command. Of course, there are multiple possible purposes for thinking, and multiple possible domains or fields into which thinking may venture. Therefore, how we discipline our thinking, how we self-direct our thinking, varies according to purpose and domain. To become a proficient critical thinker is not simply to become well trained in a variety of loosely connected disciplines, but more precisely to develop an over-arching commitment to think beyond specialized techniques and technical concepts to take command of one's cognitions overall, to grasp global or universal obstacles to independence of thought, and to develop generalizable insights and skills across multiple domains of human thought and action.

With these thoughts in mind, I offer the following definition:

> Critical thinking is disciplined, rational, self-directed thinking that skillfully pursues the purpose for thinking within some domain of knowledge or human concern.

Now let me take this definition apart and indicate my understanding of its various elements. First, critical thinking is *disciplined* and *self-directed*. Everyone thinks. It is of the very nature of the mind to think. Whether we like it or not, will it or not, our minds are continually engaged in acts of cognition: conceptualizing, interpreting, and evaluating aspects of our lives, our values, and our experiences. Indeed, experiences and meaning are constructed by the mind, continuously and automatically. Nonetheless, despite the pervasiveness of thinking in human life, much of it is undisciplined and therefore not under the direction of ourselves — the thinker.

Thus, we interpret the world in ways that we do not consciously realize. We make assumptions of which we are unaware. We judge without knowing how we are judging, without conscious reflection on our criteria for judgment. We make inferences without any sense of the movement of the mind from premise to conclusion, without any sense of the need to validate evidence or justify our line of reasoning. We choose and use concepts to shape our experiences and organize them within our point of view. We often don't realize we have created the very points of view that dominate our thinking. We sometimes assume that what we have created through our thinking — our interpretations, beliefs, points of view — are not simply various ways of getting at reality, but are reality itself. We uncritically assume we are in touch with things as they are in themselves, with no sense of our involvement in mental selectiveness or distortion. We think, in other words, largely in an undisciplined and unself-directed fashion. In a word, we typically think uncritically.

We do this because we never learned how to do otherwise. We do this because those who raised and shaped us did not realize that conscious and deliberate *thinking about thinking* is essential to the fullest development of thinking. We do this because most people around us think uncritically. Most of our teachers were given subject content to learn, but little insight into how content must be organized and shaped to be genuinely, deeply, or rationally learned. Our teachers learned content just as we did from them, without deeply understanding, without grasping it in relation to other things learned inside and outside of school, without testing what they were learning within the crucible of their own experiences, without discipline or self-directedness of thought.

Of course, the best students and learners stumble upon some standards for thinking simply by being exposed to organized content. Because academic content itself has been thought-out and organized by disciplined minds, the best students pick up something of that discipline merely because they try to take that content into their minds and keep it there for testing purposes. Furthermore, some students are exposed to other people (parents, teachers, peers) who do have some command of critical thought, and so pick up some intellectual skills from the give-and-take of discussion and debate with them.

But most students go through school largely on the outside looking in, largely alienated from intellectual discipline and skills of self-directed thinking; they do not know how to make learning exciting, powerful, and educational. Most students never know the power of bringing their thinking under their control. They are like people trying to learn to dance by looking at hundreds of still pictures of people dancing, with no more than a faint sense of music in the background, with little vision of how picture and music come together, and with little grasp of how to move their own bodies to the beat of the music. Somehow knowledge is discovered. Somehow it gets put into categories and subject fields. Somehow it gets into books and teachers' heads. And then somehow it is there before them waiting to be "learned". It's all discontinuous still pictures. There is no beat or rhythm to it. There is no power or beauty in it. There is no theme or harmony within it.

Classrooms are, on the whole, fairly dull and boring places to most students precisely because most students do not know how to make them otherwise. Yet all teachers should be skilled in helping students discover the nature and power of learning, for that is precisely what all classrooms and schools ought to be — centers of skilled and significant learning. Indeed, it is paradoxical that we should need learning centers at institutionally established centers of learning. We do need them precisely because students have not learned how to make their own minds, and teachers have not learned how to make their classrooms, *true* centers of learning.

It all comes down to the virtual impossibility for the mind to become disciplined and self-directed, unless it is systematically stimulated to turn inward upon itself and so become consciously aware of its own operations, its own powers and disabilities. In its natural state, the mind unconsciously absorbs beliefs and sets up pathways of thought through mere association and what Freud called pleasure-principle thinking. We believe what we want to believe, what people around us believe, what we are rewarded for believing, what *seems* or appears to be true. Raised in the U.S., we believe what U.S. citizens believe. Raised in Iran, we would believe what Iranians believe. Raised in the Soviet Union, we would believe what Soviets believe. We do not individually reason our way to our basic beliefs. They are, in essence, given to us, insinuated, repeated, and approved of so often by those with influence over us that we find them in possession of our minds. Rather than running our minds, our minds typically run us. This uncritical process of belief-absorption is the natural state of affairs in societies as we know them. Rational belief formation is not automatic or natural — the propensity to question what those around you believe, to do your own thinking, to form your own beliefs, to withhold assent to beliefs until you have adequate reason or evidence to support them.

So we should not be surprised that most students lack discipline and self-direction in their thinking, that they are not in command of the shaping forces in their own minds, and that they do not know how to achieve self-command. At the same time, it is possible to describe what students need to learn to become more rational, to transform their thinking from passive, undisciplined, other-directedness to disciplined self-command. They need three things: *1)* explicit standards or criteria for assessing their thought, *2)* insight into the elements of thought, and *3)* practice orchestrating those elements to improve their thinking, to take charge of it.

Let us look first at the standards for, or perfections of, thinking, implicit in what may properly be called universal ideals of thought:

1)	clarity	*6)*	breadth
2)	accuracy	*7)*	fairness
3)	relevance	*8)*	logicalness
4)	consistency	*9)*	significance
5)	depth	*10)*	adequacy

We don't often think of perfections of thought, even though we consciously recognize perfection or its lack in most other human activities. We recognize perfection in dance, in playing musical instruments, in sports, in the manual arts, in the fitness of the body. We recognize in a skilled dancer command of physical movements. We recognize that skilled dancers can do with their bodies what others cannot. We also recognize that to develop that command one has to self-monitor one's body movements and practice extensively. We line dance studios with mirrors so students can watch their own dancing in process, and notice their relative perfection or lack of perfection of line and form.

We don't generally recognize the parallel facts for the mind. We don't know, as it were, how to bring mirrors for the mind into classes. We don't know how to help students monitor their own thinking. We don't know how to demonstrate mental moves so that students can usefully practice them. We are quite unclear about the kind of time and energy necessary for disciplined thinking to be fostered, practiced, and refined.

We need to bring the perfections of thought into central focus in education. Classrooms should become places where teachers and students routinely talk about clarity of thought, precision of thought, exactness, specificity, logicalness, reflectiveness, fairness, depth, consistency of thought — these universal standards for thought. Teachers and students need to recognize that in any context we may be more or less clear or unclear, more or less precise or imprecise, exact or inexact, relevant or irrelevant, logical or illogical in our thinking. As we recognize the possibility of achieving or failing to achieve these ideals or perfections, we grasp the basis for the critique and improvement of thinking. I can fault your thinking if, and to the degree that, I can show that it is unclear, vague, inexact, irrelevant, illogical, inconsistent, superficial, narrow, or inadequate to the purpose at hand.

Needless to say, most students do not scan their thinking, speech, writing, or reading to see whether it is clear, precise, accurate, relevant, consistent, logical, or fair. They do not, in other words, have these standards intelligibly available to them. They do not aspire to these ideals. And unfortunately most teachers and professors are not clear enough in their own thinking about thinking to help students grasp these standards. Most assume they are learned more or less automatically simply by exposing students to, and questioning them on, content in their field.

Before I continue, I should draw attention to two importantly different forms of critical thinking: what I call "weak sense" and "strong sense" critical thinking. This distinction is based on two fundamentally different ends that can underlie the critical thinking of any individual: selfish interests or fairmindedness. In all critical thinking we discipline our thinking, gain command over it, direct it toward serving our purposes. But purposes may be narrow and selfish or broad and fairminded. And there is a significant difference in the educational strategies one must use to achieve these qualitatively different ends.

As things now stand in the world at large, it is *selfish* critical thinking that is most valued and practiced, skilled thinking that serves some special interest, whether commercial, political, religious, or personal. So if one works for the Democratic or Republican parties, one is expected to develop skilled defenses of party policy and practice. In neither case is a party member to publically acknowledge significant insights on the other side. Similarly, if you are a "patriotic American", in the vulgar sense of the term, you are to defend official governmental practices, not concede insight or justification in the thinking of countries that might oppose them. Finally, if you work for one company you are not expected to admit equal quality in the products of competing companies.

In each case, weak sense critical thinking is fostered, thinking that is at once skilled, narrowminded, and one-sided, thinking that lends itself to propaganda, public relations, advertisements, rationalizations, and other forms of selfish, manipulative thought. Skill in it is highly prized and paid for. A world of special interests struggling for power and advantage needs an army of skilled thinkers to defend and advance those interests.

Strong sense critical thinking is harder to develop, for it requires that one apply the same standards, the same rules of assessment, to one's own thinking as one applies to one's enemies or opposition. It requires that one think *broadly* as well as *skillfully*. To this end, students need to learn to think sympathetically and accurately within a wide variety of divergent points of view, especially within points of view to which they are most unsympathetic. To accurately represent, to appreciate, the insights of one's opponents is a necessary challenge to face in developing one's fairmindedness. Only by extensive practice in empathic reconstruction of opposing points of view does it become possible. There is virtually no emphasis on it in schooling today. This is the single most significant flaw in schooling today.

Having considered the perfections of critical thought, as well as its possible dual functions, I shall briefly review the elements of thought, the various basic structures that a disciplined thinker orchestrates and uses when achieving self-command and self-directedness in thought. They are:

1)	beliefs	*7)*	ideas/concepts
2)	inferences	*8)*	purposes/goal
3)	reasons	*9)*	issues
4)	evidence	*10)*	implications
5)	experiences	*11)*	consequences
6)	assumptions	*12)*	points of view

None of these terms, as you can see, are specialized, technical terms. They are all available in what might be called the critical, analytic vocabulary of the English language. Integrated into one's thinking about thinking, they enable a thinker to focus attention now on one, now on another, aspect or dimension of thought. They are essential terms of reference to translate the general perfections of thought into workable standards for the analysis and assessment of thought.

I can't get very far in understanding your thinking if I don't understand your basic *beliefs*. But, to understand whether to accept your beliefs, I have to understand what supports them, what *reasons,* what *evidence,* what *experiences* you would cite to support them. Thinking about these reasons, evidence, and experiences I should look for *assumptions* you may have made as you thought out your reasons, gathered your evidence, and interpreted your experience. You may have taken something for granted which should have been questioned. You may have assumed when you should have verified or tested. Furthermore, I cannot understand your thought unless I know your *purposes* or *goals*. What are you trying to accomplish and under what conditions and constraints? How are you conceiving the *issues(s)* or *problem(s)*? Are there other ways to conceive them? What *ideas* or *concepts* are you using? What are the relationships between them? How do you apply them? Are you applying them appropriately?

Then, where is your thinking taking us, what are its *implications* and *consequences?* If we accept this or that of what you claim, what else are we committed to accepting? What are some of the practical consequences that follow from this acceptance?

Finally, within what *point of view* or *frame of reference* are you thinking? Are you looking at the problem from the perspective of a particular discipline (biology, psychology, anthropology), or with a special focus (moral, economic, political)? Are you thinking within the perspective of some ideology or overarching system of beliefs (as a Christian, Muslim, Capitalist, Marxist)? Your point of view serves as a screen and selective organizer of thought and information. I should notice how your point of view is structuring your thought. Finally, I should notice how mine is doing the same.

My ability to refocus my analysis on different dimensions of thinking, my ability to analyze the elements in some process of thought, puts me in the best position to understand its strengths and weaknesses. Of course, the spirit in which I do all of the above is crucial, whether I proceed empathically and fairmindedly, or narrowly and selfishly. If I analyze your thinking only to destroy or defeat it, I will doubtless distort it, exaggerating its weaknesses while underestimating its strengths. Much of our personal experience of people critically analyzing others' thought is, as I have said, of this narrowminded sort. Most of us have had more than our fair share of egocentric argument, emotional charge and counter-charge, skilled stereotyping and intellectual sleight-of-hand. One of the difficulties we face, therefore, is giving students a different paradigm for intellectual give-and-take, helping them to grasp the nature and importance of fairminded critical thought.

✦ Deciding Between a Maximalist and a Minimalist Approach

Having roughly laid out my conception of critical thinking, I will now turn my attention to your circumstances and problems. Of what relevance is critical thinking to those who run learning centers? This question cannot be answered except in the light of some further ones. Under what conditions or circumstances do you operate? What level of support do you have? What are you expected to accomplish, and under the circumstances, what is it reasonable to try to accomplish? What are your personal goals for your learning center? What would you like it to be and how much time and energy are you willing to expend to make it that? Does the faculty support you strongly or weakly? Has your school, college, or university made a real commitment to critical thinking? Different centers exist under different circumstances, and it is therefore unreasonable for all to be structured the same way, or to have the same goals and obligations.

From this point on, I shall draw a distinction between a *minimalist* and a *maximalist* approach to education, to critical thinking, and to conceiving of and structuring a learning center. If your college's commitment to critical thinking is minimal, if your are minimally funded, if your students are minimally motivated, if you have the minimum amount of time to spend with each student, then you have little choice but to work from a minimalist conception of your center and education. Working from such a minimalist conception, there will be a minimal role for critical thinking to play. Perhaps I can make this clearer by putting a couple of these conceptions into formal definitions:

1. *A minimalist conception of education:* education is passing courses, and passing courses is memorizing enough of what the teachers and professors want to satisfy them on tests and assignments.

2. *A minimalist conception of critical thinking:* strategies for studying to survive classes, regardless of whether or not one becomes educated in the process.

3. *A minimalist learning center:* a center which helps disadvantaged or slower students to learn minimalist study skills to survive their classes.

Most students today are much more minimalist than maximalist in their orientation toward education, much more concerned with surviving than with learning deeply. There are different skills appropriate to being a minimalist and maximalist student. A minimalist student needs survival skills, and academic survival skills differ from in-depth learning skills. You can get through college and learn very little in-depth; such deep learning is unnecessary, unfortunately, to get through most courses in college. In fact, a lot of research by cognitive psychologists demonstrates the superficiality of learning, even that of some of our best students. This has led some distinguished educators, like Alan Schoenfeld, to say that most instruction (he refers to mathematics instruction) is deceptive and fraudulent in that it leads us and the students to believe that they understand subjects in more than a superficial way.

Let me give you an example. Alan Schoenfeld gave his senior math majors at the University of California, Berkeley, — a most prestigious university, — a tenth grade geometry problem on a test. Only 20% got it right. First, they didn't recognize it as a tenth grade geometry problem, then they used the wrong math trying to solve it. Schoenfeld believes that most students would get the wrong answers if we put problems on their tests from previous math courses they had taken, problem types they did not expect. This is because most mathematics instruction is structured in a patterned, predictable way: from algorithm to practice to test. Students perform reasonably well because they are programmed to use particular algorithms and formulas. They know basically what to expect on each test.

Other studies have been done in other subject areas. For example, in one study, physics students were asked questions like, "If you were driving down the freeway and threw a piece of paper out the window, what would happen to that piece of paper and why. Explain using physics." Analysis of the responses by graduate students tells us that most of them use Aristotelian physics to answer the question, a physics they'd never studied in school because it was obsolete after Newton. The thinking they used spontaneously was inconsistent with the thinking they presumably learned in class. This leads people in this area of research to distinguish "gut knowledge", beliefs learned outside of school, from school knowledge. The mind is schizophrenic, as it were — inert, academic knowledge over here and activated ignorance over there. We rarely *use* our academic knowledge because deep down, experientially, we don't *believe* it. We believe what we personally experienced, even if what we experienced was biased and distorted. When inert academic knowledge is in a contest with activated ignorance, activated ignorance wins. What cognitive psychologists are telling us is that what we think the students are learning and what they really are learning are radically different.

If this problem concerns you, you are a maximalist at heart, for you are concerned with the problem of transfer, of making academic learning effective in the real world, not just in the contrived world of academic assignments and tests. But if you feel that your first responsibility is to help students do their assignments and pass their tests, irrespective of whether those assignments and tests generate *real* knowledge, you are a minimalist.

Once again, there are often political and/or budgetary reasons for being a minimalist. There are reasons why a person might say, "I am a minimalist, but a good minimalist, and my program does help students survive, and that is all that I can realistically hope to achieve. I don't have the budget, I don't have the staff, I don't have the credibility, I don't have the respect, I don't have the conditions to be a maximalist." That makes sense to me, and so I say be a good minimalist if you are going to be a minimalist; but call a spade a spade, don't say that you are teaching higher order critical thinking skills when you aren't, when you are focused only on low level academic survival skills.

Academic survival skills are a grab bag of strategies tailor-made for specific purposes. I learned many of them when I was going through college, yet most students struggle along oblivious of them. For example, the student survivalist pays considerable attention to the prejudices of the instructors; this is an important survival skill. As an undergraduate, I took a course in Shakespeare and wrote an essay on *Romeo and Juliet*. My thesis was that the play was flawed as a tragedy because it depended too much on chance. I went through it and found all the events that turned on chance happenings — a person arrives a minute too late or too early. I systematically laid out the flaws. I turned my paper in, very happy with it, got my paper back and read words to the effect, "You reason very well for your conclusions, but I disagree: C–". I got an "A" on every subsequent paper; I learned not to disagree with my instructor. I learned a student survival skill.

I was in another course, a sociology course, and on all of my exams I put "according to the lectures," and then wrote what I was going to say. The instructor was a wonderful fellow, very bright and insightful in many respects, but he seemed to me to overestimate the scientificness of sociology. Sociology was everything, all human behavior could be explained by it. It seemed to me then, and it seems to me now, that though sociology sheds important light on human behavior, it is far from explaining it totally. In any case, my professor took me aside one day and asked me why I kept writing "according to the lectures" before I wrote out my answers to the test questions. In this case, he was quite understanding. He was willing to accept some level of dissent as long as I gave the "correct" answers on the tests. I got my "A" though I had taken a bit of a chance by revealing to the professor that I did not fully believe what was taught in class.

One can learn a variety of basic study skills that help one survive in courses, skills which do not involve anything but the lowest level of critical thinking. To give you another example, I routinely put my notes on a tape recorder, emphasizing the fundamental points made in the lectures. Then I played them back while washing the dishes or otherwise passing the time in my apartment. By maximizing my exposure to what the professor said, I did better. This, again, is not in-depth learning. This is not critical thinking, in the fullest sense of the words; it is academic survival. Techniques like these made me a better, but not a less prejudiced, student. If what I was taught was prejudiced or distorted, then what I internalized was prejudiced or distorted. It didn't teach me to go into depth in what I was learning, it didn't lead to my taking seriously what I was learning, nor relate it to my experience, but it certainly made it a lot easier to get an "A" and so was functional. This is what I have in mind by the distinction between academic survival skills and in-depth learning skills. I think students have the right to learn academic survival skills. But if this is all that school is about, then we are in a sorry mess because education, rightly conceived, is a much higher conception than that embodied in surviving a scholastic rat race. After all, at the end of a rat race everyone is still a rat. And we would like education to do more than teach people to survive mazes that others devise for them.

✦ *Critical Thinking as In-Depth Learning Skills*

As we begin to take command of our own thinking, as we learn to recognize and to focus upon the basic structures present in our thinking, we begin to study and learn in a new way. We become aware of how the majority of ideas and beliefs we have imbibed we have not formed through an independent, rational process. We become attuned to the need to critique our own ideas as well as those of others. In learning anything, we seek to find, to analyze, to relate basic ideas to our own experience. For example, in a history course, we seek to come to terms with the very concept of history. We break this idea down to its simplest terms, for example, into that of a process whereby people select an infinitesimal number of facts or events from the past, and organize them by a perspective or point of view into a narrative for others to accept as "true". We key in on each essential feature. First, that it is highly selective. Out of the countless actual events, only some few hundreds will be cited in books. Secondly, that this selectivity presupposes value judgments as to which facts are most important. Thirdly, that value judgments presuppose a point of view which generates standards of value.

Recognizing this much about the basic logic of history, we are in a position to recognize that there will be many possible histories of any given era, just as there are many possible points of view from which we could approach each. Seeing this, we are in a position to appreciate the nature of historical thinking and so can see where we need to focus our attention, both in understanding and assessing historical writing. Armed with critical insights, we then look for what was *left out*. We look specifically for the interpretations in the text that reveal the point of view and the value judgments of the historian. We read other historians, especially those who approach the same period from alternative points of view.

Finally, we begin to notice the presence of historical thinking in everyday life. We recognize in our memories of things past something analogous to the construction of history: the selectivity, the point of view, the value judgments. We recognize the analogy between history and everyday activities such as gossip. We recognize the analogy between history and "the news". The daily news becomes for us the history of yesterday: highly selective, structured within a point of view, embodying value judgments. Our mode of reading the news is transformed as is our mode of listening to gossip — by our transformed reading and understanding of history.

We critically analyze the basic concept of history and that analysis has a profound influence on how we relate to history and to its everyday analogues. Critical analysis in this sense takes us far beyond academic survival skills.

We gain similar insights into the nature of reading, writing, speaking, and listening. To speak or to write, if we think critically, is not simply to follow a stream of conscious associations. It is not simply to say or write everything that pops into our heads. It is a selective process that organizes thought within a disciplined point of view in order to accomplish a particular purpose with a particular audience. As we better understand our purpose, what exactly we want to accomplish, we see more clearly what we need to include and exclude. We also recognize that we must organize, shape, and order what we have to say. We recognize that our listeners or readers will not have precisely the same experiences, the same ideas, the same points of view that we do. We will therefore need to find ways to elaborate our ideas to maximize connections between what we want to say and what our audience has experienced. We seek out, therefore, common experiences; we look for everyday examples. We do this to build bridges for our readers or listeners to make contact with our thoughts, to enter our point of view, to think our thoughts.

When we read or listen as critical thinkers, we recognize special problems. We recognize the difficulty of entering into and appreciating the thoughts, the experiences, the point of view of others. We recognize the need to engage in a dialogue with the text we are reading or the person to whom we are listening. We recognize at the outset that there are many different points of view from which different people experience and inwardly organize the world. We recognize the need to read and listen actively to enter into the mind of another, especially if that person thinks differently from us. We immediately recognize the difficulty of re-creating in our own mind the thoughts of others based simply on hearing their words. Knowing the elements universally present in all thinking, we know, however, how to begin; we know what to look for, and how to look for it. We know how to question the structure of other people's thought, how to probe for their points of view, how to look into their reasons, their experiences, the evidence that underlies their ideas, beliefs, and conclusions. We know how to clarify and draw out their thought, how to generate examples which may make their thinking more concrete, how to dig for their assumptions and underlying ideas and values. We know how to identify possible problems or objections that might be raised to their thinking, and how to contrast their thinking with other thinking. We know, in short, how to actively engage in the give-and-take of intellectual exchange.

Reading, writing, speaking, and listening are all recognized by us to be forms of *thought,* and we appreciate the arts necessary to coming to terms with thought. Through these arts, we recognize ourselves to be getting an education, to be sharpening, deepening, and refining our own skills and insights while we progressively lessen our prejudices and biases. In the process we acquire a vast deal of information, not inert or scattered about in our minds, but organized within a framework that integrates academic learning with everyday experiences, information we can screen, structure, and restructure from multiple points of view. We can use the information we gather to reason within diverse frames of reference. We can take information apart to consider the same situations from different points of view: psychologically, sociologically, historically, philosophically, and personally. We are not dominated by information, rather we are in command of it.

✦ *Learning Centers and In-Depth Learning*

Learning centers can lead in heightening faculty and student awareness of the need for higher order thinking and in-depth learning. They can play a significant role, not simply in helping students get by in the standard routines of lower order learning, but also in generating campus-wide awareness of the nature of and need for in-depth higher order learning. Unfortunately, most academic departments are too myopic to interest themselves in the question of generalized in-depth learning. Most academic departments see the whole of education merely from the perspective of their own part in it, and they see their part mainly in narrow academic terms. Few faculty concern themselves with developing students' general critical thinking, with helping students go beyond technical vocabularies, academic jargon, standard formulas, routine procedures, isolated facts, and narrow professionalism. They do not think in these terms. No one has clear or significant academic responsibility for the education of the whole person and for the conditions under which that education takes place. Academicians continually assume that students will put the parts together automatically, and that specialized training in intradisciplinary skills and perspectives provides everything students need for generalized integration. Nothing could be further from the truth.

Specialized training, wherein terminology and technical procedures emphasize distinctiveness within a traditional discipline, impedes rather than encourages generalization and synthesis. We live in fragmented societies, and colleges and universities unambiguously reflect and serve that fragmentation, that atomism of daily life. We need structures in higher education that function college-wide to provide an impetus for synthesis, built upon in-depth learning and generalized critical thinking skills. Very specific skills and insights are needed to accomplish this foundational educational end. Unfortunately, critical thinking is now nothing more than a vague idea in the minds of most faculty, one they cannot translate into concrete teaching and testing practices.

✦ Evaluating a Learning Center

I would evaluate a minimalist center differently from a maximalist center; I would not expect the same things. It's not fair to expect a center to accomplish maximalist ends with a minimalist budget. One can only do what one is budgeted to do, unless, of course, one chooses to donate extensive time and energy to what one is not paid for. So one should begin with a clear conception of what a particular center can and cannot do, whether it can merely provide for minimalist survival skills of a few students or provide for maximalist in-depth learning skills for most. Is it possible for the center staff to work directly with faculty, or are faculty largely uninterested in the center and in the generalized critical thinking skills of the students?

Of course, all campuses have some faculty members concerned with in-depth critical thinking, who recognize the failure of college instruction to produce liberally educated persons. They will also have a few administrators willing to move in this direction if supported by the faculty. Herein lies the opportunity to move in a maximalist direction. In principle, any director of a learning center could take an interest in galvanizing interested faculty and administrators and hence provide some impetus for a concerted "maximalist" effort on campus. A clear definition of objectives for a learning center should in any case be coordinated with clearly defined goals of the college, and, in my view, every institution of higher education should take the time to clarify and specify goals and objectives. Consider the following hypothetical statement:

All students are expected to take responsibility for their own learning. This means that students are expected to learn the art of independent study and develop sound intellectual and occupational skills and habits. All work turned in should reflect care, thoroughness, and precision, should reveal command of the processes of critical reading, writing, speaking, and listening, and should demonstrate independent critical thought. Students should not approach their classes as so many unconnected fields, each with a mass of information to be blindly memorized, but rather as organized systems for thinking clearly, accurately, and precisely about interconnected domains of human life and experience. In science classes, students should learn to think scientifically, in math classes to think mathematically, in history classes to think historically, and so on, in such a way that if later called upon to respond to an issue in one of these domains, students will know how to begin to interpret and analyze it, to find and organize information appropriate to it, to reason well concerning it, and to devise a clear and reasonable way to answer or solve it. To develop into disciplined and independent critical thinkers and learners, all students should be actively involved in their own learning, looking to find in each of their classes the most basic ideas, principles, and meanings that underlie the field and to use these as a basis for analyzing, synthesizing, and assessing all of the remaining information or content covered. Students should recognize that fundamental concepts and processes must be mastered before one can successfully understand a given domain of knowledge and that it is better to learn what is basic to a field deeply and well than to rush on to half-learn, and so mis-learn, what is less basic. Classes will be designed to emphasize in-depth learning of fundamentals as a foundation for more advanced learning. Fundamental concepts and principles will continually be used as organizers for more advanced understandings.

Some such statement could be made the basis for a campus-wide commitment to critical thinking. It could then be followed up with more specific statements from each department. For example, a history department might begin to formulate its goals, vis-a-vis critical thinking, in something like the following way:

All of the history courses have the goal of helping students learn how to think historically in a critical and insightful manner. This includes learning how to identify historical viewpoints, gather and organize historical information, distinguish basic historical facts from historical interpretations, to recognize historical relationships and patterns, and to see the relevance of historical insight to the understanding of current events and problems ....

Once there was not only a campus-wide statement but also a network of departmental statements such as that above, individual instructors could follow up with even more specific statements for their particular courses. For example, a professor teaching a course in U.S. history might follow up the departmental statement above with something like the following:

The fundamental aim of the study of U.S. history will be to aid students in thinking critically, insightfully, and knowledgeably about the U.S. historical past, focusing on the basic issues upon which historians organize and base their research and the development of their divergent viewpoints. Students will learn how to write a historical essay in which they will defend a historical interpretation based on organized, analytic, historical reasoning, reflecting their careful reading of professional historians ....

These statements could be correlated with a campus-wide effort to make students aware of the universal elements of and standards for thinking, so the learning center staff could help each student see the common goals, skills, and standards at the basis of all of their classes. A core critical thinking class could also be established to provide special emphasis on critical thinking. Additionally, the learning center could begin to disseminate the research results daily accumulating which emphasize the need for a shift in instruction from didactic, memory-oriented modes of instruction to those which more actively engage students in their own learning and challenge them to think their way critically through class material and content.

Well, I have gone on at great length and it is now time for me to close. I should like to end with a word of philosophical advice, and that is this: Take the long view of things and keep yourself continually aware of what Matthew Arnold once called "the extreme slowness of things". Classroom instruction will not be changed significantly in a short time. What happens in colleges and schools is a product of many potent forces, each with deep social and psychological roots. The deeper the reform that is needed — and in my view, as you have seen, deep reform is indeed needed — the longer the time that must be allowed for it.

On the other hand, nothing is accomplished by cynicism or defeatism. Creative critical discontent is our only dependable agent for change. So if you are moved by a maximalist conception of education yet forced to live within a minimalist budget, steel yourself for the long term by integrating intense and enthusiastic commitment into long term patience. Remember, the possibility of change is before us daily. Each new day offers to each of us another chance to begin again. But substantial change is not something that happens and is done; it is something that begins, grows, and evolves by degrees in keeping with the ever present, ever powerful, "extreme slowness of things".

Part III:

Grasping Connections —
Seeing Contrasts

Contrasting Viewpoints

Chapter 30

McPeck's Mistakes:
Why Critical Thinking Applies Across Disciplines and Domains

A review of *Critical Thinking and Education* by John E. McPeck. Martin Robinson, Oxford, 1981.

Abstract

In this paper, Richard Paul rejects John McPeck's claim in Critical Thinking and Education *that, since no one can think without thinking about something, critical thinking is nothing more than a conglomeration of subject-specific skills and insights. Paul rejects, in other words, McPeck's view that there are no general critical thinking skills. Paul's argument rests on the fact that most significant and problematic issues require dialectical thought which crosses and goes beyond any one discipline; that many interpretations and uses of discipline-specific information and procedures in exploring real-life issues are inevitably multi-logical.*

*M*ost educational commentators and the general public seem to agree on at least one thing: the schools are in *deep* trouble. Many graduates, at all levels, lack the abilities to read, write, and think with a minimal level of clarity, coherence, and critical or analytic exactitude. Most commentators also agree that a significant part of the problem is a pedagogical diet excessively rich in memorization and superficial rote performance, and insufficiently rich in, if not devoid of, autonomous critical thought. This complaint is not entirely new in North American education but the degree of concern and the quiet but growing revolution represented by those attempting to address that concern is worthy of note. (A recent ERIC computer search identified 1,849 articles in the last seven years with *critical thinking* as a major descriptor.[1])

The roots of this multi-faceted movement can be traced back in a number of directions, but one of the deepest and most important goes back as far as Ed Glaser's *An Experiment in the Development of Critical Thinking* (1941) (and his establishing with Watson of the Watson-Glaser Critical Thinking Appraisal) and Max Black's *Critical Thinking* (1946). The manner in which this root of the movement has, after a halting start, progressively built up a head of steam, has been partially chronicled by Johnson and Blair.[2] It is now firmly established at the college and university level affecting there an increasing number of courses that focus on "Critical Thinking" or "Informal Logic", courses designed to provide the kind of shot-in-the-arm for critical thinking that general composition courses are expected to provide for writing.[3] The influence of this current in the movement is being increasingly felt at lower levels of education but in a more variable, if somewhat less effective way.

Enter John McPeck with his book *Critical Thinking and Education* which promises us (on its dust jacket) "a timely critique of the major work in the field", "rigorous ideas on the proper place of critical thinking in the philosophy of education", "a thorough analysis of what the concept is", as well as "a sound basis on which the role of critical thinking in the schools can be evaluated." The book is important not only because it is the first to attempt a characterization of the recent critical thinking movement, but more so because the foundational mistakes it makes are uniquely instructive, mistakes so eminently reflective of "the spirit of the age" they are likely to show up in many more places than this book alone. Unfortunately, because of serious flaws in its theoretical underpinnings, the book doubtless will lead some of McPeck's readers down a variety of blind alleys, create unnecessary obstacles to some important programs being developed, and encourage some — not many, I hope — to dismiss the work of some central figures in the field (Scriven, D'Angelo, and Ennis most obviously). At the root of the problem is McPeck's (unwitting?) commitment to a rarefied form of logical (epistemological) atomism, a commitment which is essential if he is to rule out, as he passionately wants to, *all general skills of thought* and so to give himself *a priori* grounds to oppose all programs that try to develop or enhance such skills.

McPeck's mistakes are, from one vantage point, glaring and fundamental; from another they are seductive, and, as I have suggested above, quite natural. They bear examination from a number of points of view. Certainly most can see the fallacy in inferring that, because one cannot write without writing about something, some specific subject or other, it is therefore unintelligible "muddled nonsense" to maintain general composition courses or to talk about general, as against subject-specific, writing skills. Likewise most would think bizarre someone who argued that, because speech requires something spoken about, it therefore is senseless to set up general courses in speech, and incoherent to talk of *general* speaking skills.

Yet McPeck's keystone inference, logically parallel and equally fallacious in my view, is likely to be seductively attractive to many teachers and administrators in the form in which McPeck articulates it:

> It is a matter of conceptual truth that thinking is always thinking about X, and that X can never be "everything in general" but must always be something in particular. Thus the claim "I teach my students to think" is at worst false and at best misleading.
>
> Thinking, then, is logically connected to an X. Since this fundamental point is reasonably easy to grasp, it is surprising that critical thinking should have become reified into a curriculum subject and the teaching of it an area of expertise of its own ....

> In isolation it neither refers to nor denotes any particular skill. It follows from this that it makes no sense to talk about critical thinking as a distinct subject and that it therefore cannot profitably be taught as such. To the extent that critical thinking is not about a specific subject X, it is both conceptually and practically empty. The statement "I teach critical thinking", simpliciter, is vacuous because there is no generalized skill properly called critical thinking. (pp. 4 & 5)

Many would, I suspect, find it equally attractive to conclude with McPeck that "the real problem with uncritical students is not a deficiency in a general skill, such as logical ability, but rather a general lack of education in the traditional sense" and that "... elementary schools are fully occupied with their efforts to impart the three R's, together with the most elementary information about the world around them" and hence have no *time* to teach critical thinking as well. They might not be as comfortable with his notion that "there is nothing in the logic of education that requires that schools should engage in education" and "nothing contradictory in saying 'This is a fine school, and I recommend it to others, even though it does not engage in education.'"

Still, this latter point is mentioned only once, not endlessly repeated in an array of different forms as is his major refrain that "thinking of any kind is always about X". The "X" of this refrain, that to which McPeck believes the logic of all thought is to be relativized, is itself characterized in a litany of synonyms ("the question at issue", "the subject matter", "the parent field", "the field of research", "the specific performance", "the discipline", "the cognitive domain", and so forth) as are the various criteria (the need for "specialized and technical language", "technical information", "field-dependent concepts", "unique logic", "unique skills", "intra-field considerations", "subject-specific information", and so forth) imposed on the critical thinker by the X in question. The hypnotic effect of the continual reiteration of the truism implicit in his major refrain, alongside of a variety of formulations of his major conclusion is such that readers not used to slippery *non-sequiturs* are apt to miss the logical gap from premise to conclusion.

If nothing else, the reader is bound to feel something of the attraction — in this technological, specialists' world of ours — of McPeck's placing critical thought squarely in the center of an atomistic, information-centered model of knowledge. We are already comfortable with the notion that to learn is to amass large quantities of specialized or erudite facts and we know that facts are of different *types*. In other words, we tend to think of knowledge on the model of the computers we are so enamored of: on the one hand, a huge mass of atomic facts (our data bank), and on the other a specific set of categories, McPeck's logical domains, which organize them into higher-order generalizations by formulas and decision-procedures of various kinds. To change one of the formulas or decision-procedures requires technical information about the facts to be manipulated. Critical thought in this context requires understanding of both the data bank and the established procedures.

But it is well to remember that we cannot ask computers multi-categorical questions, especially those kinds that cut across the disciplines in such a way as to require reasoned perspective on the data from a "global" point of view.

Such questions, structuring the very warp and woof of everyday life, are typically dialectical, settled, that is, by *general* cannons of argument, by objection
(from one point of view) and reply (from another), by case and counter-case,
by debate not only about the answer to the question, but also about the question itself. Most social and world problems are of this nature, as are those
that presuppose the subject's world view.

For example, consider those social problems that call for judgments on the
equity of the distribution of wealth and power, of the causes of poverty, of the
justification and limits of welfare, of the nature or existence of the military-
industrial complex, of the value or danger of capitalism, of the character of
racism and sexism or their history and manifestations, of the nature of communism or socialism, ... The position we take on any one of these issues is
likely to reflect the position we take on the others and they are all likely to
reflect our conception of human nature (the extent of human equality and
what follows from it as so conceived, the nature and causes of human "lazi-
ness" and "ambition"), the need for "social change", or "conservatism", even
the character of the "cosmos" and "nature".

This point was brought home to me recently when I got into a lengthy disagreement with an acquaintance on the putative justification of the U.S.
invasion of Grenada. Before long we were discussing questions of morality,
the appropriate interpretation of international law, supposed rights of countries to defend their interests, spheres of influence, the character of U.S. and
Soviet foreign policies, the history of the two countries, the nature and history of the C.I.A., the nature of democracy, whether it can exist without elections, who has credibility and how to judge it, the nature of the media and
how to assess it, whether it reflects an "American" party line, sociocentrism,
our own personalities, consistency, etc. Especially illuminating and instructive was the distinctive pattern that this discussion took. It was eminently
clear that we disagreed in our respective world views, our global perspectives. Because we each conceived of the world with something like an integrated point of view, we conceptualized the problem and its elements differently. Specialized information was differently interpreted by us. There were
no discipline-specific skills to save the day.

McPeck avoids commenting on such problems except insofar as they presuppose specialized information, which he then focuses on (or dismisses them
as belonging to the realm of "common sense"). From a logical atomist's point of
view (with everything carefully placed in an appropriate logical category of its
own, and there settled by appropriate specialists) dialectical, multi-categorical
questions are anomalous, they do not fit in. When they notice them, they tend
to try to fabricate specialized categories for them or to break them down into a
summary complex of mono-categorical elements. Hence the problem of peace
in relation to the military-industrial complex would be broken down by atom-
ists into discrete sets of economic, social, ethical, historical, and psychological
problems, or what have you, each to be analyzed and settled separately. This
neat and tidy picture of the world of knowledge as a specialist's world is the

Procrustean Bed that McPeck has prepared for critical thought. To aspire to critical thought, on this view, is to recognize that it can be achieved only within narrow confines of one's life: "... there are no Renaissance men in this age of specialized knowledge". (p. 7) It is possible only in those dimensions where one can function as a "properly trained physicist, historian, ... [or] art critic," (p. 150), and so learn specialized knowledge and unique skills.

McPeck assumes that for one person to rationally address a multi-categorical problem, he or she would need to be an expert in every pertinent field, an obvious impossibility. Such universal expertise, however, is far from necessary. What *is* necessary is that the individual has a firm grasp of the basic concepts and principles of the pertinent fields, experience thinking within them, and the ability to learn new details and assess relevant details the subjects contribute to understanding the problem. One need not know everything when one takes up a question or problem. One merely needs enough background knowledge and skills to begin to gather and analyze relevant discipline information and insight.

McPeck identifies the bogey man in critical thinking in a variety of ways — "the logic approach", "formalism", "informal logic", "naive logical positivism", "logic simpliciter", and so forth — but the bulk of his book is spent in attacking scholars associated with the informal logic movement (Ennis, Johnson, Blair, D'Angelo, and Scriven). The general charge against them is, predictably, that they have failed to grasp what follows from the logic of the concept of critical thinking — that it is "muddled nonsense" to base it on general skills — and that such misguided attempts necessarily result in "the knee-jerk application of skills" and "superficial opinion masquerading as profound insight", and are thus bound to run aground.

Since McPeck rests so much on his conceptual analysis, it is appropriate to note what he leaves out of it. He does not consider the full range of uses of the word 'critical' as they relate to various everyday senses of the predicate 'thinks critically'. He does not consider the history of critical thought, the various theories of it implicit in the works of Plato, Aristotle, Kant, Hegel, Marx, Freud, Weber, Sartre, Habermas, and so forth. He does not consider the implications of such classic exemplars as Socrates, Voltaire, Rousseau, Thomas Paine, Henry David Thoreau, or even of an H. L. Mencken, or Ivan Illich, to mention a few that come to mind. He fails to ask whether their critical thinking can or cannot be explained by, or reduced to, specialized knowledge or domain-specific skills. He neglects the rich range of programs that have recently been developed in the field (he has it in mind that in principle there *cannot* be a field of research here). He ignores the possibility that, given the rich variety of programs, reflecting somewhat different emphases, interests, and priorities, it may be premature to attempt to pin down in a few words "the concept of critical thinking". He fails to consider the possibility that the scholars he criticizes may be using the term in an *inductive* sense, hence not presupposing or claiming a definitive analysis of the concept, but restricting their focus rather to some of its necessary, not sufficient, conditions (for example: aiding students in developing greater skill in identifying and formulating questions at issue, distinguishing evidence from conclusion, isolating conceptual problems, identifying problems of credibility, recognizing common fallacies, and coming to a clearer sense of what a claim or an assumption or an inference or an implication is, and so forth).

One result is that his analysis of "the concept of critical thinking" is in all essentials completed in the first thirteen pages of the book with his foundational inference in place by page four. Another is that he gives a most unsympathetic and at times highly misleading representation of most of those he criticizes (Ennis, Glaser, D'Angelo, Johnson, Blair, and Scriven).

In order to have space to develop the broader implications of McPeck's analysis, I will illustrate this latter tendency solely with respect to Robert Ennis, who is at the center of most of his critical remarks in Chapter Three, "The Prevailing View of the Concept of Critical Thinking". McPeck introduces this chapter with three interrelated general charges about the "theoretical foundation" of the prevailing concept: that those who hold it subscribe "to the verifiability criterion of meaning", are "marked by a naive form of logical positivism", and have "an unquestioned faith in the efficacy of science and its methods to settle every significant controversy requiring critical thought". However, nowhere in the chapter does he back up these charges. And I myself do not find anything in the work of Ennis (or of D'Angelo for that matter) that suggest such theoretical commitments.

McPeck focuses his critique on Ennis's article, "A Concept of Critical Thinking", published in 1962, despite Ennis's subsequent published modifications. Furthermore, Ennis makes clear, even in this early article, that he does not take himself to be providing a definitive analysis of the concept; he offers but a "truncated" working definition. He describes his article as providing a "range definition" which has "vague boundaries", based on an examination of "the literature on the goals of the schools and the literature on the criterion of good thinking", and designed merely to "select" "those aspects" which come under the notion of critical thinking as "the correct assessing of statements". He makes it clear that he is leaving out at least one crucial element ("the judging of value statements is deliberately excluded"). He makes clear that his working definition does not settle the question as to how best to teach critical thinking, for example, whether as a separate subject or within subject areas. Finally, it is clear that he is concerned with critical thinking as an open-ended and complicated set of processes that can be set out in analyzed form only for the purpose of theoretical convenience, a list of "aspects" and "dimensions" that can be learned "at various levels".[4]

McPeck's motive for critiquing Ennis's concept is clearly the fact that Ennis does not define critical thinking so as to link it "conceptually with particular activities and special fields of knowledge". (p. 56) And because McPeck sees this conceptual link as necessary, as given *in* the concept, it is, to him, "impossible to conceive of critical thinking as a generalized skill". (p. 56) In other words, Ennis conceives of critical thinking in an "impossible" and therefore incoherent, muddled, and contradictory way. If we are not persuaded of this conceptual link and we read Ennis to be making more modest claims than McPeck attributes to him, most of McPeck's criticisms fall by the wayside.

Let us look more closely, then, at McPeck's model and its implications. It depends upon the plausibility of placing any line of thought into a "category", "domain", "subject area", or "field", which placement provides, implicitly or explicitly, criteria for judging that line of thought. It tacitly assumes that all thinking is in one and only one category, that we can, without appealing to an expert on experts, tell what the appropriate category is, and thus what specialized information or skills are unique to it. Each discrete category requires specialized concepts, experience, skills, etc. Thus, only some limited set of people can develop the necessary wherewithal to think critically within it. Since there are many logical domains and we can be trained only in a few of them, it follows that we must use our critical judgment mainly to suspend judgment and defer to experts when we ourselves lack expertise. It leaves little room for the classical concept of the liberally educated person as having skills of learning that are general and not domain specific. It is worthwhile therefore to set out more particularly, if somewhat abstractly, why it is unacceptable.

First, the world is not given to us sliced up into logical categories, and there is not one, but an indefinite number of ways to "divide" it, that is, experience, perceive, or think about the world, and no "detached" point of view from the supreme perspective of which we can decide on the appropriate taxonomy for the "multiple realities" of our lives. Conceptual schemes create logical domains and it is human thought, not nature, that creates them.

Second, our conceptual schemes themselves can be classified in an indefinite number of ways. To place a line of reasoning into a category and so to identify it by its "type" is heuristic, not ontological — a useful tool, not descriptive of its nature. Even concepts and lines of reasoning *clearly* within one category are also simultaneously within others. Most of what we say and think, to put it another way, is not only open-textured but *multi*-textured as well. For example, in what logical domain does the (technical?) concept of alcoholism solely belong: disease, addiction, crime, moral failing, cultural pattern, lifestyle choice, defect of socialization, self-comforting behavior, psychological escape, personal weakness, ...? How many points of view can be used to illuminate it? Then, is it *in* one or many categories? Or consider the question, "How can society ameliorate the problem of alcoholism?" It cannot be adequately addressed from *one* domain. Nor can the problem be adequately addressed by parsing out its elements and addressing each in isolation from the rest. The light shed by the experts must be synthesized.

Not only conceptualizing "things", but most especially classifying what we have conceptualized, are not matters about which we should give the final word to experts and specialists. To place something said or thought into a category, from the perspective of which we intend to judge it, is to take a potentially contentious position with respect to it. There are no specialists who have the definitive taxonomy or undebatable means for so deciding. The category a thing is in logically depends upon what it is *like,* but all things (including conceptual schemes) are like any number of other things (other conceptual schemes, for example) in any number of ways and so are *in,* any number of logical domains, depending on our purposes.

Consider for example Copernicus' statements about the earth in relation to the sun. These are, you may be tempted to say, astronomical statements and nothing else. But if they become a part of concepts and lines of thought that have radically reoriented philosophical, social, religious, economic, and personal thought, as indeed they have, are they *merely in* that one category? When we begin to think in a cross-categorical way, as the intellectual heirs of Copernicus, Darwin, Freud, and Marx, are there category-specific skills and specialists to interpret that thought and tell us what the correct synthesis of these ingredients is and how it ought to color or guide our interpretation or critical assessment of statements "within" some particular domain or other?

The most important place that knowledge has in any life is, in my view, that of shaping our concept of things overall, our system of values, meanings, and interpretive schemes. This is the domain in which critical thought is most important to us. We spend only a small percentage of our lives making judgments as specialists, and even then we typically give a broader meaning to those acts as persons and citizens.

Hence a business person may place a high value on professional acts as contributing to the social good, may interpret and assess the schools and education on the model of a business, may judge the political process in its relation to the business community and see business opportunities and freedom as conceptually interrelated, and may then unfavorably judge societies not organized so as to favor "free investment of capital" as dangerous threats to human well being. Logical synthesis, cutting across categories, extracting metaphors from one domain and using them to organize others, arguing for or against the global metaphors of others, are intellectual acts ultimately grounded, not in the criteria and skills of specialists, not in some science or any combination thereof, but in the *art* of rational-dialectical-critical thought, in the art of thinking of anything in its relationship to things overall.

Hence, to be rational agents, we must learn to think critically about how we totalize our experience and bring that total picture to bear on particular dimensions of our lives. We cannot, without forfeiting our autonomy, delegate the construction of those crucial acts to specialists or technicians. Students, teachers, and people in general, need to maintain their critical autonomy even in, *especially* in, the face of specialists and even with respect to claims made within specialized areas. If democracy is a viable form of government and way of life, then judgments not only of policy but of world view are the common task of all, not the prerogative of privileged groups of specialists. We need to pay special attention to those *general* skills of critical cross-examination, for they are what enable us to maintain our autonomous judgment in the midst of experts. These pay-off skills of civic literacy and personal autonomy can be articulated best, not in procedures that read like a technical manual, but in *principles* that will often sound platitudinous or have the ring of "general" advice — the principles of clarity, accuracy, consistency, relevance, depth, breadth, precision, completeness, fairness. Platitudes however can become insights and insights definitive of general skills when systematic, case-by-case practice is supported by careful argument for and against. It is a platitude to say, for example, that the press and the media of a nation tend to cover the news so as to foster or presuppose the correctness of the "world view" of that nation or its government. But this bit of "common knowledge" is a far cry from the very important general skill of reading a newspaper so as to note how, where, and when it is insinuating nationalistic biases. Or again, it is one thing to recognize that all "news" is news from a point of view. It is another to be able to read or hear news with the critical sensitivity to see one point of view presupposed and others ruled out. McPeck thinks otherwise:

> ... where there is only common knowledge, there can only be common criticism — which is usually plain enough for one and all to see. This view not only represents a very shallow, or superficial, understanding of the cognitive ingredients of critical thinking, but it is also forced to underestimate and play down the real complexities that usually underlie even apparently "common" or "everyday" problems. The solutions to "common", "everyday" problems, if they are in fact problems, are seldom common or everyday. In any event, the educational aspirations of our schools are (fortunately) set higher than the treatment of issues that could otherwise be solved by common sense. Where common sense can solve a problem there is hardly a need for special courses in critical thinking. And where common sense cannot solve a problem, one quickly finds the need for subject-specific information; hence, the traditional justification for subject-oriented courses. (pp. 156–157).

The principles may be "common sense" or platitudinous — "consider all and only relevant facts" — but *applying* these principles when their application is not obvious, or when the life-long habit of applying them tendentiously interferes, goes beyond "lowly" common sense. It takes guidance, extended practice, and evaluation of that practice. Far from such work being too lowly for our schools to bother with at any length, it is difficult to imagine a more worthwhile task than developing such judgment to its highest degree in each student. If you believe in democracy you must believe that citizens have the potential to judge. If you believe that one primary function of education is to prepare students for participation in democracy, you must agree that helping students refine their ability to judge social, political, and economic questions (and questions to which these subjects apply) as clearmindedly, fairly, and rationally as possible is among the most important and useful functions of education. Use of "common sense" is not inborn, but developed.

The logics we use, and which we are daily constructing and reconstructing, are far more mutable, less discrete, more general, more open-textured and multi-textured, more social, more dialectical, and even more personal — and hence far less susceptible to domain-specific skills and concepts — than McPeck dares to imagine. We need to base our model of the critical thinker, not on the domain-bound individual with subject-specific skills, but on the disciplined generalist. This means that we ought to encourage the student as soon as possible to recognize that in virtually every area of our lives, cutting across categories every which way, there are multiple conflicting view-points and theories vying for our allegiance, virtually all of whose possible truth call for shifts in our global perspective. Discipline-specific approaches to everyday problems are often partial and one-sided and need to be balanced and "corrected" by other approaches. A critical thinker must not be the captive of the concepts, criteria, or traditions in any one subject or discipline.

The general skills necessary to finding our way about in this dialectical world are more appropriately captured in the work of an Ennis, a D'Angelo, or a Scriven than a McPeck. *General* critical skills and dispositions cannot be learned without content, no doubt, but few would disagree with this point, certainly not Ennis, D'Angelo, or Scriven. The real and pressing question is not whether or not content is necessary to thought (it is), but whether "content" restricts us to thinking *within* as against *across* and *between* and *beyond* categories. If there is such a thing as having a global perspective, and if that perspective not only sets out categories but also implies their taxonomy, and if such a perspective can be assessed only by appeal to general dialectical skills, not domain or subject-specific ones, then McPeck's vision of critical thinking instruction is fundamentally flawed and the move to a greater emphasis on critical thinking in education is more challenging, and to some perhaps more threatening, than has generally been recognized until now.[5]

✦ *Footnotes*

[1] In addition, there is a growing number of national and international conferences on the subject, for example, the *First* and *Second International Symposium on Informal Logic,* the *First* and *Second National Conference on Critical Thinking, Moral Education, and Rationality,* and the *First International Conference on Critical Thinking, Education, and the Rational Person.*

[2] Blair and Johnson, eds., *Informal Logic, The Proceedings of the First International Conference on Informal Logic,* Pt. Reyes, CA: Edgepress, 1980.

[3] Such a course is now a graduation requirement for all California State College and University system students, as well as for the California Community College system.

[4] Robert Ennis, "A Concept of Critical Thinking." *Harvard Educational Review,* 1962.

[5] Something should be said in passing about McPeck's treatment of Edward de Bono to whose ideas he devotes a full chapter. This is odd, given the book's supposed focus on *critical* thinking, for de Bono has no theory of critical thinking as such, unless his stereotype of critical thinking as uncreative fault-finding qualifies. Indeed, de Bono uses the concept of critical thinking merely as a foil for "lateral" or "creative" thinking, which he of course takes to be essentially different. He holds that we already put too great an emphasis on *critical* thought. Perhaps McPeck includes him because of his celebrity. I find this inclusion inappropriate and the amount of attention devoted to him unjustified, if critical thinking is indeed McPeck's concern. Furthermore, de Bono is *clearly* not in the same league theoretically as an Ennis, D'Angelo, or Scriven, whatever his celebrity, and his kaleidoscopic, helter-skelter development of metaphors, which merely *suggest* rather than theoretically *probe* the character of "lateral" thought, is an easy target for critique.

Chapter 31

Bloom's Taxonomy and Critical Thinking Instruction:
Recall is not Knowledge

Abstract

In this brief article, Richard Paul analyses and critiques Bloom's Taxonomy from the perspective of the critical thinking movement. He points out Bloom's achievements in Cognitive Domains *and* Affective Domains: *the analysis of cognitive processes of thought and their interrelationships; the emphasis on the need for these processes (including critical thinking skills and abilities) to be explicitly and mindfully taught and used; the emphasis on critical thinking values, such as openmindedness and faith in reason.*

Dr. Paul then argues that Bloom's approach suffers from the following two flaws: 1) the attempt to be "value neutral" is impossible and incompatible with the values presupposed in critical thinking education and 2) Bloom confuses recall with knowledge.

As a result of the way the taxonomy is explained, many teachers identify learning to think critically with merely learning how to ask and answer questions in all of Bloom's categories: knowledge, comprehension, application, analysis, synthesis, and evaluation. Teachers typically take the categories to express objectives which they should teach to in strict order: first give the students "knowledge", then show them how to comprehend it, then how to apply it, etc. Paul, while recognizing that Bloom's distinctions themselves are important, argues that the common understanding of their link to critical thinking is largely misconceived. Teaching critical thinking is not a simple matter of asking questions from each of Bloom's categories; moreover, the categories themselves are not independent but interdependent. Paul shows, for example, how knowledge is not something that can be given to a student before he or she comprehends it. He explains how the critical thinking movement has properly emphasized that getting knowledge is in fact a complex achievement involving thought, *and so should be understood as the product of rational thought processes, rather than as recall. This insight needs to be brought into the heart of instruction.*

*I*t would be difficult to find a more influential work in education today than *The Taxonomy of Educational Objectives* (Bloom, et al. 1979). Developed by a committee of college and university examiners from 1949 to 1954 and published as two handbooks — *Cognitive Domain* and *Affective Domain* — its objectives were manifold. Handbook I, *Cognitive Domain*, for instance, lists four encompassing objectives.

1. To "provide for classification of the goals of our educational system ... to be of general help to all teachers, administrators, professional specialists, and research workers who deal with curricular and evaluation problems ... to help them discuss these problems with greater precision ...".

2. To "be a source of constructive help ... in building a curriculum ...".

3. To "help one gain a perspective on the emphasis given to certain behaviors ...".

4. To "specify objectives so that it becomes easier to plan learning experience and prepare evaluation devices ...". (pp. 1–2)

The authors also note that the categories of the Taxonomy below can be used "as a framework for viewing the educational process and analyzing its workings" and even for "analyzing teachers' success in classroom teaching." (p. 3)

Bloom's Taxonomy

The Taxonomy of Educational Objectives: Cognitive Domain

1.00 *Knowledge*
    1.10 Knowledge of Specifics
    1.11 Knowledge of Terminology
    1.12 Knowledge of Specific Facts
    1.20 Knowledge of Ways and Means of Dealing with Specifics
    1.21 Knowledge of Conventions
    1.22 Knowledge of Trends and Sequences
    1.23 Knowledge of Classifications and Categories
    1.24 Knowledge of Criteria
    1.25 Knowledge of Methodology
    1.30 Knowledge of the Universals and Abstractions in a Field
    1.31 Knowledge of Principles and Generalizations
    1.32 Knowledge of Theories and Structures

2.00 *Comprehension*
    2.10 Translation
    2.20 Interpretation
    2.30 Extrapolation

3.00 *Application*
    The use of abstractions in particular and concrete situations. The abstractions may be in the form of general ideas, rules of procedures, or generalized methods. The abstractions may also be technological principles, ideas, and theories which must be remembered and applied.

4.00 *Analysis*
    4.10 Analysis of Elements
    4.20 Analysis of Relationships
    4.30 Analysis of Organizational Principles

5.00 *Synthesis*
    5.10 Production of a Unique Communication
    5.20 Production of a Plan, or Proposed Set of Operations
    5.30 Derivation of a Set of Abstract Relations

6.00 *Evaluation*
    6.10 Judgments in Terms of Internal Evidence
    6.20 Judgments in Terms of External Criteria

(From the *Taxonomy of Educational Objectives,* Bloom et al. 1974 p. 201)

A generation of teachers have now come of age not only familiar with and acceptant of the general categories of the Taxonomy, but also persuaded that the Taxonomy's identified higher-order skills of analysis, synthesis, and evaluation are essential to education at all levels. For these teachers, critical thinking is essential because higher-order skills are essential. To learn how to think critically, in this view, is to learn how to ask and answer questions of analysis, synthesis, and evaluation. To help teachers incorporate critical thinking in the classroom is to help them ask questions that call for analysis, synthesis, and evaluation. In this view, then, learning to teach critical thinking is quite straightforward. The teacher's thinking does not need to be significantly altered, and no fundamental shifts in educational philosophy are required. The Taxonomy and the ability to generate a full variety of question types are all that an intelligent teacher really needs to teach critical thinking skills.

This view is seriously misleading. According to most advocates of critical thinking, no neat set of recipes can foster critical thinking in students. The single most useful thing a teacher can do is to take at least one well-designed college course in critical thinking, in which the *teacher's own* thinking skills are analyzed and nurtured in numerous ways. In other words, teachers need a solid foundation in critical thinking skills before they can teach them.

What follows is a succinct analysis and critique of Bloom's Taxonomy, from the perspective of the values and epistemological presuppositions of the critical thinking movement. I hope it will contribute to a deeper understanding of the nature and demands of critical thinking instruction.

✦ *A One-Way Hierarchy*

Though not designed to further critical thinking instruction as such, *Cognitive Domain* contains a wealth of information of use in such instruction. Reading it in its entirety is most rewarding, particularly the sections on analysis, synthesis, and evaluation. These sections disclose that most of the cognitive processes characterized as essential to higher-order questions in fact presuppose use of basic critical thinking concepts: assumption, fact, concept, value, conclusion, premise, evidence, relevant, irrelevant, consistent, inconsistent, implication, fallacy, argument, inference, point of view, bias, prejudice, authority, hypothesis, and so forth. This is clear, for example, in the explanation of analysis:

> Skill in analysis may be found as an objective of any field of study. It is frequently expressed as one of their important objectives by teachers of science, social studies, philosophy, and the arts. They wish, for example, to develop in students the ability to distinguish fact from hypothesis in a communication, to identify conclusions and supporting statements, to distinguish relevant from extraneous material, to note how one idea relates to another, to see what unstated assumptions are involved in what is said, to distinguish dominant from subordinate ideas or themes in poetry or music, to find evidence of the author's techniques and purposes .... (*Cognitive Domain*, p. 144)

In other words, if the ability to analyze usually requires students to do such things as distinguish facts from hypotheses, conclusions from evidence, relevant from irrelevant material, note relationships between concepts, and probe and detect unstated assumptions, then it seems essential that students become not only familiar with these words (by teachers introducing them frequently into classroom discussion) but also comfortable with using them as they think their way through analytic problems. This need becomes more evident if we recognize that by analysis, synthesis, and evaluation, the authors of the Taxonomy have in mind only their *explicit* (not subconscious) uses. They rightly emphasize what has become a virtual platitude in cognitive psychology — that students (and experts) who do the best analyses, syntheses, and evaluations tend to do them mindfully with a clear sense of their component elements. So, if the concepts of critical thinking are presupposed in mindful analysis, synthesis, and evaluation, we can best heighten that mindfulness by raising those component concepts to a conscious level.

Although *Affective Domain* implies that it is *value neutral,* many of the examples of higher-order valuing illustrate values intrinsic to education conceived on a critical thinking paradigm, wherein a student:

> Deliberately examines a variety of viewpoints on controversial issues with a view to forming opinions about them.
>
> [Develops] faith in the power of reason in methods of experimental discussion.
>
> Weighs alternative social policies and practices against the standards of the public welfare rather than the advantage of specialized and narrow interest groups.
>
> [Achieves] readiness to revise judgments and to change behavior in the light of evidence.
>
> Judges problems and issues in terms of situations, issues, purposes, and consequences involved rather than in terms of fixed, dogmatic precepts or emotionally wishful thinking.
>
> Develops a consistent philosophy of life. (pp. 181–185)

Along with the usefulness of Bloom's Cognitive and Affective Taxonomies, we must bear in mind their limitations for critical thinking curriculum construction. To some extent, the Taxonomies represent an attempt to achieve the impossible: a perfectly neutral classification of cognitive and affective processes that makes no educational value judgments and favors no educational philosophy over any other — one that could be used by any culture, nation, or system whatsoever, independent of its specific values or world view:

> ... to avoid partiality to one view of education as opposed to another, we have attempted to make the taxonomy neutral by avoiding terms which implicitly convey value judgments and by making the taxonomy as conclusive as possible. This means that the kinds of behavioral changes emphasized by *any* institution, educational unit, or educational philosophy can be represented in the classification. Another way of saying this is that any objective which describes an intended behavior should be classifiable in this system. (*Cognitive Domain*, p. 14)

This approach to knowledge, cognition, and education is partly irreconcilable with a commitment to critical thinking skills, abilities, and dispositions:

> To a large extent, knowledge as taught in American schools depends upon some external authority: some expert or group of experts is the arbitrator of knowledge. (*Cognitive Domain*, p. 31)
>
> ... the scheme does provide levels for the extreme inculcation of a prescribed set of values if this is the philosophy of the culture. (*Affective Domain*, p. 43)
>
> It is possible to imagine a society or culture which is relatively fixed. Such a society represents a closed system in which it is possible to predict in advance both the kinds of problems individuals will encounter and the solutions which are appropriate to those problems. Where such predictions can be made in advance, it is possible to organize the educational experience so as to give each individual the particular knowledge and specific methods needed for solving the problems he will encounter. (*Cognitive Domain*, p. 39–40)

But precisely because of this attempt at neutrality the category of "knowledge" is analyzed in such a restricted way and the relationship of the categories is assumed to be hierarchical in only one direction. For instance, according to Bloom's Taxonomy, "comprehension" presupposes "knowledge", but "knowledge" does not presuppose "comprehension". The second of these conceptual decisions would be questioned by those who hold that the basic skills and dispositions of critical thinking must be brought into schooling from the start, and that for any learning to occur, they must be intrinsic to every element of it.

✦ *Knowledge as Achievement*

The critical thinking movement has its roots in the practice and vision of Socrates, who discovered by a probing method of questioning that few people could rationally justify their confident claims to knowledge. Confused meanings, inadequate evidence, or self-contradictory beliefs often lurked beneath smooth but largely empty rhetoric. This led to a basic insight into the problem of human irrationality and to a view of knowledge and learning which holds that to believe or assent without reason, judgment, or understanding is to be prejudiced. This belief is central to the critical thinking movement. This view also holds the corollary principle that critical reflection by each learner is an essential precondition of knowledge. Put another way, those who advocate critical thinking instruction hold that knowledge is not something that can be *given* by one person to another. It cannot simply be memorized out of a book or taken whole cloth from the mind of another. Knowledge, rightly understood, is a distinctive construction by the learner, something that issues out of a *rational* use of mental processes.

To expect students to assent before they have developed the capacity to do so rationally is to indoctrinate rather than to educate them and to foster habits of thought antithetical to the educative process. Peter Kneedler (1985) observed "an unfortunate tendency to teach facts in isolation from the thinking skills" — to *give* students knowledge and some time later expect them to *think* about it. Knowledge, in any defensible sense, is an *achievement* requiring a mind slow rather than quick to believe — which waits for, expects, and weighs evidence before agreeing. The sooner a mind begins to develop rational scruples, in this view, the better.

As Quine and Ullian (1970) put it:

> ... knowledge is in some ways like a good golf score: each is substantially the fruit of something else, and there are no magic shortcuts to either one. To improve your golf score you work at perfecting the various strokes; for knowledge you work at garnering and sifting evidence and sharpening your reasoning skills ... knowledge is no more guaranteed than is a lowered golf score, but there is no better way. (p. 12)

We don't actually know whether students have achieved some knowledge until we have determined whether their beliefs represent something they actually know (have rationally assented to) or merely something they have memorized to repeat on a test. Dewey, as the authors of the Taxonomy recognize, illustrated this point with the following story in which he asked a class:

> "What would you find if you dug a hole in the earth?" Getting no response, he repeated the question: again he obtained nothing but silence. The teacher chided Dr. Dewey, "You're asking the wrong question." Turning to the class, she asked, "What is the state of the center of the earth?" The class replied in unison, "Igneous fusion."

The writers of the Taxonomy attempt to side-step this problem by defining "knowledge" as "what is currently known or accepted by the experts or specialists in a field, whether or not such knowledge, in a philosophical sense, corresponds to 'reality'". (*Cognitive Domain*, p. 32)

The writers of the Taxonomy erroneously assume that the only issue here is the relative *value* of the knowledge, not whether statements merely memorized should be called knowledge at all:

> In these latter conceptions [those which link knowledge to understanding and rational assent] it is implicitly assumed that knowledge is of little value if it cannot be utilized in new situations or in a form very different from that in which it was originally encountered. The denotations of these latter concepts would usually be close to what have been defined as "abilities and skills" in the Taxonomy. (*Cognitive Domain*, p. 29)

This inadvertently begs the question whether blindly memorized true belief can properly be called knowledge at all — and hence whether inculcation and indoctrination into true belief can properly be called education. If knowledge of any kind is to some extent a skilled, rational achievement, then we should not confuse knowledge and education with belief inculcation and indoctrination, just as we should not confuse learning more with acquiring knowledge (we *learn*, are not born with bias, prejudices, and misconceptions, for example). This point, crucial for the critical thinking movement, was well formulated by John Henry Newman (1852):

> ... knowledge is not a mere extrinsic or accidental advantage ... which may be got up from a book, and easily forgotten again, ... which we can borrow for the occasion, and carry about in our hand ... [it is] something intellectual ... which reasons upon what it sees ... the action of a formative power ... making the objects of our knowledge subjectively our own.

The reductio ad absurdum of the view that knowledge can be distinguished from comprehension and rational assent is suggested by William Graham Sumner (1906), one of the founding fathers of anthropology, commenting on the failure of the schools of his day:

> The examination papers show the pet ideas of the examiners .... An orthodoxy is produced in regard to all the great doctrines. It consists in the most worn and commonplace opinions .... It is intensely provincial and philistine ... [containing] broad fallacies, half-truths, and glib generalizations ... children [are] taught just that one thing which is "right" in the view and interest of those in control and nothing else.

Clearly, Sumner maintained that provincial, fallacious, or misleading beliefs should not be viewed as knowledge at all, however widely they are treated as such, and that inculcating them is not education, however widely described as such.

✦ *Rational Learning*

To sum up, the authors of the Taxonomy organized cognitive processes into a one-way hierarchy, leading readers to conclude that knowledge is always a simpler behavior than comprehension, comprehension a simpler behavior than application, application a simpler behavior than analysis, and so forth through synthesis and evaluation. However, this view is misleading in at least one important sense: achieving knowledge *always* presupposes at least minimal comprehension, application, analysis, synthesis, and evaluation. This counter-insight is essential for well-planned and realistic curriculum designed to foster critical thinking skills, abilities, and dispositions, and it cannot be achieved without the development of the teacher's critical thinking.

From the very start, for any learning, we should expect and encourage those rational scruples realistically within the range of student grasp, a strategy that requires critical insight into the evidentiary foundation of everything we teach. We should scrutinize our instructional strategies lest we inadvertently nurture student *irrationality,* as we do when we encourage students to believe what, from the perspective of their own thought, they have no good reason to believe. If we want rational learning (and again, *not all learning is rational*), then the process leading to belief is more important than belief itself. Everything we believe we have in some sense *judged* to be credible. If students believe something just because we or the text assert it, they learn to accept blindly.

Right-answer inculcation is not a preliminary step to critical thought. It nurtures irrational belief and unnecessarily generates a mindset that must be broken down for rational learning and knowledge acquisition to begin. The structure of our lifelong learning generally arises from our early cognitive habits. If they are irrational, then they are likely to remain so. There are twin obstacles to the development of rational learning: *1)* being told and expecting to be told what to believe (belief inculcation); and *2)* being told and expecting to be told precisely what to do (the over-proceduralization of thought). Together they fatally undermine independence of thought and comprehension.

Bloom's Taxonomy, all of the above notwithstanding, is a remarkable tour de force, a ground-breaking work filled with seminal insights into cognitive processes and their interrelations. Nevertheless, the attempt to remain neutral with respect to all educational values and philosophical issues is a one-sided hierarchical analysis of cognitive processes that limits our insight into the nature of critical thinking. (To minimize misunderstanding, let me express in another way one basic sense in which I consider it misleading to call Bloom's Taxonomy "neutral". By labeling the first category "knowledge" rather than "rote recall", the Taxonomy legitimates calling the product of rote recall "knowledge". Such labeling is educationally tendentious and therefore not neutral.) Successful critical thinking instruction requires that:

- teachers have a full range of insights into cognitive processes and their complex interrelationships.
- Bloom's hierarchy become two-sided.
- teachers see that rational learning is *process-* rather than *product-*oriented — a process that brings comprehension, analysis, synthesis, and evaluation into every act of the mind that involves the acceptance, however provisional, of beliefs or claims to truth, and that thereby fosters *rational* habits of thought and *rational* learning:

> ... the teacher's primary job is that of making clear the bases upon which he weighs the facts, the methods by which he separates facts from fancies, and the way in which he discovers and selects his ultimate norms .... This concept of teaching ... requires that the purported facts be accompanied by the reasons why they are considered the facts. Thereby the teacher exposes his methods of reasoning to test and change. If the facts are in dispute ... then the reasons why others do not consider them to be facts must also be presented, thus bringing alternative ways of thinking and believing into dialogue with each other.
>
> — Emerson Shideler

✦ *References*

Bloom, Benjamin S., and others. *The Taxonomy of Educational Objectives: Affective and Cognitive Domains.* New York: David McKay Company, Inc., 1974.

Kneedler, Peter. "Critical Thinking in History and Social Science" (pamphlet). Sacramento: California State Department of Education, 1985.

Newman, John Henry. *Idea of a University.* New York: Longmans, Green and Company, 1912.

Sumner, William Graham. *Folkways.* New York: Dover Publications, 1906.

✦✦ Chapter 32

Critical and Cultural Literacy:
Where E. D. Hirsch Goes Wrong

Abstract

In this paper, originally a talk at the Montclair State College Conference on Critical Think-ing: Focus on Social and Cultural Enquiry *(1989), Richard Paul critiques E. D. Hirsch's* Cul-tural Literacy. *Paul points out several problems with Hirsch's view, primarily that it is based on a didactic theory of education, and so depends on our giving students information to retain, and that what students need most is the ability to think clearly and fairmindedly.*

✦ Hirsch on Cultural Literacy

The term 'cultural literacy' has been popularized by E. D. Hirsch in a book of the same name. It's subtitle is "What Every American Needs to Know". The basic argument of the book is simple. Indeed, it is well character-ized in the dust jacket of the hard cover edition as a "manifesto". Hirsch's call to arms is not addressed to the workers of the world but rather to the educa-tors of the world, or, more accurately, *American* educators. Hirsch argues that there is a discrete, relatively small body of specific information pos-sessed by all literate Americans and that this information is the foundation not only of American culture but also the key to literacy and education. Hirsch reasons as follows. Because there is a "descriptive list of the informa-tion actually possessed by literate Americans" (xiv), and because "all human communities are founded upon specific shared information" (xv) and because "shared culture requires transmission of specific information to children" (xxvii), it follows that "the basic goal of education in a human community is acculturation". (xvi) Furthermore, because,

> Books and newspapers assume a 'common reader', that is, a person who knows the things known by other literate persons in the culture, ... Any read-er who doesn't possess the knowledge assumed in a piece he or she reads will in fact be illiterate with respect to that particular piece of writing. (p. 13)

In his reasoning, Hirsch links the having of a discrete body of information not only with learning to read but also with becoming educated and indeed with achieving success. ("To be culturally literate is to possess the basic information needed to thrive in the modern world.") (xiii) Hirsch plays down the need for critical thinking and emphasizes instead that the information needed for cultural literacy does not have to be deeply understood:

> The superficiality of the knowledge we need for reading and writing may be unwelcome news to those who deplore superficial learning and praise critical thinking over mere information. (p. 15)

The culturally literate, according to Hirsch, often possess common cultural content in a way that is "telegraphic, vague, and limited". (p. 26) Those concerned with critical thinking, on the other hand, Hirsch alleges, are exclusively concerned with "abstract skills" and unconcerned with "cultural content". (p. 27) Yet, he claims, it is precisely this finite quantity of "cultural content" that empowers students to read, write, and achieve success. In Hirsch's mind, therefore, it is a mistake to criticize rote learning:

> Our current distaste for memorization is more pious than realistic. At an early age when their memories are most retentive, children have an almost instinctive urge to learn specific tribal traditions. At that age they seem to be fascinated by catalogues of information and are eager to master the materials that authenticate their membership in adult society. (p. 30)

The result is that Hirsch believes himself to have discovered the "key to all other fundamental improvements in American education", (p. 2) and "the only sure avenue of opportunity for disadvantaged children", (xiii) "traditional literate knowledge", "the information attitudes, and assumptions that literate Americans share" (p. 127) which, if transmitted to students, — even superficially — will make them culturally literate. Once educators recognize these facts, Hirsch confidently believes that "a straight-forward plan" to reform education can be set out. In this plan educators would set aside "abstract formalism" and the ill-conceived focus on critical thinking, "abstract skills", and carry out instead three tasks: *1)* "reach an accord about the contents of the national vocabulary and a good sequence for presenting it", (p. 141) *2)* "shift the reading materials used in kindergarten through eighth grade to a much stronger base in factual information and traditional lores", (p. 140) and *3)* "develop general knowledge tests for three different stages of schooling". (p. 143) These simple steps, Hirsch holds, will ensure that all citizens will become not only culturally literate readers but autonomous persons as well:

> It should energize people to learn that only a few hundred pages of information stand between the literate and the illiterate, between dependence and autonomy. (p. 143)

✦ What's Wrong with Hirsch's View

There are many problems with Hirsch's reasoning. In the first place, it is simplistic. It suffers from the same faults as all panaceas, all attempts to reduce the complex and multi-faceted to the simple and uncomplicated.

Reading, culture, and education are more profound than they appear in Hirsch's neat and tidy world. There are many more distinctions to be drawn than Hirsch entertains and many of the concepts which he analyzes superficially need a more refined, a more precise analysis. To understand how to help students become empowered readers and autonomous persons who thrive in the modern world, we must lay our foundations more carefully and deeply than Hirsch suggests. We must draw careful distinctions and come to terms with complexities which he ignores.

1) We must take care to distinguish possessing information from having knowledge. Hirsch uses the terms 'information' and 'knowledge' synonymously throughout his book. Yet "information" may be false, biased, incomplete, or misleading while the word 'knowledge', in contrast, implies solid epistemic grounding. If I *know* something, I do not merely *believe* it. I grasp the evidence or reasons that account for or make intuitive its truth. 'False information' is intelligible. 'False knowledge' is not. As educators, therefore, we cannot be satisfied to merely transmit information. We must be concerned with how students receive and internalize information — if knowledge is an important end of education. As educators we want students to learn how to gain *genuine* knowledge, not simply what is commonly accepted as such. We do not want our students to become informational blotters, open to the manipulation of propagandists. We want them to learn how to question what is presented as the truth. We want them to routinely look for reasons and evidence to support, qualify, or refute what others simply accept uncritically and we want them to *understand* what they learn. This point can be put another way. There are significant differences between the processes of indoctrination, socialization, training, and education. These words should not be used synonymously. Yet apparently Hirsch sees no reason to distinguish them. He recognizes, as far as I can see, no contradiction in the sentence "Jane is very well educated with only one proviso: she cannot think for herself."

2) We must recognize the complexity of society and culture and the extent to which they are necessarily a central point of intellectual and social debate. Since both society and culture, whatever their character, are dynamic, and different groups have an interest in how they evolve and change, these same groups have an interest in how their history is told.

A conservative's account of society and culture differs from a liberal's account. Conservatives play up what liberals play down. Liberals play up what conservatives play down. Often the difference is less a disagreement about what happened, than about whether this or that happening should be included in the account at all. Moreover, after the problem of inclusion is settled, further problems arise regarding how much space to give an event, how it should be characterized, and what we should learn from it. Conservatives often emphasize how past practice is worth preserving; liberals often emphasize how it should be corrected or transformed. These opposing construals have implications for our analysis of social problems and issues.

Much depends on whether one defines culture in terms of articulated ideals (however little they were practiced) or in terms of living practices (however distant from the ideal). So when Hirsch says that "We (Americans) believe in altruism and self-help, in equality, freedom, truth telling, and respect for the national law", (p. 99) his statement is ambiguous. He does not say whether he refers to articulated ideals or living practices. And when he says,

> Besides these vague principles, American culture fosters such myths about itself as its practicality, ingenuity, inventiveness, and independent-mindedness, its connection with the frontier, and its beneficence in the world (even when its leaders do not always follow beneficent policies). (p. 98)

one does not know what status we should give to the term 'myths'. If it is part of our cultural tradition to foster false beliefs about ourselves, then it is odd to consider this dimension of our culture as a manifestation of our belief in "truth telling". Or is belief in our truth telling itself a myth to be transmitted? If so, is it to be transmitted *as a myth?* It is unclear how this dimension of our culture should be "transmitted" to the young. Hirsch tries to side-step this issue by arguing that our national culture is not coherent and therefore,

> What counts in the sphere of public discourse is simply being able to use the language of culture in order to communicate *any* point of view effectively. (p. 103)

What he fails to take into account is that *how we pass on our culture* shapes what *our culture is.* If we pass on our culture so that the young uncritically accept myths as facts, then we cultivate uncritical thinking and uncritical conformity as part of our culture. If, however, we pass on our culture so that students must face the challenge of defining our culture, so that students hear and have to respond to alternative conceptualizations of our culture, then we cultivate critical thinking and independence of thought as part of our culture. These differing approaches to one's understanding of culture and its continuity have implications for our understanding of the process of cultural literacy as manifested in reading.

3) Reading as a mode of cultural literacy is intrinsically a mode of critically questioning what one reads. Hirsch repeatedly shows that reading is intrinsically a mode of thinking:

> The reader's mind is constantly inferring meanings that are not directly stated by the words of a text but are nonetheless part of its essential content. The explicit meanings of a piece of writing are the tip of an iceberg of meaning; the larger part lies below the surface of the text and is composed of the reader's own relevant knowledge. (p. 34)

Unfortunately, Hirsch understands this process of inference to be fundamentally an uncritical or robotic process, a process that relies on "telegraphic, vague, and limited" meanings and associations. The issue, as I see it, is not "Does the extraction or construction of meaning depend on inferences based on prior knowledge?" The issue is "How does the *good* reader extract or construct meanings through inference?" Hirsch appears to forget that the information we use to construct meanings are of multiple types, some (when misused in reading) lead us to distort or misconstrue the text. Reading a text is analogous to interpreting a situation. And remember we often construct interpretations as a result of our prejudices, biases, hates, fears, stereotypes, caricatures, self-delusions, and narrowmindedness. Our experience is not then less inferential. The poor reader makes inferences just as much as the good reader. The biased person makes inferences just as much as the relatively unbiased person does. Both reading texts and interpreting situations require insight into the multiple ways we can *mis-read* and *misinterpret.*

Reading is not a good in itself but only as it contributes to our understanding, only as it enriches us, enabling us to see things more truly, more faithfully. By the same token, experience is not a good in itself. Better no experience of a person or culture than a highly distorted experience of that person or culture. If reading and interpretation are to contribute to our education, they must reflect an emerging disciplining of mind and therefore of the mind's inferences. To do this requires a lot more than information that is "telegraphic" or "vague". It requires what might be called, for want of a better term, *critical literacy.*

4) Critically literate readers must learn to distinguish the sources of the concepts they use to make inferences and most importantly must understand the logic of those concepts. The critically literate reader routinely distinguishes cultural association from empirical facts, data from interpretations, evidence from conclusions, believing from knowing, having convictions from being stubborn, having judgment from being judgmental, conversation from gossip, mastery from domination.

If in a text the word 'democracy' appears, critically literate readers do not ramble through a panoply of cultural associations, such as images of Democratic and Republican conventions, balloons, ads on T.V., apple pie, motherhood, our government, Abraham Lincoln, ... Instead they probe the conceptual essence of the word 'democracy:' "the people govern". One constructs legitimate paraphrases of the word, such as "a form of government in which political power is in the hands of the people collectively rather than concentrated in the hands of a few". One recognizes that it stands in contrast to oligarchy, monarchy, and plutocracy. One achieves, in other words, command of what the word implies to educated speakers of the English language. One distinguishes educated uses of the word from uneducated or culturally narrowminded uses.

For example, in the U.S. careless speakers often assume a necessary semantic relationship between the word 'democracy' and the word 'capitalism' or 'free enterprise'. They assume that a particular economic system — a market economy — is part of the very meaning of the word 'democratic'. With this culturally biased conceptual assumption they pre-judge a variety of empirical issues.

Critically literate persons continually distinguish undisciplined and often misleading cultural associations from educated use. The word 'love' does not imply to educated speakers of the English language what it implies in Hollywood movies and soap operas. It takes intellectual discipline for speakers of a language to free themselves from the domination of the cultural associations that surround a word or phrase and grasp the trans-cultural meaning inherent in educated use. We tend to forget, for example, that there are educated speakers of English in virtually every country of the world and that the educated use of English, and all other natural languages, is not a simple reflection of the culturally dominant images and associations of any given culture that happens to use it. Learning to speak and write educated English does not presuppose U.S. or British or Australian or New Zealand cultural conditioning.

Hirsch seems oblivious of this essential insight, of this necessary discipline. He never mentions how an uncritical following of a cultural association that flies in the face of educated usage can cause a reader to misconstrue a text.

5) Background logic, not background knowledge, is the crucial element to reading for understanding. All writing that purports to convey knowledge or insight is structured by ideas and concepts in some logical relationships to each other. There are four dimensions of background logic that the educated, critical reader can probe: *1)* the source of the ideas or concepts, *2)* the substructure of the ideas or concepts, *3)* the implications or consequences of the ideas or concepts, and *4)* the relationships of the ideas to other ideas, similar and different. Since to read we must use our own thinking to figure out another's thought, critical readers form hypotheses about the author's possible meanings by trying out models from their own thought and experience. What could be meant, what is being implied by this or that sentence? If this is implied how does that square with what appears to be implied in the next and the next sentence? Let's see, could this or that experience of mine be what the author has in mind? If so, then he or she will also imply or assume this. Does he or she? Let me look further in the text.

One begins with the assumption that writers are logical and consistent. One begins with the most charitable interpretation of what they are saying, trying to come up with the strongest most insightful construal consistent with the text. One takes on the author's standpoint imaginatively and empathically. One tries to reason from the author's assumptions. One looks for evidence and experience to support what the author is saying. Only when one cannot find such evidence and support does a critical reader entertain the possibility that the text may be flawed conceptually or empirically.

This mode of critical reading was delineated many years ago by Mortimer Adler in his excellent book, *How to Read a Book.* In it he emphasizes how disciplined critical readers can figure out the basic logic of a text even when they don't have much of the background knowledge that would make it easier to read. This analytic process was used in the circle of people who read the Great Books of the Western World without the technical background in each book's field — psychology, philosophy, economics, physics, ... Armed with good dictionaries and the conceptual resources of their own minds thousands of dedicated readers sloughed their way through culturally diverse texts with minimal background knowledge. What they did is similar to what I did when I spent three days reading technical articles in medical journals at the U.C. Medical School Library to help a family member evaluate the status of research on his medical problem. I had virtually none of the background knowledge of the typical readers (doctors), but I did know how to use a dictionary and the resources of my own mind.

With effort and struggle and some conceptual puzzlement, I was able to identify three distinguishable therapeutic approaches to the medical problem I was researching. I was also able to identify arguments that advocates of each were using in support of their own and in opposition to the other proposed treatments. I was then able to hold my own in subsequent discussions with medical proponents of those approaches. This ability to determine the basic logic of a text in the absence of the standard background knowledge of those it was written for is one of the hallmarks of critically literate readers. It enabled me to read technical articles by cognitive psychologists, anthropologists, economists, and others even though they each presupposed background knowledge within their fields that I lacked.

Having background knowledge presupposed in a text is a matter of *degree*. The less you have, the more you have to figure out. A critically literate reader, like a cryptographer, can reconstruct much of what is not given by reasoning analytically from what is given. It is more important for students to learn that good readers look up unknown references when necessary, go back and reread, and don't simply keep moving on, than for students to be given lots of background. Even the best readers do not immediately understand everything they read. Students need practice learning this kind of reading, as well as practice reading material on which they have background.

✦✦ Chapter 33

Critical Thinking and General Semantics:
On the Primacy of Natural Languages

Abstract

Given the frequent sloppiness, vagueness, and obvious irrationality of much human thought, and the rigor, clarity, and usefulness of the physical sciences, many have felt that the answer to irrationality is a more "scientific" approach to language and human problem-solving. As understandable and tempting as this approach may be, it misses some crucial insights into both the nature of human life and understanding, and the nature and value of non-technical, natural, or ordinary language. In this paper, originally presented as the Alfred Korzybski *Memorial Lecture at the Yale Club in New York (1987), Richard Paul critiques the work of the General Semanticist Alfred Korzybski and explores how General Semantics and Critical Thinking can illuminate each other. Both traditions make similar assumptions about human experience: that the meanings we create shape our experience; that irrational habits and patterns of thought are a major cause of irrational behavior; and that people can, by disciplining their thought, become more rational. Korzybski, however, used mathematics and science as models for that improvement. Paul argues for a more "informal", naturalistic model, one in which the flexibility and resources of natural languages (French, German, English, etc.) are valued over artificial or technical languages as tools of thought. Each technical language, by its nature, assumes one perspective or framework; no other can be expressed by it. Natural languages, in contrast, allow for unlimited perspectives to be intelligibly expressed. Technical languages are rigid, natural languages flexible.*

Note to the Reader

Since this paper was read at the Symposium on General Semantics, it presupposed familiarity with the work of Alfred Korzybski. For those unfamiliar with his work, a brief introduction is in order. Korzybski took science to be a model of intellectual power, and began a system designed to free men of "unsane" and "pathological" habits of using and reacting to language. Such pathology, he thought, could be traced back to Aristotle. His critique of traditional conceptions of language drew upon relativity theory, quantum mechanics, colloidal chemistry, neurology, and mathematical logic. His goal was to show that Aristotelian habits oversimplify reality and thus produce dogmatism, rigidity, and lack of emotional balance. Such habits confuse symbols and what they represent, ignore limitations of abstraction, involve excessive attachment to sharp either-or distinctions, and generate uncontrolled responses — un-sanities requiring semantic therapy. Korzybski's proposed theory includes "indexing" ('man$_1$' to indicate difference in sense from 'man$_2$'), "dating" ('Roosevelt$_{1940}$', 'Roosevelt$_{1930}$'), and adding a symbol to all statements indicating an implicit 'et cetera'.

✦ *Introduction*

$\mathcal{M}$ y fundamental objective is to make a case for shifting the emphasis in General Semantics today. For the insights of Alfred Korzybski to have significant influence today and in the future, they must be freed from the limitations of the language he often used to express them. They must also be synthesized with insights which have developed since his major works. I believe that the emphases emerging in the critical thinking field today highlight useful insights that can be incorporated into General Semantics, just as General Semantics highlights useful insights that can be incorporated into the critical thinking movement. I shall proceed as follows. I shall sketch my understandings of the overall thrust of Korzybski's thought, and then analyze what in that thought needs to be emphasized, what de-emphasized, and what added, as it were. In general, I shall argue that Korzybski had too much faith in the possibility of solving human problems by applying scientific methods to them, and too little faith in the power, richness, and flexibility of natural languages like English, French, and German.

One of the insights implicit in critical thinking is that most human problems should be approached through dialogical and dialectical reasoning in natural languages, rather than through tightly disciplined but technically narrow scientific procedures in "artificial" languages. By this I mean that *reasoned judgment,* rather than hypothesis, prediction, and controlled experiment, can solve non-scientific human problems, and ordinary languages are the best medium for discussing them. For example, the disagreement, between Thomas Jefferson and Alexander Hamilton on the interpretation of the U.S. Constitution cannot be settled by facts about the Constitution or even by facts about people and society, but rather by a reasoned assessment in ordinary language. To conduct this reasoned assessment, we must empathically enter into the logic of both of these thinkers' arguments. We must think our way back and forth between their views, consider objections from both sides, consider answers to these objections, and integrate our own insights and experiences into the process. A language like English has excellent conceptual resources for constructing the two opposing sides. We can most readily express our insights and experiences in a natural language such as English.

Moreover, although *I* may settle the issue for myself, at least tentatively, my reasoning does not substitute for the reasoning of anyone else who wants to settle it. Basic human issues must be re-thought by each human. They cannot be settled once and for all in the logic of a scientific language.

Let me put this another way. Korzybski himself raised many important issues that cannot be fundamentally settled by scientific methods expressed in scientific languages. Though he used scientific and mathematical examples throughout his works, the books he wrote did not become part of science. Korzybski did not change any of the hard sciences by his writings, nor did he directly use scientific methods as they are used in the hard sciences themselves (physics, biology, chemistry, etc.). Rather he used scientific and non-scientific insights to construct a frame of reference fundamentally expressed in ordinary language, a philosophy or point of view from which many human failings and follies can be understood. He developed a variety of imaginative and practical devices for heightening our awareness of pitfalls in human thinking. But in his major works he did not write science.

Scientific methods work best only when we focus on ultimately monological rather than multilogical issues. We must distinguish when *one* frame of reference, *one* language, *one* set of laws are the keys to settling an issue from when rationally defensible competing viewpoints must be considered. We have good reason to suppose that the laws of physics, biology, chemistry, geology, and so forth are in harmony with each other and hence capable of being unified into one *logic,* the logic of science. In that sense, all the languages of science in principle can be synthesized. But human creations, our own personalities, the structure of our social groups and cultures, our lives and traditions, our thoughts, feelings, strengths and weaknesses do not display one unified logic, but a complicated network of competing and often contradictory logics. Natural languages have the "openness" to express this contradictory thinking without begging the key questions. Issues requiring an understanding of human behavior often require, therefore, multilogical reasoning in natural languages rather than scientific methods in technical languages for their settlement. And we can often settle them only for ourselves, not for others. Scientific insights may play a role in our thinking but they cannot determine that thinking.

In arguing for greater emphasis on non-scientific, multilogical thinking, I will explain how the quality of such thinking should be assessed. The possibility for assessment, I will suggest, is grounded in universal features or dimensions which can be critically examined in all thinking whose goal is understanding. I will argue also that we need special emphasis on seven traits of mind essential to the rational application of critical thinking principles: intellectual humility, intellectual courage, intellectual empathy, intellectual integrity, intellectual perseverance, faith in reason, and fairmindedness.

People construct the meaning of things from many divergent points of view, within, if you will, the framework of diverse logics. We can insightfully and autonomously participate in that construction only by becoming proficient in multilogical thinking. Korzybski made a significant contribution to our understanding of how this construction of meaning can become more sane and emancipatory. But now we need to add further insights to the process and make contributions of our own. General Semantics of the '80's and '90's should not be General Semantics of the '30's.

✦ *General Semantics*

General Semantics is a theory of human nature, language, and science whose announced goal is virtually the same as that of the critical thinking movement, namely, the development of rational people in a rational world, of people freed from the entrapments of language, thought, and logic. The foundation for it was laid in Alfred Korzybski's two major works, *Manhood of Humanity: The Science and Art of Human Engineering* (1921) and *Science and Sanity: An Introduction to Non-Aristotelian Systems and General Semantics* (1933). These two seminal insights run throughout the whole of Korzybski's works: that human life is mainly the product of how we construct the meaning of things; and that people can assimilate this insight and reform their minds and behavior in the light of it.

To assimilate this insight, Korzybski argued, people must realize that their day-to-day lives reflect day-to-day evaluations, and that these in turn reflect deep-seated but often unscientific and inappropriate habits of thought. We erroneously and unmindfully assume that we directly observe the world about us and that how we conceptualize and talk about that world reflects reality as it is. In fact, Korzybski argues, we systematically confuse simplistic meanings and rigid absolutistic labels with complex and dynamic realities. We become entrapped in meanings and labels because we have few practical tools for coming to terms with complexity, dynamism, and multi-dimensionality. Furthermore, because our evaluations of life situations are typically one-dimensional, absolutistic, and rigid, we act in ways which are, to a reasonable person, mad, foolish, or infantile. Yet this need not be so. A practical program of education that helps us keep before our minds the complexity, the dynamism, and the multi-dimensionality of the world is possible.

The structure of science and math provides Korzybski with basic models for this program. The languages of science and math, unlike those of natural languages like English, German, Chinese, and so forth, are for Korzybski specially designed to allow for the expression of complexity, dynamism, and multi-dimensionality. Ordinary natural languages, in contrast, encourage us to atomize and dichotomize the world. This is due, Korzybski argues, to Aristotelian assumptions and Aristotelian logic, built into the structure of such language, which blind us to the limitations of abstraction. These assumptions encourage us to use sharp "either-or" distinctions. They undermine our capacity to see the world in a scientific and hence realistic and sane way.

✦ *The Need for Shift of Emphasis in General Semantics*

Korzybski, at the beginning of the second half of *Science and Sanity* (p. 367), cites the following from Augustus De Morgan:

> Of all men, Aristotle is the one of whom his followers have worshiped his defects as well as his excellencies, which is what he himself never did to any man living or dead; indeed he has been accused of the contrary fault.

I would not go so far as to claim that Korzybski has suffered the same fate as Aristotle, for Aristotle has been slavishly followed for hundreds of years while Korzybski's work is relatively recent. Nevertheless, General Semantics needs to be updated with some insights whose significance has been deeply understood only within the last 30 to 40 years. The most important of these insights are threefold: firstly, the increasing recognition of the richness, flexibility, subtlety, and power of the conceptual resources implicit in the logic of natural languages; secondly, recognition of the insufficiency of mathematical logic as a set of tools for analyzing and critiquing ordinary reasoning; and thirdly, recognition of the important implications of the multi-dimensionality of most vexing human problems. The first set of insights is developed in the later works of Ludwig Wittgenstein and in the writings of such ordinary language philosophers as John Wisdom, J. L. Austin, and Gilbert Ryle. The second set of insights is developed in the writings of informal logicians and critical thinking theorists such as Michael Scriven, Ralph Johnson, J. Anthony Blair, and others. The third set of insights is being highlighted in the critical thinking movement.

Extensive scholarly work has emerged around the first two insights: hundreds of articles and books exploring the logic of concepts embedded in natural language usage and hundreds of articles and books that place practical logic and critical thinking on the foundation of *informal* rather than *formal* logic. These insights call for a modification of Korzybski's emphasis on scientific and mathematical language as paradigms for understanding the relationships among language, thought, logic, and behavior. Indeed, scientific and mathematical languages are much too rigid and technically specialized to serve as our main source of concepts for basic human problems, while natural languages have just the framework neutrality, the subtlety, and the flexibility we need to mediate between competing views and disciplines. Scientific and mathematical languages are tailor-made for what I have called monological problems, those which can be settled by working within one conceptual framework rather than many. Each hard science operates with one evolving but tightly disciplined language. All well-trained physicists around the world share one common set of foundational concepts and foundational understandings, criteria for evaluating the relevance and strength of claims, and established procedures for settling the vast majority of problems that can be generated within the domain of physics. A Soviet and a North American physicist have no problem sharing their thinking and the results of their work.

But hard science has emerged only in the realm of the purely physical and biological domains, not in the human domain, not in the analysis and assessment of human activities and values. This is because many human problems are multilogical rather than monological. By their nature, they can be approached from multiple frames of reference. They cannot be settled within one universally accepted point of view. By their nature they admit to being understood in different ways. The reason for this difference between most problems in the biological and physical worlds and most problems in the human world is in one sense simple.

We humans have no control over the logic of biological and physical nature but we do have significant control over the logic of human nature and society. Human life, unlike chemical behavior, has many logics, not just one logic. The logic and structure of human lives vary in accordance with divergent and often conflicting meanings people bring to the act of living, through their diverse philosophies and ideologies. We of all animals create the logic we live. And we have never collectively agreed what that logic will or should be. This is not a problem created by natural languages or their various structures, for, despite thinking in the same language, there is tremendous variation among speakers regarding basic frames of reference and points of view. Soviet, Chinese, and U.S. economists, historians, and sociologists do not see eye-to-eye, not because of differences in the structure of the natural languages they speak. Economists, historians, and sociologists from the same society speaking the same natural language, approach their subjects with very different conceptual frameworks and points of view. Human multi-dimensionality is often connected with conflicting ways of thinking about and structuring the human world. Sometimes these differences have largely social roots, sometimes largely economic roots, sometimes philosophical or ideological roots, and sometimes personal roots. Most often these various roots are so intertwined and have so grown together that it is impossible to separate them.

My basic point is this: when problems are multilogical rather than monological in nature, we cannot turn to science, by its nature monological, for a model. A science of human life is not possible because human life is not now, nor will it ever be, scientific. It is not now, nor will it ever be, monological. Monological problems can, in the last analysis, be solved within a dominant frame of reference, but human problems require the ability to move back and forth between and among conflicting frames of reference. Human problems require dialogical and dialectical, rather than monological, formal, or procedural, thinking. Korzybski's involvement in science and math, his background in engineering and technical, monological disciplines hampered his ability to fully grasp this important fact. He fails to see that we must look outside the monological disciplines for our paradigms. On the other hand, he is very much aware of the unlimited number of ways the world can be conceptualized and interpreted.

The shift of emphasis I suggest in no way invalidates the various extensional devices Korzybski developed to highlight the uniqueness of every person and event, to remind us of multiple causal influences, of differences in historical and environmental conditions, and of the impossibility of any statement covering all characteristics of a situation. Neither should we forget Korzybski's concern that we keep clearly in mind the inevitable inter-connectedness of events and the ever present danger of reifying our concepts. The heuristic value of such devices to General Semanticists parallels the heuristic value of various fallacy labels developed by critical thinking theorists to heighten our awareness of the pitfalls of various simplistic patterns of thought. Finally, the shift in vision I suggest does not invalidate Korzybski's emphasis on the need to think holistically and multi-dimensionally and to be aware of assumptions hidden in our ways of thinking and talking.

Still this shift would require some basic reorientation within the Korzybskian world view and so I should explain in further detail what that shift, as I envision it, entails.

✦ Critical Thinking and the Critical Mind

If human life is by its nature multilogical, then the problem of learning to think critically includes the very difficult task of learning to think clearly, accurately, and insightfully within a variety of conflicting points of view. We must become increasingly more cognizant of how our thought is being shaped by humanly created perspectives, and of their strengths and weaknesses, insights and biases. Taking this task seriously requires us to learn the art of dialogical and dialectical thinking and develop the mental traits which enable us to hold a set of beliefs or use a set of concepts without being dominated by them. These two tasks are interrelated, because dialogical or dialectical reasoning develops the fairminded critical mind only insofar as the thinking reflects certain dispositions or traits of mind.

Let me express this in more detail while I come at it from a somewhat different point of view. As critical thinkers, we begin with the premise that all thinking whose goal is understanding has a logic which, if we develop the appropriate skills, can be explicated, understood and, at least potentially, assessed. Thinking, despite its inevitable particularity, always operates within systems that display universal features. Hence all human thinking:

1)   is defined by purposes and ends.

2)   affirms or creates meanings and values.

3)   embodies some concepts and distinctions and not others.

4)   emphasizes some things and not others (puts some things into the foreground of our attention while throwing others into the background).

5)   is based on assumptions.

6)   advances or uses reasons or evidence.

7)   generates implications or consequences.

8)   is consistent with or contradictory to other lines of thought.

9)   is developed within a point of view or perspective.

10)   formulates or highlights some problems or issues and not others.

11)   is relatively clear or unclear, elaborated or underdeveloped, deep or superficial, one-dimensional or multi-dimensional, strong or weak, insightful or prejudiced.

A skilled critical thinker is adept at probing into and explicating these dimensions of thought. Skill in Socratic questioning helps the critical thinker bring alternative and conflicting patterns of thought into explicit formulation, while skill in dialogical and dialectical exchange enables the critical thinker to gain insights into the strengths and weaknesses of those patterns.

For example, suppose I was raised in a traditional U.S. "liberal" family and have learned to reason about and interpret events from a liberal perspective. If I learn to think critically, I learn to identify the various elements of the logic of liberal thought, not as facts given in the world, but as guides and foundations in my own thinking. I recognize that others, for example conservatives, have different guides and foundations. I learn to recognize quite explicitly that I begin with some assumptions, rather than others; use some concepts, rather than others; raise some issues, rather than others; look for some kinds of causes of and explanations for social problems; and so forth. I also learn to value entering empathically into the thinking of a wide range of other competing political perspectives. I reason back and forth between them. I role play, in my own mind, various persuasions and perspectives. I learn to critically compare alternative assumptions, alternative objections, alternative implications and consequences. I ransack my experience for events that support these ways of thinking. I begin to integrate insights from other perspectives into my own. My thinking and my perspective evolves. I think of myself less and less as defined by the *substance* of my beliefs and more and more by the critical *processes* that enable me to shape and re-shape them. I realize, more and more, the importance of *how* I think, and of how I relate to that thinking.

My own intellectual traits become more important to me as I see how much the quality and value of my own thinking depends on them. Who I am and *how* I think — rather that *what* I think — become importantly united. I identify myself less and less with particular substantive beliefs. I make common cause, not with those who uncritically reinforce, nor with those who sophistically defend, my substantive beliefs, but with those who critically hold whatever beliefs they hold. I recognize that, as a critical liberal or conservative or radical or socialist or Christian or communist or feminist or atheist or capitalist, I have more in common with those who critically hold their beliefs, even though they may substantively disagree with me, than I have with those who uncritically or closedmindedly defend the substance of what I believe.

So as a critical thinker, I would suggest that Korzybski himself would not identify with the substance of his beliefs at any point in time. He would be willing to abandon, for example, his model of science and mathematics as the fundamental paradigm of knowledge if he came to see the importance of multi-logical "knowledge" and the kind of multi-logical thinking and traits of mind such knowledge requires. Korzybski, as a critical thinker, would be willing to enter empathically into this altered "non-scientific", "non-technical" way of thinking about knowledge that I am now sketching out. Furthermore, Korzybski would be willing to recognize that natural languages have advantages he failed to emphasize and scientific languages disadvantages he failed to highlight. This openness to change of view has characterized most of the great contributors to human knowledge and insight. It is reasonable to postulate then that, if Korzybski had lived to this day, his own views would have undergone significant shifts as a result.

✦ Concluding Remarks

The uncritical or sophistically critical mind is not unmotivated or without traits. The development of a critical mind through critical thinking is not a matter of placing bits and pieces of wisdom into a void. We are each born inclined toward egocentrism. We automatically and painlessly generate fantasies and beliefs that give us pleasure and satisfy our desires. We do not need to be taught how to avoid unpleasant truth nor how to distort, falsify, twist, or misrepresent situations to serve our egocentric interests. We do this quite naturally. Children display great precocity in these "skills" with no training in their backgrounds. The human egocentric mind is tailor-made for self-deception and ready-equipped with what Freud called defense mechanisms. Many of the important meanings we construct for ourselves produce powerful stereotypes, prejudices, delusions, illusions, and narrowmindedness of various kinds. We need a much more developed theory of the cultivation of intellectual traits than we now have in order to realistically combat egocentric thought.

I can reason well in domains in which I am prejudiced — hence, eventually reason my way out of my prejudices — only if I develop a set of mental benchmarks for such reasoning. Of course, one of the insights I will need is the clear recognition that when I am prejudiced, it will seem to me that I am not, and, similarly, that those who are not prejudiced as I am will nevertheless seem to me to be prejudiced. (To a prejudiced person an unprejudiced person will seem prejudiced.) I will come to this insight only to the degree that I have analyzed experiences in which I have first been intensely convinced that I was correct only to find after a series of challenges, reconsiderations, and new reasonings that my previous conviction was in fact prejudiced. I must take this experience apart in my mind, gain a clear sense of its elements and of how these elements fit together (how I became prejudiced; how I inwardly experienced that prejudice; how intensely that prejudice appeared to me to be insight; how I progressively began to break down that prejudice through serious consideration of opposing lines of reasoning; how I slowly came to new assumptions, new information, and ultimately new conceptualizations ...).

Only when one gains analyzed experiences of working one's way, reasoning one's way, out of prejudices can one gain the sort of higher order abilities a fairminded critical thinker requires. To reason one's way out of prejudices in the way suggested above requires that we recognize that our own egocentric drives are the fundamental obstacles to rational living, not forces operating outside of us, not language in itself but language as we are egocentrically inclined to use it. Our capacity to develop a critical mind develops at best alongside of our native egocentric thought. Only through critical analysis directed at our egocentrism can we hope to develop skills in isolating the irrational dimension of our experience. But this skill grows only through time and as a result of very particular educational cultivation.

One implication of the above reasoning is this: if we take seriously the traditional goals of General Semantics, we must go beyond its traditional means.

We must reshape and shift our vision somewhat of the roots of the problem. We must give up the view that the structure of natural languages is the fundamental problem. We must learn to use the language we speak with clarity, precision, and accuracy, for it is in natural rather than artificial languages that can we find the linguistic and conceptual resources to develop our critical faculties. We must learn to distinguish monological, technical issues from multi-logical, cross-disciplinary ones. We must develop the art of Socratic questioning and practice dialogical and dialectical exchange. We must empathically enter into and reason within a diversity of points of view. We must develop skill in laying out the logical features of our own thinking and that of others. We must develop our intellectual humility and courage, our intellectual empathy and integrity, our intellectual perseverance, our confidence in reason, and our fairmindedness. And we must do this as part of the very frustrating and difficult task of combatting our ever-lurking egocentric minds.

Most of all we must realize that science cannot tell us how to construct the meaning of things and certainly not how to create a humane world. We must play down the significance of disagreements concerning the substance of thought and look to find others within a diversity of perspectives who critically, rather than simplistically or sophistically, believe what they believe. We must make common cause with critical General Semanticists as well as with critical opponents of General Semantics, if any. We must beware of allegiances based on labels like "American", "Russian", "Communist", "Capitalist", "Christian", "Atheist", "Liberal", "Conservative", "Radical". Only with such a shift of emphasis and vision can the enduring insights of Korzybski be carried forward and honored in the deepest fashion, by being empathically and critically entertained by empathic critical minds.

Chapter 34

Philosophy and Cognitive Psychology:
Contrasting Assumptions

Abstract

This paper was originally written for the Association for Supervision and Curriculum Development (ASCD) meeting, held at Wingspread in 1987 to discuss the ASCD publication, Dimensions of Thinking. In it, Paul critiques the book for its pedagogical and theoretical bias toward a cognitive-psychological approach to thinking, a bias that largely ignores the contributions of philosophy, as well as those of affective and social psychology. Paul contrasts the very different assumptions that philosophers and cognitive psychologists make when analyzing the nature of thinking.

ne of the major objectives of the authors of *Dimensions of Thinking* was to produce a comprehensive, theoretically balanced, and pedagogically useful thinking skills framework. Unfortunately, the value of the present framework is limited by its bias in every important respect toward the approach of cognitive psychology. Virtually all of the research cited, the concepts and terminology used, and the recommendations made for implementation are taken from the writings of scholars working principally in cognitive psychology. The work and perspective of many of the philosophers concerned with thinking is minimally reported. Those whose work is not significantly used include these:

> Michael Scriven, Harvey Siegel, Mortimer Adler, John Passmore, Israel Scheffler, Mark Weinstein, R. S. Peters, Ralph Johnson, J. Anthony Blair, Stephen Norris, John Dewey, Vincent Ruggiero, Edward D'Angelo, Perry Weddle, Sharon Bailin, Lenore Langsdorf, T. Edward Damer, Howard Kahane, Nicholas Rescher, Paulo Freire, Robert Swartz, Max Black, James Freeman, John Hoaglund, Gerald Nosich, Jon Adler, Eugene Garver, (to name some who come readily to mind).

Nor does *Dimensions of Thinking* incorporate significant philosophical contributions to our understanding of thinking from the great philosophers of the last three hundred years. It fails to mention Immanuel Kant's work on the mind's shaping and structuring of human experience, Hegel's work on the dialectical nature of human thought, Marx's work on the economic and ideological foundations of human thought, Nietzsche's illumination of self-delusion in human thought, or Wittgenstein's work on the socio-linguistic foundations of human thought.

Another perspective conspicuously absent from *Dimensions of Thinking* is that of affective and social psychology, especially those studies that shed light on the major obstacles or blocks to rational thinking: prejudice, bias, self-deception, desire, fear, vested interest, delusion, illusion, egocentrism, sociocentrism, and ethnocentrism. The significance of this omission should be clear. The point behind the thinking skills movements (in both cognitive psychology and philosophy) is not simply to get students to think; all humans think spontaneously and continuously. The problem is to get them to think *critically* and *rationally* and this requires insight by students into the nature of uncritical and irrational thought. The massive literature in affective and social psychology bears on this problem; its seminal insights and concepts should be a significant part of any adequate framework for understanding how to reform education to cultivate rational, reflective, autonomous, empathic thought. (Philosophers, I might add, are often as guilty as cognitive psychologists of ignoring the work of affective and social psychologists.) Recently, when I did an ERIC search under the descriptors "prejudice or bias or self-deception or defense mechanism", the search turned up 8,673 articles! This then is a significant omission.

More important than the sheer numerical imbalance in scholarship cited is the imbalance in perspective. There are important differences between those features of thinking highlighted by philosophers in the critical thinking movement and the general approach to thinking fostered by cognitive psychologists and the educators influenced by them. And though there is much that each field is beginning to learn from the other, that learning can fruitfully take place only if some of their differences are clearly set out and due emphasis given to each. After I have spelled out these differences roughly, I will detail what I see as emerging common ground, what I see that gives me hope that these fields may yet work together. But first the down side.

In thinking of the relationship between the traditions of cognitive psychology and philosophy, I am reminded of a couple of remarks by the great 19th Century educator-philosopher John Henry Newman (1912) in his classic *Idea of a University*:

> I am not denying, I am granting, I am assuming, that there is reason and truth in the "leading ideas", as they are called and "large views" of scientific men; I only say that, though they speak truth, they do not speak the whole truth; that they speak a narrow truth, and think it a broad truth; that their deductions must be compared with other truths, which are acknowledged to be truths, in order to verify, complete, and correct them. (p. 178)

and:

> If different studies are useful for aiding, they are still more useful for correcting each other; for as they have their particular merits severally, so they have their defects. (p. 176)

In this case, the "scientific" views of cognitive psychologists need to be corrected by the insights of philosophers, for the whole truth to be apprehended.

Only when we see the differing emphases, assumptions, and concepts, even the differing value priorities of the two disciplines and how the work of those interested in critical thinking reflects them can we begin to appreciate the distinctive contributions of both cognitive psychology and philosophy to instruction for thinking. Few K–12 educators and their education department counterparts recognize the possible contribution of philosophy to instruction for thinking because their own educational background was heavily biased in favor of psychologically and scientistically-oriented courses. Rarely were they expected to articulate a philosophical perspective, to reason and synthesize across disciplinary lines, to formulate their philosophy. Moreover, few feel comfortable with philosophical argumentation and counter-argumentation as a means of establishing probable truth. Well-reasoned philosophical essays do not seem to them to be *research,* properly so called, because they rarely cite empirical studies.

With these thoughts in mind, let us examine 24 contrasting emphases between these two disciplines. I do not assume, of course, that all 24 are always present, but that, on the whole, there is a pattern of differences between the writings of *most* cognitive psychologists and *most* philosophers. In the case of *Dimensions of Thinking,* for example, I am confident that had the co-authors been Lipman, Ennis, Scriven, Scheffler, and Paul, a very different account of thinking would have emerged, one reflective of the contrasts which I now list.

	Tendencies of:	
With respect to:	*Cognitive Psychologists*	*Philosophers*
1. Approach to thinking	Approach thinking descriptively.	Approach thinking normatively.
2. Methodology	Focus on empirical fact-gathering. (This is not to imply that cognitive psychologists do not formulate theories or engage in conceptual analysis.)	Focus on the analysis of cases of "well-justified" thinking in contrast to cases of "poorly justified" thinking.
3. Modes of thinking studied	Focus on expert versus novice thinking, intradisciplinary thinking, and monological thinking.	Focus on rational reflective thinking, on interdisciplinary thinking, and on multilogical thinking.
4. Value emphasis	Emphasize the value of expertise.	Emphasize the values of rationality, autonomy, self-criticism, open-mindedness, truth, and empathy.

	Tendencies of:	
With respect to:	**Cognitive Psychologists**	**Philosophers**
5. Authority	Make the authority of the expert central.	Play down the authority of the expert and play up the authority of independent reason.
6. Language used	Generate more technical terminology and make their points in a technical fashion.	Take their terminology and concepts more from the critical, analytic vocabulary of a natural language (e. g., assumes, claims, implies, is consistent with, contradicts, is relevant to).
7. Role of values in thinking	Separate the cognitive from the domain of *a)* value-choices of the thinker and *b)* the overall world view of the thinker (at least when discussing basic mental skills and processes).	Emphasize the role in thinking of values and the overall conceptual framework of the thinker; hence, the significance of identifying and assessing points of view and frames of reference.
8. Place of dialogue	Play down the significance of dialogical and dialectical thinking.	Play up the significance of dialogical and dialectical thinking; view debate and argumentation as central to rational thinking.
9. View of affect	Underemphasize the affective obstacles to rational thinking; fear, desire, prejudice, bias, vested interest, conformity, self-deception, egocentrism, and ethnocentrism.	Emphasize the affective obstacles to rational thinking (this emphasis is correlated with the emphasis on the philosophical ideal of becoming a rational person).
10. Role of teacher	Play down the role of the teacher as autonomous critical thinker (this is perhaps an emerging issue in cognitive psychology).	Make central the role of the teacher as autonomous critical thinker, the need to question her own biases, prejudices, point of view, and so forth.

With respect to:	Tendencies of:	
	Cognitive Psychologists	**Philosophers**
11. Classroom climate	Play down the need to develop classrooms as communities of inquiry wherein dialogical and dialectical exchange is a matter of course.	Play up the need to develop classrooms as communities of inquiry where students learn the arts of analyzing, synthesizing, advocating, reconstructing, and challenging each other's ideas.
12. Place of intelligent skepticism	Ignore or play down the significance of the student as Socratic questioner, as intelligent skeptic (this too may be an emerging issue).	Make central the significance of questioning; view intellectual advancement more in terms of skill in the art of questioning than in the amassing of anunquestioned knowledge base (the thinker as questioner is connected by philosophers with the disposition to suspend judgment in cases in which the thinker is called upon to accept beliefs not justified by his or her own thinking.)
13. Place of empirical research	Play up the significance of empirical research in settling educational issues.	Skeptical of empirical research as capable of settling significant educational issues without argumentation between conflicting educational viewpoints or philosophies on those issues.
14. View of the teaching process	Give more weight to the significance of teaching as embodying step-by-step procedures (although there is increasing dissent within cognitive psychology on this point).	Play up the significance of dialogical approaches that involve much crisscrossing and unpredictable back-tracking in teaching and thinking; skeptical of step-by-step procedures in teaching and thinking.

	Tendencies of:	
With respect to:	***Cognitive Psychologists***	***Philosophers***
15. Identified micro-elements in thinking	Emphasize such categories as recalling, encoding and storing, and identifying relationships and patterns — all of which admit to empirical study.	Emphasize identification of issues, assumptions, relevant and irrelevant considerations, unclear concepts and terms, supported and unsupported claims, contradictions, inferences and implications — all of which shed light on thought conceived as the intellectual moves of a reasoning person.
16. Place of micro-skills	Separate the analysis of micro-skills from normative considerations.	Link the analysis of micro-skills with normative considerations since, for philosophers, micro-skills are intellectual moves which can be used to clarify, analyze, synthesize, support, elaborate, question, deduce, or induce.
17. View of macro-processes	View macro-processes from the perspective of categories of research in cognitive psychology: problem solving, decision making, concept formation, and so forth.	View macro-processes from the perspective of the overall reasoning needs of a rational person: ability to analyze issues and distinguish questions of different logical types, ability to Socratically question, ability to engage in conceptual analysis, ability to accurately reconstruct the strongest case for opposing points of view, ability to reason dialogically and dialectically (each use of a macro-process is a unique orchestration of some sequence of micro-skills in the context of some issue, problem, or objective).

	Tendencies of:	
With respect to:	**Cognitive Psychologists**	**Philosophers**
18. Teaching as a science or art	Present teaching for thinking as a quasi-science, with the assumption that there is a discrete body of information that can be "added up" or "united" and passed on "as is" to the teacher.	Present teaching for thinking as an intellectual art; play down the significance of technical, empirical information as necessary to skill in that art.
19. Place of philosophy of education	Ignore or play down the significance of teachers developing a philosophy of education into which rationality, autonomy, and self-criticism become central values.	Emphasize the importance of each teacher developing an explicit philosophy of education which is openly stated in the classroom; tend to encourage students to do the same, especially in relation to their philosophy of life.
20. Obstacles to rational thinking	Ignore the problem of prejudice and bias in parents and the community as possible obstacles to teaching for rational thinking.	Sensitive to the dangers of community and national bias as possible obstacles to teaching for rational thinking.
21. Place of virtues and passions	Underemphasize the significance of rational passions and intellectual virtues.	Emphasize rational passions (a passiona for clarity, accuracy, fairmindedness, a fervor for getting to the bottom of things or deepest root issues, for listening sympathetically to opposing perspectives, a compelling drive to seek out evidence, an intense aversion to contradiction and sloppy thinking, a devotion to truth over self-interest) and intellectual virtues (intellectual humility, intellectual courage, intellectual integrity, intellectual empathy, intellectual perseverance, faith in reason, and intellectual sense of justice).

	Tendencies of:	
With respect to:	**Cognitive Psychologists**	**Philosophers**
22. Specialized versus mundane thinking	Orient themselves toward domain-specific thinking, with the "good" thinker often associated with the successful business or professional person, or with a specialist working within a discipline.	Emphasize the link between an emphasis on rational thought and the goals of a traditional liberal education, of the ideal of the liberally educated person and on mundane generalizable skills such as the art of reading the newspaper critically, detecting propaganda and bias in public discourse, advertising, and textbooks, and in rational reorientation of personal values and beliefs.
23. Place of ethics of teaching and the rights of students	Lay insufficient stress upon the relation of teaching for thinking to the ethics of teaching and the rights of students.	Emphasize the link between teaching for critical thinking and developing moral insight, with the rights of students; with the student's "right to exercise his independent judgment and powers of evaluation"; as Siegel (1980) puts it: "To deny the student this right is to deny the student the status of person of equal worth."
24. Thinking and one's way of life	Lay insufficient stress upon the relation of modes of thinking to fundamental ethical and philosophical choices concerning a way of life.	Link emphasis on critical thinking with an attempt to initiate students, as Israel Scheffler (1965) puts it, "into the rational life, a life in which the critical quest for reasons is a dominant and integrating motive."

Those whose thinking about thinking is basically shaped by scholars in one tradition differ from those shaped by the other. They differ in style, direction, and methods for improving thinking. Inevitably problems of misunderstanding and mutual prejudice remain as residues of the historical separation of psychology from philosophy. That psychologists are sometimes skeptical of philosophical approaches to teaching for thinking is poignantly demonstrated by Al Benderson (1984) of the Educational Testing Service. In characterizing "The View From Psychology" (on philosophy's contribution to teaching for thinking) Benderson says:

> Psychologists, who have their roots in research into mental processes, tend to view thinking from a different perspective than do philosophers. ETS Distinguished Research Scientist Irving Seigel, a psychologist, views philosophers who claim to teach thinking skills as encroaching upon a field in which they have little real expertise. "These philosophers are imperialists", he charges. "They don't know the first thing about how kids think." (p. 10)

R. S. Peters and C. A. Mace (1967), two philosophers in turn commenting on the separation of psychology from philosophy for the *Encyclopedia of Philosophy,* say:

> The trouble began when psychologists claimed the status of empirical scientists. At first the philosophers were the more aggressive, deriding the young science as a bogus discipline. The psychologists hit back and made contemptuous remarks about philosophical logic-chopping and armchair psychology. The arguments were charged with emotion and neither side emerged with great credit .... Not all issues between philosophers and psychologists have been resolved, but there has been notable progress toward a policy of coexistence, and here and there some progress toward cooperation has been made. (p. 26)

In the field of teaching for thinking there has been, in my view, much more coexistence than cooperation. The largest and oldest conference tradition in the field (the Sonoma Conferences: two national and six international conferences, the last with a registration of over 1,000 with over 100 presenters and 230 sessions) has had only token participation by cognitive psychologists. The conference on *Thinking* at Harvard, in turn, had only token participation by philosophers. It appears to me that few psychologists or philosophers read widely in the other tradition. The field of education has been dominated by various psychologically-based rather than philosophically-based models of instruction. It is understandable therefore why *Dimensions of Thinking,* written by a team that included no philosophers, fails to successfully represent or integrate the distinctive approach of philosophy toward the thinking skills movement.

Having said this much about the typical failure of cognitive psychologists and philosophers to appropriate the strengths and correct for the weaknesses of their two traditions, I nevertheless want to mention the signs of common themes emerging in the two traditions which may become the basis for integration. Representatives of both traditions are developing a profound critique of what I would call a "didactic" theory of knowledge, learning, and literacy and framing a "critical" alternative. Behind this critique and reconstruction is a growing common sense of how the didactic paradigm impedes the scholastic development of critical thinkers.

✦ Conclusion

Perhaps a growing joint recognition of the need for both cognitive psychologists and philosophers to make common cause against the didactic theory of education will be the impetus for an on-going fruitful exchange of ideas across these rich traditions. It is certainly in the interest of all who consider the ability to think critically to be at the heart of education rightly conceived, for this rapprochement to take place.

✦ References

Newman, John Henry. *The Idea of a University.* London: Langman's, Green, and Co. 1912.

Benderson, Al. "The View from Psychology." *Critical Thinking: Focus 15.* 1984.

Peters, R. S. & Mace, C. A. "Psychology" *Encyclopedia of Philosophy, Vol. 7.* New York: Macmillan Publishing Co., Inc. & The Free Press. 1967.

Paul, Richard W. "Critical Thinking in North America: A New Theory of Knowledge, Learning, and Literacy." *Argumentation: North American Perspectives on Teaching Critical Thinking.* (in press).

Siegel, Harvey. "Critical Thinking as an Educational Ideal" *National Forum.* November, 1980.

Scheffler, Israel. *The Conditions of Knowledge.* Chicago: Scott Foresman. 1965.

*Critical Thinking and
Academic Subjects*

✦✦ Chapter 35

The Contribution of
Philosophy to Thinking

Abstract

In this paper, originally part of "Philosophy and Cognitive Psychology", Paul argues for the power of philosophy and philosophical thinking for intellectual autonomy. He claims that even children have a need and right to think philosophically and are very much inclined to do so, but are typically discouraged by the didactic absolutistic answers and attitudes of adults. Consequently, the inquiring minds of children soon become jaded by the self-assured absolutistic environment which surrounds them.

The potential of children to philosophize is suggested in a transcript of a 4th grade classroom discussion of a series of abstract questions. Following the transcript, Paul illustrates a variety of ways in which traditional school subjects can be approached philosophically. He closes with a discussion of the values and intellectual traits fostered by philosophical thought, the skills and processes of thought, and the relation of philosophical to critical thought.

*I*n this paper I lay the foundation for a philosophy-based, in contrast to a psychology-based, approach to teaching critical thinking across the curriculum. I lay out the general theory and provide some examples of how it could be used to transform classroom instruction and activities. Nevertheless, I want to underscore the point that I lack the space to cover my subject comprehensively. Interested readers must independently pursue the leads I provide, to see the power and flexibility of philosophy-based approaches to critical thinking instruction. I must content myself with modest goals, with a few basic insights into philosophical thinking, with a few of its advantages for instruction.

There are three overlapping senses of *philosophy* that can play a role in explicating the nature of philosophical thinking: philosophy as a field of study, philosophy as a mode of thinking, and philosophy as a framework for thinking. In what follows, I focus on philosophy as a mode of and framework for thinking and will say least about it as a field of study. Nevertheless, some characterization of the field of philosophy is useful.

Philosophy is steeped in dialogical and dialectical thought. Philosophy is an art rather than a science, a discipline that formulates issues that can be approached from multiple points of view and invites critical dialogue and reasoned discourse between conflicting viewpoints. Critical thought and dis-

554

cussion are its main instruments of learning. More so than any other field, philosophy requires all participants to think their own way to whatever system of beliefs ultimately constitute their thought within the field. This entails that all philosophers develop their own unique philosophies.

In contrast, science students are not expected to construct their own science. Sciences have emerged because of the possibility of specializiation and joint work within a highly defined shared frame of reference. Its ground rules exclude what is not subject to quantification and measurement. Sciences are cooperative, collaborative ventures whose practitioners agree to limit strictly the range of issues they consider and how they consider them.

Philosophy, on the other hand, is largely an individualistic venture wherein participants agree, only in the broadest sense on the range and nature of the issues they will consider. Philosophers have traditionally been concerned with big questions, root issues that organize the overall framework of thinking itself, in all domains, not just one. Philosophers do not typically conduct *experiments*. They rarely form *hypotheses* or make *predictions* as scientists do. Philosophical tradition gives us a tapestry rich in the development of individual syntheses of ideas across multiple subject domains: syntheses carefully and precisely articulated and elaborately argued. There is reason for this basic difference between the history of science and that of philosophy.

Some questions, by their nature, admit of collaborative treatment and solution; others do not. For example, we do not need to individually test for the chemical structure of lead or determine the appropriate theory of that structure; we can rely on the conclusions of those who have done so. But we cannot learn the structure of our own lives or the best way to plan for the future by looking up the answer in a technical manual or having an answer determined for us by a collaborative scientific effort. We must each individually analyze these questions to obtain rationally defensible answers. There is a wide range of ways human lives can be understood and a variety of strategies for living them. Rarely, if ever, can answers to philosophical questions be validated by one person for another.

The method of philosophy, or the *mode* of thinking characteristic of philosophy, is that of critical discussion, rational cross examination, and dialectical exchange. Every person who would participate in that discussion must create and elaborate a framework for thinking comprehensively. This discipline in the mode of thinking characteristic of philosophy has roots in the ideal of learning to think with a clear sense of the ultimate foundations of one's thinking, of the essential logic of one's thought, and of significant alternative, competing ways of thinking.

Consider philosophical thinking as a framework for thought. When one engages in philosophical thinking, one thinks within a self-constructed network of assumptions, concepts, defined issues, key inferences, and insights. To think philosophically as a liberal, for example, is to think within a different framework of ideas than conservatives do. What is more, to think philosophically, in this sense, is to *know* that one is thinking within a different framework of ideas than other thinkers. It is to know the foundations of liberalism compared to those of conservativism.

✦ Philosophical and Unphilosophical Minds: Philosophy as a Mode of Thinking and a Framework for Thinking

Perhaps the best way to show what lies at the heart of the uniqueness and power of philosophy is to consider the contrast in general between unphilosophical and philosophical minds. In doing so, I present the two as idealized abstractions for the purpose of clarifying a paradigm; I realize that no one perfectly illustrates these idealizations.

The unphilosophical mind thinks without a clear sense of the foundations of its own thought, without conscious knowledge of the most basic concepts, aims, assumptions, and values that define and direct it. The unphilosophical mind is unaware that it thinks within a system, within a framework, within, if you will, a *philosophy*. Consequently, the unphilosophical mind is trapped within the system it uses, unable to deeply understand alternative or competing systems. The unphilosophical mind tends toward an intra-system closedmindedness. The unphilosophical mind may learn to think within different systems of thought, if the systems are compartmentalized and apply in different contexts, but it cannot compare and contrast whole systems, because, at any given time, it thinks within a system without a clear sense of what it means to do so. This kind of intra-system thinking can be skilled, but it lacks foundational self-command. It functions well when confronted with questions and issues that fall clearly within its system, but is at its worse when facing issues that cross systems, require revising a system, or presuppose explicit critique of the system used.

Unphilosophical liberals, for example, would be hard pressed to think clearly and accurately within a conservative point of view, and hence would not do well with an issue like "What are some of the most important insights of conservatism?" Unphilosophical psychologists, to take another example, would find it difficult to integrate sociological or economic insights into their thinking. Indeed, thinking unphilosophically in almost any discipline means thinking reductionistically with respect to insights from other disciplines: one either reduces them to whatever can be absorbed into the established concepts in one's field or ignores them entirely.

An unphilosophical mind is at its best when routine methods, rules, or procedures function well and there is no need to critically reconceptualize them in the light of a broad understanding of one's framework for thinking. If one lacks philosophical insight into the underlying logic of those routines, rules, or procedures, one lacks the ability to mentally step outside of them and conceive of alternatives. As a result, the unphilosophical mind tends toward conformity to a system without grasping clearly what the system is, how it came to be thus, or how it might have been otherwise.

The philosophical mind, in contrast, routinely probes the foundations of its own thought, realizes its thinking is defined by basic concepts, aims, assumptions, and values. The philosophical mind gives serious consideration to alternative and competing concepts, aims, assumptions, and values, enters empathically into thinking fundamentally different from its own, and does not confuse its thinking with reality. By habitually thinking globally, the philosophical mind gains foundational self-command, and is comfortable when problems cross disciplines, domains, and frameworks. A philosophical mind habitually probes the basic principles and concepts that lie behind standard methods, rules, and procedures. The philosophical mind recognizes the need to refine and improve the systems, concepts, and methods it uses and does not simply conform to them. The philosophical mind deeply values gaining command over its own fundamental modes of thinking.

The discipline of philosophy is the only one at present that routinely fosters the philosophical mind, though there are philosophical minds at work in every discipline. The philosophical mind is most evident in other disciplines in those working on foundational concepts and problems. In everyday life, the philosophical mind is most evident in those who deeply value doing their own thinking about the basic issues and problems they face and giving serious reasoned consideration to the ideas and thinking of others. In everyday life, the philosophical mind is most evident in those not afraid to probe conventional thought, rules, mores, and values, those skeptical of standard answers and standard definitions of questions and problems.

In teaching, the philosophical mind is most evident in those who routinely probe the concepts, aims, assumptions, and values that underlie their teaching; who routinely raise fundamental issues through Socratic questions; who routinely encourage students to probe the foundation and source of their own ideas and those of others; and who routinely encourage students to develop their own philosophy or approach to life or learning based on their own disciplined, rational thought. Need I add that philosophical thinking is not habit for most?

✦ Why Children Need to Think Philosophically

There is a sense in which everyone has a philosophy, since human thought and actions are always embedded in a framework of foundational concepts, values, and assumptions which define a "system" of some sort. Humans are by nature inferential, meaning-creating animals. In this sense, all humans use "philosophies" and even in some sense create them. Even the thinking of very young children presupposes philosophical foundations, as Piaget so ably demonstrated. Of course, if by 'philosophy' we mean explicit and systematic reflection on the concepts, values, aims, and assumptions that structure thinking and underlie behavior, then in that sense most children do *not* philosophize. It all depends on whether one believes that one can have a philosophy without *thinking* one's way to it.

Most children have at least the impulse to philosophize and for a time seem driven by a strong desire to know the most basic *what* and *why* of things. Of course parents or teachers rarely cultivate this tendency. Usually children are given didactic answers in ways that discourage, rather than stimulate, further inquiry. Many parents and teachers seem to think that they or textbooks have appropriate and satisfactory answers to the foundational questions that children raise, and the sooner children accept these answers the better. Such authorities unwittingly encourage children to assent to, without truly understanding, basic beliefs. In effect, we teach answers to philosophical questions as though they were like answers to chemical questions. As a result, children lose the impulse to question, as they learn to mouth the standard answers of parents, peers, and other socializing groups. How many of these mouthed answers become a part of children's lived beliefs is another matter.

Children learn behaviors as well as explanations. They learn to act as well as to speak. Thus they learn to behave in ways inconsistent with much of their conscious talk and thought. Children learn to live, as it were, in different and only partially integrated worlds. They develop unconscious worlds of meaning that do not completely square with what they are told or think they believe. Some of these meanings become a source of pain, frustration, repression, fear, and anxiety. Some become a source of harmless fantasizing and day-dreaming. Some are embedded in action, albeit in camouflaged, or in tacit, unarticulated ways.

In any case, the process of unconsciously taking in or unknowingly constructing a variety of meanings outstrips the child's initial impulse to reflect on or question those meanings. In one sense, then, children become captives of the ideas and meanings whose impact on their own thought and action they do not themselves determine. They have in this sense two philosophies (only partially compatible with each other): one verbal but largely unlived; the other lived but mainly unverbalized. This split continues into adulthood. On the emotional level, it leads to anxiety and stress. On the moral level, it leads to hypocrisy and self-deception. On the intellectual level, it results in a condition in which lived beliefs and spontaneous thought are unintegrated with school learning which in turn is ignored in "real life" situations.

As teachers and parents we seldom consider the plight of children from this perspective. We tend to act as though there were no real need for children to reflect deeply about the meanings they absorb. We fail to see the conflicting meanings they absorb, the double messages that capture their minds. Typically our principal concern is that they absorb the meanings that we think are correct and act in ways that we find acceptable. Reflecting upon their thoughts and actions seems important to us only to get them to think or act correctly, that is, as we want them to think and act. We seldom question whether they deeply agree or even understand. We pay little attention as parents to whether or not conflicting meanings and double messages become an on-going problem for them.

In some sense we act as though we believe, and doubtless many do believe, that children have no significant capacity, need, or right to think for themselves. Many adults do not think that children can participate mindfully in the process which shapes their own minds and behavior. Of course, at the same time we often talk to our children as though they were somehow responsible for, or in control of, the ideas they express or act upon. This contradictory attitude toward children is rarely openly admitted. We need to deal explicitly with it.

I believe that children have the need, the capacity, and the *right* to freedom of thought, and that the proper cultivation of that capacity requires an emphasis on the philosophical dimension of thought and action. Again, by 'the philosophical dimension', I mean precisely the kind of deliberative thought that gives to thinkers the on-going disposition to mindfully create, analyze, and assess their own most basic assumptions, concepts, values, aims, and meanings, in effect to choose the very framework in which they think and on the basis of which they act. I would not go so far as to say, as Socrates was reputed to have said, that the unreflective life is not worth living, but I would say that an unreflective life is not a truly *free* life and is often a basic cause of personal and social problems. I claim at least this much, that philosophical thinking is necessary to freedom of thought and action and that freedom of thought and action are good in themselves and should be given a high priority in schooling. They are certainly essential for a democracy. How can the people rule, as the word *democracy* implies, if they do not think for themselves on issues of civic importance? And if they are not encouraged to think for themselves *in* school, why should they do so once they leave it?

Let me now discuss whether children are in fact capable of this sort of freedom of thought, reflection upon ultimate meanings, values, assumptions, and concepts. The question is both conceptual and empirical. On the conceptual side, the issue is one of *degree*. Only to the degree that children are encouraged in supportive circumstances to reflect philosophically, will they develop proficiency in it. Since few parents and teachers value this sort of reflection or are adept at cultivating it, it is understandable that children soon give up their instinctive philosophical impulses (the basic *why* and *what* questions). It would be foolish to assume that it is the *nature* of children to think and act unreflectively when indeed our experience indicates that they are socialized into unreflectiveness. Since we do not encourage children to philosophize why should they do so?

Furthermore, in many ways we penalize children for philosophizing. Children will sometimes innocently entertain an idea in conflict with the ideas of their parents, teachers, or peers. Such ideas are often ridiculed and the children made to feel ashamed of their thoughts. It is quite common, in other words, for people to penalize unconventional thought and reward conventional thought. When we think only as we are rewarded to think, however, we cease to think freely or deeply. Why should we think for ourselves if doing so may get us into trouble and if teachers, parents, and powerful peers provide authoritative didactic answers for us? Before we decide that children cannot think for themselves about basic ideas and meanings, we ought to give them a real and extended opportunity to do so. No society has yet done this. Unless we are willing to exercise some faith in freedom of thought, we will never be in a position to reap the benefits of it or to discover its true limits, if any.

Let me now explore the conceptual side of the question further by suggesting some kinds of philosophical issues embedded, not only in the lives of children, but also in the lives of adults:

> Who am I? What am I like? What are the people around me like? What are people of different backgrounds, religions, and nations like? How much am I like others? How much am I unlike them? What kind of a world do I live in? When should I trust? When should I distrust? What should I accept? What should I question? How should I understand my past, the pasts of my parents, my ethnic group, my religion, my nation? Who are my friends? Who are my enemies? What is a friend? How am I like and unlike my enemy? What is most important to me? How should I live my life? What responsibilities do I have to others? What responsibilities do they have to me? What responsibilities do I have to my friends? Do I have any responsibilities to people I don't like? To people who don't like me? To my enemies? Do my parents love me? Do I love them? What is love? What is hate? What is indifference? Does it matter if others do not approve of me? When does it matter? When should I ignore what others think? What rights do I have? What rights should I give to others? What should I do if others do not respect my rights? Should I get what I want? Should I question what I want? Should I take what I want if I am strong or smart enough to get away with it? Who comes out ahead in this world, the strong or the good person? Is it worthwhile to be good? Are authorities good or just strong?

I do not assume that children must reflect on all or even most of the questions that professional philosophers consider — although the preceding list contains many concepts that professional philosophers tackle. To cultivate philosophical thinking, one does not force students to think in a sophisticated way before they are ready. Each student can contribute to a philosophical discussion thoughts which help other students to orient themselves within a range of thoughts, some of which support or enrich and some of which conflict with other thoughts. Different students achieve different levels of understanding. There is no reason to try to force any given student to achieve a particular level of understanding. But the point is that we can lead young students into philosophical discussions which help them begin to:

1. see the significance and relevance of basic philosophical questions to understanding themselves and the world about them,

2. understand the problematic character of human thought and the need to probe deeply into it,

3. gain insights into what it takes to make thinking more rational, critical, and fairminded,

4. organize their thinking globally across subject matter divisions,

5. achieve initial command over their own thought processes, and

6. come to believe in the value and power of their own minds.

In the transcript that follows, a normal 4th grade class is led to discuss a variety of basic ideas: how the mind works, the nature of mind, why different people interpret the same events differently, the relationship between emotions and mental interpretations, the nature and origin of personality, nature versus nurture, peer group influence on the mind, cultural differences, free will versus determinism, the basis for ethical and unethical behavior, the basis for reputation, the relation of reputation to goodness, mental illness, social prejudice and sociocentrism, and the importance of thinking for oneself. This transcript represents the first philosophical discussion this particular class had and although it is clear from some of their answers that their present degree of insight into the ideas being discussed is limited, it is also clear that they are capable of pursuing those insights and of articulating important philosophical ideas that could be explored in greater and greater depth over time.

✦ Transcript

The following is a transcript of a 4th grade Socratic discussion. The discussion leader was with these particular students for the first time. The purpose was to determine the status of the children's thinking on some of the abstract questions whose answers tend to define our broadest thinking. The students were eager to respond and often seemed to articulate responses that reflected potential insights into the character of the human mind, its relation to the body, the forces that shape us, the influence of parents and peer groups, the nature of morality and of ethnocentric bias. The insights are disjointed, of course, but the questions that elicited them and the responses that articulated them could be used as the basis of future discussions or simple assignments with these students.

> ➤ *How does your mind work?*
> *Where's your mind?*

Student: In your head. (Numerous students point to their heads.)

> ➤ *Does your mind do anything?*

Student: It helps you remember and think.

Student: It helps, like, if you want to move your legs. It sends a message down to them.

Student: This side of your mind controls this side of your body and that side controls this other side.

Student: When you touch a hot oven it tells you whether to cry or say ouch.

> ➤ *Does it tell you when to be sad and when to be happy?*
> *How does your mind know when to be happy and when to be sad?*

Student: When you're hurt it tells you to be sad.

Student: If something is happening around you is sad.

Student: If there is lightning and you are scared.

Student: If you get something you want.

Student: It makes your body operate. It's like a machine that operates your body.

➤ *Does it ever happen that two people are in the same circumstance but one is happy and the other is sad? Even though they are in exactly the same circumstance?*

Student: You get the same toy. One person might like it. The other gets the same toy and he doesn't like the toy.

➤ *Why do you think that some people come to like some things and some people seem to like different things?*

Student: 'Cause everybody is not the same. Everybody has different minds and is built different, made different.

Student: They have different personalities?

➤ *Where does personality come from?*

Student: When you start doing stuff and you find that you like some stuff best.

➤ *Are you born with a personality or do you develop it as you grow up?*

Student: You develop it as you grow up.

➤ *What makes you develop one rather than another?*

Student: Like, your parents or something.

➤ *How can your parent's personality get into you?*

Student: Because you're always around them and then the way they act, if they think they are good and they want you to act the same way, then they'll sort of teach you and you'll do it.

Student: Like, if you are in a tradition. They want you to carry on something that their parents started.

➤ *Does your mind come to think at all the way the children around you think? Can you think of any examples where the way you think is like the way children around you think? Do you think you behave like other American kids?*

Student: Yes.

➤ *What would make you behave more like the kids around you than like Eskimo kids?*

Student: Because you're around them.

Student: Like, Eskimo kids probably don't even know what the word 'jump-rope' is. American kids know what it is.

➤ *And are there things that the Eskimo kids know that you don't know about?*

Student: Yes.

Student: And also we don't have to dress like them or act like them and they have to know when a storm is coming so they won't get trapped outside.

→ *O.K., so if I understand you then, parents have some influence on how you behave and the kids around you have some influence on how you behave. ... Do you have some influence on how you behave? Do you choose the kind of person you're going to be at all?*

Student: Yes.

→ *How do you do that do you think?*

Student: Well if someone says to jump off a five-story building, you won't say O.K. You wouldn't want to do that ....

→ *Do you ever sit around and say, "Let's see shall I be a smart person or a dumb one?"*

Student: Yes.

→ *But how do you decide?*

Student: Your grades.

→ *But I thought your teacher decided your grades. How do you decide?*

Student: If you don't do your homework you get bad grades and become a dumb person but if you study real hard you'll get good grades.

→ *So you decide that, right?*

Student: And if you like something at school like computers you work hard and you can get a good job when you grow up. But if you don't like anything at school you don't work hard.

Student: You can't just decide you want to be smart, you have to work for it.

Student: You got to work to be smart just like you got to work to get your allowance.

→ *What about being good and being bad, do you decide whether you're good or you're bad? How many people have decided to be bad? (Three students raise their hands.) (To first student,) Why have you decided to be bad?*

Student: Well, I don't know. Sometimes I think I've been bad too long and I want to go to school and have a better reputation but sometimes I feel like just making trouble and who cares.

→ *Let's see, is there a difference between who you are and your reputation? What's your reputation? That's a pretty big word. What's your reputation?*

Student: The way you act. If you had a bad reputation people wouldn't like to be around you and if you had a good reputation people would like to be around you and be your friend.

→ *Well, but I'm not sure of the difference between who you are and who people think you are. Could you be a good person and people think you bad? Is that possible?*

Student: Yeah, because you could try to be good. I mean, a lot of people think this one person's really smart but this other person doesn't have nice clothes but she tries really hard and people don't want to be around her.

→ *So sometimes people think somebody is real good and they're not and sometimes people think that somebody is real bad and they're not. Like if you were a crook, would you let everyone know you're a crook?*

Students: [Chorus of "NO!"]

→ *So some people are really good at hiding what they are really like. Some people might have a good reputation and be bad; some people might have a bad reputation and be good.*

Student: Like, everyone might think you were good but you might be going on dope or something.

Student: Does reputation mean that if you have a good reputation you want to keep it just like that? Do you always want to be good for the rest of your life?

→ *I'm not sure ....*

Student: So if you have a good reputation you try to be good all the time and don't mess up and don't do nothing?

→ *Suppose somebody is trying to be good just to get a good reputation — why are they trying to be good?*

Student: So they can get something they want and they don't want other people to have?

Student: They might be shy and just want to be left alone.

Student: You can't tell a book by how it's covered.

→ *Yes, some people are concerned more with their cover than their book. Now let me ask you another question. So if its true that we all have a mind and our mind helps us to figure out the world and we are influenced by our parents and the people around us, and sometimes we choose to do good things and sometimes we choose to do bad things, sometimes people say things about us and so forth and so on.... Let me ask you: Are there some bad people in this world?*

Student: Yeah.

Student: Terrorists and stuff.

Student: Nightstalker.

Student: The TWA hijackers.

Student: Robbers.

Student: Rapers.

Student: Bums.

→ *Bums, are they bad?*

Student: Well, sometimes.

Student: The Klu Klux Klan.

Student: The Bums ... not really, cause they might not look good but you can't judge them by how they look. They might be really nice and everything.

→ *O.K., so they might have a bad reputation but be good, after you care to know them. There might be good bums and bad bums.*

Student: Libyan guys and Machine gun Kelly.

→ *Let me ask you, do the bad people think they're bad?*

Student: A lot of them don't think they're bad but they are. They might be sick in the head.

→ *Yes, some people are sick in their heads.*

Student: A lot of them (bad guys) don't think they're bad.

→ *Why did you say Libyan people?*

Student: Cause they have a lot 'o terrorists and hate us and bomb us ....

→ *If they hate us do they think we are bad or good?*

Student: They think we are bad.

→ *And we think they are bad? And who is right?*

Student: Usually both of them.

Student: None of us are really bad!

Student: Really, I don't know why our people and their people are fighting. Two wrongs don't make a right.

Student: It's like if there was a line between two countries, and they were both against each other, if a person from the first country crosses over the line, they'd be considered the bad guy. And if a person from the second country crossed over the line he'd be considered the bad guy.

→ *So it can depend on which country you're from who you consider right or wrong, is that right?*

Student: Like a robber might steal things to support his family. He's doing good to his family but actually bad to another person.

→ *And in his mind do you think he is doing something good or bad?*

Student: It depends what his mind is like. He might think he is doing good for his family or he might think he is doing bad for the other person.

Student: It's like the underground railroad a long time ago. Some people thought it was bad and some people thought it was good.

→ *But if lots of people think something is right and lots of people think something is wrong, how are you supposed to figure out the difference between right and wrong?*

Student: Go by what you think!

→ *But how do you figure out what to think?*

Student: Lots of people go by other people.

➤ *But somebody has to decide for themselves, don't they?*

Student: Use your mind?

➤ *Yes, let's see, suppose I told you: "You are going to have a new classmate. Her name is Sally and she's bad." Now, you could either believe me or what could you do?*

Student: You could try to meet her and decide whether she was bad or good.

➤ *Suppose she came and said to you: "I'm going to give you a toy so you'll like me." And she gave you things so you would like her, but she also beat up on some other people, would you like her because she gave you things?*

Student: No, because she said I'll give you this so you'll like me. She wouldn't be very nice.

➤ *So why should you like people?*

Student: Because they act nice to you.

➤ *Only to you?*

Student: To everybody!

Student: I wouldn't care what they gave me. I'd see what they're like inside.

➤ *But how do you find out what's on the inside of a person?*

Student: You could ask, but I would try to judge myself.

Socratic questioning is flexible. The questions asked at any given point will depend on what the students say, what ideas the teacher wants to pursue, and what questions occur to the teacher. Generally, Socratic questions raise basic issues, probe beneath the surface of things, and pursue problematic areas of thought.

The above discussion could have gone in a number of different directions. For instance, rather than focussing on the mind's relationship to emotions, the teacher could have pursued the concept 'mind' by asking for more examples of its functions, and having students group them. The teacher could have followed up the response of the student who asked, "Does reputation mean that if you have a good reputation you want to keep it just like that?" He might, for instance, have asked the student why he asked that, and asked the other students what they thought of the idea. Such a discussion may have developed into a dialogical exchange about reputation, different degrees of goodness, or reasons for being bad. Or the concept 'bad people' could have been pursued and clarified by asking students why the examples they gave were examples of bad people. Students may then have been able to suggest tentative generalizations which could have been tested and probed through further questioning. Instead of exploring the influence of perspective on evaluation, the teacher might have probed the idea, expressed by one student, that no one is "really bad". The student could have been asked to explain the remark, and other students could have been asked for their responses. In these cases and others, the teacher has a choice between any number of equally thought provoking questions. No one question is the 'right' question.

A general discussion such as this lays the foundation for subsequent discussions by raising and briefly covering a variety of interrelated issues. This can be followed up in small group discussions or made the basis of brief writing assignments or integrated into the discussion of literature, history, or other subject areas. Note the variety of questions that were raised in the preceding discussion:

1. *Is the mind like a machine that operates your body?*

2. *How is it influenced by events?*
   If something happening around you is sad.

   If you get something you want.

3. *How is it influenced by its own interpretations and meanings?*
   You get the same toy. One person might like it. The other gets the same toy and he doesn't like the toy.

   When you start doing stuff and you find that you like some stuff best.

4. *How is it shaped by significant persons like parents?*
   Because you're always around them and then the way they act, if they think they are good and they want you to act the same way, then they'll sort of teach you and you'll do it.

5. *How is it shaped by cultural forces like peer groups?*
   Because you're around them.

   Like, Eskimo kids probably don't even know what the word 'jump-rope' is. American kids know what it is.

   And also we don't have to dress like them or act like them and they have to know when a storm is coming so they won't get trapped outside.

6. *Does free will involve more than just inwardly <u>deciding</u>?*
   You can't just decide you want to be smart, you have to work for it.

   You got to work to be smart just like you got to work to get your allowance.

   Sometimes I think I've been bad too long and I want to go to school and have a better reputation, but sometimes I feel like just making trouble and who cares.

7. *Are minds sometimes deceived by others or self-deceived?*
   Like, everyone might think you were good but you might be going on dope or something.

   You can't tell a book by how it's covered.

   The bums, ... not really 'cause they might not look good but you can't judge them by how they look. They might be really nice and everything.

   A lot of them don't think they're bad but they are. They might be sick in the head.

   A lot of them (bad guys) don't think they're bad.

It depends what his mind is like. He might think he is doing good for his family or he might think he is doing bad for the other person.

Yeah, because you could try to be good. I mean, a lot of people think this one person's really smart but this other person doesn't have nice clothes but she tries really hard and people don't want to be around her.

8. *What are people really like? Should you approach anyone as if they were evil?*

None of us are really bad!

Really, I don't know why our people and their people are fighting. Two wrongs don't make a right.

They might be shy and just want to be left alone.

9. *Should you think as others think or do your own thinking?*

Lots of people go by other people.

You could ask, but I would try to judge myself.

You could try to meet her and decide whether she was bad or good.

When teachers approach their subjects philosophically, they make it much easier for students to begin to integrate their thinking across subject matter divisions. In the preceding discussion, for example, the issues considered involved personal experience, psychology, sociology, ethics, culture, and philosophy. The issues, philosophically put, made these diverse areas relevant to each other. And just as one might inquire into a variety of issues by first asking a basic philosophical question, so one might proceed in the other direction: first asking a question within a subject area and then, by approaching it philosophically, explore its relationships to other subjects. These kinds of transitions are quite natural and unforced in a philosophical discussion, because all dimensions of human study and experience are indeed related to each other. We would see this if we could set aside the blinders that usually come with conventional discipline-specific instruction. By routinely considering root questions and root ideas philosophically, we naturally pursue those connections freed of these blinders.

As teachers teaching philosophically, we are continually interested in what the students themselves think on basic matters and issues. We continually encourage students to explore how what they think about X relates to what they think about Y and Z. This necessarily requires that students' thought moves back and forth between their own basic ideas and those presented in class by other students, between their own ideas and those expressed in a book, between their thinking and their experiences, between ideas within one domain and those in another.

This *dialogical* process (moving back and forth between divergent domains and points of view) will sometimes become *dialectical* (some ideas will clash or be inconsistent with others). The act of *integrating* thinking is deeply tied to the act of *assessing* thinking, because, as we consider a diversity of ideas, we discover that many of them contradict each other. Teachers should introduce the critical, analytic vocabulary of English (to be discussed presently) into classroom talk, so that students increasingly learn standards and tools they can use to make their integrative assessments. Skilled use of such terms as 'assumes', 'implies', and 'contradicts' is essential to rational assessment of thinking.

It would be unrealistic to expect students to suddenly and deeply grasp the roots of their own thinking, or to immediately be able to honestly and fairmindedly assess it — to instantly weed out all beliefs to which they have not consciously assented. In teaching philosophically, one is continually priming the pump, as it were, continually encouraging responsible autonomy of thought, and making progress in degrees across a wide arena of concerns. The key is to continually avoid forcing the student to acquiesce to authoritative answers without understanding them. To the extent that students become submissive in their thinking, they stop thinking for themselves. When they comply tacitly or passively without genuine understanding, they are set back intellectually.

To cultivate students' impulses to think philosophically, we must continually encourage them to believe that they can figure out where they stand on root issues, that they themselves have something worthwhile to say, and that what they have to say should be given serious consideration by the other students and the teacher.

All subjects, in sum, can be taught philosophically or unphilosophically. Let me illustrate by using the subject of history. Since philosophical thinking tends to make our most basic ideas and assumptions explicit, by using it we can better orient ourselves toward the subject as a whole and mindfully integrate the parts into the whole.

Students are introduced to history early in their education, and that subject area is usually required through high school and into college, and with good reason. But the unphilosophical way history is often taught fails to develop students' ability to think historically for themselves. Indeed, history books basically tell students what to believe and what to think about history. Students have little reason in most history classes to relate the material to the framework of their own ideas, assumptions, or values. Students do not know that they have a philosophy and even if they did it is doubtful that without the stimulation of a teacher who approached the subject philosophically they would see the relevance of history to it.

But consider the probable outcome of teachers raising and facilitating discussion questions such as the following:

> What is history? Is everything that happened part of history? Can everything that happened be put into a history book? Why not? If historians have to select some events to include and leave out others, how do they do this? If this requires that historians make value judgments about what is important, is it likely that they will all agree? Is it possible for people observing and recording events to be biased or prejudiced? Could a historian be biased or prejudiced? How would you find out? How do people know what caused an event? How do people know what outcomes an event

had? Would everyone agree about causes and outcomes? If events, to be given meaning, have to be interpreted from some point of view, what is the point of view of the person who wrote our text?

Do you have a history? Is there a way in which everyone develops an interpretation of the significant events in his or her own life? If there is more than one point of view that events can be considered from, could you think of someone in your life who interprets your past in a way different from you? Does it make any difference how your past is interpreted? How are people sometimes harmed by the way in which they interpret their past?

These questions would not, of course, be asked at once. But they should be the *kind* of question routinely raised as part of stimulating students to take history seriously, to connect it to their lives, minds, values, and actions. After all, many of the most important questions we face in everyday life do have a significant historical dimension, but that dimension is not given by a bare set of isolated facts. For example, arguments between spouses often involve disagreements on how to interpret events or patterns of past events or behaviors. How we interpret events in our lives depends on our point of view, basic values and interests, prejudices, and so forth.

Few of us are good historians or philosophers in the matter of our own lives. But then, no one has encouraged us to be. No one has helped us grasp these kinds of connections nor relate to our own thought or experience in these ways. We don't see ourselves as shaping our experience within a framework of meanings, because we have not learned how to isolate and identify central issues in our lives. Rather we tend to believe, quite egocentrically, that we directly and immediately grasp life as it is. The world must be the way we see it, because we see nothing standing between us and the world. We seem to see it directly and objectively. We don't really see the need therefore to consider seriously other ways of seeing or interpreting it.

As we identify our point of view (philosophy) explicitly, and deliberately put its ideas to work in interpreting our world, including seriously considering competing ideas, we are freed from the illusion of absolute objectivity. We begin to recognize egocentric subjectivity as a serious problem in human affairs. Our thought begins to grapple with this problem in a variety of ways. We begin to discover how our fears, insecurities, vested interests, frustrations, egocentricity, ethnocentricity, prejudices, and so forth, blind us. We begin to develop intellectual humility. We begin, in short, to think philosophically. Children have this need as much as adults, for children often take in and construct meanings that constrain and frustrate their development and alienate them from themselves and from healthy relationships to others.

✦ Values and Intellectual Traits

Philosophical thinking, like all human thinking, is infused with values. But those who think philosophically make it a point to understand and assent to the values that underlie their thought. One thinks philosophically because one *values* coming to terms with the meaning and significance of one's life. If we do so sincerely and well, we recognize problems that challenge us to decide the kind of person we want to make ourselves, including deciding the kind of mind we want to have. We have to make a variety of value judgments about ourselves regarding, among other things, fears, conflicts, and prejudices. This requires us to come to terms with the traits of mind we are developing. For example, to be truly open to knowledge, one must become intellectually humble. But intellectual humility is connected with other traits, such as intellectual courage, intellectual integrity, intellectual perseverance, intellectual empathy, and fairmindedness. The intellectual traits characteristic of our thinking become for the philosophical thinker a matter of personal concern. Philosophical reflection heightens this concern.

Consider this excerpt from a letter from a teacher with a Masters degree in physics and mathematics:

> After I started teaching, I realized that I had learned physics by rote and that I really did not understand all I knew about physics. My thinking students asked me questions for which I always had the standard textbook answers, but for the first time made me start thinking for myself, and I realized that these canned answers were not justified by my own thinking and only confused my students who were showing some ability to think for themselves. To achieve my academic goals I had memorized the thoughts of others, but I had never learned or been encouraged to learn to think for myself.

This is a good example of intellectual humility and, like all intellectual humility, is based on a philosophical insight into the nature of knowing. It is reminiscent of the ancient Greek insight that Socrates himself was the wisest of the Greeks because only he realized how little he really knew. Socrates developed this insight as a result of extensive, deep questioning of the knowledge claims of others. He, like all of us, had to think his way to this insight and did so by raising the same basic *what* and *why* questions that children often ask. We as teachers cannot hand this insight to children on a silver platter. All persons must do for themselves the thinking that leads to it.

Unfortunately, though intellectual virtues cannot be conditioned into people, intellectual failings can. Because of the typically unphilosophical way most instruction is structured, intellectual arrogance rather than humility is typically fostered, especially in those who have retentive minds and can repeat like parrots what they have heard or read. Students are routinely rewarded for giving standard textbook answers and encouraged to believe that they understand what has never been justified by their own thinking. To move toward intellectual humility most students (and teachers) need to think broadly, deeply, and foundationally about most of what they have "learned", as the teacher in the previous example did. Such questioning, in turn, requires intellectual courage, perseverance, and faith in one's ability to think one's way to understanding and insight.

Genuine intellectual development requires people to develop intellectual traits, traits acquired only by thinking one's way to basic philosophical insights. Philosophical thinking leads to insights which in turn shape basic skills of thought. Skills, values, insights, and intellectual traits are mutually and dynamically interrelated. It is the whole person who thinks, not some fragment of the person.

For example, intellectual empathy requires the ability to reconstruct accurately the viewpoints and reasoning of others and to reason from premises, assumptions, and ideas other than one's own. But if one has not developed the philosophical insight that different people often think from divergent premises, assumptions, and ideas, one will never appreciate the need to entertain them. Reasoning from assumptions and ideas other than our own will seem absurd to us precisely to the degree that we are unable to step back philosophically and recognize that differences exist between people in their very frameworks for thinking.

Philosophical differences are common, even in the lives of small children. Children often reason from the assumption that their needs and desires are more important than anyone else's to the conclusion that they ought to get what they want in this or that circumstance. It often seems absurd to children that they are not given what they want. They are trapped in their egocentric viewpoints, see the world from within them, and unconsciously take their viewpoints (their philosophies, if you will) to define reality. To work out of this intellectual entrapment requires time and much reflection.

To develop consciousness of the limits of our understanding we must attain the *courage* to face our prejudices and ignorance. To discover our prejudices and ignorance in turn we often have to *empathize* with and reason within points of view toward which we are hostile. To achieve this end, we must *persevere* over an extended period of time, for it takes time and significant effort to learn how to empathically enter a point of view against which we are biased. That effort will not seem justified unless we have the *faith in reason* to believe we will not be tainted or taken in by whatever is false or misleading in this opposing viewpoint. Furthermore, the belief alone that we can survive serious consideration of alien points of view is not enough to motivate most of us to consider them seriously. We must also be motivated by an *intellectual sense of justice*. We must recognize an intellectual *responsibility* to be fair to views we oppose. We must feel *obliged* to hear them in their strongest form to ensure that we do not condemn them out of ignorance or bias.

If we approach thinking or teaching for thinking atomistically, we are unlikely to help students gain the kind of global perspective and global insight into their minds, thought, and behavior which a philosophical approach to thinking can foster. Cognitive psychology tends to present the mind and dimensions of its thinking in just this atomistic way. Most importantly, it tends to leave out of the picture what should be at its very center: the active, willing, judging agent. The character of our mind is one with our moral character. How we think determines how we behave and how we behave determines who we are and who we become. We have a moral as well as an intellectual responsibility to become fairminded and rational, but we will not become so unless we cultivate these traits through specific modes of thinking. From a philosophical point of view, one does not develop students' thinking skills without in some sense simultaneously developing their autonomy, their rationality, and their character. This is not fundamentally a matter of drilling the student in a battery of skills. Rather it is essentially a matter of orchestrating activities to continually stimulate students to express and to take seriously their own thinking: what it assumes, what it implies, what it includes, excludes, highlights, and foreshadows; and to help the student do this with intellectual humility, intellectual courage, intellectual empathy, intellectual perseverance, and fairmindedness.

✦ *The Skills and Processes of Thinking*

Philosophers do not tend to approach the micro-skills and macro-processes of thinking from the same perspective as cognitive psychologists. Intellectual skills and processes are approached not from the perspective of the needs of empirical research but from the perspective of achieving personal, rational control. The philosophical is, as I have suggested, a *person-centered* approach to thinking. Thinking is always the thinking of some actual person, with some egocentric and sociocentric tendencies, with some particular traits of mind, engaged in the problems of a particular life. The need to understand one's own mind, thought, and action cannot be satisfied with information from empirical studies about aspects or dimensions of thought. The question foremost in the mind of the philosopher is not "How should I conceive of the various skills and processes of the human mind to be able to conduct empirical research on them?" but "How should I understand the elements of thinking to be able to analyze, assess, and rationally control my own thinking and accurately understand and assess the thinking of others?" Philosophers view thinking from the perspective of the needs of the thinker trying to achieve or move toward an intellectual and moral ideal of rationality and fairmindedness. The tools of intellectual analysis result from philosophy's 2,500 years of thinking and thinking about thinking.

Since thinking for one's self is a fundamental presupposed value for philosophy, the micro-skills philosophers use are intellectual moves that a reasoning person continually makes, independent of the subject matter of thought. Hence, *whenever one is reasoning,* one is reasoning about some issue or problem (hence needs skills for analyzing and clarifying issues and problems). Likewise, *whenever one is reasoning,* one is reasoning from some point of view or within some conceptual framework (hence needs skills for analyzing and clarifying interpretations or interpretive frameworks.) Finally, *whenever one is reasoning,* one is, in virtue of one's inferences, coming to some conclusions from some beliefs or premises which, in turn, are based on some assumptions (hence needs skills for analyzing, clarifying, and evaluating beliefs, judgments, inferences, implications, and assumptions.) For virtually any reasoning, one needs a variety of interrelated processes and skills.

Hence, from the philosophical point of view, the fundamental question is not whether one is solving problems or making decisions or engaging in scientific inquiry or forming concepts or comprehending or composing or arguing, precisely because one usually does most or all of them in *every* case. Problem solving, decision-making, concept formation, comprehending, composing, and arguing are in some sense common to all reasoning. What we as reasoners need to do, from the philosophical point of view, is not to decide which of these things we are doing, but rather to orchestrate any or all of the following macro-processes:

1) *Socratic Questioning:* questioning ourselves or others so as to make explicit the salient features of our thinking:

   a) What precisely is at issue? Is this the fairest way to put the issue?

   b) From what point of view are we reasoning? Are there alternative points of view from which the problem or issue might be approached?

   c) What assumptions are we making? Are they justified? What alternative assumptions could we make instead?

   d) What concepts are we using? Do we grasp them? Their appropriateness? Their implications?

   e) What evidence have we found or do we need to find? How dependable is our source of information?

   f) What inferences are we making? Are those inferences well supported?

   g) What are the implications of our reasoning?

   h) How does our reasoning stand up to competing or alternative reasoning?

   i) Are there objections to our reasoning we should consider?

2) *Conceptual Analysis:* Any problematic concepts or uses of terms must be analyzed and their basic logic set out and assessed. Have we done so?

3) *Analysis of the Question-at-Issue:* Whenever one is reasoning, one is attempting to settle some question at issue. But to settle a question, one must understand the kind of question it is. Different questions require different modes of settlement. Do we grasp the precise demands of the question-at-issue?

4) *Reconstructing Alternative Viewpoints in their Strongest Forms:* Since whenever one is reasoning, one is reasoning from a point of view or within a conceptual framework, one must identify and reconstruct those views. Have we empathically reconstructed the relevant points of view?

5) *Reasoning Dialogically and Dialectically:* Since there are almost always alternative lines of reasoning about a given issue or problem, and since a reasonable person sympathetically considers them, one must engage in dialectical reasoning. Have we reasoned from a variety of points of view (when relevant) and rationally identified and considered the strengths and weaknesses of these points of view as a result of this process?

Implicit in the macro-processes, as suggested earlier, are identifiable micro-skills. These constitute moves of the mind while thinking in a philosophical, and hence in a rational, critically-creative way. The moves are marked in the critical-analytic vocabulary of everyday language. Hence in Socratically questioning someone we are engaging in a *process* of thought. Within that process we make a variety of moves. We can make those moves explicit by using analytic terms such as these:

> claims, assumes, implies, infers, concludes, is supported by, is consistent with, is relevant to, is irrelevant to, has the following implications, is credible, plausible, clear, in need of analysis, without evidence, in need of verification, is empirical, is conceptual, is a judgment of value, is settled, is at issue, is problematic, is analogous, is biased, is loaded, is well confirmed, is theoretical, hypothetical, a matter of opinion, a matter of fact, a point of view, a frame of reference, a conceptual framework, etc.

To put the point another way, to gain command of our thinking we must be able to take it apart and put it back together in light of its *logic,* the patterns of reasoning that support it, oppose it, and shed light on its rational acceptability. We don't need a formal or technical language to do this, but we do need a command of the critical-analytic terms available in ordinary English. Their careful use helps discipline, organize, and render self-conscious our ordinary inferences and the concepts, values, and assumptions that underlie them.

✦ *Philosophical and Critical Thinking*

Those familiar with some of my other writings will recognize that what I am here calling *philosophical* thinking is very close to what I have generally called *strong sense critical thinking.* The connection is not arbitrary. The ideal of strong sense critical thinking is implicit in the Socratic philosophical ideal of living a reflective life (and thus achieving command over one's mind and behavior). Instead of absorbing their philosophy from others, people can, with suitable encouragement and instruction, develop a critical and reflective attitude toward ideas and behavior. Their outlook and interpretations of themselves and others can be subjected to serious examination. Through this process, our beliefs become more our own than the product of our unconscious absorption of others' beliefs. Basic ideas such as 'history', 'science', 'drama', 'mind', 'imagination', and 'knowledge' become organized by the criss-crossing paths of one's reflection. They cease to be compartmentalized subjects. The philosophical questions one raises about history cut across those raised about the human mind, science, knowledge, and imagination. Only deep philosophical questioning and honest criticism can protect us from the pronounced human tendency to think in a self-serving way. It is common to question only within a fundamentally unquestioned point of view. We naturally use our intellectual skills to defend and buttress those concepts, aims, and assumptions already deeply rooted in our thought.

The roots of thinking determine the nature, direction, and quality of that thinking. If teaching for thinking does not help students understand the roots of their thinking, it will fail to give them real command over their minds. They will simply make the transition from uncritical thought to weak sense critical thought. They will make the transition from being unskilled in thinking to being narrowly, closedmindedly skilled.

David Perkins (1986) has highlighted this problem from a somewhat different point of view. In studying the relationship between people's scores on standard IQ tests and their openmindedness, as measured by their ability to construct arguments against their points of view on a public issue, Perkins found that,

> intelligence scores correlated substantially with the degree to which subjects developed arguments thoroughly on their own sides of the case. However, there was no correlation between intelligence and elaborateness of arguments on the other side of the case. In other words, the more intelligent participants invested their greater intellectual endowment in bolstering their own positions all the more, not in exploring even-handedly the complexities of the issue.

Herein lies the danger of an approach to thinking that relies fundamentally, as cognitive psychology often does, on the goal of technical competence, without making central the deeper philosophical or normative dimensions of thinking. Student skill in thinking may increase, but whatever narrowness of mind or lack of insight, whatever intellectual closedmindedness, intellectual arrogance, or intellectual cowardice the students suffer, will be supported by that skill. It is crucial therefore that this deeper consideration of the problem of thinking be highlighted and addressed in a significant and global manner. Whether one labels it 'philosophical' thinking or 'strong sense critical thinking' or 'thinking that embodies empathy and openmindedness' is insignificant.

A similar point can be made about the thinking of teachers. If we merely provide teachers with exercises for their students that do no more than promote technical competence in thinking, if inservice is not long-term and designed to develop the critical thinking of teachers, they will probably be ineffective in fostering the thinking of their students.

Teachers need to move progressively from a didactic to a critical model of teaching. In this process, many old assumptions will have to be abandoned and new ones taken to heart as the basis for teaching and learning. This shift can be spelled out systematically as follows.

	Theory of Knowledge, Learning, and Literacy	
Assumption about	*Didactic Theory*	*Critical Theory*
1. The fundamental needs of students	That students need to be taught more or less *what* to think, not *how* to think; they will learn the "how" if they learn the "what".	That students need to be taught *how* not *what* to think; they should learn significant content by considering live issues that stimulate them to gather, analyze, and assess that content.
2. The nature of knowledge	That knowledge is independent of the thinking that generates, organizes, and applies it.	That all knowledge of "content" is generated, organized, applied, analyzed, synthesized, and assessed by thinking; that one must *think* to truly gain knowledge.
3. Model of the educated person	That an educated, literate person is fundamentally analogous to an encyclopedia or a data bank, directly comparing situations in the world with facts that he or she has absorbed.	That an educated, literate person is fundamentally a repository of strategies, principles, concepts, and insights embedded in processes of thought rather than in atomic facts.
4. The nature of knowledge	That knowledge, truth, and understanding can be transmitted from one person to another by verbal statements in the form of lectures or didactic teaching.	That knowledge and truth can rarely, and insight never, be transmitted from one person to another by the transmitter's verbal statements alone.
5. The nature of listening	That students do not need to be taught skills of listening to learn to pay attention — fundamentally a matter of self-discipline and will power.	That students need to be taught how to listen critically — an active and skilled process that can be learned by degrees with various levels of proficiency.
6. The relationship of basic skills to thinking skills	That the basic skills of reading and writing can be taught without emphasis on higher order critical thinking.	That the basic skills of reading and writing are inferential and require critical thinking; that critical reading and writing involve raising and answering probing critical questions.

| Assumption about | *Theory of Knowledge, Learning, and Literacy* | |
	Didactic Theory	*Critical Theory*
7. The status of questioning	That students who have no questions typically are learning well, while students with a lot of questions are experiencing difficulty in learning; that doubt and questioning weaken belief.	That students who have no questions typically are not learning — while having pointed and specific questions is a significant sign of learning. Doubt and questioning, by deepening understanding, strengthen belief by putting it on more solid ground.
8. The desirable classroom environment	That quiet classes with little student talk are typically reflective of students learning while classes with a lot of student talk are typically disadvantaged in learning.	That quiet classes with little student talk are typically classes with little learning while classes with much student talk focused on live issues is a sign of learning.
9. The view of knowledge (atomistic vs. holistic)	That knowledge and truth can typically be learned best by being broken down into elements, and the elements into sub-elements, each taught sequentially and atomically. Knowledge is additive.	That knowledge and truth is heavily systemic and holistic and can be learned only by many acts of synthesis, moving from wholes to parts.
10. The place of values	That people can gain significant knowledge without seeking or valuing it, and hence that education can take place without significant transformation of values for the learner.	That people gain only the knowledge they seek and value. All other learning is superficial and transitory. All genuine education transforms the basic values of the person educated.
11. The importance of being aware of one's own learning processes	That understanding the mind and how it functions, its epistemological health and pathology, are not important or necessary parts of learning.	That understanding the mind and how it functions, its health and pathology, are important and necessary parts of learning.

	Theory of Knowledge, Learning, and Literacy	
Assumption about	*Didactic Theory*	*Critical Theory*
12. The nature and correction of misconceptions	That ignorance is a vacuum or simple lack, and that student prejudices, biases, misconceptions, and ignorance are automatically replaced by their being given knowledge.	That prejudices, biases, and misconceptions are built up through actively constructed inferences embedded in experience and must be broken down through a similar process.
13. The level of understanding desired	That students need not understand the rational ground or deeper logic of what they learn in order to absorb knowledge.	That rational assent is essential for any genuine learning and that an in-depth understanding of basic concepts and principles is essential for rational learning.
14. Depth versus breadth	That it is more important to cover a great deal of knowledge or information superficially than a smaller amount in depth.	That it is more important to cover a small amount of knowledge or information in depth than to cover a great deal of knowledge superficially.
15. Role definition for teacher and student	That the roles of teacher and learner are distinct and should not be blurred.	That people learn best by teaching or explaining to others what they know.
16. The correction of ignorance	That the teacher should correct the students' ignorance by telling them what they do not know.	That students need to learn to distinguish for themselves what they know from what they do not.
17. The responsibility for learning	That the teacher has the fundamental responsibility for student learning. Teachers and texts provide information, questions, and drill.	That progressively the student should be given increasing responsibility for his or her own learning.
18. The transfer of learning to everyday situations	That students will automatically transfer the knowledge that they learn in didactically taught courses to relevant real-life situations.	That most of what students learn in didactically taught courses is either forgotten or rendered "inert", and that the most significant transfer is achieved by in-depth learning which focuses on experiences meaningful to the student.

	Theory of Knowledge, Learning, and Literacy	
Assumption about	Didactic Theory	Critical Theory
19. Status of personal experiences	That the personal experience of the student has no essential role to play in education.	That the personal experience of the student is essential to all schooling at all levels and in all subjects; that it is a crucial part of the content to be processed.
20. The assessment of knowledge acquisition	That a student who can correctly answer questions, provide definitions, and apply formulae while taking tests has proven his or her knowledge or understanding of those details.	That students can often provide correct answers, repeat definitions, and apply formulae while yet not *understanding* those questions, definitions, or formulae.
21. The authority validating knowledge	That learning is essentially a private monological process in which learners can proceed more or less directly to established truth under the guidance of an expert in such truth. The authoritative answers that the teacher has are the fundamental standards for assessing students' learning.	That learning is essentially public, communal, dialogical, and dialectical. Learners must engage in much back-tracking, misconception, self-contradiction, and frustration in the process. The fundamental standards for assessing student learning are not authoritative answers but authoritative standards.

✦ Bringing a Philosophical Approach into the Classroom

Unfortunately a general case for the contribution of philosophy to thinking and to teaching for thinking, such as this one, must of necessity lack a good deal of the concrete detail regarding how one would, as a practical matter, translate the generalities discussed here into action in the classroom or in everyday thinking. There are two basic needs. The first is an ample supply of concrete models that bridge the gap between theory and practice. These models should come in a variety of forms: video tapes, curriculum materials, handbooks, etc. Second, most teachers need opportunities to work on their own philosophical thinking skills and insights. These two needs are best met in conjunction with each other. It is important for the reader to review particular philosophy-based strategies in detail.

The most extensive program available is *Philosophy for Children,* developed by Matthew Lipman in association with the *Institute for the Advancement of Philosophy for Children.* It is based on the notion that philosophy ought to be brought into schools as a separate subject, and philosophical reflection and ideas used directly as an occasion for teaching thinking skills. The program introduces philosophy in the form of children's novels. Extensive teachers' handbooks are provided and a thorough inservice required to ensure that teachers develop the necessary skills and insights to encourage classroom discussion of root ideas in such a way that students achieve philosophical insights and reasoning skills. In a year-long experiment conducted by the *Educational Testing Service* significant improvements were recorded in reading, mathematics, and reasoning. *Philosophy for Children* achieves transfer of reasoning skills into the standard curriculum but is not designed to directly infuse philosophical reflection into it.

In contrast, the *Center for Critical Thinking and Moral Critique* at Sonoma State University in California is developing a philosophy-based approach focused on directly infusing philosophical thinking across the curriculum. Handbooks of lesson plans K–12 have been remodelled by the Center staff to demonstrate that, with redesign, philosophically-based critical thinking skills and processes can be integrated into the lessons presently in use, if teachers learn to remodel the lessons they presently use with critical thinking in mind.

We provide a 'before' and 'after', (the lesson plan before remodelling and after remodelling); a critique of the unremodelled lesson plan to clarify how the remodel was achieved; a list of specific objectives; and the particular strategies used in the remodel. Here is one such example:

Two Ways to Win

(Language Arts — 2nd Grade)

Objectives of the remodelled lesson

The student will:

- use analytic terms such as assume, infer, and imply to analyze and assess story characters' reasoning
- make inferences from story details
- clarify 'good sport' by contrasting it with its opposite, 'bad sport' and exploring its implications

Original Lesson Plan

Abstract

Students read a story about a brother and sister named Cleo and Toby. Cleo and Toby are new in town and worried about making new friends. They ice skate at the park every day after school, believing that winning an upcoming race can help them make new friends (and that they won't make friends if they don't win). Neither of them wins; Cleo, because she falls, Toby, because he forfeits his chance to win by stopping to help a boy who falls. Some children come over after the race to compliment Toby on his good sportsmanship and Cleo on her skating.

Most of the questions about the story probe the factual components. Some require students to infer. Questions ask what 'good sport' means and if Cleo's belief about meeting people is correct.

from *Mustard Seed Magic,*
Theodore L. Harris et al. Economy Company. © 1972. pp. 42–46

Critique

The original lesson has several good questions which require students to make inferences, for example, "Have Toby and Cleo lived on the block all their lives?" The text also asks students if they know who won the race. Since they do not, this question encourages students to suspend judgment. Although 'good sportsmanship' is a good concept for students to discuss and clarify, the text fails to have students practice techniques for clarifying it in sufficient depth. Instead, students merely list the characteristics of a good sport (a central idea in the story) with no discussion of what it means to be a bad sport or sufficient assessment of specific examples. The use of opposite cases to clarify concepts helps students develop fuller and more accurate concepts. With such practice a student can begin to recognize borderline cases as well — where someone was a good sport in some respects, bad in others, or not clearly either. This puts students in a position to develop criteria for judging behavior.

Strategies used to remodel
S-10 clarifying the meanings of words or phrases
S-28 supplying evidence for a conclusion
S-23 using critical vocabulary
S-25 examining assumptions

Remodelled Lesson Plan

Where the original lesson asks, "What does 'a good sport' mean?" we suggest an extension. **S-10** The teacher should make two lists on the board of the students' responses to the question "How do good sports and bad sports behave?" Students could go back over the story and apply the ideas on the list to the characters in the story, giving reasons to support any claims they make regarding the characters' sportsmanship. *S–28* In some cases there might not be enough information to determine whether a particular character is a good or bad sport. Or they might find a character who is borderline, having some characteristics of both good and bad sports. Again, students should cite evidence from the story to support their claims.

The students could also change details of the story to make further points about the nature of good and bad sportsmanship. (If the girl had pushed Cleo down to win the race, that would have been very bad sportsmanship.) To further probe the concept of good sportsmanship, ask questions like the following: How did Toby impress the other children? Why did they think he did a good thing? If you had seen the race, what would you have thought of Toby? Why do we value the kind of behavior we call 'good sportsmanship'? Why don't we like bad sportsmanship? Why are people ever bad sports? *S–10*

There are a number of places in the lesson where the teacher could introduce, or give students further practice using critical thinking vocabulary. Here are a few examples "What can you *infer* from the story title and picture? What parts of the story *imply* that Toby and Cleo will have some competition in the race? What do Toby and Cleo *assume* about meeting new people and making new friends? Is this a good or a bad *assumption?* Why? Why do you think they made this assumption? Have you ever made similar assumptions? Why? *S–25* What can you infer that Cleo felt at the end of the story? How can you tell?" *S–23*

Only after close examination of specific classroom materials and teaching strategies, can teachers begin to understand how to translate philosophically-based approaches into classroom practice. This requires long-term staff development with ample provision for peer collaboration and demonstration teaching. Only then can one reasonably assess the value and power of a philosophical approach.

✦ *Summary and Conclusion*

A strong case can be made for a philosophically-based approach to thinking and teaching for thinking. Such an approach differs fundamentally from most cognitive psychology-based approaches. Philosophy-based approaches reflect the historic emphases of philosophy as a field, as a mode of thinking, and as a framework for thinking. The field is historically committed to specific intellectual and moral ideals, and presupposes people's capacity to live reflective lives and achieve an understanding of and command over the most basic ideas that rule their lives. To achieve this command, people must critically examine the ideas on which they act and replace those ideas when, in their own best judgment, they can no longer rationally assent to them. Such an ideal of freedom of thought and action requires that individuals have a range of intellectual standards by which they can assess thought. These standards, implicit in the critical-analytic terms that exist in every natural language, must be applied in a certain spirit — a spirit of intellectual humility, empathy, and fairmindedness. To develop insight into proper intellectual judgment, one must engage in and become comfortable with dialogical and dialectical thinking. Such thinking is naturally stimulated when one asks basic questions, inquires into root ideas, and invites and honestly considers a variety of responses. It is further stimulated when one self-reflects. The reflective mind naturally moves back and forth between a variety of considerations and sources. The reflective mind eventually learns how to inwardly generate alternative points of view and lines of reasoning, even when others are not present to express them.

A teacher who teaches philosophically brings these ideals and practices into the classroom whatever the subject matter, for all subject matter is grounded in ideas which must be understood and related to ideas pre-existing in the students' minds. The philosophically-oriented teacher wants all content to be critically and analytically processed by all students in such a way that they can integrate it into their own thinking, rejecting, accepting, or qualifying it in keeping with their honest assessment. All content provides grist for the philosophical mill, an opportunity for students to think further, to build upon their previous thought. The philosophically oriented teacher is careful not to require the students to take in more than they can intellectually digest. The philosophically oriented teacher is keenly sensitive to the ease with which minds become passive and submissive. The philosophically oriented teacher is more concerned with the global state of students' minds (Are they developing their own thinking, points of view, intellectual standards and traits, etc.) than with the state of the students' minds within a narrowly defined subject competence. Hence it is much more important to such a teacher that students learn how to think historically (how to look at their own lives and experience and the lives and experiences of others from a historical vantage point) than that they learn how to recite information from a history text. History books are read as aids to historical thought, not as ends-in-themselves.

The philosophically oriented teacher continually looks for deeply rooted understanding and encourages the impulse to look more deeply into things. Hence, the philosophically oriented teacher is much more impressed with how little we as humans know than with how much information we have collected. They are much more apt to encourage students to believe that they, as a result of their own thinking, may design better answers to life's problems than have yet been devised, than they are to encourage students to submissively accept established answers.

What stands in the way of successful teaching for thinking in most classrooms is not as much the absence of technical, empirical information about mental skills and processes, as a lack of experience of and commitment to teaching philosophically. As students, most teachers, after all, were not themselves routinely encouraged to think for themselves. They were not exposed to teachers who stimulated them to inquire into the roots of their own ideas or to engage in extended dialogical and dialectical exchange. They have had little experience in Socratic questioning, in taking an idea to its roots, in pursuing its ramifications across domains and subject areas, in relating it critically to their own experience, or in honestly assessing it from other perspectives.

To appreciate the power and usefulness of a philosophy-based approach, one must understand not only the general case that can be made for it but also how it translates into specific classroom practices. One will achieve this understanding only if one learns how to step outside the framework of assumptions of cognitive psychology and consider thinking, thinking about thinking, and teaching for thinking from a different and fresh perspective. If we look at thinking only from the perspective of cognitive psychology, we will likely fall into the trap which Gerald W. Bracey (1987) recently characterized as,

> ... the long and unhappy tendency of American psychology to break learning into discrete pieces and then treat the pieces in isolation. From James Mill's "mental mechanics", through Edward Titchener's structuralism, to behavioral objectives and some "componential analysis" in current psychology, U.S. educators have acted as if the whole were never more than the sum of its parts, as if a house were no more than the nails and lumber and glass that went into it, as if education were no more than the average number of discrete objectives mastered. We readily see that this is ridiculous in the case of a house, but we seem less able to recognize its absurdity in the case of education. (p. 684)

In thinking, if nowhere else, the whole is greater than the sum of its parts, and cannot be understood merely by examining its psychological leaves, branches, or trunk. We must also dig up its philosophical roots and study its seed ideas as ideas: the "stuff" that determines the very nature of thought itself.

✦ References

Bracey, Gerald W. "Measurement-Driven Instruction: Catchy Phrase, Dangerous Practice." *Phi Delta Kappan.* May, 1987. pp. 683–688.

Paul, Richard W., Binker, A. J. A., & Charbonneau, Marla. *Critical Thinking Handbook: K–3, A Guide for Remodelling Lesson Plans in Language Arts, Social Studies, and Science.* Rohnert Park, California: Center for Critical Thinking and Moral Critique. 1987.

Paul, Richard W., Binker, A. J. A., Jensen, Karen, & Kreklau, Hiedi. *Critical Thinking Handbook: 4th–6th Grades, a Guide for Remodelling Lesson Plans in Language Arts,*

Social Studies, and Science. Rohnert Park, California: Center for Critical Thinking and Moral Critique. 1987.

Perkins, David. "Reasoning as it Is and Could Be: An Empirical Perspective." Paper given at *American Educational Research Association* Conference, San Francisco. April, 1986.

✦✦ **Chapter 36**

Critical Thinking and Social Studies

with A. J. A. Binker

Abstract

In this paper, originally published as a chapter in the Critical Thinking Handbooks *6ᵗʰ–9ᵗʰ Grades, and High School, Paul and Binker outline a critical approach to teaching social studies emphasizing the need to focus instruction on the basic questions of social studies. They first argue that thinking about social studies is multi-dimensional or dialogical and that students must think their way to knowledge, then they list common flaws in social studies texts (both in general and within the fields of history, politics, economics, anthropology, and geography). They then provide recommendations for educational reform. Finally they list key questions, first in the various disciplines of social studies, and then basic questions which suggest their overlap and interrelationships, which can help teachers and students unify social studies.*

✦ Introduction

*T*he major problem to overcome in remodelling social studies units and lessons is that of transforming didactic instruction within one point of view into dialogical instruction within multiple points of view. As teachers, we should see ourselves not as dispensers of absolute truth nor as proponents of relativity, but as careful reflective seekers after truth, a search in which we invite our students to participate. We continually need to remind ourselves that each person responds to social issues from one of many mutually inconsistent points of view. Each point of view rests on assumptions about human nature. Thinking of one point of view as *the truth* limits our understanding of issues. Practice entering into and coming to understand divergent points of view, on the other hand, heightens our grasp of the real problems of our lives. Children, in their everyday lives, already face the kinds of issues studied in social studies and are engaged in developing assumptions on questions like the following:

> What does it mean to belong to a group? Does it matter if others do not approve of me? Is it worthwhile to be good? What is most important to me? How am I like and unlike others? Whom should I trust? Who are my friends and enemies? What are people like? What am I like? How do I fit in with others? What are my rights and responsibilities? What are others' rights and responsibilities?

Humans live in a world of humanly constructed meanings. There is always more than one way to conceptualize human behavior. Humans create points of view, ideologies, and philosophies that often conflict with each other. Students need to understand the implications of these crucial insights: that all accounts of human behavior are expressed within a point of view; that no one account of what happened can possibly cover all the facts; that each account stresses some facts over others; that when an account is given (by a teacher, student, or textbook author), the point of view in which it is given should be identified and, where possible, alternative points of view considered; and finally, that points of view need to be critically analyzed and assessed.

Adults, as well as children, tend to assume the truth of their own unexamined points of view. People often unfairly discredit or misinterpret ideas based on assumptions differing from their own. To address social issues critically, students must continually evaluate their beliefs by contrasting them with opposing beliefs. From the beginning, social studies instruction should encourage dialogical thinking, that is, the fairminded discussion of a variety of points of view and their underlying beliefs. Of course, this emphasis on the diversity of human perspectives should not be covered in a way that implies that all points of view are equally valid. Rather, students should learn to value critical thinking skills as tools to help them distinguish truth from falsity, insight from prejudice, accurate conception from misconception.

Dialogical experience in which students begin to use critical vocabulary to sharpen their thinking and their sense of logic, is crucial. Words and phrases such as 'claims', 'assumes', 'implies', 'supports', 'is evidence for', 'is inconsistent with', 'is relevant to' should be integrated into such discussions. Formulating their own views of historical events and social issues enables students to synthesize data from divergent sources and to grasp important ideas. Too often, students are asked to recall details with no synthesis, no organizing ideas, and no distinction between details and basic ideas or between facts and common U.S. interpretations of them.

Students certainly need opportunities to explicitly learn basic principles of social analysis, but more importantly they need opportunities to *apply* them to real and imagined cases and to develop insight into social analysis. They especially need to come to terms with the pitfalls of human social analyses, to recognize the ease with which we mask self-interest or egocentric desires with "social scientists'" language. For any particular instance of social judgment or reasoning, students should learn the art of distinguishing *perspectives on the world* from *facts* (which provide the specific information or occasion for a particular social judgment).

As people, students have an undeniable right to develop their own social perspective — whether conservative or liberal, whether optimistic or pessimistic — but they should also be able to analyze their perspectives, compare them accurately with other perspectives, and scrutinize the facts they conceptualize and judge in the social domain with the same care required in any other domain of knowledge. They should, in other words, become as adept in using critical thinking principles in the social domain as we expect them to be in scientific domains of learning.

Traditional lessons cover several important subjects within social studies: politics, economics, history, anthropology, and geography. Critical education in social studies focuses on basic questions in each subject, and prepares students for their future economic, political, and social roles.

✦ *Some Common Problems with Social Studies Texts*

- End-of-chapter questions often ask for recall of a random selection of details and key facts or ideas. Minor details are often given the same emphasis as important events and principles. Students come away with collections of sentences but little sense of how to distinguish major from minor points. The time and space given to specifics should reflect their importance.

- Often the answers to review questions are found in the text in bold or otherwise emphasized type. Thus, students need not even understand the question, let alone the answer, to complete their assignments.

- Timelines, maps, charts and graphs are presented and read as mere drill rather than as aids to understanding deeper issues. Students do not learn to *read* them or *use* them. Students do not develop useful schemas of temporal or spatial relationships — timelines and globes in their heads.

- Texts rarely have students extend insights to analogous situations in other times and places. Students do not learn to *use* insights or principles to understand specifics. They do not learn to recognize recurring patterns.

- Although texts treat diversity of opinion as necessary, beliefs are not presented as subject to examination or critique. Students are encouraged to accept that others have different beliefs but are not encouraged to understand why. Yet only by understanding *why* others think as they do, can students profit from considering other points of view. The text writers' emphasis on simple tolerance serves to end discussion, whereas students should learn to consider judgments as subject to rational assessment.

- Students are not encouraged to recognize and combat their own natural ethnocentricity. Texts encourage ethnocentricity in many ways. They often present U.S. ideals as uniquely ours when, in fact, every nation shares at least some of them. Although beliefs about the state of the world and about how to achieve ideals vary greatly, the U.S. version of these is often treated as universal or self-evident. Students should learn not to confuse their limited perspective with universal belief.

- Ethnocentricity is reflected in word choices that assume a U.S. or Western European perspective. For example, cultures are described as "isolated" rather than as "isolated from Europe". Christian missionaries are described as spreading or teaching "religion" rather than "Christianity". Cultures are evaluated as "modern" according to their similarity to ours. In addition, texts often assume, imply, or clearly state that most of the world would prefer to be just like us. The "American Way of Life" and policies, according to the world view implied in standard texts, is the pinnacle of human achievement and presents the best human life has to offer. That others might believe the same of their own cultures is rarely mentioned or considered.

- Texts often wantonly omit crucial concepts, relationships, and details. For example, in discussing the opening of trade relations between Japan and the U.S., one text failed to mention why the Japanese had cut off relations with the West. Another text passed over fossil fuels and atomic energy in two sentences.

- Most texts treat important subjects superficially. There seems to be more concern for the outward appearance of things and trivial details than for their underlying dynamics. Texts often cover different political systems by merely listing the titles of political offices. Most discussions of religion reflect the same superficiality. Texts emphasize names of deities, rituals, and practices. But beliefs are not explored in depth; the inner life is ignored, the personal dimension omitted. Geography texts are filled with such trivia as names of currencies, colors of flags, vegetation, and so on. Students do not learn important information about other countries. Important information that is covered is usually lost amidst the trivia and so soon forgotten.

- Many texts also tend to approach the heart of the matter and then stop short. Important topics are introduced, treated briefly, and dropped. History, for instance, is presented as merely a series of events. Texts often describe events briefly but seldom mention how people perceived them, why they accepted or resisted them, or what ideas and assumptions influenced them. Problems are dismissed with, "This problem is very complicated. People will have to work together to solve it." In effect, this tells students that when something is complicated, they shouldn't think about it or try to understand it. Students do not learn how to sort out the contributing factors or develop and assess specific solutions.

- Texts often encourage student passivity by providing all the answers. They are not held accountable for providing significant answers on their own. Texts usually err by asking questions students should be able to answer on their own, and then immediately providing the answer. Once students understand the system, they know that they don't have to stop and think for themselves because the text will do it for them in the next sentence.

- After lengthy map skills units, students are asked to apply those skills to answer simple questions. ("Find the following cities:") Students practice reading maps in their texts for reasons provided by the texts. They are not required to determine for themselves what questions a map can answer, what sort of map is required, or how to find it. Map reading practice could be used to develop students' confidence in their abilities to reason and learn for themselves, but rarely is. Graphs and charts are treated similarly.

- Although the rich selections of appendices are convenient for the students, they discourage students from discovering where to find information on their own. In real life, problems are not solved by referring to a handy chart neatly labeled and put into a book of information on the subject. In fact few, if any, complex issues are resolved by perusing one book. Instead we should teach students to decide what kind of information is necessary and how to get it. In addition, many of the appendices are neatly correlated, designed and labeled to answer precisely those questions asked in the text. Students therefore do not develop the strategies they need to transfer their knowledge to the issues, problems, and questions they will have as adults.

- Texts often emphasize the ideal or theoretical models of government, economic systems, and institutions without exploring real (hidden) sources of power and change. Texts rarely distinguish ideals from the way a system might really operate in a given situation. They often give people's *stated* reasons as the *real* reasons for their actions.

- Explanations are often abstract and lack detail or connection to that which they explain, leaving students with a vague understanding. Texts fail to address such questions as: *How* did this bring about that? What was going on in people's minds? Why? How did that relate to the rest of society? Why is this valued? Without context, the bits have little meaning and therefore, if remembered at all, serve no function and cannot be recalled for use.

✦ Subject-Specific Problems

There are somewhat different problems which emerge in each of the areas of social studies. It is important to identify them.

HISTORY

- Although texts *mention* that to understand the present one must understand the past, they fail to *show* students the necessity of knowing historical background. They fail to illustrate *how* current situations, events, problems, conflicts, and so on can be better understood and addressed by those who understand how they came to be. "It is important to understand the past" becomes a vague slogan rather than a crucial insight which guides thought.

- Although texts refer to past problems, give the solutions attempted, and mention results, students don't evaluate them *as solutions.* They don't look at what others did about the same problem, nor do they analyze causes or evaluate solutions for themselves. We recommend that teachers ask, "To what extent and in what ways did this solve the problem? Fail to solve it? Create new problems?" Students should assess solutions tried and argue for their own solutions.

- When discussing causes and results of historical events, texts present the U.S. interpretation as though it were fact. They often treat historical judgment and interpretation as though they were facts on the order of dates. Thus, students gain little or no insight into historical reasoning, into how one reasonably decides that this caused that.

- When texts present negative information about the U.S., they don't encourage students to explore its consequences or implications. Students are not encouraged to refine their judgment by judging past actions and policies.

• Primary sources, when used or referred to at all, are not examined as sources of information or as explications of important attitudes and beliefs which shaped events. Their assessment is not discussed, nor are influences which shape that assessment. Texts fail to mention, for example, that most history was written by victors of wars and by the educated few. Much information about other points of view has been lost. Most selections from primary sources are trivial narratives.

POLITICS

• Traditional lessons stress that we should all be good citizens, but fail to explore what that entails (for example, the importance of assessing candidates and propositions before voting).

• Texts tend to make unfair comparisons, such as comparing the *ideal* of governments of the U.S. and its allies to the *real* Soviet government.

• Important ideals, such as freedom of speech, are taught as mere slogans. Students read, recall, and repeat vague justifications for ideals rather than deepen their understanding of them and of the difficulty in achieving them. In effect, such ideas are taught as though they were facts on the order of the date a treaty was signed. Texts do not, for example, have students discuss the positive aspects of dissent such as the need to have a wide-ranging open market of ideas.

• Texts often confuse facts with ideals and genuine patriotism with show of patriotism or false patriotism. The first confusion discourages us from seeing ourselves, others, and the world accurately; we fail to see the gap between how we want to be and how we are. The second encourages us to reject constructive criticism. The concept of love of one's country is reduced to a pep rally.

ECONOMICS

• Texts assume a capitalist perspective on economics. They fail to explain how other systems work. Students are ill-prepared to understand how the economies of other countries work.

• Texts generally contrast *ideal* capitalism with *real* socialism. Students come away with the idea that what we have needs no improvement and with a set of overly negative stereotypes of others.

• Texts cover economic systems superficially, neglecting serious and in-depth coverage of *how* they are supposed to work (for example, in our system, people must make rational choices as consumers, employers, employees, and voters). Students are left with vague slogans rather than realistic understanding and the ability to *use* principles to understand issues, problems, and specific situations.

ANTHROPOLOGY

• Cultural differences are often reduced to holidays and foods rather than values, perspectives, habits, and more significant customs, giving students little more than a superficial impression of this field. Students fail to learn how much people (themselves included) are shaped by their cultures, that their culture is only one way of understanding or behaving, or how much hostility is generated by culture clashes. For example, what happens when someone from a culture wherein looking someone in the eye is rude meets someone from a culture wherein avoiding another's eye is rude? Each feels offended, becomes angry at the other who breaks the rules. Are "Germans cold", or do "Americans smile too much?" Texts overemphasize tolerance for food and clothing differences but often neglect developing insight into more important or problematic differences.

GEOGRAPHY

- Texts more often use maps to show such trivialities as travelers' and explorers' routes than to illuminate the history and culture of the place shown and the lives of the people who actually live there.

- Texts fail to explain *why* students should know specific details. For example, texts mention chief exports, but don't have students explore their implications or consequences: What does this tell us about this country? The people there? It's relationships with other countries? Environmental problems? Economic problems? International and domestic politics?

What ties many of these criticisms together and points to their correction is the understanding that study of each subject should teach students how to *reason* in that subject, and this requires that students learn how to synthesize their insights into each subject to better understand their world. The standard didactic approach, with its emphasis on giving students as much information as possible, neglects this crucial task. Even those texts which attempt to teach geographical or historical reasoning do so only occasionally, rather than systematically. By conceptualizing education primarily as passing data to students, texts present *products* of reasoning. A critical approach, emphasizing root questions and independent thought, on the other hand, helps students get a handle on the facts and ideas and offers students crucial tools for thinking through the problems they will face throughout their lives.

Students need assignments that challenge their ability to assess actual political behavior. Such assignments will, of course, produce divergent conclusions by students depending on their present leanings. And don't forget that student thinking, speaking, and writing should be graded not on some authoritative set of substantive answers, but rather on the clarity, cogency, and intellectual rigor of their work. All students should be expected to learn the art of social and political analysis — the art of subjecting political behavior and public policies to critical assessment — based on an analysis of relevant facts and on consideration of reasoning within alternative political viewpoints.

✦ *Some Recommendations for Action*

Students in social studies, regardless of level, should be expected to begin to take responsibility for their own learning. This means that they must develop the art of independent thinking and study and cultivate intellectual and study skills. This includes the ability to critique the text one is using, discovering how to learn from even a poor text. And since it is unreasonable to expect the classroom teacher to remodel the format of a textbook, the teacher must choose how to use the text as given.

Discussions and activities should be designed or remodelled by the teacher to develop the students' use of critical reading, writing, speaking, and listening. Furthermore, students should begin to get a sense of the interconnecting fields of knowledge within social studies, and the wealth of connections between these fields and others, such as math, science, and language arts. The students should not be expected to memorize a large quantity of unrelated facts, but rather to think in terms of interconnected domains of human life and experience. This includes identifying and evaluating various viewpoints; gathering and organizing information for interpretation; distinguishing facts from ideals, interpretations, and judgments; recognizing relationships and patterns; and applying insights to current events and problems.

Students should repeatedly be encouraged to identify the perspective of their texts, imagine or research other perspectives, and compare and evaluate them. This means, among other things, that words like 'conservatism' and 'liberalism', the 'right' and 'left', must become more than vague jargon; they must be recognized as names of different ways of thinking about human nature and society. Students need experience actually thinking within diverse political perspectives. No perspective, not even one called 'moderate', should be presented as *the* correct one. By the same token, we should be careful not to lead the students to believe that all perspectives are equally justified or that important insights are equally found in all points of view. Beware especially of the misleading idea that the truth always lies in the middle of two extremes. We should continually encourage and stimulate our students to think and never do their thinking for them. We should, above all, teach, not preach.

HISTORY

History lessons should show students how to reason historically and why historical reasoning is necessary to understanding the present and to making rational decisions regarding the future. To learn to reason historically, students must discuss issues dialogically, generating and assessing multiple interpretations of events they study. This requires students to distinguish facts from interpretations. It also requires that they develop a point of view of their own.

- Many crucial historical insights have analogies in students' lives which you can use to clarify historical events. For example, as with wars between nations, relatively few childhood conflicts are entirely caused by *one* participant. Most result from an escalation of hostilities in which both sides participate.

- Dates are useful not so much as things-in-themselves, but as markers placing events in relation to each other and within a context (historical, political, anthropological, technological, etc.). To reason with respect to history, we need to orient ourselves to events in relation to each other. So when you come across a particular date, you might ask the students to discuss in pairs what events came before and after it and to consider the significance of this sequence. They might consider the possible implications of different conceivable sequences. (Suppose dynamite had been invented 50 years earlier. What are some possible consequences of that?)

* What do we know about this time? What was happening in other parts of the world? What countries or empires were around? What technology existed? What didn't exist? What were things like then?

* Why is this date given in the text? What dates are the most significant according to the text? To us? To others? Notice that many dates significant to other groups, such as to Native Americans, are not mentioned. All dates that are mentioned result from a value judgment about the significance of that event.

All students should leave school with a timeline in their heads of basic eras and a few important dates with a deeply held and thoroughly understood conviction that all history is history from a point of view, and that one needs to understand how things came to be and why.

ECONOMICS

When reasoning economically, North Americans reason not only from a capitalist perspective, but also as liberals, conservatives, optimists, or pessimists. Lessons on economics should stress not only how our system is supposed to work but also how liberals, conservatives, etc. tend to interpret the same facts differently. Students should routinely consider questions like the following: "What can I learn from conservative and liberal readings of these events? What facts support each interpretation?" They should also have an opportunity to imagine alternative economic systems and alternative incentives, other than money, to motivate human work. Students should analyze and evaluate their own present and future participation in the economy by exploring reasoning and values underlying particular actions, and the consequences of those actions.

✦ *Some Key Questions in Subject Areas*

Instruction for each subject should be designed to highlight the basic or root questions of that subject and help students learn how to reason within each field. To help you move away from the didactic, memorization-oriented approach found in most texts, we have listed below some basic questions, to suggest what sort of background issues could be used to unify and organize instruction and relate it to students' lives. We have made no attempt to provide a comprehensive list. Consider the questions as suggestions only.

HISTORY

Why are things the way they are now? What happened in the past? Why? What was it like to live then? How has it influenced us now? What kinds of historical events are most significant? Why? How do I learn what happened in the past? How do I reconcile conflicting accounts? How can actions of the past best be understood? Evaluated? How does study of the past help me understand present situations and problems? To understand this present-day problem, what sort of historical background do I need, and how can I find and assess it? Is there progress? Is the world getting better? Worse? Always the same? Do people shape their times or do the times shape people?

ANTHROPOLOGY

Why do people have different cultures? What shapes culture? How do cultures change? How have you been influenced by our culture? By ideas in movies and TV? How does culture influence people? What assumptions underlie my culture? Others' cultures? To what extent are values universal? Which of our values are universal? To what extent do values vary between cultures? Within cultures? How can cultures be categorized? What are some key differences between cultures that have writing and those that don't? What are the implications and consequences of those differences? How might a liberal critique our culture? A socialist? Is each culture so unique and self-contained, and so thoroughly defining of reality that cultures cannot be compared or evaluated? How is your peer group like a culture? How are cultures like and unlike other kinds of groups — clubs, nations, groups of friends, families, generations?

GEOGRAPHY

How do people adapt to where they live? What kinds of geographical features influence people the most? How? How do people change their environment? What effects do different changes have? How can uses of land be evaluated? How can we distinguish geographical from cultural influences? (Are Swedes hardy as a result of their geography or as a result of their cultural values?) Which geographical features in our area are the most significant? Does our climate influence our motivation? How so? Would you be different if you had been raised in the desert? Explain how. Why is it important to know what products various countries export? What does that tell us about that country, its relationships to other countries, its problems, its strengths?

POLITICS

What kinds of governments are there? What is government for? What should governments do? What shouldn't they do? What is my government like? What are other governments like? How did they come to be that way? Who has power? Who should have power? What ways can power be used? How is our system designed to prevent abuse of power? To what extent is that design successful? What assumptions underlie various forms of government? What assumptions underlie ours? On what values are they theoretically based? What values are actually held? How is the design of this government supposed to achieve its ideals? To what extent should a country's political and economic interests determine its foreign relations? To what extent should such ideals as justice and self-determination influence foreign policy decisions? Take a particular policy and analyze the possible effects of vested interests. How can governments be evaluated? How much should governments do to solve political, social, or economic, problems?

ECONOMICS

What kinds of economic decisions do you make? What kinds will you make in the future? On what should you base those decisions? How should you decide where your money goes? When you spend money, what are you telling manufacturers? How is a family like an economic system? What kinds of economies are there? In this economy, who makes what kinds of decisions? What values underlie this economy? What does this economic system assume about people and their relationship to their work — why people work? According to proponents of this economic system, who should receive the greatest rewards? Why? Who should receive less reward? How can economic systems be evaluated? What problems are there in our economy according to liberals? Conservatives? Socialists? What features of our economy are capitalistic? Socialistic? How does ideal capitalism (socialism) work? In what ways do we depart from ideal capitalism? Are these departures justified? What kinds of things are most important to produce? Why? What kinds of things are less important? Why?

✦ *Unifying Social Studies Instruction*

Although it makes sense to say that someone is reasoning historically, anthropologically, geographically, etc., it does not make the same sense to say that someone is reasoning socio-scientifically. There is no *one* way to put all of these fields together. Yet, understanding the interrelationships between each field and being able to integrate insights gained from each field is crucial to social studies. We must recognize the need for students to develop their own unique perspectives on social events and arrangements. This requires that questions regarding the interrelationships between the fields covered in social studies be frequently raised and that lessons be designed to require students to apply ideas from various fields to one topic or problem. Keep in mind the following questions:

- What are people like? How do people come to be the way they are? How does society shape the individual? How does the individual shape society?

- Why do people disagree? Where do people get their points of view? Where do I get my point of view?

- Are some people more important than others?

- How do people and groups of people solve problems? How can we evaluate solutions?

- What are our biggest problems? What has caused them? How should we approach them?

- What are the relationships between politics, economics, culture, psychology, history, and geography? How do each of these influence the rest? How does the economy of country X influence its political decisions? How does the geography of this area affect its economy? How is spending money like voting?

- How can governments, cultures, and economic systems be evaluated?

- Could you have totalitarian capitalism? Democratic communism?

- Are humans subject to laws and, hence, ultimately predictable?

In raising these questions beware the tendency to assume a "correct" answer from our social conditioning as U.S. citizens, especially on issues dealing with socialism or communism. Remember, we, like all peoples, have biases and prejudices. Our own view of the world must be critically analyzed and questioned.

Try to keep in mind that it takes a long time to develop a person's *thinking*. Our thinking is connected with every other dimension of us. All of our students enter our classes with many "mindless" beliefs, ideas which they have unconsciously picked up from TV, movies, small talk, family background, and peer groups. Rarely have they been encouraged to think for themselves. Thinking their way through these beliefs takes time. We therefore need to proceed very patiently. We must accept small payoffs at first. We should expect many confusions to arise. We must not despair in our role as cultivators of independent critical thought. In time, students will develop new modes of thinking. In time they will become more clear, more accurate, more logical, more openminded — if only we stick to our commitment to nurture these abilities. The social studies provide us with an exciting opportunity, since they address issues central to our lives and well-being. It is not easy to shift the classroom from a didactic-memorization model, but, if we are willing to pay the price of definite commitment, it can be done.

✦✦ Chapter 37

Critical Thinking and Language Arts

with A. J. A. Binker

Abstract

In this paper, originally published as a chapter in the Critical Thinking Handbooks *for 6ᵗʰ–9ᵗʰ Grades and High School, Paul and Binker outline a critical approach to teaching language arts, emphasizing the need to help students gain command over language. Binker and Paul outline the essential disciplined and questioning attitude of the ideal student of the language arts (as critical reader, writer, and listener), outline characteristics and goals of language arts instruction (emphasizing mastery of the logic of language), point out common flaws in standard texts, and list generic questions students could learn to raise about the aspects of language arts (reading, writing, listening, and grammar).*

✦ Introduction

*L*anguage arts, as a domain of learning, mainly covers the study of literature and the arts of reading and writing. All three areas — literature, reading and writing — deal with the art of conceptualizing and representing *in language* how people live and might live their lives. All three are primarily concerned with gaining command of language and expression. Of course, there is no command of language separate from command of thought and no command of thought without command of language.

Very few students will ever publish novels, poems, or short stories, but presumably all should develop insight into what can be learned from literature. Students should develop a sense of the art involved in writing a story and, hence, of putting experiences into words. At its root is the need everyone has to make sense of human life. This requires command of our own ideas, which requires command over the words in which we express them.

In words and ideas there is power — power to understand and describe, to take apart and put together, to create systems of beliefs and multiple conceptions of life. Literature displays this power, and reading apprehends it. Students lack insight into these processes. Few have command of the language they use or a sense of how to gain that command. Not having a command of their own language, they typically struggle when called upon to read literature. They often find reading and writing frustrating and unrewarding. And worse, they rarely see the value of achieving such command. Literature seems a frill, something artificial, irrelevant, and bookish, outside of the important matters of life. Reading, except in its most elementary form, seems expendable as a means of learning. Writing is often viewed as a painful bore and, when attempted, reduced to something approaching stream-of-consciousness verbalization.

The task of turning students around, stimulating them to cultivate a new and different conception of literature, of reading, and of writing, is a profound challenge. If we value students thinking for themselves, we cannot ignore this challenge. If a basic goal of English classes is to instill the love of lifelong reading, we must seriously confront why most students have little or no interest in literature. We need to think seriously about the life-world in which they live: the music they listen to, the TV programs and movies they watch, the desires they follow, the frustrations they experience, the values they live for.

Most teachers can probably enumerate the most common features and recurring themes of, say, students' favorite movies: danger, excitement, fun, sex, romance, rock music, car chases, exploding planets, hideous creatures, mayhem, stereotypes, cardboard characters, and so on. The lyrics and values of most popular music are equally accessible, expressing as they do an exciting, fast-moving, sentimentalized, superficial world. Much student talk consists in slang. Though sometimes vivid it is more often vague, imprecise, and superficial. (He, like totally freaked out! It was awesome. He got totally weird.) Most quality literature seems dull to students in comparison.

Good English instruction must respect and challenge students' attitudes. Ignoring student preferences doesn't alter them. Students must assess for themselves the relative worth of popular entertainment and quality works. Students need opportunities to scrutinize and evaluate the forms of entertainment they prefer. They need to assess the messages they receive from them, the conceptions of life they presuppose, and the values they manifest. As instruction is now designed, students typically ignore what they hear, read, and reiterate in school work and activities. They may follow the teacher's request to explain why a particular classic has lasted many generations, but this ritual performance has little influence on students' real attitudes. Critical thinking can help encourage students to refine their tastes, and we should encourage it with this end in mind. Nevertheless, under no conditions should we try to order or force students to say what they don't believe. A well-reasoned, if wrong-headed, rejection of Shakespeare is better than mindless praise of him.

✦ The Ideal English Student

In addition to the need to enter sympathetically into the life-world of our students, appreciating how and why they think, speak, and act as they do, we must also have a clear conception of what changes we want to cultivate in them. We must clearly see the ideals we are striving for as teachers. Consider language itself and the way in which an ideal student might approach it. We want students to be sensitive to their language, striving to understand it and use it thoughtfully, accurately, and clearly. We want them to become autonomous thinkers and so command, rather than be commanded by, language.

As Critical Reader

Critical readers of literature approach literature as an opportunity to live within another's world or experience, to consider someone else's view of human nature, relationships, and problems. Critical readers familiarize themselves with different uses of language to enhance their understanding and appreciation of literature. They choose to read literature because they recognize its worth. They can intelligently discuss it with others, considering the interpretations of others as they support their own.

Critical readers approach a piece of nonfiction with a view to entering a silent dialogue with the author. They realize they must actively reconstruct the author's meaning. They read because there is much that they know they do not know, much to experience that they have not experienced. Thus, critical readers do not simply pass their eyes over the words with the intention of filling their memories. They question, organize, interpret, synthesize, and digest what they read. They question, not only what was said, but also what was implied and presupposed. They organize the details, not only around key ideas in the work, but also around their own key ideas. They not only interpret, they recognize their interpretations *as interpretations,* and consider alternative interpretations. Recognizing their interpretations as such, they revise and refine them. They do not simply accept or reject; they work to make ideas their own, accepting what makes most sense, rejecting what is ill-thought-out, distorted, and false, fitting their new understanding into their existing frameworks of thought.

As Critical Writer

Command of reading and command of writing go hand-in-hand. All of the understanding, attitudes, and skills we have just explored have parallels in writing. When writing, critical writers recognize the challenge of putting their ideas and experiences into words. They recognize that inwardly many of our ideas are a jumble, some supporting and some contradicting other ideas, some vague, some clear, some true, some false, some expressing insights, some reflecting prejudices or mindless conformity. Since critical writers recognize that they only partially understand and only partially command their own ideas and experiences, they recognize a double difficulty in making those ideas and experiences accessible to others.

As readers they recognize they must *actively* reconstruct an author's meaning; as writers they recognize the parallel need to *actively* construct their own meanings as well as the probable meanings of their readers. In short, critical writers engage in parallel tasks when writing to those of reading. Both are challenging. Both organize, engage, and develop the mind. Both require the full and heightened involvement of critical and creative thought.

AS CRITICAL LISTENER

The most difficult condition in which to learn is in that of a listener. People naturally become passive when listening, leave to the speaker the responsibility to express and clarify, to organize and exemplify, to develop and conclude. The art of becoming a critical listener is therefore the hardest and the last art that students develop. Of course, most students never develop this art. Most students remain passive and impressionistic in their listening throughout their lives.

Yet this need not be the case. If students can come to grasp the nature of critical reading and writing, they can also grasp the nature of critical listening. Once again, each of the understandings, attitudes, and skills of reading and writing have parallels in listening. There is the same challenge to sort out, to analyze, to consider possible interpretations, the same need to ask questions, to raise possible objections, to probe assumptions, to trace implications. As listeners we must follow the path of another person's thought. Listening is every bit as dialogical as reading and writing, though harder, since we cannot go back over the words of the speaker as we can when reading.

What is more, our students face a special problem in listening to a teacher, for if they listen so as to take seriously what is being said, they may appear to their peers to be playing up to the teacher, or may appear foolish if they seem to say a wrong or dumb thing. Student peer groups often expect students to listen with casual indifference, even with passive disdain. To expect students to become active classroom listeners is, therefore, to expect them to rise above the domination of the peer group. This is very difficult for most students.

The ideal English student, as you can see, is quite like the ideal learner in other areas of learning, in that critical reading, writing, and listening are required in virtually all subject areas. Yet the language arts are more central to education than perhaps any other area. Without command of one's native language, no significant learning can take place. Other domains of learning rely on this command. The ideal English student should therefore come close to being the ideal learner, and while helping our students to gain command of reading, writing, and listening we should see ourselves as laying the foundation for all thought and learning.

✦ Ideal Instruction

Considering the ideal reader, writer, and listener paves the way for a brief overview of ideal instruction. We should use our understanding of the ideal as a model to move toward, as an organizer for our behavior, not as an empty or unrealistic dream. Reading, writing, and listening, as critical thinking activities, help organize and develop learning. Each depends on recognizing that if we actively probe and analyze, dialogue and digest, question and synthesize, we will begin to understand alternative schemes of meaning and belief. The world of Charles Dickens is not the same as that of George Eliot, nor are either the same as those of Hemingway or Faulkner. Similarly, each of us lives in a somewhat different world. Each of us has somewhat different ideas, goals, values, and experiences. Each of us constructs somewhat different meanings to live by. In ideal instruction, we want students to discover and understand different worlds so that they can better understand and develop their own. We want them to struggle to understand the meanings of others so they can better understand their own.

Unfortunately, most texts do not have a unified approach toward this goal. They are often a patchwork, as if constructed by a checklist mentality, as if each act of learning were independent of the one that precedes or follows it. Texts typically lack a global concept of literature, language, reading, writing, and listening. Even grammar is treated as a separate, unconnected set of rules and regulations. This is not what we want, and this is not how we should design our instruction. Rather, we should look for opportunities to tie dimensions of language arts instruction together. There is no reason for treating any dimension of language arts instruction as unconnected to the rest.

Thus far, we have talked about reading, writing, listening, and literature as ways of coming to terms with constructing and organizing meanings. We can now use this central concept to show how one can tie grammar to the rest of language arts instruction, for clearly grammar itself can be understood as an organized system for expressing meanings. Each "subject" of each sentence, after all, represents a focus for the expression of meaning, something that we are thinking or talking about. Each "predicate" represents what is said about, the meaning we are attributing to, the subject. All adjectives and adverbs qualify or render more precise the meanings we express in subjects and predicates. By the same token, each sentence we write has some sort of meaningful relationship to the sentences that precede and follow it. The same principle holds for the paragraphs we write. In each paragraph, there must be some unifying thing that we are talking about and something that we are saying about it.

To put this another way, at each level of language arts instruction we should aim at helping the student gain insight into the idea that there is a "logic" to the language arts. This key insight builds upon the idea of constructing and organizing meanings; it makes even clearer how we can tie all of the language arts together. It reminds us of the established uses for all facets and dimensions of language, and that the reasons behind these uses can be made intelligible. Basic grammar has a logic to it, and that logic can be understood. Individual words and phrases also have a logic to them, and, therefore, they too can be understood. When we look into use of language realizing that there is intelligible structure to be understood, our efforts are rewarded. Unfortunately, we face a special obstacle in accomplishing this purpose.

Usually, students treat the meanings of words as "subjective" and "mysterious". I have my meanings of words, and you have your meanings of them. On this view, problems of meaning are settled by asking people for their personal definitions. What do *you* mean by 'love', 'hate', 'democracy', 'friendship',

etc.? Each of us is then expected to come forward with a "personal definition". *My* definition of love is this .... *My* definition of friendship is that ....

To persuade students that it is possible to use words precisely, we must
demonstrate to them every word in the language had an established use with
established *implications* that they must learn to respect. For example, consider the words 'rise', 'arise', 'spring', 'originate', 'derive', 'flow', 'issue',
'emanate', and 'stem'. They cannot be used however one pleases, according to
a merely personal definition in mind. Each has different implications:

> 'Rise' and 'arise' both imply a coming into being, action, notice,
> etc., but 'rise' carries an added implication of ascent (empires *rise*
> and fall) and 'arise' is often used to indicate causal relationship
> (accidents *arise* from carelessness); 'spring' implies sudden emer-
> gence (weeds *sprang* up in the garden); 'originate' is used in indi-
> cating a definite source, beginning, or prime cause (psychoanalysis
> *originated* with Freud); 'derive' implies a proceeding or developing
> from something else that is the source (this word *derives* from the
> Latin) 'flow' suggests a streaming from a source like water ("Praise
> God, from whom all blessings *flow"*); 'issue' suggests emergence
> through an outlet (not a word *issued* from his lips); 'emanate'
> implies the flowing forth from a source of something that is non-
> material or intangible (rays of light *emanating* from the sun);
> 'stem' implies outgrowth as from a root or a main stalk (modern
> detective fiction *stems* from Poe).

Or consider the words 'contract', 'shrink', 'condense', 'compress', and
'deflate'. Each of them, too, has definite implications in use:

> 'Contract' implies a drawing together of surface or parts and a
> resultant decrease in size, bulk, or extent; to 'shrink' is to contract
> so as to be short of the normal or required length, amount, extent,
> etc. (those shirts have *shrunk*); 'condense' suggests reduction of
> something into a more compact or more dense form without loss of
> essential content (*condensed* milk); to 'compress' is to press or
> squeeze into a more compact, orderly form (a lifetime's work *com-
> pressed* into one volume); 'deflate' implies a reduction in size or
> bulk by the removal of air, gas, or in extended use, anything insub-
> stantial (to *deflate* a balloon, one's ego, etc.)

There is a parallel insight necessary for understanding how to arrange
sentences in logical relationships to each other. Our language provides a
wide variety of adverbial phrases that can make connections between our
sentences clearer. Here, as above, students need to learn and respect this
established logic.

Connectives	How they are used
besides	To add another thought
what's more	
furthermore	
moreover	
in addition	

for example for instance in other words	To add an illustration or explanation.
therefore consequently accordingly	To connect an idea with another one that follows from it.
of course to be sure although though	To grant an exception or limitation.
still however on the other hand nevertheless rather	To connect two contrasting ideas.
first next finally meanwhile later afterwards nearby eventually above beyond in front	To arrange ideas in order, time, or space.
in short in brief to sum up in summary in conclusion	To sum up several ideas.

✦ *Common Problems With Texts*

A critical thinking approach to language arts instruction, with its emphasis on helping students understand the *logic* of what they study, can provide a strong unifying force in all of the basic dimensions of the language arts curriculum: reading, writing, language, grammar, and appreciation of literature. Unfortunately, this unifying stress is rare in language arts textbooks. Consequently, the emphases in reading, writing, language, grammar, and literature do not "add-up" for students. They don't recognize common denominators between reading and writing. They don't grasp how words in language have established uses and so can be used precisely or imprecisely, clearly or vaguely. Their lack of understanding of the logic of language in turn undermines their clarity of thought when reading and writing.

Similarly, grammar seems to students to be nothing more than a set of arbitrary rules. Most texts take a didactic approach. They introduce principles or concepts, then provide drills. Specific skills are often torn from their proper contexts and practiced merely for the sake of practice. Yet, without context, skills have little or no meaning. An occasional simple reiteration of basic purposes or ideas is insufficient. Students need to see for themselves when, how, and why each skill is used specifically as it is.

Texts rarely even mention that most crucial distinction: well written versus poorly written. Students rarely, if ever, evaluate what they read. Students do not explore their standards for evaluating written material, or distinguish for themselves when a written work is clear or unclear, engaging or dull, profound or superficial, realistic or unrealistic, well-organized or disjointed, and so on.

Texts occasionally have a short lesson or activity on "describing plot", "identifying theme", and "finding the main point". But students are rarely, if ever, called upon to describe the plots of selections they read. Yet these basic concepts are worthy of frequent discussion. Students should continually be required to describe the plot and state the theme of literature they read or state the main point of nonfiction passages.

Unfortunately, texts seldom have students examine work for themselves, discovering strengths and flaws, distinguishing main points from details, exploring the use of various techniques, formulating their conceptions of theses, plots, and themes.

SOME QUESTIONS TO RAISE ABOUT THE LOGIC OF LANGUAGE AND GRAMMAR

Keeping in mind the idea that language and grammar are, on the whole, logical, we should ask questions that help students discover this logic. Students should learn *how* to use grammatical distinctions, and *why*. For example, though students "cover" the distinction between transitive and intransitive verbs, they see no reason to make this distinction when they read or write. They should learn to supply implied objects of transitive verbs when they read or write. They should *use* grammatical analysis to help them read vague or difficult writing and to edit writing, not merely practice parsing sentences as drill.

"What is a sentence? How is it different from a group of words? What is a paragraph? How is it different from a group of sentences? What are words for? What do they do? How? How are words alike? Different? What kinds of words are there? How is each used? Why are some ways of using a word right and others wrong? What different kinds of sentences are there? When and how should each be used? Why follow the rules of grammar? How does punctuation help the reader? How does knowing about grammar help me write? Read? When do I need to know this distinction or concept? How should I use it? How does knowing this help me as a writer? A reader? Why and how do different types of writing differ? What do they have in common?"

SOME QUESTIONS TO RAISE ABOUT THE LOGIC OF LITERATURE

Stories have their own logic. Events don't just happen. They make sense within the meanings and thinking of their authors. When we ask a question, there should be method to it. The questions should lead students to discover how to come to terms with the logic of the story. We should always have students support their answers by reference to passages in the story. It is not their particular answers that are of greatest importance, but rather how they support their answers with reasons and references to the story.

"What happened? Why? What is the author trying to convey? Why is this important? What is the main character like? How do you know? What parts of the book gave you that idea? What has shaped the main character? How has this person shaped others? Why do the characters experience their worlds as they do? How do those experiences relate to my experience or to those of people around me? How realistic are the characters? How consistent? If they aren't (realistic, consistent) why not? Is it a flaw in the work, or does it serve some purpose? What conflicts occur in the story? What is the nature of this conflict? What is its deeper meaning? What relationship does it have to my life? What meaning does that conflict have for the character? For me? Though the world, society, lifestyle, or characters are obviously different than what I know, what does this work tell me about my world, society, life, character, and the characters of those around me? What needs, desires, and ideas govern these characters? Can I identify with them? Should I? How does the view presented in this work relate to my view? To what extent do I accept the conception of humanity and society expressed or implicit in this work? To what extent or in what way is it misleading? How does it relate to conceptions I've found in other works? How good is this work?"

SOME QUESTIONS TO RAISE ABOUT THE LOGIC OF PERSUASIVE WRITING

Persuasive writing has a straightforward logic. In it, an author attempts to describe some dimension of real life and hopes to persuade us to take it seriously. We, as readers, need to grasp what is being said and judge whether it does make sense or in what way or to what degree it makes sense.

"What parts of this work do I seem to understand? What parts don't I understand? What, exactly, is the author trying to say? Why? How does the author support what is said with reasons, evidence, or experiences? What examples can I give to further illuminate these ideas? What counter-examples can I cite? How could the author respond to my counter-examples? What are the basic parts of this work? How are the pieces organized? Which claims or ideas support which other claims or ideas? What beliefs does this claim presuppose? What does it imply? What are the consequences of believing or doing as the author says? What kind of writing is this? How has the writer attempted to achieve this purpose? Given that this is what I think is meant, how does this statement fit in? Could this be meant instead? Which of these interpretations makes more sense? How does the writer know what he or she claims to know? Have I good reason to accept these claims? Doubt them?

How could I check, or better evaluate what it says? How are such questions settled, or such claims evaluated? What deeper meaning does this work have? What criticisms can I make? What is left out? Distorted? How are opponents addressed? Are these opponents represented fairly? Does the evidence support exactly the conclusions drawn? If not, am I sure I understand the conclusions and evidence? What is the source of the evidence? How should I evaluate it? What is left unexplained? What would the writer say about it? Of all the ideas or concepts, which is the most fundamental or basic? How are these concepts used? To what other concepts are they related? How does the writer's use of concepts relate to mine and to that of others? Should other concepts have been used instead? How can I reconcile what has been said with what others have said?"

SOME QUESTIONS TO ASK WHILE WRITING

Writing has a logic. Good substance poorly arranged loses most of its value. Whatever the principle of order chosen, thought must progress from somewhere to somewhere else. It must follow a definite direction, not ramble aimlessly. In the entire piece, as well as in section and paragraph, ideally, each sentence should have a place so plainly its own that it could not be shifted to another place without losing coherence. Remember, disorderly thinking produces disorderly writing, and, conversely, orderly thinking produces orderly writing.

"What do I want to communicate? Why? What am I talking about? What do I want to say about it? What else do I want to say about it and why? What else do I know or think about this? How is what I am saying like and unlike what others have said? What am I sure of? What questions do I have? What must I qualify? How can I divide my ideas into intelligible parts? What are the relationships between the parts? How can I show those relationships? How does this detail fit in? How does that claim illuminate my main point? What form of expression best gets this idea across? Would the reader accept this? What questions would the reader have? How can I answer those questions? If I word it this way, would the reader understand it the way I intended? How can I clarify my meaning? How could someone judge this idea or claim? How can it be supported? How would others refute it? Which of those criticisms should I take into account? How can I reconcile the criticisms with my ideas? How should I change what I've said? Will the support seem to the reader to justify the conclusion? Should I change the conclusion, or beef up the support? What counter-examples or problems would occur to the reader here? What do I want to say about them? How am I interpreting my sources? How would someone else interpret them? How can I adjust or support my interpretation? What implications do I want the reader to draw? How can I help the reader see that I mean this and not that? Which of all of the things I'm saying is the most important? How will the reader know which is most important? Why is this detail important? Have I assumed the reader knows something he or she may not know?"

✦ Conclusion

As a teacher of language arts, you should develop a clear sense of the logic of language and of the unity of the language arts. If you model the insight that every dimension of language and literature makes sense, can be figured out, can be brought under our command, can be made useful to us, your students will be much more apt to make this same discovery for themselves. Remember that students are not used to unifying what they study. They are more used to fragmented learning. They are used to forgetting, for everything to begin anew, for each part to be self-contained.

Furthermore, they are not used to clear and precise use of language. They are usually satisfied with any words that occur to them to say or write. They are unfamiliar with good writing. Disciplined thinking is something foreign to their lives and being. Therefore, don't expect the shift from a didactic approach ("The teacher tells us and we repeat it back" "We do the sentences in chapter one, then in chapter two.") to a critical one ("We figure it out for ourselves and integrate it into our own thought") to occur quickly and painlessly. Expect a slow transition. Expect the students to experience many frustrations along the way. Expect progress to come by degrees over time. Commit yourself to the long view, to what Matthew Arnold called "the extreme slowness of things", and you will have the attitude necessary for success. Teaching critically, with a critical spirit, is a global transformation. Global transformations take a long time to achieve, but their effect is then often permanent. And that is what we want — students who learn to use language clearly and precisely for the rest of their lives, students who listen and read critically for the rest of their lives, students who become critical and creative persons for the rest of their lives.

Chapter 38

Critical Thinking and Science

with A. J. A. Binker

Abstract

In this brief paper, originally published as a chapter in the Critical Thinking Handbook
*4th–6th Grades, Paul and Binker discuss the key features of education in science. They
argue for the need to teach students to think scientifically and to examine and critique
their preconceptions of science and the physical world. They then point out common flaws
in standard instructional practices, and provide generic questions students can consider
when studying science.*

$\mathcal{A}$ critical approach to teaching science is concerned less with students
accumulating undigested facts and scientific definitions and procedures, than with students learning to *think scientifically*. As students learn
to think scientifically they inevitably do organize and internalize facts,
learn terminology, and use scientific procedures. But they learn them
deeply, tied into ideas they have thought through, and hence do not have to
"re-learn" them again and again.

The biggest obstacle to science education is students' previous misconceptions. Although there are well-developed, defensible methods for settling many
scientific questions, educators should recognize that students have developed
their own ideas about the physical world. Merely presenting established methods to the student does not usually affect those beliefs; they continue to exist in
an unarticulated and therefore unchallenged form. Rather than transferring
the knowledge they learn in school to new settings, students continue to use
their pre-existing frameworks of knowledge. Students' own emerging egocentric conceptions about events in their immediate experience seem much more
real and true to them than what they have superficially picked up in school.

For example, in one study, few college physics students could correctly
answer the question, "What happens to a piece of paper thrown out of a moving car's window?" They reverted to a naive physics inconsistent with what
they learned in school; they used Aristotelian rather than Newtonian physics.
The *Proceedings of the International Seminar on Misconceptions in Science
and Mathematics* offers another example. A student was presented with evidence about current flow incompatible with his articulated beliefs. In response

to the instructor's demonstration, the student replied, "Maybe that's the case here, but if you come home with me you'll see it's different there."[1] This student's response graphically illustrates one way students can retain their own beliefs while simply juxtaposing them with a new belief. Unless students practice expressing and defending their own beliefs, and listening critically to those of others, they will not critique their own beliefs and modify them in light of what they learn, a process essential for genuine understanding.

> As children discover they have different solutions, different methods, different frameworks, and they try to convince each other, or at least to understand each other, they revise their understanding in many small but important ways.[2]

Science texts suffer from serious flaws which give students false and misleading ideas about science. Scientists are not given experiments; they begin with a problem or question, and have to figure out, through trial and error, how to solve it. Typical science texts, however, present the student with the finished products of science. These texts present information, and tell students how to conduct experiments. They have students sort things into given categories, rather than stimulating students to discover and assess their own categories. Texts require students to practice the skills of measuring, graphing, and counting, often for no reason but practice or mindless drill. Such activities merely reinforce the stereotype that scientists are people who run around counting and measuring and mixing bizarre liquids together for no recognizable reason.

Texts also introduce scientific concepts. But students must understand scientific concepts through ordinary language and ordinary concepts. After a unit on photosynthesis, a student who was asked, "Where do plants get their food?" replied, "From water, soil, and all over." The student misunderstood what the concept 'food' means for plants and missed the crucial idea that *plants make their own food.* He was using his previous (ordinary, human) concept of 'food'. Confusion often arises when science concepts that have another meaning in ordinary language (e.g. 'work') are not distinguished in a way that highlights how purpose affects use of language. Students need to see that the each concept is correct for its purpose.

Students are rarely called upon to understand the reasons for doing their experiments or for doing them in a particular way. Students have little opportunity to come to grips with the concept of 'the controlled experiment' or understand the reasons for the particular controls used. Furthermore texts often fail to make the link between observation and conclusion explicit. "How do scientists get from *that* observation to *that* conclusion?" Sometimes the experiment or study is not obviously related to the question it's supposed to answer. Scientific reasoning remains a mystery to students, whereas education in science should combat the common assumption that, "Only scientists and geniuses can understand science."

To learn from a science activity, students should understand its purpose. A critical approach to science education would allow students to ponder questions, propose solutions, and develop and conduct their own experiments.

Although many of their experiments would fail, the attempt and failure provide a valuable learning experience which more accurately parallels what scientists do. When an experiment designed by students fails, those students are stimulated to amend their beliefs.

Many texts also treat the concept of "*the* scientific method" in a misleading way. Scientific thinking is not a matter of running through a set of steps once. Rather it is a kind of thinking in which we continually move back and forth between questions we ask about the world and observations we make and experiments we devise to test out various hypotheses, guesses, hunches, and models. We continually think in a hypothetical fashion: "If this idea of mine is true, then what will happen under these or those conditions? Let me see, suppose we try this. What does this result tell me? Why did this happen? If *this* is why, then *that* should happen when I ...." We have to do a lot of critical thinking in the process, because we must ask clear and precise questions in order to devise experiments that can give us clear and precise answers. Typically the results of experiments — especially those devised by students — will be open to more than one interpretation. What one student thinks the experiment has shown often differs from what another student thinks. Here then is another opportunity to try to get students to be clear and precise in what they are saying. Exactly how are these two different interpretations different? Do they agree at all? If so, where do they agree?

Furthermore, not all scientists do the same kinds of things — some experiment, others don't, some do field observations, others develop theories. Compare what chemists, theoretical physicists, zoologists, and paleontologists do.

As part of learning to think scientifically, clearly, and precisely, students need opportunities to transfer ideas to new contexts. This can be linked with the scientific goal of bringing different kinds of phenomena under one scientific law, and the process of clarifying our thinking through analogies. Students should seek connections, and assess explanations and models. "How do the concepts of gravity, mass, and air resistance explain the behavior of pebbles and airplanes, boulders and feathers?"

Finally, although science is much more monological than social studies, students should learn to do their own thinking about scientific questions from the beginning. Once students give up on trying to do their own scientific thinking and start passively taking in what their textbooks tell them, the spirit of science, the scientific attitude and frame of mind, is lost. Never forget the importance of "I can figure this out for myself! I can find some way to *test* this!" as an essential scientific stance for students in relationship to how they think about themselves as *knowers*. If they reach the point of believing that knowledge is something in books that other people smarter than them figured out, then they have lost the fundamental drive that ultimately distinguishes the educated from the uneducated person. Unfortunately this shift commonly occurs in the thinking of most students some time during elementary school. We need to teach science, and indeed all subjects, in such a way that this shift never occurs, so that the drive to figure out things for oneself does not die, but is continually fed and supported.

Students often mindlessly do their science work. We should look for opportunities that call upon them to explain or make intelligible what they are doing and why it is necessary or significant.

When students perform experiments, we should ask questions such as these:

• What exactly are you doing? Why? What results do you expect? Why? Have you designed any controls for this experiments? (Why do you have to use the same amount of liquid for both tests? Why do these have to be the same temperature? Size? What would happen if they weren't?) What might happen if we ... instead?

When students make calculations or take measurements, we should ask questions like these:

• What are you measuring? Why? What will that tell you? What numbers do you need to record? In what units? Why? What equation are you using? Why? Which numbers go where in the equation? What does the answer tell you? What would a different answer mean?

When studying anatomy, students can apply what they learn by considering such questions as these:

• If this part of the body has this function, what would happen if it no longer functioned fully or at all? Why do you say so? What would that be like for the person? What if it functioned on "overdrive"? What other parts of the body would such breakdowns affect? Why?

When students use theoretical concepts in biology or zoology, for example, they could be asked to explain the purpose and significance of those concepts by answering questions like these:

• How important is this distinction? Let's look at our chart of categories of living things. Where on the chart is this distinction? Why? What distinction is more important? Why? Less important? Why? (Why is the distinction between vertebrates and invertebrates more important to zoologists than the distinction between warm-blooded and cold-blooded animals?)
• Did any categorizations surprise you or seem strange? Do zoologists group together animals that seem very different to you? Which? How can we find out why they are grouped this way?

In general, students should be asked to explain the justification for scientific claims.

• Why does your text say this? How did scientists find this out? How would that prove this conclusion? Could we explain these results another way? What? Then how could we tell which was right? What would we have to do? Why? What results would you expect if this were so, rather than that hypothesis?

Whenever possible, students should be encouraged to express their ideas and try to convince each other to adopt them. Having to listen to their fellow students' ideas, to take those ideas seriously, and to try to find ways to test those ideas with observations and experiments are necessary experiences. Having to listen to their fellow students' objections will facilitate the process of self critique in a more fruitful way than if they are merely corrected by teachers who are typically taken as absolute authorities on "textbook" matters. Discussion with peers should be used to make reasoning from observation to conclusion explicit, help students learn how to state their own assumptions and to recognize the assumptions of others.

✦ Footnotes

[1] Hugh Helm & Joseph D. Novak, "A Framework for Conceptual Change with Special Reference to Misconceptions," *Proceedings of the International Seminar on Misconceptions in Science and Mathematics,* Cornell University, Ithaca, NY, June 20–22, 1983, p. 3.

[2] Jack Easley, "A Teacher Educator's Perspective on Students' and Teachers' Schemes: Or Teaching by Listening," *Proceedings of the Conference on Thinking, Harvard Graduate School of Education,* August, 1984, p. 8.

Chapter 39

Critical Thinking, Human Development, and Rational Productivity

Abstract

In this paper, originally presented at the Annual Rupert N. Evans Symposium *at the University of Illinois in 1985, Paul argues that productivity, development, and thinking are deeply interrelated. Consequently, societies concerned with their development and productivity must concern themselves with the nature of their educational systems, especially with whether or not the mass of citizens learn to think critically. Paul distinguishes rational from irrational productivity and argues that critical thinking is essential to rational productivity in a democratic world.*

Irrational production, in Paul's view, is productivity which "fails to serve the public good, insofar as it is production wasteful of non-renewable resources, destructive of public health, or at the expense of basic human needs". As both capitalism and democracy develop as world forces, it is important that we recognize the struggle "between the ideal of democracy and protection of the public good, on the one hand, and the predictable drive on the part of vested interests to multiply their wealth and power irrespective of the public need or good, on the other .... To the extent that it is possible for concentrations of wealth to saturate the media with images and messages that manipulate the public against its own interest, the forms of democracy become mere window dressing, mere appearance with no substantial reality."

Paul believes that the human world we have created has been created with a minimum of critical thought, a minimum of public rationality. He is convinced, however, that we can no longer afford mass irrationality. For Paul, the tensions between democracy, unbridled capitalism, and the public good must be increasingly resolved by a genuinely educated, rational, citizenry.

*W*hen we look upon learning in itself or productivity in itself or any other dimension of human life in itself, we look upon it with a partial view, as an abstraction from the real world in which all things exist in relationship. We then fail to see how it derives from relationship its true qualities. We view our object uncritically and narrowly. We fail to achieve the comprehensiveness all genuine and deep understanding presupposes. In this paper, I emphasize the intimate reciprocal relation between learning and productivity, arguing that what we learn about the nature and problems of learning sheds light on the nature and problems of productivity. Hence, just as learning can be rational or irrational, so, too, can productivity. Just as learning can be assessed not only in terms of quantity but quality as well, so, too, can productivity. Finally, I will argue that the nature and quality of life in society is intimately dependent on the nature and quality of human learning which in turn determines the nature and quality of productivity.

A free and rational society requires free and rational learning and thus generates free and rational production. Education, rightly conceived, has as its fundamental end the nurturing of free and rational learning and hence aims to contribute and will contribute to free and rational production. Vocational education should not, then, be seen as independent of the fundamental aims and ends of all education. It should proceed with the same liberating comprehensiveness, the same excellence, and the same command of mind and behavior that we typically think of as the desired hallmarks of a liberal education. My fundamental questions are these:

What is the nature of irrational human learning?

What is the nature of irrational human productivity?

What is the significance for education of irrational learning and irrational productivity as social phenomena?

✦ What is the Nature of
Irrational Human Learning?

All learning has social and psychological as well as epistemological roots. Whatever we learn, we learn in some social setting and in the light of the inborn constitution of the human mind. There is a natural reciprocity between the nature of the human mind as we know it and society as we know it. The human mind — and we must understand it as it is, not as we may judge it ought to be — has a profound and natural tendency toward egocentrism. Human society in turn, has a profound and natural tendency toward ethnocentrism. Both egocentrism and ethnocentrism are powerful impediments to rational learning and rational production. An irrational society tends to spawn irrational learning and inevitably generates irrational productivity. Both socially and individually, irrationality is the normal state of affairs in human life. It represents our primary nature, the side of us that needs no cultivation, that emerges willy-nilly in our earliest behaviors.

No one needs to teach young children to focus on their own interests and desires (to the relative exclusion of the rights, interests, and desires of others), to experience their desires as self-evidently "justified", and to structure experience with their own egos at the center. They do this quite naturally and spontaneously. They and we are spontaneously motivated to learn what gets us what we want. They and we are instinctively motivated to believe whatever justifies our getting what we want. It is not *natural* for us to step outside our egocentric point of view. It is not natural for us to take into account the interests, needs, or points of view of others. We do so only insofar as we are compelled as we experience the force and power of others who require us to respond to their interests and desires and to take into account their point of view. We do so, then, often grudgingly and with limited understanding. We acquire and extinguish beliefs, knowledge, habits, and behaviors insofar as they seem to us to further our, typically unexamined, desires. We begin with visceral learning that is functional in the most immediate and spontaneous way. We learn without knowing we are learning, without making any conscious choice about the conditions of our learning, without recognizing the pitfalls of our learning, without recognizing its selective, its epistemologically naive, its narrow foundations. And, as long as what we learn "works", as long as we can get by with it, we tend not to discover the longer range value of self-critique.

Socialization, which comes close on the heels of egocentric experience, builds upon, rather than significantly modifies, egocentrism. Our egocentrism is partially transformed into ethnocentrism. We spontaneously and subconsciously internalize the world view that is dominant in our society. And just as we don't as individuals recognize the egocentrism of our personal point of view, we don't as members of social groups recognize the ethnocentrism of our collective world view. We take that world view to be as objective, as completely a mirror-image of the world, as we take our personal point of view to be. Indeed, it is a rare individual who can tell where the one ends and the other begins.

The capacity to think critically — to penetrate our egocentrism and ethnocentrism, to give credence to points of view other than our own, to recognize ourselves as *having* a point of view (rather than simply grasping the nature of the world directly and objectively), to seek evidence for our beliefs, to monitor and assess the component elements in our reasoning — is not spontaneous as is our primary egocentrism, but must be laboriously cultivated through education. When we develop abilities to think critically we develop our capacity to function as free agents. As they develop, we come to analyze, assess, and take command of our learning and so of the actions that issue from that learning, including our own productions and productivity. As rational agents, we bring a new dimension to learning and production. We open the way for our own rational production and the collective development of a rational society. We can understand this better by considering the nature of human productivity.

✦ What Is the Nature of Human Productivity?

Production is, quite simply, the creation of some *utility*. The first question to ask, then, in probing the roots of productivity is, *whose utility?* Beyond production for sheer survival, utility must be judged from a human point of view; and all of the diversity and opposition that exists between conflicting points of view is reflected in judgments of the relative utility of diverse forms and modes of production and productivity.

Production and productivity can be looked at both quantitatively and qualitatively. Of greatest significance are the standards we use to assess production qualitatively. I suggest that *the most pressing problem the world faces today* is the problem of irrational production, of that production which wastefully expends human labor and precious resources for ends that would not be valued by rational persons nor be given priority in a rational society.

The modes and nature of production within any given society reflect the nature, development, and values of that society. Insofar as a society is democratic, the modes and nature of production will reflect democratic decision making regarding production. This reflects not only individual decisions that one might make as an autonomous "consumer" and vocational decision-maker but also collective decisions as a citizen who supports some given social and economic philosophy or other. For example, the decision to provide many hundreds of millions of dollars to subsidize the development of nuclear energy rather than solar energy was a "collective" decision, heavily dependent on public funds and resources. So, too, were the development of railroad systems, the airline industries, the public highways, and sewer systems. These general decisions and the precise ways in which they were implemented can be analyzed for their implications for the use of public resources and the meeting of public interest and need. Indeed, there are very few "political" or "social" decisions which do not have economic and moral implications. Every expenditure of public or private resources represents both an economic trade-off (in that other possible uses cannot, then, be furthered) and some implementation of a judgment of value for public or private good. A society is not democratic if its citizens are not disposed to participate in this economic and social decision making in such a way as to knowingly and effectively protect the public good and interest.

✦ What Is Irrational Production?

It is a platitude, but an important platitude to keep in mind, that the productive resources of society should be marshalled to serve public need and public good, as against the vested interests of a relative few at the expense of the public good. *Production is irrational to the extent that it fails to serve the public good, insofar as it is production wasteful of non-renewable resources, destructive of public health, or at the expense of basic human needs.* One valuable rule of thumb is this: any economic practice is of questionable rationality if it can be maintained only by keeping the public in ignorance as to specific nature and modes of operation. The public cannot be understood to sanction that which it does not comprehend.

Production and productivity are to be viewed as collective as well as individual decisions in a functioning democracy. For these decisions to be made in a rational fashion, the public must have been educated to think critically, for when some narrow interest group seeks to maintain some form of irrational production (either as a whole or in part), it is inevitable that public relations and lobbying efforts will be launched which function, at least in part, to obfuscate public recognition of its own interests. For instance, it was in the narrow egocentric interest of asbestos manufacturers to minimize public disclosure of the health hazards of working and building with asbestos. The asbestos industry obscured the public interest to serve its own. As a result of the industry successfully protecting its vested interest, a mode of production was maintained for decades at great expense and loss in public health.

Since it is unrealistic to expect industries with narrow vested interests to abandon those interests for the public good, it becomes necessary that the public be armed with the critical, analytic, fact-finding, and reasoning abilities that critical thinking provides, that they may judge where, when, and to what degree the pursuit of a vested interest is consistent with the public good.

It is easy to find innumerable historical examples in which the public good was flagrantly sacrificed precisely because the public was kept in the dark about the manner in which and the extent to which private interest was secured. Adam Smith himself was well aware of the tendency of private interest to seek its own advancement at the expense of the public good:

> People of the same trade seldom meet together, even for merriment and diversion, but the conversation ends in a conspiracy against the public, or in some contrivance to raise prices. (*Wealth of Nations,* Book 1, Ch 10.)

It is extremely difficult to maintain genuine competition that serves the public good in the face of ever-changing market structures and ever-growing concentrations of economic wealth and power. Multi-national corporations, for example, are increasingly able to function as quasi-monopolies, or, in their capacity to move their productive facilities and great concentrations of wealth from one country to another, as to function as quasi-oligopolies. For example, when a foreign dictator prevents the development of free labor unions and preserves both "political stability" and "low wages" by effective and organized instruments of social and political repression, then the "free" labor force economically competing in "democratic" countries loses effective bargaining power at home. Free labor cannot effectively compete against unorganized repressed labor. A market economy cannot function in the public good when increasing concentrations of wealth produce conditions of radically inequitable bargaining power.

Again and again, questions intrinsic to the nature and mode of production and productivity turn upon decisions and policies that can be argued from divergent points of view and in which the relation of private and public interest are in need of critical explication. The individual citizen's capacity to penetrate the rationalizing smoke screens that can be generated to undermine the public good in service of private gain is a profound on-going problem of public life.

Consider, for example, an argument in the London *Economist* of July 13, 1850, criticizing the "sanitary movement" which was urging that government support the development of a pure water supply and proper sewage disposal. The *Economist* argued that poor housing and high urban death rates,

> sprung from two causes, both of which will be aggravated by these new laws. The first is the poverty of the masses, which if possible, will be

increased by the taxation inflicted by the new laws. The second is that the people have never been allowed to take care of themselves. They have always been treated as serfs or children and they have to a great extent become in respect to those objects which the government has undertaken to perform for them, imbeciles .... There is a worse evil than typhus or cholera or impure water, and that is mental imbecility.

Here the public good is defined as allowing poor water treatment and supply to continue. To correct them, say these editors, would *harm* the poor.

As Adam Smith recognized, private vested interests naturally try to increase their wealth regardless of the public good. Hence, ironically, no private interest is in favor of more, but rather in favor of less competition in its own industry (unless an increase in competition would increase its own profits). When it is possible to take advantage of the public, private interests will almost inevitably do so. Thus, during OPEC's oil embargo, U.S. oil companies raised their own prices at home as well as abroad even though internal consumption of Arab oil was no more than 10% of our market. The OPEC action, in other words, provided a convenient excuse to join in a monopolistic practice of a special interest cartel. The result was windfall profits extracted from the U.S. public under artificially created, non-competitive conditions. The public, on the other hand, was continually led to believe that "Arabs" were exclusively to blame, as though U.S. companies hadn't taken advantage of the situation to advance their own interests, irrespective of the public good.

I am arguing that the nature and conditions of production and productivity are never things-in-themselves, forces independent of political and social decisions, but rather intimately bound to such decisions. These decisions may be rational (in the public interest) or irrational (against the public interest). Whether they are the one or the other, can only be determined by full and fair public argument. If a nation is to function as a democracy, then its citizens must be armed with the critical thinking skills which enable them to penetrate the propagandistic arguments which are creatively and adroitly developed by private interests to keep violations of the public good from public recognition. The history of the country is shot through with cases in which the public was deceived into supporting policies in which public interest was sacrificed to private greed. A tremendous price in lives and resources has been paid as a result of the public's inability to think critically to a sufficient degree to protect itself from irrational modes of production. We are, in my opinion, very far from the sort of educational system which nurtures the economic survival skills the public needs to protect itself against highly sophisticated propaganda which routinely advances private greed against public good.

It is crucial that we grasp the inevitable struggle that will continue to be played out between the ideal of democracy and protection of the public good, on the one hand, and the predictable drive on the part of vested interests to multiply their wealth and power irrespective of public need or good, on the other. In a society based not only on the ideal of democracy but also on a market economy that produces large concentrations of capital and vested interest, the power of the voting public is only as great as the information upon which the public can base its votes. To the extent that it is possible for concentrations of wealth to saturate the media with images and messages that manipulate the public against its own interests, the forms of democracy become mere window dressing, mere appearance with no substantial reality. As John Dewey remarked in *Individualism, Old and New,* "financial and industrial power, corporately organized, can deflect economic consequences away from the advantage of the many to serve the privilege of the few". Unfortunately, but predictably, the political parties, heavily dependent for their success upon the raising of large amounts of capital, "have been eager accomplices in maintaining the confusion and unreality". (p. 114) Dewey saw the issue as fundamental to whether the democratic ideal would be achieved, and as being determined by whether *force* or *intelligence* would prevail:

> The question is whether force or intelligence is to be the method upon which we consistently rely and to whose promotion we devote our energies. Insistence that the use of force is inevitable limits the use of available intelligence .... There is an undoubted objective clash of interests between finance-capitalism that controls the means of production and whose profit is served by maintaining relative scarcity, and idle workers and hungry consumers. But what generates violent strife is failure to bring the conflict into the light of intelligence where the conflicting interests can be adjudicated in behalf of the interests of the great majority. (p. 79f)

✦ What Is the Significance for Education of Irrational Learning and Irrational Production as Social Phenomena?

Wentworth Eldredge has put part of the background of the problem in a stark light:

> The traditional democratic assumption is that rational adults in a rational society have the necessary hereditary intelligence and social training, coupled with a determined interest and sufficient time, to absorb the available facts which will enable them to make in the political process wise decisions among offered choices and upon occasion to invent and make real alternate choices. A majority vote of such reasoning citizens shall constitute the truth and the ship of state will sail a true course .... Most adults have completely inadequate training to understand even remotely the complexity of the contemporary scene. They lack interest and feel hopeless to think and act correctly in other than purely private concerns; and moreover, they have neither the time nor the information — assuming they could cope with the latter if by chance it were made available. They are merely carrying out the trite inculcated orders of their culture which have been drilled into them formally and informally since birth. Most adults are feeble reeds in the wild, whistling storm of a dangerous world they neither made nor could ever understand. To ask for the people's reasoned decision and advice on weighty matters of policy would

seem to be a waste of everyone's time and energy, including their own. One might as well inquire of a five-year-old if he wanted polio vaccine injections.

In a rational society three general conditions would prevail:

1) The modes of production would be rational; that is, the bulk of production would be designed to satisfy basic human needs in a manner minimally wasteful of human and natural resources.

2) There would be, as a result, a multiplicity of jobs available to individuals whose performance would have a self-fulfilling quality based on the realization that it contributes to production in the public good.

3) Education would be oriented toward providing citizens with the critical thinking skills to make informed judgments with regard to the social and political decisions that ultimately shape and determine the economic destiny of the nation.

I am arguing that we are far from this democratic ideal of a rational society. If we are committed to it, we must devise means to achieve it. The only satisfactory strategy available to educators lies in making *rational learning* the hallmark of schooling. We can no longer afford the kind of schooling that at best transforms students into narrow specialists or experts who function as *tools* subject to additional *retooling* as dictated by the needs of production narrowly defined and narrowly controlled, and at worst leaves them without either specialized job skills or a general capacity to learn. The ordinary citizen needs the critical thinking skills of a person able to probe the evidential grounds for belief, a person who is swayed not by appeals to fear, prejudice, or ego but rather by the weight of evidence and reason, who is capable of suspending his judgment until such reasonable grounds for beliefs are forthcoming; a person eager to hear reasons and evidence against his or her beliefs if they become available, and to modify his or her views in accordance with them. Today's industrial technology is complex, specialized, and interdependent, but the social uses to which it is put and the human decision-making needed to maintain and direct it must be flexible, analytic, and humane — "ends" as well as "means" oriented.

✦ *Two Objections*

Before concluding, I should air a couple of obvious objections. One may be put as follows:

> So far you have not dealt with the most obvious problem of productivity, the unproductive worker, the employee who, through lack of knowledge, training, or motivation, fails to perform in an optimal or adequate fashion. What employers want are dedicated, motivated, conscientious, and skilled employees who carry out their tasks as prescribed, not reflective thinkers who ponder the global problems of society.

This objection, you should note, assumes that the fundamental problem of productivity is "the worker". This is, of course, a natural assumption to make if the role one has played is one of traditional management in U.S. industry. From that vantage point, it is natural to key in on employee performance standards and to see those standards as a function of employees in themselves. Studies have demonstrated, however, that in most of the Western world, management and labor both operate with a strong caricature or stereotype of each other. The fact is that each tends to function with a narrow view of its own immediate vested interest. Hence, while it may be in the immediate vested interest of employers to get the most labor from the least investment of capital, it is also in the immediate vested interest of employees to get the highest pay for the least labor. There is minimal incentive in the system to cooperate toward mutual advantage, and maximal incentive to compete as adversaries for available capital.

The Japanese system of management with its guarantees to the worker of life-long employment and its provision for child care, recreation, profit-sharing, and job-retraining (if necessary) suggests the possibility of the accent being focused on cooperation rather than adversarial competition. It seems to me more reasonable to assume that there are no genetic or "moral" differences between Japanese, and say, U.S. workers, but that the differences in productivity are more a function of radically different philosophies of management/employee relations. I don't believe that any significant increase in worker productivity will occur unless, and only to the degree that, the interest of workers is more structurally linked to the interests of employers. This is both a global problem and one that can be addressed at the level of individual companies. One reason for the success of high-tech industries, it seems to me, has been a management/employee model closer to the "Japanese" than to the traditional "American" one. Much worker inefficiency arises from these two interrelated causes: workers don't seem to think; workers don't seem to care.

Present instructional practices and management/employee relations seem perfectly designed to produce the first cause. Students are neither taught nor expected to *think*. Such practices as mindless, purposeless drill, over-proceduralization (first do this, then this, then that — don't worry about understanding it) seem suited to what employers want: workers who keep moving, look busy, *seem* efficient, and don't question. But this very training-for-mindlessness produces workers who don't use their heads. Education and industry encourage "going through the motions."

Regarding the second cause, why *should* workers care about mindless tasks over which they have no control, which they are not encouraged to understand or value, and for which they often get little recognition or reward?

Here is a second objection:

> The dominant trend in business is toward giant corporations. Within them relations are direct, hierarchical, and bureaucratic. Directions flow from the top down. There is minute specialization of tasks. The entire task is accomplished by orchestrating the diverse specialized contributions. Very few specialists are in a position to judge the contributions of other specialists, or to judge the productive

process as a whole. What we need are specialists who know their own specialty well, not generalists who judge this process as a whole.

My argument is not an argument against specialization but rather an argument for how to teach specialized skills. It is an argument in favor of specialists with the skills of generalists. There are two different modes of specialization, a narrowing and a broadening one. Most tools nowadays have a narrow specialized function. They are increasingly designed to serve a specific purpose in a specific process. But, as such, they are quickly rendered obsolete. We cannot afford vocational education or training that renders workers obsolete. Precisely because information and technology are quickly being replaced and transformed, we need workers who can adapt to profound changes.

Mindless, routine jobs are quickly being automated. The jobs that remain require increasing ability to adapt, to abandon old and adopt new ways. The same kinds of general critical thinking skills and abilities required for the global decisions of a citizen and consumer are required by specialists to adapt to new information, new technologies, and new procedures. This has been attested to in the call for new emphasis on critical thinking skills in vocational and professional education by the Educational Commission of the States, The National Academy of Sciences, and the Association of American Medical Colleges. As one business leader put it, we do not need "a steady supply of drones moving in a huge beehive". What we do need he suggested with the following example:

> My company took a contract to extract beryllium from a mine in Arizona.
> I called in several consulting engineers and asked, "Can you furnish a chemical or electrolytic process that can be used at the mine site to refine directly from the ore?" Back came a report saying that I was asking for the impossible — a search of the computer tapes had indicated that no such process existed. I paid the engineers for their report. Then I hired a student from Stanford University who was home for the summer. He was majoring in Latin American history with a minor in philosophy. I gave him an airplane ticket and a credit card and told him, "Go to Denver and research the Bureau of Mines archives and locate a chemical process for the recovery of beryllium." He left on Monday. I forgot to tell him that I was sending him for the impossible. He came back on Friday. He handed me a pack of notes and booklets and said, "Here is the process. It was developed 33 years ago at a government research station at Rolla, Mo." He then continued, "And here also are other processes for the recovery of mica, strontium, columbium and yttrium, which also exist as residual ores that contain beryllium." After one week of research, he was making sounds like a metallurgical expert.

Whereas the specialists' preconceptions, intellectual arrogance, and algorithmic thought prevented them from solving the problem, the student's open mind and general skills enabled him to do so. It is clear that the age of changing specializations needs specialists skilled in the art of changing their specialty, not specialists who, like tools and machines, become obsolete. Those corporations, giant or otherwise, who recognize this will thrive. Those who seek drones with specialities will continually be in trouble and, eventually, I would guess, out of business.

✦ Conclusion

We do not live in a disembodied world of objects and physical laws. Neither do we live in a world of nature-created economic laws. We live in a world of people. The fundamental institutional structures, the rules, laws, principles, mores, and folkways are, consciously or unconsciously, created by people. The conditions for and the nature of productivity are not things-in-themselves, but products of multitudes of human decisions embodied in human activity and behavior. The benefits yielded by any mode of production can be viewed narrowly or broadly. They can be treated technically as a function of production curves, of so much raw material and labor costs, of product output and input factors, of production standards expressible in time per unit or units per hour. They can, of course, be viewed from the perspective of management as skill in using labor and equipment or of maximizing profits for investors. In many settings, the narrow view will inevitably prevail as determined by pressing agendas and the imperatives that result from functioning essentially in the service of narrow vested interests. Stockholders do not gather together to hear reports of service to the broader public good but to hear what the balance sheets say, what the present profits are and, given intelligent projections, can be expected to be in the near future.

But educators, whether concerned with "liberal", "professional", or "vocational", programs, should not function as representatives of any vested interest but rather as public servants working to advance the public good. Such a responsibility requires a broad, a comprehensive, and a critical view of society as a whole. Our understanding of the role of our specialization must be determined by our vision of its place in service of a critically sophisticated view of the problems of working to achieve a society that serves the public rather than private interests. Our global vision must shape our understanding of our specialty; our specialty as a thing-in-itself, as a system of narrow loyalties must not be used as a model for generalizing our vision of the world as a whole. The vocational or professional educator who adopts the philosophy, "What's good for General Motors is good for the United States" uncritically confuses vested and public interest.

A market economy is compatible with democracy only insofar as large accumulations of capital cannot be used to harness mass communications to manipulate the public into the service of vested interest and private greed. There is no way to prevent such practices except through the development of sophisticated critical thinking processes on the part of the electorate as a whole. Such processes must be honed in school on complex, controversial issues that force one to deal with opposing points of view and the subtle devices of propaganda and mass manipulation. The result of instruction in critical thinking is independence of thought and flexibility of mind, the very features essential to the metamorphosis of work from routine, mechanical functions (more and more to be automated) to complex problem-solving functions that presuppose the ability to question and redefine the basic problems themselves. Our view should not then be "What's good for General Motors is good for the United States", but "What's good for the United States is good for General Motors", whether it realizes it or not.

Appendix

✦✦ Chapter 40

What Critical Thinking Means to Me:
The Views of Teachers

Abstract

The following passages were written by teachers from Greensboro School District following a workshop on critical thinking.

Critical thinking is a process through which one solves problems and makes decisions. It is a process that can be improved through practice, though never perfected. It involves self-discipline and structure. Sometimes it can make your head hurt, but sometimes it comes naturally. I believe, for critical thinking to be its most successful, it must be intertwined with creative thinking.

Kathryn Haines
Grade 5

Thinking critically gives me an organized way of questioning what I hear and read in a manner that goes beyond the surface or literal thought. It assists me in structuring my own thoughts such that I gain greater insight into how I feel and appreciation for the thoughts of others, even those with which I disagree. It further enables me to be less judgmental in a negative way and to be more willing to take risks.

Patricia Wiseman
Grade 3

Critical thinking is being able and willing to examine all sides of an issue or topic, having first clarified it; supporting or refuting it with either facts or reasoned judgment; and in this light, exploring the consequences or effects of any decision or action it is possible to take.

Kim V. DeVaney
Facilitator, WATTS

All of us think, but critical thinking has to do with becoming more aware of how we think and finding ways to facilitate clear, reasoned, logical, and better-informed thinking. Only when our thoughts are backed with reason and logic, and are based on a process of careful examination of ideas and evidence, do they become critical and lead us in the direction of finding what is true. In order to do this, it seems of major importance to maintain an openminded willingness to look at other points of view. In addition, we can utilize various skills which will enable us to become more proficient at thinking for ourselves.

Nancy Johnson
Kindergarten

627

Critical thinking is necessary to a happy and full life. It provides me the opportunity to analyze and evaluate my thoughts, beliefs, ideas, reasons, and feelings as well as those of other individuals. Utilizing this process, it helps me to understand and respect others as total persons. It helps me in instructing my students and in my personal life. Critical thinking extends beyond the classroom setting and has proven to be valid in life other than the school world.

Veronica Richmond
Grade 6

Critical thinking is the ability to analyze and evaluate feelings and ideas in an independent, fairminded, rational manner. If action is needed on these feelings or ideas, this evaluation motivates meaningfully positive and useful actions. Applying critical thinking to everyday situations and classroom situations is much like Christian growth. If we habitually evaluate our feelings and ideas based on reasonable criteria, we will become less likely to be easily offended and more likely to promote a positive approach as a solution to a problem. Critical thinking, like Christian growth, promotes confidence, creativity, and personal growth.

Carolyn Tarpley
Middle School
Reading

Critical thinking is a blend of many things, of which I shall discuss three: independent thinking; clear thinking; and organized Socratic questioning.

As for the first characteristic mentioned above, a critical thinker is an independent thinker. He doesn't just accept something as true or believe it because he was taught it as a child. He analyzes it, breaking it down into its elements; he checks on the author of the information and delves into his or her background; he questions the material and evaluates it; and then he makes up his own mind about its validity. In other words, he thinks independently.

A second criterion of critical thinking is clarity. If a person is not a clear thinker, he can't be a critical thinker. I can't say that I agree or disagree with you if I can't understand you. A critical thinker has to get very particular, because people are inclined to throw words around. For example, they misuse the word 'selfish'. A person might say: "You're selfish, but I'm motivated!" A selfish person is one who systematically ignores the rights of others and pursues his own desires. An unselfish one is a person who systematically considers the rights of others while he pursues his own desires. Thus, clarity is important. We have to be clear about the meanings of words.

The most important aspect of critical thinking is its spirit of Socratic questioning. However, it is important to have the questioning organized in one's mind and to know in general the underlying goals of the discussion. If you want students to retain the content of your lesson, you must organize it and help them to see that ideas are connected. Some ideas are derived from basic ideas. We need to help students to organize their thinking around basic ideas and to question. To be a good questioner, you must be a wonderer — wonder

aloud about meaning and truth. For example, "I wonder what Jack means." "I wonder what this word means?" "I wonder if anyone can think of an example?" "Does this make sense?" "I wonder how true that is?" "Can anyone think of an experience when that was true?" The critical thinker must have the ability to probe deeply, to get down to basic ideas, to get beneath the mere appearance of things. We need to get into the very spirit, the "wonderment" of the situation being discussed. The students need to feel, "My teacher really wonders; and really wants to know what we think." We should wonder aloud. A good way to stimulate thinking is to use a variety of types of questions. We can ask questions to get the students to elaborate, to explain, to give reasons, to cite evidence, to identify their points of view, to focus on central ideas, and to raise problems. Socratic questioning is certainly vital to critical thinking.

Thus, critical thinking is a blend of many characteristics, especially independent thinking, clear thinking, and Socratic questioning. We all need to strive to be better critical thinkers.

Holly Touchstone
Middle School
Language Arts

Critical thinking is wondering about that which is not obvious, questioning in a precise manner to find the essence of truth, and evaluating with an open mind. As a middle school teacher, critical thinking is a way to find out where my stdents are coming from (a way of being with-it). Because of this "withitness", produced by bringing critical thinking into the classroom, student motivation will be produced. This motivation fed by fostering critical thinking will produce a more productive thinker in society. Thus, for me, critical thinking is a spirit I can infuse into society by teaching my students to wonder, question, and evaluate in search of truth while keeping an open mind.

Malinda McCuiston
Middle School
Language Arts, Reading

Critical thinking means thinking clearly about issues, problems, or ideas, and questioning or emphasizing those that are important to the "thinker". As a teacher, I hope to develop Socratic questioning so that my students will feel comfortable discussing why they believe their thoughts to be valid. I hope that they will develop language skills to communicate with others and that they will be open to ideas and beliefs of others.

Jessie Smith
Grade 1

The spirit of critical thinking is a concept that truly excites me. I feel the strategies of critical thinking, implemented appropriately in my classroom, can enable me to become a more effective teacher. By combining this thinking process with my sometimes overused emotions and intuitive power, I can critically examine issues in my classroom as well as in my personal life. I feel it is of grave importance for us as educators to provide a variety of opportunities for our students to think critically by drawing conclusions, clarifying ideas, evaluating assumptions, drawing inferences, and giving reasons and examples to support ideas. Also, Socratic dialogue is an effective means of enabling the students to discover ideas, contradictions, implications, etc., instead of being told answers and ideas by the teacher. Critical thinking is an excellent tool for the teacher to help the students learn *how* to think rather than just *what* to think. Hopefully critical thinking will help me be a more effective teacher as well as excite my students.

> Beth Sands
> Middle School
> Language Arts

Critical thinking is what education should be. It is the way I wish I had been taught. Although I left school with a wealth of facts, I had never learned how to connect them or to use them. I loved learning but thought that being learned meant amassing data. No one ever taught me how to contrast and compare, analyze, and dissect. I believed that all teachers knew everything, all printed material was true and authority was always right. It took me years to undo the habits of "good behavior" in school. I want to save my students the wasted time, the frustration, the doubts that I encountered during and after my school years. And teaching and using critical thinking is the way to do that.

> Nancy Poueymirou
> High School
> Language Arts

For me, critical thinking is a combination of learning and applying a database of learning to evaluate and inter-relate concepts from diverse academic disciplines. Critical thinking is understanding that knowledge, wisdom, and education are not divided into math, science, English, etc. It is the fairness of tolerance combined with a strong sense of ethics and morals. It is the fun of feeling your mind expand as you accomplish intellectual challenges that attain your own standards. It is the zest of life.

> Joan Simons
> High School
> Biology

Both as teacher and individual, I find critical thinking skills essential elements of a full and enjoyable life. With the ability to think critically, one can both appreciate and cope with all aspects of life and learning. When dealing with problems, from the most mundane to the most complex, the ability to think critically eliminates confusion, dispels irrational emotion, and enables one to arrive at an appropriate conclusion. At the same time, as we ponder the beauty and creativity of our environment, we are free to "wonder" and enjoy the complexity around us, rather than be perplexed or intimidated by it, because we have the mental capability to understand it. To live is to be ever curious, ever learning, ever investigating. Critical thinking enables us to do this more fully and pleasurably.

> Mary Lou Holoman
> High School
> Language Arts

A critical thinker never loses the joy of learning, never experiences the sadness of not caring or not wondering about the world. The essence of the truly educated person is that of being able to question, inquire, doubt, conclude, innovate. And beyond that, to spread that enthusiasm to those around him, obscuring the lines that divide teacher and student, enabling them to travel together, each learning from the other.

Jane Davis-Seaver
Grade 3

Critical thinking is a means of focusing energy to learn. The learning may be academic (proscribed by an institutional curriculum or self-directed) or non-academic (determined by emotional need). It provides a systematic organization for gathering information, analyzing that information, and evaluating it to reach reasonable, acceptable conclusions for yourself.

Blair Stetson
Elementary
Academically Gifted

Critical thinking is the ability to reason in a clear and unbiased way. It is necessary to consider concepts or problems from another's point of view and under varying circumstances in order to make reasoned judgments. Awareness of one's own reasoning processes enables one to become a more fairminded and objective thinker.

Karen Marks
Elementary
Academically Gifted

Critical thinking is questioning, analyzing, and making thoughtful judgments about questions, ideas, issues, or concepts. It refines thoughts to more specific or definite meanings. The critical thinker must be an active listener who does not simply accept what he or she hears or reads at face value without questioning, but looks for deeper meaning. Critical thinking also involves evaluating the ideas explored or problems addressed and better prepares a student to be able to think about the world around him or her.

Becky Hampton
Grade 6

Critical thinking has given me a broader means of evaluating my daily lesson plans. It has helped me better understand the thinking principles of each student I teach. It has also enabled me to practice strategies in lesson planning and to become a more effective classroom teacher.

Pearl Norris Booker
Grade 2

Critical thinking provides me the opportunity to broaden the thinking process of my students. It can be used to have the students reason and think about different ideas of a problem or a given situation.

Portia Staton
Grade 3

Critical thinking is a process that takes all the ideas, questions, and problems that we are faced with each day and enables us to come up with solutions. It is the process by which we are able to search for evidence that supports already-existing answers, or better yet, to come up with new solutions to problems. Through critical thinking, one begins to realize that many times there is more than one solution whereupon decisions can be made. To me, critical thinking has helped and will continue to help me understand myself and the world around me.

Debbie Wall
Grade 4

Critical thinking is a skill that involves the expansion of thoughts and the art of questioning. This skill must be developed over a period of time. It is a way of organizing your thoughts in a logical sequence. Knowledge is gained through this process.

Carolyn Smith
Grade 5

Critical thinking is questioning, analyzing, and evaluating oral or written ideas. A critical thinker is disciplined, self-directed, and rational in problem solving. Reaching conclusions of your own rather than accepting everything as it is presented, is internalizing critical thinking.

Denise Clark
Grade 2

To think critically, one must analyze and probe concepts or ideas through reasoning. It makes one an active reasoner, not a passive accepter of ideas (or facts). It turns one into a doer, an evaluater, or re-evaluater. Critical thinking occurs everywhere, is applicable everywhere, and while it can be tedious, need not be, because as one thinks critically, new ideas are formed, conclusions are drawn, new knowledge is acquired.

Janell Prester
Grade 3

Critical thinking means to think through and analyze a concept or idea. You are able to back up your reasoning and think through an idea in a manner which allows an over-all focus. If a person is a critical thinker, a yes-no answer is too brief. An answer to a problem or idea must have an explanation and reasoning backing it.

Donna Phillips
Grade 4

Critical thinking is a tool that teachers can use to offer a new dimension of education to their students: that of thinking about, questioning, and exploring the concepts in the curriculum. When critical thinking is an integral part of the teaching-learning process, children learn to apply thinking skills throughout the curriculum as well as in their daily lives. Socratic dialogue fosters critical thinking and motivates the teacher and learner to share and analyze experiences and knowledge. Critical thinking involves the child in the learning process and makes education more meaningful to the individual, thus facilitating learning.

> Andrea Allen
> Grade 1

The most important part of critical thinking, to me, is discovery. We discover a deeper level of thinking. We discover the reasons for ideas instead of just accepting ideas. We are motivated by action, interaction, and involvement. We discover we have the ability to expand our thoughts to include all aspects and perspectives of our beliefs.

> Mandy Ryan
> Grade 5

Critical thinking, to me, is the process of analyzing new and old information to arrive at solutions. It's the process of learning to question information that you may have taken for granted. It's being independent. Critical thinking is letting people think for themselves and make judgments for themselves.

> Leigh Ledet
> Grade 4

Critical thinking is the process of taking the knowledge you have gained through past experience or education and re-evaluating conclusions on a certain situation or problem. Because students must evaluate the reasons for their beliefs, they become actively involved in learning through the teacher's use of Socratic questioning. Allowing students to clarify their reasons through the writing process further stimulates the students to become critical thinkers. The ultimate goal for students in using critical thinking is to become active thinkers for themselves.

> Robin Thompson
> Middle School
> Language Arts

Critical thinking, to me, is to be open-ended in my thoughts. It is like opening a door which leads to many other doors through which ideas may evolve, move about, change, and come to rest. It is like a breath of freshness in which one can gain new insight over long-established opinions. It stimulates and generates endless new possibilities.

> Eutha M. Godfrey
> Grades 2–3

Critical thinking is thinking that demonstrates an extension of an idea or concern beyond the obvious. A critical thinker's values are significant to his learning.

> Frances Jackson
> Grade 2

To me, critical thinking means independence. It gives me a tool which lets me explore my own mind extending beyond basic recall to a higher level of reasoning. I then feel more in touch with myself and my own inner feelings. This results in my becoming a better decision-maker.

> Jean Edwards
> Grade 5

Critical thinking is the process of working your mind through different channels. It is the process of thinking logically. Critical thinking is analyzing your thoughts through questions. It is the process of seeing that your ideas and concepts may not be the same as another's. It is opening your mind to those who have different views and looking at their views.

Cathy L. Smith
Grade 3

Critical thinking is to question in-depth at every possible angle or point of view, to look at someone else's point of view without making hasty judgments. Critical thinking is to logically and fairly re-orient your own personal point of view, if necessary. To think critically, you are self-directed in your thinking process, as well as disciplined.

Mary Duke
Grade 1

Critical thinking is the vehicle by which I encourage students to become active participants in the learning process. I allow more time for and become more aware of the need for students to express ideas verbally and in written form to clarify ideas in their own minds. I recognize the importance of developing skills for analyzing and evaluating. Ultimately, once students become comfortable using critical thinking skills, they assume greater responsibility for their learning.

Dora McGill
Grade 6

Critical thinking is clear, precise thinking. I believe that all human actions and expressions involve in some way, thinking. For example, I believe that feelings, emotions, and intuitions are much the results of earlier thought (reactions to stimuli). I think that this, in one way, explains the variations of emotional responses in some people to similar stimuli. Thus, I believe that critical thinking not only has the potential to clarify new and former conscious thoughts but also to affect/change likely (future) emotive and intuitive reactions/responses.

More concrete and less theoretical outcomes of critical thinking may be more relevant to me as an educator. Better questioning skills on the part of the students and the teacher is an obvious outcome. There seem to be several positive outcomes of better questioning: more opportunity for in-depth understanding of content, a natural (built-in) process for assessing the effectiveness of lessons, and more opportunity for student participation, self-assessment, and direction are three apparent outcomes. There are, of course, many other outcomes of developing better questioning skills, and from the other skills of critical thinking.

I simply believe that critical thinking improves the overall integrity of the individual and the collective group, class, school, community, etc.

Richard Tuck
High School
Art

I perceive critical thinking in teaching as a tool for my learning. As I attempt to develop the critical thinker, I will become more aware of the students' thoughts, values, and needs. I must learn from what students offer, and develop acceptance and sensitivity to the individual. The knowledge I gain from the student will determine what I utilize as strategies or principles of critical thinking.

> Loretta Jennings
> Grade 1

Critical thinking is the ability to look at a problem or issue with a spirit of openmindedness and to take that problem and analyze or evaluate it based on the facts or good, "educated" hypotheses. Critical thinking is being flexible enough to suspend one's bias towards an issue in order to study all sides to formulate an opinion or evaluation.

> Mark Moore
> Grade 4

Critical thinking to me involves mental conversations and dialogues with myself. I try first to establish the facts. Then I try to search for criteria to examine my "facts". The next question is whether or not there are distortions and irrelevancies. I have to examine whether I have a personal bias which has led me to select only certain facts and leave others out.

I then try to mentally list facts and arguments on both sides of a question and, finally, draw logical questions and conclusions.

> Barbara Neller
> Middle School
> Social Studies

Critical thinking is a systematic, logical approach to life in which an individual, using this method, truly learns and understands a concept rather than imitates or mimics. Knowledge and intellectual growth are achieved by a variety of strategies which include examining a variety of viewpoints, making assumptions based on viable evidence and forming well thought out conclusions.

> Jane S. Thorne
> High School
> Math

Critical thinking allows students to become active participants in their learning. Socratic dialogue stimulates communication between teacher and students, thus creating an atmosphere where everyone is encouraged to become risk-takers. A teacher needs to become a model of critical thinking for the students. Through this interaction, content can be analyzed, synthesized, and evaluated with thinking.

> Carol Thanos
> Grade 6

Critical thinking is the complex process of exploring an issue, concept, term, or experience which requires verbal as well as non-verbal involvement from the participant. It involves listing ideas related to the subject, so that the person involved can objectively examine the relationship of the ideas thought of. It demands that the person involved in the process investigates the issue, concept, or process from varied vantage points, in order that intuitions, assumptions, and conclusions are presented with reasoned opinions or experienced evidences. Critical thinking is a task that involves the participant's in-depth assessment of his or her body of knowledge, experience, and emotions on the subject in question.

Ariel Collins
High School
Language Arts

Critical thinking is thinking that is clear, fairminded, and directed. It is not sloppy or self-serving thinking, but deep and probing thought aimed at finding the truth. It is skillful thinking aimed at genuine understanding, not superficial head-shaking. It is the tool used by and descriptive of an educated person whose mantra would be "veritas".

Helen Cook
Middle School
Science

Critical thinking is a process of questioning and seeking truth and clarity. It is a continual endeavor as one is constantly exposed to new knowledge which must be reconciled with prior conclusions. As one's body of knowledge grows, it is all the more important to be able to critically consider and determine what is truth.

Critical thinking demands certain prerequisites: openmindedness, willingness to withhold snap judgments, commitment to exploring new ideas. The development of such qualities empowers me to participate in the various facets of critical thinking, e.g., clarifying ideas, engaging in Socratic discussions. These skills are not nearly so difficult as achieving the mindset which must precede them. Only a commitment to question and persevere and honestly pursue truth will supply the impetus necessary to delve beneath the surface of issues and concepts. Yet this predisposition is difficult to achieve, because it necessitates taking risks, making mistakes, being wrong, and being corrected — activities very threatening to our safe ego-boundaries.

Only in transcending these ego-boundaries does growth occur and genuine learning transpire. Critical thinking is comprised of a sense of wonderment, daring, and determination. It is undergirded by a value for truth and personal growth. It is the continual learning process of the individual.

Deborah Norton
High School
Social Studies

The definition of critical thinking that I now hold is one that explains some things that I have felt for some time. I am convinced that everything that I know, that is a part of my education, I have figured or found out for myself. I have had close to twenty years of formal, didactic education, but I could tell you very little about anything that was presented to me in lecture through all those classes, except perhaps some trivia. In college, I did my real learning through the writing that I did, either from research or from contemplation. I have felt that this was true, but a lot of my own teaching has continued to be didactic and students have learned to be very accepting and non-questioning and to expect to be told what the right answer is, what someone else has decided the right answer is. I hope that I can change that now. I now feel that it is imperative that my students learn to be critical thinkers, and I hope that I can model that belief and, through all my activities in class, lead them in that direction. We all need to be openminded, to realize that there are often many sides to a problem, many points of view, and that there are strategies and techniques for analyzing, making decisions, and making learning our own. I want to be, and I want my students to be, questioning, openminded, fairminded, synthesizing individuals — in other words, critical thinkers.

Liza Burton
High School
Language Arts

Chapter 41

Glossary:
An Educator's Guide to
Critical Thinking Terms and Concepts

with A. J. A. Binker

accurate: Free from errors, mistakes, or distortion. *Correct* connotes little more than absence of error; *accurate* implies a positive exercise of one to obtain conformity with fact or truth; *exact* stresses perfect conformity to fact, truth, or some standard; *precise* suggests minute accuracy of detail. Accuracy is an important goal in critical thinking, though it is almost always a matter of degree. It is also important to recognize that making mistakes is an essential part of learning and that it is far better that students make their own mistakes, than that they parrot the thinking of the text or teacher. It should also be recognized that some distortion usually results whenever we think within a point of view or frame of reference. Students should think with this awareness in mind, with some sense of the limitations of their own, the text's, the teacher's, the subject's perspective. See *perfections of thought.*

ambiguous: A sentence having two or more possible meanings. Sensitivity to ambiguity and vagueness in writing and speech is essential to good thinking. *A continual effort to be clear and precise in language usage is fundamental to education.* Ambiguity is a problem more of sentences than of individual words. Furthermore, not every sentence that can be construed in more than one way is problematic and deserving of analysis. Many sentences are clearly intended one way; any other construal is obviously absurd and not meant. For example, "Make me a sandwich." is never seriously intended to request metamorphic change. It is a poor example for teaching genuine insight into critical thinking. For an example of a problematic ambiguity, consider the statement, "Welfare is corrupt." Among the possible meanings of this sentence are the following: Those who administer welfare programs take bribes to administer welfare policy unfairly; Welfare policies are written in such a way that much of the money goes to people who don't deserve it rather than to those who do; A government that gives money to people who haven't earned it corrupts both the giver and the recipient. If two people are arguing about whether or not welfare is corrupt, but interpret the claim differently, they can make little or no progress; they aren't arguing about the same point. Evidence and considerations relevant to one interpretation may be irrelevant to others.

analyze: To break up a whole into its parts, to examine in detail so as to determine the nature of, to look more deeply into an issue or situation. *All learning presupposes some analysis of what we are learning,* if only by categorizing or labelling things in one way rather than another. Students should continually be asked to analyze their ideas, claims, experiences, interpretations, judgments, and theories and those they hear and read. See *elements of thought.*

argue: There are two meanings of this word that need to be distinguished: *1)* to argue in the sense of *to fight* or to emotionally disagree; and *2)* to give reasons for or against a proposal or proposition. In emphasizing critical thinking, we continually try to get our students to move from the first sense of the word to the second; that is, we try to get them to see the importance of *giving reasons* to support their views without getting their egos involved in what they are saying. This is a fundamental problem in human life. To argue in the critical thinking sense is to use logic and reason, and to bring forth facts to support or refute a point. It is done in a spirit of cooperation and good will.

argument: A reason or reasons offered for or against something, the offering of such reasons. This term refers to a discussion in which there is disagreement and suggests the use of logic and bringing forth of facts to support or refute a point. See *argue.*

to assume: To take for granted or to presuppose. Critical thinkers can and do make their assumptions explicit, assess them, and correct them. Assumptions can vary from the mundane to the problematic: I heard a scratch at the door. I got up to let the cat in. I assumed that only the cat makes that noise, and that he makes it only when he wants to be let in. Someone speaks gruffly to me. I feel guilty and hurt. I assume he is angry *at me,* that he is only angry at me when I do something bad, and that if he's angry at me, he dislikes me. *Notice that people often equate making assumptions with making false assumptions.* When people say, "Don't assume", this is what they mean. In fact, we cannot avoid making assumptions and some are justifiable. (We have assumed that people who buy this book can read English.) Rather than saying "Never assume", we say, "Be aware of and careful about the assumptions you make, and be ready to examine and critique them." See *assumption, elements of thought.*

assumption: A statement accepted or supposed as true without proof or demonstration; an unstated premise or belief. *All human thought and experience is based on assumptions.* Our thought must begin with something we take to be true in a particular context. We are typically unaware of what we assume and therefore rarely question our assumptions. Much of what is wrong with human thought can be found in the uncritical or unexamined assumptions that underlie it. For example, we often experience the world in such a way as to assume that we are observing things just as they are, as though we were seeing the world without the filter of a point of view. People we disagree with, of course, we recognize as *having a point of view.* One of the key dispositions of critical thinking is the on-going sense that as humans we always think within a perspective, that we virtually never experience things totally and absolutistically. There is a connection therefore between thinking so as to be *aware of our assumptions* and being *intellectually humble.*

authority: *1)* The power or supposed right to give commands, enforce obedience, take action, or make final decisions. *2)* A person with much knowledge and expertise in a field, hence reliable. Critical thinkers recognize that ultimate authority rests with reason and evidence, since it is only on the assumption that purported experts have the backing of reason and evidence that they rightfully gain authority. Much instruction discourages critical thinking by encouraging students to believe that whatever the text or teacher says is true. As a result, students do not learn how to assess authority. See *knowledge.*

bias: A mental leaning or inclination. We must clearly distinguish two different senses of the word 'bias'. One is neutral, the other negative. In the neutral sense we are referring simply to the fact that, *because of one's point of view, one notices some things rather than others,* emphasizes some points rather than others, and thinks in one direction rather than others. This is not in itself a criticism because *thinking within a point of view is unavoidable.* In the negative sense, we are implying *blindness or irrational resistance to weaknesses within one's own point of view* or to the strength or insight within a point of view one opposes. Fairminded critical thinkers try to be aware of their bias (in sense one) and try hard to avoid bias (in sense two). Many people confuse these two senses. Many confuse bias with emotion or with evaluation, perceiving any expression of emotion or any use of evaluative words to be biased (sense two). Evaluative words that can be justified by reason and evidence are not biased in the negative sense. See *criteria, evaluation, judgment, opinion.*

clarify: To make easier to understand, to free from confusion or ambiguity, to remove obscurities. *Clarity* is a fundamental perfection of thought and *clarification* a fundamental aim in critical thinking. Students often do not see why it is important to write and speak clearly, why it is so important to *say what you mean and mean what you say*. The key to clarification is *concrete, specific* examples. See *accurate, ambiguous, logic of language, vague.*

concept: An idea or thought, especially a generalized idea of a thing or of a class of things. Humans think within concepts or ideas. *We can never achieve command over our thoughts unless we learn how to achieve command over our concepts or ideas.* Thus we must learn how to identify the concepts or ideas we are using, contrast them with alternative concepts or ideas, and clarify what we include and exclude by means of them. For example, most people say they believe strongly in democracy, but few can clarify with examples what that word does and does not imply. *Most people confuse the meaning of words with cultural associations,* with the result that 'democracy' means to people whatever we do in running our government — any country that is different is undemocratic. We must distinguish the concepts implicit in the English language from the psychological associations surrounding that concept in a given social group or culture. The failure to develop this ability is a major cause of uncritical thought and selfish critical thought. See *logic of language.*

conclude/conclusion: To decide by reasoning, to infer, to deduce. The last step in a reasoning process. A judgment, decision, or belief formed after investigation or reasoning. All beliefs, decisions, or actions are based on human thought, but rarely as the result of conscious reasoning or deliberation. *All that we believe is,* one way or another, *based on conclusions* that we have come to during our lifetime. Yet, we rarely monitor our thought processes, we don't critically assess the conclusions we come to, to determine whether we have sufficient grounds or reasons for accepting them. People seldom recognize when they have come to a conclusion. They confuse their conclusions with evidence, and so cannot assess the reasoning that took them from evidence to conclusion. Recognizing that *human life is inferential,* that we continually come to conclusions about ourselves and the things and persons around us, is essential to thinking critically and reflectively.

consistency: To think, act, or speak in agreement with what has already been thought, done, or expressed; to have intellectual or moral integrity. Human life and thought is filled with inconsistency, hypocrisy, and contradiction. We often say one thing and do another, judge ourselves and our friends by one standard and our antagonists by another, lean over backwards to justify what we want or negate what does not serve our interests. Similarly, we often confuse desires with needs, treating our desires as equivalent to needs, putting what we want above the basic needs of others. *Logical and moral consistency are fundamental values of fairminded critical thinking.* Social conditioning and native egocentrism often obscure social contradictions, inconsistency, and hypocrisy. See *personal contradiction, social contradiction, intellectual integrity, human nature.*

contradict/contradiction: To assert the opposite of; to be contrary to, go against; a statement in opposition to another; a condition in which things tend to be contrary to each other; inconsistency; discrepancy; a person or thing containing or composed of contradictory elements. See *personal contradiction, social contradiction.*

criterion (criteria, pl): A standard, rule, or test by which something can be judged or measured. Human life, thought, and action are based on human values. The standards by which we determine whether those values are achieved in any situation represent criteria. Critical thinking depends upon making explicit the standards or criteria for rational or justifiable thinking and behavior. See *evaluation.*

critical listening: A mode of monitoring how we are listening so as to maximize our accurate understanding of what another person is saying. By understanding the logic of human communication — that *everything spoken expresses point of view,* uses some ideas and not others, has implications, etc. — critical thinkers can listen so as to enter sympathetically and analytically into the perspective of others. See *critical speaking, critical reading, critical writing, elements of thought, intellectual empathy.*

critical person: One who has mastered a range of intellectual skills and abilities. If that person generally uses those skills to advance his or her own selfish interests, that person is a critical thinker only in a weak or qualified sense. If that person generally uses those skills fairmindedly, entering empathically into the points of view of others, he or she is a critical thinker in the strong or fullest sense. See *critical thinking.*

critical reading: *Critical reading is an active, intellectually engaged process* in which the reader participates in an inner dialogue with the writer. Most people read uncritically and so miss some part of what is expressed while distorting other parts. A critical reader realizes the way in which *reading, by its very nature, means entering into a point of view other than our own,* the point of view of the writer. A critical reader actively looks for assumptions, key concepts and ideas, reasons and justifications, supporting examples, parallel experiences, implications and consequences, and any other structural features of the written text, to interpret and assess it accurately and fairly. See *elements of thought.*

critical society: A society which rewards adherence to the values of critical thinking and hence *does not use indoctrination and inculcation as basic modes of learning* (rewards reflective questioning, intellectual independence, and reasoned dissent). Socrates is not the only thinker to imagine a society in which independent critical thought became embodied in the concrete day-to-day lives of individuals; William Graham Sumner, North America's distinguished anthropologist, explicitly formulated the ideal:

> The critical habit of thought, if usual in a society, will pervade all its mores, because it is a way of taking up the problems of life. Men educated in it cannot be stampeded by stump orators and are never deceived by dithyrambic oratory. They are slow to believe. They can hold things as possible or probable in all degrees, without certainty and without pain. They can wait for evidence and weigh evidence, uninfluenced by the emphasis or confidence with which assertions are made on one side or the other. They can resist appeals to their dearest prejudices and all kinds of cajolery. Education in the critical faculty is the only education of which it can be truly said that it makes good citizens. (Folkways, 1906)

Until critical habits of thought pervade our society, however, there will be a tendency for schools as social institutions to transmit the prevailing world view more or less uncritically, to transmit it as reality, not as a picture of reality. Education for critical thinking, then, requires that the school or classroom become a microcosm of a critical society. See *didactic instruction, dialogical instruction, intellectual virtues, knowledge.*

critical thinking: 1) Disciplined, self-directed thinking which exemplifies the perfections of thinking appropriate to a particular mode or domain of thinking. 2) Thinking that displays mastery of intellectual skills and abilities. 3) The art of thinking about your thinking while you are thinking in order to make your thinking better: more clear, more accurate, or more defensible. Critical thinking can be distinguished into two forms: "selfish" or "sophistic", on the one hand, and "fairminded", on the other. In thinking critically we use our command of the elements of thinking to adjust our thinking successfully to the logical demands of a type or mode of thinking. See *critical person, critical society, critical reading, critical listening, critical writing, perfections of thought, elements of thought, domains of thought, intellectual virtues.*

critical writing: To express oneself in language requires that one arrange ideas in some relationships to each other. When accuracy and truth are at issue, then we must understand what our thesis is, how we can support it, how we can elaborate it to make it intelligible to others, what objections can be raised to it from other points of view, what the limitations are to our point of view, and so forth. *Disciplined writing requires disciplined thinking; disciplined thinking is achieved through disciplined writing.* See *critical listening, critical reading, logic of language.*

critique: An objective judging, analysis, or evaluation of something. The purpose of critique is the same as the purpose of critical thinking: to appreciate strengths as well as weakness, virtues as well as failings. *Critical thinkers critique in order to redesign, remodel, and make better.*

cultural association: Undisciplined thinking often reflects associations, personal and cultural, absorbed or uncritically formed. If a person who was cruel to me as a child had a particular tone of voice, I may find myself disliking a person who has the same tone of voice. Media advertising juxtaposes and joins logically unrelated things to influence our buying habits. Raised in a particular country or within a particular group within it, we form any number of mental links which, if they remain unexamined, unduly influence our thinking. See *concept, critical society.*

cultural assumption: Unassessed (often implicit) belief adopted by virtue of upbringing in a society. Raised in a society, we unconsciously take on its point of view, values, beliefs, and practices. At the root of each of these are many kinds of assumptions. Not knowing that we perceive, conceive, think, and experience within assumptions we have taken in, we take ourselves to be perceiving "things as they are", not "things as they appear from a cultural vantage point". Becoming aware of our cultural assumptions so that we might critically examine them is a crucial dimension of critical thinking. It is, however, a dimension almost totally absent from schooling. Lip service to this ideal is common enough; a realistic emphasis is virtually unheard of. See *ethnocentricity, prejudice, social contradiction.*

data: Facts, figures, or information from which conclusions can be inferred, or upon which interpretations or theories can be based. As critical thinkers we must make certain to distinguish hard data from the inferences or conclusions we draw from them.

dialectical thinking: Dialogical thinking (thinking within more than one perspective) conducted to test the strengths and weaknesses of opposing points of view. (Court trials and debates are, in a sense, dialectical.) When thinking dialectically, reasoners pit two or more opposing points of view in competition with each other, developing each by providing support, raising objections, countering those objections, raising further objections, and so on. Dialectical thinking or discussion can be conducted so as to "win" by defeating the positions one disagrees with — using critical insight to support one's own view and point out flaws in other views (associated with critical thinking in the restricted or weak sense), or fairmindedly, by conceding points that don't stand up to critique, trying to integrate or incorporate strong points found in other views, and using critical insight to develop a fuller and more accurate view (associated with critical thinking in the fuller or strong sense). See *monological problems.*

dialogical instruction: Instruction that fosters dialogical or dialectic thinking. Thus, when considering a question, the class brings all relevant subjects to bear and considers the perspectives of groups whose views are not canvassed in their texts — for example, "What did King George think of the *Declaration of Independence,* the Revolutionary War, the Continental Congress, Jefferson and Washington, etc.?" or, "How would an economist analyze this situation? A historian? A psychologist? A geographer?" See *critical society, didactic instruction, higher order learning, lower order learning, Socratic questioning, knowledge.*

dialogical thinking: Thinking that involves a dialogue or extended exchange between different points of view or frames of reference. Students learn best in dialogical situations, in circumstances in which they continually express their views to others and try to fit other's views into their own. See *Socratic questioning, monological thinking, multilogical thinking, dialectical thinking.*

didactic instruction: Teaching by telling. In didactic instruction the teacher directly tells the student what to believe and think about a subject. The students' task is to remember what the teacher said and reproduce it on demand. In its most common form, this mode of teaching falsely assumes that one can directly give a person knowledge without that person having to think his or her way to it. It falsely assumes that knowledge can be separated from understanding and justification. It confuses the ability to *state* a principle with *understanding* it, the ability to *supply* a definition with *knowing* a new word, and the act of *saying* that something is important with *recognizing* its importance. See *critical society, knowledge.*

domains of thought: Thinking can be oriented or structured with different issues or purposes in view. *Thinking varies in accordance with purpose and issue.* Critical thinkers learn to discipline their thinking to take into account the nature of the issue or domain. We see this most clearly when we consider the difference between issues and thinking within different academic disciplines or subject areas. Hence mathematical thinking is quite different from, say, historical thinking. Mathematics and history, we can say then, represent different domains of thought. See the *logic of questions.*

egocentricity: A tendency to view everything in relationship to oneself; to confuse immediate perception (how things *seem)* with reality. One's desires, values, and beliefs (seeming to be self-evidently correct or superior to those of others) are often uncritically used as the norm of all judgment and experience. Egocentricity is one of the fundamental impediments to critical thinking. As one learns to think critically in a strong sense, one learns to become more rational, in contrast to being egocentric. See *human nature, strong sense critical thinker, ethnocentrism, sociocentrism, personal contradiction.*

elements of thought: All thought has a universal set of elements, each of which can be monitored for possible problems: Are we clear about our *purpose or goal?* about the *problem or question at issue?* about our *point of view or frame of reference?* about our *assumptions?* about the *claims* we are making? about the *reasons or evidence* upon which we are basing our claims? about our *inferences and line of reasoning?* about the *implications and consequences* that follow from our reasoning? Critical thinkers develop skills of identifying and assessing these elements in their thinking and in the thinking of others.

emotion: A feeling aroused to the point of awareness, often a strong feeling or state of excitement. When our egocentric emotions or feelings get involved, when we are excited by infantile anger, fear, jealousy, etc., our objectivity often decreases. Critical thinkers need to be able to monitor their egocentric feelings and use their rational passions to reason themselves into feelings appropriate to the situation as it really is, rather than to how it seems to their infantile ego. Emotions and feelings themselves are not irrational; however, it is common for people to feel strongly when their ego is stimulated. One way to understand the goal of strong sense critical thinking is as the attempt to develop rational feelings and emotions at the expense of irrational, egocentric ones. See *rational passions, intellectual virtues.*

empirical: Relying or based on experiment, observation, or experience rather than on theory or meaning. *It is important to continually distinguish those considerations based on experiment, observation, or experience from those based on the meaning of a word or concept or the implications of a theory.* One common form of uncritical or selfish critical thinking involves distorting facts or experience in order to preserve a preconceived meaning or theory. For example, a conservative may distort the facts that support a liberal perspective to prevent empirical evidence from counting against a theory of the world that he or she holds rigidly. Indeed, within all perspectives and belief systems many will distort the facts before they will admit to a weakness in their favorite theory or belief. See *data, fact, evidence.*

empirical implication: That which follows from a situation or fact, not due to the logic of language, but from experience or scientific law. The redness of the coil on the stove empirically implies dangerous heat.

ethnocentricity: A tendency to view one's own race or culture as central, based on the deep-seated belief that one's own group is superior to all others. Ethnocentrism is a form of egocentrism extended from the self to the group. Much uncritical or selfish critical thinking is either egocentric or ethnocentric in nature. ('Ethnocentrism' and 'sociocentrism' are used synonymously, for the most part, though 'sociocentricity' is broader, relating to *any* group, including, for example, sociocentricity regarding one's profession.) The "cure" for ethnocentrism or sociocentrism is empathic thought within the perspective of opposing groups and cultures. Such empathic thought is rarely cultivated in the societies and schools of today. Instead, many people develop an empty rhetoric of tolerance, saying that others have different beliefs and ways, but without seriously considering those beliefs and ways, what they mean to those others, and their reasons for maintaining them.

evaluation: To judge or determine the worth or quality of. *Evaluation has a logic and should be carefully distinguished from mere subjective preference.* The elements of its logic may be put in the form of questions which may be asked whenever an evaluation is to be carried out: *1)* Are we clear about *what precisely we are evaluating?; 2)* Are we clear about *our purpose?* Is our purpose legitimate?; *3)* Given our purpose, what are the *relevant criteria or standards* for evaluation?; *4)* Do we have *sufficient information* about that which we are evaluating? Is that *information relevant to the purpose?;* and *5)* Have we *applied our criteria accurately and fairly to the facts* as we know them? Uncritical thinkers often treat evaluation as mere preference or treat their evaluative judgments as direct observations not admitting of error.

evidence: The data on which a judgment or conclusion might be based or by which proof or probability might be established. Critical thinkers distinguish the evidence or raw data upon which they base their interpretations or conclusions from the inferences and assumptions that connect data to conclusions. Uncritical thinkers treat their conclusions as something given to them in experience, as something they directly observe in the world. As a result, they find it difficult to see why anyone might disagree with their conclusions. After all, the truth of their views is, they believe, right there for everyone to see! Such people find it difficult or even impossible to describe the evidence or experience without coloring that description with their interpretation.

explicit: Clearly stated and leaving nothing implied; *explicit* is applied to that which is so clearly stated or distinctly set forth that there should be no doubt as to the meaning; *exact and precise* in this connection both suggest that which is strictly defined, accurately stated, or made unmistakably clear; *definite* implies precise limitations as to the nature, character, meaning, etc. of something; *specific* implies the pointing up of details or the particularizing of references. Critical thinking often requires the ability to be explicit, exact, definite, and specific. Most students cannot make what is implicit in their thinking explicit. This deficiency affects their ability to monitor and assess their thinking.

fact: What actually happened, what is true; verifiable by empirical means; distinguished from interpretation, inference, judgment, or conclusion; the raw data. There are distinct senses of the word 'factual:' "True", (as opposed to "claimed to be true"); and "empirical" (as opposed to conceptual or evaluative). You may make many "factual claims" in one sense, that is, claims which can be verified or disproven by observation or empirical study, but I must evaluate those claims to determine if they are true. People often confuse these two senses, even to the point of accepting as true, statements which merely "seem factual", for example, "29.23 % of Americans suffer from depression." Before I accept this as true, I should assess it. I should ask such questions as "How do you know? How *could* this be known? Did you merely ask people if they were depressed and extrapolate those results? How exactly did you arrive at this figure?" Purported facts should be assessed for their accuracy, completeness, and relevance to the issue. Sources of purported facts should be assessed for their qualifications, track records, and impartiality. Education which stresses retention and repetition of factual claims stunts students' desire and ability to assess alleged facts, leaving them open to manipulation. Activities in which students are asked to "distinguish fact from opinion" often confuse these two senses. They encourage students to accept *as true* statements which merely "look like" facts. See *intellectual humility, knowledge.*

fair: Treating both or all sides alike, without reference to one's own feelings or interests; *just* implies adherence to a standard of rightness or lawfulness without reference to one's own inclinations; *impartial* and *unbiased* both imply freedom from prejudice for or against any side; *dispassionate* implies the absence of passion or strong emotion, hence, connotes cool, disinterested judgment; *objective* implies a viewing of persons or things without reference to oneself, one's interests, etc.

faith: *1)* Unquestioning belief in anything. *2)* Confidence, trust, or reliance. A critical thinker does not accept faith in the first sense, for every belief is reached on the basis of some thinking, which may or may not be justified. Even in religion one believes in one religion rather than another, and in doing so implies that there are good reasons for accepting one rather than another. A Christian, for example, believes that there are good reasons for not being an atheist, and Christians often attempt to persuade non-Christians to change their beliefs. In some sense, then, everyone has confidence in the capacity of his or her own mind to judge rightly on the basis of good reasons, and does not believe simply on the basis of blind faith.

fallacy/fallacious: An error in reasoning; flaw or defect in argument; an argument which doesn't conform to rules of good reasoning (especially one that appears to be sound). Containing or based on a fallacy; deceptive in appearance or meaning; misleading; delusive.

higher order learning: Learning through exploring the foundations, justification, implications, and value of a fact, principle, skill, or concept. *Learning so as to deeply understand.* One can learn in keeping with the rational capacities of the human mind or in keeping with its irrational propensities, cultivating the capacity of the human mind to discipline and direct its thought through commitment to intellectual standards, or one can learn through mere association. Education for critical thought produces higher order learning by helping students actively think their way to conclusions; discuss their thinking with other students and the teacher; entertain a variety of points of view; analyze concepts, theories, and explanations in their own terms; actively question the meaning and implications of what they learn; compare what they learn to what they have experienced; take what they read and write seriously; solve non-routine problems; examine assumptions; and gather and assess evidence. Students should learn each subject by engaging in thought within that subject. They should learn history by thinking historically, mathematics by thinking mathematically, etc. See *dialogical instruction, lower order learning, critical society, knowledge, principle, domains of thought.*

human nature: The common qualities of all human beings. People have both a primary and a secondary nature. Our primary nature is spontaneous, egocentric, and strongly prone to irrational belief formation. It is the basis for our instinctual thought. People need no training to believe what they want to believe: what serves their immediate interests, what preserves their sense of personal comfort and righteousness, what minimizes their sense of inconsistency, and what presupposes their own correctness. People need no special training to believe what those around them believe: what their parents and friends believe, what is taught to them by religious and school authorities, what is repeated often by the media, and what is commonly believed in the nation in which they are raised. People need no training to think that those who disagree with them are wrong and probably prejudiced. People need no training to assume that their own most fundamental beliefs are self-evidently true or easily justified by evidence. People naturally and spontaneously identify with their own beliefs, and experience most disagreement as personal attack. The resulting defensiveness interferes with their capacity to empathize with or enter into other points of view.

On the other hand, *people need extensive and systematic practice to develop their secondary nature, their implicit capacity to function as rational persons.* They need extensive and systematic practice to recognize the tendencies they have to form irrational beliefs. They need extensive practice to develop a dislike of inconsistency, a love of clarity, a passion to seek reasons and evidence and to be fair to points of view other than their own. People need extensive practice to recognize that they indeed have a point of view, that they live inferentially, that they do not have a direct pipeline to reality, that it is perfectly possible to have an overwhelming inner sense of the correctness of one's views and still be wrong. See *intellectual virtues.*

idea: Anything existing in the mind as an object of knowledge or thought; *concept* refers to generalized idea of a class of objects, based on knowledge of particular instances of the class; *conception,* often equivalent to concept, specifically refers to something conceived in the mind or imagined; *thought* refers to any idea, whether or not expressed, that occurs to the mind in reasoning or contemplation; *notion* implies vagueness or incomplete intention; *impression* also implies vagueness of an idea provoked by some external stimulus. Critical thinkers are aware of what ideas they are using in their thinking, where those ideas came from, and how to assess them. See *clarify, concept, logic, logic of language.*

imply/implication: A claim or truth which follows from other claims or truths. One of the most important skills of critical thinking is the ability to distinguish between what is actually implied by a statement or situation from what may be carelessly inferred by people. Critical thinkers try to *monitor their inferences to keep them in line with what is actually implied* by what they know. When speaking, critical thinkers *try to use words that imply only what they can legitimately justify.* They recognize that there are established word usages which generate established implications. To say of an act that it is murder, for example, is to imply that it is unjustified. See *clarify, precision, logic of language, critical listening, critical reading, elements of thought.*

infer/inference: An inference is a step of the mind, an intellectual act by which one concludes that something is so in light of something else's being so, or seeming to be so. If you come at me with a knife in your hand, I would probably infer that you mean to do me harm. Inferences can be strong or weak, justified or unjustified. Inferences are based upon assumptions. See *imply/implication.*

insight: The ability to see and clearly and deeply understand the inner nature of things. Instruction for critical thinking fosters insight rather than mere performance; it cultivates the achievement of deeper knowledge and understanding through insight. *Thinking one's way into and through a subject leads to insights* as one synthesizes what one is learning, relating one subject to other subjects and all subjects to personal experience. Rarely is insight formulated as a goal in present curricula and texts. See *dialogical instruction, higher order learning, lower order learning, didactic instruction, intellectual humility.*

intellectual autonomy: Having rational control of ones beliefs, values, and inferences. The ideal of critical thinking is to learn to think for oneself, to gain command over one's thought processes. Intellectual autonomy does not entail willfulness, stubbornness, or rebellion. It entails a commitment to analyzing and evaluating beliefs on the basis of reason and evidence, to question when it is rational to question, to believe when it is rational to believe, and to conform when it is rational to conform. See *know, knowledge.*

(intellectual) confidence in reason: Confidence that in the long run *one's own higher interests and those of humankind at large will best be served by giving the freest play to reason* — by encouraging people to come to their own conclusions through a process of developing their own rational faculties; faith that (with proper encouragement and cultivation) people can learn to think for themselves, form rational viewpoints, draw reasonable conclusions, think coherently and logically, persuade each other by reason, and become reasonable, despite the deep-seated obstacles in the native character of the human mind and in society. Confidence in reason is developed through experiences in which one reasons one's way to insight, solves problems through reason, uses reason to persuade, is persuaded by reason. Confidence in reason is undermined when one is expected to perform tasks without understanding why, to repeat statements without having verified or justified them, to accept beliefs on the sole basis of authority or social pressure.

intellectual courage: The willingness to face and fairly assess ideas, beliefs, or viewpoints to which we have not given a serious hearing, regardless of our strong negative reactions to them. This courage arises from the recognition that *ideas considered dangerous or absurd are sometimes rationally justified* (in whole or in part), and that *conclusions or beliefs espoused by those around us or inculcated in us are sometimes false or misleading.* To determine for ourselves which is which, we must not passively and uncritically "accept" what we have "learned". Intellectual courage comes into play here, because inevitably we will come to see some truth in some ideas considered dangerous and absurd and some distortion or falsity in some ideas strongly held in our social group. It takes courage to be true to our own thinking in such circumstances. Examining cherished beliefs is difficult, and the penalties for non-conformity are often severe.

intellectual empathy: Understanding the need to imaginatively put oneself in the place of others to genuinely understand them. We must recognize our egocentric tendency to identify truth with our immediate perceptions or longstanding beliefs. Intellectual empathy correlates with the ability to accurately reconstruct the viewpoints and reasoning of others and to *reason from premises, assumptions, and ideas other than our own.* This trait also requires that we remember occasions when we were wrong, despite an intense conviction that we were right, and consider that we might be similarly deceived in a case at hand.

intellectual humility: Awareness of the limits of one's knowledge, including sensitivity to circumstances in which one's native egocentrism is likely to function self-deceptively; sensitivity to bias and prejudice in, and limitations of one's viewpoint. Intellectual humility is based on the recognition that *no one should claim more than he or she actually knows.* It does not imply spinelessness or submissiveness. It implies the lack of intellectual pretentiousness, boastfulness, or conceit, combined with insight into the strengths or weaknesses of the logical foundations of one's beliefs.

intellectual integrity: Recognition of the need to be true to one's own thinking, to be consistent in the intellectual standards one applies, to hold oneself to the same rigorous standards of evidence and proof to which one holds one's antagonists, to practice what one advocates for others, and to honestly admit discrepancies and inconsistencies in one's own thought and action. This trait develops best in a supportive atmosphere in which people feel secure and free enough to honestly acknowledge their inconsistencies, and can develop and share realistic ways of ameliorating them. It requires honest acknowledgment of the difficulties of achieving greater consistency.

intellectual perseverance: Willingness and consciousness of the need to pursue intellectual insights and truths despite difficulties, obstacles, and frustrations; firm adherence to rational principles despite irrational opposition of others; a sense of the need to struggle with confusion and unsettled questions over an extended period of time in order to achieve deeper understanding or insight. This trait is undermined when teachers and others continually provide the answers, do students' thinking for them or substitute easy tricks, algorithms, and short cuts for careful, independent thought.

intellectual sense of justice: Willingness and consciousness of the need to entertain all viewpoints sympathetically and to assess them with the same intellectual standards, without reference to one's own feelings or vested interests, or the feelings or vested interests of one's friends, community, or nation; implies adherence to intellectual standards without reference to one's own advantage or the advantage of one's group.

intellectual virtues: The traits of mind and character necessary for right action and thinking; the traits of mind and character essential for fairminded rationality; the traits that distinguish the narrowminded, self-serving critical thinker from the openminded, truth-seeking critical thinker. These *intellectual traits are interdependent.* Each is best developed while developing the others as well. They cannot be imposed from without; they must be cultivated by encouragement and example. People can come to deeply understand and accept these principles by analyzing their experiences of them: learning from an unfamiliar perspective, discovering you don't know as much as you thought, and so on. They include: intellectual sense of justice, intellectual perseverance, intellectual integrity, intellectual humility, intellectual empathy, intellectual courage, (intellectual) confidence in reason, and intellectual autonomy.

interpret/interpretation: To give one's own conception of, to place in the context of one's own experience, perspective, point of view, or philosophy. Interpretations should be distinguished from the facts, the evidence, the situation. (I may interpret someone's silence as an expression of hostility toward me. Such an interpretation may or may not be correct. I may have projected my patterns of motivation and behavior onto that person, or I may have accurately noticed this pattern in the other.) The best interpretations take the most evidence into account. Critical thinkers recognize their interpretations, distinguish them from evidence, consider alternative interpretations, and reconsider their interpretations in the light of new evidence. *All learning involves personal interpretation, since whatever we learn we must integrate into our own thinking and action.* What we learn must be given a meaning by us, must be meaningful to us, and hence involves interpretive acts on our part. Didactic instruction, in attempting to directly implant knowledge in students' minds, typically ignores the role of personal interpretation in learning.

intuition: The direct knowing or learning of something without the conscious use of reasoning. We sometimes seem to know or learn things without recognizing how we came to that knowledge. When this occurs, we experience an inner sense that what we believe is true. The problem is that sometimes we are correct (and have genuinely experienced an intuition) and sometimes we are incorrect (having fallen victim to one of our prejudices). A critical thinker does not blindly accept that what one thinks or believes but cannot account for is necessarily true. A critical thinker realizes how easily we confuse intuitions and prejudices. Critical thinkers may follow their inner sense that something is so, but only with a healthy sense of intellectual humility.

irrational/irrationality: 1) Lacking the power to reason. 2) Contrary to reason or logic. 3) Senseless, absurd. Uncritical thinkers have failed to develop the ability or power to reason well. Their beliefs and practices, then, are often contrary to reason and logic, and are sometimes senseless or absurd. It is important to recognize, however, that in societies with irrational beliefs and practices, it is not clear whether challenging those beliefs and practices — and therefore possibly endangering oneself — is rational or irrational. Furthermore, suppose one's vested interests are best advanced by adopting beliefs and practices that are contrary to reason. Is it then rational to follow reason and negate one's vested interests or follow one's interests and ignore reason? These very real dilemmas of everyday life represent on-going problems for critical thinkers. Selfish critical thinkers, of course, face no dilemma here because of their consistent commitment to advance their narrow vested interests. Fairminded critical thinkers make these decisions self-consciously and honestly assess the results.

irrational learning: All rational learning presupposes rational assent. And, though we sometimes forget it, not all learning is automatically or even commonly rational. *Much that we learn in everyday life is quite distinctively irrational.* It is quite possible — and indeed the bulk of human learning is unfortunately of this character — *to come to believe any number of things without knowing how or why.* It is quite possible, in other words, to believe for irrational reasons: because those around us believe, because we are rewarded for believing, because we are afraid to disbelieve, because our vested interest is served by belief, because we are more comfortable with belief, or because we have ego identified ourselves, our image, or our personal being with belief. In all of these cases, our beliefs are without rational grounding, without good reason and evidence, without the foundation a rational person demands. We become rational, on the other hand, to the extent that our beliefs and actions are grounded in good reasons and evidence; to the extent that we recognize and critique our own irrationality; to the extent that we are not moved by bad reasons and a multiplicity of irrational motives, fears, and desires; to the extent that we have cultivated a passion for clarity, accuracy, and fairmindedness. These global skills, passions, and dispositions, integrated into behavior and thought, characterize the rational, the educated, and the critical person. See *higher and lower order learning, knowledge, didactic instruction.*

judgment: *1)* The act of judging or deciding. *2)* Understanding and good sense. A person has good judgment when they typically judge and decide on the basis of understanding and good sense. Whenever we form a belief or opinion, make a decision, or act, we do so on the basis of implicit or explicit judgments. All thought presupposes making judgments concerning what is so and what is not so, what is true and what is not. To cultivate people's ability to think critically is to foster their judgment, to help them to develop the habit of judging on the basis of reason, evidence, logic, and good sense. Good judgment is developed, not by merely learning about principles of good judgment, but by frequent practice judging and assessing judgments.

justify/justification: The act of showing a belief, opinion, action, or policy to be in accord with reason and evidence, to be ethically acceptable, or both. Education should foster reasonability in students. This requires that both teachers and students develop the disposition to ask for and give justifications for beliefs, opinions, actions, and policies. Asking for a justification should not, then, be viewed as an insult or attack, but rather as a normal act of a rational person. Didactic modes of teaching that do not encourage students to question the justification for what is asserted fail to develop a thoughtful environment conducive to education.

know: To have a clear perception or understanding of, be sure of, to have a firm mental grasp of; *information* applies to data that are gathered in any way, as by reading, observation, hearsay, etc. and does not necessarily connote validity; *knowledge* applies to any body of facts gathered by study, observation, etc. and to the ideas inferred from these facts, and connotes an *understanding* of what is known. Critical thinkers need to distinguish knowledge from opinion and belief. See *knowledge.*

knowledge: The act of having a clear and justifiable grasp of what is so or of how to do something. Knowledge is based on understanding or skill, which in turn are based on thought, study, and experience. 'Thoughtless knowledge' is a contradiction. 'Blind knowledge' is a contradiction. 'Unjustifiable knowledge' is a contradiction. Knowledge implies justifiable belief or skilled action. Hence, when students blindly memorize and are tested for recall, they are not being tested for knowledge. *Knowledge is continually confused with recall in present-day schooling.* This confusion is a deep-seated impediment to the integration of critical thinking into schooling. *Genuine knowledge is inseparable from thinking minds.* We often wrongly talk of knowledge as though it could be divorced from thinking, as though it could be gathered up by one person and given to another in the form of a collection of sentences to remember. When we talk in this way, we forget that knowledge, by its very nature, depends on thought. Knowledge is produced by thought, analyzed by thought, comprehended by thought, organized, evaluated, maintained, and transformed by thought. Knowledge exists, properly speaking, only in minds that have comprehended and justified it through thought. Knowledge is not to be confused with belief nor with symbolic representation of belief. Humans easily and frequently believe things that are false or believe things to be true without knowing them to be so. A book contains knowledge only in a derivative sense, only because minds can thoughtfully read it and through that process gain knowledge.

logic: 1) Correct reasoning or the study of correct reasoning and its foundations. 2) The relationships between propositions (supports, assumes, implies, contradicts, counts against, is relevant to ...). 3) The system of principles, concepts, and assumptions that underlie any discipline, activity, or practice. 4) The set of rational considerations that bear upon the truth or justification of any belief or set of beliefs. 5) The set of rational considerations that bear upon the settlement of any question or set of questions. The word 'logic' covers a range of related concerns all bearing upon the question of rational justification and explanation. *All human thought and behavior is to some extent based on logic* rather than instinct. Humans try to figure things out using ideas, meanings, and thought. Such intellectual behavior inevitably involves "logic" or considerations of a logical sort: some sense of what is relevant and irrelevant, of what supports and what counts against a belief, of what we should and should not assume, of what we should and should not claim, of what we do and do not know, of what is and is not implied, of what does and does not contradict, of what we should or should not do or believe. *Concepts have a logic* in that we can investigate the conditions under which they do and do not apply, of what is relevant or irrelevant to them, of what they do or don't imply, etc. *Questions have a logic* in that we can investigate the conditions under which they can be settled. *Disciplines have a logic* in that they have purposes and a set of logical structures that bear upon those purposes: assumptions, concepts, issues, data, theories, claims, implications, consequences, etc. The concept of logic is a seminal notion in critical thinking. Unfortunately, it takes a considerable length of time before most people become comfortable with its multiple uses. In part, this is due to people's failure to monitor their own thinking in keeping with the standards of reason and logic. This is not to deny, of course, that logic is involved in all human thinking. It is rather to say that the logic we use is often implicit, unexpressed, and sometimes contradictory. See *knowledge, higher and lower order learning.*

the logic of a discipline: The notion that every technical term has logical relationships with other technical terms, that some terms are logically more basic than others, and that every discipline relies on concepts, assumptions, and theories, makes claims, gives reasons and evidence, avoids contradictions and inconsistencies, has implications and consequences, etc. Though all students study disciplines, most are ignorant of the logic of the disciplines they study. This severely limits their ability to grasp the discipline as a whole, to think independently within it, to compare and contrast it with other disciplines, and to apply it outside the context of academic assignments. Typically now, students do not look for seminal terms as they study an area. They do not strive to translate technical terms into analogies and ordinary words they understand or distinguish technical from ordinary uses of terms. They do not look for the basic assumptions of the disciplines they study. Indeed, on the whole, they do not know what assumptions are nor why it is important to examine them. What they have in their heads exists like so many BB's in a bag. Whether one thought supports or follows from another, whether one thought elaborates another, exemplifies, presupposes, or contradicts another, are matters students have not learned to think about. They have not learned to use thought to understand thought, which is another way of saying that they have not learned how to use thought to gain knowledge. *Instruction for critical thinking cultivates the students' ability to make explicit the logic of what they study.* This emphasis gives depth and breath to study and learning. It lies at the heart of the differences between lower order and higher order learning. See *knowledge.*

the logic of language: For a language to exist and be learnable by persons from a variety of cultures, it is necessary that *words have definite uses and defined concepts that transcend particular cultures.* The English language, for example, is learned by many peoples of the world unfamiliar with English or North American cultures. Critical thinkers must learn to use their native language with precision, in keeping with educated usage. Unfortunately, many students do not understand the significant relationship between precision in language usage and precision in thought. Consider, for example, how most students relate to their native language. If one questions them about the meanings of words, their account is typically incoherent. They often say that people have their own meanings for all the words they use, not noticing that, were this true, we could not understand each other. Students speak and write in vague sentences because they have no rational criteria for choosing words — they simply write whatever words pop into their heads. They do not realize that every language has a highly refined logic one must learn to express oneself precisely. They do not realize that even words similar in meaning typically have different implications. Consider, for example, the words explain, expound, explicate, elucidate, interpret, and construe. *Explain* implies the process of making clear and intelligible something not understood or known. *Expound* implies a systematic and thorough explanation, often by an expert. *Explicate* implies a scholarly analysis developed in detail. *Elucidate* implies a shedding of light upon by clear and specific illustration or explanation. *Interpret* implies the bringing out of meanings not immediately apparent. *Construe* implies a particular interpretation of something whose meaning is ambiguous. See *clarify, concept.*

the logic of questions: The range of rational considerations that bear upon the settlement of a given question or group of questions. A critical thinker is adept at analyzing questions to determine what, precisely, a question asks and how to go about rationally settling it. A critical thinker recognizes that different kinds of questions often call for different modes of thinking, different kinds of considerations, and different procedures and techniques. Uncritical thinkers often confuse distinct questions and use considerations irrelevant to an issue while ignoring relevant ones.

lower order learning: Learning by rote memorization, association, and drill. There are a variety of forms of lower order learning in the schools which we can identify by understanding the relative *lack of logic informing them.* Paradigmatically, lower order learning is learning by sheer association or rote. Hence students come to think of history class, for example, as a place where you hear names, dates, places, events, and outcomes; where you try to remember them and state them on tests. Math comes to be thought of as numbers, symbols, and formulas — mysterious things you mechanically manipulate as the teacher told you in order to get the right answer. Literature is often thought of as uninteresting stories to remember along with what the teacher said is important about them. Consequently, students leave with a jumble of undigested fragments, scraps left over after they have forgotten most of what they stored in their short-term memories for tests. Virtually never do they grasp the logic of what they learn. Rarely do they relate what they learn to their own experience or critique each by means of the other. Rarely do they try to test what they learn in everyday life. Rarely do they ask "Why is this so? How does this relate to what I already know? How does this relate to what I am learning in other classes?" To put the point in a nutshell, very few students think of what they are learning as worthy of being arranged logically in their minds or have the slightest idea of how to do so. See *didactic instruction, monological and multilogical problems and thinking.*

monological (one-dimensional) problems: Problems that can be solved by reasoning exclusively within one point of view or frame of reference. For example, consider the following problems: *1)* Ten full crates of walnuts weigh 410 pounds, whereas an empty crate weighs 10 pounds. How much do the walnuts alone weigh?; and *2)* In how many days of the week does the third letter of the day's name immediately follow the first letter of the day's name in the alphabet? I call these problems and the means by which they are solved 'monological'. They are settled within one frame of reference with a definite set of logical moves. When the right set of moves is performed, the problem is settled. The answer or solution proposed can be shown by standards implicit in the frame of reference to be the "right" answer or solution. *Most important human problems are multilogical rather than monological,* nonatomic problems inextricably joined to other problems, with some conceptual messiness to them and very often with important values lurking in the background. When the problems have an empirical dimension, that dimension tends to have a controversial scope. In multilogical problems it is often arguable how some facts should be considered and interpreted, and how their significance should be determined. When they have a conceptual dimension, there tend to be arguably different ways to pin the concepts down. Though life presents us with predominantly multilogical problems, schooling today over-emphasizes monological problems. Worse, and more frequently, present instructional practices treat multilogical problems as though they were monological. The posing of multilogical problems, and their consideration from multiple points of view, play an important role in the cultivation of critical thinking and higher order learning.

monological (one-dimensional) thinking: Thinking that is conducted exclusively within one point of view or frame of reference: figuring our how much this $67.49 pair of shoes with a 25% discount will cost me; learning what signing this contract obliges me to do; finding out

when Kennedy was elected President. A person can think monologically whether or not the question is genuinely monological. (For
example, if one considers the question, "Who caused the Civil War?"
only from a Northerner's perspective, one is thinking monologically
about a multilogical question.) The strong sense critical thinker
avoids monological thinking when the question is multi-logical.
Moreover, higher order learning requires multi-logical thought, even
when the problem is monological (for example, learning a concept in
chemistry), since students must explore and assess their original
beliefs to develop insight into new ideas.

multilogical (multi-dimensional) problems: Problems that can be analyzed and approached from more than one, often from conflicting,
points of view or frames of reference. For example, many ecological
problems have a variety of dimensions to them: historical, social, economic, biological, chemical, moral, political, etc. A person comfortable
thinking about multilogical problems is comfortable thinking within
multiple perspectives, in engaging in dialogical and dialectical thinking, in practicing intellectual empathy, in thinking across disciplines
and domains. See *monological problems, the logic of questions, the
logic of disciplines, intellectual empathy, dialogical instruction.*

multilogical thinking: Thinking that sympathetically enters, considers,
and reasons within multiple points of view. See *multilogical problems, dialectical thinking, dialogical instruction.*

national bias: Prejudice in favor of one's country, it's beliefs, traditions,
practices, image, and world view; a form of sociocentrism or ethnocentrism. It is natural, if not inevitable, for people to be favorably
disposed toward the beliefs, traditions, practices, and world view
within which they were raised. Unfortunately, this favorable inclination commonly becomes a form of prejudice: a more or less rigid,
irrational ego-identification which significantly distorts one's view of
one's own nation and the world at large. It is manifested in a tendency to mindlessly take the side of one's own government, to uncritically accept governmental accounts of the nature of disputes with
other nations, to uncritically exaggerate the virtues of one's own
nation while playing down the virtues of "enemy" nations. National
bias is reflected in the press and media coverage of every nation of
the world. Events are included or excluded according to what
appears significant within the dominant world view of the nation,
and are shaped into stories to validate that view. Though constructed to fit into a particular view of the world, the stories in the news
are presented as neutral, objective accounts, and uncritically accepted as such because people tend to uncritically assume that their own
view of things is the way things really are. To become responsible

critically thinking citizens and fairminded people, students must practice identifying national bias in the news and in their texts, and to broaden their perspective beyond that of uncritical nationalism. See *ethnocentrism, sociocentrism, bias, prejudice, world view, intellectual empathy, critical society, dialogical instruction, knowledge.*

opinion: A belief, typically one open to dispute. Sheer unreasoned opinion should be distinguished from reasoned judgment — beliefs formed on the basis of careful reasoning. See *evaluation, judgment, justify, know, knowledge, reasoned judgment.*

the perfections of thought: Thinking, as an attempt to understand the world as it is, has a natural excellence or fitness to it. This excellence is manifest in its *clarity, precision, specificity, accuracy, relevance, consistency, logicalness, depth, completeness, significance, fairness, and adequacy.* These perfections are general canons for thought; they represent legitimate concerns irrespective of the discipline or domain of thought. To develop one's mind and discipline one's thinking with respect to these standards *requires extensive practice and long-term cultivation.* Of course, achieving these standards is a relative matter and varies somewhat among domains of thought. Being *precise* while doing mathematics is not the same as being precise while writing a poem, describing an experience, or explaining a historical event. Furthermore, one perfection of thought may be periodically incompatible with the others: adequacy to purpose. Time and resources sufficient to thoroughly analyze a question or problem is all too often an unaffordable luxury. Also, since the social world is often irrational and unjust, because people are often manipulated to act against their interests, and because skilled thought often serves vested interest, thought adequate to these manipulative purposes may require *skilled violation of the common standards for good thinking.* Skilled propaganda, skilled political debate, skilled defense of a group's interests, skilled deception of one's enemy may require the violation or selective application of any of the above standards. Perfecting one's thought as an instrument for success in a world based on power and advantage differs from perfecting one's thought for the apprehension and defense of fairminded truth. *To develop one's critical thinking skills merely to the level of adequacy for social success is to develop those skills in a lower or <u>weaker</u> sense.*

personal contradiction: An inconsistency in one's personal life, wherein one says one thing and does another, or uses a double standard, judging oneself and one's friends by an easier standard than that used for people one doesn't like. Typically a form of hypocrisy accompanied by self-deception. Most personal contradictions remain

unconscious. People too often ignore the difficulty of becoming intellectually and morally consistent, preferring instead to merely
admonish others. Personal contradictions are more likely to be discovered, analyzed, and reduced in an atmosphere in which they can
be openly admitted and realistically considered without excessive
penalty. See *egocentricity, intellectual integrity.*

perspective (point of view): Human thought is relational and selective. It
is impossible to understand any person, event, or phenomenon from
every vantage point simultaneously. Our purposes often control how
we see things. Critical thinking requires that this fact be taken into
account when analyzing and assessing thinking. This is not to say
that human thought is incapable of truth and objectivity, but only
that human truth, objectivity, and insight is virtually always limited
and partial, virtually never total and absolute. The hard sciences
are themselves a good example of this point, since qualitative realities are systematically ignored in favor of quantifiable realities.

precision: The quality of being accurate, definite, and exact. The standards
and modes of precision vary according to subject and context. See
the logic of language, elements of thought.

prejudice: A judgment, belief, opinion, point of view — favorable or unfavorable — formed before the facts are known, resistant to evidence and
reason, or in disregard of facts which contradict it. Self-announced
prejudice is rare. Prejudice almost always exists in obscured, rationalized, socially validated, functional forms. It enables people to
sleep peacefully at night even while flagrantly abusing the rights of
others. It enables people to get more of what they want, or to get it
more easily. It is often sanctioned with a superabundance of pomp
and self-righteousness. Unless we recognize these powerful tendencies toward selfish thought in our social institutions, even in what
appear to be lofty actions and moralistic rhetoric, we will not face
squarely the problem of prejudice in human thought and action.
Uncritical and selfishly critical thought are often prejudiced. Most
instruction in schools today, because students do not think their way
to what they accept as true, tends to give students prejudices rather
than knowledge. For example, partly as a result of schooling, people
often accept as authorities those who liberally sprinkle their statements with numbers and intellectual-sounding language, however
irrational or unjust their positions. This prejudice toward psuedo-
authority impedes rational assessment. See *insight, knowledge.*

premise: A proposition upon which an argument is based or from which a
conclusion is drawn. A starting point of reasoning. For example, one
might say, in commenting on someone's reasoning, "You seem to be

reasoning from the premise that everyone is selfish in everything they do. *Do* you hold this belief?"

principle: A fundamental truth, law, doctrine, value, or commitment, upon which others are based. Rules, which are more specific, and often superficial and arbitrary, are based on principles. Rules are more algorithmic; they needn't be understood to be followed. Principles must be understood to be appropriately applied or followed. Principles go to the heart of the matter. Critical thinking is dependent on principles, not rules and procedures. Critical thinking is principled, not procedural, thinking. Principles cannot be truly grasped through didactic instruction; they must be practiced and applied to be internalized. See *higher order learning, lower order learning, judgment.*

problem: A question, matter, situation, or person that is perplexing or difficult to figure out, handle, or resolve. Problems, like questions, can be divided into many types. Each has a (particular) logic. See *logic of questions, monological problems, multilogical problems.*

problem-solving: Whenever a problem cannot be solved formulaically or robotically, critical thinking is required: first, to determine the nature and dimensions of the problem, and then, in the light of the first, to determine the considerations, points of view, concepts, theories, data, and reasoning relevant to its solution. Extensive practice in independent problem-solving is essential to developing critical thought. Problem-solving is rarely best approached procedurally or as a series of rigidly followed steps. For example, problem-solving schemas typically begin, "State the problem." Rarely can problems be precisely and fairly stated prior to analysis, gathering of evidence, and dialogical or dialectical thought wherein several provisional descriptions of the problem are proposed, assessed, and revised.

proof (prove): Evidence or reasoning so strong or certain as to demonstrate the validity of a conclusion beyond a reasonable doubt. How strong evidence or reasoning have to be to demonstrate what they purport to prove varies from context to context, depending on the significance of the conclusion or the seriousness of the implications following from it. See *domain of thought.*

rational/rationality: That which conforms to principles of good reasoning, is sensible, shows good judgment, is consistent, logical, complete, and relevant. Rationality is a summary term like 'virtue' or 'goodness'. It is manifested in an unlimited number of ways and depends on a host of principles. There is some ambiguity in it, depending on whether one considers only the logicalness and effectiveness by which one pursues one's ends, or whether it includes the assessment of ends themselves. There is also ambiguity in whether one considers selfish ends to be rational, even when they conflict with what is just. Does a rational person have to be just or only skilled in pursuing his or her interests? Is it rational to be rational in an irrational world? See *perfections of thought, irrational/irrationality, logic, intellectual virtues, weak sense critical thinking, strong sense critical thinking.*

rational emotions/passions: R. S. Peters has explained the significance of the affective side of reason and critical thought in his defense of the necessity of "rational passions:"

> There is, for instance, the hatred of contradictions and inconsistencies, together with the love of clarity and hatred of confusion without which words could not be held to relatively constant meanings and testable rules and generalizations stated. A reasonable man cannot, without some special explanation, slap his sides with delight or express indifference if he is told that what he says is confused, incoherent and perhaps riddled with contradictions.
>
> Reason is the antithesis of arbitrariness. In its operation it is supported by the appropriate passions which are mainly negative in character — the hatred of irrelevance, special pleading and arbitrary fiat. The more developed emotion of indignation is aroused when some excess of arbitrariness is perpetuated in a situation where people's interests and claims are at stake. The positive side of this is the passion for fairness and impartial consideration of claims....
>
> A man who is prepared to reason must feel strongly that he must follow the arguments and decide things in terms of where they lead. He must have a sense of the giveness of the impersonality of such considerations. In so far as thoughts about persons enter his head they should be tinged with the respect which is due to another who, like himself, may have a point of view which is worth considering, who may have a glimmering of the truth which has so far eluded himself. A person who proceeds in this way, who is influenced by such passions, is what we call a reasonable man.

rational self: Our character and nature to the extent that we seek to base our beliefs and actions on good reasoning and evidence. Who we are, what our true character is, or our predominant qualities are, is always somewhat or even greatly different from who we think we are. Human egocentrism and accompanying self-deception often stand in the way of our gaining more insight into ourselves. We can develop a rational self, become a person who gains significant insight into what our true character is, only by reducing our egocentrism and self-deception. Critical thinking is essential to this process.

rational society: See *critical society.*

reasoned judgment: Any belief or conclusion reached on the basis of careful thought and reflection, distinguished from mere or unreasoned opinion on the one hand, and from sheer fact on the other. Few people have a clear sense of which of their beliefs are based on reasoned judgment and which on mere opinion.

reasoning: The mental processes of those who reason; especially the drawing of conclusions or inferences from observations, facts, or hypotheses. The evidence or arguments used in this procedure. A critical thinker tries to develop the capacity to transform thought into reasoning at will, or rather, the ability to make his or her inferences explicit, along with the assumptions or premises upon which those inferences are based. Reasoning is a form of explicit inferring, usually involving multiple steps. When students write a persuasive paper, for example,we want them to be clear about their reasoning.

reciprocity: The act of entering empathically into the point of view or line of reasoning of others; learning to think as others do and by that means sympathetically assessing that thinking. (Reciprocity requires creative imagination as well as intellectual skill and a commitment to fairmindedness.)

relevant: Bearing upon or relating to the matter at hand; *relevant* implies close logical relationship with, and importance to, the matter under consideration; *germane* implies such close natural connection as to be highly appropriate or fit; *pertinent* implies an immediate and direct bearing on the matter at hand (a pertinent suggestion); *apposite* applies to that which is both relevant and happily suitable or appropriate; *applicable* refers to that which can be brought to bear upon a particular matter or problem. Students often have problems sticking to an issue and distinguishing information that bears upon a problem from information that does not. Merely reminding students to limit themselves to relevant considerations fails to solve this problem. The usual way of teaching students the term 'relevant' is to mention only clear-cut cases of relevance and irrelevance. Consequently, students do not learn that not everything that *seems* relevant is, or that some things which do not *seem* relevant are. Sensitivity to (ability to judge) relevance can only be developed with continual practice — practice distinguishing relevant from irrelevant, evaluating or judging relevance, arguing for and against the relevance of facts and considerations.

self-deception: Deceiving one's self about one's true motivations, character, identity, etc. One possible definition of the human species is "The Self-Deceiving Animal". Self-deception is a fundamental problem in human life and the cause of much human suffering. Overcoming self-deception through self-critical thinking is a fundamental goal of strong sense critical thinking. See *egocentric, rational self, personal contradiction, social contradiction, intellectual virtues.*

social contradiction: An inconsistency between what a society preaches and what it practices. In every society there is some degree of inconsistency between its image of itself and its actual character. Social contradiction typically correlates with human self-deception on the social or cultural level. Critical thinking is essential for the recognition of inconsistencies, and recognition is essential for reform and eventual integrity.

sociocentricity: The assumption that one's own social group is inherently and self-evidently superior to all others. When a group or society sees itself as superior and so considers its views about the world as correct or as the only reasonable or justifiable views, and all its actions justified, there is a tendency to presuppose this superiority in all of its thinking and thus to think closedmindedly. All dissent and doubt are considered disloyal, and rejected without consideration. Few people recognize the sociocentric nature of much of their thought.

Socratic questioning: A mode of questioning that deeply probes the meaning, justification, or logical strength of a claim, position, or line of reasoning. Socratic questioning can be carried out in a variety of ways and adapted to many levels of ability and understanding. See *elements of thought, dialogical instruction, knowledge.*

specify/specific: To mention, describe, or define in detail. Limiting or limited; specifying or specified; precise; definite. Student thinking, speech, and writing tend to be vague, abstract, and ambiguous rather than specific, concrete, and clear. Learning how to state one's views specifically is essential to learning how to think clearly, precisely, and accurately. See *perfections of thought.*

strong sense critical thinker: One who is predominantly characterized by the following traits: *1)* an ability to question deeply one's own framework of thought; *2)* an ability to reconstruct sympathetically and imaginatively the strongest versions of points of view and frameworks of thought opposed to one's own; and *3)* an ability to reason dialectically (multilogically) in such a way as to determine when one's own point of view is at its weakest and when an opposing point of view is at its strongest. Strong sense critical thinkers are not routinely blinded by their own points of view. They know they have points of view and therefore recognize on what framework of assumptions and ideas their own thinking is based. They realize the necessity of putting their own assumptions and ideas to the test of the strongest objections that can be leveled against them. Teaching for critical thinking in the strong sense is teaching so that students explicate, understand, and critique their own deepest prejudices, biases, and misconceptions, thereby discovering and contesting their own egocentric and sociocentric tendencies. Only if we contest our inevitable egocentric and sociocentric habits of thought can we hope to think in a genuinely rational fashion. Only dialogical thinking about basic issues that genuinely matter to the individual provides the kind of practice and skill essential to strong sense critical thinking.

Students need to develop all critical thinking skills in dialogical settings to achieve ethically rational development, that is, genuine fairmindedness. If critical thinking is taught simply as atomic skills separate from the empathic practice of entering into points of view that students are fearful of or hostile toward, they will simply find additional means of rationalizing prejudices and preconceptions, or convincing people that their point of view is the correct one. They will be transformed from vulgar to sophisticated (but not to strong sense) critical thinkers.

teach: The basic inclusive word for the imparting of knowledge or skills. It usually connotes some individual attention to the learner; *instruct* implies systematized teaching, usually in some particular subject; *educate* stresses the development of latent faculties and powers by formal, systematic teaching, especially in institutions of higher learning; *train* implies the development of a particular faculty or skill or instruction toward a particular occupation, as by methodical discipline, exercise, etc. See *knowledge.*

theory: A systematic statement of principles involved in a subject; a formulation of apparent relationships or underlying principles of certain observed phenomena which has been verified to some degree. Often without realizing it, we form theories that help us make sense of the people, events, and problems in our lives. Critical thinkers put their theories to the test of experience and give due consideration to the theories of others. Critical thinkers do not take their theories to be facts.

think: The general word meaning to exercise the mental faculties so as to form ideas, arrive at conclusions, etc.; *reason* implies a logical sequence of thought, starting with what is known or assumed and advancing to a definite conclusion through the inferences drawn; *reflect* implies a turning of one's thoughts on or back on a subject and connotes deep or quiet continued thought; *speculate* implies a reasoning on the basis of incomplete or uncertain evidence and therefore stresses the conjectural character of the opinions formed; *deliberate* implies careful and thorough consideration of a matter in order to arrive at a conclusion. Though everyone thinks, few people think critically. We don't need instruction to think; we think spontaneously. We need instruction to learn how to discipline and direct our thinking on the basis of sound intellectual standards. See *elements of thought, perfections of thought.*

truth: Conformity to knowledge, fact, actuality, or logic: a statement proven to be or accepted as true, not false or erroneous. Most people uncritically assume their views to be correct and true. Most people, in other words, assume themselves to possess the truth. Critical thinking is essential to avoid this, if for no other reason.

uncritical person: One who has not developed intellectual skills (naive, conformist, easily manipulated, dogmatic, easily confused, unclear, closedminded, narrowminded, careless in word choice, inconsistent, unable to distinguish evidence from interpretation). Uncriticalness is a fundamental problem in human life, for when we are uncritical we nevertheless think of ourselves as critical. The first step in becoming a critical thinker consists in recognizing that we are uncritical. Teaching for insight into uncriticalness is an important part of teaching for criticalness.

vague: Not clearly, precisely, or definitely expressed or stated; not sharp, certain, or precise in thought, feeling, or expression. Vagueness of thought and of language usage is a major obstacle to the development of critical thinking. We cannot begin to test our beliefs until we recognize clearly what they are. We cannot disagree with what someone says until we are clear about what they mean. Students need much practice in transforming vague thoughts into clear ones. See *ambiguous, clarify, concept, logic, logic of questions, logic of language.*

verbal implication: That which follows, according to the logic of the language. If I say, for example, that someone used flattery on me, I *imply* that the compliments were insincere and given only to make me feel positively toward that person, to manipulate me against my reason or interest for some end.

weak sense critical thinkers: *1)* Those who do not hold themselves or those with whom they ego-identify to the same intellectual standards to which they hold "opponents". *2)* Those who have not learned how to reason empathically within points of view or frames of reference with which they disagree. *3)* Those who tend to think monologically. *4)* Those who do not genuinely accept, though they may verbally espouse, the values of critical thinking. *5)* Those who use the intellectual skills of critical thinking selectively and self-deceptively to foster and serve their vested interests (at the expense of truth); able to identify flaws in the reasoning of others and refute them; able to shore up their own beliefs with reasons.

world view: All human action takes place within a way of looking at and interpreting the world. As schooling now stands very little is done to help students to grasp how they are viewing the world and how those views determine the character of their experience, their interpretations, their conclusions about events and persons, etc. In teaching for critical thinking in a strong sense, we make the discovery of one's own world view and the experience of other people's world views a fundamental priority. See *bias, interpret.*

✦✦ Appendix

Recommended Readings in Critical Thinking

The General Case for Critical Thinking

Bailin, Sharon. *Achieving Extraordinary Ends: An Essay of Creativity.* Kluwer-Academic Publishers, Norwell, MA, 1988.

Baron, Joan and Robert Sternberg. *Teaching Thinking Skills: Theory and Practice.* W. H. Freeman Co., New York, NY, 1987.

Blair, J. Anthony and Ralph H. Johnson, eds. *Informal Logic (First International Symposium).* Edgepress, Point Reyes, CA, 1980.

Glaser, Edward M. *An Experiment in the Development of Critical Thinking.* AMS Press, New York, NY, reprint of 1941 edition.

Kennedy, Mary. "Policy Issues in Teacher Education." *Phi Delta Kappan.* May, 1991

Mill, John Stuart. *On Liberty.* AHM Publishing Corp., Arlington Heights, IL, 1947.

Resnick, Lauren. *Education and Learning to Think.* National Academy Press, Washington, D.C., 1987.

Scriven, Michael. *Evaluation Thesaurus.* Point Reyes, CA, Edge Press, 1991

Scheffler, Israel. *Reason and Teaching.* Hackett Publishing, Indianapolis, IN, 1973.

Siegel, Harvey. *Educating Reason: Rationality, Critical Thinking, & Education.* Routledge Chapman & Hall, Inc., New York, NY, 1988.

Sumner, William G. *Folkways.* Ayer Co., Publishing, Salem, NH, 1979.

Toulmin, Stephen E. *The Uses of Argument.* Cambridge University Press, New York, NY, 1958.

Critical Thinking Pedagogy

Brookfield, Stephen D. *Developing Critical Thinkers.* Jossey-Bass, San Francisco, CA, 1987.

Costa, Arthur L. *Developing Minds: A Resource Book for Teaching Thinking.* Revised Edition, Volume 1. Alexandria, VA: ASCD, 1991.

D'Angelo, Edward. *The Teaching of Critical Thinking.* B. R. Grüner, N. V., Amsterdam, 1971.

Lipman, Matthew. *Ethical Inquiry.* Institute for the Advancement of Philosophy for Children, Upper Montclair, N.J., 1977.

Lipman, Matthew. *Harry Stottlemeier's Discovery.* Institute for the Advancement of Philosophy for Children, Upper Montclair, N.J., 1982.

Lipman, Matthew. *Lisa*. Institute for the Advancement of Philosophy for Children, Upper Montclair, N.J., 1976.

Lipman, Matthew. *Mark*. Institute for the Advancement of Philosophy for Children, Upper Monclair, N.J., 1980.

Lipman, Matthew, Ann M. Sharp, and Frederick S. Oscanyan. *Philosophical Inquiry*. University Press of America, Lanham, MD, 1979.

Lipman, Matthew, and Ann M. Sharp. *Philosophy in the Classroom*. 2ⁿᵈ edition, Temple University Press, Philadelphia, PA, 1980.

Lipman, Matthew. *Social Inquiry*. Institute for the Advancement of Philosophy for Children, Upper Montclair, N.J., 1980.

Meyers, Chet. *Teaching Students to Think Critically: A Guide for Faculty in all Disciplines*. Jossey-Bass, San Francisco, CA, 1986.

Norris, Stephen P, and Ennis, Robert H. *Evaluating Critical Thinking*. Pacific Grove, CA: Midwest Publications, 1989.

Paul, Richard, Binker, A. J. A., et al. *Critical Thinking Handbook: K–3ʳᵈ Grades. A Guide for Remodelling Lesson Plans in Language Arts, Social Studies, & Science*. 2ⁿᵈ edition, Santa Rosa, CA: Foundation for Critical Thinking 1990.

Paul, Richard, Binker, A. J. A., et al. *Critical Thinking Handbook: 4ᵗʰ–6ᵗʰ Grades. A Guide for Remodelling Lesson Plans in Language Arts, Social Studies, & Science*. 2ⁿᵈ edition, Santa Rosa, CA: Foundation for Critical Thinking, 1990.

Paul, Richard, Binker, A. J. A., et al. *Critical Thinking Handbook: 6ᵗʰ–9ᵗʰ Grades. A Guide for Remodelling Lesson Plans in Language Arts, Social Studies, & Science*. Rohnert Park, CA: Center for Critical Thinking and Moral Critique 1989.

Paul, Richard, Binker, A. J. A., et al. *Critical Thinking Handbook: High School A Guide for Redesigning Instruction,* Rohnert Park, CA: Center for Critical Thinking and Moral Critique 1989.

Raths, Louis. *Teaching for Thinking: Theories, Strategies, and Activities for the Classroom*. 2ⁿᵈ edition, Teachers College Press, New York, NY, 1986.

Ruggiero, Vincent. *Thinking Across the Curriculum*. Harper & Row, New York, NY, 1988.

Ruggiero, Vincent. *Art of Thinking*. 2ⁿᵈ edition, Harper & Row, New York, NY, 1988.

Williamson, Janet L. *The Greensboro Plan: Infusing Reasoning and Writing into the K–12 Curriculum*. Santa Rosa, CA, Foundation for Critical Thinking 1990.

College Textbooks (Not Focused on a Specific Discipline)

Barker, Evelyn M. *Everyday Reasoning*. Prentice-Hall, Englewood Cliffs, NJ, 1981.

Barry, Vincent E., and Joel Rudinow. *Invitation to Critical Thinking*. 2ⁿᵈ edition, Holt, Rinehart & Winston, New York, NY, 1990.

Brown, Neil and Stuart Keely. *Asking the Right Questions: A Guide to Critical Thinking*. 2ⁿᵈ edition, Prentice-Hall, Englewood Cliffs, NJ, 1986.

Capaldi, Nicholas. *The Art of Deception*. 2ⁿᵈ edition, Prometheus Books, Buffalo, New York, 1979.

Cederblom, Jerry. *Critical Reasoning*. 2ⁿᵈ edition, Wadsworth Publishing Co., Belmont, CA, 1986.

Chaffee, John. *Thinking Critically*. 2ⁿᵈ edition, Houghton Mifflin, Boston, MA, 1988.

Damer, T. Edward. *Attacking Faulty Reasoning.* 2nd edition, Wadsworth Publishing Co., Belmont, CA, 1987.

Engel, Morris. *Analyzing Informal Fallacies.* Prentice-Hall, Englewood Cliffs, NJ, 1980.

Engel, Morris. *With Good Reason: An Introduction to Informal Fallacies.* 3rd edition, St. Martin's Press, New York, NY, 1986.

Fahnestock, Jeanne and Marie Secor. *Rhetoric of Argument.* McGraw-Hill Book Co., New York, NY, 1982.

Fisher, Alec. *The Logic of Real Arguments.* Cambridge University Press, New York, NY, 1988.

Govier, Trudy. *A Practical Study of Argument.* 2nd edition, Wadsworth Publishing Co., Belmont, CA, 1988.

Hitchcock, David. *Critical Thinking: A Guide to Evaluating Information.* Methuan Publications, Toronto, Canada, 1983.

Hoagland, John. *Critical Thinking.* Vale Press, Newport News, VA, 1984.

Johnson, Ralph H. and J. A. Blair. *Logical Self-Defense.* 2nd edition, McGraw-Hill, New York, NY, 1983.

Kahane, Howard. *Logic and Contemporary Rhetoric.* 5th edition, Wadsworth Publishing Co., Belmont, CA, 1988.

Meiland, Jack W. *College Thinking: How to Get the Best Out of College.* New American Library, New York, NY, 1981.

Michalos, Alex C. *Improving Your Reasoning.* Prentice-Hall, Englewood Cliffs, NJ, 1986.

Miller, Robert K. *Informed Argument.* 2nd edition, Harcourt, Brace, Jovanovich, San Diego, CA, 1989.

Missimer, Connie. *Good Arguments: An Introduction to Critical Thinking.* 2nd edition, Prentice-Hall, Englewood Cliffs, NJ, 1986.

Moore, Brooke N. *Critical Thinking: Evaluating Claims and Arguments in Everyday Life.* 2nd edition, Mayfield Publishing Co., Palo Alto, CA, 1989.

Moore, Edgar. *Creative and Critical Reasoning.* 2nd edition, Houghton Mifflin, Boston, MA, 1984.

Nickerson, Raymond S. *Reflections on Reasoning.* L. Erlbaum, Assoc., Hillsdale, NJ, 1986.

Nosich, Gerald. *Reasons and Arguments.* Belmont, CA Wadsworth 1981.

Ruggiero, Vincent. *Moral Imperative.* Mayfield Publishing, Palo Alto, CA, 1984.

Scriven, Michael. *Reasoning.* McGraw-Hill Book Co., New York, NY, 1976.

Seech, Zachary. *Logic in Everyday Life: Practical Reasoning Skills.* Wadsworth Publishing Co., Belmont, CA, 1988.

Shor, Ira. *Critical Teaching & Everyday Life.* University of Chicago Press, Chicago, IL, 1987.

Toulmin, Stephen E., Richard Rieke, and Alan Janik. *An Introduction to Reasoning.* Macmillan Publishing Co., New York, NY, 1979.

Weddle, Perry. *Argument: A Guide to Critical Thinking.* McGraw-Hill, New York, NY, 1978.

Wilson, John. *Thinking with Concepts.* 4th edition, Cambridge University Press, New York, NY, 1987.

Mathematics and Critical Thinking

Schoenfeld, Alan. *Mathematical Problem Solving: Issues in Research.* Lester, F.K. and Garofalo, J., ed's. Philadelphia, PA: The Franklin Institute Press 1982.

Curriculum and Evaluation Standards for School Mathematics, by the Working Groups of the Commission on Standards for School Mathematics of the National Council of Teachers of Mathematics, Reston, VA 1989.

Science and Critical Thinking

Giere, Ronald N. *Understanding Scientific Reasoning.* Holt, Rinehart, and Winston, New York, NY, 1979. (Out of print.)

Radner, Daisie and Radner, Michael. *Science and Unreason.* Wadsworth Publishing Co., Belmont, CA, 1982.

Language Arts and Critical Thinking

Adler, Mortimer. *How to Read a Book.* Simon and Schuster, New York, NY, 1972.

Horton, Susan. *Thinking Through Writing.* Johns Hopkins, Baltimore, MD, 1982.

Kytle, Ray. *Clear Thinking for Composition.* 5th edition, McGraw-Hill Book Co., New York, NY, 1987.

Mayfield, Marlys. *Thinking for Yourself: Developing Critical Thinking Skills Through Writing.* Wadsworth Publishing Co., Belmont, CA, 1987.

Rosenberg, Vivian. *Reading, Writing, and Thinking: Critical Connections.* McGraw-Hill Book Co., New York, NY, 1989.

Scull, Sharon. *Critical Reading and Writing for Advanced ESL Students.* Prentice-Hall, Englewood Cliffs, NJ, 1987.

Critical Thinking and the Media

Lazere, Donald. *American Media & Mass Culture.* University of California Press, Berkeley, CA, 1987.

Also of Interest

Baker, Paul J., and Louis Anderson. *Social Problems: A Critical Thinking Approach.* Wadsworth Publishing Co., Belmont, CA, 1987.

Bloom, Benjamin. *Taxonomy of Educational Objectives.* David McKay Co., Inc., New York, 1956.

Goffman, Erving. *Presentation of Self in Everyday Life.* Doubleday & Co., New York, NY, 1959.

Lappé, Francis Moore. *Rediscovering America's Values.* Ballantine Books, New York, NY, 1989.

Siegel, Harvey. *Relativism Refuted.* Kluwer-Academic Publishers, Norwell, MA, 1987.

Tavris, Carol. *Anger: The Misunderstood Emotion.* Simon & Schuster, New York, NY, 1987.

Wilson, Barrie. *The Anatomy of Argument.* University Press of America, Lanham, Maryland, 1980.